Granger Inde

CHOICE READINGS

CHOICE READINGS

FROM

STANDARD AND POPULAR AUTHORS

EMBRACING

A COMPLETE CLASSIFICATION OF SELECTIONS, A COMPREHENSIVE DIAGRAM OF THE PRINCIPLES OF VOCAL EXPRESSION, AND INDEXES TO THE CHOICEST READINGS

FROM

SHAKESPEARE, THE BIBLE, AND THE HYMN-BOOKS

COMPILED AND ARRANGED BY

ROBERT I. FULTON

AND

THOMAS C. TRUEBLOOD

Granger Index Reprint Series

BOOKS FOR LIBRARIES PRESS
FREEPORT, NEW YORK

First Published 1884
Reprinted 1972

Library of Congress Cataloging in Publication Data

Fulton, Robert Irving, 1855-1916.
Choice readings from standard and popular authors.

(Granger index reprint series)
1. Recitations. I. Trueblood, Thomas Clarkson, 1856-1951, joint comp. II. Title.
PN4201.F88 1972 808.85'4 72-5590
ISBN 0-8369-6383-0

PRINTED IN THE UNITED STATES OF AMERICA

TO

Our Mothers

AND

OUR PUPILS

This Volume is Affectionately Inscribed

BY

THE COMPILERS.

PREFACE.

IN publishing this volume we make no apology for its appearance among so many similar books now in the market. We believe there is a demand for it in the place it attempts to supply. Some features are novel. Many selections are new; others are old and standard. We invite a careful examination of the class of pieces employed, their arrangement under the fourteen divisions, the Diagram of the Elements of Vocal Expression, and the Indexes to Readings from Shakespeare, the Bible, and the Hymn-books.

The pieces have been selected with regard to their literary merit and their adaptation to elocutionary purposes. The book contains only those selections which, if correctly delivered, will prove entertaining and instructive as public and private readings. The fourteen classes or divisions are comprehensive, covering the entire range of thought, and at once indicate the character of the selections placed under them. To be sure, many shades of sentiment often occur in one piece; but it is believed that each selection, *as a whole*, is correctly classified, so that the classification will be a safe guide to the pupil. The Diagrams of the Principles, which are based upon the philosophy of Dr. James Rush, will prove valuable to any student of the art of expression, but they are intended more particularly to assist our own pupils in the interpretation and correct reading of the contents of this volume, and also to accompany "*Fulton and Trueblood's New Chart of the Principles of Expression.*" The Indexes are a feature which has not, we believe, been presented in any other book of readings. By them we are enabled to use a wide field of matter without reprinting so much that is already published in a cheap form and is universally accessible. In short, the book is intended for use in our growing profession, in social and reading circles, and in schools and colleges; and we leave it upon its own merits to find its proper place in public favour.

In compiling we have drawn from a number of sources, all of which have, in some form, been duly recognized. We here acknowledge our indebtedness for the valuable criticisms and suggestions of the Rev. Henry N. Hudson, the well-known Shakespearian, who has revised and approved the selections, and has himself furnished some of them, and has also superintended and corrected the printing throughout; which of itself should be endorsement enough to satisfy the most critical.

We also wish to acknowledge the courtesy extended to us by the following well-known publishing firms in allowing us the use of selections of which they hold the copyright: — D. Appleton & Co., New York; Clark & Maynard, New York, S. C. Griggs & Co., Chicago; Harper Brothers, New York; Houghton, Mifflin, & Co., Boston; J. B. Lippincott & Co., Philadelphia; Robert Clark & Co., Cincinnati.

F. AND T.

KANSAS CITY, MO.,
July 24, 1884.

ANALYSIS OF THE CONTENTS.

CONTENTS.

I.

NARRATIVE, DESCRIPTIVE, DIDACTIC.

II.

LOVE, BEAUTY, TRANQUILLITY.

III.

GRAVE, SOLEMN, SERIOUS, PATHETIC.

IV.

REVERENCE, DEVOTION, ADORATION.

V.

GRAND, BOLD, SUBLIME.

VI.

PATRIOTIC, SENATORIAL, ORATORICAL.

VII.

INVECTIVE, VEHEMENT, INDIGNANT.

VIII.

LIVELY, JOYOUS, GAY.

IX.

HUMOROUS, COMIC.

X.

DIALECTIC.

COCKNEY.

FRENCH.

GERMAN.

IRISH.

ITALIAN.

NEGRO.

SCOTCH.

SPANISH.

XIV.

SCENES FROM POPULAR DRAMAS.

XI.

ONOMATOPOETIC.

XII.

FOR YOUNG FOLKS.

XIII.

DRAMATIC, NOT IN THE DRAMA.

DIAGRAM

OF

THE ELEMENTS OF VOCAL EXPRESSION.

[NOTE.—The object of this Diagram is to present at a glance all the Principles of vocal expression, and to show in a brief and convenient form the kinds of thought they express. There is no attempt here to give *all* the sentiments expressed by each Element, but only such *representative* words are used as will direct the thoughts of the pupil into the right channel. The different shades and changes of sentiment, as they occur in a selection, will at once be understood by the context; and, by reference to this Diagram, the student can easily determine the Elements required for a correct and natural expression.]

I. TIME	***a.* QUANTITY**	LONG	Pathos. Sorrow. Solemnity. Sublimity. Awe. Reverence. Adoration. Apostrophe. Commanding. Calling.
		MODERATE	Narrative, didactic, bold, and lofty thought. Secrecy. Alarm. Courage. Grandeur.
		SHORT	Joy. Mirth. Laughter. Exciting appeal. Impatience. Detestation. Fright. Anger. Contempt.
	***b.* PAUSE**	INTERSYLLABIC	Used between syllables of very emphatic words for articulative enforcement.
		PROSODIAL	Used to mark the prosody of verse only when the emphasis and measure of speech coincide.
		RHETORICAL	Used in phrasing spoken discourse to make the sense apparent to the ear.
		GRAMMATICAL	Used to show the grammatical construction of written discourse, and represented to the eye by the punctuation marks.
		EMOTIONAL	Used before and after a word, or group of words, expressing very strong emotion.
	***c.* MOVEMENT**	VERY RAPID	Ecstatic joy. Laughter. Fright. Lyric description. Wrath. Anxiety. Excitement.
		RAPID	Gladness. Exciting appeal. Mirth. Animated description. Anger. Defiance. Alarm.
		MODERATE	Ordinary conversation. Didactic and oratorical thought. Grandeur. Seriousness. Secrecy. Hate.
		SLOW	Gravity. Solemn narration. Pathos. Reverence. Awe. Sublimity. Command.
		VERY SLOW	Melancholy. Gloom. Despair. Adoration. Profound repose. Deepest awe and sublimity.
	***d.* RHYTHMUS.**		

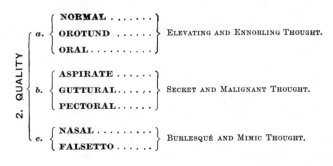

2. QUALITY

- *a.* **NORMAL**, **OROTUND**, **ORAL** — Elevating and Ennobling Thought.
- *b.* **ASPIRATE**, **GUTTURAL**, **PECTORAL** — Secret and Malignant Thought.
- *c.* **NASAL**, **FALSETTO** — Burlesqué and Mimic Thought.

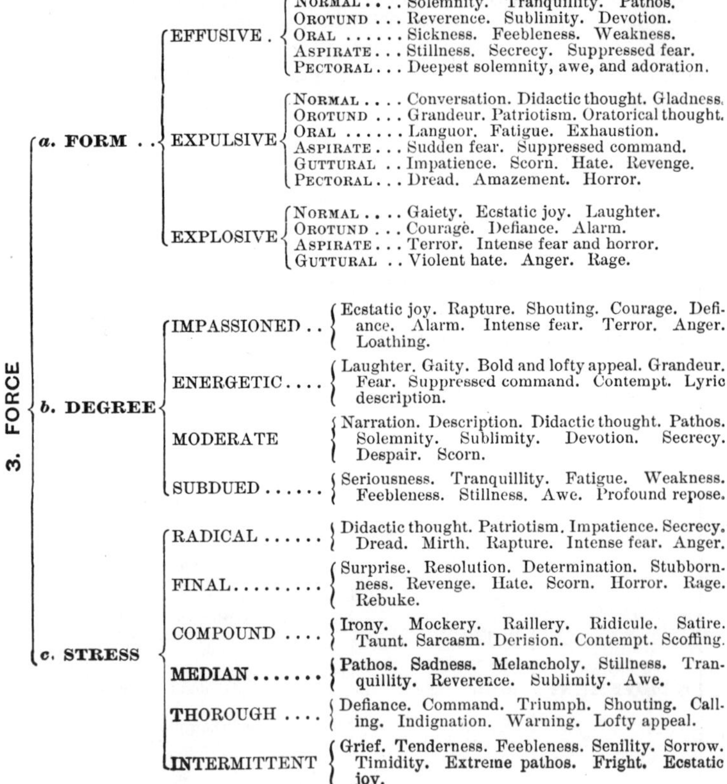

3. FORCE
a. FORM
EFFUSIVE
NORMAL . . . . Solemnity. Tranquillity. Pathos.
OROTUND . . . Reverence. Sublimity. Devotion.
ORAL . . . . . . Sickness. Feebleness. Weakness.
ASPIRATE . . . Stillness. Secrecy. Suppressed fear.
PECTORAL . . . Deepest solemnity, awe, and adoration.
EXPULSIVE
NORMAL . . . . Conversation. Didactic thought. Gladness.
OROTUND . . . Grandeur. Patriotism. Oratorical thought.
ORAL . . . . . . Languor. Fatigue. Exhaustion.
ASPIRATE . . . Sudden fear. Suppressed command.
GUTTURAL . . Impatience. Scorn. Hate. Revenge.
PECTORAL . . . Dread. Amazement. Horror.
EXPLOSIVE
NORMAL . . . . Gaiety. Ecstatic joy. Laughter.
OROTUND . . . Couragė. Defiance. Alarm.
ASPIRATE . . . Terror. Intense fear and horror.
GUTTURAL . . Violent hate. Anger. Rage.
b. DEGREE
IMPASSIONED . . Ecstatic joy. Rapture. Shouting. Courage. Defiance. Alarm. Intense fear. Terror. Anger. Loathing.
ENERGETIC . . . . Laughter. Gaity. Bold and lofty appeal. Grandeur. Fear. Suppressed command. Contempt. Lyric description.
MODERATE Narration. Description. Didactic thought. Pathos. Solemnity. Sublimity. Devotion. Secrecy. Despair. Scorn.
SUBDUED . . . . . . Seriousness. Tranquillity. Fatigue. Weakness. Feebleness. Stillness. Awe. Profound repose.
c. STRESS
RADICAL . . . . . . Didactic thought. Patriotism. Impatience. Secrecy. Dread. Mirth. Rapture. Intense fear. Anger.
FINAL . . . . Surprise. Resolution. Determination. Stubbornness. Revenge. Hate. Scorn. Horror. Rage. Rebuke.
COMPOUND . . . . Irony. Mockery. Raillery. Ridicule. Satire. Taunt. Sarcasm. Derision. Contempt. Scoffing.
MEDIAN . . . . Pathos. Sadness. Melancholy. Stillness. Tranquillity. Reverence. Sublimity. Awe.
THOROUGH . . . . Defiance. Command. Triumph. Shouting. Calling. Indignation. Warning. Lofty appeal.
INTERMITTENT Grief. Tenderness. Feebleness. Senility. Sorrow. Timidity. Extreme pathos. Fright. Ecstatic joy.

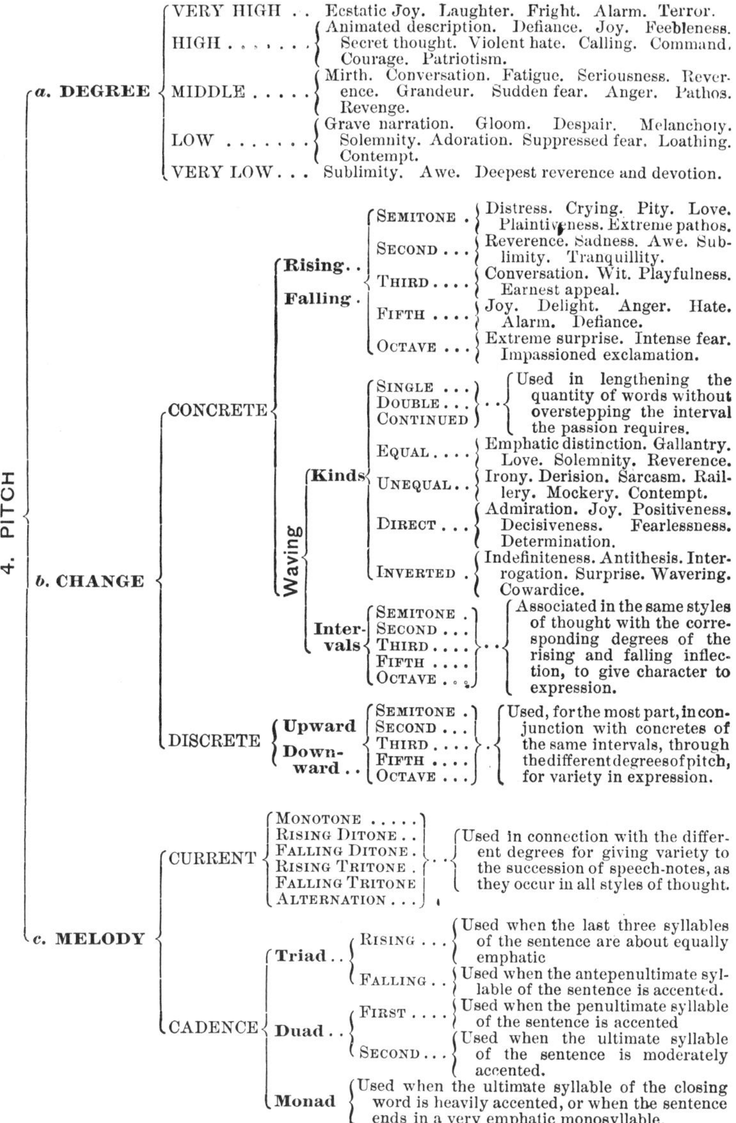

- **4. PITCH**
  - ***a.* DEGREE**
    - VERY HIGH . . Ecstatic Joy. Laughter. Fright. Alarm. Terror.
    - HIGH . . . . Animated description. Defiance. Joy. Feebleness. Secret thought. Violent hate. Calling. Command. Courage. Patriotism.
    - MIDDLE . . . . . Mirth. Conversation. Fatigue. Seriousness. Reverence. Grandeur. Sudden fear. Anger. Pathos. Revenge.
    - LOW . . . . Grave narration. Gloom. Despair. Melancholy. Solemnity. Adoration. Suppressed fear. Loathing. Contempt.
    - VERY LOW . . . Sublimity. Awe. Deepest reverence and devotion.
  - ***b.* CHANGE**
    - CONCRETE
      - **Rising. .** / **Falling .**
        - SEMITONE . Distress. Crying. Pity. Love. Plaintiveness. Extreme pathos.
        - SECOND . . . Reverence. Sadness. Awe. Sublimity. Tranquillity.
        - THIRD . . . . Conversation. Wit. Playfulness. Earnest appeal.
        - FIFTH . . . . Joy. Delight. Anger. Hate. Alarm. Defiance.
        - OCTAVE . . . Extreme surprise. Intense fear. Impassioned exclamation.
      - **Waving**
        - **Kinds**
          - SINGLE . . . / DOUBLE . . . / CONTINUED . . Used in lengthening the quantity of words without overstepping the interval the passion requires.
          - EQUAL . . . . Emphatic distinction. Gallantry. Love. Solemnity. Reverence.
          - UNEQUAL . . Irony. Derision. Sarcasm. Raillery. Mockery. Contempt.
          - DIRECT . . . Admiration. Joy. Positiveness. Decisiveness. Fearlessness. Determination.
          - INVERTED . Indefiniteness. Antithesis. Interrogation. Surprise. Wavering. Cowardice.
        - **Intervals**
          - SEMITONE . / SECOND . . . / THIRD . . . . / FIFTH . . . . / OCTAVE . . . . . Associated in the same styles of thought with the corresponding degrees of the rising and falling inflection, to give character to expression.
    - DISCRETE
      - **Upward** / **Downward . .**
        - SEMITONE . / SECOND . . . / THIRD . . . . / FIFTH . . . . / OCTAVE . . . . . Used, for the most part, in conjunction with concretes of the same intervals, through the different degrees of pitch, for variety in expression.
  - ***c.* MELODY**
    - CURRENT
      - MONOTONE . . . . . / RISING DITONE . . / FALLING DITONE . / RISING TRITONE . / FALLING TRITONE / ALTERNATION . . . . . Used in connection with the different degrees for giving variety to the succession of speech-notes, as they occur in all styles of thought.
    - CADENCE
      - **Triad . .**
        - RISING . . . Used when the last three syllables of the sentence are about equally emphatic
        - FALLING . . Used when the antepenultimate syllable of the sentence is accented.
      - **Duad . .**
        - FIRST . . . . Used when the penultimate syllable of the sentence is accented
        - SECOND . . . Used when the ultimate syllable of the sentence is moderately accented.
      - **Monad** Used when the ultimate syllable of the closing word is heavily accented, or when the sentence ends in a very emphatic monosyllable.

CHOICE READINGS.

I.

NARRATIVE, DESCRIPTIVE, DIDACTIC.

KNOWLEDGE AND WISDOM.

WILLIAM COWPER.

KNOWLEDGE and wisdom, far from being one,
Have ofttimes no connection. Knowledge dwells
In heads replete with thoughts of other men,
Wisdom in minds attentive to their own.
Knowledge, a rude unprofitable mass,
The mere materials with which wisdom builds,
Till smooth'd and squared and fitted to its place,
Does but encumber whom it seems t' enrich.
Knowledge is proud that he has learn'd so much;
Wisdom is humble that he knows no more.
Books are not seldom talismans and spells,
By which the magic art of shrewder wits
Holds an unthinking multitude enthrall'd.
Some to the fascination of a name
Surrender judgment hoodwink'd. Some the style
Infatuates, and through labyrinths and wilds
Of error leads them, by a tune entranced;
While sloth seduces more, too weak to bear
The insupportable fatigue of thought,
And swallowing therefore, without pause or choice,
The total grist unsifted, husks and all.
But trees, and rivulets whose rapid course

Defies the check of Winter, haunts of deer,
And sheepwalks populous with bleating lambs,
And lanes in which the primrose ere her time
Peeps through the moss that clothes the hawthorn root,
Deceive no student. Wisdom there, and Truth,
Not shy as in the world, and to be won
By slow solicitation, seize at once
The roving thought, and fix it on themselves.

ADAM'S ACCOUNT OF HIS CREATION.

JOHN MILTON.

FOR man to tell how human life began,
Is hard; for who himself beginning knew?
Desire with thee still longer to converse
Induced me. As new-waked from soundest sleep,
Soft on the flowery herb I found me laid,
In balmy sweat; which with his beams the Sun
Soon dried, and on the reeking moisture fed.
Straight towards heaven my wondering eyes I turn'd,
And gazed awhile the ample sky; till, raised
By quick instinctive motion, up I sprung,
As thitherward endeavouring, and upright
Stood on my feet. About me round I saw
Hill, dale, and shady woods, and sunny plains,
And liquid lapse of murmuring streams; by these,
Creatures that lived and moved, and walk'd or flew;
Birds on the branches warbling; all things smiled;
With fragrance and with joy my heart o'erflow'd.
Myself I then perused, and limb by limb
Survey'd; and sometimes went, and sometimes ran
With supple joints, as lively vigour led:
But who I was, or where, or from what cause,
Knew not. To speak I tried, and forthwith spake;
My tongue obey'd, and readily could name

Whate'er I saw. "Thou Sun," said I, "fair light,
And thou, enlighten'd Earth, so fresh and gay;
Ye hills and dales; ye rivers, woods, and plains;
And ye that live and move, fair creatures! tell,
Tell, if ye saw, how came I thus? how here?"

ADAM DESCRIBING THE CREATION OF EVE.

JOHN MILTON.

MINE eyes he closed, but open left the cell
Of fancy, my internal sight, by which
Abstract, as in a trance, methought I saw,
Though sleeping, where I lay, and saw the shape
Still glorious before whom awake I stood;
Who, stooping, open'd my left side, and took
From thence a rib, with cordial spirits warm,
And life-blood streaming fresh; wide was the wound,
But suddenly with flesh fill'd up and heal'd:
The rib he form'd and fashion'd with his hands;
Under his forming hands a creature grew,
Man-like, but different sex, so lovely fair,
That what seem'd fair in all the world seem'd now
Mean, or in her summ'd up, in her contain'd,
And in her looks; which from that time infused
Sweetness into my heart unfelt before,
And into all things, from her air, inspired
The spirit of love and amorous delight.
She disappear'd, and left me dark; I waked
To find her, or for ever to deplore
Her loss, and other pleasures all abjure;
When out of hope, behold her, not far off,
Such as I saw her in my dream, adorn'd
With all that Earth or Heaven could bestow
To make her amiable. On she came,
Led by her heavenly Maker, though unseen,

And guided by his voice; nor uninform'd
Of nuptial sanctity and marriage rites:
Grace was in all her steps, Heaven in her eye,
In every gesture dignity and love.
I, overjoy'd, could not forbear aloud:
"This turn hath made amends; Thou hast fulfill'd
Thy words, Creator bounteous and benign,
Giver of all things fair! but fairest this
Of all Thy gifts; nor enviest. I now see
Bone of my bone, flesh of my flesh, myself
Before me: Woman is her name, of man
Extracted: for this cause he shall forego
Father and mother, and to his wife adhere;
And they shall be one flesh, one heart, one soul."

ADVICE TO YOUNG LAWYERS.

JUDGE STORY.

WHENE'ER you speak, remember every cause
Stands not on eloquence, but stands on laws;
Pregnant in matter, in expression brief,
Let every sentence stand with bold relief;
On trifling points nor time nor talents waste,
A sad offense to learning and to taste;
Nor deal with pompous phrase, nor e'er suppose
Poetic flights belong to reasoning prose.

Loose declamation may deceive the crowd,
And seem more striking as it grows more loud;
But sober sense rejects it with disdain,
As nought but empty noise, and weak as vain.

The froth of words, the schoolboy's vain parade
Of books and cases, — all his stock in trade, —
The pert conceits, the cunning tricks and play
Of low attorneys, strung in long array,

Th' unseemly jest, the petulant reply,
That chatters on, and cares not how or why,
Strictly avoid; — unworthy themes to scan,
They sink the speaker and disgrace the man;
Like the false lights by flying shadows cast,
Scarce seen when present, and forgot when past.

Begin with dignity; expound with grace
Each ground of reasoning in its time and place;
Let order reign throughout; each topic touch,
Nor urge its power too little nor too much;
Give each strong thought its most attractive view,
In diction clear and yet severely true;
And, as the arguments in splendour grow,
Let each reflect its light on all below:
When to the close arrived, make no delays
By petty flourishes or verbal plays,
But sum the whole in one deep, solemn strain,
Like a strong current hastening to the main.

A CHILD'S DREAM OF A STAR.

CHARLES DICKENS.

THERE was once a child, and he strolled about a good deal, and thought of a number of things. He had a sister who was a child too, and his constant companion. They wondered at the beauty of flowers; they wondered at the height and blueness of the sky; they wondered at the depth of the water; they wondered at the goodness and power of God, who made them lovely.

They used to say to one another sometimes: Supposing all the children upon Earth were to die, would the flowers, and the water, and the sky be sorry? They believed they would be sorry. For, said they, the buds are the children of the flowers, and the little playful streams that gambol down the hillsides are the children of the water, and the smallest bright specks playing at hide and seek in the sky all night must surely be the children of the stars; and they would all be grieved to see their playmates, the children of men, no more.

There was one clear shining star that used to come out in the sky before the rest, near the church spire, above the graves. It was larger and more beautiful, they thought, than all the others, and every night they watched for it, standing hand-in-hand at a window. Whoever saw it first, cried out, "I see the star." And after that, they cried out both together, knowing so well when it would rise, and where. So they grew to be such friends with it that, before laying down in their bed, they always looked out once again to bid it good night; and when they were turning around to sleep, they used to say, "God bless the star!"

But while she was still very young, O, very young, the sister drooped, and came to be so weak that she could no longer stand in the window at night, and then the child looked sadly out by himself, and, when he saw the star, turned round and said to the patient pale face on the bed, "I see the star!" and then a smile would come upon the face, and a little weak voice used to say, "God bless my brother and the star!"

And so the time came, all too soon, when the child looked out all alone, and when there was no face on the bed, and when there was a grave among the graves, not there before, and when the star made long rays down toward him as he saw it through his tears.

Now these rays were so bright, and they seemed to make such a shining way from Earth to Heaven, that when the child went to his solitary bed, he dreamed about the star; and dreamed that, laying where he was, he saw a train of people taken up that sparkling road by angels; and the star, opening, showing him a great world of light, where many more such angels waited to receive them.

All these angels, who were waiting, turned their beaming eyes upon the people who were carried up into the star; and some came out from the long rows in which they stood, and fell upon the people's necks, and kissed them tenderly, and went away with them down avenues of light, and were so happy in their company, that lying in his bed he wept for joy.

But there were many angels who did not go with them, and among them one he knew. The patient face that once had lain upon the bed was glorified and radiant, but his heart found out his sister among all the host.

His sister's angel lingered near the entrance of the star, and said to the leader among those who had brought the people thither,

"Is my brother come?"

And he said, "No!"

She was turning hopefully away, when the child stretched out his arms, and cried, "O, sister, I am here! Take me!" And then she turned her beaming eyes upon him,—and it was night; and the star was shining into the room, making long rays down towards him as he saw it through his tears.

From that hour forth, the child looked out upon the star as the home he was to go to when his time should come; and he thought that he did not belong to the Earth alone, but to the star too, because of his sister's angel gone before.

There was a baby born to be a brother to the child, and, while he was so little that he never yet had spoken a word, he stretched out his tiny form on his bed, and died.

Again the child dreamed of the opened star, and of the company of angels, and the train of people, and the rows of angels, with their beaming eyes all turned upon those people's faces.

Said his sister's angel to the leader,

"Is my brother come?"

And he said, "Not that one, but another!"

As the child beheld his brother's angel in her arms, he cried, "O, my sister, I am here! Take me!" And she turned and smiled upon him,—and the star was shining.

He grew to be a young man, and was busy at his books, when an old servant came to him and said,

"Thy mother is no more. I bring her blessing on her darling son."

Again at night he saw the star, and all that former company. Said his sister's angel to the leader, "Is my brother come?"

And he said, "Thy mother!"

A mighty cry of joy went forth through all the star, because the mother was re-united to her two children. And he stretched out his arms and cried, "O, mother, sister, and brother, I am here! Take me!" And they answered him, "Not yet!"—and the star was shining.

He grew to be a man, whose hair was turning gray, and he was sitting in his chair by the fireside, heavy with grief, and with his face bedewed with tears, when the star opened once again.

Said his sister's angel to the leader, "Is my brother come?"

And he said, "Nay, but his maiden daughter!"

And the man who had been the child saw his daughter,

newly lost to him, a celestial creature among those three, and he said, "My daughter's head is on my sister's bosom, and her arm is around my mother's neck, and at her feet is the baby of old time, and I can bear the parting from her, God be praised!"—And the star was shining.

Thus the child came to be an old man, and his once smooth face was wrinkled, and his steps were slow and feeble, and his back was bent. And one night as he lay upon his bed, his children standing round, he cried, as he cried so long ago, "I see the star!"

They whispered one another, "He is dying." And he said, "I am. My age is falling from me like a garment, and I move towards the star as a child. And, O my Father, now I thank Thee that it has so often opened to receive those dear ones who await me!"

And the star was shining; and it shines upon his grave.

DESTRUCTION OF POMPEII.

LORD EDWARD BULWER-LYTTON.

THE cloud, which had scattered so deep a murkiness over the day, had now settled into a solid and impenetrable mass. It resembled less even the thickest gloom of a night in the open air than the close and blind darkness of some narrow room. But, in proportion as the blackness gathered, did the lightnings around Vesuvius increase in their vivid and scorching glare. Nor was their horrible beauty confined to the usual hues of fire; no rainbow ever rivalled their varying and prodigal dyes. Now brightly blue as the most azure depth of a southern sky,—now of a livid and snake-like green, darting restlessly to and fro as the folds of an enormous serpent, — now of a lurid and intolerable crimson, gushing forth through the columns of smoke, far and wide, and lighting up the whole city from arch to arch, — then suddenly dying into a sickly paleness, like the ghost of their own life!

In the pauses of the showers you heard the rumbling of the earth beneath, and the groaning waves of the tortured sea; or, lower still, and audible but to the watch of intensest fear, the grinding and hissing murmur of the escaping gases through the chasms of the distant mountain. Sometimes the cloud appeared to break from its solid mass, and, by the lightning, to assume quaint and vast mimicries of human or of monster shapes, striding across the gloom, hurtling one upon the other, and vanishing swiftly into the turbulent abyss of shade; so that, to the eyes and fancies of the affrighted wanderers, the unsubstantial vapours were as the bodily forms of gigantic foes, — the agents of terror and death.

The ashes in many places were already knee-deep; and the boiling showers which came from the steaming breath of the volcano forced their way into the houses, bearing with them a strong and suffocating vapour. In some places immense fragments of rock, hurled upon the house roofs, bore down along the streets masses of confused ruin, which yet more and more, with every hour, obstructed the way; and, as the day advanced, the motion of the earth was more sensibly felt; the footing seemed to slide and creep, nor could chariot or litter be kept steady, even on the most level ground.

Sometimes the huger stones, striking against each other as they fell, broke into countless fragments, emitting sparks of fire, which caught whatever was combustible within their reach; and along the plain beyond the city the darkness was now terribly relieved; for several houses, and even vineyards, had been set on flames; and at various intervals the fires rose sullenly and fiercely against the solid gloom. To add to this partial relief of the darkness, the citizens had, here and there, in the more public places, such as the porticos of temples and the entrances to the forum, endeavoured to place rows of torches; but these rarely continued long; the showers and the winds extinguished them, and the sudden darkness into which their fitful light was converted had something in it doubly terrible and doubly impressive on the impotence of human hopes, the lesson of despair.

Frequently, by the momentary light of these torches, parties of fugitives encountered each other, some hurrying towards the sea, others flying from the sea back to the land; for the ocean had retreated rapidly from the shore; an utter darkness lay over it, and, upon its groaning and tossing waves, the storm of cinders and rocks fell without the protection which the streets and roofs afforded to the land. Wild, haggard, ghastly with supernatural fears, these groups encountered each other, but without the leisure to speak, to consult, to advise; for the showers fell now frequently, though not continuously, extinguishing the lights, which showed to each band the death-like faces of the other, and hurrying all to seek refuge beneath the nearest shelter.

The whole elements of civilization were broken up. Ever and anon, by the flickering lights, you saw the thief hastening by the most solemn authorities of the law, laden with, and fearfully chuckling over the produce of his sudden gains. If, in the darkness, wife was separated from husband, or parent from child, vain was the hope of reunion. Each hurried blindly and confusedly on. Nothing in all the various and complicated machinery of social life was left save the primal law of self-preservation.

A BEE-HUNT IN THE FAR WEST.

WASHINGTON IRVING.

WE had not been long in the camp when a party set out in quest of a bee-tree, and, being curious to witness the sport, I gladly accepted an invitation to accompany them. The party was headed by a veteran bee-hunter, a tall, lank fellow in home-spun garb that hung loosely about his limbs, and a straw hat shaped not unlike a bee-hive; a comrade, equally uncouth in garb, and without a hat, straddled along at his heels, with a long rifle on his shoulder. To these succeeded half a dozen others, some with axes and some with rifles, for no one stirs far from the camp without his firearm, so as to be ready either for wild deer or wild Indian.

After proceeding some distance we came to an open glade on the skirts of the forest. Here our leader halted, and then advanced quietly to a low bush, on the top of which I perceived a piece of honey-comb. This I found was the bait or lure for the wild bees. Several were humming about it, and diving into its cells. When they had laden themselves with honey they would rise into the air, and dart off in a straight line almost with the velocity of a bullet. The hunters watched attentively the course they took, and then set off in the same direction, stumbling along over twisted roots and fallen trees, with their eyes turned up to the sky. In this way they traced the honey-laden bees to their hive, in the hollow trunk of a blasted oak, where, after buzzing about for a moment, they entered a hole about sixty feet from the ground.

Two of the bee-hunters now plied their axes vigorously at the foot of the tree, to level it with the ground. The mere spectators and amateurs, in the meantime, drew off to a cautious distance, to be out of the way of the falling of the tree and the vengeance of its inmates. The jarring blows of the axe seemed to have no effect in alarming or disturbing this most industrious community. They continued to ply at their usual occupations, some arriving full-freighted into port, others sallying forth on new expeditions, like so many merchantmen in a money-making metropolis, little suspicious of impending bankruptcy and downfall. Even a loud crack which announced the disrupture of the trunk failed to divert their attention from the intense pursuit of gain; at length down came the tree with a tremendous crash, bursting open from end to end, and displaying all the hoarded treasures of the commonwealth.

One of the hunters immediately ran up with a wisp of lighted hay as a defense against the bees. The latter, however, made no attack and sought no revenge; they seemed stupefied by the catastrophe and unsuspicious of its cause, and remained crawling and buzzing about the ruins without offering us any molestations. Every one of the party now fell to, with spoon and hunting-knife, to scoop out the flakes of honey-comb with which the hollow trunk was stored. Some of them were of old date and a deep brown color; others were beautifully white, and the honey in their cells was almost limpid. Such of the combs as were entire were placed in camp-kettles, to be conveyed to the encampment; those which had been shivered in the fall were devoured upon the spot. Every stark bee-hunter was to be seen with a rich morsel in his hand, dripping about his fingers, and disappearing as rapidly as a cream tart before the holiday appetite of a school-boy.

Nor was it the bee-hunters alone that profited by the downfall of this industrious community; as if the bees would carry through the similitude of their habits with those of laborious and gainful man. I beheld numbers from rival hives arriving on eager wing, to enrich themselves with the ruins of their neighbours. These busied themselves as eagerly and cheerfully as so many wreckers on an Indiaman that has been driven on shore; plunging into the cells of the broken honey-combs, banqueting greedily on the spoil, and then winging their way full-freighted to their homes. As to the poor proprietors of the ruin, they seemed to have no heart to do any thing, not even to taste the nectar that flowed around them; but crawled backwards and forwards, in vacant desolation, as I have seen a poor fellow with his hands in his pockets, whistling vacantly and despondingly about the ruins of his house that had been burnt.

It is difficult to describe the bewilderment and confusion of the bees of the bankrupt hive who had been absent at the time of the catastrophe, and who arrived from time to time with full cargoes from abroad. At first they wheeled about in the air, in the place where the fallen tree had once reared its head, astonished at finding it all a vacuum. At length, as if comprehending their disaster, they settled down in clusters on a dry branch of a neighbouring tree, whence they seemed to contemplate the prostrate ruin, and to buzz forth doleful lamentations over the downfall of their republic.

A GOOD CONSCIENCE.

ANONYMOUS.

MY mind to me a kingdom is;
  Such perfect joy therein I find
As far exceeds all earthly bliss,
  That God or Nature hath assign'd:
Though much I want, that most would have,
Yet still my mind forbids to crave.

Content I live, this is my stay;
  I seek no more than may suffice:
I press to bear no haughty sway;
  Look, what I lack, my mind supplies.
Lo! thus I triumph like a king,
Content with what my mind doth bring.

I see how plenty surfeits oft,
  And hasty climbers soonest fall;
I see that such as sit aloft
  Mishap doth threaten most of all:
These get with toil, and keep with fear;
Such cares my mind could never bear.

Some have too much, yet still they crave;
  I little have, yet seek no more:
They are but poor, though much they have;
  And I am rich with little store:
They poor, I rich; they beg, I give;
They lack, I lend; they pine, I live.

I laugh not at another's loss,
  I grudge not at another's gain;
No worldly wave my mind can toss,
  I brook what is another's bane:
I fear no foe, nor fawn on friend:
I loathe not life, nor dread my end.

I wish but what I have at will;
  I wander not to seek for more;
I like the plain, I climb no hill:
  In greater storms I sit on shore,
And laugh at them that toil in vain
To get what must be lost again.

I kiss not where I wish to kill;
  I feign not love where most I hate;
I break no sleep to win my will;
  I wait not at the mighty's gate;
I scorn no poor, I fear no rich;
I feel no want, nor have too much.

My wealth is health and perfect ease;
  My conscience clear my chief defence:
I never seek by bribes to please,
  Nor by desert to give offence.
Thus do I live, thus will I die;
Would all did live so well as I!

ELEGY WRITTEN IN A COUNTRY CHURCHYARD.

THOMAS GRAY.

THE curfew tolls the knell of parting day,
The lowing herd winds slowly o'er the lea,
The ploughman homeward plods his weary way,
And leaves the world to darkness and to me.

Now fades the glimmering landscape on the sight,
And all the air a solemn stillness holds,
Save where the beetle wheels his droning flight,
And drowsy tinklings lull the distant folds;

Save that, from yonder ivy-mantled tower,
The moping owl does to the Moon complain
Of such as, wandering near her secret bower,
Molest her ancient solitary reign.

Beneath those rugged elms, that yew-tree's shade,
Where heaves the turf in many a mouldering heap,
Each in his narrow cell for ever laid,
The rude forefathers of the hamlet sleep.

The breezy call of incense-breathing morn,
The swallow twittering from the straw-built shed,
The cock's shrill clarion, or the echoing horn,
No more shall rouse them from their lowly bed.

For them no more the blazing hearth shall burn,
Or busy housewife ply her evening care;
No children run to lisp their sire's return,
Or climb his knees, the envied kiss to share.

Oft did the harvest to their sickle yield,
Their furrow oft the stubborn glebe has broke;
How jocund did they drive their team afield!
How bow'd the woods beneath their sturdy stroke!

Let not Ambition mock their useful toil,
Their homely joys and destiny obscure;
Nor Grandeur hear with a disdainful smile
The short and simple annals of the poor.

The boast of heraldry, the pomp of power,
And all that beauty, all that wealth e'er gave,
Await alike th' inevitable hour:—
The paths of glory lead but to the grave.

Nor you, ye proud, impute to these the fault,
If memory o'er their tomb no trophies raise,
Where through the long-drawn aisle and fretted vault
The pealing anthem swells the note of praise.

Can storied urn or animated bust
Back to its mansion call the fleeting breath?
Can Honour's voice provoke the silent dust,
Or Flattery soothe the dull, cold ear of Death?

Perhaps in this neglected spot is laid
Some heart once pregnant with celestial fire;
Hands that the rod of empire might have sway'd,
Or waked to ecstasy the living lyre.

But Knowledge to their eyes her ample page,
Rich with the spoils of time, did ne'er unroll;
Chill Penury repress'd their noble rage,
And froze the genial current of the soul.

Full many a gem of purest ray serene
The dark, unfathom'd caves of ocean bear;
Full many a flower is born to blush unseen,
And waste its sweetness on the desert air.

Some village Hampden, that with dauntless breast
The little tyrant of his fields withstood,
Some mute, inglorious Milton here may rest;
Some Cromwell, guiltless of his country's blood.

Th' applause of listening senates to command,
The threats of pain and ruin to despise,
To scatter plenty o'er a smiling land,
And read their history in a nation's eyes,

Their lot forbade; nor circumscribed alone
Their growing virtues, but their crimes confined;
Forbade to wade through slaughter to a throne,
And shut the gates of mercy on mankind;

The struggling pangs of conscious truth to hide,
To quench the blushes of ingenuous shame,
Or heap the shrine of luxury and pride
With incense kindled at the Muse's flame.

Far from the madding crowd's ignoble strife,
Their sober wishes never learn'd to stray;
Along the cool, sequester'd vale of life
They kept the noiseless tenour of their way.

Yet e'en these bones from insult to protect,
Some frail memorial still erected nigh,
With uncouth rhymes and shapeless sculpture deck'd,
Implores the passing tribute of a sigh.

Their names, their years, spelt by th' unletter'd Muse,
The place of fame and elegy supply;
And many a holy text around she strews,
That teach the rustic moralist to die.

For who, to dumb forgetfulness a prey,
Their pleasing, anxious being e'er resign'd,
Left the warm precincts of the cheerful day,
Nor cast one longing, lingering look behind?

On some fond breast the parting soul relies,
Some pious drops the closing eye requires;
E'en from the tomb the voice of Nature cries,
E'en in our ashes live their wonted fires.

For thee, who, mindful of th' unhonour'd dead,
Dost in these lines their artless tale relate,
If, 'chance, by lonely contemplation led,
Some kindred spirit shall inquire thy fate, —

Haply some hoary-headed swain may say,
"Oft have we seen him, at the peep of dawn,
Brushing with hasty steps the dews away,
To meet the Sun upon the upland lawn.

There, at the foot of yonder nodding beech
That wreathes its old fantastic roots so high,
His listless length at noontide would he stretch,
And pore upon the brook that babbles by.

Hard by yon wood, now smiling as in scorn,
Muttering his wayward fancies, he would rove,
Now drooping, woeful-wan, like one forlorn,
Or crazed with care, or cross'd in hopeless love.

One morn I miss'd him on the custom'd hill,
Along the heath, and near his favourite tree:
Another came; nor yet beside the rill,
Nor up the lawn, nor at the wood was he:

The next, with dirges due, in sad array,
Slow through the churchway-path we saw him borne.
Approach, and read (for thou canst read) the lay
Graved on the stone beneath yon agèd thorn."

There scatter'd oft, the earliest of the year,
By hands unseen, are showers of violets found;
The redbreast loves to build and warble there,
And little footsteps lightly print the ground.

THE EPITAPH.

Here rests his head, upon the lap of Earth,
A youth to fortune and to fame unknown;
Fair Science frown'd not on his humble birth,
And Melancholy mark'd him for her own.

Large was his bounty, and his soul sincere;
Heaven did a recompense as largely send:
He gave to misery, all he had, a tear, —
He gain'd from Heaven ('twas all he wish'd) a friend.

No further seek his merits to disclose,
Or draw his frailties from their dread abode,
(There they alike in trembling hope repose,)
The bosom of his Father and his God.

THE FIRST SETTLER'S STORY.

WILL CARLETON.

WELL, when I first infested this retreat,
Things to my view look'd frightful incomplete;
But I had come with heart-thrift in my song,
And brought my wife and plunder right along;

I hadn't a round-trip ticket to go back,
And if I had there was no railroad track;
And drivin' East was what I couldn't endure:
I hadn't started on a circular tour.

My girl-wife was as brave as she was good,
And help'd me every blessèd way she could;
She seem'd to take to every rough old tree,
As sing'lar as when first she took to me.
She kep' our little log-house neat as wax,
And once I caught her fooling with my axe.
She hadn't the muscle (though she *had* the heart)
In out-door work to take an active part;
She *was* delicious, both to hear and see, —
That pretty girl-wife that kep' house for me.

Well, neighbourhoods meant counties in those days;
The roads didn't have accommodating ways;
And maybe weeks would pass before she'd see —
And much less talk with — any one but me.
The Indians sometimes show'd their sun-baked faces,
But they didn't teem with conversational graces;
Some ideas from the birds and trees she stole,
But 'twasn't like talking with a human soul;
And finally I thought that I could trace
A half heart-hunger peering from her face.

One night, when I came home unusual late,
Too hungry and too tired to feel first-rate,
Her supper struck me wrong, (though I'll allow
She hadn't much to strike with, anyhow);
And, when I went to milk the cows, and found
They'd wander'd from their usual feeding ground,
And maybe'd left a few long miles behind 'em,
Which I must copy, if I meant to find 'em,
Flash-quick the stay-chains of my temper broke,
And in a trice these hot words I had spoke:

"You ought to've kept the animals in view,
And drove 'em in; you'd nothing else to do.
The heft of all our life on me must fall;
You just lie round, and let me do it all."

That speech, — it hadn't been gone a half a minute
Before I saw the cold black poison in it;
And I'd have given all I had, and more,
To've only safely got it back in-door.
I'm now what most folks "well-to-do" would call:
I feel to-day as if I'd give it all,
Provided I through fifty years might reach
And kill and bury that half-minute speech.

She handed back no words, as I could hear;
She didn't frown; she didn't shed a tear;
Half proud, half crush'd, she stood and look'd me o'er,
Like some one she had never seen before!
But such a sudden anguish-lit surprise
I never view'd before in human eyes.
(I've seen it oft enough since in a dream;
It sometimes wakes me like a midnight scream.)

Next morning, when, stone-faced but heavy-hearted,
With dinner-pail and sharpen'd axe I started
Away for my day's work, she watch'd the door,
And follow'd me half way to it or more;
And I was just a-turning round at this,
And asking for my usual good-by kiss;
But on her lip I saw a proudish curve,
And in her eye a shadow of reserve;
And she had shown — perhaps half unawares —
Some little independent breakfast airs;
And so the usual parting didn't occur,
Although her eyes invited me to her;
Or rather half invited me, for she
Didn't advertise to furnish kisses free:

You always had — that is, I had — to pay
Full market price, and go more'n half the way.
So, with a short "Good-bye," I shut the door,
And left her as I never had before.
But, when at noon my lunch I came to eat,
Put up by her so delicately neat, —
Choicer, somewhat, than yesterday's had been,
And some fresh, sweet-eyed pansies she'd put in, —
"Tender and pleasant thoughts," I knew they meant, —
It seem'd as if her kiss with me she'd sent;
Then I became once more her humble lover,
And said, "To-night I'll ask forgiveness of her."

I went home over-early on that eve,
Having contrived to make myself believe,
By various signs I kind o' knew and guess'd,
A thunder-storm was coming from the west.
('Tis strange, when one sly reason fills the heart,
How many honest ones will take its part:
A dozen first-class reasons said 'twas right
That I should strike home early on that night.)

Half out of breath, the cabin door I swung,
With tender heart-words trembling on my tongue;
But all within look'd desolate and bare:
My house had lost its soul, — she was not there!
A pencil'd note was on the table spread,
And these are something like the words it said:
"The cows have stray'd away again, I fear;
I watch'd them pretty close; don't scold me, dear.
And where they are I think I *nearly* know;
I heard the bell not very long ago.
I've hunted for them all the afternoon;
I'll try once more, — I think I'll find them soon.
Dear, if a burden I have been to you,
And haven't help'd you as I ought to do,
Let old-time memories my forgiveness plead;
I've tried to do my best, — I have, indeed.

Darling, piece out with love the strength I lack,
And have kind words for me when I get back."

Scarce did I give this letter sight and tongue, —
Some swift-blown rain-drops to the window clung,
And from the clouds a rough, deep growl proceeded:
My thunder-storm had come, now 'twasn't needed.
I rush'd out-door. The air was stain'd with black:
Night had come early, on the storm-cloud's back:
And every thing kept dimming to the sight,
Save when the clouds threw their electric light;
When, for a flash, so clean-cut was the view,
I'd think I saw her, — knowing 'twas not true.
Through my small clearing dash'd wide sheets of spray,
As if the ocean waves had lost their way;
Scarcely a pause the thunder-battle made,
In the bold clamour of its cannonade.
And she, while I was shelter'd, dry, and warm,
Was somewhere in the clutches of this storm!
She who, when storm-frights found her at her best,
Had always hid her white face on my breast!

My dog, who'd skirmish'd round me all the day,
Now crouch'd and whimpering, in a corner lay;
I dragg'd him by the collar to the wall,
I press'd his quivering muzzle to a shawl, —
"Track her, old boy!" I shouted; and he whined,
Match'd eyes with me, as if to read my mind,
Then with a yell went tearing through the wood.
I follow'd him, as faithful as I could.
No pleasure-trip was that, through flood and flame;
We raced with death; we hunted noble game.
All night we dragg'd the woods without avail;
The ground got drench'd, — we could not keep the trail.
Three times again my cabin home I found,
Half hoping she might be there, safe and sound;
But each time 'twas an unavailing care:
My house had lost its soul; she was not there!

When, climbing the wet trees, next morning-sun
Laugh'd at the ruin that the night had done,
Bleeding and drench'd, by toil and sorrow bent,
Back to what used to be my home I went.
But, as I near'd our little clearing-ground, —
Listen! — I heard the cow-bell's tinkling sound.
The cabin door was just a bit ajar;
It gleam'd upon my glad eyes like a star.
"Brave heart," I said, "for such a fragile form!
She made them guide her homeward through the storm!"
Such pangs of joy I never felt before.
"You've come!" I shouted, and rush'd through the door.

Yes, she had come, — and gone again. She lay
With all her young life crush'd and wrench'd away, —
Lay, the heart-ruins of our home among,
Not far from where I kill'd her with my tongue.
The rain-drops glitter'd 'mid her hair's long strands,
The forest thorns had torn her feet and hands,
And 'midst the tears — brave tears — that one could trace
Upon the pale but sweetly resolute face,
I once again the mournful words could read,
"I've tried to do my best, — I have, indeed."

And now I'm mostly done; my story's o'er;
Part of it never breathed the air before.
'Tisn't over-usual, it must be allow'd,
To volunteer heart-story to a crowd,
And scatter 'mongst them confidential tears,
But you'll protect an old man with his years;
And wheresoe'er this story's voice can reach,
This is the sermon I would have it preach:

Boys flying kites haul in their white-wing'd birds:
You can't do that way when you're flying words.
"Careful with fire," is good advice we know:
"Careful with words," is ten times doubly so.

Thoughts unexpress'd may sometimes fall back dead,
But God himself can't kill them when they're said!
You have my life-grief: do not think a minute
'Twas told to take up time. There's business in it.
It sheds advice: whoe'er will take and live it,
Is welcome to the pain it costs to give it.

THE BLIND FIDDLER.

WILLIAM WORDSWORTH.

An Orpheus! an Orpheus! Yes, Faith may grow bold,
And take to herself all the wonders of old;—
Near the stately Panthéon you'll meet with the same,
In the street that from Oxford hath borrow'd its name.

His station is there; and he works on the crowd,
He sways them with harmony merry and loud;
He fills with his power all their hearts to the brim,—
Was aught ever heard like his fiddle and him?

What an eager assembly! what an empire is this!
The weary have life, and the hungry have bliss;
The mourner is cheer'd, and the anxious have rest;
And the guilt-burthen'd soul is no longer opprest.

As the Moon brightens round her the clouds of the night,
So he, where he stands, is a centre of light;
It gleams on the face, there, of dusky-brow'd Jack,
And the pale-visaged Baker's, with basket on back.

That errand-bound 'Prentice was passing in haste,—
What matter! he's caught, and his time runs to waste;
The Newsman is stopp'd, though he stops on the fret;
And the half-breathless Lamplighter, he's in the net!

The Porter sits down on the weight which he bore;
The Lass with her barrow wheels hither her store;—

If a thief could be here he might pilfer at ease;
She sees the Musician, 'tis all that she sees!

He stands, back'd by the wall; — he abates not his din;
His hat gives him vigour, with boons dropping in,
From the old and the young, from the poorest; and there!
The one-pennied Boy has his penny to spare.

O, blest are the hearers, and proud be the hand
Of the pleasure it spreads through so thankful a band;
I am glad for him, blind as he is! — all the while
If they speak, 'tis to praise, and they praise with a smile.

That tall Man, a giant in bulk and in height,
Not an inch of his body is free from delight;
Can he keep himself still, if he would? O, not he!
The music stirs in him like wind through a tree.

Mark that Cripple who leans on his crutch; like a tower
That long has lean'd forward, leans hour after hour! —
That Mother, whose spirit in fetters is bound,
While she dandles the Babe in her arms to the sound.

Now, coaches and chariots! roar on like a stream;
Here are twenty souls happy as souls in a dream:
They are deaf to your murmurs, — they care not for you,
Nor what ye are flying, nor what ye pursue!

HISTORY.

James Anthony Froude.

At the dawn of civilization, when men began to observe and think, they found themselves in possession of various faculties, — first their five senses, and then imagination, fancy, reason, and memory. They did not distinguish one from the other. They did not know why one idea of which they were conscious should be more true than another. They looked round them in continual surprise, conjecturing fantastic explanations of all they saw and heard. Their traditions and their theories blended one into another, and their cosmogonies, their philosophies, and their histories are all alike imaginative and poetical. It was never perhaps seriously believed as a scientific reality that the Sun was the chariot of Apollo, or that Saturn had devoured his children, or that Siegfred had been bathed in the dragon's blood, or that earthquakes and volcanoes were caused by buried giants, who were snorting and tossing in their sleep; but also it was not disbelieved.

The original historian and the original man of science was alike the poet. Before the art of writing was invented, exact knowledge was impossible. The poet's business was to throw into beautiful shapes the current opinions, traditions, and beliefs; and the gifts required of him were simply memory, imagination, and music. Each celebrated minstrel sang his stories in his own way, adding to them, shaping them, colouring them, as suited his peculiar genius. The *Iliad* of Homer, the most splendid composition of this kind which exists in the world, is simply a collection of ballads. The tale of Troy was the heroic story of Greece, which every tribe modified or re-arranged.

The chronicler is not a poet like his predecessor. He does not shape out consistent pictures with a beginning, a middle, and an end. He is a narrator of events and he connects them on a chronological string. He professes to be relating facts. He is not idealizing; he is not singing the praises of heroes; he means to be true in the literal and commonplace sense of that ambiguous word.

Neither history nor any other knowledge can be obtained except by scientific methods. A constructive philosophy of it, however, is as yet impossible, and for the present, and for a long time to come, we shall be confined to analysis. First one cause and then another has interfered from the beginning of time with a correct and authentic chronicling of events and actions. Superstition, hero-worship, ignorance of the laws of probability, religious, political, or speculative prejudice, — one or other of these has tended from the beginning to give us distorted pictures.

The most perfect English history which exists is to be found, in my opinion, in the historical plays of Shakespeare. In these plays, rich as they are in fancy and imagination, the main bearings of the national story are scrupulously adhered to, and, whenever attainable, with verbal correctness. Shakespeare's object was to exhibit as faithfully as he possibly could the exact character of the great actors in the national drama, the circumstances which attended them, and the motives, internal and external, by which they were influenced. Shakespeare's attitude towards human life will become again attainable to us only when intelligent people can return to an agreement on first principles; when the common sense of the wisest and best among us has superseded the theorizing of parties and factions; when the few but all-important truths of our moral condition, which can be certainly known, have become the exclusive rule of our judgments and actions.

CHRISTMAS EVE IN THE OLDEN TIME.

SIR WALTER SCOTT.

HEAP on more wood! — The wind is chill;
But, let it whistle as it will,
We'll keep our merry Christmas still:
Each age has deem'd the new-born year
The fittest time for festal cheer.

And well our Christian sires of old
Loved when the year its course had roll'd,
And brought blithe Christmas back again,
With all his hospitable train.
Domestic and religious rite
Gave honour to the holy night:
On Christmas eve the bells were rung;
On Christmas eve the Mass was sung;
The only night, in all the year,
Saw the stoled priest the chalice rear.
The damsel donn'd her kirtle sheen;
The hall was dress'd with holly green;
Forth to the wood did merry men go,
To gather in the mistletoe.

Then open'd wide the Baron's hall
To vassal, tenant, serf, and all;
Power laid his rod of rule aside,
And Ceremony doff'd her pride.
The heir, with roses in his shoes,
That night might village partner choose;
The lord, underogating, share
The regular game of "Past and Pair."
All hail'd, with uncontroll'd delight
And general voice, the happy night,
That to the cottage, as the Crown,
Brought tidings of salvation down.

The fire, with well-dried logs supplied,
Went roaring up the chimney wide;
The huge hall-table's oaken face,
Scrubb'd till it shone, the day to grace,
Bore then upon its massive board
No marks to part the squire and lord.
Then was brought in the lusty brawn,
By old blue-coated serving-man;
Then the grim boar's-head frown'd on high,
Crested with bays and rosemary.

Well can the green-garb'd ranger tell
How, when, and where the monster fell;
What dogs before his death he tore,
And all the baiting of the boar.

The vassal round, in good brown bowls
Garnish'd with ribbons, blithely trowls.
There the huge surloin reek'd; hard by
Plum-porridge stood, and Christmas pie;
Nor fail'd old Scotland to produce,
At such high tide, her savoury goose.
Then came the merry masquers in,
And carols roar'd with blithesome din;
If unmelodious was the song,
It was a hearty note, and strong.

Who lists may in their murmuring see
Traces of ancient mystery:
White shirts supplied the masquerade,
And smutted cheeks the visors made;
But, O, what masquers, richly dight,
Can boast of bosoms half so light!
England was merry England, when
Old Christmas brought his sports again.
'Twas Christmas broach'd the mightiest ale,
'Twas Christmas told the merriest tale;
A Christmas gambol oft could cheer
The poor man's heart through half the year.

NO SECTS IN HEAVEN.

Mrs. E. H. J. Cleaveland.

Talking of sects till late one eve,
Of the various doctrines the saints believe,
That night I stood, in a troubled dream,
By the side of a darkly flowing stream.

And a Churchman down to the river came;
When I heard a strange voice call his name,
"Good father, stop; when you cross this tide,
You must leave your robes on the other side."

But the agèd father did not mind;
And his long gown floated out behind,
As down to the stream his way he took,
His pale hands clasping a gilt-edged book:

"I'm bound for Heaven; and, when I'm there,
Shall want my Book of Common Prayer;
And, though I put on a starry crown,
I should feel quite lost without my gown."

Then he fix'd his eyes on the shining track,
But his gown was heavy and held him back,
And the poor old father tried in vain
A single step in the flood to gain.

I saw him again on the other side,
But his silk gown floated on the tide;
And no one ask'd, in that blissful spot,
Whether he belong'd to "*the* Church" or not.

Then down to the river a Quaker stray'd;
His dress of a sober hue was made:
"My coat and hat must all be gray, —
I cannot go any other way."

Then he button'd his coat straight up to his chin,
And staidly, solemnly, waded in,
And his broad-brimm'd hat he pull'd down tight,
Over his forehead so cold and white.

But a strong wind carried away his hat;
A moment he silently sigh'd over that;
And then, as he gazed on the further shore,
His coat slipp'd off, and was seen no more;

As he enter'd Heaven, his suit of gray
Went quietly, sailing, away, away;
And none of the angels question'd him
About the width of his beaver's brim.

Next came Dr. Watts, with a bundle of psalms
Tied nicely up in his agèd arms,
And hymns as many, — a very wise thing, —
That the people in Heaven, "all round," might sing.

But I thought that he heaved an anxious sigh,
When he saw that the river ran broad and high,
And look'd rather surprised, as one by one
The psalms and hymns in the wave went down.

And after him, with his MSS.,
Came Wesley, the pattern of godliness;
But he cried, "Dear me! what shall I do?
The water has soak'd them through and through."

And there on the river, far and wide,
Away they went down the swollen tide;
And the saint, astonish'd, pass'd through alone,
Without his manuscripts, up to the throne.

Then, gravely walking, two saints by name
Down to the river together came;
But, as they stopp'd at the river's brink,
I saw one saint from the other shrink.

"Sprinkled or plunged? may I ask you, friend,
How you attain'd to life's great end?"
"*Thus*, with a few drops on my brow."
"But *I* have been dipp'd, as you'll see me now;

And I really think it will hardly do,
As I'm 'close communion,' to cross with you:
You're bound, I know, to the realms of bliss,
But you must go that way, and I'll go this."

Then straightway plunging with all his might,
Away to the left,—his friend to the right,—
Apart they went from this world of sin,
But at last together they enter'd in.

And now, when the river was rolling on,
A Presbyterian Church went down;
Of women there seem'd an innumerable throng,
But the men I could count as they pass'd along.

And concerning the road they could never agree,
The *old* or the *new* way, which it could be,
Nor ever a moment paused to think
That both would lead to the river's brink.

And a sound of murmuring, long and loud,
Came ever up from the moving crowd:
"You're in the old way, and I'm in the new;
That is the false, and this is the true":
Or, "I'm in the old way, and you're in the new;
That is the false, and *this* is the true."

But the *brethren* only seem'd to speak:
Modest the sisters walk'd and meek,
And, if one of them ever chanced to say
What troubles she met with on the way,
How she long'd to pass to the other side,
Nor fear'd to cross over the swelling tide,
A voice arose from the brethren then:
"Let no one speak but the 'holy men';
For have ye not heard the words of Paul,
'O, let the women keep silence all'?"

I watch'd them long in my curious dream,
Till they stood by the borders of the stream:
Then, just as I thought, the two ways met;
But all the brethren were talking yet,
And would talk on till the heaving tide
Carried them over side by side,—
Side by side, for the way was one:
The toilsome journey of life was done;
And all who in Christ the Saviour died
Came out alike on the other side.

No forms or crosses or books had they;
No gowns of silk or suits of gray;
No creeds to guide them, or MSS.;
For all had put on Christ's righteousness.

EDWIN AND ANGELINA.

OLIVER GOLDSMITH.

"TURN, gentle Hermit of the dale,
And guide my lonely way,
To where yon taper cheers the vale
With hospitable ray:

For here forlorn and lost I tread,
With fainting steps and slow;
Where wilds, immeasurably spread,
Seem lengthening as I go."

"Forbear, my son," the Hermit cries,
"To tempt the dangerous gloom;
For yonder faithless phantom flies
To lure thee to thy doom.

Here to the houseless child of want
  My door is open still;
And, though my portion is but scant,
  I give it with good will.

Then turn to-night, and freely share
  Whate'er my cell bestows;
My rushy couch and frugal fare,
  My blessing and repose.

No flocks that range the valley free
  To slaughter I condemn;
Taught by that Power that pities me,
  I learn to pity them:

But from the mountain's grassy side
  A guiltless feast I bring;
A scrip with herbs and fruits supplied,
  And water from the spring.

Then, pilgrim, turn, thy cares forego;
  All earth-born cares are wrong:
Man wants but little here below,
  Nor wants that little long."

Soft as the dew from heaven descends,
  His gentle accents fell:
The modest stranger lowly bends,
  And follows to the cell.

Far in a wilderness obscure
  The lonely mansion lay,
A refuge to the neighbouring poor,
  And strangers led astray.

No stores beneath its humble thatch
  Required a master's care;
The wicket, opening with a latch,
  Received the harmless pair.

And now, when busy crowds retire
  To take their evening rest,
The Hermit trimm'd his little fire,
  And cheer'd his pensive guest;

And spread his vegetable store,
  And gaily press'd and smiled;
And, skill'd in legendary lore,
  The lingering hours beguiled.

Around in sympathetic mirth
  Its tricks the kitten tries;
The cricket chirrups in the hearth,
  The crackling faggot flies.

But nothing could a charm impart,
  To soothe the stranger's woe;
For grief was heavy at his heart,
  And tears began to flow.

His rising cares the Hermit spied,
  With answering care opprest:
"And whence, unhappy youth," he cried,
  "The sorrows of thy breast?

From better habitations spurn'd,
  Reluctant dost thou rove?
Or grieve for friendship unreturn'd,
  Or unregarded love?

Alas! the joys that fortune brings,
  Are trifling and decay;
And those who prize the paltry things,
  More trifling still than they.

And what is friendship but a name,
  A charm that lulls to sleep;
A shade that follows wealth or fame,
  But leaves the wretch to weep?

And love is still an empty sound,
  The modern fair-one's jest;
On Earth unseen, or only found
  To warm the turtle's nest.

For shame, fond youth! thy sorrows hush,
  And spurn the sex," he said:
But while he spoke, a rising blush
  His love-lorn guest betray'd.

Surprised he sees new beauties rise,
  Swift mantling to the view;
Like colours o'er the morning skies,
  As bright, as transient too.

The bashful look, the rising breast,
  Alternate spread alarms:
The lovely stranger stands confest
  A maid in all her charms.

"And, ah! forgive a stranger rude,
  A wretch forlorn," she cried;
"Whose feet unhallow'd thus intrude
  Where Heaven and you reside.

But let a maid thy pity share,
  Whom love has taught to stray;
Who seeks for rest, but finds despair
  Companion of her way.

My father lived beside the Tyne,
  A wealthy lord was he;
And all his wealth was mark'd as mine,—
  He had but only me.

To win me from his tender arms,
  Unnumber'd suitors came;
Who praised me for imputed charms,
  And felt or feign'd a flame.

Each hour a mercenary crowd
  With richest proffers strove ;
Amongst the rest young Edwin bow'd,
  But never talk'd of love.

In humblest, simplest habit clad,
  No wealth nor power had he ;
Wisdom and worth were all he had,
  But these were all to me.

And when, beside me in the dale,
  He caroll'd lays of love,
His breath lent fragrance to the gale,
  And music to the grove.

The blossom opening to the day,
  The dews of Heaven refined,
Could nought of purity display,
  To emulate his mind.

The dew, the blossom on the tree,
  With charms inconstant shine ;
Their charms were his, but, woe to me !
  Their constancy was mine.

For still I tried each fickle art,
  Importunate and vain ;
And, while his passion touch'd my heart,
  I triumph'd in his pain ;

Till, quite dejected with my scorn,
  He left me to my pride ;
And sought a solitude forlorn,
  In secret where he died.

But mine the sorrow, mine the fault,
  And well my life shall pay :
I'll seek the solitude he sought,
  And stretch me where he lay.

And there, forlorn, despairing, hid,
  I'll lay me down and die;
'Twas so for me that Edwin did,
  And so for him will I."

"Forbid it, Heaven!" the Hermit cried,
  And clasp'd her to his breast:
The wondering fair-one turn'd to chide,—
  'Twas Edwin's self that press'd.

"Turn, Angelina, ever dear,
  My charmer, turn to see
Thy own, thy long-lost Edwin here,
  Restored to love and thee.

Thus let me hold thee to my heart,
  And every care resign."
"And shall we never, never part,
  My life,—my all that's mine?"

"No, never from this hour to part,
  We'll live and love so true;
The sigh that rends thy constant heart
  Shall break thy Edwin's too."

ALPINE MINSTRELSY.

SCHILLER: *Translated by* THEODORE MARTIN.

FISHER-BOY, IN HIS BOAT.

THE clear smiling lake woo'd to bathe in its deep;
A boy on its green shore had laid him to sleep;
Then heard he a melody flowing and soft,
And sweet, as when Angels are singing aloft:
And as, thrilling with pleasure, he wakes from his rest,
The waters are murmuring over his breast;
And a voice from the deep cries, "With me thou must go;
I charm the young shepherd, I lure him below."

HERDSMAN, ON THE MOUNTAIN.

Farewell, ye green meadows, farewell, sunny shore!
The herdsman must leave you, the Summer is o'er.
We go to the hills, but you'll see us again,
When the cuckoo is calling, and wood-notes are gay,
When flowerets are blooming in dingle and plain,
And the brooks sparkle up in the sunshine of May.
Farewell, ye green meadows, farewell, sunny shore!
The herdsman must leave you, the Summer is o'er.

CHAMOIS–HUNTER, ON THE TOP OF A CLIFF.

On the heights peals the thunder, and trembles the bridge;
The huntsman bounds on by the dizzying ridge:
Undaunted he hies him o'er ice-cover'd wild,
Where leaf never budded, nor Spring ever smiled;
And beneath him an ocean of mist, where his eye
No longer the dwellings of man can espy:
Through the parting clouds only the earth can be seen,
Far down 'neath the vapour the meadows of green.

A LEGEND OF BREGENZ.

ADELAIDE A. PROCTER.

GIRT round with rugged mountains the fair Lake Constance lies;
In her blue heart reflected, shine back the starry skies;
And, watching each white cloudlet float silently and slow,
You think a piece of Heaven lies on our Earth below!

Midnight is there; and silence, enthroned in heaven, looks down
Upon her own calm mirror, upon a sleeping town:
For Bregenz, that quaint city upon the Tyrol shore,
Has stood above Lake Constance a thousand years and more.

Her battlements and towers, upon their rocky steep,
Have cast their trembling shadows for ages on the deep;

Mountain, and lake, and valley a sacred legend know,
Of how the town was saved one night, three hundred years
ago.

Far from her home and kindred, a Tyrol maid had fled,
To serve in the Swiss valleys, and toil for daily bread;
And every year that fleeted so silently and fast
Seem'd to bear further from her the memory of the past.

She served kind, gentle masters, nor ask'd for rest or change;
Her friends seem'd no more new ones, their speech seem'd
no more strange;
And, when she led her cattle to pasture every day,
She ceased to look and wonder on which side Bregenz lay.

She spoke no more of Bregenz, with longing and with tears;
Her Tyrol home seem'd faded in a deep mist of years;
She heeded not the rumours of Austrian war or strife;
Each day she rose contented, to the calm toils of life.

Yet, when her master's children would clustering round her
stand,
She sang them the old ballads of her own native land;
And, when at morn and evening she knelt before God's
throne,
The accents of her childhood rose to her lips alone.

And so she dwelt: the valley more peaceful year by year,
When suddenly strange portents of some great deed seem'd
near.
The golden corn was bending upon its fragile stalk,
While farmers, heedless of their fields, paced up and down
in talk.

The men seem'd stern and alter'd, with looks cast on the
ground;
With anxious faces, one by one, the women gather'd round;
All talk of flax, or spinning, or work, was put away;
The very children seem'd afraid to go alone to play.

One day, out in the meadow with strangers from the town,
Some secret plan discussing, the men walk'd up and down.
Yet now and then seem'd watching a strange uncertain gleam,
That look'd like lances 'mid the trees that stood below the stream.

At eve they all assembled, all care and doubt were fled;
With jovial laugh they feasted, the board was nobly spread.
The elder of the village rose up, his glass in hand,
And cried, "We drink the downfall of an accursed land!

The night is growing darker; ere one more day is flown
Bregenz, our foemen's stronghold, Bregenz shall be our own!"
The women shrank in terror, (yet pride, too, had her part,)
But one poor Tyrol maiden felt death within her heart.

Before her stood fair Bregenz, once more her towers arose;
What were the friends beside her? Only her country's foes!
The faces of her kinsfolk, the days of childhood flown,
The echoes of her mountains reclaim'd her as their own!

Nothing she heard around her, (though shouts rang forth again,)
Gone were the green Swiss valleys, the pasture, and the plain;
Before her eyes one vision, and in her heart one cry,
That said, "Go forth, save Bregenz, and then, if need be, die!"

With trembling haste and breathless, with noiseless step she sped;
Horses and weary cattle were standing in the shed;
She loosed the strong white charger, that fed from out her hand,
She mounted and she turn'd his head toward her native land.

Out — out into the darkness — faster, and still more fast;
The smooth grass flies behind her, the chestnut wood is pass'd;
She looks up; clouds are heavy: Why is her steed so slow? —
Scarcely the wind beside them can pass them as they go.

"Faster!" she cries, "O, faster!" Eleven the church-bells chime:
"O God," she cries, "help Bregenz, and bring me there in time!"
But louder than bells' ringing, or lowing of the kine,
Grows nearer in the midnight the rushing of the Rhine.

Shall not the roaring waters their headlong gallop check?
The steed draws back in terror, she leans above his neck
To watch the flowing darkness, the bank is high and steep;
One pause, — he staggers forward, and plunges in the deep.

She strives to pierce the blackness, and looser throws the rein;
Her steed must breast the waters that dash above his mane:
How gallantly, how nobly, he struggles through the foam,
And see, in the far distance shine out the lights of home!

Up the steep bank he bears her, and now they rush again
Towards the heights of Bregenz, that tower above the plain.
They reach the gate of Bregenz, just as the midnight rings,
And out come serf and soldier to meet the news she brings.

Bregenz is saved! Ere daylight her battlements are mann'd;
Defiance greets the army that marches on the land:
And, if to deeds heroic should endless fame be paid,
Bregenz does well to honour the noble Tyrol maid.

Three hundred years are vanish'd, and yet upon the hill
An old stone gateway rises, to do her honour still.
And there, when Bregenz women sit spinning in the shade,
They see in quaint old carving the charger and the maid.

And when, to guard old Bregenz, by gateway, street, and tower,
The warder paces all night long, and calls each passing hour:
"Nine," "ten," "eleven," he cries aloud, and then (O crown of fame!)
When midnight pauses in the skies he calls the maiden's name.

THE RIDE OF JENNIE M'NEAL.

WILL CARLETON.

PAUL REVERE was a rider bold,—
Well has his valorous deed been told;
Sheridan's ride was a glorious one,—
Often it has been dwelt upon;
But why should men do all the deeds
On which the love of a patriot feeds?
Hearken to me, while I reveal
The dashing ride of Jennie M'Neal.

On a spot as pretty as might be found
In the dangerous length of the Neutral Ground,
In a cottage, cozy, and all their own,
She and her mother lived alone.
Safe were the two, with their frugal store,
From all the many who pass'd their door;
For Jennie's mother was strange to fears,
And Jennie was large for fifteen years:
With vim her eyes were glistening,
Her hair was the hue of a blackbird's wing;
And, while her friends who knew her well
The sweetness of her heart could tell,
A gun that hung on the kitchen wall
Look'd solemnly quick to heed her call;
And they who were evil-minded knew
Her nerve was strong and her aim was true.
So all kind words and acts did deal
To generous, black-eyed Jennie M'Neal.

One night, when the Sun had crept to bed,
And rain-clouds linger'd overhead,
And sent their surly drops for proof
To drum a tune on the cottage roof,

Close after a knock at the outer door
There enter'd a dozen dragoons or more.
Their red coats, stain'd by the muddy road,
That they were British soldiers show'd:
The captain his hostess bent to greet,
Saying, "Madam, please give us a bit to eat;
We will pay you well, and, if may be,
This bright-eyed girl for pouring our tea;
Then we must dash ten miles ahead,
To catch a rebel colonel a-bed.
He is visiting home, as doth appear;
We will make his pleasure cost him dear."
And they fell on the hasty supper with zeal,
Close-watch'd the while by Jennie M'Neal.

For the gray-hair'd colonel they hover'd near
Had been her true friend, kind and dear;
And oft, in her younger days, had he
Right proudly perch'd her upon his knee,
And told her stories many a one
Concerning the French war lately done.
And oft together the two friends were,
And many the arts he had taught to her;
She had hunted by his fatherly side,
He had shown her how to fence and ride;
And once had said, "The time may be,
Your skill and courage may stand by me."
So sorrow for him she could but feel,
Brave, grateful-hearted Jennie M'Neal.

With never a thought or a moment more,
Bare-headed she slipp'd from the cottage door,
Ran out where the horses were left to feed,
Unhitch'd and mounted the captain's steed,
And down the hilly and rock-strewn way
She urged the fiery horse of gray.
Around her slender and cloakless form
Patter'd and moan'd the ceaseless storm;
Secure and tight a gloveless hand
Grasp'd the reins with stern command;
And full and black her long hair stream'd,
Whenever the ragged lightning gleam'd.
And on she rush'd for the colonel's weal,
Brave, lioness-hearted, Jennie M'Neal.

Hark! from the hills, a moment mute,
Came a clatter of hoofs in hot pursuit;
And a cry from the foremost trooper said,
"Halt! or your blood be on your head!"

She heeded it not, and not in vain
She lash'd the horse with the bridle rein;
So into the night the gray horse strode;
His shoes hew'd fire from the rocky road;
And the high-born courage that never dies
Flash'd from his rider's coal-black eyes:
The pebbles flew from the fearful race;
The rain-drops grasp'd at her glowing face.
"On, on, brave beast!" with loud appeal,
Cried eager, resolute Jennie M'Neal.
"Halt!" once more came the voice of dread;
"Halt! or your blood be on your head!"
Then, no one answering to the calls,
Sped after her a volley of balls.
They pass'd her in her rapid flight,
They scream'd to her left, they scream'd to her right:
But, rushing still o'er the slippery track,
She sent no token of answer back,
Except a silvery laughter peal,
Brave, merry-hearted Jennie M'Neal.

So on she rush'd, at her own good will,
Through wood and valley, o'er plain and hill:
The gray horse did his duty well,
Till all at once he stumbled and fell,
Himself escaping the nets of harm,
But flinging the girl with a broken arm.
Still undismay'd by the numbing pain,
She clung to the horse's bridle rein,
And gently bidding him to stand,
Petted him with her able hand;
Then sprung again to the saddle-bow,
And shouted, "One more trial now!"
As if ashamed of the heedless fall,
He gather'd his strength once more for all,
And, galloping down a hill-side steep,
Gain'd on the troopers at every leap;
No more the high-bred steed did reel,
But ran his best for Jennie M'Neal.

They were a furlong behind, or more,
When the girl burst through the colonel's door,—
Her poor arm helpless hanging with pain,
And she all drabbled and drench'd with rain,
But her cheeks as red as fire-brands are,
And her eyes as bright as a blazing star,—
And shouted, "Quick! be quick, I say!
They come! they come! Away! away!"

Then sunk on the rude white floor of deal
Poor, brave, exhausted Jennie M'Neal.

The startled colonel sprung, and press'd
The wife and children to his breast,
And turn'd away from his fireside bright,
And glided into the stormy night;
Then soon and safely made his way
To where the patriot army lay.
But first he bent, in the dim fire-light,
And kiss'd the forehead broad and white,
And bless'd the girl who had ridden so well
To keep him out of a prison-cell.
The girl roused up at the martial din,
Just as the troopers came rushing in,
And laugh'd, e'en in the midst of a moan,
Saying, "Good sirs, your bird has flown:
'Tis I who have scared him from his nest;
So deal with me now as you think best."
But the grand young captain bow'd, and said,
"Never you hold a moment's dread:
Of womankind I must crown you queen;
So brave a girl I have never seen:
Wear this gold ring as your valour's due;
And when peace comes I will come for you."
But Jennie's face an arch smile wore,
As she said, "There's a lad in Putnam's corps,
Who told me the same, long time ago;
You two would never agree, I know:
I promised my love to be true as steel,"
Said good, sure-hearted Jennie M'Neal.

MAUD MULLER.

J. G. Whittier.

Maud Muller, on a Summer's day,
Raked the meadows sweet with hay:

Beneath her torn hat glow'd the wealth
Of simple beauty and rustic health:

Singing, she wrought, and her merry glee
The mock-bird echo'd from his tree.

But, when she glanced to the far-off town,
White from its hill-slope looking down,

The sweet song died, and a vague unrest
And a nameless longing fill'd her breast, —

A wish, that she hardly dared to own,
For something better than she had known.

The Judge rode slowly down the lane,
Smoothing his horse's chestnut mane.

He drew his bridle in the shade
Of the apple-trees, to greet the maid,

And ask a draught from the spring that flow'd
Through the meadow across the road.

She stoop'd where the cool spring bubbled up,
And fill'd for him her small tin cup,

And blush'd as she gave it, looking down
On her feet so bare, and her tatter'd gown.

"Thanks!" said the Judge; "a sweeter draught
From a fairer hand was never quaff'd."

He spoke of the grass and flowers and trees,
Of the singing birds and the humming bees;

Then talk'd of the haying, and wonder'd whether
The cloud in the west would bring foul weather.

And Maud forgot her brier-torn gown,
And her graceful ankles bare and brown;

And listen'd, while a pleased surprise
Look'd from her long-lash'd hazel-eyes.

At last, like one who for delay
Seeks a vain excuse, he rode away.

Maud Muller look'd and sigh'd: "Ah, me!
That I the Judge's bride might be!

He would dress me up in silks so fine,
And praise and toast me at his wine.

My father should wear a broadcloth coat;
My brother should sail a painted boat.

I'd dress my mother so grand and gay;
And the baby should have a new toy each day.

And I'd feed the hungry and clothe the poor,
And all should bless me who left our door."

The Judge look'd back as he climb'd the hill,
And saw Maud Muller standing still.

"A form more fair, a face more sweet,
Ne'er hath it been my lot to meet.

And her modest answer and graceful air
Show her wise and good as she is fair.

Would she were mine, and I to-day,
Like her a harvester of hay:

No doubtful balance of rights and wrongs,
Nor weary lawyers with endless tongues,

But low of cattle and song of birds,
And health and quiet and loving words."

But he thought of his sisters proud and cold,
And his mother vain of her rank and gold.

So, closing his heart, the Judge rode on,
And Maud was left in the field alone.

But the lawyers smiled that afternoon,
When he humm'd in court an old love-tune;

And the young girl mused beside the well,
Till the rain on the unraked clover fell.

He wedded a wife of richest dower,
Who lived for fashion, as he for power.

Yet oft, in his marble hearth's bright glow,
He watch'd a picture come and go;

And sweet Maud Muller's hazel eyes
Look'd out in their innocent surprise.

Oft, when the wine in his glass was red,
He long'd for the wayside well instead;

And closed his eyes on his garnish'd rooms,
To dream of meadows and clover-blooms.

And the proud man sigh'd, with a secret pain:
"Ah, that I were free again!

Free as when I rode that day,
Where the barefoot maiden raked her hay."

She wedded a man unlearn'd and poor,
And many children play'd round her door.

And oft, when the summer Sun shone hot
On the new-mown hay in the meadow lot,

And she heard the little spring brook fall
Over the roadside, through the wall,

In the shade of the apple-tree again
She saw a rider draw his rein.

And, gazing down with timid grace,
She felt his pleased eyes read her face.

Sometimes her narrow kitchen walls
Stretch'd away into stately halls;

The weary wheel to a spinnet turn'd,
The tallow candle an astral burn'd,

And for him who sat by the chimney lug,
Dozing and grumbling o'er pipe and mug,

A manly form at her side she saw,
And joy was duty and love was law.

Then she took up her burden of life again,
Saying only, "It might have been."

Alas for maiden, alas for Judge,
For rich repiner and household drudge!

God pity them both! and pity us all,
Who vainly the dreams of youth recall.

For of all sad words of tongue or pen,
The saddest are these, "It might have been!"

Ah, well! for us all some sweet hope lies
Deeply buried from human eyes;

And, in the hereafter, angels may
Roll the stone from its grave away!

MONA'S WATERS.

O, Mona's waters are blue and bright
  When the Sun shines out like a gay young lover;
But Mona's waves are dark as night
  When the face of heaven is clouded over.
The wild wind drives the crested foam
  Far up the steep and rocky mountain,
And booming echoes drown the voice,
  The silvery voice, of Mona's fountain.

Wild, wild against that mountain's side
  The wrathful waves were up and beating,
When stern Glenvarloch's chieftain came:
  With anxious brow and hurried greeting
He bade the widow'd mother send
  (While loud the tempest's voice was raging)
Her fair young son across the flood,
  Where winds and waves their strife were waging.

And still that fearful mother pray'd,
  "O, yet delay, delay till morning,
For weak the hand that guides our bark,
  Though brave his heart, all danger scorning."
Little did stern Glenvarloch heed:
  "The safety of my fortress-tower
Depends on tidings he must bring
  From Fairlee bank, within the hour.

See'st thou, across the sullen wave,
  A blood-red banner wildly streaming?
That flag a message brings to me
  Of which my foes are little dreaming.
The boy *must* put his boat across,
  (Gold shall repay his hour of danger,)
And bring me back, with care and speed,
  Three letters from the light-brow'd stranger."

The orphan boy leap'd lightly in;
  Bold was his eye and brow of beauty,
And bright his smile as thus he spoke:
  "I do but pay a vassal's duty;
Fear not for me, O mother dear!
  See how the boat the tide is spurning;
The storm will cease, the sky will clear,
  And thou wilt watch me safe returning."

His bark shot on, now up, now down,
  Over the waves, — the snowy-crested;

Now like a dart it sped along,
  Now like a white-wing'd sea-bird rested;
And ever, when the wind sank low,
  Smote on the ear that woman's wailing,
As long she watch'd with streaming eyes
  That fragile bark's uncertain sailing.

He reach'd the shore, — the letters claim'd;
  Triumphant, heard the stranger's wonder
That one so young should brave alone
  The heaving lake, the rolling thunder.
And once again his snowy sail
  Was seen by her, that mourning mother;
And once she heard his shouting voice,
  That voice the waves were soon to smother.

Wild burst the wind, wide flapp'd the sail,
  A crashing peel of thunder follow'd;
The gust swept o'er the water's face,
  And caverns in the deep lake hollow'd.
The gust swept past, the waves grew calm,
  The thunder died along the mountain;
But where was he who used to play,
  On sunny days, by Mona's fountain?

His cold corpse floated to the shore,
  Where knelt his lone and shrieking mother;
And bitterly she wept for him,
  The widow's son, who had no brother!
She raised his arm, — the hand was closed;
  With pain his stiffen'd fingers parted,
And on the sand three letters dropp'd! —
  His last dim thought, — the faithful-hearted.

Glenvarloch gazed, and on his brow
  Remorse with pain and grief seem'd blending;
A purse of gold he flung beside
  That mother o'er her dead child bending.

O, wildly laugh'd that woman then:
  "Glenvarloch! would ye dare to measure
The holy life that God has given
  Against a heap of golden treasure?

Ye spurn'd my prayer, for we were poor;
  But know, proud man, that God hath power
To smite the king on Scotland's throne,
  The chieftain in his fortress-tower.
Frown on! frown on! I fear ye not;
  We've done the last of chieftain's bidding;
And cold he lies, for whose young sake
  I used to bear your wrathful chiding.

Will gold bring back his cheerful voice,
  That used to win my heart from sorrow?
Will silver warm the frozen blood,
  Or make my heart less lone to-morrow?
Go back and seek your mountain home,
  And when ye kiss your fair-hair'd daughter,
Remember him who died to-night
  Beneath the waves of Mona's water."

Old years roll'd on, and new ones came, —
  Foes dare not brave Glenvarloch's tower;
But nought could bar the sickness out
  That stole within fair Annie's bower.
The o'erblown floweret in the sun
  Sinks languid down, and withers daily,
And so she sank, — her voice grew faint,
  Her laugh no longer sounded gayly.

Her step fell on the old oak floor
  As noiseless as the snow-shower's drifting;
And from her sweet and serious eyes
  They seldom saw the dark lid lifting.
"Bring aid! Bring aid!" the father cries;
  "Bring aid!" each vassal's voice is crying;

"The fair-hair'd beauty of the isles,
  Her pulse is faint, her life is flying!"

He call'd in vain; her dim eyes turn'd
  And met his own with parting sorrow;
For well she knew, that fading girl,
  That he must weep and wail the morrow.
Her faint breath ceased; the father bent
  And gazed upon his fair-hair'd daughter.
What thought he on? The widow's son,
  And the stormy night by Mona's water.

AN ODE TO THE PASSIONS.

WILLIAM COLLINS.

WHEN Music, heavenly maid, was young,
Ere yet in early Greece she sung,
The Passions oft, to hear her shell,
Throng'd around her magic cell;
Exulting, trembling, raging, fainting,
Possess'd beyond the Muse's painting,
By turns they felt the glowing mind,
Disturb'd, delighted, raised, refined;
Till once, 'tis said, when all were fired,
Fill'd with fury, rapt, inspired,
From the supporting myrtles round,
They seized her instruments of sound;
And, as they oft had heard, apart,
Sweet lessons of her forceful art,
Each — for madness ruled the hour —
Would prove his own expressive power.

First Fear, his hand, its skill to try,
  Amid the chords bewilder'd laid;
And back recoil'd — he knew not why —
  E'en at the sound himself had made!

Next Anger rush'd, his eyes on fire,
  In lightnings own'd his secret stings;
In one rude clash he struck the lyre,
  And swept with hurried hand the strings.

With woeful measure, wan Despair —
  Low sullen sounds — his grief beguiled;
A solemn, strange, and mingled air,
  'Twas sad by fits, by starts 'twas wild!

But thou, O Hope, with eyes so fair,
  What was thy delighted measure?
  Still it whisper'd promised pleasure,
And bade the lovely scenes at distance hail!
Still would her touch the strain prolong,
  And from the rocks, the woods, the vale,
She call'd on Echo still through all the song;
And, where her sweetest themes she chose,
A soft responsive voice was heard at every close;
And Hope, enchanted, smiled, and waved her golden hair:
And longer had she sung, — but, with a frown,
  Revenge impatient rose;
He threw his blood-stain'd sword in thunder down,
  And, with a withering look,
  The war-denouncing trumpet took,
And blew a blast so loud and dread,
Were ne'er prophetic sounds so full of woe;
  And ever and anon he beat
  The doubling drum with furious heat;
And though sometimes, each dreary pause between,
  Dejected Pity, at his side,
  Her soul-subduing voice applied,
Yet still he kept his wild unalter'd mien,
While each strain'd ball of sight seem'd bursting from his head!

Thy numbers, Jealousy, to nought were fix'd,
  Sad proof of thy distressful state;
Of differing themes, the veering song was mix'd;
And now it courted Love, now raving call'd on Hate!

With eyes upraised, as one inspired,
Pale Melancholy sat retired;
And from her wild sequester'd seat,
In notes by distance made more sweet,
Pour'd through the mellow horn her pensive soul;
  And, dashing soft from rocks around,
  Bubbling runnels join'd the sound:
Through glades and glooms the mingled measure stole,
Or o'er some haunted stream, with fond delay,
  Round a holy calm diffusing,
  Love of peace and lonely musing,
In hollow murmurs died away.

But, O, how alter'd was its sprightlier tone!
  When Cheerfulness, a nymph of healthiest hue,
Her bow across her shoulder flung,
  Her buskins gemm'd with morning dew,
  Blew an inspiring air, that dale and thicket rung,
The hunter's call, to Faun and Dryad known.

The oak-crown'd sisters and their chaste-eyed Queen,
Satyrs and sylvan boys were seen,
Peeping from forth their alleys green;
Brown Exercise rejoiced to hear,
And Sport leap'd up, and seized his beechen spear.

Last came Joy's ecstatic trial:
He, with viny crown advancing,
First to the lively pipe his hand address'd;
But soon he saw the brisk, awakening viol,
Whose sweet entrancing voice he loved the best.

They would have thought, who heard the strain,
  They saw in Tempe's vale her native maids,
  Amidst the festal-sounding shades,
To some unwearied minstrel dancing;
While, as his flying fingers kiss'd the strings,
Love framed with Mirth a gay fantastic round;

Loose were her tresses seen, her zone unbound;
And he, amidst his frolic play, —
As if he would the charming air repay, —
Shook thousand odours from his dewy wings.

AN ORDER FOR A PICTURE.

ALICE CARY.

O GOOD painter, tell me true,
  Has your hand the cunning to draw
  Shapes of things that you never saw?
Ay? Well, here is an order for you.

Woods and cornfields, a little brown, —
  The picture must not be over-bright,
  Yet all in the golden and gracious light
Of a cloud, when the summer Sun is down.
  Alway and alway, night and morn,
  Woods upon woods, with fields of corn
    Lying between them, not quite sere,
And not in the full, thick, leafy bloom,
When the wind can hardly find breathing-room
    Under their tassels, — cattle near,
Biting shorter the short green grass,
And a hedge of sumach and sassafras,
With bluebirds twittering all around, —
(Ah, good painter, you can't paint sound!)
  These, and the house where I was born,
Low and little, and black and old,
With children, many as it can hold,
All at the windows, open wide, —
Heads and shoulders clear outside,
And fair young faces all ablush:
  Perhaps you may have seen, some day,
  Roses crowding the self-same way,
Out of a wilding, wayside bush.

Listen closer: When you have done
With woods and cornfields and grazing herds,
A lady, the lovliest ever the Sun
Look'd down upon, you must paint for me;
O, if I only could make you see
The clear blue eyes, the tender smile,
The sovereign sweetness, the gentle grace,
The woman's soul, and the angel's face,
That are beaming on me all the while,
I need not speak these foòlish words:
Yet one word tells you all I would say, —
She is my mother: you will agree
That all the rest may be thrown away.

Two little urchins at her knee
You must paint, sir; one like me,
The other with a clearer brow,
And the light of his adventurous eyes
Flashing with boldest enterprise:
At ten years old he went to sea, —
God knoweth if he be living now;
He sail'd in the good ship Commodore;
Nobody ever cross'd her track
To bring us news, and she never came back.
Ah, 'tis twenty long years and more
Since that old ship went out of the bay
With my great-hearted brother on her deck:
I watch'd him till he shrank to a speck,
And his face was toward me all the way.
Bright his hair was, a golden brown,
The time we stood at our mother's knee:
That beauteous head, if it did go down,
Carried sunshine into the sea!

Out in the fields one summer night
We were together, half afraid
Of the corn-leaves' rustling, and of the shade
Of the high hills, stretching so still and far, —

Loitering till after the low little light
Of the candle shone through the open door;
And over the haystack's pointed top,
All of a tremble, and ready to drop,
The first half-hour, the great yellow star,
That we, with staring, ignorant eyes,
Had often and often watch'd to see,
Propp'd and held in its place in the skies
By the fork of a tall red mulberry tree,
Which close in the edge of our flax-field grew,—
Dead at the top,—just one branch full
Of leaves, notch'd round, and lined with wool,
From which it tenderly shook the dew
Over our heads, when we came to play
In its handbreadth of shadow, day after day.
Afraid to go home, sir; for one of us bore
A nest full of speckled and thin-shell'd eggs;
The other, a bird, held fast by the legs,
Not so big as a straw of wheat:
The berries we gave her she wouldn't eat,
But cried and cried, till we held her bill,
So slim and shining, to keep her still.

At last we stood at our mother's knee.
Do you think, sir, if you try,
You can paint the look of a lie?
If you can, pray have the grace
To put it solely in the face
Of the urchin that is likest me:
I think 'twas solely mine, indeed:
But that's no matter,—paint it so;
The eyes of our mother, (take good heed,)
Looking not on the nestful of eggs,
Nor the fluttering bird, held so fast by the legs,
But straight through our faces down to our lies,
And, O, with such injured, reproachful surprise!
I felt my heart bleed where that glance went, as though
A sharp blade struck through it.

You, sir, know
That you on the canvas are to repeat
Things that are fairest, things most sweet, —
Woods and cornfields and mulberry tree, —
The mother, — the lads, with their bird, at her knee:
But, O, that look of reproachful woe!
High as the heavens your name I'll shout,
If you paint me the picture, and leave that out.

THE PAINTER OF SEVILLE.

SUSAN WILSON.

Sebastian Gomez, better known by the name of the Mulatto of Murillo, was one of the most celebrated painters of Spain. There may yet be seen in the churches of Seville the celebrated picture which he was found painting, by his master, a St. Anne, and a holy Joseph, which are extremely beautiful, and others of the highest merit. The incident related occurred about the year 1630.

'TWAS morning in Seville; and brightly beam'd
The early sunlight in one chamber there;
Showing where'er its glowing radiance gleam'd,
Rich, varied beauty. 'Twas the study where
Murillo, the famed painter, came to share
With young aspirants his long-cherish'd art,
To prove how vain must be the teacher's care,
Who strives his unbought knowledge to impart,
The language of the soul, the feeling of the heart.

The pupils came; and, glancing round,
Mendez upon his canvas found,
Not his own work of yesterday,
But, glowing in the morning ray,
A sketch so rich, so pure, so bright,
It almost seem'd that there were given,
To glow before his dazzled sight,
Tints and expression warm from Heaven.

*   *   *   *   *   *

'Twas but a sketch, — the Virgin's head;
Yet was unearthly beauty shed
Upon the mildly beaming face:
The lip, the eye, the flowing hair,
Had separate, yet blended grace, —
  A poet's brightest dream was there!

Murillo enter'd, and, amazed,
On the mysterious painting gazed:
"Whose work is this? — speak, tell me! — he
  Who to his aid such power can call,"
Exclaim'd the teacher eagerly,
  "Will yet be master of us all:
Would I had done it! — Ferdinand!
Isturitz! Mendez! — say, whose hand
Among ye all?" — with half-breathed sigh,
Each pupil answer'd, "'Twas not I!"

"How came it, then?" impatiently
Murillo cried: "but we shall see,
Ere long, into this mystery. —
Sebastian!"
                    At the summons came
  A bright-eyed slave,
Who trembled at the stern rebuke
  His master gave.
For, order'd in that room to sleep,
And faithful guard o'er all to keep,
Murillo bade him now declare
What rash intruder had been there;
And threaten'd — if he did not tell
The truth at once — the dungeon-cell.
  "Thou answer'st not," Murillo said;
(The boy had stood in speechless fear.)
  "Speak on!" — At last he raised his head
And murmur'd, "No one has been here."
"'Tis false!" Sebastian bent his knee,
  And clasp'd his hands imploringly,
And said, "I swear it. none but me!"

"List!" said his master: "I would know
  Who enters here; there have been found,
  Before, rough sketches strewn around,
By whose bold hand, 'tis yours to show:
  See that to-night strict watch you keep,
  Nor dare to close your eyes in sleep.
If on to-morrow morn you fail
  To answer what I ask,
The lash shall force you; do you hear?
  Hence! to your daily task."

'Twas midnight in Seville; and faintly shone,
  From one small lamp, a dim uncertain ray
Within Murillo's study; all were gone
  Who there, in pleasant tasks or converse gay,
Pass'd cheerfully the morning hours away.
  'Twas shadowy gloom, and breathless silence, save
That, to sad thoughts and torturing fear a prey,
  One bright-eyed boy was there,—Murillo's little slave.

Almost a child, that boy had seen
  Not thrice five Summers yet,
But genius mark'd the lofty brow,
  O'er which his locks of jet
Profusely curl'd; his cheek's dark hue
Proclaim'd the warm blood flowing through
Each throbbing vein, a mingled tide,
To Africa and Spain allied.

"Alas! what fate is mine!" he said.
  "The lash, if I refuse to tell
Who sketch'd those figures; if I do,
  Perhaps e'en more, — the dungeon-cell!"
He breathed a prayer to Heaven for aid;
It came, — for, soon in slumber laid,
He slept, until the dawning day
Shed on his humble couch its ray.

"I'll sleep no more!" he cried; "and now
  Three hours of freedom I may gain,
Before my master comes; for then
  I shall be but a slave again.
Three blessèd hours of freedom! how
Shall I employ them?— ah! e'en now
The figure on that canvas traced
Must be — yes, it must be effaced."

He seized a brush; the morning light
  Gave to the head a soften'd glow:
Gazing enraptured on the sight,
  He cried, "Shall I efface it?—No!
That breathing lip! that beaming eye!
Efface them? — I would rather die!"

The terror of the humble slave
  Gave place to the o'erpowering flow
Of the high feelings Nature gave,—
  Which only gifted spirits know.

He touch'd the brow — the lip; it seem'd
  His pencil had some magic power:
The eye with deeper feeling beam'd;
  Sebastian then forgot the hour!
Forgot his master, and the threat
  Of punishment still hanging o'er him;
For, with each touch, new beauties met
  And mingled in the face before him.

At length 'twas finish'd: rapturously
He gazed, — could aught more beauteous be?
Awhile absorb'd, entranced he stood,
Then started; horror chill'd his blood!
His master and the pupils all
  Were there e'en at his side!
The terror-stricken slave was mute, —
  Mercy would be denied,

E'en could he ask it; so he deem'd,
And the poor boy half lifeless seem'd.

Speechless, bewilder'd, for a space
They gazed upon that perfect face,
  Each with an artist's joy;
At length Murillo silence broke,
And with affected sternness spoke, —
  "Who is your master, boy?"
"You, Senior," said the trembling slave.
"Nay, who, I mean, instruction gave,
Before that Virgin's head you drew?"
Again he answer'd, "Only you."
"I gave you none," Murillo cried!
"But I have heard," the boy replied,
  "What you to others said."
"And more than heard," (in kinder tone,
The painter said;) "'tis plainly shown
  That you have profited."

"What" (to his pupils) "is his meed?
  Reward or punishment?"
"Reward, reward!" they warmly cried.
  (Sebastian's ear was bent
To catch the sounds he scarce believed,
But with imploring look received.)
"What shall it be?" They spoke of gold
  And of a splendid dress;
But still unmoved Sebastian stood,
  Silent and motionless.

"Speak!" said Murillo, kindly; "choose
  Your own reward: what shall it be?
Name what you wish, I'll not refuse;
  Then speak at once and fearlessly."
"O, if I dared!" — Sebastian knelt,
  And feelings he could not control,
(But fear'd to utter even then,)
  With strong emotion shook his soul.

"Courage!" his master said, and each
Essay'd, in kind, half-whisper'd speech,
To soothe his overpowering dread.
He scarcely heard, till some one said,
"Sebastian, — ask, — you have your choice, —
Ask for your *freedom!*" — At the word,
The suppliant strove to raise his voice:
At first but stifled sobs were heard,
And then his prayer, breathed fervently,
"O master, make my *father* free!"
"Him and thyself, my noble boy!"
Warmly the painter cried:
Raising Sebastian from his feet,
He press'd him to his side.
"Thy talents rare, and filial love,
E'en more have fairly won;
Still be thou mine by other bonds, —
My pupil and my son."

Murillo knew, e'en when the words
Of generous feeling pass'd his lips,
Sebastian's talents soon must lead
To fame, that would his own eclipse;
And, constant to his purpose still,
He joy'd to see his pupil gain,
Beneath his care, such matchless skill
As made his name the pride of Spain.

POTENCY OF ENGLISH WORDS.

JOHN S. McINTOSH.

SEEK out "acceptable words"; and as ye seek them turn to our English stores. Seeking to be rich in speech, you will find that in the broad ocean of our English literature there are pearls of great price, our potent English words; words that are wizards more mighty than the old Scotch magician; words that are pictures bright and moving with all the colouring and circumstances of life; words that go down the century like battle cries; words that sob like litanies, sing like larks, sigh like zephyrs, shout like seas. Seek amid our exhaustless stores and you will find words that flash like the stars of the frosty sky, or are melting and tender like Love's tear-filled eyes; words that are fresh and crisp like the mountain breeze in Autumn, or are mellow and rich as an old painting; words that are sharp, unbending, and precise like Alpine needle-points, or are heavy and rugged like great nuggets of gold; words that are glittering and gay like imperial gems, or are chaste and refined like the face of a Muse. Search and ye shall find words that crush like the battle-axe of Richard, or cut like the scimetar of Saladin; words that sting like a serpent's fangs, or soothe like a mother's kiss; words that can unveil the nether depths of Hell, or paint out the heavenly heights of purity and peace; words that can recall a Judas; words that reveal the Christ.

Here, then, you have to stir, enrich, control, and cultivate your plastic minds, a literature that embodies, in the most perfect forms of Elizabethan words, the peerless gentleness of a Sidney, the unquailing bravery of a Glanville, the quiet majesty of a Cecil, the dashing hardihood of a Raleigh, and the sublime dignity of a Howard. What a rich field of supply is here! Here is a literature that is marked by terseness and clearness, by soberness and majesty, by sweetness and fullness of expression never surpassed, rarely equalled. Here you have for your guidance and enrichment as speakers a field of literature marked in one department by the pureness, thoroughness, and calmness of the sage who loves rich, deep, but strongly ruled speech, and shuns with holy scorn all strain after the startling or striking; a literature marked in another department by the white glow of fiery zeal, the rapid rush of the dauntless will, and by the passionate, piercing cry of the deeply stirred but despairing seer; a literature marked in another department by short, sharp sentences, by pointed antitheses, striking outbursts, flashing images. This is the literature that presents to you the gathered wealth of the English tongue; and yet this vast and noble library into which I would introduce you, far from exhausting, only half reveals the marvellous riches of that language whose inexhaustible stores and manifold resources scarcely one amid a thousand speakers ever more than touches. Before us stands a grand instrument of countless strings, of myriad notes and keys, and we are content with some few hundreds, and these not the purest, richest, deepest, sweetest. If you would be strong of speech, master more of these notes; let your vocabulary be rich, varied, pure, and proportionate will be your power and attractiveness as speakers. I would have you deeply impressed by the force, fullness, and flexibility of our noble tongue, where, if anywhere, the gigantic strength of thought and truth is wedded to the seraphic beauty of perfect utterance. I would have you fling yourselves unhesitatingly out into this great fresh sea, like bold swimmers into the rolling waves of ocean. It will make you healthy, vigorous, supple, and equal to a hundred calls of duty. I would have you cherish sacredly this goodly heritage, won by centuries of English thought and countless lives of English toil. I would have you jealous, like the apostle over the Church, over these pure wells of English undefiled: de grade not our sacred tongue by slang; defile not its crystal streams with the foul waters of careless speech; honour its stern old parentage, obey its simple yet severe grammar, watch its perfect rhythm, and never mix its blue blood, the gift of noblest sires, with the base puddle of any mongrel race; never speak half the language of Ashdod and half of Canaan, but be ye of a pure English lip.

THE BLIND HIGHLAND BOY.

William Wordsworth.

Part I.

A highland boy! — why call him so?
Because, my children, ye must know
That, under hills which rise like towers,
Far higher than these hills of ours,
  He from his birth had lived.

He ne'er had seen one earthly sight,—
The Sun, the day, the stars, the night;
Or tree, or butterfly, or flower,
Or fish in stream, or bird in bower,
  Or woman, man, or child.

And yet he neither droop'd nor pined,
Nor had a melancholy mind;
For God took pity on the boy,
And was his friend, and gave him joy
  Of which we nothing know.

His mother, too, no doubt, above
Her other children him did love:
For, was she here, or was she there,
She thought of him with constant care,
  And more than mother's love.

And proud she was of heart, when, clad
In crimson stockings, tartan plaid,
And bonnet with a feather gay,
To kirk he on the Sabbath day
   Went hand in hand with her.

A dog, too, had he; not for need,
But one to play with and to feed;
Which would have led him, if bereft
Of company or friends, and left
   Without a better guide.

And then the bagpipes he could blow,
And thus from house to house would go;
And all were pleased to hear and see,
For none made sweeter melody
   Than did the poor blind boy.

Yet he had many a restless dream;
Both when he heard the eagles scream,
And when he heard the torrents roar,
And heard the water beat the shore
   Near which their cottage stood.

Beside a lake this cottage stood,
Not small like ours, a peaceful flood;
But one of mighty size, and strange;
That, rough or smooth, is full of change,
   And stirring in its bed.

For to this lake, by night and day,
The great sea-water finds its way
Through long, long windings of the hills,
And drinks up all the pretty rills,
   And rivers large and strong:

Then hurries back the way it came, —
Returns, on errand still the same:
This did it when the Earth was new;
And this for evermore will do
   As long as Earth shall last.

And, with the coming of the tide,
Come boats and ships that safely ride
Between the woods and lofty rocks;
And to the shepherds with their flocks
  Bring tales of other lands.

And of those tales, whate'er they were,
The blind boy always had his share;
Whether of mighty towers, or vales
With warmer suns and softer gales,
  Or wonders of the Deep.

Yet more it pleased him, more it stirr'd,
When from the water-side he heard
The shouting, and the jolly cheers;
The bustle of the mariners
  In stillness or in storm.

But what do his desires avail?
For *he* must never handle sail;
Nor mount the mast, nor row, nor float
In sailor's ship, or fisher's boat,
  Upon the rocking waves.

Thus lived he by Lock-Leven's side
Still sounding with the sounding tide,
And heard the billows leap and dance,
Without a shadow of mischance,
  Till he was ten years old.

PART II. — THE BLIND BOY'S SAIL ON THE LAKE.

And then, one day, (now mark me well,
Ye soon shall know how this befell,)
He, in a vessel of his own,
On the swift flood is hurrying down,
  Down to the mighty Sea.

But, say, what bears him? — Ye have seen
The Indian's bow, his arrows keen,
Rare beasts, and birds with plumage bright;
Gifts which, for wonder or delight,
Are brought in ships from far.

Such gifts had those seafaring men
Spread round that haven in the glen;
Each hut, perchance, might have its own;
And to the boy they all were known, —
He knew and prized them all.

The rarest was a turtle-shell
Which he, poor child, had studied well.
He'd heard how, in a shell like this,
An English boy, O thought of bliss!
Had stoutly launch'd from shore.

Our Highland boy oft visited
The house that held this prize; and, led
By choice or chance, did thither come
One day when no one was at home,
And found the door unbarr'd.

While there he sate, alone and blind,
That story flash'd upon his mind:
A bold thought roused him; and he took
The shell from out its secret nook,
And bore it on his head.

He launch'd his vessel; and in pride
Of spirit, from Lock-Leven's side,
Stepp'd into it; his thoughts all free
As the light breezes that with glee
Sang through th' adventurer's hair.

Awhile he stood upon his feet;
He felt the motion, — took his seat;

Still better pleased, as more and more
The tide retreated from the shore,
  And suck'd, and suck'd him in.

And there he is in face of Heaven.
How rapidly the child is driven!
The fourth part of a mile, I ween,
He thus had gone, ere he was seen
  By any human eye.

But, when he first was seen, O me,
What shrieking and what misery!
For many saw: among the rest
His mother, she who loved him best,
  She saw her poor blind boy.

But, for the child, the sightless boy,
It is the triumph of his joy!
The bravest traveller in balloon,
Mounting as if to reach the Moon,
  Was never half so blest.

And let him, let him go his way,
Alone, and innocent and gay!
For, if good Angels love to wait
On the forlorn unfortunate,
  This child will take no harm.

But quickly with a silent crew
A boat is ready to pursue;
And from the shore their course they take,
And swiftly down the running lake
  They follow the blind boy.

With sound, the least that can be made,
They follow, more and more afraid,
More cautious as they draw more near;
But in his darkness he can hear,
  And guesses their intent.

"*Lei-gha, lei-gha!*" he then cried out,
"*Lei-gha, lei-gha!*" with eager shout:
Thus did he cry, and thus did pray,
And what he meant was, "Keep away,
  And leave me to myself!"

Alas! and when he felt their hands, —
You've often heard of magic wands,
That with a motion overthrow
A palace of the proudest show,
  Or melt it into air:

So all his dreams, — that inward light
With which his soul had shone so bright,
All vanish'd: 'twas a heartfelt cross
To him, a heavy, bitter loss,
  As ever he had known.

But, hark! a gratulating voice,
With which the very hills rejoice:
'Tis from the crowd, who tremblingly
Have watch'd th' event, and now can see
  That he is safe at last.

And in the general joy of heart
The blind boy's little dog took part:
He leapt about, and oft did kiss
His master's hands in sign of bliss,
  With sound like lamentation.

But, most of all, his mother dear,
She who had fainted with her fear,
Rejoiced when, waking, she espies
The child; when she can trust her eyes,
  And touches the blind boy,

She led him home, and wept amain
When he was in the house again:
Tears flow'd in torrents from her eyes;
She kiss'd him, — how could she chastise?
  She was too happy far.

SIR WALTER SCOTT AND HIS DOGS.

WASHINGTON IRVING.

As we sallied forth, every dog in the establishment turned out to attend us. There was the old staghound, Maida, a noble animal; and Hamlet, the black greyhound, a wild, thoughtless youngster, not yet arrived at the years of discretion; and Finette, a beautiful setter, with soft, silken hair, long pendent ears, and a mild eye, the parlour favourite. When in front of the house, we were joined by a superannuated greyhound, who came from the kitchen wagging his tail, and was cheered by Scott as an old friend and comrade. In our walks, he would frequently pause in conversation, to notice his dogs, and speak to them as if rational companions: and, indeed, there appears to be a vast deal of rationality in these faithful attendants on man, derived from their close intimacy with him.

Maida deported himself with a gravity becoming his age and size, and seemed to consider himself called upon to preserve a great degree of dignity and decorum in our society. As he jogged along a little distance ahead of us, the young dogs would gambol about him, leap on his neck, worry at his ears, and endeavour to tease him into a gambol. The old dog would keep on for a long time with imperturbable solemnity, now and then seeming to rebuke the wantonness of his young companions. At length he would make a sudden turn, seize one of them, and tumble him in the dust; then, giving a glance at us, as much as to say, "You see, gentlemen, I can't help giving way to this nonsense," he would resume his gravity, and jog on as before.

Scott amused himself with these peculiarities. "I make no doubt," said he, "when Maida is alone with these young dogs he throws gravity aside, and plays the boy as much as any of them; but he is ashamed to do so in our company, and seems to say, 'Have done with your nonsense, youngsters: what will the laird and that other gentleman think of me if I give way to such foolery?'"

Scott amused himself with the peculiarities of another of his dogs, a little shamefaced terrier, with large glassy eyes, one of the most sensitive little bodies to insult and indignity in the world. If ever he whipt him, he said, the little fellow would sneak off and hide himself from the light of day in a lumber-garret, from whence there was no drawing him forth but by the sound of the chopping-knife, as if chopping up his victuals, when he would steal forth with humiliated and downcast look, but would skulk away again if any one regarded him.

While we were discussing the humours and peculiarities of our canine companions, some object provoked their spleen, and produced a sharp and petulant barking from the smaller fry; but it was some time before Maida was sufficiently roused to ramp forward two or three bounds, and join the chorus with a deep-mouthed *bow wow*. It was but a transient outbreak, and he returned instantly, wagging his tail, and looking up dubiously in his master's face, uncertain whether he would receive censure or applause. "Ay, ay, old boy!" cried Scott, "you have done wonders; you have shaken Eildon hills with your roaring: you may now lay by your artillery for the rest of the day." — "Maida," continued he, "is like the great gun at Constantinople: it takes so long to get it ready, that the smaller guns can fire off a dozen times first; but when it does go off it plays the very devil."

These simple anecdotes may serve to show the delightful play of Scott's humours and feelings in private life. His domestic animals were his friends. Everything about him seemed to rejoice in the light of his countenance.

MORNING.

DANIEL WEBSTER.

RICHMOND, April 29, 5 A.M., 1847.

WHETHER it be a favour or an annoyance, you owe this letter to my habit of early rising. From the hour marked at the top of the page, you will naturally conclude that my companions are not now engaging my attention, as we have not calculated on being early travellers to-day.

This city has "a pleasant seat." It is high; the James river runs below it; and when I went out an hour ago nothing was heard but the roar of the falls. The air is tranquil, and its temperature mild.

It is morning; and a morning sweet and fresh and delightful. Everybody knows the morning in its metaphorical sense, applied to so many objects, and on so many occasions. The health, strength, and beauty of early years lead us to call that period "the morning of life." Of a lovely young woman we say, she is "bright as the morning"; and no one doubts why Lucifer is called "son of the morning."

But the morning itself, few people, inhabitants of cities, know anything about. Among all our good people of Boston, not one in a thousand sees the Sun rise once a-year. They know nothing of the morning. Their idea of it is, that it is that part of the day which comes along after a cup of coffee and a beefsteak, or a piece of toast. With them, morning is not a new issuing of light; a new bursting-forth of the Sun; a new waking-up of all that has life, from a sort of temporary death, to behold again the works of God, the heavens and the earth: it is only a part of the domestic day, belonging to breakfast, to reading the newspapers, answering notes, sending the children to school, and giving orders for dinner. The first faint streaks of light purpling the East, which the lark springs up to greet, and the deeper and deeper colouring into orange and red, till at length "the glorious Sun is seen, regent of the day," — this they never enjoy, for this they never see.

Beautiful descriptions of the morning abound in all languages; but they are the strongest perhaps in those of the East, where the Sun is so often an object of worship. King David speaks of taking to himself "the wings of the morning." This is highly poetical and beautiful. The "wings of the morning" are the beams of the rising Sun. Rays of light are wings. It is thus said that the Sun of Righteousness shall arise "with healing in his wings"; — a rising Sun, which shall scatter light and health and joy throughout the Universe. Milton has fine descriptions of morning, but not so many as Shakespeare, from whose writings pages of the most beautiful images, all founded on the glory of the morning, might be gathered.

I never thought that Adam had much advantage of us, from having seen the world while it was new. The manifestations of the power of God, like His mercies, are "new every morning," and "fresh every evening." We see as fine risings of the Sun as ever Adam saw; and its risings are as much a miracle now as they were in his day, and, I think, a good deal more, because it is now a part of the miracle that for thousands and thousands of years he has come at his appointed time, without the variation of a millionth part of a second. Adam could not tell how this might be!

I know the morning; I am acquainted with it, and I love it, fresh and sweet as it is, a daily new creation, breaking forth, and calling all that have life and breath and being to new adoration, new enjoyments, and new gratitude.

FRIDAY'S FROLIC WITH A BEAR.

DANIEL DEFOE.

As the bear is a heavy, clumsy creature, and does not gallop as the wolf does, who is swift and light, so he has two particular qualities, which generally are the rule of his actions: first, as to men, who are not his proper prey, if you do not meddle with him, he will not meddle with you: but then you must take care to be very civil to him and give him the road, for he is a very nice gentleman; he will not go a step out of his way for a prince; nay, if you are really afraid, your best way is to look another way, and keep going on; for sometimes, if you stop and stand still, and look steadfastly at him, he takes it for an affront; but, if you throw or toss anything at him, and it hits him, though it were but a bit of stick as big as your finger, he thinks himself abused, and sets all other business aside to pursue his revenge, and will have satisfaction in point of honour. This is his first quality: the next is, if he be once affronted, he will never leave you night nor day, till he has his revenge, but follows, at a good round rate, till he overtakes you.

My man Friday had delivered our guide, and, when

we came up to him, on a sudden, we espied the bear come out of the wood, and a vast, monstrous one it was, the biggest by far that ever I saw. We were all a little surprised when we saw him; but, when Friday saw him, it was easy to see joy and courage in the fellow's countenance: O, O, O! says Friday, three times, pointing to him; O master! you give me te leave, me shakee te hand with him; me makee you good laugh.

I was surprised to see the fellow so well pleased: You fool, says I, he will eat you up.—Eatee me up! eatee me up! says Friday, twice over again; me eatee him up; me makee you good laugh: you all stay here, me show you good laugh. So down he sits, and gets off his boots in a moment, and puts on a pair of pumps, gives my other servant his horse, and with his gun away he flew, swift like the wind.

The bear was walking slowly on, and offered to meddle with nobody, till Friday coming pretty near, calls to him, as if the bear could understand him, Hark ye, hark ye, says Friday, me speakee with you. We followed at a distance; for now we were entered a great forest, where the country was plain and pretty open, though it had many trees in it scattered here and there. Friday, who had, as we say, the heels of the bear, came up with him quickly, and takes up a great stone and throws it at him, and hit him just on the head, but did him no more harm than if he had thrown it against a wall; but it answered Friday's end, for the rogue was so void of fear that he did it purely to make the bear follow him, and show us some laugh as he called it.

As soon as the bear felt the blow, and saw him, he turns about, and comes after him, taking long strides, and shuffling on at a strange rate, such as would have put a horse to a middling gallop; away runs Friday, and takes his course as if he run towards us for help; so we all resolved to fire at once upon the bear, and deliver my man; though I was angry at him heartily for bringing the bear back upon us, when he was going about his own business another way; and especially I was angry that he had turned the bear upon us, and then run away; and I called out, You dog, is this your making us laugh? Come away, and take your horse, that we may shoot the creature.

He heard me, and cried out, No shoot, no shoot; stand still, and you get much laugh; and as the nimble creature ran two feet for the bear's one, he turned on a sudden, on one side of us, and, seeing a great oak tree fit for his purpose, he beckoned to us to follow; and doubling his pace, he gets nimbly up the tree, laying his gun down upon the ground, at about five or six yards from the bottom of the tree. The bear soon came to the tree, and we followed at a distance: the first thing he did, he stopped at the gun, smelt to it, but let it lie, and up he scrambles into the tree, climbing like a cat, though so monstrous heavy. I was amazed at the folly, as I thought it, of my man, and could not for my life see any thing to laugh at yet, till, seeing the bear get up the tree, we all rode near to him.

When we came to the tree, there was Friday got out to the small end of a large branch, and the bear got about half way to him. As soon as the bear got out to that part where the limb of the tree was weaker, — Ha! says he to us, now you see me teachee the bear dance: so he falls a-jumping and shaking the bough, at which the bear began to totter, but stood still, and began to look behind him, to see how he should get back; then, indeed, we did laugh heartily. But Friday had not done with him by a great deal; when, seeing him stand still, he calls out to him again, as if he had supposed the bear could speak English, What, you come no further? pray you come further: so he left jumping and shaking the tree; and the bear, just as if he understood what he said, did come a little further; then he fell a-jumping again, and the bear stopped again.

We thought now was a good time to knock him on the head, and called to Friday to stand still, and we would shoot the bear: but he cried out earnestly, O pray! O pray! no shoot, me shoot by-and-then; he would have said by-and-by. However, Friday danced so much, and the bear stood so ticklish, that we had laughing enough, but still could not imagine what the fellow would do: for first we thought he depended upon shaking the bear off; and we found the bear was too cunning for that too; for he would not go out far enough to be thrown down, but clings fast with his great broad claws and feet, so that we could not imagine what would be the end of it, and what the jest would be at last.

But Friday puts us out of doubt quickly: for, seeing the bear cling fast to the bough, and that he would not come any further, Well, well, says Friday, you no come further, me go; you no come to me, me come to you: and, upon this, he goes out to the smaller end of the bough, where it would bend with his weight, and gently lets himself down by it, till he came near enough to jump down on his feet, and away he runs to his gun, takes it up, and stands still. Well, said I to him, Friday, what will you do now? Why don't you shoot him? —No shoot, says Friday, no yet; me no shoot now, me no kill; me stay, give you one more laugh; and, indeed, so he did: for when the bear saw his enemy gone, he comes back from the bough where he stood, but did it mighty cautiously, looking behind him every step, and coming backward till he got into the body of the tree; then, with the same hinder-end foremost, he came down the tree, grasping it with his claws, and moving one foot at a time, very leisurely. At this juncture, and just before he could set his hind-foot on the ground, Friday stepped up close to him, clapped the muzzle of his piece into his ear, and shot him dead. Then the rogue turned about, to see if we did not laugh; and when he saw we were pleased, by our looks, he falls a laughing himself very loud. So we kill bear in my country, says Friday. So you kill them? says I: why, you have no guns.— No, says he, no gun, but shoot great much long arrow.

CRUSOE'S FIGHT WITH WOLVES.

DANIEL DEFOE.

THE ground was still covered with snow, though not so deep and dangerous as on the mountains; and the ravenous creatures were come down into the forest and plain country to seek for food, and had done a great deal of mischief in the villages, where they killed a great many sheep and horses, and some people too. We had one dangerous place to pass, of which our guide told us, if there were more wolves in the country we should find them there; and this was a small plain, surrounded with woods on every side, and a long narrow defile, or lane, which we were to pass to get through the wood, and then we should come to the village where we were to lodge. It was within half an hour of sunset when we entered the first wood, and a little after sunset when we came into the plain.

We met with nothing in the first wood, except that,

in a little plain within the wood, which was not above two furlongs over, we saw five great wolves cross the road, full speed one after another, as if they had been in chase of some prey, and had it in view; they took no notice of us, and were gone out of sight in a few moments. Upon this our guide, who, by the way, was but a faint-hearted fellow, bid us keep in a ready posture, for he believed there were more wolves a-coming. We kept our arms ready, and our eyes about us; but we saw no more wolves till we came through that wood, which was near half a league, and entered the plain.

As soon as we came into the plain, we had occasion enough to look about us: the first object we met with was a dead horse, that is to say, a poor horse which the wolves had killed, and at least a dozen of them at work, we could not say eating of him, but picking of his bones rather; for they had eaten up all the flesh before. We did not think fit to disturb them at their feast; neither did they take much notice of us. Friday would have let fly at them, but I would not suffer him by any means; for I found we were like to have more business upon our hands than we were aware of.

We were not gone half over the plain, when we began to hear the wolves howl in the wood on our left in a frightful manner, and presently after we saw about a hundred coming on directly towards us, all in a body, and most of them in a line, as regularly as an army drawn up by an experienced officer. I scarce knew in what manner to receive them, but found to draw ourselves in a close line was the only way: so we formed in a moment: but, that we might not have too much interval, I ordered that only every other man should fire, and that the others who had not fired should stand ready to give them a second volley immediately, if they continued to advance upon us; and then that those who had fired at first should not pretend to load their fusees again, but stand ready every one with a pistol, for we were all armed with a fusee and a pair of pistols each man: so we were, by this method, able to fire six volleys, half of us at a time.

However, at present we had no necessity: for, upon the first volley, the enemy made a full stop, being terrified as well with the noise as with the fire; four of them, being shot in the head, dropped; several others were wounded, and went bleeding off, as we could see by the snow. I found they stopped, but did not immediately retreat; whereupon, remembering that the fiercest creatures were terrified at the voice of a man, I caused all the company to halloo as loud as we could; and, upon our shout, they began to retire, and turn about. I then ordered a second volley to be fired in their rear, which put them to the gallop, and away they went to the woods. This gave us leisure to charge our pieces again; and we had but little more than loaded our fusees, and put ourselves in readiness, when we heard a terrible noise in the same wood, on our left, only that it was further onward, the same way we were to go.

The night was coming on, and the light began to be dusky, which made it worse on our side; but, the noise increasing, we could easily perceive that it was the howling and yelling of those hellish creatures; and on a sudden we perceived two or three troops of wolves, one on our left, one behind us, and one in our front, so that we seemed to be surrounded with them: however, as they did not fall upon us, we kept our way forward, as fast as we could make our horses go, which, the way being very rough, was only a good hard trot. In this manner we came in view of the entrance of the wood, through which we were to pass, at the further side of the plain; but we were greatly surprised, when, coming nearer the lane or pass, we saw a confused number of wolves standing just at the entrance.

This filled us with horror, and we knew not what course to take; but the creatures resolved us soon, for they gathered about us presently, in hopes of prey; and I verily believe there were three hundred of them. It happened very much to our advantage, that at the entrance into the wood, there lay some large timber trees, which had been cut down the Summer before, and I suppose lay there for carriage. I drew my little troop in among those trees, and, placing ourselves in a line behind one long tree, I advised them all to alight, and, keeping that tree before us for a breastwork, to stand in a triangle or three fronts enclosing our horses in the centre. We did so, and it was well we did; for never was a more furious charge than the creatures made upon us in this place. They came on with a growling kind of noise, and mounted the piece of timber, which was our breastwork, as if they were only rushing upon their prey; and this fury of theirs, it seems, was principally occasioned by their seeing our horses behind us. I ordered our men to fire as before, every other man; and they took their aim so sure, that they killed several of the wolves at the first volley; but there was a necessity to keep a continual firing, for they came on like devils, those behind pushing on those before.

When we had fired a second volley of our fusees, we thought they stopped a little, and I hoped they would go off; but it was but a moment, for others came forward again: so we fired two volleys of our pistols; and I believe in these four firings we killed seventeen or eighteen of them, and lamed twice as many, yet they came on again. I was loth to spend our shot too hastily; so I called my servant, and, giving him a horn of powder, I bade him lay a train all along the piece of timber, and let it be a large train.

He did so; and had but just time to get away, when the wolves came up to it, and some got upon it, when I, snapping an uncharged pistol close to the powder, set it on fire: those that were upon the timber were scorched with it; and six or seven of them fell or rather jumped in among us, with the force and fright of the fire: we dispatched these in an instant, and the rest were so frightened with the light, which the night, for it was now very near dark, made more terrible, that they drew back a little; upon which I ordered our last pistols to be fired off in one volley, and after that we gave a shout: upon this the wolves turned tail, and we sallied immediately upon near twenty lame ones, that we found struggling on the ground, and fell a cutting them with our swords, which answered our expectation; for the crying and howling they made was better understood by their fellows; so that they all fled and left us.

We had, first and last, killed about threescore of them; and, had it been daylight, we had killed many more. The field of battle being thus cleared, we made forward again, for we had still near a league to go. We heard the ravenous creatures howl and yell in the woods as we went, several times, and sometimes we fancied we saw some of them, but, the snow dazzling our eyes, we were not certain: in about an hour more we came to the town where we were to lodge, which we found in a terrible fright, and all in arms; for, the night before, the wolves and some bears had broke into the village, and put them in such terror, that they were obliged to keep guard night and day, but especially in the night, to preserve their cattle, and, indeed, their people.

LADY CLARA VERE DE VERE.

ALFRED TENNYSON.

LADY Clara Vere de Vere,
Of me you shall not win renown:
You thought to break a country heart
For pastime, ere you went to town.
At me you smiled, but unbeguiled
I saw the snare, and I retired:
The daughter of a hundred Earls,
You are not one to be desired.

Lady Clara Vere de Vere,
I know you proud to bear your name;
Your pride is yet no mate for mine,
Too proud to care from whence I came:
Nor would I break for your sweet sake
A heart that dotes on truer charms.
A simple maiden in her flower
Is worth a hundred coats-of-arms.

Lady Clara Vere de Vere,
Some meeker pupil you must find;
For, were you queen of all that is,
I could not stoop to such a mind.
You sought to prove how I could love,
And my disdain is my reply:
The lion on your old stone gates
Is not more cold to you than I.

Lady Clara Vere de Vere,
You put strange memories in my head:
Not thrice your branching limes have blown
Since I beheld young Laurence dead.

O, your sweet eyes, your low replies!
A great enchantress you may be;
But there was that across his throat
Which you had hardly cared to see.

Lady Clara Vere de Vere,
When thus he met his mother's view,
She had the passions of her kind,
She spake some certain truths of you:
Indeed I heard one bitter word
That scarce is fit for you to hear;
Her manners had not that repose
Which stamps the cast of Vere de Vere.

Lady Clara Vere de Vere,
There stands a spectre in your hall:
The guilt of blood is at your door;
You changed a wholesome heart to gall.
You held your course without remorse,
To make him trust his modest worth;
And, last, you fix'd a vacant stare,
And slew him with your noble birth.

Trust me, Clara Vere de Vere,
From yon blue heavens above us bent
The grand old gardener and his wife
Smile at the claims of long descent.
Howe'er it be, it seems to me
'Tis only noble to be good:
Kind hearts are more than coronets,
And simple faith than Norman blood.

I know you, Clara Vere de Vere:
You pine among your halls and towers;
The languid light of your proud eyes
Is wearied of the rolling hours.
In glowing health, with boundless wealth,
But sickening of a vague disease,

You know so ill to deal with time,
You needs must play such pranks as these.

Clara, Clara Vere de Vere,
If Time be heavy on your hands,
Are there no beggars at your gate,
Nor any poor about your lands?
O! teach the orphan-boy to read,
Or teach the orphan-girl to sew;
Pray Heaven for a human heart,
And let the foolish yeoman go.

OUR TRAVELLED PARSON.

WILL CARLETON.

FOR twenty years and over our good parson had been toiling
To chip the bad meat from our hearts, and keep the good from spoiling;
But finally he wilted down, and went to looking sickly,
And the doctor said that something must be put up for him quickly.

So we kind of clubb'd together, each according to his notion,
And bought a circular ticket in the lands across the ocean;
Wrapp'd some pocket money in it, — what we thought would easy do him, —
And appointed me committee-man to go and take it to him.

I found him in his study, looking rather worse than ever,
And told him 'twas decided that his flock and he should sever:
Then his eyes grew wide with wonder, and it seem'd almost to blind 'em;
And some tears look'd out o' window, with some others close behind 'em.

Then I handed him the ticket, with a little bow of deference;
And he studied quite a little ere he got his proper reference;
And then the tears that waited, great unmanageable creatures,
Let themselves quite out o' window, and came trickling down his features.

I wish you could ha' seen him, coming back all fresh and glowing,
His clothes so worn and seedy, and his face so fat and knowing;
I wish you could have heard him when he pray'd for us who sent him
And paid us back twice over all the money we had lent him.

'Twas a feast to all believers, 'twas a blight on contradiction,
To hear one just from Calvary talk about the crucifixion;
'Twas a damper on those fellows who pretended they could
doubt it,
To have a man, who'd been there, stand and tell them all about it

Paul, maybe, beat our pastor in the Bible knots unravelling,
And establishing new churches; but he couldn't touch him trav
elling;
Nor in his journeys pick up half the general information;
But then he hadn't the railroads and the steamboat navigation.

And every foot of Scripture whose location used to stump us
Was now regularly laid out, with the different points of compass
When he undertook a picture, he quite natural would draw it;
He would paint it out so honest that it seem'd as if you saw it.

An' the way he chisell'd Europe, — O, the way he scamper'd
through it!
Not a mountain dodged his climbing, not a city but he knew it:
There wasn't any subject to explain in all creation,
But he could go to Europe and bring back an illustration.

So we crowded out to hear him, much instructed and delighted;
'Twas a picture-show, a lecture, and a sermon, all united;
And my wife would wipe her glasses, and serenely pat her Test'
ment,
And whisper, "That ere ticket was a very good investment."

Now, after six months' travel we were most of us all ready
To settle down a little, so's to live more staid and steady;
To develop home resources, with no foreign cares to fret us,
Using home-made faith more frequent; but the parson wouldn't
let us.

To view the self-same scenery time and time again he'd call us;
Over rivers, plains, and mountains he would any minute haul us;
He slighted our home sorrows, and our spirits' aches and ailings,
To get the cargoes ready for his reg'lar Sunday sailings.

He would take us off a-touring in all spiritual weather,
Till we at last got homesick-like, and seasick altogether;
And "I wish to all that's peaceful," said one free-expression'd
brother,
"That the Lord had made one cont'nent, and then never made
another!"

Sometimes, indeed, he'd take us into sweet, familiar places,
And pull along quite steady in the good old gospel traces;
But soon my wife would shudder, just as if a chill had got her,
Whispering, "O, my goodness gracious! he's a-takin' to the
water!"

And it wasn't the same old comfort when he call'd around to see us;
On a branch of foreign travel he was sure at last to tree us:
All unconscious of his error, he would sweetly patronize us,
And with oft-repeated stories still endeavour to surprise us.

And the sinners got to laughing; and that fin'lly gall'd and stung us
To ask him, "Would he kindly once more settle down among us?
Didn't he think that more home-produce would improve our souls' digestions?"
They appointed me committee-man to go and ask the questions.

I found him in his garden, trim an' buoyant as a feather;
He press'd my hand, exclaiming, "This is quite Italian weather;
How it 'minds me of the evenings when, your distant hearts caressing,
Upon my benefactors I invoked the heavenly blessing!"

I went and told the brothers, "No, I cannot bear to grieve him;
He's so happy in his exile, it's the proper place to leave him.
I took that journey to him, and right bitterly I rue it;
But I cannot take it from him: if you want to, go and do it."

Now a new restraint entirely seem'd next Sunday to infold him,
And he look'd so hurt and humbled that I knew some one had told him.
Subdued-like was his manner, and some tones were hardly vocal;
But every word he utter'd was pre-eminently local.

The sermon sounded awkward, and we awkward felt who heard it:
'Twas a grief to see him hedge it, 'twas a pain to hear him word it:
"When I was in—" was, maybe, half a dozen times repeated,
But that sentence seem'd to scare him, and was always uncompleted.

As weeks went on, his old smile would occasionally brighten,
But the voice was growing feeble, and the face began to whiten:
He would look off to the eastward with a listful, weary sighing;
And 'twas whisper'd that our pastor in a foreign land was dying.

The coffin lay 'mid garlands smiling sad as if they knew us;
The patient face within it preach'd a final sermon to us:
Our parson had gone touring on a trip he'd long been earning,
In that wonder-land whence tickets are not issued for returning.

O tender, good-soul'd shepherd! your sweet smiling lips, half-parted,
Told of scenery that burst on you just the minute that you started!
Could you preach once more among us, you might wander without fearing;
You could give us tales of glory we would never tire of hearing.

HAPPINESS OF ANIMALS.

WILLIAM COWPER.

HERE unmolested, through whatever sign
The Sun proceeds, I wander; neither mist,
Nor freezing sky nor sultry, checking me,
Nor stranger intermeddling with my joy.
Even in the Spring and playtime of the year,
That calls th' unwonted villager abroad
With all her little ones, a sportive train,
To gather kingcups in the yellow mead,
These shades are all my own. The timorous hare,
Grown so familiar with her frequent guest,
Scarce shuns me; and the stockdove unalarm'd
Sits cooing in the pine-tree, nor suspends
His long love-ditty for my near approach.
Drawn from his refuge in some lonely elm
That age or injury has hollow'd deep,
Where on his bed of wool and matted leaves
He has outslept the Winter, ventures forth,
To frisk awhile, and bask in the warm sun,
The squirrel, flippant, pert, and full of play.
He sees me, and at once, swift as a bird,
Ascends the neighbouring beech; there whisks his brush,
And perks his ears, and stamps and scolds aloud,
With all the prettiness of feign'd alarm,
And anger insignificantly fierce.

The heart is hard in nature, and unfit
For human fellowship, as being void
Of sympathy, and therefore dead alike
To love and friendship both, that is not pleased
With sight of animals enjoying life,
Nor feels their happiness augment his own.
The bounding fawn that darts across the glade
When none pursues, through mere delight of heart

And spirits buoyant with excess of glee;
The horse, as wanton and almost as fleet,
That skims the spacious meadow at full speed,
Then stops and snorts, and, throwing high his heels,
Starts to the voluntary race again;
The very kine that gambol at high noon,
The total herd receiving first, from one
That leads the dance, a summons to be gay,
Though wild their strange vagaries, and uncouth
Their efforts, yet resolved with one consent
To give such act and utterance as they may
To ecstasy too big to be suppress'd;—
These, and a thousand images of bliss,
With which kind Nature graces every scene
Where cruel man defeats not her design,
Impart to the benevolent, who wish
All that are capable of pleasure pleased,
A far superior happiness to theirs,—
The comfort of a reasonable joy.

II.

LOVE, BEAUTY, TRANQUILLITY.

GENEVIEVE.

S. T. Coleridge.

Maid of my Love, sweet Genevieve!
In Beauty's light you glide along;
Your eye is like the star of eve,
And sweet your Voice as Seraph's song.
Yet not your heavenly Beauty gives
This heart with passion soft to glow:
Within your soul a Voice there lives!
It bids you hear the tale of Woe.
When sinking low the Sufferer wan
Beholds no hand outstretch'd to save,
Fair, as the bosom of the Swan
That rises graceful o'er the wave,
I've seen your breast with pity heave,
And therefore love I you, sweet Genevieve!

All thoughts, all passions, all delights,
Whatever stirs this mortal frame,
All are but ministers of Love,
  And feed his sacred flame.

Oft in my waking dreams do I
Live o'er again that happy hour,
When midway on the mount I lay,
  Beside the ruin'd tower.

The moonshine, stealing o'er the scene,
Had blended with the lights of eve;
And she was there, my hope, my joy,
  My own dear Genevieve!

She lean'd against the armèd man,
The statue of the armèd knight;
She stood and listen'd to my lay,
  Amid the lingering light.

Few sorrows hath she of her own,
My hope, my joy, my Genevieve!
She loves me best, whene'er I sing
  The songs that make her grieve.

I play'd a soft and doleful air,
I sang an old and moving story, —
An old rude song, that suited well
  That ruin wild and hoary.

She listen'd with a flitting blush,
With downcast eyes and modest grace;
For well she knew I could not choose
  But gaze upon her face.

I told her of the Knight that wore
Upon his shield a burning brand;
And that for ten long years he woo'd
  The Lady of the Land.

I told her how he pined; and, ah!
The deep, the low, the pleading tone
With which I sang another's love
  Interpreted my own.

She listen'd with a flitting blush,
With downcast eyes and modest grace;
And she forgave me, that I gazed
  Too fondly on her face!

But when I told the cruel scorn
That crazed that bold and lovely Knight,
And that he cross'd the mountain-woods,
  Nor rested day nor night;

That sometimes from the savage den,
And sometimes from the darksome shade,
And sometimes starting up at once
  In green and sunny glade, —

There came and look'd him in the face
An angel beautiful and bright;
And that he knew it was a Fiend,
  This miserable Knight;

And that, unknowing what he did,
He leap'd amid a murderous band,
And saved from outrage worse than death
  The Lady of the Land; —

And how she wept, and clasp'd his knees;
And how she tended him in vain, —
And ever strove to expiate
  That scorn that crazed his brain; —

And that she nursed him in a cave;
And how his madness went away,
When on the yellow forest-leaves
  A dying man he lay; —

His dying words, — but when I reach'd
That tenderest strain of all the ditty,
My faltering voice and pausing harp
  Disturb'd her soul with pity!

All impulses of soul and sense
Had thrill'd my guileless Genevieve;
The music and the doleful tale,
  The rich and balmy eve;

And hopes, and fears that kindle hope,
And undistinguishable throng,
And gentle wishes long subdued,
  Subdued and cherish'd long!

She wept with pity and delight,
She blush'd with love and virgin-shame;
And, like the murmur of a dream,
  I heard her breathe my name.

Her bosom heaved, — she stepp'd aside,
As conscious of my look she stepp'd, —
Then suddenly, with timorous eye,
  She fled to me and wept.

She half enclosed me with her arms,
She press'd me with a meek embrace;
And, bending back her head, look'd up,
  And gazed upon my face.

'Twas partly love, and partly fear,
And partly 'twas a bashful art,
That I might rather feel than see
  The swelling of her heart.

I calm'd her fears, and she was calm,
And told her love with virgin-pride;
And so I won my Genevieve,
  My bright and beauteous Bride.

SEEN, LOVED, WEDDED.

WILLIAM WORDSWORTH.

SHE was a Phantom of delight
When first she gleam'd upon my sight;
A lovely Apparition, sent
To be a moment's ornament:

Her eyes as stars of twilight fair;
Like twilight's, too, her dusky hair;
But all things else about her drawn
From May-time and the cheerful Dawn;
A dancing Shape, an Image gay,
To haunt, to startle, and waylay.

I saw her upon nearer view,
A Spirit, yet a Woman too!
Her household motions light and free,
And steps of virgin liberty;
A countenance in which did meet
Sweet records, promises as sweet;
A creature not too bright or good
For human nature's daily food;
For transient sorrows, simple wiles,
Praise, blame, love, kisses, tears, and smiles.

And now I see with eye serene
The very pulse of the machine;
A Being breathing thoughtful breath,
A Traveller between life and death;
The reason firm, the temperate will,
Endurance, foresight, strength, and skill;
A perfect Woman, nobly plann'd
To warn, to comfort, and command;
And yet a Spirit still, and bright
With something of an angel light.

MR. GRAHAM AND LADY CLEMENTINA.

George MacDonald.

Him only in all London must she see to bid good-bye. As usual now, she was shown into his room,—his only one. As usual also, she found him poring over his Greek Testament. The gracious, graceful woman looked lovelily strange in that mean chamber, like an opal in a brass ring. There was no such contrast between the room and its occupant. His bodily presence was too weak to "stick fiery off" from its surroundings; and, to the eye that saw through the bodily presence to the inherent grandeur, that grandeur suggested no discrepancy, being of the kind that lifts everything to its own level, casts the mantle of its own radiance over its surroundings. Still, to the eye of love and reverence, it was not pleasant to see him in such *entourage*, and, now that Clementina was going to leave him, the ministering spirit that dwelt in the woman was troubled.

"Ah!" he said, and rose as she entered, "this is then the angel of my deliverance!" But with such a smile he did not look as if he had much to be delivered from. "You see," he went on, "old man as I am, and peaceful, the Summer will lay hold upon me. She stretches out a long arm into this desert of houses and stones, and sets me longing after the green fields and the living air — it seems dead here — and the face of God, as much as one may behold of the Infinite through the revealing veil of earth and sky and sea. I was even getting a little tired of that glorious God-and-man lover, Saul of Tarsus: no, not of him, never of *him*, only of his shadow in his words. Yet perhaps — yes, I think so — it is God alone of whom a man can never get tired. Well, no matter: tired I was, when, lo! here comes my pupil, with more of God in her face than all the worlds and their skies He ever made."

"I would my heart were as full of Him too, then, sir," answered Clementina. "But, if I am anything of a comfort to you, I am more than glad; therefore the more sorry to tell you that I am going to leave you, though for a little while only, I trust."

"You do not take me by surprise, my lady. I have of course been looking forward for some time to my loss and your gain. The world is full of little deaths,—deaths of all sorts and sizes, rather let me say. For this one I was prepared. The good summer-land calls you to its bosom, and you must go."

"Come with me," cried Clementina, her eyes eager with the light of a sudden thought, while her heart reproached her grievously that only now first had it come to her.

"A man must not leave the most irksome work for the most peaceful pleasure," answered the schoolmaster. "I am able to live—yes, and do my work—without you, my lady," he added with a smile, "though I shall miss you sorely."

"But you do not know where I want you to come," she said.

"What difference can that make, my lady, except indeed in the amount of pleasure to be refused, seeing this is not a matter of choice? I must be with the children whom I have engaged to teach, and whose parents pay me for my labour; not with those who, besides, can do well without me."

"I cannot, sir,—not for long at least."

"What! not with Malcolm to supply my place?"

Clementina blushed, but only like a white rose. She did not turn her head aside: she did not lower their lids to veil the light she felt mount into her eyes: she looked him gently in the face as before, and her aspect of entreaty did not change. "Ah! do not be unkind, master," she said.

"Unkind!" he repeated. "You know I am not. I have more kindness in my heart than my lips can tell. You do not know, you could not yet imagine, the half of what I hope of and for and from you."

"I *am* going to see Malcolm," she said with a little sigh. "That is, I am going to visit Lady Lossie at her place in Scotland, — your own old home, where so many must love you. *Can't* you come? I shall be travelling alone, quite alone, except my servants."

A shadow came over the schoolmaster's face: "You do not *think*, my lady, or you would not press me. It pains me that you do not see at once it would be dishonest to go without timely notice to my pupils, and to the public too. But, beyond that, I go not where I wish, but where I seem to be called or sent. I never even wish much, except when I pray to Him in whom are hid all the treasures of wisdom and knowledge. After what He wants to give me I am wishing all day long. I used to build many castles, not without a beauty of their own, — that was when I had less understanding, — now I leave them to God to build for me: He does it better, and they last longer. See now, this very hour, when I needed help, could I have contrived a more lovely annihilation of the monotony that threatened to invade my weary spirit than this inroad of light in the person of my Lady Clementina? Nor will He allow me to get overwearied with vain efforts. I do not think He will keep me here long, for I cannot do much for these children. They are but some of His many pagans, — not yet quite ready to receive Christianity, I think, — not like children with some of the old seeds of the truth buried in them, that want to be turned up nearer to the light. True, I *might* be happier where I could hear the larks; but I do not know that anywhere I have been more peaceful than in this little room, in which I see you so often cast round your eyes curiously, perhaps pitifully, my lady."

"It is not at all a fit place for *you*," said Clementina, with a touch of indignation.

"Softly, my lady, lest, without knowing it, your love should make you sin. Who set thee, I pray, for a guardian angel over my welfare? I could scarce have a lovlier, true; but where is thy brevet? No, my lady: it is a greater than thou that sets me the bounds of my habitation. Perhaps He may give me a palace one day. If I might choose, it would be things that belong to a cottage,—the whiteness and the greenness and the sweet odours of cleanliness. But the Father has decreed for His children that they shall know the thing that is neither their ideal nor His. But perhaps, my lady, you would not pity my present condition so much, if you had seen the cottage in which I was born, and where my father and mother loved each other, and died happier than on their wedding-day. When do you go?"

"To-morrow morning, as I purpose."

"Then God be with thee! He *is* with thee, only my prayer is that thou mayst know it."

"Tell me one thing before I go," said Clementina: "are we not commanded to bear each other's burdens, and so fulfil the law of Christ? I read it to-day."

"Then why ask me?"

"For another question: does not that involve the command to those who have burdens, that they should allow others to bear them?"

"Surely, my lady. But *I* have no burden to let you bear."

"Why should I have everything and you nothing? Answer me that."

"My lady, I have millions more than you, for I have been gathering the crumbs under my Master's table for thirty years."

"You are a king," answered Clementina. "But a king needs a handmaiden somewhere in his house: that let me be in yours. No, I will be proud, and assert my rights: I am your daughter. If not, why am I here? You cannot cast me off if you would. Why should you be poor when I am rich? You *are* poor; you cannot deny it," she concluded with a serious playfulness.

"I will not deny my privileges," said the schoolmaster, with a smile such as might have acknowledged the possession of some exquisite and envied rarity.

"I believe," insisted Clementina, "you are just as poor as the apostle Paul when he sat down to make a tent, or as our Lord himself after He gave up carpentering."

"You are wrong there, my lady. I am not so poor as they must often have been."

"But I don't know how long I may be away, and you may fall ill, or — or — see some — some book you want very much, or — "

"I never do," said the schoolmaster.

"What! never see a book you want to have?"

"No, not now. I have my Greek Testament, my Plato, and my Shakespeare, and one or two little books besides whose wisdom I have not yet quite exhausted."

"I can't bear it!" cried Clementina, almost on the point of weeping. "*Let* me be your servant." As she spoke she rose, and, walking softly to him where he sat, kneeled at his knees and held out suppliantly a little bag of white silk tied with crimson. "Take it, — father," she said, hesitating; "take your daughter's offering, — a poor thing to show her love, but something to ease her heart."

He took it, and weighed it up and down in his hand with an amused smile, bent his eyes full on her tears. It was heavy. He emptied it on the seat of a chair. "I never saw so much gold in my life, if it were all taken together," he said. "But I don't want it, my dear. It would trouble me." As he spoke he began to put it in the bag again. "You will want it for your journey," he said.

"I have plenty in my reticule," she answered. "That is a mere nothing to what I could have for writing a cheque. Tell me true: how much money have you?" She said this with such an earnest look of simple love, that the schoolmaster made haste to rise, that he might conceal his growing emotion.

"Rise, my dear lady," he said as he rose himself, "and I will show you." He gave her his hand, and she obeyed, but troubled and disappointed, and so stood looking after him while he went to a drawer. Thence, searching in a corner of it, he brought a half-sovereign, a few shillings, and some coppers, and held them out to her on his hand with the smile of one who has proved his point. "There!" he said, "do you think Saint Paul would have stopped preaching to make a tent so long as he had as much as that in his pocket?"

Clementina had been struggling with herself: now she burst into tears.

"Why, what a misspending of precious sorrow!" exclaimed the schoolmaster. "Do you think because a man has not a gold-mine he must die of hunger?" As he spoke he took her handkerchief from her hand, and dried her tears with it. But he had enough to do to keep back his own. "Because I won't take a bag full of gold from you when I don't want it," he went on, "do you think I should let myself starve without coming to you? I promise you I will let you know — come to you if I can — the moment I get too hungry to do my work well, and have no money left. Should I think it a disgrace to take money from *you?* That would show a poverty of spirit such as I hope never to fall into. My *sole* reason for refusing now is that I do not need it."

But for all his loving words and assurances Clementina could not stay her tears.

"See, then, for your tears are hard to bear, my daughter," he said, "I will take one of these golden ministers; and, if it has flown from me ere you come, I will ask you for another. It *may* be God's will that you should feed me for a time."

A moment of silence followed, broken only by Clementina's failures in quieting herself.

"To me," he resumed, "the sweetest fountain of money is the hand of love, but a man has no right to take it from that fountain except he is in want of it. I am not."

He opened again the bag, and slowly, reverentially indeed, drew from it one of the new sovereigns, put it in his pocket, and laid the bag on the table.

"But your clothes are shabby, sir," said Clementina, looking at him with a sad little shake of the head.

"Are they?" he returned, and looked down at his lower garments, reddening and anxious. "If you tell me, my lady, if you honestly tell me, that my garments" — and he looked at the sleeve of his coat — "are unsightly, I will take of your money to buy me a new suit." Over his coat-sleeve he regarded her, questioning.

"Everything about you is beautiful," she burst out. "You want nothing but a body that lets the light through." She took the hand still raised in his survey of his sleeve, pressed it to her lips, and walked slowly from the room.

He took the bag of gold from the table, and followed

her down the stair. Her chariot was waiting for her at the door. He handed her in, and laid the bag on the little seat in front.

THE BRIDGE.

H. W. Longfellow.

I stood on the bridge at midnight,
  As the clocks were striking the hour,
And the Moon rose o'er the city,
  Behind the dark church-tower.

I saw her bright reflection
  In the waters under me,
Like a golden goblet falling
  And sinking into the sea.

And, far in the hazy distance
  Of that lovely night in June,
The blaze of the flaming furnace
  Gleam'd redder than the Moon.

Among the long, black rafters
  The wavering shadows lay,
And the current that came from the ocean
  Seem'd to lift and bear them away;

As, sweeping and eddying through them,
  Rose the belated tide,
And, streaming into the moonlight,
  The sea-weed floated wide.

And, like those waters rushing
  Among the wooden piers,
A flood of thoughts came o'er me
  That fill'd my eyes with tears.

How often, O, how often,
  In the days that had gone by,
I had stood on that bridge at midnight,
  And gazed on that wave and sky!

How often, O, how often,
  I had wish'd that the ebbing tide
Would bear me away on its bosom
  O'er the ocean wild and wide!

For my heart was hot and restless,
  And my life was full of care,
And the burden laid upon me
  Seem'd greater than I could bear.

But now it has fallen from me,
  It is buried in the sea;
And only the sorrow of others
  Throws its shadow over me.

Yet, whenever I cross the river
  On its bridge with wooden piers,
Like the odour of brine from the ocean
  Comes the thought of other years.

And I think how many thousands
  Of care-encumber'd men,
Each bearing his burden of sorrow,
  Have cross'd the bridge since then.

I see the long procession
  Still passing to and fro,
The young heart hot and restless,
  And the old subdued and slow!

And forever and forever,
  As long as the river flows,
As long as the heart has passions,
  As long as life has woes:

The Moon and its broken reflection
  And its shadows shall appear,
As the symbol of love in Heaven,
  And its wavering image here.

THE CHILDREN.

CHARLES DICKENS.

WHEN the lessons and tasks are all ended,
  And the school for the day is dismiss'd,
And the little ones gather around me,
  To bid me "good night" and be kiss'd;
O, the little white arms that encircle
  My neck in a tender embrace;
O, the smiles that are halos of Heaven,
  Shedding sunshine of love on my face.

And when they are gone I sit dreaming
  Of my childhood too lovely to last;
Of love that my heart will remember,
  While it wakes to the pulse of the past,—
Ere the world and its wickedness made me
  A partner of sorrow and sin;
When the glory of God was about me,
  And the glory of gladness within.

O, my heart grows as weak as a woman's,
  And the fountains of feeling will flow,
When I think of the paths steep and stony
  Where the feet of the dear ones must go;
Of the mountains of sin hanging o'er them,
  Of the tempest of fate blowing wild;
O, there's nothing on Earth half so holy
  As the innocent heart of a child.

They are idols of hearts and of households;
  They are angels of God in disguise;

His sunlight still sleeps in their tresses;
  His glory still gleams in their eyes.
O, those truants from home and from Heaven,
  They have made me more manly and mild,
And I know now how Jesus could liken
  The Kingdom of God to a child.

I ask not a life for the dear ones
  All radiant, as others have done;
But that life may have just enough shadow
  To temper the glare of the Sun;
I would pray God to guard them from evil,
  But my prayer would bound back to myself;
O, a seraph may pray for a sinner,
  But a sinner must pray for himself.

The twig is so easily bended,
  I have banish'd the rule and the rod;
I have taught them the goodness of knowledge,
  They have taught me the wisdom of God.
My heart is a dungeon of darkness,
  Where I shut them from breaking a rule;
My frown is sufficient correction;
  My love is the law of the school.

I shall leave the old house in the Autumn,
  To traverse its threshold no more;
Ah! how I shall sigh for the dear ones
  That muster'd each morn at the door!
I shall miss the "good-nights" and the kisses,
  And the gush of their innocent glee,
The group on the green, and the flowers
  That are brought every morning to me.

I shall miss them at morn and at eve,
  Their song in the school and the street;
I shall miss the low hum of their voices,
  And the tramp of their delicate feet.

When the lessons and tasks are all ended,
And Death says, "the school is dismiss'd!"
May the little ones gather around me,
To bid me "good night" and be kiss'd.

[It is stated that the above Poem was found in the desk of Charles Dickens after his death.]

IMMORTALITY OF LOVE.

ROBERT SOUTHEY.

THREE happy beings are there here,
The Sire, the Maid, the Glendoveer:
A fourth approaches; — Who is this
That enters in the Bower of Bliss?
No form so fair might painter find
Among the daughters of mankind;
For death her beauties hath refined,
And unto her a form hath given
Framed of the elements of Heaven, —
Pure dwelling-place for perfect mind.
She stood and gazed on Sire and Child;
Her tongue not yet had power to speak,
The tears were streaming down her cheek;
And when those tears her sight beguiled,
And still her faltering accents fail'd,
The Spirit, mute and motionless,
Spread out her arms for the caress,
Made still and silent with excess
Of love and painful happiness.

The Maid that lovely form survey'd;
Wistful she gazed, and knew her not,
But Nature to her heart convey'd
A sudden thrill, a startling thought,
A feeling many a year forgot,
Now like a dream anew recurring,

As if again in every vein
Her mother's milk were stirring.
With straining neck and earnest eye
She stretch'd her hands imploringly,
As if she fain would have her nigh,
Yet fear'd to meet the wish'd embrace,
At once with love and awe opprest.
Not so Ladurlad: he could trace,
Though brighten'd with angelic grace,
His own Yedillian's earthly face:
He ran and held her to his breast.
O joy above all joys of Heaven,
By death alone to others given,
This moment hath to him restored
The early-lost, the long-deplored!

They sin who tell us Love can die:
With life all other passions fly,
All others are but vanity:
In Heaven Ambition cannot dwell,
Nor Avarice in the vaults of Hell;
Earthly these passions of the Earth,
They perish where they have their birth;
But Love is indestructible.
Its holy flame forever burneth,
From Heaven it came, to Heaven returneth:
Too oft on Earth a troubled guest,
At times deceived, at times opprest,
It here is tried and purified,
Then hath in Heaven its perfect rest:
It soweth here with toil and care,
But th' harvest time of Love is there.

THE ASTROLOGICAL TOWER.

SCHILLER: *Translated by* COLERIDGE.

It was a strange
Sensation that came o'er me, when at first
From the broad sunshine I stepp'd in; and now
The narrowing line of daylight, that ran after
The closing door, was gone; and all about me
'Twas pale and dusky night, with many shadows
Fantastically cast. Here six or seven
Colossal statues, and all kings, stood round me
In a half-circle. Each one in his hand
A sceptre bore, and on his head a star;
And in the tower no other light was there
But from these stars: all seem'd to come from them.
"These are the planets," said that low old man;
"They govern worldly fates, and for that cause
Are imaged here as kings. He farthest from you,
Spiteful and cold, an old man melancholy,
With bent and yellow forehead, he is Saturn.
He opposite, the king with the red light,
An arm'd man for the battle, that is Mars;
And both these bring but little luck to man."
But at his side a lovely lady stood;
The star upon her head was soft and bright,
And that was Venus, the bright star of joy.
On the left hand, lo! Mercury, with wings:
Quite in the middle glitter'd silver bright
A cheerful man, and with a monarch's mien;
And this was Jupiter, my father's star:
And at his side I saw the Sun and Moon.

O, never rudely will I blame his faith
In the might of stars and angels! 'Tis not merely
The human being's Pride that peoples space
With life and mystical predominance;
Since likewise for the stricken heart of Love

This visible Nature, and this common world,
Is all too narrow; yea, a deeper import
Lurks in the legend told my infant years
Than lies upon that truth, we live to learn.
For fable is Love's world, his home, his birth-place;
Delightedly dwells he 'mong fays and talismans
And spirits; and delightedly believes
Divinities, being himself divine.
Th' intelligible forms of ancient poets,
The fair humanities of old religion,
The Power, the Beauty, and the Majesty,
That had their haunts in dale, or piny mountain,
Or forest by slow stream, or pebbly spring,
Or chasms and watery depths, — all these have vanish'd;
They live no longer in the faith of reason!
But still the heart doth need a language, still
Doth the old instinct bring back the old names;
And to yon starry world they now are gone,
Spirits or gods, that used to share this Earth
With man as with their friend; and to the lover
Yonder they move, from yonder visible sky
Shoot influence down: and even at this day
'Tis Jupiter who brings whate'er is great,
And Venus who brings everything that's fair.

A LOST CHORD.

ADELAIDE ANNE PROCTOR.

SEATED one day at the organ,
  I was weary and ill at ease,
And my fingers wander'd idly
  Over the noisy keys.

I do not know what I was playing,
  Or what I was dreaming then,
But I struck one chord of music,
  Like the sound of a great Amen.

It flooded the crimson twilight,
  Like the close of an angel's psalm,
And it lay on my fever'd spirit,
  With a touch of infinite calm.

It quieted pain and sorrow,
  Like love overcoming strife;
It seem'd the harmonious echo
  From our discordant life.

It link'd all perplex'd meanings
  Into one perfect peace,
And trembled away into silence,
  As if it were loth to cease.

I have sought, but I seek it vainly,
  That one lost chord divine,
That came from the soul of the organ,
  And enter'd into mine.

It may be that Death's bright angel
  Will speak in that chord again;
It may be that only in Heaven
  I shall hear that grand Amen.

MEMORY.

JAMES A. GARFIELD.

'TIS beauteous night; the stars look brightly down
Upon the Earth, deck'd in her robe of snow.
No light gleams at the windows, save my own,
Which gives its cheer to midnight and to me.
And now, with noiseless step, sweet memory comes
And leads me gently through her twilight realms.
What poet's tuneful lyre has ever sung,
Or delicatest pencil e'er portray'd
Th' enchanted, shadowy land where memory dwells?

It has its valleys, cheerless, lone, and drear,
Dark-shaded by the mournful cypress-tree;
And yet its sunlit mountain-tops are bathed
In heaven's own blue. Upon its craggy cliffs,
Robed in the dreamy light of distant years,
Are cluster'd joys serene of other days.
Upon its gently sloping hillsides bend
The weeping willows o'er the sacred dust
Of dear departed ones; yet in that land,
Where'er our footsteps fall upon the shore,
They that were sleeping rise from out the dust
Of death's long, silent years, and round us stand
As erst they did before the prison-tomb
Received their clay within its voiceless halls.
The heavens that bend above that land are hung
With clouds of various hues. Some dark and chill,
Surcharged with sorrow, cast their somber shade
Upon the sunny, joyous land below.
Others are floating through the dreamy air,
White as the falling snow, their margins tinged
With gold and crimson'd hues; their shadows fall
Upon the flowery meads and sunny slopes,
Soft as the shadow of an angel's wing.
When the rough battle of the day is done,
And evening's peace falls gently on the heart,
I bound away, across the noisy years,
Unto the utmost verge of memory's land,
Where earth and sky in dreamy distance meet,
And memory dim with dark oblivion joins;
Where woke the first remember'd sounds that fell
Upon the ear in childhood's early morn;
And, wandering thence along the rolling years,
I see the shadow of my former self
Gliding from childhood up to man's estate.
The path of youth winds down through many a vale,
And on the brink of many a dread abyss,
From out whose darkness comes no ray of light,

Save that a phantom dances o'er the gulf
And beckons toward the verge. Again the path
Leads o'er the summit where the sunbeams fall;
And thus in light and shade, sunshine and gloom,
Sorrow and joy, this life-path leads along.

TEARS, IDLE TEARS.

ALFRED TENNYSON.

TEARS, idle tears, I know not what they mean,
Tears from the depth of some divine despair
Rise in the heart, and gather to the eyes,
In looking on the happy autumn fields,
And thinking of the days that are no more.

Fresh as the first beam glittering on a sail,
That brings our friends up from the under-world;
Sad as the last which reddens over one
That sinks with all we love below the verge, —
So sad, so fresh, the days that are no more.

Ah, sad and strange as in dark summer dawns
The earliest pipe of half-awaken'd birds
To dying ears, when unto dying eyes
The casement slowly grows a glimmering square;
So sad, so strange, the days that are no more.

Dear as remember'd kisses after death,
And sweet as those by hopeless fancy feign'd
On lips that are for others; deep as love,
Deep as first love, and wild with all regret, —
O Death in Life, the days that are no more!

OVER THE RIVER.

NANCY A. W. PRIEST.

OVER the river they beckon to me,
Loved ones who cross'd to the other side;

The gleam of their snowy robes I see,
  But their voices are lost in the dashing tide.
There's one with ringlets of sunny gold,
  And eyes the reflection of heaven's own blue;
He cross'd in the twilight gray and cold,
  And the pale mist hid him from mortal view.
We saw not the angels who met him there, —
  The gates of the city we could not see;
Over the river, over the river,
  My brother stands, waiting to welcome me.

Over the river the boatman pale
  Carried another, the household pet;
Her brown curls waved in the gentle gale, —
  Darling Minnie! I see her yet!
She closed on her bosom her dimpled hands,
  And fearlessly enter'd the phantom bark;
We felt it glide from the silver sands,
  And all our sunshine grew strangely dark.
We know she is safe on the farther side,
  Where all the ransom'd and angels be;
Over the river, the mystic river,
  My childhood's idol is waiting for me.

For none return from those quiet shores,
  Who cross with the boatman cold and pale;
We hear the dip of the golden oars,
  And catch a gleam of the snowy sail;
And, lo! they have pass'd from our yearning hearts, —
  They cross the stream and are gone for aye.
We may not sunder the veil apart
  That hides from our vision the gates of day;
We only know that their barks no more
  Sail with us o'er life's stormy sea;
Yet somewhere, I know, on the unseen shore,
  They watch, and beckon, and wait for me.

And I sit and think when the sunset's gold
  Is flushing river, hill, and shore,
I shall one day stand by the water cold
  And list for the sound of the boatman's oar.
I shall watch for a gleam of the flapping sail;
  I shall hear the boat as it gains the strand;
I shall pass from sight with the boatman pale
  To the better shore of the spirit-land.
I shall know the loved who have gone before,
  And joyfully sweet will the meeting be,
When over the river, the peaceful river,
  The angel of death shall carry me.

PICTURES OF MEMORY.

ALICE CARY.

AMONG the beautiful pictures
  That hang on Memory's wall,
Is one of a dim old forest,
  That seemeth best of all.
Not for its gnarl'd oaks olden,
  Dark with the mistletoe;
Not for the violets golden
  That sprinkle the vale below;
Not for the milk-white lilies
  That lean from the fragrant ledge,
Coquetting all day with the sunbeams,
  And stealing their golden edge;
Not for the vines on the upland
  Where the bright red berries rest,
Nor the pinks, nor the pale, sweet cowslip,
  It seemeth to me the best.

I once had a little brother
  With eyes that were dark and deep;
In the lap of that dim old forest,
  He lieth in peace asleep.

Light as the down of the thistle,
  Free as the winds that blow,
We roved there, the beautiful summers,
  The summers of long ago;
But his feet on the hills grew weary,
  And, one of the autumn eves,
I made for my little brother
  A bed of the yellow leaves.

Sweetly his pale arms folded
  My neck in a meek embrace,
As the light of immortal beauty
  Silently cover'd his face;
And when the arrows of sunset
  Lodged in the tree-tops bright,
He fell, in his saint-like beauty,
  Asleep by the gates of light.

Therefore, of all the pictures
  That hang on Memory's wall,
The one of the dim old forest
  Seemeth the best of all.

SANDALPHON.

H. W. Longfellow.

Have you read in the Talmud of old,
In the Legends the Rabbins have told
  Of the limitless realms of the air,
Have you read it, — the marvellous story
Of Sandalphon, the Angel of Glory,
  Sandalphon, the Angel of Prayer?

How, erect, at the outermost gates
Of the City Celestial he waits,
  With his feet on the ladder of light,
That, crowded with angels unnumber'd,
By Jacob was seen, as he slumber'd
  Alone in the desert at night?

The Angels of Wind and of Fire
Chant only one hymn, and expire
  With the song's irresistible stress;
Expire in their rapture and wonder,
As harp-strings are broken asunder
  By music they throb to express.

But, serene in the rapturous throng,
Unmoved by the rush of the song,
  With eyes unimpassion'd and slow,
Among the dead angels, the deathless
Sandalphon stands listening, breathless,
  To sounds that ascend from below; —

From the spirits on Earth that adore,
From the souls that entreat and implore
  In the fervour and passion of prayer;
From the hearts that are broken with losses,
And weary with dragging the crosses
  Too heavy for mortals to bear.

And he gathers the prayers as he stands,
And they change into flowers in his hands,
  Into garlands of purple and red;
And beneath the great arch of the portal,
Through the streets of the City Immortal
  Is wafted the fragrance they shed.

It is but a legend, I know, —
A fable, a phantom, a show,
  Of the ancient Rabbinical lore:
Yet the old mediæval tradition,
The beautiful, strange superstition,
  But haunts me and holds me the more.

When I look from my window at night,
And the welkin above is all white,
  All throbbing and panting with stars,
Among them majestic is standing
Sandalphon the angel, expanding
  His pinions in nebulous bars.

And the legend, I feel, is a part
Of the hunger and thirst of the heart,
  The frenzy and fire of the brain,
That grasps at the fruitage forbidden,
The golden pomegranates of Eden,
  To quiet its fever and pain.

ODE TO TRANQUILLITY.

S. T. Coleridge.

Tranquillity! thou better name
Than all the family of Fame!
Thou ne'er wilt leave my riper age
To low intrigue or factious rage;
For, O dear child of thoughtful Truth!
To thee I gave my early youth,
And left the bark, and blest the steadfast shore,
Ere yet the tempest rose and scared me with its roar.

Who late and lingering seeks thy shrine,
On him but seldom, Power divine,
Thy spirit rests! Satiety
And Sloth, poor counterfeits of thee,
Mock the tired worldling. Idle hope
And dire remembrance interlope,
To vex the feverish slumbers of the mind:
The bubble floats before, the spectre stalks behind.

But me thy gentle hand will lead
At morning through th' accustom'd mead;
And in the sultry Summer's heat
Will build me up a mossy seat;
And, when the gusty Autumn crowds
And breaks the busy moonlit clouds,
Thou best the thought canst raise, the heart attune,
Light as the busy clouds, calm as the gliding Moon.

The feeling heart, the searching soul,
To thee I dedicate the whole!
And, while within myself I trace
The greatness of some future race,
Aloof with hermit-eye I scan
The present works of present man, —
A wild and dream-like trade of blood and guile,
Too foolish for a tear, too wicked for a smile!

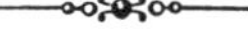

MEMORY.

William Wordsworth.

A pen — to register; a key —
That winds through secret wards;
Are well assign'd to Memory
By allegoric Bards.

As aptly, also, might be given
A Pencil to her hand;
That, softening objects, sometimes even
Outstrips the heart's demand;

That smoothes foregone distress, the lines
Of lingering care subdues,
Long-vanish'd happiness refines,
And clothes in brighter hues;

Yet, like a tool of Fancy, works
Those Spectres to dilate
That startle Conscience, as she lurks
Within her lonely seat.

O, that our lives, which flee so fast,
In purity were such,
That not an image of the past
Should fear that pencil's touch!

Retirement then might hourly look
Upon a soothing scene,
Age steal to his allotted nook
Contented and serene;

With heart as calm as lakes that sleep,
In frosty moonlight glistening;
Or mountain rivers, where they creep
Along a channel smooth and deep,
To their own far-off murmurs listening.

TRANQUILLITY! the sovereign aim wert thou
In heathen schools of philosophic lore;
Heart-stricken by stern destiny of yore
The Tragic Muse thee served with thoughtful vow;
And what of hope Elysium could allow
Was fondly seized by Sculpture, to restore
Peace to the mourner. But, when He who wore
The crown of thorns around His bleeding brow
Warm'd our sad being with celestial light,
Then Arts which still had drawn a softening grace
From shadowy fountains of the Infinite
Communed with that Idea face to face;
And move around it now, as planets run
Each in its orbit round the central Sun.

III.

GRAVE, SOLEMN, SERIOUS, PATHETIC.

THE ANGELS OF BUENA VISTA.

JOHN G. WHITTIER.

SPEAK and tell us, our Ximena, looking northward far away,
O'er the camp of the invaders, o'er the Mexican array,
Who is losing? who is winning? are they far or come they near?
Look abroad, and tell us, sister, whither rolls the storm we hear.

"Down the hills of Angostura still the storm of battle rolls;
Blood is flowing, men are dying; God have mercy on their souls!"
Who is losing? who is winning? "Over hill and over plain,
I see but smoke of cannon clouding through the mountain rain."

Holy Mother, keep our brothers! Look, Ximena, look once more:
"Still I see the fearful whirlwind rolling darkly as before,
Bearing on, in strange confusion, friend and foeman, foot and horse,
Like some wild and troubled torrent sweeping down its mountain course."

Look forth once more, Ximena! "Ah! the smoke has roll'd away;
And I see the Northern rifles gleaming down the ranks of gray.

Hark! that sudden blast of bugles! there the troop of Minon wheels;
There the Northern horses thunder, with the cannon at their heels.

"Jesu, pity! how it thickens! now retreat and now advance!
Right against the blazing cannon shivers Puebla's charging lance!
Down they go, the brave young riders; horse and foot together fall;
Like a ploughshare in the fallow, through them ploughs the Northern ball."

Nearer came the storm, and nearer, rolling fast and frightful on.
Speak, Ximena, speak, and tell us who has lost and who has won?
"Alas! alas! I know not; friend and foe together fall;
O'er the dying rush the living: pray, my sisters, for them all!"

"Lo! the wind the smoke is lifting: Blessèd Mother, save my brain!
I can see the wounded crawling slowly out from heaps of slain;
Now they stagger, blind and bleeding; now they fall, and strive to rise:
Hasten, sisters, haste and save them, lest they die before our eyes!

"O my heart's love! O my dear one! lay thy poor head on my knee;
Dost thou know the lips that kiss thee? Canst thou hear me? canst thou see?
O my husband, brave and gentle! O my Bernal, look once more
On the blessèd cross before thee! Mercy! mercy! all is o'er."

Dry thy tears, my poor Ximena; lay thy dear one down to rest;
Let his hands be meekly folded, lay the cross upon his breast;
Let his dirge be sung hereafter, and his funeral masses said:
To-day, thou poor bereaved one, the living ask thy aid.

Close beside her, faintly moaning, fair and young, a soldier lay,
Torn with shot and pierced with lances, bleeding slow his life away;
But, as tenderly before him the lorn Ximena knelt,
She saw the Northern eagle shining on his pistol belt.

With a stifled cry of horror straight she turn'd away her head;
With a sad and bitter feeling look'd she back upon her dead;
But she heard the youth's low moaning, and his struggling breath of pain,
And she raised the cooling water to his parching lips again.

Whisper'd low the dying soldier, press'd her hand, and faintly smiled:
Was that pitying face his mother's? did she watch beside her child?
All his stranger words with meaning her woman's heart supplied;
With her kiss upon his forehead, "Mother!" murmur'd he, and died.

"A bitter curse upon them, poor boy, who led thee forth
From some gentle, sad-eyed mother, weeping, lonely, in the North!"
Spake the mournful Mexic woman, as she laid him with her dead,
And turn'd to soothe the living still, and bind the wounds which bled.

Look forth once more, Ximena! "Like a cloud before the wind
Rolls the battle down the mountains, leaving blood and death behind;
Ah! they plead in vain for mercy; in the dust the wounded strive;
Hide your faces, holy angels! O, thou Christ of God, forgive!"

Sink, O Night, among thy mountains! let the cool, gray shadows fall;
Dying brothers, fighting demons, — drop thy curtain over all!
Through the thickening winter twilight, wide apart the battle roll'd,
In its sheath the sabre rested, and the cannon's lips grew cold.

But the noble Mexic women still their holy task pursued,
Through that long, dark night of sorrow, worn and faint and lacking food;
Over weak and suffering brothers with a tender care they hung,
And the dying foeman bless'd them in a strange and Northern tongue.

Not wholly lost, O Father! is this evil world of ours;
Upward, through its blood and ashes, spring afresh the Eden flowers;
From its smoking hell of battle Love and Pity send their prayer,
And still Thy white-wing'd angels hover dimly in our air.

THANATOPSIS.

W. C. Bryant.

To him who in the love of Nature holds
Communion with her visible forms, she speaks

A various language. For his gayer hours
She has a voice of gladness, and a smile
And eloquence of beauty; and she glides
Into his darker musings, with a mild
And gentle sympathy, that steals away
Their sharpness ere he is aware. When thoughts
Of the last bitter hour come like a blight
Over thy spirit, and sad images
Of the stern agony, and shroud and pall,
And breathless darkness, and the narrow house,
Make thee to shudder, and grow sick at heart,
Go forth under the open sky, and list
To Nature's teachings, while from all around —
Earth and her waters, and the depths of air —
Comes a still voice, — Yet a few days, and thee
The all-beholding Sun shall see no more
In all his course; nor yet in the cold ground,
Where thy pale form was laid, with many tears,
Nor in th' embrace of ocean, shall exist
Thy image. Earth, that nourish'd thee, shall claim
Thy growth, to be resolved to earth again;
And, lost each human trace, surrendering up
Thine individual being, shalt thou go
To mix for ever with the elements,
To be a brother to th' insensible rock,
And to the sluggish clod which the rude swain
Turns with his share, and treads upon. The oak
Shall send his roots abroad, and pierce thy mould.
Yet not to thine eternal resting-place
Shalt thou retire alone; nor couldst thou wish
Couch more magnificent. Thou shalt lie down
With patriarchs of the infant world; with kings,
The powerful of the Earth, — the wise, the good,
Fair forms, and hoary seers of ages past, —
All in one mighty sepulchre. The hills
Rock-ribb'd and ancient as the Sun; the vales
Stretching in pensive quietness between;

The venerable woods; rivers that move
In majesty, and the complaining brooks
That make the meadows green; and, pour'd round all,
Old ocean's gray and melancholy waste, —
Are but the solemn decorations all
Of the great tomb of man. The golden Sun,
The planets, all the infinite host of heaven,
Are shining on the sad abodes of death,
Through the still lapse of ages. All that tread
The globe are but a handful to the tribes
That slumber in its bosom. Take the wings
Of morning, and the Barcan desert pierce;
Or lose thyself in the continuous woods
Where rolls the Oregon, and hears no sound
Save his own dashings, — yet the dead are there;
And millions in those solitudes, since first
The flight of years began, have laid them down
In their last sleep, — the dead reign there alone.
So shalt thou rest; and what if thou shalt fall
Unnoticed by the living, and no friend
Take note of thy departure? All that breathe
Will share thy destiny. The gay will laugh
When thou art gone, the solemn brood of care
Plod on, and each one, as before, will chase
His favourite phantom; yet all these shall leave
Their mirth and their employments, and shall come
And make their bed with thee. As the long train
Of ages glide away, the sons of men,
The youth in life's green spring, and he who goes
In the full strength of years, matron, and maid,
The bow'd with age, the infant in the smiles
And beauty of its innocent age cut off,
Shall, one by one, be gather'd to thy side
By those who in their turn shall follow them.
  So live that when thy summons comes to join
Th' innumerable caravan, that moves
To the pale realms of shade, where each shall take

His chamber in the silent halls of death,
Thou go not, like the quarry-slave at night
Scourged to his dungeon; but, sustain'd and soothed
By an unfaltering trust, approach thy grave,
Like one who wraps the drapery of his couch
About him, and lies down to pleasant dreams.

THE HERMIT.

JAMES BEATTIE.

AT the close of the day, when the hamlet is still,
And mortals the sweets of forgetfulness prove,
When nought but the torrent is heard on the hill,
And nought but the nightingale's song in the grove;
'Twas thus, by the cave of the mountain afar,
While his harp rung symphonious, a hermit began:
No more with himself or with Nature at war,
He thought as a sage, though he felt as a man.

"Ah! why, all abandon'd to darkness and woe,
Why, lone Philomela, that languishing fall?
For Spring shall return, and a lover bestow,
And sorrow no longer thy bosom enthrall.
But, if pity inspire thee, renew the sad lay,
Mourn, sweetest complainer, man calls thee to mourn:
O, soothe him whose pleasures like thine pass away:
Full quickly they pass, — but they never return.

Now, gliding remote on the verge of the sky,
The Moon, half extinguish'd, her crescent displays;
But lately I mark'd when majestic on high
She shone, and the planets were lost in her blaze.
Roll on, thou fair orb, and with gladness pursue
The path that conducts thee to splendour again.
But man's faded glory what change shall renew?
Ah, fool! to exult in a glory so vain!

'Tis night, and the landscape is lovely no more;
I mourn, but, ye woodlands, I mourn not for you;
For morn is approaching, your charms to restore,
Perfumed with fresh fragrance, and glittering with dew:
Nor yet for the ravage of Winter I mourn;
Kind Nature the embryo blossom will save.
But when shall Spring visit the mouldering urn?
O, when shall it dawn on the night of the grave?

'Twas thus, by the glare of false Science betray'd,
That leads to bewilder, and dazzles to blind;
My thoughts wont to roam from shade onward to shade,
Destruction before me, and sorrow behind.
'O, pity, great Father of light,' then I cried,
'Thy creature, who fain would not wander from Thee:
Lo, humbled in dust, I relinquish my pride:
From doubt and from darkness Thou only canst free.'

And darkness and doubt are now flying away;
No longer I roam in conjecture forlorn:
So breaks on the traveller, faint, and astray,
The bright and the balmy effulgence of morn.
See Truth, Love, and Mercy in triumph descending,
And Nature all glowing in Eden's first bloom!
On the cold cheek of Death smiles and roses are blending
And Beauty immortal awakes from the tomb."

THE LADDER OF SAINT AUGUSTINE.

H. W. Longfellow.

Saint Augustine! well hast thou said,
That of our vices we can frame
A ladder, if we will but tread
Beneath our feet each deed of shame.

All common things, each day's events,
That with the hour begin and end,
Our pleasures and our discontents,
Are rounds by which we may ascend.

The low desire, the base design,
That makes another's virtues less;
The revel of the ruddy wine,
And all occasions of excess;

The longing for ignoble things;
The strife for triumph more than truth;
The hardening of the heart, that brings
Irreverence for the dreams of youth;

All thoughts of ill; all evil deeds,
That have their root in thoughts of ill;
Whatever hinders or impedes
The action of the nobler will; —

All these must first be trampled down
Beneath our feet, if we would gain
In the bright fields of fair renown
The right of eminent domain.

We have not wings, we cannot soar;
But we have feet to scale and climb
By slow degrees, by more and more,
The cloudy summits of our time.

The mighty pyramids of stone
That wedge-like cleave the desert airs,
When nearer seen and better known,
Are but gigantic flights of stairs.

The distant mountains, that uprear
Their solid bastions to the skies,
Are cross'd by pathways, that appear
As we to higher levels rise.

The heights of great men reach'd and kept
Were not attain'd by sudden flight;
But they, while their companions slept,
Were toiling upward in the night.

Standing on what too long we bore
With shoulders bent and downcast eyes,
We may discern — unseen before —
A path to higher destinies.

Nor deem th' irrevocable Past
As wholly wasted, wholly vain,
If, rising on its wrecks, at last
To something nobler we attain.

CHRISTMAS-DAY.

Samuel Richards.

Though rude winds usher thee, sweet day,
 Though clouds thy face deform,
Though Nature's grace is swept away
 Before thy sleety storm;
Even in thy sombrest wintry vest,
Of blessèd days thou art most blest.

Nor frigid air nor gloomy morn
 Shall check our jubilee:
Bright is the day when Christ was born,
 No sun need shine but He:
Let roughest storms their coldest blow,
With love of Him our hearts shall glow.

Inspired with high and holy thought,
 Fancy is on the wing:
It seems as to mine ear it brought
 Those voices carolling, —
Voices through Heaven and Earth that ran,—
"Glory to God, good-will to man!"

I see the Shepherds gazing wild
 At those fair Spirits of light;
I see them bending o'er the Child
 With that untold delight

Which marks the face of those who view
Things but too happy to be true.

Oft as this joyous morn doth come
  To speak our Saviour's love,
O, may it bear our spirits home
  Where He now reigns above!
That day which brought Him from the skies
So man restores to Paradise.

Then let winds usher thee, sweet day,
  Let clouds thy face deform:
Though Nature's grace is swept away
  Before thy sleety storm,
Even in thy sombrest wintry vest,
Of blessèd days thou art most blest.

WINIFREDA.

Away! let nought to love displeasing,
  My Winifreda, move your care;
Let nought delay the heavenly blessing,
  Nor squeamish pride, nor gloomy fear.

What though no grants of royal donors
  With pompous titles grace our blood;
We'll shine in more substantial honours,
  And to be noble we'll be good.

Our name, while virtue thus we tender,
  Will sweetly sound where'er 'tis spoke;
And all the great ones they shall wonder
  How they respect such little folk.

What though from fortune's lavish bounty
  No mighty treasures we possess;
We'll find within our pittance plenty,
  And be content without excess.

And still shall each returning season
  Sufficient for our wishes give;
For we will live a life of reason,
  And that's the only life to live.

Through youth and age in love excelling,
  We'll hand in hand together tread;
Sweet-smiling peace shall crown our dwelling,
  And babes, sweet-smiling babes, our bed.

How I should love the pretty creatures,
  While round my knees they fondly clung!
To see them look their mother's features,
  To hear them lisp their mother's tongue.

And when with envy time transported
  Shall think to rob us of our joys,
You'll in your girls again be courted,
  And I'll go wooing in my boys.

THE BLACKSMITH'S STORY.

FRANK OLIVE.

WELL, No! My wife ain't dead, sir, but I've lost her all the same;
She left me voluntarily, and neither was to blame.
It's rather a queer story, and I think you will agree —
When you hear the circumstances — 'twas rather rough on me.

She was a soldier's widow. He was kill'd at Malvern Hill;
And when I married her she seem'd to sorrow for him still;
But I brought her here to Kansas, and I never want to see
A better wife than Mary was for five bright years to me.

The change of scene brought cheerfulness, and soon a rosy glow
Of happiness warm'd Mary's cheeks and melted all their snow.

I think she loved me some, — I'm bound to think that of her, sir;
And as for me, — I can't begin to tell how I loved her!

Three years ago the baby came our humble home to bless;
And then I reckon I was nigh to perfect happiness;
'Twas hers, — 'twas mine; but I've no language to explain to you,
How that little girl's weak fingers our hearts together drew!

Once we watch'd it through a fever, and with each gasping breath,
Dumb with an awful, wordless woe, we waited for its death;
And, though I'm not a pious man, our souls together there,
For Heaven to spare our darling, went up in voiceless prayer.

And, when the doctor said 'twould live, our joy what words could tell?
Clasp'd in each other's arms, our grateful tears together fell.
Sometimes, you see, the shadow fell across our little nest,
But it only made the sunshine seem a doubly welcome guest.

Work came to me a plenty, and I kept the anvil ringing;
Early and late you'd find me there a-hammering and singing;
Love nerved my arm to labour, and moved my tongue to song,
And, though my singing wasn't sweet, it was tremendous strong!

One day a one-arm'd stranger stopp'd to have me nail a shoe,
And, while I was at work, we pass'd a compliment or two;
I ask'd him how he lost his arm. He said 'twas shot away
At Malvern Hill. "Malvern Hill! Did you know Robert May?"

"That's me," said he. "You, you!" I gasp'd, choking with horrid doubt;
"If you're the man, just follow me; we'll try this mystery out!"
With dizzy steps, I led him to Mary. God! 'Twas true!
Then the bitterest pangs of misery, unspeakable, I knew.

Frozen with deadly horror, she stared with eyes of stone,
And from her quivering lips there broke one wild, despairing moan.
'Twas he! the husband of her youth, now risen from the dead,
But all too late; and, with bitter cry, her senses fled.

What could be done? He was reported dead. On his return
He strove in vain some tidings of his absent wife to learn.
'Twas well that he was innocent! Else I'd have kill'd him, too,
So dead he never would have riz till Gabriel's trumpet blew!

It was agreed that Mary then between us should decide,
And each by her decision would sacredly abide.
No sinner, at the judgment-seat, waiting eternal doom,
Could suffer what I did, while waiting sentence in that room.

Rigid and breathless, there we stood, with nerves as tense as steel,
While Mary's eyes sought each white face, in piteous appeal.
God! could not woman's duty be less hardly reconciled
Between her lawful husband and the father of her child?

Ah, how my heart was chill'd to ice, when she knelt down and said, —
"Forgive me, John! He is my husband! Here! Alive! not dead!
I raised her tenderly, and tried to tell her she was right,
But somehow, in my aching breast, the prison'd words stuck tight!

"But, John, I can't leave baby." — "What! wife and child!" cried I;
"Must I yield all! Ah, cruel fate! Better that I should die.
Think of the long, sad, lonely hours, waiting in gloom for me, —
No wife to cheer me with her love, — no babe to climb my knee!

And yet — you are her mother, and the sacred mother-love
Is still the purest, tenderest tie that Heaven ever wove.
Take her; but promise, Mary, — for that will bring no shame, —
My little girl shall bear, and learn to lisp, her father's name!"

It may be, in the life to come, I'll meet my child and wife;
But yonder, by my cottage gate, we parted for this life;
One long hand-clasp from Mary, and my dream of love was done!
One long embrace from baby, and my happiness was gone!

HOW HE SAVED ST. MICHAEL'S.

It was long ago it happen'd, ere ever the signal gun
That blazed above Fort Sumpter had waken'd the North as one;
Long ere the wondrous pillar of battle-cloud and fire
Had mark'd where the unchain'd millions march'd on to their heart's desire.

On the roofs and the glittering turrets, that night, as the Sun went down,
The mellow glow of the twilight shone like a jewell'd crown;
And, bathed in the living glory, as the people lifted their eyes,
They saw the pride of the city, the spire of St. Michael's rise

High over the lesser steeples, tipp'd with a golden ball,
That hung like a radiant planet caught in its earthward fall, —
First glimpse of home to the sailor who made the harbour-round,
And last slow-fading vision dear to the outward bound.

The gently gathering shadows shut out the waning light;
The children pray'd at their bedsides, as you will pray to-night;
The noise of buyer and seller from the busy mart was gone;
And in dreams of a peaceful morrow the city slumber'd on.

But another light than sunrise aroused the sleeping street;
For a cry was heard at midnight, and the rush of trampling feet;
Men stared in each other's faces through mingled fire and smoke,
While the frantic bells went clashing, clamorous stroke on stroke.

By the glare of her blazing roof-tree the houseless mother fled,
With the babe she press'd to her bosom shrieking in nameless dread,
While the fire-king's wild battalions scaled wall and capstone high,
And planted their flaring banners against an inky sky.

From the death that raged behind them, and the crash of ruin loud,
To the great square of the city were driven the surging crowd;
Where yet, firm in all the tumult, unscathed by the fiery flood,
With its heavenward-pointing finger the Church of St. Michael stood.

But e'en as they gazed upon it there rose a sudden wail, —
A cry of horror, blended with the roaring of the gale,
On whose scorching wings up-driven, a single flaming brand
Aloft on the towering steeple clung like a bloody hand.

"Will it fade?" The whisper trembled from a thousand
whitening lips;
Far out on the lurid harbour, they watch'd it from the
ships, —
A baleful gleam that brighter and ever brighter shone,
Like a flickering, trembling will-o'-wisp to a steady beacon
grown.

"Uncounted gold shall be given to the man whose brave
right hand,
For the love of the perill'd city, plucks down yon burning
brand!"
So cried the mayor of Charleston, that all the people heard;
But they look'd each one at his fellow; and no man spoke a
word.

Who is it leans from the belfry, with face upturn'd to the
sky,
Clings to a column, and measures the dizzy spire with his
eye?
Will he dare it, the hero undaunted, that terrible sickening
height?
Or will the hot blood of his courage freeze in his veins at the
sight?

But, see! he has stepp'd on the railing; he climbs with his
feet and his hands;
And firm on a narrow projection, with the belfry beneath
him, he stands;
Now once, and once only, they cheer him, — a single tem-
pestuous breath, —
And there falls on the multitude gazing a hush like the stillness of death.

Slow, steadily mounting, unheeding aught save the goal of
the fire,
Still higher and higher, an atom, he moves on the face of
the spire.
He stops! Will he fall? Lo! for answer, a gleam like a
meteor's track,
And, hurl'd on the stones of the pavement, the red brand
lies shatter'd and black.

Once more the shouts of the people have rent the quivering
air:
At the church-door mayor and council wait with their feet
on the stair;
And the eager throng behind them press for a touch of his
hand,—
The unknown hero, whose daring could compass a deed so
grand.

But why does a sudden tremor seize on them while they
gaze?
And what meaneth that stifled murmur of wonder and
amaze?
He stood in the gate of the temple he had perill'd his life
to save;
And the face of the hero undaunted was the sable face of
a slave.

With folded arms he was speaking, in tones that were clear,
not loud,
And his eyes, ablaze in their sockets, burnt into the eyes of
the crowd:
"You may keep your gold; I scorn it!—but answer me,
ye who can,
If the deed I have done before you be not the deed of a
man?"

He stepp'd but a short space backward; and from all the
women and men

There were only sobs for answer; and the mayor call'd for
a pen,
And the great seal of the city, that he might read who ran:
And the slave who saved St. Michael's went out from its
door, a man.

CURFEW MUST NOT RING TO-NIGHT.

ROSE A. HARTWICK THORPE.

ENGLAND'S Sun was slowly setting o'er the hills so far away,
Filling all the land with beauty at the close of one sad day;
And the last rays kiss'd the forehead of a man and maiden
fair,
He with step so slow and weaken'd, she with sunny, floating
hair;
He with sad bow'd head, and thoughtful, she with lips so
cold and white,
Struggling to keep back the murmur, "Curfew must not
ring to-night."

"Sexton," — Bessie's white lips falter'd, pointing to the
prison old,
With its walls so dark and gloomy, walls so dark and damp
and cold, —
"I've a lover in that prison, doom'd this very night to die
At the ringing of the Curfew, and no earthly help is nigh.
Cromwell will not come till sunset"; and her face grew
strangely white,
As she spoke in husky whispers, "Curfew must not ring to-
night."

"Bessie," calmly spoke the sexton, — every word pierced
her young heart
Like a thousand gleaming arrows, like a deadly poison'd
dart, —
"Long, long years I've rung the Curfew from that gloomy
shadow'd tower;

Every evening, just at sunset, it has told the twilight hour;
I have done my duty ever, tried to do it just and right;
Now I'm old, I will not miss it; girl, the Curfew rings to-night!"

Wild her eyes and pale her features, stern and white her thoughtful brow,
And within her heart's deep centre Bessie made a solemn vow:
She had listen'd while the judges read, without a tear or sigh,
"At the ringing of the Curfew Basil Underwood *must die*."
And her breath came fast and faster, and her eyes grew large and bright, —
One low murmur, scarcely spoken, "Curfew *must not* ring to-night!"

She with light step bounded forward, sprang within the old church-door,
Left the old man coming slowly, paths he'd trod so oft before;
Not one moment paused the maiden, but, with cheek and brow aglow,
Stagger'd up the gloomy tower, where the bell swung to and fro:
Then she climb'd the slimy ladder, dark, without one ray of light,
Upward still, her pale lips saying, "Curfew *must not* ring to-night."

She has reach'd the topmost ladder, o'er her hangs the great dark bell,
And the awful gloom beneath her, like the pathway down to Hell;
See, the ponderous tongue is swinging, 'tis the hour of Curfew now;
And the sight has chill'd her bosom, stopp'd her breath and paled her brow.

Shall she let it ring? No, never! her eyes flash with sudden light,
As she springs and grasps it firmly, "Curfew *shall not* ring to-night!"

Out she swung, far out; the city seem'd a tiny speck below;
There 'twixt heaven and earth suspended, as the bell swung to and fro;
And the half-deaf Sexton ringing, (years he had not heard the bell,)
And he thought the twilight Curfew rang young Basil's funeral knell:
Still the maiden clinging firmly, cheek and brow so pale and white,
Still'd her frighten'd heart's wild beating, "*Curfew shall not ring to-night.*"

It was o'er; the bell ceased swaying, and the maiden stepp'd once more
Firmly on the damp old ladder, where for hundred years before
Human foot had not been planted; and what she this night had done
Should be told in long years after: as the rays of setting Sun
Light the sky with mellow beauty, agèd sires, with heads of white,
Tell their children why the Curfew did not ring that one sad night.

O'er the distant hills came Cromwell; Bessie saw him, and her brow,
Lately white with sickening terror, glows with sudden beauty now:
At his feet she told her story, show'd her hands all bruised and torn;
And her sweet young face so haggard, with a look so sad and worn,

Touch'd his heart with sudden pity, lit his eyes with misty light:
"Go, your lover lives!" cried Cromwell; "Curfew shall not ring to-night."

Wide they flung the massive portals, led the prisoner forth to die,
All his bright young life before him. 'Neath the darkening English sky,
Bessie came with flying footsteps, eyes aglow with love-light sweet;
Kneeling on the turf beside him, laid his pardon at his feet.
In his brave, strong arms he clasp'd her, kiss'd the face up-turn'd and white,
Whisper'd, "Darling, you have saved me; Curfew must not ring to-night."

THE DEATH OF MR. BERTRAM.

Sir Walter Scott.

Mr. Bertram, paralytic, and almost incapable of moving, occupied his easy chair, attired in his night-cap and a loose camlet coat, his feet wrapped in blankets. Behind him, with his hands crossed on the cane upon which he rested, stood Dominie Sampson, whom Mannering recognized at once. Time had made no change upon him, unless that his black coat seemed more brown, and his gaunt cheeks more lank, than when Mannering last saw him. On one side of the old man was a sylph-like form, — a young woman of about seventeen, whom Colonel Mannering accounted to be his daughter.

She was looking, from time to time, anxiously towards the avenue, as if expecting a post-chaise; and between whiles busied herself in adjusting the blankets, so as to protect her father from the cold, and in answering inquiries, which he seemed to make with a captious and querulous manner. She did not trust herself to look towards the Place, although the hum of the assembled crowd must have drawn her attention in that direction. The fourth person of the group was a handsome and genteel young man, who seemed to share Miss Bertram's anxiety, and her solicitude to soothe and accommodate her parent.

This young gentleman was the first who observed Colonel Mannering, and immediately stepped forward to meet him, as if politely to prevent his drawing nearer to the distressed group. Mannering instantly paused and explained. "He was," he said, "a stranger, to whom Mr. Bertram had formerly shown kindness and hospitality: he would not have intruded himself upon him at a period of distress, did it not seem to be in some degree a moment also of desertion; he wished merely to offer such services as might be in his power to Mr. Bertram and the young lady."

He then paused at a little distance from the chair. His old acquaintance gazed at him with lack-lustre eye, that intimated no tokens of recognition; the Dominie seemed too deeply sunk in distress even to observe his presence. The young man spoke aside with Miss Bertram, who advanced timidly, and thanked Colonel Mannering for his goodness; "but," she said, the tears gushing fast into her eyes, "her father, she feared, was not so much himself as to be able to remember him."

She then retreated towards the chair, accompanied by the Colonel. "Father," she said, "this is Mr. Mannering, an old friend, come to inquire after you."

"He's very heartily welcome," said the old man, raising himself in his chair, and attempting a gesture of courtesy, while a gleam of hospitable satisfaction seemed to pass over his faded features.

"But, Lucy, my dear, let us go down to the house; you should not keep the gentleman here in the cold.—Dominie, take the key of the wine-cooler. Mr.—the gentleman will surely take something after his ride."

Mannering was unspeakably affected by the contrast which his recollection made between this reception and that with which he had been greeted by the same individual when they last met. He could not restrain his tears, and his evident emotion at once attained him the confidence of the friendless young lady.

"Alas!" she said, "this is distressing even to a stranger; but it may be better for my poor father to be in this way, than if he knew and could feel all."

The sound of voices was now heard from the ruins. "Good God!" said Miss Bertram hastily to Sampson, "'tis that wretch Glossin's voice! if my father sees him, it will kill him outright!"

Sampson wheeled perpendicularly round, and moved with long strides to confront the attorney, as he issued from beneath the portal arch of the ruin. "Avoid ye!" he said, "avoid ye! Wouldst thou kill and take possession?"

"Come, come, Master Dominie Sampson," answered Glossin, insolently, "if ye cannot preach in the pulpit, we'll have no preaching here. We'll go by the law, my good friend; we leave the Gospel to you."

The very mention of this man's name had been of late a subject of the most violent irritation to the unfortunate patient. The sound of his voice now produced an instantaneous effect. Mr. Bertram started up without assistance, and turned round towards him; the ghastliness of his features forming a strange contrast with the violence of his exclamations. "Out of my sight, ye viper! ye frozen viper, that I warmed till ye stung me! Art thou not afraid that the walls of my father's dwelling should fall and crush thee, limb and bone? Are ye not afraid the very lintels of the door of Ellangowan-castle should break open and swallow you up? Were ye not friendless, — houseless, — penniless, when I took ye by the hand? and are ye not expelling me — me, and that innocent girl, — friendless, houseless, and penniless, from the house that has sheltered us and ours for a thousand years?"

Had Glossin been alone, he would probably have slunk off; but the consciouness that a stranger was present determined him to resort to impudence. The task, however, was almost too hard, even for his effrontery. Sir, — sir, — Mr. Bertram, — sir, you should not blame me, but your own imprudence, sir, — "

The indignation of Mannering was mounting very high. "Sir," he said to Glossin, "without entering into the merits of this controversy, I must inform you that you have chosen a very improper place, time, and presence for it. And you will oblige me by withdrawing without more words."

Glossin, being a tall, strong, muscular man, was not unwilling rather to turn upon a stranger, whom he hoped to bully, than maintain his wretched cause against his injured patron. "I do not know who you are, sir," he said, "and I shall permit no man to use such freedom with me."

Mannering was naturally hot-tempered; his eyes flashed a dark light; he compressed his nether lip so closely that the blood sprung; and, approaching Glossin, "Look you, sir," he said, "that you do not know me, is of little consequence: *I know you;* and, if you do not instantly descend that bank, without uttering a single syllable, by the Heaven that is above us, you shall make but one step from the top to the bottom!"

The commanding tone of rightful anger silenced at once the ferocity of the bully. He hesitated, turned on his heel, and, muttering something between his teeth about his unwillingness to alarm the lady, relieved them of his hateful company.

Mrs. Mac-Candlish's postillion, who had come up in time to hear what passed, said aloud, "If he had stuck by the way, I would have lent him a heezie, the dirty scoundrel, as willingly as ever I pitched a boddle." He then stepped forward to announce that his horses were in readiness for the invalid and his daughter. But they were no longer necessary. The debilitated frame of Mr. Bertram was exhausted by this last effort of indignant anger, and, when he sunk again upon his chair, he expired almost without a struggle or groan. So little alteration did the extinction of the vital spark make upon his external appearance, that the screams of his daughter, when she saw his eyes fix and felt his pulse stop, first announced his death to the spectators.

LUCY BERTRAM AND DOMINIE SAMPSON.

Sir Walter Scott.

The funeral of the late Mr. Bertram was performed with decent privacy, and the unfortunate young lady was now to consider herself as but the temporary tenant of the house in which she had been born, and where her patience and soothing attentions had so long "rocked the cradle of declining age." Her communication with Mr. Mac-Morlan encouraged her to hope that she would not be suddenly or unkindly deprived of this asylum; but fortune had ordered otherwise.

For two days before the appointed day for the sale of the land and estate of Ellangowan, Mac-Morlan daily expected the appearance of Colonel Mannering, or at least a letter containing powers to act for him. But none such arrived. "Could I have foreseen this," he said, "I would have travelled Scotland over, but I would have found some one to bid against Glossin." Alas! such reflections were too late. The appointed hour arrived. Mac-Morlan spent as much time in preliminaries as decency would permit, and read over the articles of sale as slowly as if he had been reading his own death-warrant. He turned his eye every time the door of the room opened, with hopes which grew fainter and fainter. He listened to every noise in the street of the village, and endeavoured to distinguish in it the sound of hoofs or wheels. It was all in vain. After a solemn pause, Mr. Glossin offered the upset price for the lands and barony of Ellangowan. No reply was made, and no competitor appeared: so, after a lapse of the usual interval by the running of a sand-glass, upon the intended purchaser entering the proper sureties, Mr. Mac-Morlan was obliged, in technical terms, to "find and declare the sale lawfully completed, and to prefer the said Gilbert Glossin as the purchaser of the said lands and estates."

An express arrived about six o'clock at night, "very particularly drunk," the maid servant said, with a packet from Colonel Mannering, dated four days back, at a town about a hundred miles distance, containing full powers to Mr. Mac-Morlan, or any one whom he might employ, to make the intended purchase, and stating that some family business of consequence called the

Colonel himself to Westmoreland, where a letter would find him.

Mac-Morlan, in the transports of his wrath, flung the power of attorney at the head of the innocent maid-servant, and was only forcibly withheld from horse-whipping the rascally messenger, by whose sloth and drunkenness the disappointment had taken place.

Miss Bertram no sooner heard this painful and of late unexpected intelligence, than she proceeded in the preparations she had already made for leaving the mansion-house immediately. Mr. Mac-Morlan assisted her in these arrangements, and pressed upon her so kindly the hospitality of his roof, until she should be enabled to adopt some settled plan of life, that she felt there would be unkindness in refusing an invitation urged with such earnestness. A home, therefore, and a hospitable reception were secured to her, and she went on, with better heart, to pay the wages and receive the adieus of the few domestics of her father's family.

Where there are estimable qualities on either side, this task is always affecting; the present circumstances rendered it doubly so. All received their due, and even a trifle more; and, with thanks and good wishes, to which some added tears, took farewell of their young mistress. There remained in the parlour only Mr. Mac-Morlan, who came to attend his guest to his house, Dominie Sampson, and Miss Bertram. "And now," said the poor girl, "I must bid farewell to one of my oldest and kindest friends.— God bless you, Mr. Sampson! and requite to you all the kindness of your instructions to your poor pupil, and your friendship to him that is gone! I hope I shall often see you." She slid into his hand a paper containing some gold pieces, and rose, as if to leave the room.

Dominie Sampson also rose; but it was to stand aghast with utter astonishment. The idea of parting from Miss Lucy, go where she might, had never once occurred to the simplicity of his understanding. He laid the money on the table. "It is certainly inadequate," said Mac-Morlan, mistaking his meaning; "but the circumstances" —

Mr. Sampson waved his hand impatiently, — "It is not the lucre, it is not the lucre; but that I, that have ate of her father's loaf, and drunk of his cup, for twenty years and more, — to think that I am going to leave her, — and to leave her in distress and dolour! — No, Miss Lucy, you need never think of it; while I live, I will not separate from you. I'll be no burden; I have thought how to prevent that. But, as Ruth said unto Naomi, 'Entreat me not to leave thee, nor to depart from thee; for wither thou goest I will go, and where thou dwellest I will dwell: thy people shall be my people, and thy God shall be my God. Where thou diest will I die, and there will I be buried. The Lord do so to me, and more also, if aught but death do part thee and me!'"

During this speech, the longest ever Dominie Sampson was known to utter, the affectionate creature's eyes streamed with tears; and neither Lucy nor Mac-Morlan could refrain from sympathizing with this unexpected burst of feeling and attachment. "Mr. Sampson," said Mac-Morlan, after having had resource to his snuff-box and handkerchief alternately, "my house is large enough, and if you will accept of a bed there, while Miss Bertram honours us with her residence, I shall think myself very happy, and my roof much favoured by receiving a man of your worth and fidelity." And then, with a delicacy which was meant to remove any objection on Miss Bertram's part, he added, "My business requires frequently a better accountant than any of my present clerks, and I should be glad to have recourse to your assistance in that way now and then."

"Of a surety, of a surety," said Sampson eagerly; "I understand book-keeping by double entry and the Italian method."

Our postillion had thrust himself into the room to announce his chaise and horses: he tarried, unobserved, during this extraordinary scene, and assured Mrs. Mac-Candlish it was the most moving thing he ever saw; "the death of the gray mare, puir Lizzie, was naething till't."

The visitors were hospitably welcomed by Mrs. Mac-Morlan, to whom, as well as to others, her husband intimated that he had engaged Dominie Sampson's assistance to disentangle some perplexed accounts; during which occupation he would, for convenience-sake, reside with the family.

Dominie Sampson achieved with great zeal such tasks as Mr. Mac-Morlan chose to intrust him with; but it was speedily observed that at a certain hour after breakfast he regularly disappeared, and returned again about dinner-time. The evening he occupied in the labour of the office. On Saturday, he appeared before Mr. Mac-Morlan with a look of great triumph, and laid on the table two pieces of gold.

"What is this for, Dominie?" said Mr. Mac-Morlan.

"First, to indemnify you of your charges in my behalf, worthy sir; and the balance for the use of Miss Lucy Bertram."

"But, Mr. Sampson, your labour in the office much more than recompenses me; I am your debtor, my good friend."

"Then be it all," said the Dominie, waving his hand, "for Miss Lucy Bertram's behoof."

"Well, but, Dominie, this money"—

"It is honestly come by, Mr. Mac-Morlan; it is the bountiful reward of a young gentleman to whom I am teaching the tongues; reading with him three hours daily."

A few more questions extracted from the Dominie, that this liberal pupil was young Hazlewood, and that he met his preceptor daily at the house of Mrs. Mac-Candlish, whose proclamation of Sampson's disinterested attachment to the young lady had procured him this indefatigable and bounteous scholar.

Mac-Morlan was much struck with what he heard. Little art was necessary to sift the Dominie, for the honest man's head never admitted any but the most direct and simple ideas. "Dces Miss Bertram know how your time is engaged, my good friend?"

"Surely not as yet; Mr. Charles recommended it should be concealed from her, lest she should scruple to accept of the small assistance arising from it; but," he added, "it would not be possible to conceal it long, since Mr. Charles proposed taking lessons occasionally at this house."

"O, he does!" said Mac-Morlan: "yes, yes, I can understand that better. And pray, Mr. Sampson, are these three hours entirely spent in construing and translating?"

"Doubtless, no; we have also colloquial intercourse to sweeten study."

The querist proceeded to elicit from him what their discourse chiefly turned upon.

"Upon our past meetings at Ellangowan; and, truly, I think, very often we discourse concerning Miss Lucy;

for Mr. Charles Hazlewood, in that particular, resembleth me, Mr. Mac-Morlan. When I begin to speak of her I never know when to stop; and, as I say, (jocularly,) she cheats us out of half our lessons."

THE ISLE OF LONG AGO.

BENJ. F. TAYLOR.

O A WONDERFUL stream is the river Time,
As it runs through the realm of tears,
With a faultless rhythm and a musical rhyme,
And a boundless sweep and a surge sublime,
As it blends with the Ocean of Years.

How the Winters are drifting, like flakes of snow,
And the Summers like buds between,
And the year in the sheaf; so they come and they go,
On the river's breast, with its ebb and flow,
As it glides in the shadow and sheen.

There's a magical isle up the river Time,
Where the softest of airs are playing;
There's a cloudless sky and a tropical clime,
And a song as sweet as a vesper chime,
And the Junes with the roses are straying.

And the name of that Isle is the Long Ago,
And we bury our treasures there;
There are brows of beauty and bosoms of snow;
There are heaps of dust, — but we loved them so!
There are trinkets and tresses of hair;

There are fragments of song that nobody sings,
And a part of an infant's prayer;
There's a lute unswept, and a harp without strings;
There are broken vows and pieces of rings,
And the garments that she used to wear.

There are hands that are waved when the fairy shore
By the mirage is lifted in air;
And we sometimes hear through the turbulent roar
Sweet voices we heard in the days gone before,
When the wind down the river is fair.

O, remember'd for aye be the blessèd Isle,
All the day of our life until night;
When the evening comes with its beautiful smile,
And our eyes are closing to slumber awhile,
May that "Greenwood" of Soul be in sight!

THE PAUPER'S DEATH-BEAD.

C. B. Southey.

Tread softly; bow the head,
In reverent silence bow;
No passing-bell doth toll,
Yet an immortal soul
Is passing now.

Stranger, however great,
With lowly reverence bow:
There's one in that poor shed,
One by that paltry bed,
Greater than thou.

Beneath that beggar's roof,
Lo! Death does keep his state:
Enter, — no crowds attend;
Enter, — no guards defend
This palace-gate.

That pavement, damp and cold,
No smiling courtiers tread;
One silent woman stands,
Lifting with meagre hands
A dying head.

No mingling voices sound, —
An infant wail alone;
A sob suppress'd, — again
That short, deep gasp, and then
The parting groan.

O change! O wondrous change!
Burst are the prison-bars;
This moment there, so low,
So agonized, and now
Beyond the stars!

O change, stupendous change!
  There lies the soulless clod!
The Sun eternal breaks, —
The new immortal wakes, —
  Wakes with his God!

OUR WILLIE.

Lie lightly on our Willie, earth!
  Press gently on his side:
Eight years he grew beside our hearth,
  Then laid him down and died.

And let his sleep be peaceful there,
  Whose life was wrong'd with pain,
For sweet his spirit was and fair,
  His talk like gentle rain.

And he was brave of soul and true,
  His thoughts they knew no guile;
Nor ever fell more soft the dew
  Than did his loving smile.

Patient he was, from murmur free,
  Though hard his childish lot;
'Twould grieve you much his pangs to see,
  And yet he murmur'd not.

For on his trusting spirit fell
  The peace that passes thinking;
He knew the love of Christ to tell,
The love that worketh all things well,
  And holds the meek from sinking.

" Thy rod and staff my comfort are,"
  Thus sang our precious boy: —
" Christ leads me forth with tender care,
To freshest streams He guides my feet,
At His own table bids me eat, —
  Christ lights my path with joy.

"What though the vale be dark and drear," —
So ran our Willie's song, —
"I'll pass it still, and feel no fear,
For Christ will make me strong."

We miss him here, we miss him there;
Nought breaks his deep reposing:
His voice no more in song or prayer,
No more his talk by day we share,
Nor kiss when day is closing.

We call, — he answers not the while;
His thoughts we cannot measure;
"This home is best," he seems to smile,
Our lost yet living treasure.

FORTY YEARS AGO.

I've wander'd to the village, Tom,
I've sat beneath the tree,
Upon the school-house play-ground,
That shelter'd you and me;
But none were left to greet me, Tom,
And few were left to know,
Who play'd with us upon that green
Just forty years ago.

The grass was just as green, Tom,
Barefooted boys at play
Were sporting, just as we did then,
With spirits just as gay:
But the master sleeps upon the hill,
Which, coated o'er with snow,
Afforded us a sliding-place
Some forty years ago.

The old school-house is alter'd some,
  The benches are replaced
By new ones, very like the same
  Our jack-knives had defaced;
But the same old bricks are in the wall,
  And the bell swings to and fro,
It's music just the same, dear Tom,
  'Twas forty years ago.

The boys were playing some old game
  Beneath that same old tree;
I do forget the name just now,—
  You've play'd the same with me
On that same spot; 'twas play'd with knives,
  By throwing so and so;
The loser had a task to do
  There forty years ago.

The river's running just as still;
  The willows on its side
Are larger than they were, Tom;
  The stream appears less wide;
But the grape-vine swing is miss'd now,
  Where once we play'd the beau,
And swung our sweethearts — pretty girls —
  Just forty years ago.

The spring that bubbled 'neath the hill,
  Close by the spreading beech,
Is very low; 'twas once so high
  That we could scarcely reach;
And kneeling down to take a drink,
  Dear Tom, I started so,
To think how very much I've changed
  Since forty years ago.

Near by that spring, upon an elm,
  You know, I cut your name;

Your sweetheart's just beneath it, Tom,
  And you did mine the same.
Some heartless wretch has peel'd the bark;
  'Twas dying sure, but slow,
Just as she died whose name you cut
  There forty years ago.

My lids have long been dry, Tom,
  But tears came in my eyes;
I thought of her I loved so well,
  Those early broken ties.
I visited the old church-yard,
  And took some flowers to strow
Upon the graves of those we loved
  Just forty years ago.

Some are in the church-yard laid,
  Some sleep beneath the sea;
But none are left of our old class
  Excepting you and me.
And when our time shall come, Tom,
  And we are call'd to go,
I hope we'll meet with those we loyed
  Some forty years ago.

NEARER HOME.

PHŒBE CARY.

ONE sweetly solemn thought
  Comes to me o'er and o'er:
I'm nearer my home to-day
  Than I ever have been before;

Nearer my Father's house,
  Where the many mansions be;

Nearer the great white throne;
  Nearer the crystal sea;

Nearer the bound of life,
  Where we lay our burdens down;
Nearer leaving the cross,
  Nearer gaining the crown!

But the waves of that silent sea
  Roll dark before my sight,
That brightly the other side
  Break on a shore of light.

O, if my mortal feet
  Have almost gain'd the brink;
If it be I am nearer home
  Even to-day than I think;

Father, perfect my trust;
  Let my spirit feel in death,
That her feet are firmly set
  On the Rock of a living faith!

MICHAEL AND HIS SON.

William Wordsworth.

Near the tumultuous brook of Green-head Ghyll,
In that deep valley, Michael had design'd
To build a Sheep-fold; and, before he heard
The tidings of his melancholy loss,
For this same purpose he had gather'd up
A heap of stones, which by the streamlet's edge
Lay thrown together, ready for the work.
With Luke that evening thitherward he walk'd;
And soon as they had reach'd the place he stopp'd,
And thus the old man spake to him: "My son,
To-morrow thou wilt leave me: with full heart

I look upon thee, for thou art the same
That wert a promise to me ere thy birth,
And all thy life hast been my daily joy.
I will relate to thee some little part
Of our two histories; 'twill do thee good
When thou art from me, even if I should touch
On things thou canst not know of. — After thou
First camest into the world, — as oft befalls
To new-born infants, — thou didst sleep away
Two days, and blessings from thy father's tongue
Then fell upon thee. Day by day pass'd on,
And still I loved thee with increasing love.
Never to living ear came sweeter sounds
Than when I heard thee by our own fire-side
First uttering, without words, a natural tune;
While thou, a feeding babe, didst in thy joy
Sing at thy mother's breast. Month follow'd month,
And in the open fields my life was pass'd,
And on the mountains; else I think that thou
Hadst been brought up upon thy Father's knees.
But we were playmates, Luke: among these hills,
As well thou know'st, in us the old and young
Have play'd together, nor with me didst thou
Lack any pleasure which a boy can know."
Luke had a manly heart; but at these words
He sobb'd aloud. The old man grasp'd his hand,
And said, "Nay, do not take it so, — I see
That these are things of which I need not speak.
Even to the utmost I have been to thee
A kind and a good father: and herein
I but repay a gift which I myself
Received at others' hand; for, though now old
Beyond the common life of man, I still
Remember them who loved me in my youth.
Both of them sleep together: here they lived,
As all their forefathers had done; and, when
At length their time was come, they were not loth

To give their bodies to the family mould.
I wish'd that thou shouldst live the life they lived:
But 'tis a long time to look back, my son,
And see so little gain from threescore years.
These fields were burden'd when they came to me;
Till I was forty years of age, not more
Than half of my inheritance was mine.
I toil'd and toil'd; God bless'd me in my work,
And till these three weeks past the land was free.
It looks as if it never could endure
Another master. Heaven forgive me, Luke,
If I judge ill for thee, but it seems good
That thou shouldst go."
At this the old man paused;
Then, pointing to the stones near which they stood,
Thus, after a short silence, he resumed:
"This was a work for us; and now, my son,
It is a work for me. But, lay one stone, —
Here, lay it for me, Luke, with thine own hands.
Nay, boy, be of good hope; — we both may live
To see a better day. At eighty-four
I still am strong and hale; — do thou thy part;
I will do mine. — I will begin again
With many tasks that were resign'd to thee:
Up to the heights, and in among the storms,
Will I without thee go again, and do
All works which I was wont to do alone,
Before I knew thy face. — Heaven bless thee, boy!
Thy heart these two weeks has been beating fast
With many hopes; it should be so, — yes — yes; —
I knew that thou couldst never have a wish
To leave me, Luke: thou hast been bound to me
Only by links of love: when thou art gone,
What will be left to us? — But I forget
My purposes. Lay now the corner-stone,
As I requested; and hereafter, Luke,
When thou art gone away, should evil men

Be thy companions, think of me, my son,
And of this moment; hither turn thy thoughts,
And God will strengthen thee: amid all fear
And all temptation, Luke, I pray that thou
Mayst bear in mind the life thy fathers lived,
Who, being innocent, did for that cause
Bestir them in good deeds. Now, fare thee well!
When thou return'st, thou in this place wilt see
A work which is not here: a covenant
'Twill be between us; but, whatever fate
Befall thee, I shall love thee to the last,
And bear thy memory with me to the grave."
  The Shepherd ended here; and Luke stoop'd down,
And, as his father had requested,
Laid the first stone of the Sheep-fold. At the sight
The old man's grief broke from him; to his heart
He press'd his son, he kissèd him and wept;
And to the house together they return'd.
Hush'd was that house in peace, or seeming peace,
Ere the night fell: with morrow's dawn the boy
Began his journey, and when he had reach'd
The public way, he put on a bold face;
And all the neighbours, as he pass'd their doors,
Came forth with wishes and with farewell prayers,
That follow'd him till he was out of sight.

LEONARD AND MARGARET.

ROBERT SOUTHEY.

LEONARD was not more than eight-and-twenty when he obtained a living, a few miles from Doncaster. He took his bride with him to the vicarage. The house was as humble as the benefice, which was worth less than fifty pounds a-year; but it was soon made the neatest cottage in the country round, and upon a happier dwelling the Sun never shone. A few acres of good glebe were attached to it; and the garden was large enough to afford healthful and pleasureable employment to the owners. The course of true love never ran more smoothly; but its course was short. Little more than five years from the time of their marriage had elapsed, before a head-stone in the adjacent churchyard told where the remains of Margaret Bacon had been deposited in the thirtieth year of her age.

When the stupor and the agony of that bereavement had passed away, the very intensity of Leonard's affection became a source of consolation. Margaret had been to him purely an ideal object during the years of his youth: death had again rendered her such. Imagination had beautified and idolized her then; faith sanctified and glorified her now. She had been to him all that he had fancied, all that he had hoped, all that he had desired. She would again be so in Heaven. And this second union nothing could impede, nothing could interrupt, nothing could dissolve. He had only to keep himself worthy of it by cherishing her memory, hallowing his heart to it while he performed a parent's duty to their child; and, so doing, to await his own summons, which must one day come, which was every day brought nearer, and which any day might bring.

The same feeling which from his childhood had refined Leonard's heart, keeping it pure and undefiled, had also corroborated the natural strength of his character, and made him firm of purpose. It was a saying of Bishop Andrewes that "good husbandry is good divinity"; "the truth whereof," says Fuller, "no wise man will deny." Frugality he had always practised as a needful virtue, and found that in an especial manner it brings with it its own reward. He now resolved upon scrupulously setting apart a fourth of his small income, to make a provision for his child, in case of her surviving him, as in the natural course of things might be expected. If she should be removed before him,—for this was an event the possibility of which he always bore in mind,—he resolved that whatever had been accumulated with this intent should be disposed of to some other pious purpose; for such, within the limits to which his poor means extended, he properly considered this. And, having entered on this prudential course with a calm reliance upon Providence in case his hour should come before that purpose could be accomplished, he was without any earthly hope or fear,—those alone excepted, from which no parent can be free.

The child had been christened Deborah, after her maternal grandmother, for whom Leonard ever retained a most affectionate and reverential remembrance. She was a healthy, happy creature; at first

> One of those little prating girls
> Of whom fond parents tell such tedious stories;

afterwards, as she grew up, a favourite with the village school-mistress, and with the whole parish; docile, good-natured, lively, and yet considerate, always gay as a lark and busy as a bee. One of the pensive pleasures in which Leonard indulged was to gaze on her unperceived, and trace the likeness of her mother.

That resemblance, which was strong in childhood, lessened as the child grew up; for Margaret's countenance had acquired a cast of meek melancholy during those years in which the bread of bitterness had been her portion; and when hope came to her, it was that "hope deferred" which takes from the cheek its bloom, even when the heart, instead of being made sick, is sustained by it. But no unhappy circumstances depressed the constitutional buoyancy of her daughter's spirits. Deborah brought into the world the happiest of all Nature's endowments, an easy temper and a light heart Resemblant, therefore, as the features were, the dissimilitude of expression was more apparent; and, when Leonard contrasted in thought the sunshine of hilarity that lit up his daughter's face, with the sort of moonlight loveliness which had given a serene and saint-like character to her mother's, he wished to persuade himself that, as the early translation of the one seemed to have been thus prefigured, the other might be destined to live for the happiness of others till a good old age, while length of years in these should ripen her for Heaven.

THE STABILITY OF VIRTUE.

T. MARSHALL.

THE sturdy rock, for all his strength,
  By raging seas is rent in twain;
The marble stone is pierced at length
  With little drops of drizzling rain;
The ox doth yield unto the yoke,
The steel obeys the hammer-stroke:

The stately stag, that seems so stout,
  By yelping hounds at bay is set;
The swiftest bird that flies about
  Is caught at length in fowler's net;
The greatest fish, in deepest brook,
Is soon deceived with subtle hook:

Yea, man himself, unto whose will
  All things are bounden to obey,
For all his wit and worthy skill,
  Doth fade at length, and fall away:

There is no thing but time doth waste;
The heavens, the Earth consume at last.

But virtue sits triumphing still
  Upon the throne of glorious fame:
Though spiteful death man's body kill,
  Yet hurts he not his virtuous name:
By life or death whate'er betides,
The state of virtue never slides.

THE OCEAN BURIAL.

CAPT. WM. H. SAUNDERS (U. S. A.).

[My brother, Capt. Wm. H. Saunders, wrote "Bury me not in the deep sea" nearly forty years ago, published it in the "New Orleans Picayune," gave a copy to a lady; after his death (at least five or six years after) she, I think, claimed to be the authoress of it, but I had the original manuscript and knew it to be his own production.
LEESBURGH, VA., June 26th, '83. H. SAUNDERS.]

"O, BURY me not in the deep, deep sea!"
These words came low and mournfully,
From the pallid lips of a youth, who lay
On his cabin couch, at the close of day.
He had wasted and pined, 'till o'er his brow
The death-shade had slowly pass'd; and now,
When the land and his fond-loved home were nigh,
They had gather'd around to see him die.

"O, bury me not in the deep, deep sea,
Where the billowy shroud will roll over me,
Where no light will break through the dark cold wave,
And no sunbeam rest upon my grave!
It matters not, I have oft been told,
Where the body shall lie when the heart is cold;
Yet grant ye, O, grant ye this one boon to me,
O, bury me not in the deep, deep sea!

For in fancy I've listen'd to the well-known words,
The free wild winds, and the songs of the birds;
I have thought of home, of cot and bower,
And of scenes that I loved in childhood's hour:
I have even hoped to be laid, when I died,
In the church-yard there, on the green hill-side;
By the bones of my fathers my grave should be:
O, bury me not in the deep, deep sea.

Let my death-slumbers be where a mother's prayer
And a sister's tear shall be mingled there:
O, 'twill be sweet, ere the heart's throb is o'er,
To know, when its fountains shall gush no more,
That those it so fondly hath yearn'd for will come
To plant the first wild flowers of Spring on my tomb;
Let me lie where those loved ones will weep o'er me:
O, bury me not in the deep, deep sea.

And there is another; her tears would be shed
For him who lay far in the deep ocean-bed:
In hours that it pains me to think of now,
She hath twined these locks and hath kiss'd this brow:
In the hair she hath wreathed shall the sea-snake hiss,
And the brow she hath press'd shall the cold wave kiss!
For the sake of the bright one that waiteth for me,
O, bury me not in the deep, deep sea.

She hath been in my dreams," — his voice fail'd there.
They gave no heed to his dying prayer;
They lower'd him slow o'er the vessel's side;
Above him has closed the dark, cold tide,
Where to dip their light wings the sea-fowls rest,
Where the blue waves dance o'er the ocean's crest,
Where billows bound, and the winds sport free:
They have buried him there in the deep, deep sea.

THE GOOD SON.

R. H. Dana.

There is no virtue without a characteristic beauty to make it particularly loved of the good, and to make the bad ashamed of their neglect of it. To do what is right, argues superior taste as well as morals; and those whose practice is evil feel an inferiority of intellectual power and enjoyment, even where they take no concern for a principle. Doing well has something more in it than the fulfilling of a duty. It is a cause of a just sense of elevation of character; it clears and strengthens the spirits; it gives higher reaches of thought; it widens our benevolence, and makes the current of our peculiar affections swift and deep.

A sacrifice was never yet offered to a principle, that was not made up to us by self-approval, and the consideration of what our degradation would have been had we done otherwise. Certainly, it is a pleasant and a wise thing, then, to follow what is right, when we only go along with our affections, and take the easy way of the virtuous propensities of our nature.

The world is sensible of these truths, let it act as it may. It is not because of his integrity alone that it relies on an honest man; but it has more confidence in his judgment and wise conduct, in the long run, than in the schemes of those of greater intellect, who go at large without any landmarks of principle. So that virtue seems of a double nature, and to stand oftentimes in the place of what we call talent.

This reasoning, or rather feeling, of the world, is all right; for the honest man only falls in with the order of Nature, which is grounded in truth, and will endure along with it. And such a hold has a good man upon the world, that, even where he has not been called upon to make a sacrifice to a principle, or to take a stand against wrong, but has merely avoided running into vices, and suffered himself to be borne along by the delightful and virtuous affections of private life, and has found his pleasure in practising the duties of home, he is looked up to with respect, as well as regarded with kindness. We attach certain notions of refinement to his thoughts, and of depth to his sentiment. The impression he makes on us is beautiful and peculiar. Other men in his presence, though we have nothing to object to them, and though they may be very well in their way, affect us as lacking something, — we can hardly tell what, — a certain sensitive delicacy of character and manner, without which they strike us as more or less vulgar.

No creature in the world has this character so finely marked in him as a respectful and affectionate son, — particularly in his relation to his mother. Every little attention he pays her is not only an expression of filial attachment, and a grateful acknowledgment of past cares, but is an evidence of a tenderness of disposition which moves us the more, because not looked on so much as an essential property in a man's character, as an added grace, which is bestowed only upon a few. His regards do not appear like mere habits of duty, nor does his watchfulness of his mother's wishes seem like taught submission to her will. They are the native courtesies of a feeling mind, showing themselves amidst stern virtues and masculine energies, like gleams of light on points of rocks. They are delightful as evidences of power yielding voluntary homage to the delicacy of the soul. The armed knee is bent, and the heart of the mailed man laid bare.

Feelings that would seem to be at variance with each other meet together and harmonize in the breast of a son. Every call of the mother which he answers to, and every act of submission which he performs, are not only so many acknowledgments of her authority, but also so many instances of kindness and marks of protecting regard. The servant and defender, the child and guardian, are all mingled in him. The world looks on him in this way; and to draw upon a man the confidence, the respect, and the love of the world, it is enough to say of him, he is an excellent son.

THE WIDOW AND HER SON.

WASHINGTON IRVING.

DURING my residence in the country, I used frequently to attend at the old village church, which stood in a country filled with ancient families, and contained, within its cold and silent aisles, the congregated dust of many noble generations. Its shadowy aisles, its mouldering monuments, its dark oaken panelling, all reverend with the gloom of departed years, seemed to fit it for the haunt of solemn meditation. A Sunday, too, in the country, is so holy in its repose; such a pensive quiet reigns over the face of Nature, that every restless passion is charmed down, and we feel all the natural religion of the soul gently springing up within us:

> Sweet day, so pure, so calm, so bright,
> The bridal of the Earth and Sky!

I do not pretend to be what is called a devout man: but there are feelings that visit me in a country church, amid the beautiful serenity of Nature, which I experience nowhere else; and, if not a more religious, I think I am a better man on Sunday than on any other day of the seven.

But in this church I felt myself continually thrown back upon the world by the frigidity and pomp of the poor worms around me. The only being that seemed thoroughly to feel the humble and prostrate piety of a true Christian, was a poor decrepit old woman, bending under the weight of years and infirmities. She bore the trace of something better than abject poverty. The lingerings of decent pride were visible in her appearance. Her dress, though humble in the extreme, was scrupulously clean. Some trivial respect, too, had been awarded her, for she did not take her seat among the village poor, but sat alone on the steps of the altar. She seemed to have survived all love, all friendship, all society; and to have nothing left her but the hopes of Heaven. When I saw her feebly rising and bending her aged form in prayer, — habitually conning her prayer-book, which her palsied hand and failing eyes would not permit her to read, but which she evidently knew by heart, — I felt persuaded that the faltering voice of that poor woman arose to Heaven far before the responses of the clerk, the swell of the organ, or the chanting of the choir.

I am fond of loitering about country churches, and this was so delightfully situated, that it frequently attracted me. It stood on a knoll, round which a stream made a beautiful bend, and then wound its way through a long reach of soft meadow scenery. The church was surrounded by yew-trees, which seemed almost coeval with itself. Its tall Gothic spire shot up lightly from among them, with rooks and crows generally wheeling about it. I was seated there one still, sunny morning, watching two labourers who were digging a grave. They had chosen one of the most remote and neglected corners of the church-yard, where, from the number of nameless graves around, it would appear that the indigent and friendless were huddled into the earth. I was told that the new-made grave was for the only son of a poor widow.

While I was meditating on the distinctions of wordly rank, which extend thus down into the very dust, the toll of the bell announced the approach of the funeral. They were the obsequies of poverty, with which pride had nothing to do. A coffin of the plainest materials, without pall or other covering, was borne by some of the villagers. The sexton walked before with an air of cold indifference. There were no mock mourners in the trappings of affected woe; but there was one real mourner who feebly tottered after the corpse. It was the aged mother of the deceased,— the poor old woman whom I had seen seated on the steps of the altar. She was supported by an humble friend, who was endeavouring to comfort her. A few of the neighbouring poor had joined the train, and some children of the village were running hand in hand, now shouting with unthinking mirth, and now pausing to gaze, with childish curiosity, on the grief of the mourner.

As the funeral train approached the grave, the parson issued from the church porch, arrayed in the surplice, with prayer-book in hand, and attended by the clerk. The service, however, was a mere act of charity. The deceased had been destitute, and the survivor was penniless. It was shuffled through, therefore, in form, but coldly and unfeelingly. The well-fed priest moved but a few steps from the church-door; his voice could scarcely be heard at the grave; and never did I hear the funeral service, that sublime and touching ceremony, turned into such a frigid mummery of words.

I approached the grave. The coffin was placed on the ground. On it was inscribed the name and age of the deceased, "George Somers, aged 26 years." The poor mother had been assisted to kneel down at the head of it. Her withered hands were clasped as if in prayer, but I could perceive, by a feeble rocking of the body, and a convulsive motion of the lips, that she was gazing on the last relics of her son with the yearnings of a mother's heart.

The service being ended, preparations were made to deposit the coffin in the earth. There was that bustling stir which breaks so harshly on the feelings of grief and affection: directions given in the cold tones of business; the striking of spades into sand and gravel; which, at the grave of those we love, is, of all sounds, the most withering. The bustle around seemed to waken the mother from a wretched revery. She raised her glazed eyes, and looked about with a faint wildness. As the men approached with cords to lower the coffin into the grave, she wrung her hands and broke into an agony of grief. The poor woman who attended her took her by the arm, endeavouring to raise her from the earth, and to whisper something like consolation, "Nay, now, — nay, now, — don't take it so sorely to heart!" She could only shake her head, and wring her hands, as one not to be comforted.

As they lowered the body into the earth, the creaking of the cords seem to agonize her; but when, on some accidental obstruction, there was a justling of the coffin, all the tenderness of the mother burst forth; as if any harm could come to him who was far beyond the reach of worldly suffering.

I could see no more; my heart swelled into my throat, my eyes filled with tears; I felt as if I were acting a barbarous part, in standing by and gazing idly on this scene of maternal anguish. I wandered to another part of the church-yard, where I remained until the funeral train had dispersed.

When I saw the mother slowly and painfully quitting the grave, leaving behind her the remains of all that was dear to her on Earth, and returning to silence and destitution, my heart ached for her. What, thought I, are the distresses of the rich! they have friends to soothe, pleasures to beguile, a world to divert and dissipate their griefs. What are the sorrows of the young! Their growing minds soon close above the wound; their elastic spirits soon rise beneath the pressure; their green and ductile affections soon twine round new objects. But the sorrows of the poor, who have no outward appliances to soothe; the sorrows of the aged, with whom life at best is but a wintry day, and who can look for no after-growth of joy; the sorrows of a widow, aged, solitary, destitute, mourning over an only son, the last solace of her years; — these are indeed sorrows which make us feel the impotency of consolation.

RIVERMOUTH ROCKS.

John G. Whittier.

Rivermouth Rocks are fair to see,
  By dawn or sunset shone across,
When the ebb of the sea has left them free,
  To dry their fringes of gold green moss:
For there the river comes winding down
From salt sea-meadows and uplands brown,

And waves on the outer rocks afoam
Shout to its waters, "Welcome home!"

And fair are the sunny isles in view
  East of the grisly Head of the Boar,
And Agamenticus lifts its blue
  Disk of a cloud the woodlands o'er;
And southerly, when the tide is down,
'Twixt white sea-waves and sand-hills brown,
The beach-birds dance and the gray gulls wheel
Over a floor of burnish'd steel.

Once in the old Colonial days,
  Two hundred years ago and more,
A boat sail'd down through the winding ways
  Of Hampton River to that low shore,
Full of a goodly company
Sailing out on the summer sea,
Veering to catch the land-breeze light,
With the Boar to left and the Rocks to right.

In Hampton meadows, where mowers laid
  Their scythes to the swaths of salted grass,
"Ah, well-a-day! our hay must be made!"
  A young man sigh'd, who saw them pass.
Loud laugh'd his fellows to see him stand
Whetting his scythe with a listless hand,
Hearing a voice in a far-off song,
Watching a white hand beckoning long.

"Fie on the witch!" cried a merry girl,
  As they rounded the point where Goody Cole
Sat by her door with her wheel atwirl,
  A bent and blear-eyed poor old soul.
"Oho!" she mutter'd, "ye're brave to-day!
But I hear the little waves laugh and say,
'The broth will be cold that waits at home;
For it's one to go, but another to come!'"

"She's cursed," said the skipper; "speak her fair:
  I'm scary always to see her shake
Her wicked head, with its wild gray hair,
  And nose like a hawk, and eyes like a snake."
But merrily still, with laugh and shout,
From Hampton River the boat sail'd out,
Till the huts and the flakes on the Star seem'd nigh,
And they lost the scent of the pines of Rye.

They dropp'd their lines in the lazy tide,
  Drawing up haddock and mottled cod;
They saw not the shadow that walk'd beside,
  They heard not the feet with silence shod:
But thicker and thicker a hot mist grew,
Shot by the lightnings through and through;
And muffled growls, like the growl of a beast,
Ran along the sky from west to east.

Then the skipper look'd from the darkening sea
  Up to the dimm'd and wading Sun;
But he spake like a brave man cheerily,
  "Yet there is time for our homeward run."
Veering and tacking, they backward wore;
And, just as a breath from the woods ashore
Blew out to whisper of danger past,
The wrath of the storm came down at last!

The skipper haul'd at the heavy sail:
  "God be our help," he only cried,
As the roaring gale, like the stroke of a flail,
  Smote the boat on its starboard side.
The shoalsmen look'd, but saw alone
Dark films of rain-cloud slantwise blown,
Wild rocks lit up by the lightning's glare,
The strife and torment of sea and air.

Goody Cole look'd out from her door:
  The Isles of Shoals were drown'd and gone,

Scarcely she saw the Head of the Boar
  Toss the foam from tusks of stone.
She clasp'd her hands with a grip of pain,
The tear on her cheek was not of rain:
"They are lost," she mutter'd, "boat and crew!
Lord, forgive me! my words were true!"

Suddenly seaward swept the squall;
  The low Sun smote through cloudy rack;
The shoals stood clear in the light, and all
  The trend of the coast lay hard and black:
But, far and wide as eye could reach,
No life was seen upon wave or beach;
The boat that went out at morning never
Sail'd back again into Hampton River.

O mower, lean on thy bended snath,
  Look from the meadows green and low:
The wind of the sea is a waft of death,
  The waves are singing a song of woe!
By silent river, by moaning sea,
Long and vain shall thy watching be:
Never again shall the sweet voice call,
Never the white hand rise and fall!

O Rivermouth Rocks, how sad a sight
  Ye saw in the light of breaking day!
Dead faces looking up cold and white
  From sand and sea-weed where they lay.
The mad old witch-wife wail'd and wept,
And cursed the tide as it backward crept:
"Crawl back, crawl back, blue water-snake!
Leave your dead for the hearts that break!"

Solemn it was in that old day
  In Hampton town and its log-built church,
Where side by side the coffins lay
  And the mourners stood in aisle and porch:

In the singing-seats young eyes were dim,
The voices falter'd that raised the hymn,
And Father Dalton, grave and stern,
Sobb'd through his prayer and wept in turn.

And the Sun set paled, and warm'd once more
With a softer, tenderer after-glow;
In the east was moonrise with boats off-shore
And sails in the distance drifting slow:
The beacon glimmer'd from Portsmouth bar,
The White Isle kindled its great red star;
And life and death in my old-time lay
Mingled in peace like the night and day!

SONG OF THE MYSTIC.

FATHER A. J. RYAN.

I WALK down the valley of silence, —
Down the dim voiceless valley, — alone;
And I hear not the fall of a footstep
Around me, — save God's and my own;
And the hush of my heart is as holy
As hours when angels have flown!

Long ago, was I weary of voices
Whose music my heart could not win;
Long ago, I was weary of noises
That fretted my soul with their din;
Long ago, was I weary of places
Where I met but the human, — and sin.

I walk'd through the world with the worldly,
I craved what the world never gave,
And I said, "In the world each ideal,
That shines like a star on life's wave,
Is toss'd on the shore of the real,
And sleeps like a dream in a grave."

And still did I pine for the perfect,
  And still found the false with the true;
I sought not the human for Heaven,
  But caught a mere glimpse of the blue:
And I wept when the clouds of the mortal
  Veil'd even that glimpse from my view.

And I toil'd on, heart-tired of the human,
  And I mourn'd not the mazes of men,
Till I knelt long ago at an altar,
  And heard a voice call me: since then
I walk down the valley of silence
  That lies far beyond mortal ken.

Do you ask what I found in the valley?
  'Tis my trysting-place with the Divine;
And I fell at the feet of the Holy,
  And above me a voice said "Be mine."
Then rose from the depths of my spirit
  An echo, "My heart shall be thine."

Do you ask how I live in the valley?
  I weep, and I dream, and I pray;
But my tears are as sweet as the dewdrops
  That fall on the roses of May:
And my prayer like a perfume from censers
  Ascendeth to God night and day.

In the hush of the valley of silence
  I dream all the songs that I sing;
And the music floats down the dim valley
  Till each finds a word for a wing
That to men, like the dove of the deluge,
  The message of peace they may bring.

But far on the deep there are billows
  That never shall break on the beach,

And I have heard songs in the silence
  That never shall float into speech;
And I have had dreams in the valley
  Too lofty for language to reach.

And I have seen thoughts in the valley, —
  Ah me! how my spirit was stirr'd!
And they wore holy veils on their faces,
  Their footsteps can scarcely be heard;
They pass through the valley like virgins,
  Too pure for the touch of a word.

Do you ask me the place of the valley,
  Ye hearts that are harrow'd by care?
It lieth afar between mountains,
  And God and His angels are there;
And one is the dark mount of sorrow,
  And one the bright mountain of prayer.

LUCY GRAY.

William Wordsworth.

Oft I had heard of Lucy Gray;
And, when I cross'd the wild,
I chanced to see at break of day
The solitary child.

No mate, no comrade Lucy knew;
She dwelt on a wide moor, —
The sweetest thing that ever grew
Beside a human door!

You yet may spy the fawn at play,
The hare upon the green;
But the sweet face of Lucy Gray
Will never more be seen.

"To-night will be a stormy night,—
You to the town must go;
And take a lantern, Child, to light
Your mother through the snow."

"That, Father, will I gladly do:
'Tis scarcely afternoon;
The minster-clock has just struck two,
And yonder is the Moon!"

At this the Father raised his hook,
And snapp'd a fagot-band;
He plied his work;—and Lucy took
The lantern in her hand.

Not blither is the mountain roe:
With many a wanton stroke
Her feet disperse the powdery snow,
That rises up like smoke.

The storm came on before its time:
She wander'd up and down;
And many a hill did Lucy climb,
But never reach'd the town.

The wretched parents all that night
Went shouting far and wide;
But there was neither sound nor sight
To serve them for a guide.

At day-break on a hill they stood
That overlook'd the moor;
And thence they saw the bridge of wood,
A furlong from their door.

They wept; and, turning homeward, cried,
"In Heaven we all shall meet";
When in the snow the mother spied
The print of Lucy's feet.

Then downwards from the steep hill's edge
They track'd the footmarks small;
And through the broken hawthorn hedge,
And by the long stone-wall;

And then an open field they cross'd:
The marks were still the same;
They track'd them on, nor ever lost;
And to the bridge they came.

They follow'd from the snowy bank
Those footmarks, one by one,
Into the middle of the plank;
And further there were none!

Yet some maintain that to this day
She is a living child;
That you may see sweet Lucy Gray
Upon the lonesome wild.

O'er rough and smooth she trips along,
And never looks behind;
And sings a solitary song
That whistles in the wind.

OUR FOLKS.

ETHEL LYNN.

"Hi! Harry Holly! Halt; and tell
  A fellow just a thing or two:
You've had a furlough, been to see
  How all the folks in Jersey do.
It's months ago since I was there, —
  I, and a bullet from Fair Oaks:
When you were home, — old comrade, say,
  Did you see any of our folks?

You did? Shake hands; — O, ain't I glad?
  For, if I do look grim and rough,
I've got some feelin' —
                    People think
  A soldier's heart is mighty tough;
But, Harry, when the bullets fly,
  And hot saltpetre flames and smokes,
While whole battalions lie afield,
  One's apt to think about his folks.

And so you saw them, — when? and where?
  The old man, — is he hearty yet?
And mother, — does she fade at all?
  Or does she seem to pine and fret
For me? And Sis? — has she grown tall?
  And did you see her friend, — you know
That Annie Moss —
                    (How this pipe chokes!)
Where did you see her? — tell me, Hal,
  A lot of news about our folks.

You saw them in the church, — you say;
  It's likely, for they're always there.
Not Sunday? no? A funeral? Who?
  Who, Harry? how you shake and stare!
All well, you say, and all were out;
  What ails you, Hal? Is this a hoax?
Why don't you tell me, like a man,
  What is the matter with our folks?"

"I said all well, old comrade, true;
  I say all well, for He knows best
Who takes the young ones in His arms,
  Before the Sun goes to the west.
The axe-man Death deals right and left,
  And flowers fall as well as oaks;
And so —
            Fair Annie blooms no more!
  And that's the matter with your folks.

See, this brown curl was kept for you;
  And this white blossom from her breast;
And here, — your sister Bessie wrote
  A letter, telling all the rest.
Bear up, old friend."
                    Nobody speaks;
Only the old camp raven croaks,
  And soldiers whisper:
                    "Boys, be still;
There's some bad news from Grainger's folks."

He turns his back — the only foe
  That ever saw it — on this grief,
And, as men will, keeps down the tears
  Kind Nature sends to Woe's relief.
Then answers he:
                    "Ah, Hal, I'll try;
  But in my throat there's something chokes,
Because, you see, I've thought so long
  To count her in among our folks.

I s'pose she must be happy now;
  But still I will keep thinking too,
I could have kept all trouble off,
  By being tender, kind, and true;
But maybe not.
                    She's safe up there;
  And when His Hand deals other strokes,
She'll stand by Heaven's gate, I know,
  And wait to welcome in our folks."

POOR LITTLE JOE.

PELEG ARKWRIGHT.

PROP yer eyes wide open Joey,
  Fur I've brought you sumpin' great.
Apples? No, a heap sight better!

Don't you take no int'rest? Wait!
Flowers, Joe, — I know'd you'd like 'em, —
Ain't them scrumptious? Ain't them high?
Tears, my boy? Wot's them fur, Joey?
There, — poor little Joe! — don't cry!

I was skippin' past a winder,
Where a bang-up lady sot,
All amongst a lot of bushes, —
Each one climbin' from a pot;
Every bush had flowers on it, —
Pretty? Mebbe not! O, no!
Wish you could a seen 'em growin',
It was sich a stunnin' show.

Well, I thought of you, poor feller,
Lyin' here so sick and weak,
Never knowin' any comfort;
And I puts on lots o' cheek,
"Missus," says I, "if you please, mum,
Could I ax you for a rose?
For my little brother, missus, —
Never seed one, I suppose."

Then I told her all about you, —
How I bring'd you up, poor Joe!
(Lackin' women folks to do it:)
Sich a' imp you was, you know, —
Till yer got that awful tumble,
Jist as I had broke yer in,
(Hard work, too,) to earn yer livin'
Blackin' boots for honest tin.

How that tumble crippled of you,
So's you couldn't hyper much!
Joe, it hurted when I seen you
Fur the first time with yer crutch.
"But," I says, "he's laid up now, mum,

'Pears to weaken every day":
Joe, she up and went to cuttin',—
That's the how of this bokay.

Say! It seems to me, ole feller,
You is quite yerself to-night;
Kind o' chirk; it's been a fortnit
Sence yer eyes has been so bright.
Better? Well, I'm glad to hear it!
Yes, they're mighty pretty, Joe.
Smellin' of 'em's made you happy?
Well, I thought it would, you know!

Never see the country, did you?
Flowers growin' everywhere!
Sometime when you're better, Joey,
Mebbe I kin take you there.
Flowers in Heaven? 'M — I s'pose so;
Dunno much about it, though;
Ain't as fly as wot I might be
On them topics, little Joe.

But I've heard it hinted somewheres
That in Heaven's golden gates
Things is everlastin' cheerful,—
B'lieve that's wot the Bible states.
Likewise, there folks don't git hungry;
So good people, when they dies,
Finds themselves well fix'd forever,—
Joe, my boy, wot ails yer eyes?

Thought they look'd a little sing'ler.
O, no! don't you have no fear;
Heaven was made fur such as you is,—
Joe, wot makes you look so queer?
Here, wake up! O, don't look that way!
Joe! My boy! Hold up yer head!
Here's yer flowers,—you dropp'd 'em Joey!—
O my God! can Joe be *dead?*

IV.

REVERENCE, DEVOTION, ADORATION.

CATO'S SOLILOQUY ON THE IMMORTALITY OF THE SOUL.

JOSEPH ADDISON.

It must be so, — Plato, thou reason'st well! —
Else, whence this pleasing hope, this fond desire,
This longing after immortality?
Or whence this secret dread and inward horror
Of falling into nought? Why shrinks the soul
Back on herself, and startles at destruction? —
'Tis the Divinity that stirs within us;
'Tis Heaven itself that points out an Hereafter,
And intimates Eternity to man.
Eternity! — thou pleasing, dreadful thought!
Through what variety of untried being,
Through what new scenes and changes must we pass!
The wide, th' unbounded prospect lies before me;
But shadows, clouds and darkness rest upon it.
Here will I hold. If there's a Power above us, —
And that there is, all Nature cries aloud
Through all her works, — He must delight in virtue;
And that which He delights in must be happy.
But when? or where? This world — was made for Cæsar.
I'm weary of conjectures, — this must end them.
Thus am I doubly arm'd. My death and life,
My bane and antidote, are both before me.
This, in a moment, brings me to an end;
But this informs me I shall never die!

The soul, secured in her existence, smiles
At the drawn dagger, and defies its point. —
The stars shall fade away, the Sun himself
Grow dim with age, and Nature sink in years;
But thou shalt flourish in immortal youth,
Unhurt amid the war of elements,
The wreck of matter, and the crash of worlds!

TO THE SUPREME BEING.

MICHAEL ANGELO: *Translated by* WORDSWORTH.

THE prayers I make will then be sweet indeed
If Thou the spirit give by which I pray:
My unassisted heart is barren clay,
That of its native self can nothing feed:
Of good and pious works Thou art the seed,
That quickens only where Thou say'st it may:
Unless Thou shew to us Thine own true way
No man can find it; Father, Thou must lead.
Do Thou, then, breathe those thoughts into my mind
By which such virtue may in me be bred
That in Thy holy footsteps I may tread;
The fetters of my tongue do Thou unbind,
That I may have the power to sing of Thee,
And sound Thy praises everlastingly.

Eternal Lord! eased of a cumbrous load,
And loosen'd from the world, I turn to Thee;
Shun, like a shatter'd bark, the storm, and flee
To Thy protection for a safe abode.
The crown of thorns, hands pierced upon the tree,
The meek, benign, and lacerated face,
To a sincere repentance promise grace,
To the sad soul give hope of pardon free.
With justice mark not Thou, O Light divine!
My fault, nor hear it with Thy sacred ear;

Neither put forth that way Thy arm severe;
Wash with thy blood my sins; thereto incline
More readily the more my years require
Help, and forgiveness speedy and entire.

A HYMN.

S. T. Coleridge.

My Maker! of Thy power the trace
In every creature's form and face
  The wondering soul surveys:
Thy wisdom, infinite above
Seraphic thought, a Father's love
  As infinite displays!

From all that meets or eye or ear,
There falls a genial holy fear
Which, like the heavy dew of morn,
Refreshes while it bows the heart forlorn.

Great God, Thy works how wondrous fair!
Yet sinful man didst Thou declare
  The whole Earth's voice and mind:
Lord, even as Thou all-present art,
O, may we still with heedful heart
  Thy presence know and find!
Then, come what will of weal or woe,
Joy's bosom-spring shall steady flow;
For, though 'tis Heaven Thyself to see,
Where but Thy *Shadow* falls, Grief cannot be!

THE CLOSING YEAR.

GEORGE D. PRENTICE.

'TIS midnight's holy hour, and silence now
Is brooding like a gentle spirit o'er
The still and pulseless world. Hark! on the winds
The bell's deep tones are swelling, — 'tis the knell
Of the departed year. No funeral train
Is sweeping past; yet, on the stream and wood,
With melancholy light, the moon-beams rest
Like a pale, spotless shroud; the air is stirr'd
As by a mourner's sigh; and on yon cloud,
That floats so still and placidly through heaven,
The spirits of the seasons seem to stand, —
Young Spring, bright Summer, Autumn's solemn form,
And Winter with its aged locks, — and breathe,
In mournful cadences that come abroad
Like the far wind-harp's wild and touching wail,
A melancholy dirge o'er the dead year,
Gone from the Earth forever.
'Tis a time
For memory and for tears. Within the deep,
Still chambers of the heart, a spectre dim,
Whose tones are like the wizard voice of Time
Heard from the tomb of ages, points its cold
And solemn finger to the beautiful
And holy visions that have pass'd away,
And left no shadow of their loveliness
On the dead waste of life. That spectre lifts
The coffin-lid of Hope, and Joy, and Love,
And, bending mournfully above the pale,
Sweet forms that slumber there, scatters dead flowers
O'er what has pass'd to nothingness.
The year
Has gone, and, with it, many a glorious throng
Of happy dreams. Its mark is on each brow,
Its shadow in each heart. In its swift course,

It waved its sceptre o'er the beautiful, —
And they are not. It laid its pallid hand
Upon the strong man, — and the haughty form
Is fallen, and the flashing eye is dim.
It trod the hall of revelry, where throng'd
The bright and joyous, — and the tearful wail
Of stricken ones, is heard where erst the song
And reckless shout resounded. It pass'd o'er
The battle-plain, where sword, and spear, and shield
Flash'd in the light of mid-day, — and the strength
Of serried hosts is shiver'd, and the grass,
Green from the soil of carnage, waves above
The crush'd and moldering skeleton. It came,
And faded like a wreath of mist at eve;
Yet, ere it melted in the viewless air,
It heralded its millions to their home
In the dim land of dreams.

Remorseless Time!
Fierce spirit of the glass and scythe! what power
Can stay him in his silent course, or melt
His iron heart to pity? On, still on,
He presses, and forever. The proud bird,
The condor of the Andes, that can soar
Through heaven's unfathomable depths, or brave
The fury of the northern Hurricane,
And bathe his plumage in the thunder's home,
Furls his broad wings at nightfall, and sinks down
To rest upon his mountain crag: but Time
Knows not the weight of sleep or weariness,
And night's deep darkness has no chain to bind
His rushing pinions.

Revolutions sweep
O'er Earth, like troubled visions o'er the breast
Of dreaming sorrow; cities rise and sink
Like bubbles on the water; fiery isles
Spring blazing from the Ocean, and go back
To their mysterious caverns; Mountains rear

To heaven their bald and blacken'd cliffs, and bow
Their tall heads to the plain; new Empires rise,
Gathering the strength of hoary centuries,
And rush down like the Alpine avalanche,
Startling the nations; and the very stars,
Yon bright and burning blazonry of God,
Glitter awhile in their eternal depths,
And, like the Pleiad, loveliest of their train,
Shoot from their glorious spheres, and pass away
To darkle in the trackless void; — yet Time,
Time, the tomb-builder, holds his fierce career,
Dark, stern, all-pitiless, and pauses not
Amid the mighty wrecks that strew his path,
To sit and muse, like other conquerors,
Upon the fearful ruin he has wrought.

DEVOTIONAL INCITEMENTS.

William Wordsworth.

Where will they stop, those breathing Powers,
The Spirits of the new-born flowers?
They wander with the breeze, they wind
Where'er the streams a passage find;
Up from their native ground they rise
In mute aërial harmonies:
From humble violet — modest thyme —
Exhaled, th' essential odours climb,
As if no space below the sky
Their subtle flight could satisfy:
Heaven will not tax our thoughts with pride
If like ambition be *their* guide.
  Roused by this kindliest of May-showers,
The spirit-quickener of the flowers,
That with moist virtue softly cleaves
The buds, and freshens the young leaves,
The birds pour forth their souls in notes

Of rapture from a thousand throats, —
Here check'd by too impetuous haste,
While there the music runs to waste,
With bounty more and more enlarged,
Till the whole air is overcharged:
Give ear, O Man! to their appeal,
And thirst for no inferior zeal,
Thou, who canst *think*, as well as feel.
Mount from the Earth; aspire! aspire!
So pleads the town's cathedral quire,
In strains that from their solemn height
Sink, to attain a loftier flight;
While incense from the altar breathes
Rich fragrance in embodied wreaths;
Or, flung from swinging censer, shrouds
The taper-lights, and curls in clouds
Around angelic Forms, the still
Creation of the painter's skill,
That on the service wait conceal'd
One moment, and the next reveal'd. —
Cast off your bonds, awake, arise,
And for no transient ecstasies!
What else can mean the visual plea
Of still or moving imagery, —
The iterated summons loud,
Not wasted on th' attendant crowd,
Nor wholly lost upon the throng
Hurrying the busy streets along?
Yet evermore, through years renew'd
In undisturbed vicissitude
Of seasons balancing their flight
On the swift wings of day and night,
Kind Nature keeps a heavenly door
Wide open for the scatter'd Poor.
Where flower-breathed incense to the skies
Is wafted in mute harmonies;
And ground fresh-cloven by the plough

Is fragrant with a humbler vow;
Where birds and brooks from leafy dells
Chime forth unwearied canticles,
And vapours magnify and spread
The glory of the Sun's bright head, —
Still constant in her worship, still
Conforming to th' eternal Will,
Whether men sow or reap the fields,
Divine monition Nature yields,
That not by bread alone we live,
Or what a hand of flesh can give;
That every day should leave some part
Free for a sabbath of the heart:
So shall the seventh be truly blest,
From morn to eve, with hallow'd rest.

THE INSPIRATION OF THE BIBLE.

EDWARD WINTHROP.

SUCH is the intrinsic excellence of Christianity that it is adapted to the wants of all, and it provides for all, not only by its precepts and by its doctrines, but also by its evidence.

The poor man may know nothing of history, or science, or philosophy; he may have read scarcely any book but the Bible; he may be totally unable to vanquish the skeptic in the arena of public debate; but he is, nevertheless, surrounded by a panoply which the shafts of infidelity can never pierce.

You may go to the home of the poor cottager, whose heart is deeply imbued with the spirit of vital Christianity, you may see him gather his little family around him. He expounds to them the wholesome doctrines and principles of the Bible, and, if they want to know the evidence upon which he rests his faith of the divine origin of his religion, he can tell them upon reading the book which teaches Christianity he finds not only a perfectly true description of his own natural character, but in the provisions of this religion a perfect adaptation to all his needs.

It is a religion by which to live, a religion by which to die; a religion which cheers in darkness, relieves in perplexity, supports in adversity, keeps steadfast in prosperity, and guides the inquirer to that blessed land where "the wicked cease from troubling, and the weary are at rest."

We entreat you, therefore, to give the Bible a welcome, a cordial reception; obey its precepts, trust its promises, and rely implicitly upon that Divine Redeemer whose religion brings glory to God in the highest, and on Earth peace and good-will to men.

Thus will you fulfill the noble end of your existence, and the great God of the Universe will be your father and your friend; and, when the last mighty convulsion shall shake the earth and the sea and the sky, and the fragments of a thousand barks, richly freighted with intellect and learning, are scattered on the shores of error and delusion, your vessel shall in safety outride the storm, and enter in triumph the haven of eternal rest.

BREAK, BREAK, BREAK.

ALFRED TENNYSON.

BREAK, break, break,
  On thy cold gray stones, O Sea!
And I would that my tongue could utter
  The thoughts that arise in me.

O, well for the fisherman's boy,
  That he shouts with his sister at play!
O, well for the sailor-lad,
  That he sings in his boat on the bay!

And the stately ships go on
  To their haven under the hill;
But, O, for the touch of a vanish'd hand,
  And the sound of a voice that is still!

Break, break, break,
  At the foot of thy crags, O Sea!
But the tender grace of a day that is dead
  Will never come back to me.

GOD.

DERZHAVIN.

O THOU eternal One, whose presence bright
  All space doth occupy, all motion guide;
Unchanged through time's all-devastating flight!
  Thou only God, — there is no God beside!
Being above all beings! mighty One,
  Whom none can comprehend and none explore;
Who fill'st existence with Thyself alone,
  Embracing all, supporting, ruling o'er;
  Being whom we call God, and know no more!

In its sublime research philosophy
  May measure out the ocean deep, may count
The sands or the Sun's rays; but, God! for Thee
  There is no weight nor measure; none can mount
Up to Thy mysteries; Reason's brightest spark,
  Though kindled by Thy light, in vain would try
To trace Thy counsels, infinite and dark;
  And thought is lost ere thought can soar so high,
  Even like past moments in eternity.

Thou from primeval nothingness didst call
  First chaos, then existence; Lord, on Thee
Eternity hath its foundation; all
  Sprung forth from Thee, — of light, joy, harmony,
Sole origin, — all life, all beauty Thine;
  Thy word created all, and doth create;
Thy splendour fills all space with rays divine;
  Thou art and wert and shalt be! Glorious! Great!
  Light-giving, life-sustaining Potentate!

Thy chains th' unmeasured universe surround, —
  Upheld by Thee, by Thee inspired with breath!
Thou the beginning with the end hast bound,
  And beautifully mingled life and death!
As sparks mount upward from the fiery blaze,
  So suns are born, so worlds spring forth from Thee;
And, as the spangles in the sunny rays
  Shine round the silver snow, the pageantry
Of heaven's bright army glitters in Thy praise.

A million torches, lighted by Thy hand,
  Wander unwearied through the blue abyss;
They own Thy power, accomplish Thy command,
  All gay with life, all eloquent with bliss.
What shall we call them? Piles of crystal light, —
  A glorious company of golden streams, —
Lamps of celestial ether burning bright, —
  Suns lighting systems with their joyous beams?
But Thou to these art as the noon to night.

Yes, as a drop of water in the sea,
  All this magnificence in Thee is lost:
What are ten thousand worlds compared to Thee?
  And what am I then? Heaven's unnumber'd host,
Though multiplied by myriads, and array'd
  In all the glory of sublimest thought,
Is but an atom in the balance, weigh'd

Against Thy greatness, — is a cipher brought
Against infinity! What am I then? Nought!

Nought! but the effluence of Thy light divine,
Pervading worlds, hath reach'd my bosom too;
Yes, in my spirit doth Thy spirit shine
As shines the sunbeam in a drop of dew.
Nought! but I live, and on hope's pinions fly
Eager toward Thy presence; for in Thee
I live and breathe and dwell; aspiring high,
Even to the throne of Thy divinity.
I am, O God! and surely Thou must be.

Thou art — directing, guiding all — Thou art!
Direct my understanding then to Thee;
Control my spirit, guide my wandering heart;
Though but an atom 'midst immensity,
Still I am something, fashion'd by Thy hand:
I hold a middle rank 'twixt Heaven and Earth,
On the last verge of mortal being stand,
Close to the realms where angels have their birth,
Just on the boundaries of the spirit-land!

The chain of being is complete in me,
In me is matter's last gradation lost,
And the next step is spirit, — Deity!
I can command the lightning, and am dust!
A monarch and a slave, a worm, a god!
Whence came I here, and how? so marvellously
Constructed and conceived? unknown! this clod
Lives surely through some higher energy;
For from itself alone it could not be!

Creator, yes: Thy wisdom and thy word
Created me; Thou source of life and good:
Thou spirit of my spirit, and my Lord,
Thy light, Thy love, in their bright plenitude
Fill'd me with an immortal soul, to spring

Over the abyss of death, and bade it wear
The garments of eternal day, and wing
Its heavenly flight beyond this little sphere,
Even to its source — to Thee — its Author there.

O thoughts ineffable! O visions blest!
Though worthless our conceptions all of Thee,
Yet shall Thy shadow'd image fill our breast,
And waft its homage to Thy Deity.
God! thus alone my lowly thoughts can soar,
Thus seek Thy presence, — Being wise and good!
'Midst Thy vast works admire, obey, adore;
And when the tongue is eloquent no more
The soul shall speak in tears of gratitude.

GOD'S FIRST TEMPLES.

W. C. Bryant.

The groves were God's first temples. Ere man learn'd
To hew the shaft, and lay the architrave,
And spread the roof above them, ere he framed
The lofty vault, to gather and roll back
The sound of anthems, in the darkling wood,
Amidst the cool and silence, he knelt down
And offer'd to the Mightiest solemn thanks
And supplication. For his simple heart
Might not resist the sacred influences
That, from the stilly twilight of the place,
And from the gray old trunks, that, high in heaven,
Mingled their mossy boughs, and from the sound
Of the invisible breath, that sway'd at once
All their green tops, stole over him, and bow'd
His spirit with the thought of boundless Power
And inaccessible Majesty. Ah, why
Should we, in the world's riper years, neglect
God's ancient sanctuaries, and adore

Only among the crowd, and under roofs
That our frail hands have raised? Let me, at least,
Here, in the shadow of the ancient wood,
Offer one hymn ; thrice happy, if it find
Acceptance in His ear.
                                        Father, thy hand
Hath reared these venerable columns : Thou
Didst weave this verdant roof. Thou didst look down
Upon the naked earth, and forthwith rose
All these fair ranks of trees. They in Thy sun
Budded, and shook their green leaves in Thy breeze,
And shot toward heaven. The century-living crow,
Whose birth was in their tops, grew old and died
Among their branches, till at last they stood,
As now they stand, massy and tall and dark,
Fit shrine for humble worshipper to hold
Communion with his Maker.
                                        Here are seen
No traces of man's pomp or pride ; no silks
Rustle, no jewels shine, nor envious eyes
Encounter ; no fantastic carvings show
The boast of our vain race to change the form
Of Thy fair works. But Thou art here ; Thou fill'st
The solitude. Thou art in the soft winds
That run along the summits of these trees
In music ; Thou art in the cooler breath,
That, from the inmost darkness of the place,
Comes, scarcely felt ; the barky trunks, the ground,
The fresh, moist ground, are all instinct with Thee.
   Here is continual worship ; Nature here,
In the tranquillity that Thou dost love,
Enjoys Thy presence. Noiselessly around,
From perch to perch the solitary bird
Passes ; and yon clear spring, that, 'midst its herbs,
Wells softly forth, and visits the strong roots
Of half the mighty forest, tells no tale
Of all the good it does.

Thou hast not left
Thyself without a witness, in these shades,
Of Thy perfections. Grandeur, strength and grace
Are here to speak of Thee. This mighty oak, —
By whose immovable stem I stand, and seem
Almost annihilated, — not a prince,
In all the proud old world beyond the deep,
Ere wore his crown as loftily as he
Wears the green coronal of leaves with which
Thy hand has graced him. Nestled at his root
Is beauty, such as blooms not in the glare
Of the broad Sun. That delicate forest flower,
With scented breath, and looks so like a smile,
Seems, as it issues from the shapeless mould,
An emanation of th' indwelling life,
A visible token of the upholding love,
That are the soul of this wide Universe.

My heart is awed within me when I think
Of the great miracle that still goes on,
In silence, round me, — the perpetual work
Of Thy creation, finish'd, yet renew'd
Forever. Written on Thy works I read
The lesson of Thy own eternity.
Lo! all grow old and die; but see, again,
How, on the faltering footsteps of decay,
Youth presses — ever gay and beautiful youth —
In all its beautiful forms. These lofty trees
Wave not less proudly that their ancestors
Moulder beneath them.

O, there is not lost
One of Earth's charms: upon her bosom yet,
After the flight of untold centuries,
The freshness of her far beginning lies,
And yet shall lie. Life mocks the idle hate
Of his arch enemy Death; yea, seats himself
Upon the sepulchre, and blooms and smiles,
And of the triumphs of his ghastly foe

Makes his own nourishment. For he came forth
From Thine own bosom, and shall have no end.
There have been holy men who hid themselves
Deep in the woody wilderness, and gave
Their lives to thought and prayer, till they outlived
The generation born with them, nor seem'd
Less agèd than the hoary trees and rocks
Around them; and there have been holy men
Who deem'd it were not well to pass life thus.
But let me often to these solitudes
Retire, and, in Thy presence, re-assure
My feeble virtue. Here, its enemies,
The passions, at Thy plainer footsteps, shrink,
And tremble, and are still.
O God, when Thou
Dost scare the world with tempests, set on fire
The heavens with falling thunderbolts, or fill,
With all the waters of the firmament,
The swift, dark whirlwind, that uproots the woods
And drowns the villages; when, at Thy call,
Uprises the great deep, and throws himself
Upon the continent, and overwhelms
Its cities; who forgets not, at the sight
Of these tremendous tokens of Thy power,
His pride, and lays his strifes and follies by!
O, from these sterner aspects of Thy face
Spare me and mine; nor let us need the wrath
Of the mad, unchain'd elements, to teach
Who rules them. Be it ours to meditate,
In these calm shades, Thy milder majesty,
And to the beautiful order of Thy works
Learn to conform the order of our lives.

THE PRIMROSE OF THE ROCK.

WILLIAM WORDSWORTH.

A ROCK there is whose homely front
The passing traveller slights;
Yet there the glow-worms hang their lamps,
Like stars, at various heights;
And one coy Primrose to that Rock
The vernal breeze invites.

What hideous warfare hath been raged,
What kingdoms overthrown,
Since first I spied that Primrose-tuft
And mark'd it for my own;
A lasting link in Nature's chain
From highest Heaven let down!

The flowers, still faithful to the stems,
Their fellowship renew;
The stems are faithful to the root,
That worketh out of view;
And to the rock the root adheres,
In every fibre true.

Close clings to earth the living rock,
Though threatening still to fall;
The Earth is constant in her sphere;
And God upholds them all:
So blooms this lonely Plant, nor dreads
Her annual funeral.

Here closed the meditative strain;
But air breathed soft that day,
The hoary mountain-heights were cheer'd,
The sunny vale look'd gay;
And to the Primrose of the Rock
I gave this after-lay.

I sang, — Let myriads of bright flowers,
  Like thee, in field and grove
Revive unenvied; — mightier far
  Than tremblings, that reprove
Our vernal tendencies to hope,
  Is God's redeeming love; —

That love which changed — for wan disease,
  For sorrow that had bent
O'er hopeless dust, for wither'd age —
  Their moral element,
And turn'd the thistles of a curse
  To types beneficent.

Sin-blighted though we are, we too,
  The reasoning Sons of Men,
From one oblivious winter call'd
  Shall rise, and breathe again;
And in eternal summer lose
  Our threescore years and ten.

To humbleness of heart descends
  This prescience from on high,
The faith that elevates the just,
  Before and when they die;
And makes each soul a separate heaven,
  A court for Deity.

V.

GRAND, BOLD, SUBLIME.

APOSTROPHE TO THE OCEAN.

LORD BYRON.

THERE is a pleasure in the pathless woods,
There is a rapture on the lonely shore,
There is society, where none intrudes,
By the deep sea, and music in its roar:
I love not man the less, but Nature more,
From these our interviews, in which I steal
From all I may be, or have been before,
To mingle with the universe, and feel
What I can ne'er express, yet cannot all conceal.

Roll on, thou deep and dark blue Ocean, roll!
Ten thousand fleets sweep over thee in vain;
Man marks the earth with ruin, — his control
Stops with the shore: upon the watery plain,
The wrecks are all thy deed, nor doth remain
A shadow of man's ravage, save his own,
When for a moment, like a drop of rain,
He sinks into thy depths with bubbling groan,
Without a grave, unknell'd, uncoffin'd, and unknown

The armaments, which thunderstrike the walls
Of rock-built cities, bidding nations quake,
And monarchs tremble in their capitals;
The oak leviathans, whose huge ribs make
Their clay creator the vain title take

Of lord of thee, and arbiter of war;
These are thy toys, and, as the snowy flake,
They melt into thy yeast of waves, which mar
Alike th' Armada's pride or spoils of Trafalgar.

Thy shores are empires, changed in all save thee:
Assyria, Greece, Rome, Carthage, — what are they?
Thy waters wasted them while they were free,
And many a tyrant since; their shores obey
The stranger, slave, or savage; their decay
Has dried up realms to deserts: not so thou;
Unchangeable, save to thy wild waves' play,
Time writes no wrinkles on thine azure brow;
Such as creation's dawn beheld, thou rollest now.

Thou glorious mirror, where th' Almighty's form
Glasses itself in tempests; in all time,
Calm or convulsed, — in breeze, or gale, or storm,
Icing the pole, or in the torrid clime
Dark heaving; — boundless, endless, and sublime, —
The image of Eternity, — the throne
Of the Invisible; even from out thy slime
The monsters of the deep are made; each zone
Obeys thee: thou go'st forth, dread, fathomless, alone.

And I have loved thee, Ocean! and my joy
Of youthful sports was on thy breast to be
Borne, like thy bubbles, onward: from a boy
I wanton'd with thy breakers, — they to me
Were a delight; and, if the freshening sea
Made them a terror, 'twas a pleasing fear;
For I was, as it were, a child of thee,
And trusted to thy billows far and near,
And laid my hand upon thy mane, — as I do here.

HYMN TO THE NIGHT.

H. W. LONGFELLOW.

I HEARD the trailing garments of the Night
Sweep through her marble halls!
I saw her sable skirts all fringed with light
From the celestial walls!

I felt her presence, by its spell of might,
Stoop o'er me from above;
The calm, majestic presence of the Night,
As of the one I love.

I heard the sounds of sorrow and delight,
The manifold, soft chimes,
That fill the haunted chambers of the Night,
Like some old poet's rhymes.

From the cool cisterns of the midnight air
My spirit drank repose;
The fountain of perpetual peace flows there, —
From those deep cisterns flows.

O holy Night! from thee I learn to bear
What man has borne before!
Thou lay'st thy finger on the lips of Care,
And they complain no more.

Peace! Peace! Orestes-like I breathe this prayer!
Descend with broad-winged flight,
The welcome, the thrice-pray'd for, the most fair,
The best-belovèd Night!

A VISION OF MIST-SPLENDOURS.

WILLIAM WORDSWORTH.

A SINGLE step, that freed me from the skirts
Of the blind vapour, open'd to my view

Glory beyond all glory ever seen
By waking sense or by the dreaming soul!
Th' appearance, instantaneously disclosed,
Was of a mighty city, — boldly say
A wilderness of building, sinking far
And self-withdrawn into a boundless depth,
Far sinking into splendour, — without end!
Fabric it seem'd of diamond and of gold,
With alabaster domes, and silver spires,
And blazing terrace upon terrace, high
Uplifted; here, serene pavilions bright,
In avenues disposed; there, towers begirt
With battlements that on their restless fronts
Bore stars, — illumination of all gems!
By earthly nature had th' effect been wrought
Upon the dark materials of the storm
Now pacified; on them, and on the coves
And mountain-steeps and summits, whereunto
The vapours had receded, taking there
Their station under a cerulean sky.
O, 'twas an unimaginable sight!
Clouds, mists, streams, watery rocks and emerald turf,
Clouds of all tincture, rocks and sapphire sky,
Confused, commingled, mutually inflamed,
Molten together, and composing thus,
Each lost in each, that marvellous array
Of temple, palace, citadel, and huge
Fantastic pomp of structure without name,
In fleecy folds voluminous, enwrapp'd.
Right in the midst, where interspace appear'd
Of open court, an object like a throne
Under a shining canopy of state
Stood fix'd; and fix'd resemblances were seen
To implements of ordinary use,
But vast in size, in substance glorified;
Such as by Hebrew Prophets were beheld
In vision, — forms uncouth of mightiest power

For admiration and mysterious awe.
This little Vale, a dwelling-place of Man,
Lay low beneath my feet; 'twas visible, —
I saw not, but I felt that it was there.
That which I *saw* was the reveal'd abode
Of Spirits in beatitude.

HYMN TO MONT BLANC.

S. T. Coleridge.

Hast thou a charm to stay the morning-star
In his steep course? — so long he seems to pause
On thy bald awful head, O sovereign Blanc!
The Arvè and Arveiron at thy base
Rave ceaselessly; but thou, most awful Form,
Risest from forth thy silent sea of pines,
How silently! Around thee and above
Deep is the air and dark, substantial, black,
An ebon mass: methinks thou piercest it,
As with a wedge! But, when I look again,
It is thine own calm home, thy crystal shrine,
Thy habitation from eternity.
O dread and silent Mount! I gazed upon thee,
Till thou, still present to the bodily sense,
Didst vanish from my thought: entranced in prayer,
I worshipp'd the Invisible alone.

Yet, like some sweet beguiling melody,
So sweet, we know not we are listening to it,
Thou, the meanwhile, wast blending with my thought,
Yea, with my life and life's own secret joy;
Till the dilating Soul — enrapt, transfused,
Into the mighty Vision passing — there,
As in her natural form, swell'd vast to Heaven!

Awake, my soul! not only passive praise
Thou owest; not alone these swelling tears,

Mute thanks, and secret ecstasy. Awake,
Voice of sweet song! Awake, my heart, awake!
Green vales and icy cliffs, all join my Hymn!

Thou first and chief, sole sovereign of the Vale!
O, struggling with the darkness all the night,
And visited all night by troops of stars,
Or when they climb the sky or when they sink;
Companion of the morning-star at dawn,
Thyself Earth's rosy star, and of the dawn
Co-herald; wake, O, wake, and utter praise!
Who sank thy sunless pillars deep in earth?
Who fill'd thy countenance with rosy light?
Who made thee parent of perpetual streams?

And you, ye five wild torrents fiercely glad!
Who call'd you forth from night and utter death,
From dark and icy caverns call'd you forth,
Down those precipitous, black, jagged rocks,
For ever shatter'd and the same for ever?
Who gave you your invulnerable life,
Your strength, your speed, your fury, and your joy,
Unceasing thunder and eternal foam?
And who commanded, (and the silence came,)
Here let the billows stiffen, and have rest?

Ye ice-falls! ye that from the mountain's brow
Adown enormous ravines slope amain,—
Torrents, methinks, that heard a mighty Voice,
And stopp'd at once amid their maddest plunge!
Motionless torrents! silent cataracts!
Who made you glorious as the gates of Heaven
Beneath the keen full Moon? Who bade the Sun
Clothe you with rainbows? Who, with living flowers
Of loveliest blue, spread garlands at your feet?—
God! let the torrents, like a shout of nations,
Answer! and let the ice-plains echo, God!
God! sing ye meadow-streams with gladsome voice!

Ye pine-groves, with your soft and soul-like sounds!
And they too have a voice, yon piles of snow,
And in their perilous fall shall thunder, God!

Ye living flowers that skirt th' eternal frost;
Ye wild goats sporting round the eagle's nest;
Ye eagles, play-mates of the mountain-storm;
Ye lightnings, the dread arrows of the clouds;
Ye signs and wonders of the element, —
Utter forth God, and fill the hills with praise!

Thou too, hoar Mount, with thy sky-pointing peaks,
Oft from whose feet the avalanche, unheard,
Shoots downward, glittering through the pure serene
Into the depth of clouds, that veil thy breast, —
Thou too again, stupendous Mountain! thou
That, as I raise my head, awhile bow'd low
In adoration, upward from thy base
Slow travelling with dim eyes suffused with tears,
Solemnly seemest, like a vapoury cloud,
To rise before me, — rise, O, ever rise,
Rise like a cloud of incense, from the Earth!
Thou kingly Spirit throned among the hills,
Thou dread ambassador from Earth to Heaven,
Great hierarch! tell thou the silent Sky,
And tell the stars, and tell yon rising Sun,
Earth, with her thousand voices, praises God.

MARCO BOZZARIS.

Fitz Greene Halleck.

At midnight, in his guarded tent,
  The Turk was dreaming of the hour
When Greece, her knee in suppliance bent,
  Should tremble at his power;
In dreams, through camp and court he bore
The trophies of a conqueror;

In dreams, his song of triumph heard;
Then wore his monarch's signet ring;
Then press'd that monarch's throne — a king:
As wild his thoughts, and gay of wing,
As Eden's garden bird.

At midnight, in the forest shades,
Bozzaris ranged his Suliote band,
True as the steel of their tried blades,
Heroes in heart and hand.
There had the Persian's thousands stood,
There had the glad earth drunk their blood,
On old Platæa's day;
And now there breathed that haunted air
The sons of sires who conquer'd there,
With arm to strike, and soul to dare,
As quick, as far, as they.

An hour pass'd on: the Turk awoke:
That bright dream was his last.
He woke to hear his sentries shriek,
"To arms! they come! the Greek! the Greek!"
He woke, to die 'midst flame and smoke,
And shout, and groan, and sabre-stroke,
And death-shots falling thick and fast
As lightnings from the mountain cloud,
And heard, with voice as trumpet loud,
Bozzaris cheer his band:
"Strike! — till the last arm'd foe expires;
Strike! — for your altars and your fires;
Strike! — for the green graves of your sires;
God, and your native land!"

They fought like brave men, long and well;
They piled that ground with Moslem slain;
They conquer'd; — but Bozzaris fell,
Bleeding at every vein.

His few surviving comrades saw
His smile when rang their loud hurrah,
  And the red field was won ;
Then saw in death his eyelids close,
Calmly as to a night's repose, —
  Like flowers at set of Sun.

Come to the bridal chamber, Death!
  Come to the mother's, when she feels,
For the first time, her first-born's breath;
  Come when the blessèd seals
That close the pestilence are broke,
And crowded cities wail its stroke;
Come in consumption's ghastly form,
The earthquake shock, the ocean storm;
Come when the heart beats high and warm
  With banquet song and dance and wine;
And thou art terrible: — the tear,
The groan, the knell, the pall, the bier,
And all we know, or dream, or fear,
  Of agony, are thine.

But to the hero, when his sword
  Has won the battle for the free,
Thy voice sounds like a prophet's word,
And in its hollow tones are heard
  The thanks of millions yet to be.
Come when his task of fame is wrought ;
Come, with her laurel-leaf, blood-bought;
  Come in her crowning hour, — and then
Thy sunken eye's unearthly light,
To him is welcome as the sight
  Of sky and stars to prison'd men;
Thy grasp is welcome as the hand
Of brother in a foreign land;
Thy summons welcome as the cry
That told the Indian isles were nigh

To the world-seeking Genoese,
When the land-wind, from woods of palm,
And orange-groves, and fields of balm,
Blew o'er the Haytien seas.

Bozzaris! with the storied brave
Greece nurtured in her glory's time,
Rest thee: there is no prouder grave,
Even in her own proud clime.
She wore no funeral weeds for thee,
Nor bade the dark hearse wave its plume,
Like torn branch from death's leafless tree,
In sorrow's pomp and pageantry,
The heartless luxury of the tomb;
But she remembers thee as one
Long loved, and for a season gone;
For thee her poet's lyre is wreathed,
Her marble wrought, her music breathed;
For thee she rings the birthday bells;
Of thee her babes' first lisping tells;
For thine her evening prayer is said,
At palace couch and cottage bed:
Her soldier, closing with the foe,
Gives for thy sake a deadlier blow;
His plighted maiden, when she fears
For him, the joy of her young years,
Thinks of thy fate, and checks her tears:
And she, the mother of thy boys,
Though in her eye and faded cheek
Is read the grief she will not speak,
The memory of her buried joys, —
And even she who gave thee birth
Will, by their pilgrim-circled hearth,
Talk of thy doom without a sigh;
For thou art Freedom's now, and Fame's,
One of the few, th' immortal names
That were not born to die.

THE LAUNCHING OF THE SHIP.

H. W. Longfellow.

"Build me straight, O worthy Master!
 Staunch and strong, a goodly vessel,
That shall laugh at all disaster,
 And with wave and whirlwind wrestle!"

The merchant's word,
Delighted, the Master heard;
For his heart was in his work, and the heart
Giveth grace unto every art:
And, with a voice that was full of glee,
He answer'd, "Ere long we will launch
A vessel as goodly and strong and staunch
As ever weather'd a wintry sea!"

All is finish'd! and at length
Has come the bridal day
Of beauty and of strength:
To-day the vessel shall be launch'd!
With fleecy clouds the sky is blanch'd;
And o'er the bay,
Slowly, in all his splendours dight,
The great Sun rises to behold the sight.

The ocean old,
Centuries old,
Strong as youth, as uncontroll'd,
Paces restless to and fro,
Up and down the sands of gold.
His beating heart is not at rest;
And far and wide,
With ceaseless flow,
His beard of snow
Heaves with the heaving of his breast:
He waits impatient for his bride.

There she stands,
With her foot upon the sands,
Deck'd with flags and streamers gay,
In honour of her marriage-day,
Her snow-white signals fluttering, blending,
Round her like a veil descending,
Ready to be
The bride of the gray old sea.

Then the Master,
With a gesture of command,
Waved his hand;
And at the word
Loud and sudden there was heard,
All around them and below,
The sound of hammers, blow on blow,
Knocking away the shores and spurs:
And see! she stirs!
She starts, — she moves, — she seems to feel
The thrill of life along her keel,
And, spurning with her feet the ground,
With one exulting, joyous bound,
She leaps into the ocean's arms!

And, lo! from the assembled crowd
There rose a shout, prolong'd and loud,
That to the ocean seem'd to say,
"Take her, O bridegroom, old and gray;
Take her to thy protecting arms,
With all her youth and all her charms!"

How beautiful she is! how fair
She lies within those arms that press
Her form with many a soft caress
Of tenderness and watchful care!
Sail forth into the sea, O ship!
Through wind and wave, right onward steer!

The moisten'd eye, the trembling lip,
Are not the signs of doubt or fear.

Thou, too, sail on, O Ship of State!
Sail on, O UNION, strong and great!
Humanity, with all its fears,
With all the hopes of future years,
Is hanging breathless on thy fate!
We know what Master laid thy keel,
What Workmen wrought thy ribs of steel,
Who made each mast and sail and rope,
What anvils rang, what hammers beat,
In what a forge, and what a heat,
Were shaped the anchors of thy hope!

Fear not each sudden sound and shock;
'Tis of the wave, and not the rock;
'Tis but the flapping of the sail,
And not a rent made by the gale!
In spite of rock and tempest's roar,
In spite of false lights on the shore,
Sail on, nor fear to breast the sea!
Our hearts, our hopes, are all with thee;
Our hearts, our hopes, our prayers, our tears,
Our faith triumphant o'er our fears,
Are all with thee, — are all with thee!

ODE TO APOLLO.

JOHN KEATS.

IN thy western halls of gold
When thou sittest in thy state,
Bards, that erst sublimely told
Heroic deeds, and sang of fate,
With fervour seize their adamantine lyres,
Whose chords are solid rays, and twinkle radiant fires.

Here Homer with his nervous arms
Strikes the twanging harp of war;
And even the western splendour warms,
While the trumpets sound afar:
But, what creates the most intense surprise,
His soul looks out through renovated eyes.

Then, through thy temple wide, melodious swells
The sweet majestic tones of Maro's lyre:
The soul delighted on each accent dwells, —
Enraptured dwells, — not daring to respire,
The while he tells of grief around a funeral pyre.

'Tis awful silence then again;
Expectant stand the spheres;
Breathless the laurell'd peers,
Nor move, till ends the lofty strain, —
Nor move, till Milton's tuneful thunders cease,
And leave once more the ravish'd heavens in peace.

Thou biddest Shakespeare wave his hand,
And quickly forward spring
The Passions, — a terrific band, —
And each vibrates the string
That with its tyrant temper best accords,
While from their Master's lips pour forth th' inspiring words.

A silver trumpet Spenser blows,
And, as its martial notes to silence flee,
From a virgin chorus flows
A hymn in praise of spotless Chastity.
'Tis still! Wild warblings from th' Æolian lyre
Enchantment softly breathe, and tremblingly expire.

Next Tasso's ardent numbers
Float along the pleasèd air,
Calling youth from idle slumbers,
Rousing them from Pleasure's lair:

Then o'er the strings his fingers gently move,
And melt the heart to pity and to love.

But, when *Thou* joinest with the Nine,
And all the powers of song combine,
We listen here on Earth:
The dying tones that fill the air,
And charm the ear of evening fair,
From thee, great God of Bards, receive their heavenly birth

ST. PETER'S CHURCH AT ROME.

LORD BYRON.

BUT lo! the dome, — the vast and wondrous dome,
To which Diana's marvel was a cell, —
Christ's mighty shrine above His martyr's tomb!
I have beheld th' Ephesian miracle, —
Its columns strew the wilderness, and dwell
Th' hyæna and the jackal in their shade:
I have beheld Sophia's bright roofs swell
Their glittering mass i' the sun, and have survey'd
Its sanctuary the while th' usurping Moslem pray'd:

But thou, of temples old, or altars new,
Standest alone, — with nothing like to thee, —
Worthiest of God, the holy and the true.
Since Zion's desolation, when that He
Forsook His former city, what could be,
Of earthly structures in His honour piled,
Of a sublimer aspect? Majesty,
Power, Glory, Strength, and Beauty, all are aisled
In this eternal ark of worship undefiled.

Enter: its grandeur overwhelms thee not;
And why? it is not lessen'd; but thy mind,
Expanded by the genius of the spot,
Has grown colossal, and can only find

A fit abode wherein appear enshrined
Thy hopes of immortality; and thou
Shalt one day, if found worthy, so defined,
See thy God face to face, as thou dost now
His Holy of Holies, nor be blasted by His brow.

Thou movest, but increasing with th' advance,
Like climbing some great Alp, which still doth rise,
Deceived by its gigantic elegance;
Vastness which grows, but grows to harmonize,
All musical in its immensities;
Rich marbles, richer paintings, shrines where flame
The lamps of gold, the haughty dome which vies
In air with Earth's chief structures, though their frame
Sits on the firm-set ground, and this the cloud must claim.

Thou seest not all; but piecemeal thou must break,
To separate contemplation, the great whole;
And as the ocean many bays will make,
That ask the eye, so here condense thy soul
To more immediate objects, and control
Thy thoughts, until thy mind hath got by heart
Its eloquent proportions, and unroll
In mighty graduations, part by part,
The glory which at once upon thee did not dart, —

Not by its fault, but thine. Our outward sense
Is but of gradual grasp; and as it is
That what we have of feeling most intense
Outstrips our faint expression; even so this
Outshining and o'erwhelming edifice
Fools our fond gaze, and, greatest of the great,
Defies at first our nature's littleness,
Till, growing with its growth, we thus dilate
Our spirits to the size of that they contemplate.

GOD IN NATURE.

WILLIAM WORDSWORTH.

AND what are things eternal? — Powers depart,
Possessions vanish, and opinions change,
And passions hold a fluctuating seat:
But, by the storms of circumstance unshaken,
And subject neither to eclipse nor wane,
Duty exists; — immutably survive,
For our support, the measures and the forms
Which an abstract intelligence supplies;
Whose kingdom is where time and space are not.
Of other converse which mind, soul, and heart
Do, with united urgency, require,
What more that may not perish? — Thou, dread source,
Prime, self-existing cause and end of all
That in the scale of being fill their place,
Above our human region, or below,
Set and sustain'd; Thou, who didst wrap the cloud
Of infancy around us, that Thyself,
Therein, with our simplicity awhile
Mightst hold, on Earth, communion undisturb'd;
Who from the anarchy of dreaming sleep,
Or from its death-like void, with punctual care,
And touch as gentle as the morning light,
Restorest us, daily, to the powers of sense
And reason's steadfast rule, — Thou, Thou alone
Art everlasting, and the blessèd Spirits
Which Thou includest, as the sea her waves:
For adoration Thou endurest; endure
For consciousness the motions of Thy will;
For apprehension those transcendent truths
Of the pure intellect, that stand as laws
(Submission constituting strength and power)
Even to Thy Being's infinite majesty!
This Universe shall pass away, — a work

Glorious, because the shadow of Thy might,
A step, or link, for intercourse with Thee.
Ah! if the time must come in which my feet
No more shall stray where meditation leads,
By flowing stream, through wood, or craggy wild,
Loved haunts like these; the unimprison'd Mind
May yet have scope to range among her own,
Her thoughts, her images, her high desires.
If the dear faculty of sight should fail,
Still it may be allow'd me to remember
What visionary powers of eye and soul
In youth were mine; when, station'd on the top
Of some huge hill, expectant, I beheld
The Sun rise up, from distant climes return'd
Darkness to chase, and sleep; and bring the day,
His bounteous gift! or saw him toward the deep
Sink, with a retinue of flaming clouds
Attended: then my spirit was entranced
With joy exalted to beatitude;
The measure of my soul was fill'd with bliss,
And holiest love; as earth, sea, air, with light,
With pomp, with glory, with magnificence!

VI.

PATRIOTIC, SENATORIAL, ORATORICAL.

THE SEVEN GREAT ORATORS OF THE WORLD.*

FORTUNE OF ÆSCHINES.

DEMOSTHENES.

FOR my part, I regard any one, who reproaches his fellow-man with fortune, as devoid of sense. He that is best satisfied with his condition, he that deems his fortune excellent, cannot be sure that it will remain so until the evening: how then can it be right to bring it forward, or upbraid another man with it? As Æschines, however, has on this subject (besides many others) expressed himself with insolence, look, men of

*We here give a representative selection from each of these orators. The following extract from the Rev. Henry N. Hudson's Discourse delivered in Boston on the hundredth anniversary of the birth of Daniel Webster will explain why we do so: "Sage and venerable Harvard, on mature consideration no doubt, has spoken Webster for one of the seven great orators of the world. At the theatre end of her Memorial Hall, which has the form of a semicircular polygon, in as many gablets or niches rising above the cornice, the seven heads, of gigantic size, stand forth to public view. First, of course, is Demosthenes the Greek; second, also of course, Cicero the Roman; third, Saint John Chrysostom, an Asiatic Greek, born about the middle of the fourth century; fourth, Jaques Benigne Bossuet, the great French divine and author, contemporary with Louis the Fourteenth; fifth, William Pitt the elder, Earl of Chatham, an Englishman; sixth, Edmund Burke, an Irishman, probably the greatest genius of them all, though not the greatest orator; seventh, Daniel Webster. How authentic the likenesses may be, I cannot say, except in the case of Webster: here the likeness is true; and, to my sense, Webster's head is the finest of the seven, unless that of Bossuet may be set down as its peer."

Athens, and observe how much more truth and humanity there shall be in my discourse upon fortune than in his.

If you are determined, Æschines, to scrutinize my fortune, compare it with your own; and, if you find mine better than yours, cease to revile it. Look, then, from the very beginning. And I pray and entreat that I may not be condemned for bad taste. I don't think any person wise who insults poverty, or who prides himself on having been bred in affluence: but by the slander and malice of this cruel man I am forced into such a discussion; which I will conduct with all the moderation that circumstances allow.

I had the advantage, Æschines, in my boyhood of going to proper schools, and having such allowance as a boy should have who is to do nothing mean from indigence. Arrived at man's estate, I lived suitably to my breeding; was choir-master, ship-commander, ratepayer; backward in no acts of liberality, public or private, but making myself useful to the commonwealth and to my friends. When I entered upon State affairs, I chose such a line of politics, that both by my country and many people of Greece I have been crowned many times, and not even you my enemies venture to say that the line I chose was not honourable. Such, then, has been the fortune of my life: I could enlarge upon it, but I forbear, lest what I pride myself in should give offence.

But you, the man of dignity, who spit upon others, look what sort of fortune is yours compared with mine. As a boy you were reared in abject poverty, waiting with your father on the school, grinding the ink, sponging the benches, sweeping the room, doing the duty of a menial rather than a freeman's son. After you were grown up, you attended your mother's initiations, reading her books and helping in all the ceremonies: at night wrapping the noviciates in fawn-skin, swilling, purifying, and scouring them with clay and bran, raising them after the lustration, and bidding them say, "Bad I have scaped, and better I have found"; priding yourself that no one ever howled so lustily, — and I believe him! for don't suppose that he who speaks so loud is not a splendid howler! In the daytime you led your noble orgiasts, crowned with fennel and poplar, through the highways, squeezing the big-cheeked serpents, and lifting them over your head, and shouting and capering, saluted by the beldames as Leader, Conductor, Chest-bearer, Fan-bearer, and the like; getting as your reward tarts and biscuits and rolls; for which any man might well bless himself and his fortune!

When you were enrolled among your fellow-townsmen, — by what means I stop not to inquire, — you immediately selected the most honourable of employments, that of clerk and assistant to our petty magistrates. From this you were removed after a while, having done yourself all that you charge others with; and then, sure enough, you disgraced not your antecedents by your subsequent life, but, hiring yourself to those ranting players, as they were called, Simylus and Socrates, you acted third parts, collecting figs and grapes and olives like a fruiterer, and getting more from them than from the playing, in which the lives of your whole company were at stake: for there was an implacable and incessant war between them and the audience, from whom you received so many wounds, that no wonder you taunt as cowards people inexperienced in such encounters.

But, passing over what may be imputed to poverty,

I will come to the direct charges against your character. You espoused such a line of politics, (when at last you thought of taking to them,) that, if your country prospered, you lived the life of a hare, fearing and trembling, and ever expecting to be scourged for the crimes of which your conscience accused you; though all have seen how bold you were during the misfortunes of the rest. A man who took courage at the death of a thousand citizens, — what does he deserve at the hands of the living? A great deal more that I could say about him I shall omit: for it is not all I can tell of his turpitude and infamy which I ought to let slip from my tongue, but only what is not disgraceful to myself to mention.

Contrast now the circumstances of your life and mine, gently and with temper, Æschines, and then ask these people whose fortune they would each of them prefer. You taught reading, I went to school; you performed initiations, I received them; you danced in the chorus, I furnished it; you were assembly-clerk, I was a speaker; you acted third parts, I heard you; you broke down, and I hissed; you have worked as a statesman for the enemy, I for my country. I pass by the rest; but this very day I am on my probation for a crown, and am acknowledged to be innocent of all offence; whilst you are already judged to be a pettifogger, and the question is, whether you shall continue that trade or at once be silenced by not getting a fifth part of the votes. A happy fortune, do you see, you have enjoyed, that you should denounce mine as miserable!

Panegyric on Julius Cæsar.

Marcus Tullius Cicero.

This day, Conscript Fathers, has brought with it an end to the long silence in which I have of late indulged; not out of any fear, but partly from sorrow, partly from modesty; and at the same time it has revived in me my ancient habit of saying what my wishes and opinions are. For I cannot by any means pass over in silence such great humanity, such unprecedented and unheard-of clemency, such moderation in the exercise of supreme and universal power, such incredible and almost godlike wisdom. For, now that Marcus Marcellus, Conscript Fathers, has been restored to you and the Republic, I think that not only his voice and authority are preserved and restored to you and to the Republic, but my own also.

For I was concerned, Conscript Fathers, and most exceedingly grieved, when I saw such a man as he is, who had espoused the same cause which I had, not enjoying the same good fortune as myself; nor could I persuade myself to think it right or fair that I should be going on in my usual routine, while that rival and imitator of my zeal and labours, who had been a companion and comrade of mine throughout, was separated from me. You, therefore, Caius Cæsar, have reopened to me my former habits of life, which were closed up, and have raised, as it were, a standard to all these men, as a sort of token to lead them to entertain hopes of the general welfare of the Republic. For it was seen by me before in many instances, and especially in my own, and now it is clearly understood by everybody, since you have granted Marcus Marcellus to the Senate and people of Rome, in spite of your recollection of all the injuries you have received at his hands, that you prefer the authority of this order and the dignity of the Republic to the indulgence of your own resentment or suspicions.

No one is blest with such a stream of genius, no one is endowed with such vigour and richness of eloquence, either as a speaker or a writer, as to be able, I will not say to extol, but even plainly to relate, O Cæsar, all your achievements. Nevertheless I assert, and with your leave I maintain, that in all of them you never gained greater and truer glory than you have acquired this day. I am accustomed often to keep this idea before my eyes, and to affirm it in conversation, that all the exploits of our own generals, all those of foreign nations and of the most powerful States, all the mighty deeds of the most illustrious monarchs, can be compared with yours neither in the magnitude of your wars, nor in the variety of countries which you have conquered, nor in the rapidity of your conquests, nor in the great difference of character with which your wars have been marked; and that those countries the most remote from each other could not be travelled over more rapidly by any one in a journey than they have been visited by your, I will not say journeys, but victories.

And if I were not to admit that those actions are so great that scarcely any man's mind or comprehension is capable of doing justice to them, I should be very senseless. But there are other actions greater than those. For some people are in the habit of disparaging military glory, and of denying the whole of it to the generals, and of giving the multitude a share of it also, so that it may not be the peculiar property of the commanders. And no doubt, in the affairs of war, the valour of the troops, the advantages of situation, the assistance of allies, fleets, and supplies, have great influence; and a most important share in all such transactions Fortune claims for herself, as of her right; and whatever has been done successfully she considers almost entirely as her own work.

But in this glory, Caius Cæsar, which you have just earned you have no partners. The whole of this, however great it may be, — and surely it is as great as possible, — the whole of it, I say, is your own. The centurion can claim for himself no share of that praise, neither can the prefect, nor the battallion, nor the squadron. Nay, even that very mistress of all human affairs, Fortune herself, cannot thrust herself into any participation in that glory: she yields to you; she confesses that it is all your own, your peculiar private desert. For rashness is never united with wisdom, nor is chance ever admitted to regulate affairs conducted with prudence.

You have subdued nations savage in their barbarism, countless in their numbers, boundless, if we regard the extent of country peopled by them, and rich in every kind of resource; but still you were only conquering things the nature and condition of which were such that they could be overcome by force. For there is no strength so great that it cannot be weakened and broken by arms and violence. But, to subdue one's inclinations, to master one's angry feelings, to be moderate in the hour of victory, not merely to raise from the ground a prostrate adversary, eminent for noble birth, for genius and for virtue, but even to increase his previous dignity, — these are actions of such a nature that I do not compare the author of them to the most illustrious man, but consider him equal to a god.

Therefore, O Cæsar, those military glories of yours will be celebrated not only in our own literature and language, but in those of almost all nations; nor will any age ever be silent about your praises. But still, deeds of that sort, somehow or other, even when they are read, appear to be overwhelmed with the cries of the soldiers and the sound of the trumpets. But, when we hear or read of anything that has been done with clemency, with humanity, with justice, with moderation, and with wisdom, especially in a time of anger, which is very adverse to prudence, and in the hour of victory, which is naturally insolent and haughty; with what ardour are we then inflamed, (even if the actions have not really been performed, but are only fabulous,) so as often to love those whom we have never seen! But as for you, whom we behold present among us, whose mind and heart and countenance we at this moment see to be such, that you wish to preserve everything which the fortune of war has left to the Republic, O, with what praises must we extol you! with what zeal must we follow you! with what affection must we devote ourselves to you! The very walls, I declare, the very walls of this Senate-house seem to me eager to return you thanks; because, in a short time, you will have restored their ancient authority to this venerable abode of themselves and of their ancestors.

Divine Providence in Nature.

Saint John Chrysostom.

Dost thou not perceive how this body wastes away, withers, and perishes on the flight of the soul, and each of the elements thereof returns to its own proper abode? This very same thing, indeed, would also happen to the world, if the Power which always governs it had left it devoid of its own providence. For, if a ship does not hold on its way without a pilot, but soon founders, how could the world have subsisted so long a time with no one to govern its course? And, that I may not enlarge, suppose the world to be a ship; the earth to be placed below as the keel; the sky to be the sail; men to be the passengers; the subjacent abyss, the sea. How is it, then, that, during so long a time, no shipwreck has taken place? Now, let a ship go one day without a pilot and seamen, and thou wilt see it straightway overwhelmed! But the world, though subsisting now five thousand years, and many more, hath suffered nothing of the kind.

But why do I talk of a ship? Suppose one hath pitched a small hut in the vineyards; and, when the fruit is gathered, leaves it vacant: it stands, however, scarce two or three days, but goes to pieces, and quickly falls down destroyed! Could not a hut, forsooth, stand without superintendence? How, then, could the workmanship of the world, so fair and marvellous? the laws of the night and day? the interchanging dances of the seasons? the course of Nature chequered and varied as it is in every way throughout the earth, the sea, the sky? in plants, and in animals that fly, swim, walk, creep? and in the race of men, far more dignified than any of these; — how could all continue, yet unbroken, during so long a period, without some kind of providence?

But, in addition to what has been said, follow me whilst I enumerate the meadows, the gardens, the flowery tribes; all sorts of herbs, and their uses; their odours, forms, disposition, yea, but their very names; the trees which are fruitful, and the barren; the nature of metals, — that of animals, — in the sea, or on the land; of those that swim, and those that traverse the air; the mountains, the forests, the groves; the meadow below, and the meadow above, — for there is a meadow on the earth, and a meadow too in the sky; the various flowers of the stars; the rose below, and the rainbow above! Would you have me point out also the meadow of the birds? Consider the variegated body of the peacock, surpassing every dye, and the fowls of purple plumage.

Contemplate with me the beauty of the sky: how it has been preserved so long without being dimmed; and remains as bright and clear as if it had been fabricated to-day; moreover, the power of the Earth, how it has not become effete by bringing forth during so long a time! Contemplate with me the fountains: how they burst forth and fail not, since the time they were begotten, to flow forth continually throughout the day and night! Contemplate with me the sea, receiving so many rivers, yet never exceeding its measure! But how long might we continue to pursue things incomprehensible! It is fit, indeed, that, over every one of these which have been spoken of, we should say, "O Lord, how hast Thou magnified Thy works! in wisdom hast Thou made them all."

But what is the sapient answer of the unbelievers, when we go over all these particulars with them, — the magnitude, the beauty of creation, the richness, the munificence everywhere displayed? This very thing, say they, is the worst fault, that God hath made the world so beautiful and so vast. For, if he had not made it beautiful and vast, we should not have made a god of it; but now, being struck with its grandeur, and marvelling at its beauty, we have thought it to be a deity. But such an argument is good for nothing. For, that neither the magnitude nor beauty of the world is the cause of this impiety, but their own absurdity, is what we are prepared to show, proved by the case of ourselves, who have never been so affected.

Why, then, have *we* not made a deity of it? Do we not see it with the same eyes as themselves? Do we not enjoy the same advantage from the creation with themselves? Do we not possess the same soul? Have we not the same body? Do we not tread the same earth? How comes it that this beauty and magnitude have not persuaded us to think the same as they do? But this will be evident not from this proof only, but from another besides. For, as a proof that it is not for its beauty they have made a deity of it, but by reason of their own folly, why do they adore the ape, the crocodile, the dog, and the vilest of animals? Truly, "they became vain in their imaginations, and their foolish heart was darkened. Professing themselves to be wise, they became fools."

Eulogium upon St. Paul.

Jaques Benigne Bossuet.

Christians, do not expect that the apostle will flatter your ears by harmonious cadences, or charm them by gratifiying your vain curiosity; listen to what he says of himself. We preach hidden wisdom, — we preach a crucified God. Do not let us seek to add vain ornaments to that God who rejects the things of this world. If our lowliness is displeasing to the great, let them know that we covet their disdain, for Jesus Christ despises their ostentatious indolence, and desires only to be known to the humble. The discourses of St. Paul, far from flowing with that agreeable sweetness, that calm equality which we admire in other orators, appear unequal and unfinished to those who do not study them deeply; and the delicate ones of this Earth whose ears, as they say, are so refined, are often offended by his irregular style.

But do not let us blush for this. The words of the apostle are simple, but his thoughts are divine. If he is ignorant of rhetoric and despises philosophy, Jesus Christ takes the place of all, and His name, which is ever in his mouth, and His mysteries, which he describes in such a tone of inspiration, render his simplicity all-powerful.

This man, unacquainted with fine language, whose elocution was rude, and who spoke like a stranger, goes into polished Greece, the mother of philosophy and oratory; and notwithstanding the opposition of the people he there established more churches than Plato had acquired disciples, by an eloquence which was thought divine. He pushed his conquests still further: he brought the majesty of the Roman fasces to the feet of Jesus, in the person of a proconsul, and caused the judges, before whom he was cited, to tremble on their judgment-seats. Rome even listened to his voice; and the day will yet arrive when this ancient mistress of the world will deem herself more honoured by an epistle of Paul, addressed to her citizens, than all the far-famed harrangues delivered in the forum by Cicero.

And from whence, Christians, is this? It is that St. Paul had resources of persuasion that Greece could not teach, and Rome had not yet acquired, — an inspired power which delights in extolling what the great despise, and which is spread over and mingled with the august simplicity of his words.

It is this which causes us to admire, in his epistles, a sentiment of superhuman virtue which prevails above ordinary rules, or rather does not persuade so much as it captivates the understanding, — which does not flatter the ear, but goes direct to the heart; just as we see a great river retain, when flowing through the plain, that violent and impetuous force which it had acquired in the mountains from whence it derived its source. Thus the holy virtue which is contained in the writings of St. Paul, even in the simplicity of his style, preserves all the vigour it brings from the Heavens whence it has descended.

Against the Stamp Act.

William Pitt, Earl of Chatham.

Gentlemen, Sir, have been charged with giving birth to sedition in America. Several have spoken their sentiments with freedom against this unhappy Act, and that freedom has become their crime. Sorry I am to hear the liberty of speech in this House imputed as a crime. But this imputation shall not discourage me. It is a liberty I mean to exercise. No gentleman ought to be afraid to exercise it. It is a liberty by which the gentleman who calumniates it might have profited. He ought to have profited. He ought to have desisted from his project.

The gentleman tells us America is obstinate; America is almost in open rebellion. I rejoice that America has resisted. Three millions of people so dead to all the feelings of liberty, as voluntarily to let themselves be made slaves, would have been fit instruments to make slaves of all the rest. I come not here armed at all points with law cases and Acts of Parliament, with the statute-book doubled down in dogs' ears, to defend the cause of liberty. I would not debate a point of law with the gentleman: I know his abilities. I have been obliged to his diligent researches. But, for the defence of liberty, upon a general principle, upon a constitutional principle, it is a ground on which I stand firm; on which I dare meet any man.

Since the accession of King William, many Ministers, some of great, others of moderate abilities, have taken the lead of Government. None of these thought or even dreamed of robbing the colonies of their constitutional rights. That was reserved to mark the era of the late administration: not that there were wanting some, when I had the honour to serve his Majesty, to propose to me to burn my fingers with an American Stamp Act. With the enemy at their back, with our bayonets at their breasts, in the depth of their distress perhaps the Americans would have submitted to the imposition; but it would have been taking an ungenerous and unjust advantage.

The gentleman boasts of his bounties to America! Are not those bounties intended finally for the benefit of this kingdom? If they are not, he has misapplied the national treasures. I am no courtier for America, — I stand up for this kingdom. I maintain that the Parliament has a right to bind, to restrain America. Our legislative power over the colonies is sovereign and supreme. When two countries are connected, like England and her colonies, without being incorporated, the one must necessarily govern; the greater must rule the less; but so rule it as not to contradict the fundamental principles that are common to both.

The gentleman asks, "When were the colonies emancipated?" I desire to know when they were made slaves. But I will not dwell upon words. When I had the honour of serving his Majesty, I availed myself of the means of information which I derived from my office: I speak, therefore, from knowledge. My materials were good; I was at pains to collect, to digest, to consider them; and I will be bold to affirm that the profits of Great Britain from the trade of the colonies, through all its branches, are two millions a-year. This is the fund that carried you triumphantly through the last war. The estates that were rented at two thousand pounds a-year, threescore years ago, are at three thousand pounds at present. These estates sold then for from fifteen to eighteen years' purchase; the same may now be sold for thirty.

You owe this to America. This is the price America pays for her protection. And shall a miserable financier come with a boast, that he can fetch a peppercorn into the Exchequer by the loss of millions to the nation? I dare not say how much higher these profits may be augmented. Omitting the immense increase of people by natural population in the northern colonies, and the emigration from every part of Europe, I am convinced that the whole commercial system of America may be altered to advantage. You have prohibited where you ought to have encouraged; and you have encouraged where you ought to have prohibited. Improper restraints have been laid on the continent in favour of the islands. You have but two nations to trade with in America. Would you had twenty!

A great deal has been said without doors of the power, of the strength, of America. It is a topic that ought to be cautiously meddled with. In a good cause, on a sound bottom, the force of this country can crush America to atoms. I know the valour of your troops; I know the skill of your officers. There is not a company of foot that has served in America, out of which you may not pick a man of sufficient knowledge and experience to make a governor of a colony there. But, on this ground, — on the Stamp Act, — when so many here will think it a crying injustice, I am one who will lift up my hands against it.

In such a cause even your success would be hazardous. America, if she fell, would fall like a strong man. She would embrace the pillars of the State, and pull down the Constitution along with her. Is this your boasted peace? — to sheathe the sword, not in its scabbard, but in the bowels of your countrymen? Will you quarrel with yourselves now that the whole House of Bourbon is united against you? — while France disturbs your fisheries in Newfoundland, and withholds from your subjects in Canada their property stipulated by treaty? while the ransom for the Manillas is denied by Spain, and its gallant conqueror basely traduced into a mean plunderer, — a gentleman whose noble and generous spirit would do honour to the proudest grandee of the country?

The Americans have not acted in all things with prudence and temper. The Americans have been wronged. They have been driven to madness by injustice. Will you punish them for the madness which you have occasioned? Rather let prudence and temper come first from this side. I will undertake for America that she will follow the example. — Upon the whole, I will beg leave to tell the House what is really my opinion. It is, that the Stamp Act be *repealed, absolutely, totally, and immediately.*

Impeachment of Hastings Finished.

Edmund Burke.

My Lords, I have done; the part of the Commons is concluded. With a trembling solicitude we consign this product of our long, long labours to your charge. Take it!—take it! It is a sacred trust. Never before was a cause of such magnitude submitted to any human tribunal.

My Lords, at this awful close, in the name of the Commons, and surrounded by them, I attest the retiring, I attest the advancing generations, between which, as a link in the great chain of eternal order, we stand. We call this nation, we call the world to witness, that the Commons have shrunk from no labour, that we have been guilty of no prevarication, that we have made no compromise with crime, that we have not feared any odium whatsoever, in the long warfare which we have carried on with the crimes, with the vices, with the exorbitant wealth, with the enormous and overpowering influence of Eastern corruption. This war we have waged for twenty-two years, and the conflict has been fought at your Lordships' bar for the last seven years. My Lords, twenty-two years is a great space in the scale of the life of man; it is no inconsiderable space in the history of a great nation.

A business which has so long occupied the councils and the tribunals of Great Britain cannot possibly be huddled over in the course of vulgar, trite, and transitory events. Nothing but some of those great revolutions that break the traditionary chain of human memory, and alter the very face of Nature itself, can possibly obscure it. My Lords, we are all elevated to a degree of importance by it; the meanest of us will, by means of it, more or less become the concern of posterity, — if we are yet to hope for such a thing, in the present state of the world, as a recording, retrospective, civilized posterity: but this is in the hands of the great Disposer of events; it is not ours to settle how it shall be.

My Lords, your House yet stands, — it stands as a great edifice; but let me say that it stands in the midst of ruins, — in the midst of the ruins that have been made by the greatest moral earthquake that ever convulsed and shattered this globe of ours. My Lords, it has pleased Providence to place us in such a state, that we appear every moment to be upon the verge of some great mutations. There is one thing, and one thing only, which defies all mutation, — that which existed before the world, and will survive the fabric of the world itself: I mean justice, — that justice which, emanating from the Divinity, has a place in the breast of every one of us, given us for our guide with regard to ourselves and with regard to others, and which will stand, after this globe is burned to ashes, our advocate or accuser before the great Judge.

My Lords, the Commons will share in every fate with your Lordships; there is nothing sinister which can happen to you, in which we shall not be involved. And if it should so happen that we shall be subjected to some of those frightful changes which we have seen; if it should happen that your Lordships, stripped of all the decorous distinctions of human society, should, by hands at once base and cruel, be led to those scaffolds and machines of murder upon which great kings and glorious queens have shed their blood, amidst the prelates, amidst the nobles, amidst the magistrates who supported their thrones, may you, in those moments, feel that consolation which I am persuaded they felt in the critical moments of their dreadful agony!

My Lords, there is a consolation, — and a great consolation it is! — which often happens to oppressed virtue and fallen dignity. It often happens that the very oppressors and perscutors themselves are forced to bear testimony in its favour. I do not like to go for instances a great way back into antiquity. I know very well that length of time operates so as to give an air of the fabulous to remote events, which lessens the interest and weakens the application of examples. I wish to come nearer the present time.

Your Lordships know and have heard (for which of us has not known and heard?) of the Parliament of Paris. The Parliament of Paris had an origin very, very similar to that of the great Court before which I stand; the Parliament of Paris continued to have a great resemblance to it in its constitution, even to its fall. The Parliament of Paris, my Lords, WAS; it is gone! It has passed away; it has vanished like a dream! It fell, pierced by the sword of the Comte de Mirabeau. And yet I will say that that man, at the time of his inflicting the death-wound of that Parliament, produced at once the shortest and the grandest funeral oration that ever was or could be made upon the departure of a great court of magistracy. Though he had himself smarted under its lash, as every one knows who knows his history, (and he was elevated to dreadful notoriety in history,) yet, when he pronounced the death-sentence upon that Parliament, and inflicted the mortal wound, he declared that his motives for doing it were merely political, and that their hands were as pure as those of justice itself, which they administered.

A great and glorious exit, my Lords, of a great and glorious body! And never was an eulogy pronounced upon a body more deserved. They were persons, in nobility of rank, in amplitude of fortune, in weight of authority, in depth of learning, inferior to few of those that hear me. My Lords, it was but the other day that they submitted their necks to the axe; but their honour was unwounded. Their enemies, the persons who sentenced them to death, were lawyers full of subtlety, they were enemies full of malice; yet, lawyers full of subtlety, and enemies full of malice, as they were, they did not dare to reproach them with having supported the wealthy, the great, and powerful, and of having oppressed the weak and feeble, in any of their judgments, or of having perverted justice, in any one instance whatever, through favour, through interest, or cabal.

My Lords, if you must fall, may you so fall! But, if you stand, — and stand I trust you will, together with the fortune of this ancient monarchy, together with the ancient laws and liberties of this great and illustrious kingdom, — may you stand as unimpeached in honour as in power! May you stand, not as a substitute for virtue, but as an ornament of virtue, as a security for virtue! May you stand long, and long stand the terror of tyrants! May you stand the refuge of afflicted nations! May you stand a sacred temple, for the perpetual residence of an inviolable justice!

Supposed Speech of John Adams.

Daniel Webster.

Sink or swim, live or die, survive or perish, I give my hand and my heart to this vote. It is true indeed that in the beginning we aimed not at independence. But there's a Divinity which shapes our ends. The injustice of England has driven us to arms; and, blinded to her own interest for our good, she has obstinately persisted, till independence is now within our grasp. We have but to reach forth to it, and it is ours. Why then should we defer the declaration? Is any man so weak as now to hope for a reconciliation with England, which shall leave either safety to the country and its liberties, or safety to his life and his own honour? Are not you, Sir, who sit in that chair, is not he, our venerable colleague near you, are you not both already the proscribed and predestined objects of punishment and of vengeance? Cut off from all hope of royal clemency, what are you, what can you be, while the power of England remains, but outlaws?

If we postpone independence, do we mean to carry on, or to give up, the war? Do we mean to submit to the measures of Parliament, Boston-Port Bill and all? Do we mean to submit, and consent that we ourselves shall be ground to powder, and our country and its rights trodden down in the dust? I know we do not mean to submit. We never shall submit. Do we mean to violate that most solemn obligation ever entered into by men, that plighting, before God, of our sacred honour to Washington, when, putting him forth to incur the dangers of war, as well as the political hazards of the times, we promised to adhere to him, in every extremity, with our fortunes and our lives? I know there is not a man here, who would not rather see a general conflagration sweep over the land, or an earthquake sink it, than one jot or tittle of that plighted faith fall to the ground. For myself, having, twelve months ago, in this place, moved you, that George Washington be appointed commander of the forces raised, or to be raised, for defence of American liberty, may my right hand forget her cunning, and my tongue cleave to the roof of my mouth, if I hesitate or waver in the support I give him.

The war, then, must go on. We must fight it through. And if the war must go on, why put off longer the Declaration of Independence? That measure will strengthen us. It will give us character abroad. The nations will then treat with us, which they never can do while we acknowledge ourselves subjects in arms against our sovereign. Nay, I maintain that England herself will sooner treat for peace with us on the footing of independence than consent, by repealing her Acts, to acknowledge that her whole conduct toward us has been a course of injustice and oppression. Her pride will be less wounded by submitting to that course of things which now predestinates our independence than by yielding the points in controversy to her rebellious subjects. The former she would regard as the result of fortune; the latter she would feel as her own deep disgrace. Why then, why then, Sir, do we not as soon as possible change this from a civil to a national war? And, since we must fight it through, why not put ourselves in a state to enjoy all the benefits of victory, if we gain the victory?

If we fail, it can be no worse for us. But we shall not fail. The cause will raise up armies; the cause will create navies. The people, the people, if we are true to them, will carry us, and will carry themselves, gloriously through the struggle. I care not how fickle other people have been found. I know the people of these Colonies, and I know that resistance to British aggression is deep and settled in their hearts, and cannot be eradicated. Every Colony, indeed, has expressed its willingness to follow, if we but take the lead.

Sir, the Declaration will inspire the people with increased courage. Instead of a long and bloody war for restoration of privileges, for redress of grievances, for chartered immunities, held under a British King, set before them the glorious object of entire independence, and it will breathe into them anew the breath of life. Read this Declaration at the head of the army; every sword will be drawn from its scabbard, and the solemn vow uttered, to maintain it, or to perish on the bed of honour. Publish it from the pulpit; religion will approve it, and the love of religious liberty will cling round it, resolved to stand with it, or fall with it. Send it to the public halls; proclaim it there; let them hear it who heard the first roar of the enemy's cannon; let them see it who saw their brothers and their sons fall on the field of Bunker Hill, and in the streets of Lexington and Concord, and the very walls will cry out in its support.

Sir, I know the uncertainty of human affairs, but I see, I see clearly, through this day's business. You and I indeed may rue it. We may not live to the time when this Declaration shall be made good. We may die; die, colonists; die, slaves; die, it may be, ignominiously and on the scaffold. Be it so; be it so! If it be the pleasure of Heaven that my country shall require the poor offering of my life, the victim shall be ready at the appointed hour of sacrifice, come when that hour may. But, while I do live, let me have a country, or at least the hope of a country, and that a free country.

But, whatever may be our fate, be assured, be assured, that this Declaration will stand. It may cost treasure, and it may cost blood; but it will stand, and it will richly compensate for both. Through the thick gloom of the present, I see the brightness of the future, as the Sun in heaven. We shall make this a glorious, an immortal day. When we are in our graves, our children will honour it. They will celebrate it with thanksgiving, with festivity, with bonfires, and illuminations. On its annual return they will shed tears, copious, gushing tears, not of subjection and slavery, not of agony and distress, but of exultation, of gratitude, and of joy. Sir, before God, I believe the hour is come. My judgment approves this measure, and my whole heart is in it. All that I have, and all that I am, and all that I hope, in this life, I am now ready here to stake upon it: and I leave off, as I began, that, live or die, survive or perish, I am for the Declaration. It is my living sentiment, and by the blessing of God it shall be my dying sentiment, Independence *now*, and INDEPENDENCE FOR EVER.

COMPOSED AT CORA LINN,*

IN SIGHT OF WALLACE'S TOWER.

LORD of the vale! astounding Flood,
The dullest leaf in this thick wood
Quakes, conscious of thy power;
The caves reply with hollow moan;
And vibrates, to its central stone,
Yon time-cemented Tower!

And yet how fair the rural scene!
For thou, O Clyde, hast ever been
Beneficent as strong;
Pleased in refreshing dews to steep
The little trembling flowers that peep
Thy shelving rocks among.

* *Linn* is Scottish for *waterfall* or *cascade*.

Hence all who love their country, love
To look on thee, — delight to rove
Where they thy voice can hear;
And, to the patriot-warrior's Shade,
Lord of the vale! to Heroes laid
In dust, that voice is dear!

Along thy banks, at dead of night,
Sweeps visibly the Wallace Wight;
Or stands, in warlike vest,
Aloft, beneath the Moon's pale beam,
A Champion worthy of the stream,
Yon gray tower's living crest!

But clouds and envious darkness hide
A Form not doubtfully descried:
Their transient mission o'er,
O, say to what blind region flee
These Shapes of awful phantasy?
To what untrodden shore?

Less than divine command they spurn;
But this we from the mountains learn,
And this the valleys show,—
That never will they deign to hold
Communion where the heart is cold
To human weal and woe.

The man of abject soul in vain
Shall walk the Marathonian plain;
Or thrid the shadowy gloom,
That still invests the guardian Pass
Where stood, sublime, Leonidas
Devoted to the tomb.

Nor deem that it can aught avail
For such to glide with oar or sail
Beneath the piny wood,

Where Tell once drew, by Uri's lake,
His vengeful shafts, — prepared to slake
Their thirst in tyrant's blood.

PATRIOTISM.

SIR WALTER SCOTT.

BREATHES there the man, with soul so dead,
Who never to himself hath said,
  This is my own, my native land!
Whose heart hath ne'er within him burn'd,
As home his footsteps he hath turn'd,
  From wandering on a foreign strand!
If such there breathe, go, mark him well:
For him no minstrel raptures swell;
High though his titles, proud his name,
Boundless his wealth as wish can claim;
Despite those titles, power, and pelf,
The wretch, concentred all in self,
Living, shall forfeit fair renown,
And, doubly dying, shall go down
To the vile dust, from whence he sprung,
Unwept, unhonour'd, and unsung.
O Caledonia! stern and wild,
Meet nurse for a poetic child!
Land of brown heath and shaggy wood,
Land of the mountain and the flood,
Land of my sires! what mortal hand
Can e'er untie the filial band,
That knits me to thy rugged strand!
Still, as I view each well-known scene,
Think what is now, and what hath been,
Seems as, to me, of all bereft,
Sole friends thy woods and streams were left;
And thus I love them better still,
Even in extremity of ill.

By Yarrow's stream still let me stray,
Though none should guide my feeble way;
Still feel the breeze down Ettrick break,
Although it chill my wither'd cheek;
Still lay my head by Teviot stone,
Though there, forgotten and alone,
The Bard may draw his parting groan.

PAUL REVERE'S RIDE.

H. W. LONGFELLOW.

LISTEN, my children, and you shall hear
Of the midnight ride of Paul Revere,
On the eighteenth of April, in Seventy-Five:
Hardly a man is now alive
Who remembers that famous day and year.

He said to his friend, — "If the British march
By land or sea from the town to-night,
Hang a lantern aloft in the belfry-arch
Of the North-Church tower, as a signal-light, —
One if by land, and two if by sea;
And I on the opposite shore will be,
Ready to ride and spread the alarm
Through every Middlesex village and farm,
For the country-folk to be up and to arm."

Then he said good-night, and with muffled oar
Silently row'd to the Charlestown shore,
Just as the Moon rose over the bay,
Where swinging wide at her moorings lay
The Somerset, British man-of-war:
A phantom ship, with each mast and spar
Across the Moon, like a prison-bar,
And a huge, black hulk, that was magnified
By its own reflection in the tide.

Meanwhile his friend, through alley and street
Wanders and watches with eager ears,
Till in the silence around him he hears
The muster of men at the barrack-door,
The sound of arms, and the tramp of feet,
And the measured tread of the grenadiers
Marching down to their boats on the shore.

Then he climb'd to the tower of the church,
Up the wooden stairs, with stealthy tread,
To the belfry-chamber overhead,
And startled the pigeons from their perch
On the sombre rafters, that round him made
Masses and moving shapes of shade;
Up the light ladder, slender and tall,
To the highest window in the wall,
Where he paused to listen and look down
A moment on the roofs of the quiet town,
And the moonlight flowing over all.

Beneath, in the church-yard, lay the dead
In their night-encampment on the hill,
Wrapp'd in silence so deep and still,
That he could hear, like a sentinel's tread,
The watchful night-wind as it went
Creeping along from tent to tent,
And seeming to whisper, "All is well!"
A moment only he feels the spell
Of the place and the hour, the secret dread
Of the lonely belfry and the dead;
For suddenly all his thoughts are bent
On a shadowy something far away,
Where the river widens to meet the bay, —
A line of black, that bends and floats
On the rising tide, like a bridge of boats.

Meanwhile, impatient to mount and ride,
Booted and spurr'd, with a heavy stride,

On the opposite shore walk'd Paul Revere.
Now he patted his horse's side,
Now gazed on the landscape far and near,
Then impetuous stamp'd the earth,
And turn'd and tighten'd his saddle-girth;
But mostly he watch'd with eager search
The belfry-tower of the old North Church,
As it rose above the graves on the hill,
Lonely, and spectral, and sombre, and still.

And, lo! as he looks, on the belfry's height,
A glimmer, and then a gleam of light!
He springs to the saddle, the bridle he turns,
But lingers and gazes, till full on his sight
A second lamp in the belfry burns!

A hurry of hoofs in a village-street,
A shape in the moonlight, a bulk in the dark,
And beneath from the pebbles, in passing, a spark
Struck out by a steed that flies fearless and fleet:
That was all! And yet, through the gloom and the light,
The fate of a nation was riding that night;
And the spark struck out by that steed, in his flight,
Kindled the land into flame with its heat.

It was twelve by the village-clock,
When he cross'd the bridge into Medford town,
He heard the crowing of the cock,
And the barking of the farmer's dog,
And felt the damp of the river-fog,
That rises when the Sun goes down.

It was one by the village-clock,
When he rode into Lexington.
He saw the gilded weathercock
Swim in the moonlight as he pass'd,
And the meeting-house windows, blank and bare,
Gaze at him with a spectral glare,

As if they already stood aghast
At the bloody work they would look upon.

It was two by the village clock,
When he came to the bridge in Concord town.
He heard the bleating of the flock,
And the twitter of birds among the trees,
And felt the breath of the morning-breeze
Blowing over the meadows brown.
And one was safe and asleep in his bed
Who at the bridge would be first to fall,
Who that day would be lying dead,
Pierced by a British musket-ball.

You know the rest. In the books you have read
How the British regulars fired and fled;
How the farmers gave them ball for ball,
From behind each fence and farmyard-wall,
Chasing the red-coats down the lane,
Then crossing the fields to emerge again
Under the trees at the turn of the road,
And only pausing to fire and load.

So through the night rode Paul Revere;
And so through the night went his cry of alarm
To every Middlesex village and farm, —
A cry of defiance, and not of fear, —
A voice in the darkness, a knock at the door,
And a word that shall echo for evermore!
For, borne on the night-wind of the Past,
Through all our history, to the last,
In the hour of darkness, and peril, and need,
The people will waken and listen to hear
The hurrying hoof-beat of that steed,
And the midnight-message of Paul Revere.

HORATIUS AT THE BRIDGE.

LORD MACAULAY.

Now the Consul's brow was sad,
And the Consul's speech was low,
And darkly look'd he at the wall,
And darkly at the foe:
"Their van will be upon us
Before the bridge goes down;
And, if they once may win the bridge,
What hope to save the town?"

Then outspake brave Horatius,
The captain of the gate:
"To every man upon this Earth
Death cometh soon or late.
And how can man die better
Than facing fearful odds
For the ashes of his fathers
And the temples of his gods?

Hew down the bridge, Sir Consul,
With all the speed ye may;
I, with two more to help me,
Will hold the foe in play, —
In yon strait path a thousand
May well be stopp'd by three.
Now who will stand on either hand,
And keep the bridge with me?"

Then outspake Spurius Lartius, —
A Ramnian proud was he:
"Lo, I will stand at thy right hand,
And keep the bridge with thee."
And outspake strong Herminius, —
Of Titian blood was he:
"I will abide on thy left side,
And keep the bridge with thee."

"Horatius," quoth the Consul,
  "As thou say'st, so let it be."
And straight against that great array
  Forth went the dauntless Three.
Now, while the Three were tightening
  Their harness on their backs,
The Consul was the foremost man
  To take in hand an axe;
And Fathers mix'd with Commons
  Seized hatchet, bar, and crow,
And smote upon the planks above,
  And loosed the props below.

Meanwhile the Tuscan army,
  Right glorious to behold,
Came flashing back the noonday light,
Rank behind rank, like surges bright
  Of a broad sea of gold.
Four hundred trumpets sounded
  A peal of warlike glee,
As that great host, with measured tread,
And spears advanced, and ensigns spread,
Roll'd slowly towards the bridge's head,
  Where stood the dauntless Three.

But now no sound of laughter
  Was heard amongst the foes.
A wild and wrathful clamour
  From all the vanguard rose.
Six spears' lengths from the entrance
  Halted that mighty mass,
And for a space no man came forth
  To win the narrow pass.

But, hark! the cry is Astur:
  And, lo! the ranks divide;
And the great lord of Luna
  Comes with his stately stride.

Quoth he, "The she-wolf's litter
  Stand savagely at bay;
But will ye dare to follow,
  If Astur clears the way?"

Then, whirling up his broadsword
  With both hands to the height,
He rush'd against Horatius,
  And smote with all his might.
With shield and blade Horatius
  Right deftly turn'd the blow;
The blow, though turn'd, came yet too nigh;
It miss'd his helm, but gash'd his thigh.
The Tuscans raised a joyful cry
  To see the red blood flow.

He reel'd, and on Herminius
  He lean'd one breathing-space,
Then, like a wild-cat mad with wounds,
  Sprang right at Astur's face.
Through teeth and skull and helmet
  So fierce a thrust he sped,
The good sword stood a handbreadth out
  Behind the Tuscan's head.

But meanwhile axe and lever
  Have manfully been plied,
And now the bridge hangs tottering
  Above the boiling tide.
"Come back, come back, Horatius!"
  Loud cried the Fathers all;
"Back, Lartius! back, Herminius!
  Back, ere the ruin fall!"

Back darted Spurius Lartius;
  Herminius darted back;
And, as they pass'd, beneath their feet
  They felt the timbers crack;

But, when they turn'd their faces,
  And on the further shore
Saw brave Horatius stand alone,
  They would have cross'd once more.
But, with a crash like thunder,
  Fell every loosen'd beam,
And, like a dam, the mighty wreck
  Lay right athwart the stream;
And a long shout of triumph
  Rose from the walls of Rome,
As to the highest turret-tops
  Was splash'd the yellow foam.

Alone stood brave Horatius,
  But constant still in mind, —
Thrice thirty thousand foes before,
  And the broad flood behind.
"Down with him!" cried false Sextus,
  With a smile on his pale face;
"Now yield thee," cried Lars Porsena,
  "Now yield thee to our grace!"

Round turn'd he, as not deigning
  Those craven ranks to see;
Nought spake he to Lars Porsena,
  To Sextus nought spake he;
But he saw on Palatinus
  The white porch of his home;
And he spake to the noble river
  That rolls by the towers of Rome:

"O Tiber! Father Tiber!
  To whom the Romans pray,
A Roman's life, a Roman's arms,
  Take thou in charge this day!"
So he spake, and, speaking, sheathed
  The good sword by his side,

And, with his harness on his back,
  Plunged headlong in the tide.

No sound of joy or sorrow
  Was heard from either bank,
But friends and foes in dumb surprise,
With parted lips and straining eyes,
  Stood gazing where he sank;
And, when above the surges
  They saw his crest appear,
All Rome sent forth a rapturous cry,
And even the ranks of Tuscany
  Could scarce forbear to cheer.

But fiercely ran the current,
  Swoll'n high by months of rain,
And fast his blood was flowing;
  And he was sore in pain,
And heavy with his armour,
  And spent with changing blows;
And oft they thought him sinking,
  But still again he rose.

And now he feels the bottom; —
  Now on dry earth he stands;
Now round him throng the Fathers
  To press his gory hands.
And, now with shouts and clapping,
  And noise of weeping loud,
He enters through the River Gate,
  Borne by the joyous crowd.

WALPOLE'S ATTACK ON PITT.

I WAS unwilling to interrupt the course of this debate while it was carried on, with calmness and decency, by men who do not suffer the ardour of opposition to cloud their reason or transport them to such expressions as the dignity of this assembly does not admit. I have hitherto deferred answering the gentleman who declaimed against the bill with such fluency of rhetoric and such vehemence of gesture; who charged the advocates for the expedients now proposed with having no regard to any interests but their own, and with making laws only to consume paper, and threatened them with the defection of their adherents, and the loss of their influence, upon this new discovery of their folly and ignorance. Nor do I now answer him for any other purpose than to remind him how little the clamours of rage and the petulancy of invective contribute to the end for which this assembly is called together; how little the discovery of truth is promoted, and the security of the nation established by pompous diction and theatrical emotion. Formidable sounds and furious declamation, confident assertions and lofty periods, may affect the young and inexperienced; and perhaps the gentleman may have contracted his habits of oratory by conversing more with those of his own age than with such as have more opportunities of acquiring knowledge, and more successful methods of communicating their sentiments. If the heat of his temper would permit him to attend to those whose age and long acquaintance with business give them an indisputable right to deference and superiority, he would learn, in time, to reason rather than declaim, and to prefer justness of argument, and an accurate knowledge of facts, to sounding epithets and splendid superlatives, which may disturb the imagination for a moment, but leave no lasting impression on the mind. He will learn that to accuse and prove are very different; and that reproaches, unsupported by evidence, affect only the character of him that utters them. Excursions of fancy and flights of oratory are, indeed, pardonable in young men, but in no other; and it would surely contribute more, even to the purpose for which some gentlemen appear to speak, (that of depreciating the conduct of the administration,) to prove the inconveniences and injustice of this bill, than barely to assert them, with whatever magnificence of language or appearance of zeal, honesty, or compassion.

PITT'S REPLY TO WALPOLE.

SIR, — The atrocious crime of being a young man, which the honourable gentleman has, with such spirit and decency, charged upon me, I shall neither attempt to palliate nor deny; but content myself with wishing that I may be one of those whose follies may cease with their youth, and not of that number who are ignorant in spite of experience. Whether youth can be imputed to any man as a reproach, I will not, sir, assume the province of determining; but surely age may become justly contemptible, if the opportunities which it brings have passed away without improvement, and vice appears to prevail when the passions have subsided.

The wretch who, after having seen the consequences of a thousand errors, continues still to blunder, and whose age has only added obstinacy to stupidity, is surely the object either of abhorrence or contempt, and deserves not that his gray hairs should secure him from insult. Much more, Sir, is *he* to be abhorred who, as he has advanced in age, has receded from virtue, and become more wicked with less temptation; who prostitutes himself for money which he cannot enjoy, and spends the remains of his life in the ruin of his country.

But youth, Sir, is not my only crime; I have been accused of acting a theatrical part. A theatrical part may either imply some peculiarities of gesture, or a dissimulation of my real sentiments, and an adoption of the opinions and language of another man.

In the first sense, Sir, the charge is too trifling to be confuted, and deserves only to be mentioned, that it may be despised. I am at liberty, like every other man, to use my own language; and, though perhaps I may have some ambition to please this gentleman, I shall not lay myself under any restraint, nor very solicitously copy his diction or his mien, however matured by age or modelled by experience.

But if any man shall, by charging me with theatrical behaviour imply that I utter any sentiments but my own, I shall treat him as a calumniator and a villain; nor shall any protection shelter him from the treatment he deserves. I shall, on such an occasion, without scruple, trample upon all those forms with which wealth and dignity intrench themselves; nor shall anything but age restrain my resentment, — age, which always brings *one* privilege, that of being insolent and supercilious, without punishment.

But with regard, Sir, to those whom I have offended, I am of opinion that, if I had acted a borrowed part, I should have avoided their censure; the heat that offended them is the ardour of conviction, and that zeal for the service of my country which neither hope nor fear shall influence me to suppress. I will not sit unconcerned while my liberty is invaded, nor look in silence upon public robbery. I will exert my endeavours, at whatever hazard, to repel the aggressor, and drag the thief to justice, whoever may protect him in his villainy, and whoever may partake of his plunder.

OUR DUTIES TO THE REPUBLIC.

JUDGE STORY.

THE Old World has already revealed to us, in its unsealed books, the beginning and end of all its own marvellous struggles in the cause of liberty. Greece, lovely Greece, "the land of scholars and the nurse of arms," where sister republics, in fair procession, chanted the praises of liberty and the gods, — where and what is she? For two thousand years the oppressor has ground her to the earth. Her arts are no more. The last sad relics of her temples are but the barracks of a ruthless soldiery. The fragments of her columns and her palaces are in the dust, yet beautiful in ruins. She fell not when the mighty were upon her. Her sons were united at Thermopylæ and Marathon; and the tide of her triumph rolled back upon the Hellespont. She was conquered by her own factions. She fell by the hands of her own people. The man of Macedonia did not the work of destruction. It was already done by her own corruptions, banishments, and dissensions.

Rome, republican Rome, whose eagles glanced in the rising and setting Sun, — where and what is she? The eternal city yet remains, proud even in her desolation, noble in her decline, venerable in the majesty of religion, and calm as in the composure of death. The malaria has but travelled in the paths worn by her destroyers. More than eighteen centuries have mourned over the loss of her empire. A mortal disease was upon her vitals before Cæsar crossed the Rubicon; and Brutus did not restore her health by the deep probings of the Senate-chamber. The Goths and Vandals and Huns, the swarms of the North, completed only what was already begun at home. Romans betrayed Rome.

The legions were bought and sold; but the people offered the tribute money.

We stand the latest, — and, if we fail, probably the last, — experiment of self-government by the people. We have begun it under circumstances of the most auspicious nature. We are in the vigour of youth. Our growth has never been checked by the oppressions of tyranny. Our constitutions have never been enfeebled by the vices or luxuries of the old world. Such as we are, we have been from the beginning, — simple, hardy, intelligent, accustomed to self-government and to self-respect. The Atlantic rolls between us and any formidable foe. Within our own territory, stretching through many degrees of latitude and longitude, we have the choice of many products and many means of independence. The government is mild. The Press is free. Religion is free. Knowledge reaches or may reach every home. What fairer prospect of success could be presented? What means more adequate to accomplish the sublime end? What more is necessary than for the people to preserve what they have themselves created? Already has the age caught the spirit of our institutions. It has already ascended the Andes, and snuffed the breezes of both oceans. It has infused itself into the life-blood of Europe, and warmed the sunny plains of France and the low lands of Holland. It has touched the philosophy of Germany and the North; and, moving onward to the South, has opened to Greece the lessons of her better days. Can it be that America, under such circumstances, can betray herself? Can it be that she is to be added to the catalogue of republics, the inscription upon whose ruins is: "They were, but they are not"? Forbid it, my countrymen! Forbid it, Heaven!

LIBERTY AND UNION.

DANIEL WEBSTER.

I PROFESS, Sir, in my career hitherto, to have kept steadily in view the prosperity and honour of the whole country, and the preservation of our Federal Union. It is to that Union we owe our safety at home, and our consideration and dignity abroad. It is to that Union that we are chiefly indebted for whatever makes us most proud of our country. That Union we reached only by the discipline of our virtues in the severe school of adversity. It had its origin in the necessities of disordered finance, prostrate commerce, and ruined credit. Under its benign influences, these great interests immediately awoke, as from the dead, and sprang forth with newness of life. Every year of its duration has teemed with fresh proofs of its utility and its blessings; and, although our territory has stretched out wider and wider, and our population spread further and further, they have not outrun its protection or its benefits. It has been to us all a copious fountain of national, social, and personal happiness.

I have not allowed myself, Sir, to look beyond the Union, to see what might lie hidden in the dark recess behind. I have not coolly weighed the chances of preserving liberty when the bonds that unite us together shall be broken asunder. I have not accustomed myself to hang over the precipice of disunion, to see whether, with my short sight, I can fathom the depth of the abyss below; nor could I regard him as a safe counsellor in the affairs of this government, whose thoughts should be mainly bent on considering, not how the Union may be best preserved, but how tolerable might be the condition of the people when it shall be broken up and destroyed.

While the Union lasts, we have high, exciting, gratifying prospects spread out before us, for us and our children. Beyond that I seek not to penetrate the veil. God grant that, in my day at least, that curtain may not rise! God grant that on my vision never may be opened what lies behind! When my eyes shall be turned to behold, for the last time, the Sun in heaven, may I not see him shining on the broken and dishonoured fragments of a once glorious Union; on States dissevered, discordant, belligerent; on a land rent with civil feuds, or drenched, it may be, in fraternal blood! Let their last feeble and lingering glance rather behold the gorgeous ensign of the republic, now known and honoured throughout the Earth, still full high advanced, its arms and trophies streaming in their original lustre, not a stripe erased or polluted, nor a single star obscured; bearing for its motto, no such miserable interrogatory as, "What is all this worth?" nor those other words of delusion and folly, "Liberty first, and Union afterwards"; but everywhere, spread all over in characters of living light, blazing on all its ample folds, as they float over the sea and over the land, and in every wind under the whole heavens, that other sentiment, dear to every true American heart, — Liberty *and* Union, now and for ever, one and inseparable!

INDEPENDENCE BELL. — JULY 4, 1776.

[When the Declaration of Independence was adopted by Congress, the event was announced by ringing the old State-House bell, which bore the inscription "Proclaim liberty throughout the land, to all the inhabitants thereof!" The old bellman stationed his little grandson at the door of the hall, to await the instructions of the door-keeper when to ring. At the word, the young patriot rushed out, and clapping his hands, shouted: — "*Ring!* RING! **RING!**"]

There was a tumult in the city,
  In the quaint old Quaker town,
And the streets were rife with people
  Pacing restless up and down, —
People gathering at the corners,
  Where they whisper'd each to each,
And the sweat stood on their temples
  With the earnestness of speech.

As the bleak Atlantic currents
  Lash the wild Newfoundland shore,
So they beat against the State-House,
  So they surged against the door;
And the mingling of their voices
  Made a harmony profound,
Till the quiet street of Chestnut
  Was all turbulent with sound.

"Will they do it?" "Dare they do it?"
  "Who is speaking?" "What's the news?"
"What of Adams?" "What of Sherman?"
  "O, God grant they won't refuse!"
"Make some way there!" "Let me nearer!"
  "I am stifling!" "Stifle, then!
When a nation's life's at hazard,
  We've no time to think of men!"

So they surged against the State-House,
  While all solemnly inside
Sat the Continental Congress,
  Truth and reason for their guide.
O'er a simple scroll debating,
  Which, though simple it might be,
Yet should shake the cliffs of England
  With the thunders of the free.

Far aloft in that high steeple
  Sat the bellman, old and gray;

He was weary of the tyrant
  And his iron-scepter'd sway,
So he sat, with one hand ready
  On the clapper of the bell,
When his eye could catch the signal,
  The long-expected news, to tell.

See, see! the dense crowd quivers
  Through all its lengthen'd line,
As the boy beside the portal
  Hastens forth to give the sign!
With his little hands uplifted,
  Breezes dallying with his hair,
Hark! with deep, clear intonation,
  Breaks his young voice on the air:

Hush'd the people's swelling murmur,
  Whilst the boy cries joyously;
"Ring!" he shouts, "Ring! grandpapa,
  Ring! O, ring for Liberty!"
Quickly, at the given signal,
  The old bellman lifts his hand,
Forth he sends the good news, making
  Iron music through the land.

How they shouted! What rejoicing!
  How the old bell shook the air,
Till the clang of freedom ruffled
  The calmly-gliding Delaware!
How the bonfires and the torches
  Lighted up the night's repose,
And from the flames, like fabled Phœnix,
  Our glorious liberty arose!

That old State-House bell is silent,
  Hush'd is now its clamorous tongue;
But the spirit it awaken'd
  Still is living, — ever young;

And, when we greet the smiling sunlight
  On the fourth of each July,
We will ne'er forget the bellman
  Who, betwixt the earth and sky,
Rung out, loudly, "Independence";
  Which, please God, shall never die!

THE AMERICAN FLAG.

JOSEPH RODMAN DRAKE.

WHEN Freedom, from her mountain height,
  Unfurl'd her standard to the air,
She tore the azure robe of night,
  And set the stars of glory there!
She mingled with its gorgeous dyes
The milky baldric of the skies,
And striped its pure celestial white
With streakings of the morning light;
Then, from his mansion in the Sun,
She call'd her eagle bearer down,
And gave into his mighty hand
The symbol of her chosen land!

Majestic monarch of the cloud!
  Who rear'st aloft thy regal form,
To hear the tempest-trumpings loud,
And see the lightning lances driven,
  When strive the warriors of the storm,
And rolls the thunder-drum of heaven,—
Child of the Sun! to thee 'tis given
  To guard the banner of the free,
To hover in the sulphur smoke,
To ward away the battle-stroke,
  And bid its blendings shine afar,
  Like rainbows on the cloud of war,
    The harbingers of victory!

Flag of the brave! thy folds shall fly,
The sign of hope and triumph high!
When speaks the signal-trumpet tone,
And the long line comes gleaming on,
Ere yet the life-blood, warm and wet,
Has dimm'd the glistening bayonet,
Each soldier's eye shall brightly turn
To where thy sky-born glories burn,
And, as his springing steps advance,
Catch war and vengeance from the glance.
And when the cannon-mouthings loud
Heave in wild wreaths the battle shroud,
And gory sabres rise and fall
Like shoots of flame on midnight's pall,
Then shall thy meteor glances glow,
  And cowering foes shall shrink beneath
Each gallant arm that strikes below
  That lovely messenger of death.

Flag of the seas! on ocean wave
Thy stars shall glitter o'er the brave;
When death, careering on the gale,
Sweeps darkly round the bellied sail,
And frighten'd waves rush wildly back
Before the broadside's reeling rack,
Each dying wanderer of the sea
Shall look at once to heaven and thee,
And smile to see thy splendours fly
In triumph o'er his closing eye.

Flag of the free heart's hope and home,
  By angel-hands to valour given,
Thy stars have lit the welkin dome,
  And all thy hues were born in heaven.
Forever float that standard sheet,
  Where breathes the foe but falls before us,
With Freedom's soil beneath our feet,
  And Freedom's banner streaming o'er us!

THE RISING OF 1776.

THOMAS BUCHANAN READ.

Out of the North the wild news came,
Far flashing on its wings of flame,
Swift as the boreal light which flies
At midnight through the startled skies.
And there was tumult in the air,
  The fife's shrill note, the drum's loud beat,
And through the wide land everywhere
  The answering tread of hurrying feet;
While the first oath of Freedom's gun
Came on the blast from Lexington;
And Concord roused, no longer tame,
Forgot her old baptismal name,
Made bare her patriot arm of power,
And swell'd the discord of the hour.

Within its shade of elm and oak
  The church of Berkley Manor stood;
There Sunday found the rural folk,
  And some esteem'd of gentle blood.
  In vain their feet with loitering tread
Pass'd 'mid the graves where rank is nought;
All could not read the lesson taught
  In that republic of the dead.

How sweet the hour of Sabbath talk,
  The vale with peace and sunshine full,
Where all the happy people walk,
  Deck'd in their homespun flax and wool;
  Where youth's gay hats with blossoms bloom;
And every maid, with simple art,
Wears on her breast, like her own heart,
  A bud whose depths are all perfume;
While every garment's gentle stir
Is breathing rose and lavender.

The pastor came: his snowy locks
  Hallow'd his brow of thought and care;
And calmly, as shepherds lead their flocks,
  He led into the house of prayer.
Then soon he rose; the prayer was strong;
The Psalm was warrior David's song;
The text, a few short words of might—
"The Lord of hosts shall arm the right!"
He spoke of wrongs too long endured,
Of sacred rights to be secured;
Then from his patriot tongue of flame
The startling words for Freedom came.
The stirring sentences he spake
Compell'd the heart to glow or quake,
And, rising on his theme's broad wing,
  And grasping in his nervous hand
  Th' imaginary battle-brand,
In face of death he dared to fling
Defiance to a tyrant king.

Even as he spoke, his frame, renew'd
In eloquence of attitude,
Rose, as it seem'd, a shoulder higher;
Then swept his kindling glance of fire
From startled pew to breathless choir;
When suddenly his mantle wide
His hands impatient flung aside,
And, lo! he met their wondering eyes
Complete in all a warrior's guise.

A moment there was awful pause,
When Berkley cried, "Cease, traitor! cease!
God's temple is the house of peace!"
  The other shouted, "Nay, not so,
When God is with our righteous cause;
His holiest places then are ours,
His temples are our forts and towers

That frown upon the tyrant foe;
In this, the dawn of Freedom's day,
There is a time to fight and pray!"

And now before the open door—
The warrior priest had order'd so—
Th' enlisting trumpet's sudden roar
Rang through the chapel, o'er and o'er,
Its long reverberating blow,
So loud and clear, it seem'd the ear
Of dusty death must wake and hear.

And there the startling drum and fife
Fired the living with fiercer life;
While overhead, with wild increase,
Forgetting its ancient toll of peace,
The great bell swung as ne'er before:
It seem'd as it would never cease;
And every word its ardour flung
From off its jubilant iron tongue
Was, "War! War! WAR!"

"Who dares"—this was the patriot's cry,
As striding from the desk he came—
"Come out with me, in Freedom's name,
For her to live, for her to die?"
A hundred hands flung up reply,
A hundred voices answer'd, "I!"

REPLY TO MR. CORRY.

H. Grattan.

Has the gentleman done? Has he completely done? He was unparliamentary from the beginning to the end of his speech. There was scarce a word he uttered that was not a violation of the privileges of the House. But

I did not call him to order, — why? because the limited talents of some men render it impossible for them to be severe without being unparliamentary. But before I sit down I shall show him how to be severe and parliamentary at the same time.

On any other occasion, I should think myself justifiable in treating with silent contempt anything which might fall from that honourable member; but there are times when the insignificance of the accuser is lost in the magnitude of the accusation. I know the difficulty the honourable gentleman laboured under when he attacked me, conscious that, on a comparative view of our characters, public and private, there is nothing he could say which would injure me. The public would not believe the charge. I despise the falsehood. If such a charge were made by an honest man, I would answer it in the manner I shall do before I sit down. But I shall first reply to it when *not* made by an honest man.

The right-honourable gentleman has called me "an unimpeached traitor." I ask why not "traitor," unqualified by any epithet? I will tell him: it was because he durst not. It was the act of a coward, who raises his arm to strike, but has not courage to give the blow. I will not call him villain, because it would be unparliamentary, and he is a Privy Counsellor. I will not call him fool, because he happens to be Chancellor of the Exchequer. But I say, he is one who has abused the privilege of parliament and the freedom of debate, by uttering language which, if spoken out of the House, I should answer only with a blow. I care not how high his situation, how low his character, how contemptible his speech; whether a Privy Counsellor or a parasite, my answer would be a blow.

He has charged me with being connected with the rebels. The charge is utterly, totally, and meanly false. Does the honourable gentleman rely on the report of the House of Lords for the foundation of his assertion? If he does, I can prove to the committee there was a physical impossibility of that report being true. But I scorn to answer any man for my conduct, whether he be a political coxcomb, or whether he brought himself into power by a false glare of courage or not.

I have returned, — not, as the right-honourable member has said, to raise another storm, — I have returned to discharge an honourable debt of gratitude to my country, that conferred a great reward for past services, which, I am proud to say, was not greater than my desert. I have returned to protect that Constitution of which I was the parent and founder, from the assassination of such men as the right-honourable gentleman and his unworthy associates. They are corrupt, they are seditious, and they, at this very moment, are in a conspiracy against their country. I have returned to refute a libel, as false as it is malicious, given to the public under the appellation of a report of the committee of the Lords. Here I stand, ready for impeachment or trial. I dare accusation. I defy the honourable gentleman; I defy the Government; I defy their whole phalanx: let them come forth! I tell the Ministers, I will neither give quarter nor take it. I am here to lay the shattered remains of my constitution on the floor of this house, in defence of the liberties of my country.

WISDOM DEARLY PURCHASED.

EDMUND BURKE.

THE British Parliament, in a former session, frightened into a limited concession by the menaces of Ireland, frightened out of it by the menaces of England, was now frightened back again, and made an universal surrender of all that had been thought the peculiar, reserved, uncommunicable rights of England. No reserve, no exception; no debate, no discussion. A sudden light broke in upon us all. It broke in, not through well-contrived and well-disposed windows, but through flaws and breaches, — through the yawning chasms of our ruin. We were taught wisdom by humiliation. No town in England presumed to have a prejudice, or dared to mutter a petition. What was worse, the whole Parliament of England, which retained authority for nothing but surrenders, was despoiled of every shadow of its superintendence. It was, without any qualification, denied in theory, as it had been trampled upon in practice.

What, Gentlemen! was I not to foresee, or, foreseeing, was I not to endeavour to save you from all these multiplied mischiefs and disgraces? Would the little, silly, canvass prattle of obeying instructions, and having no opinions but yours, and such idle, senseless tales, which amuse the vacant ears of unthinking men, have saved you from "the pelting of that pitiless storm" to which the loose improvidence, the cowardly rashness, of those who dare not look danger in the face so as to provide against it in time, and therefore throw themselves headlong into the midst of it, have exposed this degraded nation, beat down and prostrate on the earth, unsheltered, unarmed, unresisting? Was I an Irishman on that day that I boldly withstood our pride? or on the day that I hung down my head, and wept in shame and silence over the humiliation of Great Britain? I became unpopular in England for the one, and in Ireland for the other. What then? What obligation lay on me to be popular? I was bound to serve both kingdoms. To be pleased with my service was their affair, not mine.

I was an Irishman in the Irish business, just as much as I was an American, when, on the same principles, I wished you to concede to America at a time when she prayed concession at our feet. Just as much was I an American, when I wished Parliament to offer terms in victory, and not to wait the ill-chosen hour of defeat, for making good by weakness and by supplication a claim of prerogative, preëminence, and authority.

Instead of requiring it from me, as a point of duty, to kindle with your passions, had you all been as cool as I was, you would have been saved disgraces and distresses that are unutterable. Do you remember our commission? We sent out a solemn embassy across the Atlantic Ocean, to lay the crown, the peerage, the commons of Great Britain at the feet of the American Congress. That our disgrace might want no sort of brightening and burnishing, observe who they were that composed this famous embassy. My Lord Carlisle is among the first ranks of our nobility. He is the identical man who, but two years before, had been put forward, at the opening of a session, in the House of Lords, as the mover of an haughty and rigorous address against America. He was put in the front of the embassy of submission. Mr. Eden was taken from the office of Lord Suffolk, to whom he was then Under-Secretary of State, — from the office of that Lord Suffolk who but a few weeks before, in his place in Parliament, did not deign to inquire where a congress of vagrants was to be found.

They enter the capital of America only to abandon it; and these assertors and representatives of the dignity of England, at the tail of a flying army, let fly their Parthian shafts of memorials and remonstrances at random behind them. Their promises and their offers, their flatteries and their menaces, were all despised; and we were saved the disgrace of their formal reception only because the Congress scorned to receive them; whilst the State-house of independent Philadelphia opened her doors to the public entry of the ambassador of France. From war and blood we went to submission, and from submission plunged back again to war and blood, to desolate and be desolated, without measure, hope, or end. I am a Royalist: I blushed for this degradation of the Crown. I am a Whig: I blushed for the dishonour of Parliament. I am a true Englishman: I felt to the quick for the disgrace of England. I am a man: I felt for the melancholy reverse of human affairs in the fall of the first power in the world.

To read what was approaching in Ireland, in the black and bloody characters of the American war, was a painful, but it was a necessary part of my public duty. For, Gentlemen, it is not your fond desires or mine that can alter the nature of things; by contending against which, what have we got, or ever shall get, but defeat and shame? I did not obey your instructions. No. I conformed to the instructions of truth and Nature, and maintained your interest, against your opinions, with a constancy that became me. A representative worthy of you ought to be a person of stability.

I am to look, indeed, to your opinions, — but to such opinions as you and I *must* have five years hence. I was not to look to the flash of the day. I knew that you chose me, in my place, along with others, to be a pillar of the State, and not a weathercock on the top of the edifice, exalted for my levity and versatility, and of no use but to indicate the shiftings of every fashionable gale. Would to God the value of my sentiments on Ireland and on America had been at this day a subject of doubt and discussion! No matter what my sufferings had been, so that this kingdom had kept the authority I wished it to maintain, by a grave foresight, and by an equitable temperance in the use of its power.

"MATCHES AND OVERMATCHES."

DANIEL WEBSTER.

BUT the gentleman inquires why *he* was made the object of such a reply. Why was *he* singled out? If an attack has been made on the East, he, he assures us, did not begin it: it was made by the gentleman from Missouri. Sir, I answered the gentleman's speech because I happened to hear it; and because, also, I chose to give an answer to that speech which, if unanswered, I thought most likely to produce injurious impressions. I did not stop to inquire who was the original drawer of the bill. I found a responsible indorser before me, and it was my purpose to hold him liable, and to bring him to his just responsibility without delay. But, Sir, this interrogatory of the honourable member was only introductory to another. He proceeded to ask me whether I had turned upon him, in this debate, from the consciousness that I should find an overmatch, if I ventured on a contest with his friend from Missouri.

If, Sir, the honourable member, *modestiæ gratia*, had chosen thus to defer to his friend, and to pay him a compliment, without intentional disparagement to others, it would have been quite according to the friendly courtesies of debate, and not at all ungrateful to my own feelings. I am not one of those, Sir, who esteem any tribute of regard, whether light and occasional, or more serious and deliberate, which may be bestowed on others, as so much unjustly withholden from themselves. But the tone and manner of the gentleman's question forbid me thus to interpret it. I am not at liberty to consider it as nothing more than a civility to his friend. It had an air of taunt and disparagement, something of the loftiness of asserted superiority, which does not allow me to pass it over without notice. It was put as a question for me to answer, and so put as if it were difficult for me to answer, whether I deemed the member from Missouri an overmatch for myself in debate here. It seems to me, Sir, that this is extraordinary language, and an extraordinary tone, for the discussions of this body.

Matches and overmatches! Those terms are more applicable elsewhere than here, and fitter for other assemblies than this. Sir, the gentleman seems to forget where and what we are. This is a Senate, a Senate of equals, of men of individual honour and personal character, and of absolute independence. We know no masters, we acknowledge no dictators. This is a hall for mutual consultation and discussion; not an arena for the exhibition of champions. I offer myself, Sir, as a match for no man; I throw the challenge of debate at no man's feet. But then, Sir, since the honourable member has put the question in a manner that calls for an answer, I will give him an answer; and I tell him that, holding myself to be the humblest of the members here, I yet know nothing in the arm of his friend from Missouri, either alone or when aided by the arm of *his* friend from South Carolina, that need deter even me from espousing whatever opinions I may choose to espouse, from debating whenever I may choose to debate, or from speaking whatever I may see fit to say, on the floor of the Senate.

Sir, when uttered as matter of commendation or compliment, I should dissent from nothing which the honourable member might say of his friend. Still less do I put forth any pretensions of my own. But, when put to me as matter of taunt, I throw it back, and say to the gentleman that he could possibly say nothing more likely than such a comparison to wound my pride of personal character. The anger of its tone rescued the remark from intentional irony, which otherwise, probably, would have been its general acceptation. But, Sir, if it be imagined that by this mutual quotation and commendation; if it be supposed that, by casting the characters of the drama, assigning to each his part, to one the attack, to another the cry of onset; or if it be thought that, by a loud and empty vaunt of anticipated victory, any laurels are to be won here; if it be imagined, especially, that any, or all these things will shake any purpose of mine, I can tell the honourable member, once for all, that he is greatly mistaken, and that he is dealing with one of whose temper and character he has yet much to learn.

Sir, I shall not allow myself, on this occasion, I hope on no occasion, to be betrayed into any loss of temper: but, if provoked, as I trust I never shall be, into crimination and recrimination, the honourable member may perhaps find that, in that contest, there will be blows to take as well as blows to give; that others can state comparisons as significant, at least, as his own; and that his impunity may possibly demand of him whatever powers of taunt and sarcasm he may possess. I commend him to a prudent husbandry of his resources.

EULOGY ON LAFAYETTE.

EDWARD EVERETT.

THERE have been those who have denied to Lafayette the name of a great man. What is greatness? Does goodness belong to greatness, and make an essential part of it? If it does, who, I would ask, of all the prominent names in history, has run through such a career with so little reproach, justly or unjustly bestowed? Are military courage and conduct the measure of greatness? Lafayette was intrusted by Washington with all kinds of service, — the laborious and complicated, which required skill and patience; the perilous, that demanded nerve; and we see him performing all with entire success and brilliant reputation. Is the readiness to meet vast responsibilities a proof of greatness? The memoirs of Mr. Jefferson show us that there was a moment, in 1789, when Lafayette took upon himself, as the head of the military force, the entire responsibility of laying down the basis of the Revolution. Is the cool and brave administration of gigantic power a mark of greatness? In all the whirlwind of the Revolution, and when, as commander-in-chief of the National Guard, an organized force of three millions of men, who, for any popular purpose, needed but a word, a look, to put them in motion, we behold him ever calm, collected, disinterested; as free from affectation as selfishness; clothed not less with humility than with power. Is the voluntary return, in advancing years, to the direction of affairs, at a moment like that when, in 1815, the ponderous machinery of the French Empire was flying asunder, —stunning, rending, crushing thousands on every side, —a mark of greatness? Lastly, is it any proof of greatness, to be able, at the age of seventy-three, to take the lead in a successful and bloodless revolution; to change the dynasty; to organize, exercize, and abdicate a military command of three and a half millions of men; to take up, to perform, and lay down the most momentous, delicate, and perilous duties, without passion, without hurry, without selfishness? Is it great to disregard the bribes of title, office, money; to live, to labour, and suffer for great public ends alone; to adhere to principle under all circumstances; to stand before Europe and America conspicuous, for sixty years, in the most responsible stations, the acknowledged admiration of all good men?

But it is more than time, fellow-citizens, that I commit the memory of this great and good man to your unprompted contemplation. On his arrival among you, ten years ago, when your civil fathers, your military, your children, your whole population, poured itself out, in one throng, to salute him; when your cannons proclaimed his advent with joyous salvos, and your acclamations were answered, from steeple to steeple, by festal bells, — with what delight did you not listen to his cordial and affectionate words, — "I beg of you all, beloved citizens of Boston, to accept the respectful and warm thanks of a heart which has for nearly half a century been devoted to your illustrious city!"

That noble heart, — to which, if any object on Earth was dear, that object was the country of his early choice, of his adoption, and his more than regal triumph, — that noble heart will beat no more for your welfare. Cold and still, it is already mingling with the dust. While he lived, you thronged with delight to his presence; you gazed with admiration on his placid features and venerable form, not wholly unshaken by the rude storms of his career; and now, that he has departed, you have assembled in this cradle of the liberties for which, with your fathers, he risked his life, to pay the last honours to his memory. You have thrown open these consecrated portals to admit the lengthened train, which has come to discharge the last public offices of respect to his name. You have hung these venerable arches, for the second time since their erection, with the sable badges of sorrow. You have thus associated the memory of Lafayette in those distinguished honours, which but a few years since you paid to your Adams and Jefferson.

There is not, throughout the world, a friend of liberty who has not dropped his head when he has heard that Lafayette is no more. Poland, Italy, Greece, Spain, Ireland, the South American republics, — every country where man is struggling to recover his birthright, — have lost a benefactor, a patron in Lafayette. And what was it, fellow-citizens, which gave to our Lafayette his spotless fame? The love of liberty. What has consecrated his memory in the hearts of good men? The love of liberty. What nerved his youthful arm with strength, and inspired him, in the morning of his days, with sagacity and counsel? The living love of liberty. To what did he sacrifice power, and rank, and country, and freedom itself? To the horror of licentiousness, —

— to the sanctity of plighted faith, — to the love of liberty protected by law. Thus the great principle of your Revolutionary fathers, and of your Pilgrim sires, was the rule of his life, — *the love of liberty protected by law.*

You have now assembled within these celebrated walls, to perform the last duties of respect and love, on the birthday of your benefactor. The spirit of the departed is in high communion with the spirit of the place, — the temple worthy of the new name which we now behold inscribed on its walls. Listen, Americans, to the lesson which seems borne to us on the very air we breathe, while we perform these dutiful rites! Ye winds, that wafted the Pilgrims to the land of promise, fan, in their children's hearts, the love of freedom! Blood, which our fathers shed, cry from the ground! Echoing arches of this renowned hall, whisper back the voices of other days! Glorious Washington, break the long silence of that votive canvas! Speak, speak, marble lips; teach us THE LOVE OF LIBERTY PROTECTED BY LAW.

RIENZI'S ADDRESS TO THE ROMANS.

MISS M. R. MITFORD.

FRIENDS, I come not here to talk. Ye know too well
The story of our thraldom; — we are slaves!
The bright Sun rises to his course, and lights
A race of slaves! He sets, and his last beam
Falls on a slave! — not such as, swept along
By the full tide of power, the conqueror leads
To crimson glory and undying fame;
But base, ignoble slaves, — slaves to a horde
Of petty tyrants, feudal despots, lords,
Rich in some dozen paltry villages, —
Strong in some hundred spearmen, — only great

In that strange spell, a name! Each hour, dark fraud,
Or open rapine, or protected murder,
Cries out against them. But this very day,
An honest man, my neighbour, — there he stands, —
Was struck — struck like a dog, by one who wore
The badge of Ursini! because, forsooth,
He toss'd not high his ready cap in air,
Nor lifted up his voice in servile shouts,
At sight of that great ruffian! Be we men,
And suffer such dishonour? men, and wash not
The stain away in blood? Such shames are common.
I have known deeper wrongs. I, that speak to you, —
I had a brother once, — a gracious boy,
Full of all gentleness, of calmest hope,
Of sweet and quiet joy; there was the look
Of Heaven upon his face, which limners give
To the beloved disciple. How I loved
That gracious boy! Younger by fifteen years,
Brother at once and son! He left my side,
A summer bloom on his fair cheeks, a smile
Parting his innocent lips. In one short hour,
The pretty, harmless boy was slain! I saw
The corse, the mangled corse, and then I cried
For vengeance! Rouse, ye Romans! rouse, ye slaves!
Have ye brave sons? Look, in the next fierce brawl,
To see them die! Have ye daughters fair? Look
To see them live, torn from your arms, distain'd,
Dishonour'd! and, if ye dare call for justice,
Be answer'd by the lash! Yet this is Rome,
That sat on her seven hills, and from her throne
Of beauty ruled the world! Yet we are Romans!
Why, in that elder day, to be a Roman
Was greater than a king! — and once again, —
Hear me, ye walls, that echo'd to the tread
Of either Brutus! — once again I swear,
Th' eternal city shall be free! her sons
Shall walk with princes!

LOCHIEL'S WARNING.

THOMAS CAMPBELL.

Seer. Lochiel, Lochiel, beware of the day
When the Lowlands shall meet thee in battle array!
For a field of the dead rushes red on my sight,
And the clans of Culloden are scatter'd in fight:
They rally, they bleed, for their kingdom and crown;
Woe, woe, to the riders that trample them down!
Proud Cumberland prances, insulting the slain,
And their hoof-beaten bosoms are trod to the plain.
But, hark! through the fast-flashing lightning of war,
What steed to the desert flies frantic and far?
'Tis thine, O Glenullin! whose bride shall await,
Like a love-lighted watch-fire, all night at the gate.
A steed comes at morning: no rider is there;
But its bridle is red with the sign of despair!
Weep, Albin! to death and captivity led!
O, weep! but thy tears cannot number the dead;
For a merciless sword on Culloden shall wave, —
Culloden, that reeks with the blood of the brave!
Lochiel. Go preach to the coward, thou death-telling seer!
Or, if gory Culloden so dreadful appear,
Draw, dotard, around thy old wavering sight,
This mantle, to cover the phantoms of fright!
Seer. Ha! laughest thou, Lochiel, my vision to scorn?
Proud bird of the mountain, thy plume shall be torn!
Say, rush'd the bold eagle exultingly forth
From his home in the dark-rolling clouds of the North?
Lo! the death-shot of foemen out-speeding, he rode
Companionless, bearing destruction abroad;
But down let him stoop, from his havoc on high!
Ah! home let him speed, — for the spoiler is nigh.
Why flames the far summit? Why shoot to the blast
Those embers, like stars from the firmament cast?
'Tis the fire-shower of ruin, all dreadfully driven

From his eyrie, that beacons the darkness of heaven.
O crested Lochiel! the peerless in might,
Whose banners arise on the battlements' height,
Heaven's fire is around thee, to blast and to burn;
Return to thy dwelling! all lonely return!
For the blackness of ashes shall mark where it stood,
And a wild mother scream o'er her famishing brood!
Lochiel. False wizard, avaunt! I have marshall'd my clan,
Their swords are a thousand, — their bosoms are one!
They are true to the last of their blood and their breath,
And like reapers descend to the harvest of death.
Then welcome be Cumberland's steed to the shock!
Let him dash his proud foam like a wave on the rock!
But woe to his kindred, and woe to his cause,
When Albin her claymore indignantly draws!
When her bonneted chieftains to victory crowd,
Clanranald the dauntless, and Moray the proud,
All plaided and plumed in their tartan array, —
Seer. Lochiel! Lochiel! beware of the day!
For, dark and despairing, my sight I may seal,
But man cannot cover what God would reveal.
'Tis the sunset of life gives me mystical lore,
And coming events cast their shadows before.
I tell thee, Culloden's dread echoes shall ring
With the bloodhounds that bark for thy fugitive king.
Lo! anointed by Heaven with the vials of wrath,
Behold, where he flies on his desolate path!
Now in darkness and billows he sweeps from my sight;
Rise! rise! ye wild tempests, and cover his flight! —
'Tis finish'd. Their thunders are hush'd on the moors, —
Culloden is lost, and my country deplores.
But where is the iron-bound prisoner? Where?
For the red eye of battle is shut in despair.
Say, mounts he the ocean-wave, banish'd, forlorn,
Like a limb from his country cast bleeding and torn?
Ah, no! for a darker departure is near;

The war-drum is muffled, and black is the bier;
His death-bell is tolling: O mercy, dispel
Yon sight, that it freezes my spirit to tell!
Life flutters, convulsed, in his quivering limbs,
And his blood-streaming nostril in agony swims!
Accursed be the fagots that blaze at his feet,
Where his heart shall be thrown, ere it ceases to beat,
With the smoke of its ashes to poison the gale, —
Lochiel. Down, soothless insulter! I trust not the tale!
For never shall Albin a destiny meet
So black with dishonour, so foul with retreat.
Though my perishing ranks should be strew'd in their gore,
Like ocean-weeds heap'd on the surf-beaten shore,
Lochiel, untainted by flight or by chains,
While the kindling of life in his bosom remains,
Shall victor exult, or in death be laid low,
With his back to the field, and his feet to the foe!
And, leaving in battle no blot on his name,
Look proudly to Heaven from the death-bed of fame!

SPEECH IN THE VIRGINIA CONVENTION, 1775.

PATRICK HENRY.

MR. PRESIDENT, it is natural for man to indulge in the illusions of hope. We are apt to shut our eyes against a painful truth, and listen to the song of that siren till she transforms us into beasts. Is this the part of wise men engaged in the great and arduous struggle for liberty? Are we disposed to be of the number of those who having eyes see not, and having ears hear not, the things which so nearly concern their temporal salvation? For my part, whatever anguish of spirit it may cost, I am willing to know the whole truth; to know the worst, and to provide for it.

I have but one lamp by which my feet are guided, and that is the lamp of experience. I know of no way of judging of the future but by the past. And, judging by the past, I wish to know what there has been in the conduct of the British Ministry for the last ten years to justify those hopes with which gentlemen have been pleased to solace themselves and the House. Is it that insidious smile with which our petition has been lately received? Trust it not, sir; it will prove a snare to your feet. Suffer not yourselves to be betrayed with a kiss. Ask yourselves how this gracious reception of our petition comports with those warlike preparations which cover our waters and darken our land. Are fleets and armies necessary to a work of love and reconciliation? Have we shown ourselves so unwilling to be reconciled that force must be called in to win back our love?

Let us not deceive ourselves, sir. These are the implements of war and subjugation, the last arguments to which kings resort. I ask gentlemen, sir, what means this martial array, if its purposes be not to force us to submission? Can gentlemen assign any other possible motive for it? Has Great Britain any enemy in this quarter of the world to call for all this accumulation of navies and armies? No, sir, she has none. They are meant for us. They can be meant for no other. They are sent over to bind and rivet upon us those chains which the British Ministry have been so long forging.

And what have we to oppose them? Shall we try argument? Sir, we have been trying that for the last ten years. Have we anything new to offer upon the subject? Nothing. We have held the subject up in every light of which it is capable; but it has been all in vain. Shall we resort to entreaty and supplication? What terms shall we find that have not been already exhausted? Let us not, I beseech you, sir, deceive ourselves longer. Sir, we have done everything that could have been done to avert the storm that is now coming on. We have petitioned, we have remonstrated, we have supplicated, we have prostrated ourselves before the throne, and have implored its interposition to arrest the tyrannical hands of the Ministry and Parliament.

Our petitions have been slighted, our remonstrances have produced additional violence and insult, our supplications have been disregarded, and we have been spurned with contempt from the foot of the throne. In vain, after these things, may we indulge the fond hope of peace and reconciliation. There is no longer any room for hope. If we wish to be free, if we mean to preserve inviolate those inestimable privileges for which we have been so long contending; if we mean not basely to abandon the noble struggle in which we have been so long engaged, and which we have pledged ourselves never to abandon until the glorious object of our contest shall be obtained, we must fight! I repeat it, sir, we must fight! An appeal to arms and to the God of hosts is all that is left us.

They tell us, sir, that we are weak; unable to cope with so formidable an adversary. But when shall we be stronger? Will it be the next week, or the next year? Will it be when we are totally disarmed, and when a British guard shall be stationed in every house? Shall we gather strength by irresolution and inaction? Shall we acquire the means of effectual resistance by lying supinely on our backs, and hugging the delusive phantom of hope, until our enemies shall have bound us hand and foot? Sir, we are not weak if we make a proper use of those means which the God of Nature hath placed in our power.

Three millions of people armed in the holy cause of liberty, and in such a country as that which we possess, are invincible by any force which our enemy can send against us. Besides, sir, we shall not fight our battles alone. There is a just God who presides over the destinies of nations, and who will raise up friends to fight our battles for us. The battle, sir, is not to the strong alone: it is to the vigilant, the active, the brave. Besides, sir, we have no election. If we were base enough to desire it, it is now too late to retire from the contest. There is no retreat but in submission and slavery! Our chains are forged. Their clanking may be heard on the plains of Boston! The war is inevitable, and let it come! I repeat, sir, let it come!

It is vain, sir, to extenuate the matter. Gentlemen may cry, Peace, peace! but there is no peace. The war is actually begun! The next gale that sweeps from the North will bring to our ears the clash of resounding arms! Our brethren are already in the field! Why stand we here idle? What is it that gentlemen wish? What would they have? Is life so dear, or peace so sweet, as to be purchased at the price of chains and slavery? Forbid it, Almighty God! I know not what course others may take, but as for me, give me liberty or give me death!

SPEECH OF VINDICATION.

ROBERT EMMETT.

MY LORDS: What have I to say why sentence of death should not be pronounced on me, according to law?—I have nothing to say that can alter your predetermination, nor that it will become me to say, with any view to the mitigation of that sentence which you are here to pronounce, and I must abide by. But I have that to say which interests me more than life, and which you have laboured to destroy. I have much to say, why my reputation should be rescued from the load of false accusation and calumny which has been heaped upon it.

Were I only to suffer death, after being adjudged guilty by your tribunal, I should bow in silence, and meet the fate that awaits me without a murmur. The man dies, but his memory lives. That mine may not perish,—that it may live in the respect of my countrymen,—I seize upon this opportunity to vindicate myself from some of the charges alleged against me.

I swear, by the throne of Heaven, before which I must shortly appear,—by the blood of the murdered patriots who have gone before me,—that my conduct has been, through all this peril, and all my purposes, governed only by the convictions which I have uttered, and no other view than that of the emancipation of my country from the superinhuman oppression under which she has so long, and too patiently, travailed; and that I confidently and assuredly hope, wild and chimerical as it may appear, that there is still union and strength in Ireland to accomplish this noble enterprise.

Let no man dare, when I am dead, to charge me with dishonour; let no man attaint my memory by believing that I could have engaged in any cause but that of my country's liberty and independence; or that I could have become the pliant minion of power, in the oppression or the miseries of my countrymen. I would not have submitted to a foreign oppressor, for the same reason that I would resist the domestic tyrant; in the dignity of freedom, I would have fought upon the threshold of my country, and her enemies should enter only by passing over my lifeless corpse. Am I, who lived but for my country, and who have subjected myself to the vengeance of the jealous and wrathful oppressor, and to the bondage of the grave, only to give my countrymen their rights, — am I to be loaded with calumny, and not to be suffered to resent or repel it? No! — God forbid!

If the spirits of the illustrious dead participate in the concerns and cares of those who are dear to them in this transitory life, — O ever dear and venerated shade of my departed father, look down with scrutiny on the conduct of your suffering son; and see if I have even for a moment deviated from those principles of morality and patriotism which it was your care to instil into my youthful mind, and for an adherence to which I am now to offer up my life!

My Lords, you are all impatient for the sacrifice. The blood which you seek is not congealed by the artificial terrors which surround your victim; it circulates warmly and unruffled, through the channels which God created for noble purposes, but which you are bent to destroy, for purposes so grievous that they cry to Heaven! Be yet patient! I have but a few words more to say. I am going to my silent grave; my lamp of life is nearly extinguished; my race is run; the grave opens to receive me, and I sink into its bosom. I have but one request to ask at my departure from this world, — it is the charity of its silence. Let no man write my epitaph; for, as no one who knows my motives dare now vindicate them, let not prejudice or ignorance asperse them. Let them and me repose in obscurity and peace, and my tomb remain uninscribed, until other times, and other men, can do justice to my character. When my country shall take her place among the nations of the Earth, then, and not till then, let my epitaph be written! I have done.

APPEAL IN BEHALF OF IRELAND.

S. S. PRENTISS.

FELLOW-CITIZENS: It is no ordinary cause that has brought together this vast assemblage. We have met, not to prepare ourselves for political contests; we have met, not to celebrate the achievements of those gallant men who have planted our victorious standards in the heart of an enemy's country; we have assembled, not to respond to shouts of triumph from the West; but to answer the cry of want and suffering which comes from the East. The Old World stretches out her arms to the New. The starving parent supplicates the young and vigorous child for bread.

There lies upon the other side of the wide Atlantic a beautiful island, famous in story and in song. Its area is not so great as that of the State of Louisiana, while its population is almost half that of the Union. It has given to the world more than its share of genius and of greatness. It has been prolific in statesmen, warriors, and poets. Its brave and generous sons have fought successfully all battles but their own. In wit and humour it has no equal; while its harp, like its history, moves to tears by its sweet but melancholy pathos.

Into this fair region God has seen fit to send the most terrible of all those fearful ministers that fulfil His inscrutable decrees. The earth has failed to give her increase. The common mother has forgotten her offspring, and she no longer affords them their accustomed nourishment. Famine, gaunt and ghastly famine, has seized a nation with its strangling grasp. Unhappy Ireland, in the sad woes of the present, forgets, for a moment, the gloomy history of the past.

O, it is terrible that, in this beautiful world which the good God has given us, and in which there is plenty for us all, men should die of starvation! When a man dies of disease he alone endures the pain. Around his pillow are gathered sympathizing friends, who, if they cannot keep back the deadly messenger, cover his face and conceal the horrors of his visage as he delivers his stern mandate. In battle, in the fullness of his pride and strength, little recks the soldier whether the hissing bullet sings his sudden requiem, or the cords of life are severed by the sharp steel.

But he who dies of hunger wrestles alone, day by day, with his grim and unrelenting enemy. He has no friends to cheer him in the terrible conflict; for, if he had friends, how could he die of hunger? He has not the hot blood of the soldier to maintain him; for his foe, vampire-like, has exhausted his veins. Famine comes not up, like a brave enemy, storming, by a sudden onset, the fortress that resists. Famine besieges. He draws his lines round the doomed garrison. He cuts off all supplies. He never summons to surrender, for he gives no quarter.

Alas, for poor human nature! how can it sustain this fearful warfare? Day by day the blood recedes, the flesh deserts, the muscles relax, and the sinews grow powerless. At last the mind, which at first had bravely nerved itself against the contest, gives way under the mysterious influences which govern its union with the body. Then the victim begins to doubt the existence of an overruling Providence. He hates his fellow-men, and glares upon them with the longing of a cannibal; and, it may be, dies blaspheming.

This is one of those cases in which we may without impiety assume, as it were, the function of Providence. Who knows but that one of the very objects of this calamity is to test the benevolence and worthiness of us upon whom unlimited abundance is showered? In the name, then, of common humanity, I invoke your aid in behalf of starving Ireland. Give generously and freely. Recollect that in so doing you are exercising one of the most God-like qualities of your nature, and at the same time enjoying one of the greatest luxuries of life. Go home and look at your family, smiling in rosy health, and then think of the pale, famine-pinched cheeks of the poor children of Ireland; and I know you will give, according to your store, even as a bountiful Providence has given to you, — not grudgingly, but with an open hand. He who is able, and will not aid such a cause, is not a man, and has no right to wear the form. He should be sent back to Nature's mint, and re-issued as a counterfeit on humanity of Nature's baser metal.

AMBITION OF A STATESMAN.

HENRY CLAY.

I HAVE been accused of ambition in presenting this measure, — ambition, inordinate ambition. If I had thought of myself only I should have never brought it forward. I know well the perils to which I expose myself, — the risk of alienating faithful and valued friends, with but little prospect of making new ones, if any new ones could compensate for the loss of those we have long tried and loved; and I know well the honest misconception both of friends and foes. Ambition! If I had listened to its soft and seducing whispers, if I had yielded myself to the dictates of a cold, calculating, and prudential policy, I would have stood still and unmoved. I might even have silently gazed on the raging storm, enjoyed its loudest thunders, and left those who are charged with the care of the vessel of State to conduct it as they could.

I have been heretofore often unjustly accused of ambition. Low, grovelling souls, who are utterly incapable of elevating themselves to the higher and nobler duties of pure patriotism, — beings who, forever keeping their own selfish ends in view, decide all public measures by their presumed influence or their aggrandizement, — judge me by the venal rule which they prescribe to themselves. I have given to the winds those false accusations, as I consign that which now impeaches my motives. I have no desire for office, not even the highest. The most exalted is but a prison, in which the incarcerated incumbent daily receives his cold, heartless visitants, marks his weary hours, and is cut off from the practical enjoyment of all the blessings of genuine freedom.

I am no candidate for any office in the gift of the people of these States, united or separated; I never wish, never expect, to be. Pass this bill, tranquillize the country, restore confidence and affection in the Union, and I am willing to go home to Ashland and renounce public service forever. I should there find in its groves, under its shades, on its lawns, 'mid my flocks and herds, in the bosom of my family, sincerity and truth, attachment and fidelity and gratitude, which I have not always found in the walks of public life. Yes, I have ambition; but it is the ambition of being the humble instrument, in the hands of Providence, to reconcile a divided people; once more to revive concord and harmony in a distracted land, — the pleasing ambition of contemplating the glorious spectacle of a free, united, prosperous, and fraternal people.

VALUE OF REPUTATION.

CHARLES PHILLIPS.

WHO shall estimate the cost of a priceless reputation, that impress which gives this human dross its currency, without which we stand despised, debased, depreciated? Who shall repair it if injured? Who can redeem it if lost? O, well and truly does the great philosopher of poetry esteem the world's wealth as "trash" in the comparison! Without it gold has no value; birth, no distinction; station, no dignity; beauty, no charm; age, no reverence. Without it every treasure impoverishes, every grace deforms, every dignity degrades, and all the arts, the decorations, and accomplishments of life stand, like the beacon-blaze upon a rock, warning the world that its approach is dangerous, that its contact is death.

The wretch without it is under eternal quarantine; no friend to greet, no home to harbour him. The voyage of his life becomes a joyless peril; and in the midst of all ambition can achieve, or avarice amass, or rapacity plunder, he tosses on the surge, a buoyant pestilence. But let me not degrade into the selfishness of individual safety or individual exposure this universal principle; it testifies a higher, a more ennobling origin.

It is this which, consecrating the humble circle of the hearth, will at times extend itself to the circumference of the horizon, which nerves the arm of the patriot to save his country, which lights the lamp of the philosopher to amend man, which, if it does not inspire, will at least invigorate, the martyr to merit immortality, which, when one world's agony is passed, and the glory of another is dawning, will prompt the prophet, even in his chariot of fire, and in his vision of Heaven, to bequeath to mankind the mantle of his memory! O, divine, O, delightful legacy of a spotless reputation! Rich is the inheritance it leaves; pious the example it testifies; pure, precious, and imperishable the example it inspires!

Can there be conceived a more atrocious injury than to filch from its possessor this inestimable jewel, to rob society of its charm and solitude of its solace; not only to outlaw life, but to attaint death, converting the very grave, the refuge of the sufferer, into the gate of infamy and shame? I can conceive few crimes beyond it. He who plunders my property takes from me that which can be repaired by time; but what period can repair a ruined reputation? He who maims my person affects that which medicine may remedy; but what herb has sovereignty over the wounds of slander? He who ridicules my poverty, or reproaches my profession, upbraids me with that which industry may retrieve and integrity may purify; but what riches shall redeem the bankrupt fame? What power shall blanch the sullied snow of character? There can be no injury more deadly. There can be no crime more cruel. It is without remedy. It is without antidote. It is without evasion.

The reptile, calumny, is ever on the watch. From

the fascination of its eye no activity can escape; from the venom of its fang no sanity can recover. It has no enjoyment but crime; it has no prey but virtue; it has no interval from the restlessness of its malice, save when, bloated with its victims, it grovels to disgorge them at the withered shrine where envy idolizes her own infirmities.

TOUSSAINT L'OUVERTURE.

WENDELL PHILLIPS.

IF I were to tell you the story of Napoleon, I should take it from the lips of Frenchmen, who find no language rich enough to paint the great captain of the nineteenth century. Were I to tell you the story of Washington, I should take it from your hearts, — you, who think no marble white enough on which to carve the name of the Father of his country. But I am to tell you the story of a negro, Toussaint L'Ouverture, who has left hardly one written line. I am to glean it from the reluctant testimony of his enemies, men who despised him because he was a negro and a slave, hated him because he had beaten them in battle.

Cromwell manufactured his own army. Napoleon, at the age of twenty-seven, was placed at the head of the best troops Europe ever saw. Cromwell never saw an army till he was forty; this man never saw a soldier till he was fifty. Cromwell manufactured his own army — out of what? Englishmen, — the best blood in Europe. Out of the middle class of Englishmen, — the best blood of the island. And with it he conquered what? Englishmen, — their equals. This man manufactured his army out of what? Out of what you call the despicable race of negroes, debased, demoralized by two hundred years of slavery, one hundred thousand of them imported into the island within four years, unable to speak a dialect intelligible even to each other. Yet out of this mixed, and, as you say, despicable mass he forged a thunderbolt and hurled it at what? At the proudest blood in Europe, the Spaniard, and sent him home conquered; at the most warlike blood in Europe, the French, and put them under his feet; at the pluckiest blood in Europe, the English, and they skulked home to Jamaica. Now, if Cromwell was a general, at least this man was a soldier.

Now, blue-eyed Saxon, proud of your race, go back with me to the commencement of the century, and select what statesman you please. Let him be either American or European; let him have a brain the result of six generations of culture; let him have the ripest training of university routine; let him add to it the better education of practical life; crown his temples with the silver locks of seventy years, and show me the man of Saxon lineage for whom his most sanguine admirer will wreathe a laurel, rich as embittered foes have placed on the brow of this negro, — rare military skill, profound knowledge of human nature, content to blot out all party distinctions, and trust a State to the blood of its sons, — anticipating Sir Robert Peel fifty years, and taking his station by the side of Roger Williams, before any Englishman or American had won the right; and yet this is the record which the history of rival States makes up for this inspired black of St. Domingo.

Some doubt the courage of the negro. Go to Hayti, and stand on those fifty thousand graves of the best soldiers France ever had, and ask them what they think of the negro's sword.

I would call him Napoleon, but Napoleon made his

way to empire over broken oaths and through a sea of blood. This man never broke his word. I would call him Cromwell, but Cromwell was only a soldier, and the State he founded went down with him into his grave. I would call him Washington, but the great Virginian held slaves. This man risked his empire rather than permit the slave-trade in the humblest village of his dominions.

You think me a fanatic, for you read history, not with your eyes but with your prejudices. But fifty years hence, when Truth gets a hearing, the Muse of history will put Phocion for the Greek, Brutus for the Roman, Hampden for England, Fayette for France, choose Washington as the bright consummate flower of our earlier civilization, then, dipping her pen in the sunlight, will write in the clear blue, above them all, the name of the soldier, the statesman, the martyr, TOUSSAINT L'OUVERTURE.

MASSACHUSETTS AND SOUTH CAROLINA.

DANIEL WEBSTER.

I SHALL not acknowledge that the honourable member goes before me in regard for whatever of distinguished talent, or distinguished character, South Carolina has produced. I claim part of the honour, I partake in the pride, of her great names. I claim them for countrymen, one and all; the Laurenses, the Rutledges, the Pinckneys, the Sumpters, the Marions, Americans all, whose fame is no more to be hemmed in by State lines, than their talents and patriotism were capable of being circumscribed within the same narrow limits. In their day and generation, they served and honoured the country, and the whole country; and their renown is of the treasures of the whole country. Him whose honoured name the gentleman himself bears, — does he esteem me less capable of gratitude for his patriotism, or sympathy for his sufferings, than if his eyes had first opened upon the light of Massachusetts, instead of South Carolina? Sir, does he suppose it in his power to exhibit a Carolina name so bright as to produce envy in my bosom?

No, Sir, increased gratification and delight, rather. I thank God that, if I am gifted with little of the spirit which is able to raise mortals to the skies, I have yet none, as I trust, of that other spirit which would drag Angels down. When I shall be found, Sir, in my place here in the Senate, or elsewhere, to sneer at public merit, because it happens to spring up beyond the little limits of my own State or neighbourhood; when I refuse, for any such cause, or for any cause, the homage due to American talent, to elevated patriotism, to sincere devotion to liberty and the country; or, if I see an uncommon endowment of Heaven, if I see extraordinary capacity and virtue in any son of the South, and if, moved by local prejudice or gangrened by State jealousy, I get up here to abate the tithe of a hair from his just character and just fame, may my tongue cleave to the roof of my mouth!

Sir, let me recur to pleasing recollections; let me indulge in refreshing remembrance of the past; let me remind you that, in early times, no States cherished greater harmony, both of principle and feeling, than Massachusetts and South Carolina. Would to God that harmony might again return! Shoulder to shoulder they went through the Revolution; hand in hand they stood round the administration of Washington, and felt his own great arm lean on them for support. Unkind feeling, if it exist, alienation and distrust, are the growth, unnatural to such soils, of false principles since sown. They are weeds, the seeds of which that same great arm never scattered.

Mr. President, I shall enter on no encomium upon Massachusetts; she needs none. There she is: behold her, and judge for yourselves. There is her history; the world knows it by heart. The past, at least, is secure. There is Boston, and Concord, and Lexington, and Bunker Hill; and there they will remain for ever. The bones of her sons, falling in the great struggle for Independence, now lie mingled with the soil of every State from New England to Georgia; and there they will lie for ever. And, Sir, where American Liberty raised its first voice, and where its youth was nurtured and sustained, there it still lives, in the strength of its manhood and full of its original spirit. If discord and disunion shall wound it; if party strife and blind ambition shall hawk at and tear it; if folly and madness, if uneasiness under salutary and necessary restraint, shall succeed in separating it from that Union by which alone its existence is made sure; it will stand, in the end, by the side of that cradle in which its infancy was rocked; it will stretch forth its arm, with whatever of vigour it may still retain, over the friends who gather round it; and it will fall at last, if fall it must, amidst the proudest monuments of its own glory, and on the very spot of its origin.

THE CHARGE OF THE LIGHT BRIGADE.

Alfred Tennyson.

Half a league, half a league,
 Half a league onward,
All in the valley of death
 Rode the six hundred.
Forward the Light Brigade!
Charge for the guns, he said.
Into the valley of death
 Rode the six hundred.

Forward the Light Brigade!
Was there a man dismay'd?
Not though the soldiers knew
 Some one had blunder'd.
Theirs not to make reply,
Theirs not to reason why,
Theirs but to do and die.
Into the valley of death
 Rode the six hundred.

Cannon to right of them,
Cannon to left of them,
Cannon in front of them
 Volley'd and thunder'd;
Storm'd at with shot and shell,
Boldly they rode and well,
Into the jaws of Death,
Into the mouth of Hell
 Rode the six hundred.

Flash'd all their sabres bare,
Flash'd as they turn'd in air,
Sabering the gunners there,
Charging an army, while
 All the world wonder'd:
Plunged in the battery-smoke,
Right through the line they broke;
Cossack and Russian
Reel'd from the sabre-stroke
 Shatter'd and sunder'd.
Then they rode back, but not,
 Not the six hundred.

Cannon to right of them,
Cannon to left of them,
Cannon behind them
 Volley'd and thunder'd;
Storm'd at with shot and shell,
While horse and hero fell,
They that had fought so well
Came through the jaws of Death
Back from the mouth of Hell,
All that was left of them,
 Left of six hundred.

When can their glory fade?
O, the wild charge they made!
 All the world wonder'd.
Honour the charge they made!
Honour the Light Brigade,
 Noble Six Hundred!

VII.

INVECTIVE, VEHEMENT, INDIGNANT.

CATILINE'S DEFIANCE.

GEORGE CROLY.

CONSCRIPT FATHERS:
I do not rise to waste the night in words;
Let that Plebeian talk, 'tis not my trade;
But here I stand for right, — let him show proofs, —
For Roman right, though none, it seems, dare stand
To take their share with me. Ay, cluster there!
Cling to your master, judges, Romans, slaves!
His charge is false; — I dare him to his proofs.
You have my answer. Let my actions speak!

But this I will avow, that I have scorn'd,
And still do scorn, to hide my sense of wrong.
Who brands me on the forehead, breaks my sword,
Or lays the bloody scourge upon my back,
Wrongs me not half so much as he who shuts
The gates of honour on me, — turning out
The Roman from his birthright; and for what?
To fling your offices to every slave!
Vipers, that creep where man disdains to climb,
And, having wound their loathsome track to the top
Of this huge, mouldering monument of Rome,
Hang hissing at the nobler man below. [*To the Senate.*

Come, consecrated Lictors, from your thrones;
Fling down your sceptres; take the rod and axe,
And make the murder as you make the law.

Banish'd from Rome! What's banish'd but set free
From daily contact of the things I loathe?
"Tried and convicted traitor!" Who says this?
Who'll prove it, at his peril, on my head?
Banish'd! I thank you for't: it breaks my chain!
I held some slack allegiance till this hour;
But now my sword's my own. Smile on, my Lords!
I scorn to count what feelings, wither'd hopes,
Strong provocations, bitter, burning wrongs,
I have within my heart's hot cells shut up,
To leave you in your lazy dignities.
But here I stand and scoff you! here I fling
Hatred and full defiance in your face!
Your Consul's merciful; — for this all thanks.
He dares not touch a hair of Catiline!

"Traitor!" I go; but, I return! This — trial!
Here I devote your Senate! I've had wrongs
To stir a fever in the blood of age,
Or make the infant's sinews strong as steel.
This day's the birth of sorrow; this hour's work
Will breed proscriptions! Look to your hearths, my Lords!
For there, henceforth, shall sit, for household gods,
Shapes hot from Tartarus; all shames and crimes;
Wan Treachery, with his thirsty dagger drawn;
Suspicion, poisoning his brother's cup;
Naked Rebellion, with the torch and axe,
Making his wild sport of your blazing thrones;
Till Anarchy comes down on you like night,
And Massacre seals Rome's eternal grave.

I go; but not to leap the gulf alone.
I go; but when I come, 'twill be the burst
Of ocean in the earthquake, — rolling back
In swift and mountainous ruin. Fare you well!
You build my funeral pile; but your best blood
Shall quench its flame! Back, slaves! [*To the Lictors.*
I will return.

SPARTACUS TO THE GLADIATORS AT CAPUA.

YE call me chief; and ye do well to call him chief who for twelve long years has met upon the arena every shape of man or beast the broad Empire of Rome could furnish, and who never yet lowered his arm. If there be one among you who can say that ever, in public fight or private brawl, my actions did belie my tongue, let him stand forth and say it. If there be three in all your company dare face me on the bloody sands, let them come on. And yet I was not always thus, — a hired butcher, a savage chief of still more savage men. My ancestors came from old Sparta, and settled among the vine-clad rocks and citron groves of Syrasella. My early life ran quiet as the brooks by which I sported; and when, at noon, I gathered the sheep beneath the shade, and played upon the shepherd's flute, there was a friend, the son of a neighbour, to join me in the pastime. We led our flocks to the same pasture, and partook together our rustic meal.

One evening, after the sheep were folded, and we were all seated beneath the myrtle which shaded our cottage, my grandsire, an old man, was telling of Marathon and Leuctra; and how, in ancient times, a little band of Spartans, in a defile of the mountains, had withstood a whole army. I did not then know what war was; but my cheeks burned, I know not why, and I clasped the knees of that venerable man, until my mother, parting the hair from off my forehead, kissed my throbbing temples, and bade me go to rest, and think no more of those old tales and savage wars.

That very night the Romans landed on our coast. I saw the breast that had nourished me trampled by the hoof of the war-horse, — the bleeding body of my father flung amidst the blazing rafters of our dwelling! To-day I killed a man in the arena; and, when I broke his helmet-clasps, behold! he was my friend. He knew me, smiled faintly, gasped, and died; — the same sweet smile upon his lips that I had marked, when, in adventurous boyhood, we scaled the lofty cliff to pluck the first ripe grapes, and bear them home in childish triumph! I told the prætor that the dead man had been my friend, generous and brave; and I begged that I might bear away the body, to burn it on a funeral pile, and mourn over its ashes. Ay! upon my knees, amid the dust and blood of the arena, I begged that poor boon, while all the assembled maids and matrons, and the holy virgins they call Vestals, and the rabble, shouted in derision, deeming it rare sport, forsooth, to see Rome's fiercest gladiator turn pale and tremble at sight of that piece of bleeding clay! And the prætor drew back as if I were pollution, and sternly said, "Let the carrion rot; there are no noble men but Romans."

And so, fellow-gladiators, must you, and so must I, die like dogs. O, Rome! Rome! thou hast been a tender nurse to me. Ay! thou hast given to that poor, gentle, timid shepherd lad, who never knew a harsher tone than a flute-note, muscles of iron and a heart of flint; taught him to drive the sword through plaited mail and links of rugged brass, and warm it in the marrow of his foe; — to gaze into the glaring eyeballs of the fierce Numidian lion, even as a boy upon a laughing girl! And he shall pay thee back, until the yellow Tiber is red as frothing wine, and in its deepest ooze thy life-blood lies curdled!

Ye stand here now like giants, as ye are! The strength of brass is in your toughened sinews, but to-morrow some Roman Adonis, breathing sweet perfume from his curly locks, shall with his lily fingers pat your red brawn, and bet his sesterces upon your blood. Hark! hear ye yon lion roaring in his den? 'Tis three days since he has tasted flesh; but to-morrow he shall break his fast upon yours, — and a dainty meal for him ye will be!

If ye are beasts, then stand here like fat oxen, waiting for the butcher's knife! If ye are men, follow me! Strike down yon guard, gain the mountain passes, and then do bloody work, as did your sires at old Thermopylæ! Is Sparta dead? Is the old Grecian spirit frozen in your veins, that you do crouch and cower like a belaboured hound beneath his master's lash? O, comrades! warriors! Thracians! if we must fight, let us fight for ourselves! If we must slaughter, let us slaughter our oppressors! If we must die, let it be under the clear sky, by the bright waters, in noble, honourable battle!

MARMION AND DOUGLAS.

Sir Walter Scott.

The train from out the castle drew,
But Marmion stopp'd to bid adieu:
"Though something I might plain," he said,
"Of cold respect to stranger guest,
Sent hither by your king's behest,
While in Tantallon's towers I stay'd,
Part we in friendship from your land,
And, noble Earl, receive my hand."

But Douglas round him drew his cloak,
Folded his arms, and thus he spoke:
"My manors, halls, and bowers shall still
Be open, at my sovereign's will,
To each one whom he lists, howe'er

Unmeet to be the owner's peer.
My castles are my king's alone
From turret to foundation-stone;
The hand of Douglas is his own,
And never shall in friendly grasp
The hand of such as Marmion clasp."

Burn'd Marmion's swarthy cheek like fire,
And shook his very frame for ire,
And, "This to me!" he said;
"An 'twere not for thy hoary beard,
Such hand as Marmion's had not spared
To cleave the Douglas' head!
And, first, I tell thee, haughty Peer,
He who does England's message here,
Although the meanest in her State,
May well, proud Angus, be thy mate:
And, Douglas, more I tell thee here,
Even in thy pitch of pride,
Here in thy hold, thy vassals near,
(Nay, never look upon your lord,
And lay your hands upon your sword,)
I tell thee, thou'rt defied!
And, if thou said'st I am not peer
To any lord in Scotland here,
Lowland or Highland, far or near,
Lord Angus, thou hast lied!"

On the Earl's cheek the flush of rage
O'ercame the ashen hue of age;
Fierce he broke forth, "And darest thou then
To beard the lion in his den,
The Douglas in his hall?
And hopest thou hence unscathed to go?
No, by Saint Bride of Bothwell, no!
Up drawbridge, grooms, — what, Warder, ho!
Let the portcullis fall."

Lord Marmion turn'd, — well was his need! —
And dash'd the rowels in his steed,
Like arrow through the archway sprung;
The ponderous gate behind him rung:
To pass there was such scanty room,
The bars, descending, razed his plume.

The steed along the drawbridge flies,
Just as it trembled on the rise;
Not lighter does the swallow skim
Along the smooth lake's level brim;
And, when Lord Marmion reach'd his band,
He halts, and turns with clenchèd hand,
And shout of loud defiance pours,
And shook his gauntlet at the towers.

THE SEMINOLE'S REPLY

GEORGE W. PATTEN.

BLAZE, with your serried columns!
  I will not bend the knee!
The shackles ne'er again shall bind
  The arm which now is free.
I've mail'd it with the thunder,
  When the tempest mutter'd low;
And, where it falls, ye well may dread
  The lightning of its blow!

I've scared ye in the city,
  I've scalp'd ye on the plain;
Go, count your chosen, where they fell
  Beneath my leaden rain!
I scorn your proffer'd treaty!
  The pale-face I defy!
Revenge is stamp'd upon my spear,
  And blood's my battle cry!

Some strike for hope of booty,
  Some to defend their all;
I battle for the joy I have
  To see the white man fall:
I love, among the wounded,
  To hear his dying moan,
And catch, while chanting at his side,
  The music of his groan.

Ye've trail'd me through the forest,
  Ye've track'd me o'er the stream;
And, struggling through the everglade,
  Your bristling bayonets gleam;
But I stand as should the warrior,
  With his rifle and his spear;
The scalp of vengeance still is red,
  And warns ye, — Come not here!

I loathe ye in my bosom,
  I scorn ye with mine eye,
And I'll taunt ye with my latest breath,
  And fight ye till I die!
I ne'er will ask ye quarter,
  And I ne'er will be your slave;
But I'll swim the sea of slaughter,
  Till I sink beneath its wave!

HORRORS OF SAVAGE WARFARE.

William Pitt, Earl of Chatham.

I am astonished, shocked, to hear such principles confessed, to hear them avowed in this House, or even in this country! principles equally unconstitutional, inhuman, and unchristian!

My Lords, I did not intend to trespass again upon your attention, but I cannot repress my indignation, —

I feel myself impelled by every duty. We are called upon as members of this House, as men, as Christian men, to protest against such notions, standing near the throne, polluting the ear of Majesty. "That God and Nature put into our hands!" * I know not what ideas that Lord may entertain of God and Nature; but I know that such abominable principles are equally abhorrent to religion and humanity.

What! attribute the sacred sanction of God and Nature to the massacres of the Indian scalping-knife, — to the cannibal savage, torturing, murdering, roasting, and eating, — literally, my Lords, *eating* the mangled victims of his barbarous battles! Such horrible notions shock every precept of religion revealed or natural, and every generous feeling of humanity; and, my Lords, they shock every sentiment of honour; they shock me as a lover of honourable war, and a detester of murderous barbarity.

These abominable principles, and this more abominable avowal of them, demand the most decisive indignation. I call upon the Right-Reverend Bench, those holy ministers of the Gospel, and pious pastors of our Church, — I conjure them to join in the holy work, and to vindicate the religion of their God. I appeal to the wisdom and the law of this Learned Bench to defend and support the justice of their country. I call upon the Bishops to interpose the unsullied sanctity of their lawn, upon the learned Judges to interpose the purity of their ermine, to save us from this pollution. I call upon the honour of your Lordships to reverence the

* Lord Suffolk, one of the Secretaries of State, defending the employment of Indians in the American war, had declared, in the House of Lords, that "it was perfectly justifiable to use all the means that *God and Nature put into our hands.*"

dignity of your ancestors, and to maintain your own. I call upon the spirit and humanity of my country to vindicate the national character. I invoke the genius of the Constitution.

From the tapestry that adorns these walls, the immortal ancestor of this noble Lord frowns with indignation at *the disgrace of his country!* In vain he led your victorious fleets against the boasted Armada of Spain; in vain he defended and established the honour, the liberties, the religion, the Protestant religion of his country, against the arbitrary cruelties of Popery and the Inquisition, if these worse than popish and inquisitorial practices are let loose amongst us, to turn forth into our settlements, among our ancient friends and relations, the merciless cannibal, thirsting for the blood of man, woman, and child.

To send forth the infidel savage, — against whom? Against your Protestant brethren! to lay waste their country, to desolate their dwellings, and extirpate their race and name, with these horrible hell-hounds of savage war! — *hell-hounds*, I say, *of savage war!* Spain armed herself with blood-hounds to extirpate the wretched natives of America; and we improve on the inhuman example of even Spanish cruelty: we turn loose these savage hell-hounds against our brethren and countrymen in America, of the same language, laws, liberties, and religion; endeared to us by every tie that should sanctify humanity.

My Lords, this awful subject, so important to our honour, our Constitution, and our religion, demands the most solemn and effectual inquiry. And I again call upon your Lordships, and the united powers of the State, to examine it thoroughly and decisively, and to stamp upon it an indelible stigma of the public abhorrence. And I again implore those holy prelates of our religion to do away these iniquities from among us. Let them perform a lustration; let them purify this House and this country from this sin.

My Lords, I am old and weak, and at present unable to say more; but my feelings and my indignation were too strong to have said less. I could not have slept this night in my bed, or have reposed my head on my pillow, without giving this vent to my eternal abhorrence of such preposterous and enormous principles.

ARRAIGNMENT OF MINISTERS.

EDMUND BURKE.

I CONFESS I feel a degree of disgust, almost leading to despair, at the manner in which we are acting in the great exigencies of our country. There is now a bill in this House, appointing a rigid inquisition into the minutest detail of our offices at home. The collection of sixteen millions annually, — a collection on which the public greatness, safety, and credit have their reliance; the whole order of criminal jurisprudence, which holds together society itself, — has at no time obliged us to call forth such powers; no, nor any thing like them. There is not a principle of the law and Constitution of this country that is not subverted to favour the execution of that project.

And for what is all this apparatus of bustle and terror? Is it because any thing substantial is expected from it? No. The stir and bustle itself is the end proposed. The eye-servants of a short-sighted master will employ themselves, not on what is most essential to his affairs, but on what is nearest to his ken. Great difficulties have given a just value to economy; and our Minister of the day must be an economist, whatever it may cost us. But where is he to exert his talents? At home, to be sure; for where else can he obtain a profitable credit for their exertion? It is nothing to him, whether the object on which he works under our eye be promising or not. If he does not obtain any public benefit, he may make regulations without end. Those are sure to pay in present expectation, whilst the effect is at a distance, and may be the concern of other times and other men.

On these principles he chooses to suppose (for he does not pretend more than to suppose) a naked possibility, that he shall draw some resource out of crumbs dropped from the trenchers of penury; that something shall be laid in store from the short allowance of revenue officers, overladen with duty, and famished for want of bread. From the marrowless bones of these skeleton establishments, by the use of every sort of cutting and every sort of fretting tool, he flatters himself that he may chip and rasp an empirical alimentary powder, to diet into some similitude of health and substance the languishing chimeras of fraudulent reformation.

Whilst he is thus employed according to his policy and to his taste, he has not leisure to inquire into those abuses in India that are drawing off money by millions from the treasures of this country, and are exhausting the vital juices from members of the State, where the public inanition is far more sorely felt than in the local exchequer of England. Not content with winking at these abuses, whilst he attempts to squeeze the laborious, ill-paid drudges of English revenue, he lavishes in one act of corrupt prodigality, upon those who never served the public in any honest occupation at all, an annual income equal to two-thirds of the whole collection of the revenues of this kingdom.

Actuated by the same principle of choice, he has now on the anvil another scheme, full of difficulty and desperate hazard, which totally alters the commercial relation of two kingdoms; and, what end soever it shall have, may bequeath a legacy of heart-burning and discontent to one of the countries, perhaps to both, to be perpetuated to the latest posterity. This project is also undertaken on the hope of profit. It is provided that, out of some (I know not what) remains of the Irish hereditary revenue, a fund at some time, and of some sort, should be applied to the protection of the Irish trade.

Here we are commanded again to task our faith, and to persuade ourselves that, out of the surplus of deficiency, out of the savings of habitual and systematic prodigality, the Minister of wonders will provide support for this nation, sinking under the mountainous load of two hundred and thirty millions of debt. But whilst we look with pain at his desperate and laborious trifling, whilst we are apprehensive that he will break his back in stooping to pick up chaff and straws, he recovers himself at an elastic bound, and, with a broadcast swing of his arm, he squanders over his Indian field a sum far greater than the clear produce of the whole hereditary revenue of the kingdom of Ireland.

Strange as this scheme of conduct in Ministry is, and inconsistent with all just policy, it is still true to itself, and faithful to its own perverted order. Those who are bountiful to crimes will be rigid to merit, and penurious to service. Their penury is even held out as a blind and cover to their prodigality. The economy of injustice is, to furnish resources for the fund of corruption.

Then they pay off their protection to great crimes and great criminals, by being inexorable to the paltry frailties of little men; and these modern flagellants are sure, with a rigid fidelity, to whip their own enormities on the vicarious back of every small offender.

REVOLUTIONARY DESPERADOES.

SIR JAMES MACKINTOSH.

THE French Revolution began with great and fatal errors. These errors produced atrocious crimes. A mild and feeble monarchy was succeeded by a bloody anarchy, which very shortly gave birth to military despotism. France, in a few years, described the whole circle of human society. All this was in the order of Nature. When every principle which enables some men to command, and disposes others to obey, was extirpated from the mind by atrocious theories, and still more atrocious examples; when every old institution was trampled down with contumely; and every new institution was covered in its cradle with blood; there remained only one principle strong enough to hold society together,—a principle utterly incompatible, indeed, with liberty, and unfriendly to civilization itself,—a tyrannical and barbarous principle, but, in that miserable condition of human affairs, a refuge from still more intolerable evils;—I mean the principle of military power, which gains strength from that confusion and bloodshed in which all other elements of society are dissolved, and which, in these terrible extremities, is the cement that preserves it from total destruction.

Under such circumstances, Buonaparte usurped the supreme power in France;—I say *usurped*, because an illegal assumption of power is an usurpation. But *usurpation*, in its strongest moral sense, is scarcely applicable to a period of lawless and savage anarchy. But, though the government of Buonaparte has silenced the Revolutionary factions, it has not extinguished them. No human power could re-impress upon the minds of men all those sentiments and opinions which the sophistry and anarchy of fourteen years had obliterated.

As for the wretched populace who were made the blind and senseless instrument of so many crimes,— whose frenzy can now be reviewed by a good mind, with scarcely any moral sentiment but that of compassion, — that miserable multitude of beings, scarcely human, have already fallen into a brutish forgetfulness of the very atrocities which they themselves perpetrated. They have passed from senseless rage to stupid quiet: their delirium is followed by lethargy.

In a word, Gentlemen, the great body of the people of France have been severely trained in those convulsions and proscriptions which are the school of slavery. They are capable of no mutinous, and even of no bold and manly political sentiments. But it is otherwise with those who have been the actors and leaders in the scene of blood: it is otherwise with the numerous agents of the most indefatigable, searching, multiform, and omnipresent tyranny that ever existed, which pervaded every class of society, — which had ministers and victims in every village in France.

Some of them, indeed, — the basest of the race, — the Sophists, the Rhetors, the Poet-laureates of murder, who were cruel only from cowardice and calculating selfishness, are perfectly willing to transfer their venal pens to any government that does not disdain their infamous support. These men, republicans from servility, who published rhetorical panegyrics on massacre, and who reduced plunder to a system of ethics, are as ready to preach slavery as anarchy.

But the more daring — I had almost said the more respectable — ruffians cannot so easily bend their heads under the yoke. These fierce spirits leave the luxuries of servitude to the mean and dastardly hypocrites, — to the Belials and Mammons of the infernal faction. They pursue their old end of tyranny under their old pretext of liberty. The recollections of their unbounded power renders every inferior condition irksome and vapid; and their former atrocities form, if I may so speak, a sort of moral destiny which irresistibly impels them to the perpetration of new crimes. They have no place left for penitence on Earth: they labour under the most awful proscription of opinion that ever was pronounced against human beings: they have cut down every bridge by which they could retreat into the society of men.

Awakened from their dream of democracy, — the noise subsided that deafened their ears to the voice of humanity, — the film fallen from their eyes which hid from them the blackness of their own deeds, — haunted by the memory of their inexpiable guilt, — condemned daily to look on the faces of those whom their hand has made widows and orphans, — they are goaded and scourged by these real furies, and hurried into the tumult of new crimes, to drown the cries of remorse, or, if they be too depraved for remorse, to silence the curses of mankind. Tyrannical power is their only refuge from the just vengeance of their fellow-creatures: murder is their only means of usurping power. They have no taste, no occupation, no pursuit, but power and blood. If their hands are tied, they must at least have the luxury of murderous projects. They have drunk too deeply of human blood ever to relinquish their cannibal appetite.

Such a faction exists in France: it is numerous; it is powerful; and it has a principle of fidelity stronger than any that ever held together a society. They are banded together by despair of forgiveness, — by the unanimous detestation of mankind. They are now restrained by a severe and stern government: but they still meditate the renewal of insurrection and massacre; and they are prepared to renew the worst and most atrocious of their crimes, — that crime against posterity and against human nature itself, — the crime of degrading and prostituting the sacred name of liberty. I must own that, however paradoxical it may appear, I should almost think, not worse, but more meanly of them, if it were otherwise. I must then think them destitute of that, — I will not call it courage, because that is the name of a virtue, — but of that ferocious energy which alone rescues ruffians from contempt. If they were destitute of that which is the heroism of murderers, they would be the lowest as well as the most abominable of mankind. It is impossible to conceive any thing more despicable than the wretches who, after playing the tyrannicides to women and children, become the supple and fawning slaves of the first government that knows how to wield the scourge with a firm hand.

FRAUDULENT PARTY OUTCRIES.

Daniel Webster.

Mr. President: On the great questions which occupy us, we all look for some decisive movement of public opinion. As I wish that movement to be free, intelligent, and unbiased, the true manifestation of the public will, I desire to prepare the country for another appeal, which I perceive is about to be made to popular prejudice, another attempt to obscure all distinct views of the public good, by loud cries against false danger, and by exciting the passions of one class against another. I am not mistaken in the omen; I see the magazine whence the weapons of this warfare are to be drawn. I already hear the din of the hammering of arms preparatory to the combat. They may be such arms, perhaps, as reason and justice and honest patriotism cannot resist. Every effort at resistance, it is possible, may be feeble and powerless; but, for one, I shall make an effort, — an effort to be begun now, and to be carried on and continued, with untiring zeal, till the end of the contest comes.

Sir, I see, in those vehicles which carry to the people sentiments from high places, plain declarations that the present controversy is but a strife between one part of the community and another. I hear it boasted as the unfailing security, the solid ground, never to be shaken, on which recent measures rest, *that the poor naturally hate the rich.* I know that, under the cover of the roofs of the Capitol, within the last twenty-four hours, among men sent here to devise means for the public safety and the public good, it has been vaunted forth, as matter of boast and triumph, that one cause existed powerful enough to support every thing, and to defend every thing; and that was, *the natural hatred of the poor to the rich.*

Sir, I pronounce the author of such sentiments to be guilty of attempting a detestable fraud on the community; a double fraud; a fraud which is to cheat men out of their property and out of the earnings of their labour, by first cheating them out of their understandings.

"The natural hatred of the poor to the rich!" Sir, it shall not be till the last moment of my existence, — it shall be only when I am drawn to the verge of oblivion, when I shall cease to have respect or affection for any thing on Earth, — that I will believe the people of the United States capable of being effectually deluded, cajoled, and *driven about in herds*, by such abominable frauds as this. If they shall sink to that point; if they so far cease to be men, thinking men, intelligent men, as to yield to such pretences and such clamour, — they will be slaves already; slaves to their own passions, slaves to the fraud and knavery of pretended friends. They will deserve to be blotted out of all the records of freedom; they ought not to dishonour the cause of self-government, by attempting any longer to exercise it; they ought to keep their unworthy hands entirely off from the cause of republican liberty, if they are capable of being the victims of artifices so shallow, of tricks so stale, so threadbare, so often practised, so much worn out, on serfs and slaves.

"The natural hatred of the poor against the rich!" "The danger of a moneyed aristocracy!" "A power as great and dangerous as that resisted by the Revolution!" "A call to a new Declaration of Independence!" Sir, I admonish the people against the objects of outcries like these. I admonish every industrious labourer in the country to be on his guard against such delusion. I tell him the attempt is to play off his passions against his interests, and to prevail on him, in the name of liberty, to destroy all the fruits of liberty; in the name of patriotism, to injure and afflict his country; and, in the name of his own independence, to destroy that very independence, and make him a beggar and a slave. Has he a dollar? He is advised to do that which will destroy half its value. Has he hands to labour? Let him rather fold them, and sit still, than be pushed on, by fraud and artifice, to support measures which will render his labour useless and hopeless.

INDIGNATION OF A HIGH-MINDED SPANIARD.

WORDSWORTH.

We can endure that he should waste our lands,
Despoil our temples, and by sword and flame
Return us to the dust from which we came;
Such food a Tyrant's appetite demands:
And we can brook the thought that by his hands
Spain may be overpower'd, and he possess,
For his delight, a solemn wilderness
Where all the brave lie dead. But, when of bands
Which he will break for us he dares to speak,
Of benefits, and of a future day
When our enlighten'd minds shall bless his sway;
Then, the strain'd heart of fortitude proves weak;
Our groans, our blushes, our pale cheeks declare
That he has power to inflict what we lack strength to bear.

VIII.

LIVELY, JOYOUS, GAY.

L'ALLEGRO.

JOHN MILTON.

HASTE thee, nymph, and bring with thee
Jest and youthful Jollity,
Quips, and cranks, and wanton wiles,
Nods, and becks, and wreathèd smiles,
Such as hang on Hebe's cheek,
And love to live in dimple sleek;
Sport, that wrinkled Care derides,
And Laughter holding both his sides.
Come, and trip it as you go
On the light fantastic toe;
And in thy right hand lead with thee
The mountain nymph, sweet Liberty:
And, if I give thee honour due,
Mirth, admit me of thy crew,
To live with her, and live with thee,
In unreprovèd pleasures free;
To hear the lark begin his flight,
And singing startle the dull night,
From his watch-tower in the skies,
Till the dappled dawn doth rise.

Then to come, in spite of sorrow,
And at my window bid good-morrow,
Through the sweet-brier, or the vine,
Or the twisted eglantine;

While the cock with lively din
Scatters the rear of darkness thin,
And to the stack, or the barn-door,
Stoutly struts his dames before:
Oft listening how the hounds and horn
Cheerily rouse the slumbering morn,
From the side of some hoar hill,
Through the high wood echoing shrill;
Sometimes walking not unseen
By hedgerow elms, on hillocks green,
Right against the eastern gate,
Where the great Sun begins his state,
Robed in flames and amber light,
The clouds in thousand liveries dight;
While the ploughman near at hand
Whistles o'er the furrow'd land,
And the milkmaid singeth blithe,
And the mower whets his scythe,
And every shepherd tells his tale
Under the hawthorn in the dale.

Straight mine eye hath caught new pleasures,
While the landscape round it measures;
Russet lawns and fallows gray
Where the nibbling flocks do stray;
Mountains on whose barren breast
The labouring clouds do often rest;
Meadows trim with daisies pied;
Shallow brooks, and rivers wide:
Towers and battlements it sees
Bosom'd high in tufted trees,
Where perhaps some beauty lies,
The cynosure of neighbouring eyes.
Sometimes, with secure delight,
The upland hamlets will invite,
When the merry bells ring round,
And the jocund rebecks sound

To many a youth and many a maid,
Dancing in the checker'd shade;
And young and old come forth to play
On a sunshine holiday.

Tower'd cities please us then,
And the busy hum of men,
Where throngs of knights and barons bold
In weeds of peace high triumphs hold,
With store of ladies, whose bright eyes
Rain influence, and judge the prize
Of wit or arms, while both contend
To win her grace whom all commend.
There let Hymen oft appear,
In saffron robe, with taper clear,
And pomp and feast and revelry,
With masque and antique pageantry;
Such sights as youthful poets dream
On summer eves by haunted stream.
Then to the well-trod stage anon,
If Jonson's learnèd sock be on,
Or sweetest Shakespeare, Fancy's child,
Warble his native wood-notes wild.
These delights if thou canst give,
Mirth, with thee I mean to live.

THE DAFFODILS.

WORDSWORTH.

I WANDER'D lonely as a cloud
That floats on high o'er vales and hills,
When all at once I saw a crowd,
A host, of golden daffodils;
Beside the lake, beneath the trees,
Fluttering and dancing in the breeze.

Continuous as the stars that shine
And twinkle on the milky way,
They stretch'd in never-ending line
Along the margin of the bay:
Ten thousand saw I at a glance,
Tossing their heads in sprightly dance.

The waves beside them danced; but they
Out-did the sparkling waves in glee:
A poet could not but be gay,
In such a jocund company:
I gazed — and gazed — but little thought
What wealth the show to me had brought:

For oft, when on my couch I lie
In vacant or in pensive mood,
They flash upon that inward eye
Which is the bliss of solitude;
And then my heart with pleasure fills,
And dances with the daffodils.

YOUNG LOCHINVAR.

SIR WALTER SCOTT.

O, YOUNG Lochinvar is come out of the West!
Through all the wide border his steed was the best;
And save his good broadsword he weapons had none;
He rode all unarm'd and he rode all alone.
So faithful in love and so dauntless in war,
There never was knight like the young Lochinvar.

He stay'd not for brake, and he stopp'd not for stone;
He swam the Eske river where ford there was none;
But, ere he alighted at Netherby gate,
The bride had consented, — the gallant came late;
For a laggard in love and a dastard in war
Was to wed the fair Ellen of brave Lochinvar.

So boldly he enter'd the Netherby hall,
Among bridesmen, and kinsmen, and brothers, and all:
Then spoke the bride's father, his hand on his sword, —
For the poor craven bridegroom said never a word, —
"O come ye in peace here, or come ye in war,
Or to dance at our bridal, young Lord Lochinvar?"

"I long woo'd your daughter; — my suit you denied:
Love swells like the Solway, but ebbs like its tide;
And now I am come, with this lost love of mine,
To lead but one measure, — drink one cup of wine.
There be maidens in Scotland, more lovely by far,
That would gladly be bride to the young Lochinvar."

The bride kiss'd the goblet; the knight took it up;
He quaff'd off the wine, and he threw down the cup;
She look'd down to blush, and she look'd up to sigh,
With a smile on her lip and a tear in her eye;
He took her soft hand ere her mother could bar; —
"Now tread we a measure!" said young Lochinvar.

So stately his form and so lovely her face,
That never a hall such a galliard did grace;
While her mother did fret, and her father did fume,
And the bridegroom stood dangling his bonnet and plume,
And the bridemaidens whisper'd, "'twere better, by far,
To have match'd our fair cousin with young Lochinvar."

One touch to her hand, and one word in her ear,
When they reach'd the hall door, where the charger stood near;
So light to the croup the fair lady he swung,
So light to the saddle before her he sprung; —
"She is won! we are gone, over bank, bush, and scaur;
They'll have fleet steeds that follow!" quoth young Lochinvar.

There was mounting 'mong Græmes of the Netherby clan;
Fosters, Fenwicks, and Musgraves, they rode and they ran;

There was racing and chasing on Cannobie lea,
But the lost bride of Netherby ne'er did they see.
So daring in love, and so dauntless in war;
Have ye e'er heard of gallant like young Lochinvar?

A MORNING RIDE.

From "THE WHEELMAN."

UP with the lark in the first flush of morning,
Ere the world wakes to its work or its play;
Off for a spin to the wide-stretching country,
Far from the close, stifling city away.

A spring to the saddle, a spurt with the pedal,
The roadway is flying from under my wheel:
With motions so sprightly, with heart beating lightly,
How glorious to master this creature of steel!

Now mounting the hill-slope with slow, steady toiling,
Each turn of the wheel brings us nearer the goal;
And so on life's journey 'tis patient endeavour
That opens the path to the conquering soul.

The summit surmounted, we're now wildly dashing
Through woodland and meadow, past farm-house and dell;
Inhaling the breath of the field and the forest,
Keeping time as we glide to the tinkling cow-bell.

Lo! at length in the east, 'mid the radiant glory,
Great Phœbus Apollo looks forth, bright and fair,

Attended by cloudlets all roseate and golden;
  O, joy to be out on a morning so rare!

Now slowly; whoa, Reindeer! here comes a fair milkmaid:
  Pure milk through a straw is refreshing, I ween;
And so are the blushes of pure, happy girlhood;
  Then here's to your health and your sweetness, my queen!

Once more in the saddle, we're bounding on homeward,
  Our frame all aglow with this excellent sport;
Now coasting, now climbing, then racing and beating
  Some young rustic jockey in metre so short,

That in furious rage he whips and he lashes:
  But, 'tis useless, you see, my fine fellow, say we,
As we dash along onward still faster and faster,
  Hoping next time that he not so foolish will be.

As we mount the last hill, to the smoke-clouded city,
  Just beginning to boil with its great human tide,
It calls us to toil, and to enter the conflict;
  So endeth this morning our twenty-mile ride.

I'M WITH YOU ONCE AGAIN.

G. P. Morris.

I'm with you once again, my friends;
  No more my footsteps roam;
Where it began my journey ends,
  Amid the scenes of home.

No other clime has skies so blue,
  Or streams so broad and clear;
And where are hearts so warm and true
  As those that meet me here?

Since last, with spirits wild and free,
  I press'd my native strand,
I've wander'd many miles at sea,
  And many miles on land:
I've seen fair regions of the Earth
  With rude commotion torn,
Which taught me how to prize the worth
  Of that where I was born.

In other countries, when I heard
  The language of my own,
How fondly each familiar word
  Awoke an answering tone!
But, when our woodland songs were sung
  Upon a foreign mart,
The vows that falter'd on the tongue
  With rapture fill'd my heart.

My native land, I turn to you
  With blessing and with prayer,
Where man is brave and woman true,
  And free as mountain air.
Long may our flag in triumph wave
  Against the world combined,
And friends a welcome, foes a grave,
  Within our borders find!

THE LAST LEAF.

OLIVER WENDELL HOLMES.

I SAW him once before,
As he pass'd by the door;
    And again
The pavement-stones resound
As he totters o'er the ground
    With his cane.

They say that in his prime,
Ere the pruning-knife of Time
 Cut him down,
Not a better man was found
By the crier on his round
 Through the town.

But now he walks the streets,
And he looks at all he meets
 So forlorn;
And he shakes his feeble head,
That it seems as if he said,
 "They are gone."

The mossy marbles rest
On the lips that he has press'd
 In their bloom;
And the names he loved to hear
Have been carved for many a year
 On the tomb.

My grandmamma has said,—
Poor old lady! she is dead
 Long ago,—
That he had a Roman nose,
And his cheek was like a rose
 In the snow.

But now his nose is thin,
And it rests upon his chin
 Like a staff;
And a crook is in his back,
And a melancholy crack
 In his laugh.

I know it is a sin
For me to sit and grin
 At him here;
But the old three-corner'd hat
And the breeches, and all that,
 Are so queer!

And, if I should live to be
The last leaf upon the tree
 In the Spring,
Let them smile as I do now,
At the old forsaken bough
 Where I cling.

SONG OF THE BROOK.

ALFRED TENNYSON.

I COME from haunts of coot and hern:
 I make a sudden sally
And sparkle out among the fern,
 To bicker down a valley.

By thirty hills I hurry down,
 Or slip between the ridges,
By twenty thorps, a little town,
 And half a hundred bridges.

Till last by Philip's farm I flow
 To join the brimming river,
For men may come and men may go,
 But I go on forever.

I chatter over stony ways,
  In little sharps and trebles,
I bubble into eddying bays,
  I babble on the pebbles.

With many a curve my banks I fret
  By many a field and fallow,
And many a fairy foreland set
  With willow-weed and mallow.

I chatter, chatter, as I flow
  To join the brimming river;
For men may come and men may go,
  But I go on forever.

I wind about, and in and out,
  With here a blossom sailing,
And here and there a lusty trout,
  And here and there a grayling;

And here and there a foamy flake
  Upon me, as I travel
With many a silvery waterbreak
  Above the golden gravel;

And draw them all along, and flow
  To join the brimming river;
For men may come and men may go,
  But I go on forever.

I steal by lawns and grassy plots;
  I slide by hazel covers;
I move the sweet forget-me-nots
  That grow for happy lovers:

I slip, I slide, I gloom, I glance,
  Among my skimming swallows;
I make the netted sunbeams dance
  Against my sandy shallows:

I murmur under Moon and stars
  In brambly wildernesses;
I linger by my shingly bars;
  I loiter round my cresses;

And out again I curve and flow
  To join the brimming river;
For men may come and men may go,
  But I go on forever.

A PSALM OF LIFE.

H. W. LONGFELLOW.

TELL me not, in mournful numbers,
  "Life is but an empty dream!
For the soul is dead that slumbers,
  And things are not what they seem."

Life is real! life is earnest!
  And the grave is not its goal;
"Dust thou art, to dust returnest,"
  Was not spoken of the soul.

Not enjoyment, and not sorrow,
  Is our destined end or way;
But to act, that each to-morrow,
  Find us further than to-day.

Art is long, and Time is fleeting,
  And our hearts, though stout and brave,
Still, like muffled drums, are beating,
  Funeral marches to the grave.

In the world's broad field of battle,
  In the bivouac of Life,
Be not like dumb, driven cattle!
  Be a hero in the strife!

Trust no Future, howe'er pleasant!
  Let the dead Past bury its dead!
Act, — act in the living Present!
  Heart within, and God o'erhead.

Lives of great men all remind us
  We can make our lives sublime,
And, departing, leave behind us
  Footprints on the sands of time;

Footprints that perhaps another,
  Sailing o'er life's solemn main,
A forlorn and shipwreck'd brother,
  Seeing, shall take heart again.

Let us, then, be up and doing,
  With a heart for any fate;
Still achieving, still pursuing,
  Learn to labour and to wait.

THE BOYS.

O. W. Holmes.

Has there any old fellow got mix'd with the boys?
If he has, take him out, without making a noise.
Hang the almanac's cheat and the catalogue's spite!
Old Time is a liar! we're twenty to-night!

We're twenty! We're twenty! Who says we are more?
He's tipsy, — young jackanapes! — show him the door!
"Gray temples at twenty?" — Yes! white if we please;
Where the snow-flakes fall thickest there's nothing can freeze!

Was it snowing I spoke of? Excuse the mistake!
Look close, — you will not see a sign of a flake!
We want some new garlands for those we have shed,
And these are white roses in place of the red.

We've a trick, we young fellows, you may have been told,
Of talking, in public, as if we were old;
That boy we call "Doctor," and this we call "Judge";
It's a neat little fiction, — of course its all fudge.

That fellow's the "Speaker," the one on the right;
"Mr. Mayor," my young one, how are you to-night?
That's our "Member of Congress," we say when we chaff;
There's the "Reverend," — what's his name? — don't make
me laugh.

That boy with the grave mathematical look
Made believe he had written a wonderful book,
And the Royal Society thought it was true!
So they chose him right in, — a good joke it was too!

There's a boy, we pretend, with a three-decker brain,
That could harness a team with a logical chain;
When he spoke of our manhood in syllabled fire,
We call'd him "The Justice," but now he's the "Squire."

And there's a nice youngster of excellent pith;
Fate tried to conceal him by naming him Smith;
But he shouted a song for the brave and the free, —
Just read on his medal, "My country," "of thee!"

You hear that boy laughing? You think he's all fun;
But the angels laugh too at the good he has done;
The children laugh loud as they troop to his call,
And the poor man that knows him laughs loudest of all!

Yes, we're boys, — always playing with tongue or with pen;
And I sometimes have ask'd, Shall we ever be men?
Shall we always be youthful, and laughing, and gay,
Till the last dear companion drops smiling away?

Then here's to our boyhood, its gold and its gray!
The stars of its Winter, the dews of its May!
And, when we have done with our life-lasting toys,
Dear Father, take care of Thy children, THE BOYS!

EXPOSTULATION AND REPLY.

WORDSWORTH.

"WHY, William, on that old gray stone,
Thus for the length of half a day,
Why, William, sit you thus alone,
And dream your time away?

Where are your books? that light bequeath'd
To Beings else forlorn and blind!
Up! up! and drink the spirit breathed
From dead men to their kind.

You look round on your Mother Earth,
As if she for no purpose bore you;
As if you were her first-born birth,
And none had lived before you!"

One morning thus, by Esthwaite lake,
When life was sweet, I knew not why,
To me my good friend Matthew spake,
And thus I made reply:

"The eye — it cannot choose but see;
We cannot bid the ear be still;
Our bodies feel, where'er they be,
Against or with our will.

Nor less I deem that there are Powers
Which of themselves our minds impress;
That we can feed this mind of ours
In a wise passiveness.

Think you, 'mid all this mighty sum
Of things for ever speaking,
That nothing of itself will come,
But we must still be seeking?

Then ask not wherefore, here, alone,
Conversing as I may,
I sit upon this old gray stone,
And dream my time away."

THE TABLES TURNED.

Up! up! my Friend, and quit your books,
Or surely you'll grow double:
Up! up! my Friend, and clear your looks;
Why all this toil and trouble?

The Sun, above the mountain's head,
A freshening lustre mellow
Through all the long green fields has spread,
His first sweet evening yellow.

Books! 'tis a dull and endless strife:
Come, hear the woodland linnet,
How sweet his music! on my life,
There's more of wisdom in it.

And hark, how blithe the throstle sings!
He, too, is no mean preacher:
Come forth into the light of things,
Let Nature be your teacher.

She has a world of ready wealth,
Our minds and hearts to bless,—
Spontaneous wisdom breathed by health,
Truth breathed by cheerfulness.

One impulse from a vernal wood
May teach you more of man,
Of moral evil and of good,
Than all the sages can.

Sweet is the lore which Nature brings;
Our meddling intellect
Mis-shapes the beauteous forms of things:
We murder to dissect.

Enough of Science and of Art;
Close up those barren leaves;
Come forth, and bring with you a heart
That watches and receives.

THE PLEASURE-BOAT.

R. H. DANA.

COME, hoist the sail, the fast let go!
  They're seated side by side;
Wave chases wave in pleasant flow;
  The bay is fair and wide.

The ripples lightly tap the boat.
  Loose! Give her to the wind!
She shoots ahead; they're all afloat;
  The strand is far behind.

No danger reach so fair a crew!
  Thou goddess of the foam,
I'll ever pay thee worship due,
  If thou wilt bring them home.

Fair ladies, fairer than the spray
  The prow is dashing wide,
Soft breezes take you on your way,
  Soft flow the blessèd tide!

O, might I like those breezes be,
  And touch that arching brow,
I'd dwell for ever on the sea
  Where ye are floating now.

The boat goes tilting on the waves;
  The waves go tilting by:
There dips the duck, — her back she laves:
  O'erhead the sea-gulls fly.

Now, like the gulls that dart for prey,
  The little vessel stoops;
Now, rising, shoots along her way,
  Like them, in easy swoops.

The sunlight falling on her sheet,
  It glitters like the drift,
Sparkling, in scorn of Summer's heat,
  High up some mountain rift.

The winds are fresh; she's driving fast
  Upon the bending tide;
The crinkling sail and crinkling mast
  Go with her side by side.

Why dies the breeze away so soon?
  Why hangs the pennant down?
The sea is glass; the Sun at noon. —
  Nay, lady, do not frown;

For, see, the wingèd fisher's plume
  Is painted on the sea:
Below, a cheek of lovely bloom.
  Whose eyes look up at thee?

She smiles; thou needs must smile on her:
  And, see, beside her face
A rich white cloud that doth not stir:
  What beauty, and what grace!

And pictured beach of yellow sand,
  And peakèd rock, and hill
Change the smooth sea to fairy land:
  How lovely and how still!

From that far isle the thresher's flail
  Strikes close upon the ear;
The leaping fish, the swinging sail
  Of yonder sloop, sound near.

The parting Sun sends out a glow
  Across the placid bay,
Touching with glory all the show. —
  A breeze! Up helm! Away!

Careering to the wind, they reach,
  With laugh and call, the shore.
They've left their footprints on the beach,
  But then I hear no more.

THE NEW YEAR.

ALFRED TENNYSON.

RING out, wild bells, to the wild sky,
  The flying cloud, the frosty light;
  The year is dying in the night;
Ring out, wild bells, and let him die.

Ring out the old, ring in the new;
  Ring, happy bells, across the snow;
  The year is going; let him go;
Ring out the false; ring in the true.

Ring out the grief, that saps the mind,
  For those that here we see no more;
  Ring out the feud of rich and poor;
Ring in redress to all mankind.

Ring out a slowly dying cause,
  And ancient forms of party strife;
  Ring in the nobler modes of life,
With sweeter manners, purer laws.

Ring out the want, the care, the sin,
The faithless coldness of the times;
Ring out, ring out my mournful rhymes,
But ring the fuller minstrel in.

Ring out false pride in place and blood,
The civic slander and the spite;
Ring in the love of truth and right;
Ring in the common love of good.

Ring out old shapes of foul disease;
Ring out the narrowing lust of gold;
Ring out the thousand wars of old,
Ring in the thousand years of peace.

Ring in the valiant man and free,
The larger heart, the kindlier hand;
Ring out the darkness of the land;
Ring in the Christ that is to be.

FISH-WOMEN AT CALAIS.

'Tis said, fantastic ocean doth enfold
The likeness of whate'er on land is seen;
But, if the Nereid Sisters and their Queen,
Above whose heads the tide so long hath roll'd,
The Dames resemble whom we here behold,
How fearful were it down through opening waves
To sink and meet them in their fretted caves,
Wither'd, grotesque, immeasurably old,
And shrill and fierce in accent! — Fear it not:
For they Earth's fairest daughters do excel;
Pure undecaying beauty is their lot;
Their voices into liquid music swell,
Thrilling each pearly cleft and sparry grot,
The undisturb'd abodes where Sea-nymphs dwell!

IX.

HUMOROUS, COMIC.

AUNT TABITHA.

O. W. HOLMES.

WHATEVER I do and whatever I say,
Aunt Tabitha tells me that isn't the way;
When she was a girl, (forty Summers ago,)
Aunt Tabitha tells me they never did so.

Dear aunt! if I only would take her advice,—
But I like my own way, and I find it so nice!
And besides I forget half the things I am told;
But they will come back to me,—when I am old.

If a youth passes by, it may happen, no doubt,
He may chance to look in as I chance to look out:
She would never endure an impertinent stare;
It is horrid, she says, and I mustn't sit there.

A walk in the moonlight has pleasure, I own,
But it isn't quite safe to be walking alone;
So I take a lad's arm,—just for safety, you know;
But Aunt Tabitha tells me, *they* didn't do so.

How wicked we are, and how good they were then!
They kept at arm's length those detestable men:
What an era of virtue she lived in!—but stay,—
Were the men such rogues in Aunt Tabitha's day?

If the men *were* so wicked, — I'll ask my papa
How he dared to propose to my darling mamma?
Was he like the rest of them? goodness! who knows?
And what shall I say, if a wretch should propose?

I am thinking if aunt knew so little of sin,
What a wonder Aunt Tabitha's *aunt* must have been!
And her *grand-aunt*, — it scares me, — how shockingly sad
That we girls of to-day are so frightfully bad!

A martyr will save us, and nothing else can;
Let us perish to rescue some wretched young man!
Though, when to the altar a victim I go,
Aunt Tabitha'll tell me — she never did so.

AWFULLY LOVELY PHILOSOPHY.

A FEW days ago a Boston girl, who had been attending the School of Philosophy at Concord, arrived in Brooklyn, on a visit to a seminary chum. After canvassing thoroughly the fun and gum-drops that made up their education in the seat of learning at which their early scholastic efforts were made, the Brooklyn girl began to inquire the nature of the Concord entertainment.

"And so you are taking lessons in philosophy! How do you like it?"

"O, it's perfectly lovely! It's about science, you know, and we all just dote on science."

"It must be nice. What is it about?"

"It's about molecules as much as any thing else, and molecules are just too awfully nice for any thing. If there's any thing I really enjoy it's molecules."

"Tell me about them, my dear. What are molecules?"

"O, molecules! They are little wee things, and it takes ever so many of them. They are splendid things. Do you know, there ain't anything but what's got molecules in it. And Mr. Cook is just as sweet as he can be, and Mr. Emerson too. They explain everything so beautifully."

"How I'd like to go there!" said the Brooklyn girl, enviously.

"You'd enjoy it ever so much. They teach protoplasm, too; and if there is one thing perfectly heavenly it's protoplasm. I really don't know which I like best, protoplasm or molecules."

"Tell me about protoplasm. I know I should adore it."

"'Deed you would. It's just too sweet to live. You know it's about how things get started, or something of that kind. You ought to hear Mr. Emerson tell about it. It would stir your very soul. The first time he explained about protoplasm there wasn't a dry eye in the house. We named our hats after him. This is an Emerson hat. You see the ribbon is drawn over the crown and caught with a buckle and a bunch of flowers. Then you turn up the side with a spray of forget-me-nots. Ain't it just too sweet? All the girls in the school have them."

"How exquisitely lovely! Tell me some more science."

"O, I almost forgot about differentiation. I am really and truly positively in love with differentiation. It's different from molecules and protoplasm, but it's every bit as nice. And Mr. Cook! You should hear him go on about it. I really believe he's perfectly bound up in it. This scarf is the Cook scarf. All the girls wear them, and we named them after him, just on account of the interest he takes in differentiation."

"What is it, anyway?"

"This is mull, trimmed with Languedoc lace —"

"I don't mean that, — that other."

"O, differentiation! Ain't it sweet? It's got something to do with species. It's the way you tell one hat from another, so you'll know which is becoming. And we learn all about ascidians too. They are the divinest things! I'm absolutely enraptured with ascidians. If I only had an ascidian of my own I wouldn't ask anything else in the world."

"What do they look like, dear? Did you ever see one?" asked the Brooklyn girl, deeply interested.

"O, no; nobody ever saw one except Mr. Cook and Mr. Emerson; but they are something like an oyster with a reticule hung on its belt. I think they are just heavenly."

"Do you learn any thing else besides?"

"O, yes. We learn about common philosophy and logic, and those common things like metaphysics; but the girls don't care anything about those. We are just in ecstasies over differentiations and molecules, and Mr. Cook and protoplasms, and ascidians and Mr. Emerson, and I really don't see why they put in those vulgar branches. If anybody besides Mr. Cook and Mr. Emerson had done it, we should have told him to his face that he was too terribly, awfully mean." And the Brooklyn girl went to bed that night in the dumps, because fortune had not vouchsafed her the advantages enjoyed by her friend.

THE BALD-HEADED MAN.

THE other day a lady, accompanied by her son, a very small boy, boarded a train at Little Rock. The woman had a care-worn expression hanging over her face like a tattered veil, and many of the rapid questions asked by the boy were answered by unconscious sighs.

"Ma," said the boy, "that man's like a baby, ain't he?" pointing to a bald-headed man sitting just in front of them.

"Hush!"

"Why must I hush?"

After a few moments' silence, "Ma, what's the matter with that man's head?"

"Hush, I tell you. He's bald."

"What's bald?"

"His head hasn't got any hair on it."

"Did it come off?"

"I guess so."

"Will mine come off?"

"Some time, maybe."

"Then I'll be bald, won't I?"

"Yes."

"Will you care?"

"Don't ask so many questions."

After another silence, the boy exclaimed, "Ma, look at that fly on that man's head."

"If you don't hush, I'll whip you when we get home."

"Look! There's another fly. Look at 'em fight, look at 'em!"

"Madam," said the man, putting aside a newspaper and looking around, "what's the matter with that young hyena?"

The woman blushed, stammered out something, and attempted to smooth back the boy's hair.

"One fly, two flies, three flies," said the boy innocently, following with his eyes a basket of oranges carried by a newsboy.

"Here, you young hedgehog," said the bald-headed man, "if you don't hush, I'll have the conductor put you off the train."

The poor woman, not knowing what else to do, boxed the boy's ears, and then gave him an orange to keep him from crying.

"Ma, have I got red marks on my head?"

"I'll whip you again if you don't hush."

"Mister," said the boy, after a short silence, "does it hurt to be bald-headed?"

"Youngster," said the man, "if you'll keep quiet, I'll give you a quarter."

The boy promised, and the money was paid over.

The man took up his paper, and resumed his reading.

"This is my bald-headed money," said the boy. "When I get bald-headed, I'm goin' to give boys money. Mister, have all bald-headed men got money?"

The annoyed man threw down his paper, arose, and exclaimed, "Madam, hereafter, when you travel, leave that young gorilla at home. Hitherto, I always thought that the old prophet was very cruel for calling the bears to kill the children for making sport of his head, but now I am forced to believe that he did a Christian act. If your boy had been in the crowd he would have died first. If I can't find another seat on this train, I'll ride on the cow-catcher rather than remain here."

"The bald-headed man is gone," said the boy; and, as the woman leaned back, a tired sigh escaped from her lips.

THE BRAKEMAN AT CHURCH.

R. J. BURDETTE.

ON the road once more, with Lebanon fading away in the distance, the fat passenger drumming idly on the window pane, the cross passenger sound asleep, and the tall, thin passenger reading "Gen. Grant's Tour Around the World," and wondering why "Green's August Flower" should be printed above the doors of "A Buddhist Temple at Benares." To me comes the brakeman, and, seating himself on the arm of the seat, says, "I went to church yesterday."

"Yes?" I said, with that interested inflection that asks for more. "And what church did you attend?"

"Which do you guess?" he asked.

"Some union mission church," I hazarded.

"No," he said, "I don't like to run on these branch roads very much. I don't often go to church, and, when I do, I want to run on the main line, where your run is regular, and you go on schedule time, and don't have to wait on connections. I don't like to run on a branch. Good enough, but I don't like it.'

"Episcopal?" I guessed.

"Limited express," he said, "all palace cars and $2 extra for seat, fast time, and only stop at big stations. Nice line, but too exhaustive for a brakeman. All train men in uniform, conductor's punch and lantern silver plated, and no train boys allowed. Then the passengers are allowed to talk back at the conductor, and it makes them too free and easy. No, I couldn't stand the palace cars. Rich road, though. Don't often hear of a receiver being appointed for that line. Some mighty nice people travel on it, too."

"Universalist?" I suggested.

"Broad gauge," said the brakeman, "does too much complimentary business. Everybody travels on a pass. Conductor doesn't get a fare once in fifty miles. Stops at flag stations, and won't run into anything but a union depot. No smoking-car on the train. Train orders are rather vague though, and the train men don't get along well with the passengers. No, I don't go to the Universalist, but I know some good men who run on that road."

"Presbyterian?" I asked.

"Narrow gauge, eh?" said the brakeman, "pretty track, straight as a rule; tunnel right through a mountain rather than go around it; spirit-level grade; passengers have to show their tickets before they get on the train. Mighty strict road, but the cars are a little narrow; have to sit one in a seat, and no room in the aisle to dance. Then there is no stop-over tickets allowed; got to go straight through to the station you're ticketed for, or you can't get on at all. When the car is full, no extra coaches; cars built at the shop to hold just so many, and nobody else allowed on. But you don't often hear of an accident on that road. It's run right up to the rules."

"Maybe you joined the Free-Thinkers?" I said.

"Scrub road," said the brakeman, "dirt road-bed and no ballast; no time-card and no train-dispatcher. All trains run wild, and every engineer makes his own time, just as he pleases. Smoke if you want to; kind of go-as-you-please road. Too many side tracks, and every switch wide open all the time, with the switchman sound asleep and the target lamp dead out. Get on as you please, and get off when you want to. Don't have to show your tickets, and the conductor isn't expected to do anything but amuse the passengers. No, sir. I was offered a pass, but I don't like the line. I don't like to travel on a road that has no terminus. Do you know, sir, I asked a division-superintendent where that road run to, and he said he hoped to die if he knew. I asked him if the general superintendent could tell me, and he said he didn't believe they had a general superintendent, and if they had he didn't know any thing more about the road than the passengers. I asked him who he reported to, and he said 'nobody.' I asked a conductor who he got his orders from, and he said he didn't take orders from any living man or dead ghost. And, when I asked the engineer who he got his orders from, he said he'd like to see anybody give him orders; he'd run the train to suit himself, or he'd run it into the ditch. Now you see, sir, I'm a railroad man, and I don't care to run on a road that has no time, makes no connections, runs nowhere, and has no superintendent. It may be all right, but I've railroaded too long to understand it."

"Maybe you went to the Congregational Church?"

"Popular road," said the brakeman; "an old road, too, — one of the very oldest in the country. Good road-bed and comfortable cars. Well-managed road, too; directors don't interfere with division-superintendents and train-orders. Road's mighty popular, but its pretty independent, too. Yes, didn't one of the division superintendents down east discontinue one of the oldest stations on this line two or three years ago? But it's a mighty pleasant road to travel on, — always has such a pleasant class of passengers."

"Did you try the Methodist?" I said.

"Now you're shouting!" he said with some enthusiasm. "Nice road, eh? Fast time and plenty of passengers. Engines carry a power of steam, and don't you forget it; steam-gauge shows a hundred, and enough all the time. Lively road; when the conductor shouts 'all aboard,' you can hear him at the next station. Every train-light shines like a head-light. Stop-over checks are given on all through-tickets; passenger can drop off the train as often as he likes, do the station two or three days, and hop on the next revival train that comes thundering along. Good, wholesouled, companionable conductors; ain't a road in the country where the passengers feel more at home. No passes; every passenger pays full traffic rates for his ticket. Wesleyanhouse air-brakes on all trains, too; pretty safe road, but I didn't ride over it yesterday."

"Perhaps you tried the Baptist?" I guessed once more.

"Ah, ha!" said the brakeman, "she's a daisy, isn't she? River road; beautiful curves; sweep around any thing to keep close to the river, but it's all steel rail and rock ballast, single track all the way, and not a side track from the round house to the terminus. Takes a heap of water to run it, though; double tanks at every station, and there isn't an engine in the shops that can pull a pound or run a mile with less than two gauges. But it runs through a lovely country; those river roads always do; river on one side and hills on the other, and it's a steady climb up the grade all the way till the run ends where the fountain-head of the river begins. Yes, sir; I'll take the river road every time for a lovely trip, sure connections and a good time, and no prairie dust blowing in at the windows. And yesterday, when the conductor came around for the tickets with a little basket punch, I didn't ask him to pass me, but I paid my fare like a little man, — twenty-five cents for an hour's run, and a little concert by the passengers thrown in. I tell you, pilgrim, you take the river road when you want — "

But just here the long whistle from the engine announced a station, and the brakeman hurried to the door, shouting:

"Zionsville! The train makes no stops between here and Indianapolis!"

THE CHAMPION SNORER.

From the "BURLINGTON HAWKEYE."

IT was the Cedar Rapids sleeper. Outside, it was as dark as the inside of an ink-bottle. In the sleeping-car people slept. Or tried it.

Some of them slept like Christian men and women, peacefully, sweetly, and quietly.

Others slept like demons, malignantly, hideously, fiendishly, as though it was their mission to keep everybody else awake.

Of these the man in lower number three was the worst.

We never heard any thing snore like him. It was the most systematic snoring that was ever done, even on one of these tournaments of snoring, a sleeping-car. He didn't begin as soon as the lamps were turned down and everybody was in bed. O, no! There was more cold-blooded diabolism in his system than that. He waited until everybody had had a taste of sleep, just to see how nice and pleasant it was; and then he broke in on their slumbers like a winged, breathing demon, and they never knew what peace was again that night.

He started out with a terrific

"Gu-r-r-rt!"

that opened every eye in the car. We all hoped it was

an accident, however; and, trusting that he wouldn't do it again, we all forgave him. Then he blasted our hopes and curdled the sweet serenity of our forgiveness by a long-drawn

"Gw-a-h-h-hah!"

that sounded too much like business to be accidental. Then every head in that sleepless sleeper was held off the pillow for a minute, waiting in breathless suspense to hear the worst; and the sleeper in "lower three" went on in long-drawn, regular cadences that indicated good staying qualities,

"Gwa-a-a-h! Gwa-a-a-a-h! Gahwayway! Gahwaywah! Gahwa-a-ah!"

Evidently it was going to last all night; and the weary heads dropped back on the sleepless pillows, and the swearing began. It mumbled along in low, muttering tones, like the distant echoes of a profane thunderstorm. Pretty soon "lower three" gave us a little variation. He shot off a spiteful

"Gwook!"

which sounded as though his nose had got mad at him and was going to strike. Then there was a pause, and we began to hope he had either awakened from sleep or strangled to death,—nobody cared very particularly which. But he disappointed everybody with a guttural

"Gurroch!"

Then he paused again for breath; and when he had accumulated enough for his purpose he resumed business with a stentorious

"Kowpff!"

that nearly shot the roof off the car. Then he went on playing such fantastic tricks with his nose, and breathing things that would make the immortal gods weep, if they did but hear him. It seemed an utter, preposterous impossibility that any human being could make the monstrous, hideous noises with its breathing machine that the fellow in "lower three" was making with his. He then ran through all the ranges of the nasal gamut; he went up and down a very chromatic scale of snores; he ran through intricate and fearful variations until it seemed that his nose must be out of joint in a thousand places. All the night and all the day through he told his story;

"Gawoh! gurrah! gu-r-r-r! Kowpff! Gawaw-wah! gawah-hah! gwock! gwart! gwah-h-h-h woof!"

Just as the other passengers had consulted together how they might slay him, morning dawned, and "lower number three" awoke. Everybody watched the curtain to see what manner of man it was that made the sleeping-car a pandemonium. Presently the toilet was completed, the curtains parted, and "lower number three" stood revealed. Great Heavens!

It was a fair young girl, with golden hair, and timid, pleading eyes, like a hunted fawn.

COURTSHIP UNDER DIFFICULTIES.

Snobbleton. Yes, there is that fellow Jones, again. I declare, the man is ubiquitous. Wherever I go with my cousin Prudence we stumble across him, or he follows her like her shadow. Do we take a boating? So does Jones. Do we wander on the beach? So does Jones. Go where we will, that fellow follows or moves before. Now, that was a cruel practical joke which Jones once played upon me at college. I have never forgiven him. But I would gladly make a pretence of doing so, if I could have my revenge. Let me see. Can't I manage it? He is head over ears in love with Prudence, but too bashful to speak. I half believe she is not indifferent to him, though altogether unacquainted. It may prove a match, if I cannot spoil it. Let me think. Ha! I have it. A brilliant idea! Jones, beware! But here he comes.

Enter JONES.

Jones. (*Not seeing Snobbleton, and delightedly contemplating a flower, which he holds in his hand.*) O, rapture! what a prize! It was in her hair, — I saw it fall from her queenly head. (*Kisses it every now and then.*) How warm are its tender leaves from having touched her neck! How doubly sweet is its perfume, — fresh from the fragrance of her glorious locks! How beautiful! how — Bless me! here is Snobbleton, and we are enemies!

Snob. Good-morning, Jones, — that is, if you will shake hands.

Jones. What! you — you forgive! You really —

Snob. Yes, yes, old fellow! All is forgotten. You played me a rough trick; but let bygones be bygones. Will you not bury the hatchet?

Jones. With all my heart, my dear fellow!

Snob. What is the matter with you, Jones? You look quite grumpy, — not by any means the same cheerful, dashing, rollicking fellow you were.

Jones. Grumpy, — what is that? How *do* I look, Snobbleton?

Snob. O, not much out of the way. Only a little shaky in the shanks, — blue lips, red nose, cadaverous jaws, blood-shot eyes, yellow —

Jones. Bless me, you don't say so! (*Aside.*) Confound the man. Here have I been endeavouring to appear romantic for the last month; and now to be called grumpy, — shaky-shanked, cadaverous, — it is unbearable!

Snob. But never mind. Cheer up, old fellow! I see it all. Egad! I know what it is to be in —

Jones. Ah! you can then sympathize with me! You know what it is to be in —

Snob. *Of course* I do! Heaven preserve me from the toils! What days of bitterness!

Jones. What nights of bliss!

Snob. (*Shuddering.*) And then the letters, — the interminable letters!

Jones. O yes, the letters! the *billet doux!*

Snob. And the bills, — the endless bills!

Jones. (*In surprise.*) The bills!

Snob. Yes; and the bailiffs, the lawyers, the judge, and the jury.

Jones. Why, man, what are you talking about? I thought you said you knew what it was to be in —

Snob. In debt. *To be sure,* I did.

Jones. Bless me! I'm not in debt, — never borrowed a dollar in my life. Ah, me! (*Sighs.*) it's worse than *that.*

Snob. Worse than that! Come, now, Jones, there is only one thing worse. You're surely not in love?

Jones. Yes, I am. O Snobby, help me, help me! Let me confide in you.

Snob. Confide in me! Certainly, my dear fellow! See, I do not shrink, — I stand firm.

Jones. Snobby, I — I love her.

Snob. Whom?

Jones. Your cousin, Prudence.

Snob. Ha! Prudence Angelina Winterbottom.

Jones. Now, don't be angry, Snobby! I don't mean any harm, you know. I — I — you know how it is.

Snob. Harm! my dear fellow. Not a bit of it. Angry! Not at all. You have my consent, old fellow. Take her. She is yours. Heaven bless you both!

Jones. You are very kind, Snobby, but I haven't got her consent yet.

Snob. Well, that *is* something, to be sure. But leave it all to me. She may be a little coy, you know; but, considering your generous overlooking of her unfortunate defect, —

Jones. Defect! You surprise me.

Snob. What! and you did not know of it?

Jones. Not at all. I am astonished! Nothing serious I hope.

Snob. O, no! only a little — (*He taps his ear with his finger, knowingly.*) I see, you understand it.

Jones. Merciful Heaven! can it be? But really, is it serious?

Snob. I should think it was.

Jones. What! But is she ever dangerous?

Snob. Dangerous! Why should she be?

Jones. (*Considerably relieved.*) O, I perceive! A mere airiness of brain, — a gentle abberration, — scorning the dull world, — a mild —

Snob. Zounds, man, she's not crazy!

Jones. My dear Snobby, you relieve me. What then?

Snob. Slightly deaf. That's all.

Jones. Deaf!

Snob. As a lamp-post. That is, you must elevate your voice to a considerable pitch in speaking to her.

Jones. Is it possible! However, I think I can manage. As, for instance, if it was my intention to make her a floral offering, and I should say, (*elevating his voice considerably,*) "Miss, will you make me happy by accepting these flowers?" I suppose she could hear me, eh? How would that do?

Snob. Pshaw! Do you call that elevated?

Jones. Well, how would this do? (*Speaks very loudly.*) "Miss, will you make me happy —"

Snob. Louder, shriller, man!

Jones. "Miss, will you —"

Snob. Louder, louder, or she will only see your lips move.

Jones. (*Almost screaming.*) "Miss, will you oblige me by accepting these flowers?"

Snob. There, that *may* do. Still you want practice. I perceive the lady herself is approaching. Suppose you retire for a short time, and I will prepare her for the introduction.

Jones. Very good. Meantime I will go down to the beach and endeavour to acquire the proper pitch. Let me see: "Miss, will you oblige me —" [*Exit* JONES.]

Enter PRUDENCE.

Prud. Good-morning, cousin. Who was that speaking so loudly?

Snob. Only Jones. Poor fellow, he is so deaf that I suppose he fancies his own voice to be a mere whisper.

Prud. Why, I was not aware of this. Is he *very* deaf?

Snob. Deaf as a stone fence. To be sure, he does not use an ear-trumpet any more, but one must speak excessively high. Unfortunate, too, for I believe he is in love.

Prud. (*With some emotion.*) In love! with whom?

Snob. Can't you guess?

Prud. O, no; I haven't the slightest idea.

Snob. With yourself! He has been begging me to obtain him an introduction.

Prud. Well, I have always thought him a nice-looking young man. I suppose he would hear me if I should say, (*speaking loudly,*) "Good-morning, Mr. Jones?"

Snob. (*Compassionately.*) *Do* you think he would hear *that?*

Prud. Well, then, how would, (*speaks very loudly,*) "Good-morning, Mr. Jones!" How would that do?

Snob. Tush! he would think you were speaking under your breath.

Prud. (*Almost screaming.*) "Good-morning!"

Snob. A mere whisper, my dear cousin. But here he comes. Now, do try and make yourself audible.

Enter, JONES.

Snob. (*Speaking in a high voice.*) Mr. Jones, cousin. Miss Winterbottom, Jones. You will please excuse me for a short time. (*He retires, but remains in view.*)

Jones. (*Speaking shrill and loud, and offering some flowers.*) Miss, will you accept these flowers? I plucked them from their slumber on the hill.

Prud. (*In an equally high voice.*) Really, sir, I — I —

Jones. (*Aside.*) She hesitates. It must be that she does not hear me. (*Increasing his tone.*) Miss, will you accept these flowers — FLOWERS? I plucked them sleeping on the hill — HILL.

Prud. (*Also increasing her tone.*) Certainly, Mr. Jones. They are beautiful — BEAU-U-TIFUL.

Jones. (*Aside.*) How she screams in my ear. (*Aloud.*) Yes, I plucked them from their slumber — SLUMBER, on the hill — HILL.

Prud. (*Aside.*) Poor man, what an effort it seems to him to speak. (*Aloud.*) I perceive you are poetical. Are you fond of poetry? (*Aside.*) He hesitates. I must speak louder. (*In a scream.*) Poetry — POETRY — POETRY!

Jones. (*Aside.*) Bless me, the woman would wake the dead! (*Aloud.*) Yes, Miss, I ad-o-r-e it.

Snob. (*Solus from behind, rubbing his hands.*) Glorious! glorious! I wonder how loud they *can* scream. O, vengeance, thou art sweet!

Prud. Can you repeat some poetry — POETRY?

Jones. I only know one poem. It is this:

> You'd scarce expect one of my age — AGE,
> To speak in public on the stage — STAGE.

Prud. (*Putting her lips to his ear and shouting.*) Bravo — bravo!

Jones. (*In the same way.*) Thank you! THANK —

Prud. (*Putting her hands over her ears.*) Mercy on us! Do you think I am DEAF, sir?

Jones. (*Also stopping his ears.*) And do you fancy *me* deaf, Miss?

(*They now speak in their natural tones.*)

Prud. Are you not, sir? You surprise me!

Jones. No, Miss. I was led to believe that *you* were deaf. Snobbleton told me so.

Prud. Snobbleton! Why, he told me that *you* were deaf.

Jones. Confound the fellow! he has been making game of us.

DARIUS GREEN AND HIS FLYING-MACHINE.

J. T. TROWBRIDGE.

IF ever there lived a Yankee lad,
Wise or otherwise, good or bad,
Who, seeing the birds fly, didn't jump
With flapping arms from stake or stump,
Or, spreading the tail of his coat for a sail,
Take a soaring leap from post or rail,
And wonder why *he* couldn't fly,
And flap and flutter and wish and try, —
If ever you knew a country dunce
Who didn't try that as often as once,
All I can say is, that's a sign
He never would do for a hero of mine.

An aspiring genius was Dary Green:
The son of a farmer, — age fourteen;
His body was long and lank and lean, —
Just right for flying, as will be seen;
He had two eyes as bright as a bean,
And a freckled nose that grew between,
A little awry; for I must mention
That he had riveted his attention
Upon his wonderful invention,
Twisting his tongue as he twisted the strings,
And working his face as he work'd the wings,
And with every turn of gimlet or screw
Turning and screwing his mouth round too,

Till his nose seem'd bent to catch the scent,
Around some corner, of new-baked pies,
And his wrinkled cheeks and his squinting eyes
Grew pucker'd into a queer grimace,
That made him look very droll in the face,
And also very wise.
And wise he must have been, to do more
Than ever a genius did before,
Excepting Dædalus of yore
And his son Icarus, who wore
Upon their backs those wings of wax
He had read of in the old almanacs.
Darius was clearly of the opinion,
That the air is also man's dominion,
And that, with paddle or fin or pinion,
We soon or late shall navigate
The azure as now we sail the sea.
The thing looks simple enough to me;
And, if you doubt it,
Hear how Darius reason'd about it:

"The birds can fly, an' why can't I?
Must we give in," says he with a grin,
"That the bluebird an' phœbe are smarter'n we be?
Jest fold our hands, an' see the swaller
An' blackbird an' catbird beat us holler?
Does the little chatterin', sassy wren,
No bigge'rn my thumb, know more than men?
Jest show me that! ur prove 't the bat
Hez got more brains than's in my hat,
An' I'll back down, an' not till then!"
He argued further: "Nur I can't see
What's th' use o' wings to a bumble-bee,
Fur to git a livin' with, more'n to me; —
Ain't my business important's his'n is?
That Icarus made a pretty muss, —
Him an' his daddy Dædalus;

They might 'a' know'd that wings made o' wax
Wouldn't stand sun-heat an' hard whacks:
I'll make mine o' luther, ur suthin' ur other."

And he said to himself, as he tinker'd and plann'd,
"But I ain't goin' to show my hand
To nummies that never can understand
The fust idee that's big an' grand."
So he kept his secret from all the rest,
Safely button'd within his vest;
And in the loft above the shed
Himself he locks, with thimble and thread
And wax and hammer and buckles and screws,
And all such things as geniuses use; —
Two bats for patterns, curious fellows!
A charcoal-pot and a pair of bellows;
Some wire, and several old umbrellas;
A carriage-cover, for tail and wings;
A piece of harness; and straps and strings;
And a big strong box, in which he locks
These and a hundred other things.
His grinning brothers, Reuben and Burke
And Nathan and Jotham and Solomon, lurke
Around the corner to see him work,
Sitting cross-legg'd, like a Turk,
Drawing the wax'd-end through with a jerk,
And boring the holes with a comical quirk
Of his wise old head, and a knowing smirk.
But vainly they mounted each other's backs,
And poked through knot-holes and pried through cracks;
With wood from the pile and straw from the stacks
He plugg'd the knot-holes and calk'd the cracks;
And a dipper of water, which one would think
He had brought up into the loft to drink
When he chanced to be dry,
Stood always nigh, for Darius was sly!
And, whenever at work he happen'd to spy

At chink or crevice a blinking eye,
He let the dipper of water fly:
"Take that! an', ef ever ye git a peep,
Guess ye'll ketch a weasel asleep!"
And he sings as he locks his big strong box:

"The weasel's head is small an' trim,
An' he is little an' long an' slim,
An' quick of motion an' nimble of limb,
An', ef you'll be advised by me,
Keep wide awake when ye're ketchin' him!"

So day after day
He stitch'd and tinker'd and hammer'd away,
Till at last 'twas done, —
The greatest invention under the Sun!
"An' now," says Darius, "hooray fur some fun!"

'Twas the Fourth of July, and the weather was dry,
And not a cloud was on all the sky,
Save a few light fleeces, which here and there,
Half mist, half air,
Like foam on the ocean went floating by, —
Just as lovely a morning as ever was seen
For a nice little trip in a flying-machine.
Thought cunning Darius, "Now I shan't go
Along 'ith the fellers to see the show:
I'll say I've got sich a terrible cough!
An' then, when the folks 'ave all gone off,
I'll hev full swing fur to try the thing,
An' practise a little on the wing."

"Ain't goin' to see the celebration?"
Says brother Nate. "No; botheration!
I've got sich a cold — a toothache — I —
My gracious! — feel's though I should fly!"
Said Jotham, "'Sho! guess ye better go."
But Darius said, "No!
Shouldn't wonder 'f you might see me, though,

'Long 'bout noon, ef I git red
O' this jumpin', thumpin' pain 'n my head."
For all the while to himself he said, —

"I tell ye what!
I'll fly a few times around the lot,
To see how 't seems, then soon's I've got
The hang o' the thing, ez likely's not,
I'll astonish the nation, an' all creation,
By flyin' over the celebration!
Over their heads I'll sail like an eagle;
I'll balance myself on my wings like a sea-gull;
I'll dance on the chimbleys; I'll stand on the steeple;
I'll flop up to winders an' scare the people!
I'll light on the liberty-pole, an' crow;
An' I'll say to the gawpin' fools below,
'What world's this 'ere that I've come near?'
Fur I'll make 'em b'lieve I'm a chap f'm the Moon;
An' I'll try a race 'ith their ol' balloon!"

He crept from his bed;
And, seeing the others were gone, he said,
"I'm gittin' over the cold 'n my head."
And away he sped,
To open the wonderful box in the shed.

His brothers had walk'd but a little way,
When Jotham to Nathan chanced to say,
"What is the feller up to, hey?"
"Don'o', — the's suthin' ur other to pay,
Ur he wouldn't 'a' stay'd to hum to-day."
Says Burke, "His toothache's all 'n his eye!
He never'd miss a Fo'th-o'-July,
Ef he hedn't got some machine to try."
Then Sol, the little one, spoke: "By darn
Le's hurry back, an' hide 'n the barn,
An' pay him fur tellin' us that yarn!"
"Agreed!" Through the orchard they creep back,

Along by the fences, behind the stack,
And one by one, through a hole in the wall,
In under the dusty barn they crawl,
Dress'd in their Sunday garments all;
And a very astonishing sight was that,
When each in his cobwebb'd coat and hat
Came up through the floor like an ancient rat.
And there they hid; and Reuben slid
The fastenings back, and the door undid.
    "Keep dark!" said he,
"While I squint an' see what the' is to see.

As knights of old put on their mail, —
From head to foot an iron suit,
Iron jacket and iron boot,
Iron breeches, and on the head
No hat, but an iron pot instead,
And under the chin the bail,
(I believe they call'd the thing a helm,) —
Then sallied forth to overwhelm
The dragons and pagans that plagued the realm;
So this *modern* knight prepared for flight,
Put on his wings and strapp'd them tight, —
Jointed and jaunty, strong and light, —
Buckled them fast to shoulder and hip, —
Ten feet they measured from tip to tip!
And a helm had he, but that he wore,
Not on his head, like those of yore,
But more like the helm of a ship.

"Hush!" Reuben said, "he's up in the shed!
He's open'd the winder, — I see his head!
He stretches it out, an' pokes it about,
Lookin' to see 'f the coast is clear,
    An' nobody near; —
Guess he don'o' who's hid in here!
He's riggin' a spring-board over the sill!

Stop laffin', Solomon! Burke, keep still!
He's a climbin' out now — Of all the things!
What's he got on? I van, it's wings!
An' that t'other thing? I vum, it's a tail!
An' there he sets like a hawk on a rail!
Steppin' careful, he travels the length
Of his spring-board, and teeters to try its strength.
Now he stretches his wings, like a monstrous bat;
Peeks over his shoulder, this way an' that,
Fur to see 'f the' 's any one passin' by,
But the' 's on'y a ca'f an' a goslin' nigh.
They turn up at him wonderin' eye,
To see — The dragon! he's goin' to fly!
Away he goes! Jimminy! what a jump!
Flop — flop — an' plump to the ground with a thump!
Flutt'rin' an' flound'rin', all'n a lump!"

As a demon is hurl'd by an angel's spear,
Heels over head, to his proper sphere, —
Heels over head, and head over heels,
Dizzily down the abyss he wheels, —
So fell Darius. Upon his crown,
In the midst of the barn-yard, he came down,
In a wonderful whirl of tangled strings,
Broken braces and broken springs,
Broken tail and broken wings,
Shooting-stars, and various things, —
Barn-yard litter of straw and chaff,
And much that wasn't so sweet by half.
Away with a bellow fled the calf,
And what was that? Did the gosling laugh?
'Tis a merry roar from the old barn-door,
And he hears the voice of Jotham crying;
"Say, D'rius! how do you like flyin'?"
Slowly, ruefully, where he lay,
Darius just turn'd and look'd that way,
As he stanch'd his sorrowful nose with his cuff.

"Wal, I like flyin' well enough,"
He said; "but the' ain't sich a thunderin' sight
O' fun in't when ye come to light."

I just have room for the MORAL here:
And this is the moral, — Stick to your sphere;
Or, if you insist, as you have the right,
On spreading your wings for a loftier flight,
The moral is, — Take care how you light.

HOW "RUBY" PLAYED.

DR. G. W. BAGBY.

WELL, sir, he had the blamedest, biggest, catty-cornedest pianner you ever laid eyes on; somethin' like a distracted billiard table on three legs. The lid was hoisted, and mighty well it was. If it hadn't been, he'd a tore the entire inside clean out, and scattered 'em to the four winds of heaven.

Played well? You bet he did; but don't interrupt me. When he first sit down, he 'peared to keer mighty little 'bout playin', and wisht he hadn't come. He tweedle-leede'd a little on the treble, and twoodle-oodled some on the base, — just foolin' and boxin' the thing's jaws for bein' in his way. And I says to a man settin' next to me, says I, "What sort of fool playin' is that?" And he says, "Heish!" But presently his hands commenced chasin' one another up and down the keys, like a passel of rats scamperin' through a garret very swift. Parts of it was sweet, though, and reminded me of a sugar squirrel turnin' the wheel of a candy cage.

"Now," I says to my neighbour, "he's showin' off. He thinks he's a-doin' of it, but he ain't got no idee, no plan of nothin'. If he'd play me a tune of some kind or other I'd —"

But my neighbor says "Heish!" very impatient.

I was just about to git up and go home, bein' tired of that foolishness, when I heard a little bird waking up away off in the woods, and call sleepy-like to his mate, and I looked up, and see that Rubin was beginning to take some interest in his business, and I sit down again. It was the peep of day. The light came faint from the east, the breezes blowed gentle and fresh, some more birds waked up in the orchard, then some more in the trees near the house, and all begun singin' together. People began to stir, and the gal opened the shutters. Just then the first beam of the sun fell upon the blossoms a leetle more, and it techt the roses on the bushes, and the next thing it was broad day; the sun fairly blazed, the birds sung like they'd split their little throats; all the leaves was movin', and flashin' diamonds of dew, and the whole wide world was bright and happy as a king. Seemed to me like there was a good breakfast in every house in the land, and not a sick child or woman anywhere. It was a fine mornin'.

And I says to my neighbour, "That's music, that is."

But he glared at me like he'd like to cut my throat.

Presently the wind turned; it begun to thicken up, and a kind of gray mist came over things; I got low-spirited directly. Then a silver rain begun to fall. I could see the drops touch the ground; some flashed up like long pearl ear-rings, and the rest rolled away like round rubies. It was pretty but melancholy. Then the pearls gathered themselves into long strands and necklaces, and then they melted into thin silver streams, running between golden gravels; and then the streams joined each other at the bottom of the hill, and made a brook that flowed silent, except that you could kinder see the music, specially when the bushes on the banks moved as the music went along down the valley. I could smell the flowers in the meadow. But the Sun didn't shine, nor the birds sing; it was a foggy day, but not cold.

The most curious thing was the little white angel-boy, like you see in pictures, that run ahead of the music-brook, and led it on and on, away out of the world, where no man ever was, certain. I could see that boy just as plain as I see you. Then the moonlight came, without any sunset, and shone on the graveyards, where some few ghosts lifted their hands and went over the wall; and between the black, sharp-top trees splendid marble houses rose up, with fine ladies in the lit-up windows, and men that loved 'em, but could never get a-nigh 'em, who played on guitars under the trees, and made me that miserable I could have cried, because I wanted to love somebody, I don't know who, better than the men with the guitars did.

Then the Sun went down, it got dark, the wind moaned and wept like a lost child for its dead mother, and I could a got up then and there and preached a better sermon than any I ever listened to. There wasn't a thing in the world left to live for, not a blame thing, and yet I didn't want the music to stop one bit. It was happier to be miserable than to be happy without being miserable. I couldn't understand it. I hung my head and pulled out my handkerchief, and blowed my nose loud to keep me from cryin'. My eyes is weak anyway; I didn't want anybody to be a-gazin' at me a-snivlin', and it's nobody's business what I do with my nose. It's mine. But some several glared at me mad as blazes. Then, all of a sudden, old Rubin changed his tune. He ripped out and he rared, he tipped and he tared, he pranced and he charged like the grand entry at a circus. 'Peared to me that all the gas in the house was turned on at once, things got so bright, and I hilt up my head, ready to look any man in the face, and not afraid of nothin'. It was a circus, and a brass band, and a big ball all goin' on at the same time. He lit into them keys like a thousand of brick; he give em no rest day or night; he set every livin' joint in me a-goin'; and, not bein' able to stand it no longer, I jumped spang onto my seat, and jest hollored,

"*Go it, my Rube!*"

Every blamed man, woman, and child in the house riz on me, and shouted, "Put him out! put him out!"

"Put your great grandmother's grizzly-gray-greenish cat into the middle of next month!" I says. "Tech me if you dare! I paid my money, and you jest come a-nigh me!"

With that some several policemen run up, and I had to simmer down. But I would a fit any fool that laid hands on me, for I was bound to hear Ruby out or die.

He had changed his tune again. He hop-light ladies and tip-toed fine from end to end of the key-board. He played soft and low and solemn. I heard the church bells over the hills. The candles of heaven was lit, one by one; I saw the stars rise. The great organ of eternity began to play from the world's end to the world's end, and all the angels went to prayers. * * * * Then the music changed to water, full of feeling that couldn't be thought, and began to drop—drip, drop—drip, drop, clear and sweet, like tears of joy falling into a lake of glory. It was sweeter than that. It was as sweet as a sweet-heart sweetened with white sugar mixt with powdered silver and seed diamonds. It was too sweet. I tell you the audience cheered. Rubin he kinder bowed, like he wanted to say, "Much obleeged, but I'd rather you wouldn't interrup' me."

He stopt a moment or two to ketch breath. Then he got mad. He run his fingers through his hair, he shoved up his sleeve, he opened his coat tails a leetle further, he drug up his stool, he leaned over, and, sir, he just went for that old pianner. He slapt her face, he boxed her jaws, he pulled her nose, he pinched her ears, and he scratched her cheeks until she fairly yelled. He knockt her down and he stampt on her shameful. She bellowed like a bull, she bleated like a calf, she howled like a hound, she squealed like a pig, she shrieked like a rat, and *then* he wouldn't let her up. He run a quarter stretch down the low grounds of the base, till he got clean in the bowels of the earth, and you heard thunder galloping after thunder, through the hollows and caves of perdition; and then he fox-chased his right hand with his left till he got way out of the treble into the clouds, whar the notes was finer than the pints of cambric needles, and you couldn't hear nothin' but the shadders of 'em. And *then* he wouldn't let the old pianner go. He far'ard two'd, he crost over first gentleman, he chassade right and left, back to your places, he all-hands'd aroun', ladies to the right, promenade all, in and out, here and there, back and forth, up and down, perpetual motion, double twisted and turned and tacked and tangled into forty-eleven thousand double bow-knots.

By jinks! it was a mixtery. And then he wouldn't let the old pianner go. He fecht up his right wing, he fecht up his left wing, he fecht up his center, he fecht up his reserves. He fired by file, he fired by platoons, by company, by regiments, and by brigades. He opened his cannon, — siege guns down thar, Napoleons here, twelve-pounders yonder, — big guns, little guns, middle-sized guns, round shot, shells, shrapnels, grape, canister, mortar, mines and magazines, every livin' battery and bom a-goin' at the same time. The house trembled, the lights danced, the walls shuk, the floor come up, the ceilin' come down, the sky split, the ground rockt, — heavens and earth, creation, sweet potatoes, Moses, ninepences, glory, ten-penny nails, Sampson in a 'simmon tree, Tump, Tompson in a tumbler-cart, roodle-oodle-oodle-oodle — ruddle-uddle-uddle-uddle — raddle-addle-addle-addle — riddle-iddle-iddle-iddle — reedle-eedle-eedle-eedle — p-r-r-r-rlank! Bang! ! ! lang! perlang! p-r-r-r-r-r! ! Bang! ! !

With that bang! he lifted himself bodily into the a'r and he come down with his knees, his ten fingers, his ten toes, his elbows, and his nose, striking every single solitary key on the pianner at the same time. The thing busted and went off into seventeen hundred and fifty-seven thousand five hundred and forty-two hemi-demi-semi quivers, and I know'd no mo'.

When I come to, I were under ground about twenty foot, in a place they call Oystĕr Bay, treatin' a Yankee that I never laid eyes on before, and never expect to agin. Day was breakin' by the time I got to the St. Nicholas Hotel, and I pledge you my word I did not know my name. The man asked me the number of my room, and I told him, "Hot music on the half-shell for two!"

OUR GUIDES.

MARK TWAIN.

EUROPEAN guides know about enough English to tangle every thing up so that a man can make neither head nor tail of it. They know their story by heart, — the history of every statue, painting, cathedral, or other wonder they show you. They know it and tell it as a parrot would, — and if you interrupt, and throw them off the track, they have to go back and begin over again. All their lives long, they are employed in showing strange things to foreigners, and listening to their bursts of admiration.

It is human nature to take delight in exciting admiration. It is what prompts children to say "smart" things, and do absurd ones, and in other ways "show off" when company is present. It is what makes gossips turn out in rain and storm to go and be the first to tell a startling bit of news. Think, then, what a passion it becomes with a guide, whose privilege it is, every day, to show to strangers wonders that throw them into perfect ecstasies of admiration! He gets so that he could not by any possibility live in a soberer atmosphere.

After we discovered this, we *never* went into ecstasies any more, — we never admired any thing, — we never showed any but impassible faces and stupid indifference in the presence of the sublimest wonders a guide had to display. We had found their weak point. We have made good use of it ever since. We have made some of those people savage, at times, but we have never lost our serenity.

The doctor asks the questions generally, because he can keep his countenance, and look more like an inspired idiot, and throw more imbecility into the tone of his voice than any man that lives. It comes natural to him.

The guides in Genoa are delighted to secure an American party, because Americans so much wonder, and deal so much in sentiment and emotion before any relic of Columbus. Our guide there fidgeted about as if he had swallowed a spring mattress. He was full of animation, — full of impatience. He said:

"Come wis me, genteelmen! — come! I show you ze letter writing by Christopher Colombo! — write it himself! — write it wis his own hand! — come!"

He took us to the municipal palace. After much impressive fumbling of keys and opening of locks, the stained and aged document was spread before us. The guide's eyes sparkled. He danced about us and tapped the parchment with his finger:

"What I tell you, genteelmen! Is it not so? See! handwriting Christopher Colombo! — write it himself!"

We looked indifferent, — unconcerned. The doctor examined the document very deliberately, during a painful pause. Then he said, without any show of interest, —

"Ah, — Ferguson, — what — what did you say was the name of the party who wrote this?"

"Christopher Colombo! ze great Christopher Colombo!"

Another deliberate examination.

"Ah, — did he write it himself, or, — or how?"

"He write it himself! — Christopher Colombo! he's own handwriting, write by himself!"

Then the doctor laid the document down and said, —

"Why, I have seen boys in America only fourteen years old that could write better than that."

"But zis is ze great Christo —"

"I don't care who it is! It's the worst writing I ever saw. Now you mustn't think you can impose on us because we are strangers. We are not fools, by a good deal. If you have got any specimens of penmanship of real merit, trot them out! — and if you haven't, drive on!"

We drove on. The guide was considerably shaken up, but he made one more venture. He had something which he thought would overcome us. He said, —

"Ah, genteelmen, you come wis us! I show you beautiful, O, magnificent bust Christopher Colombo! — splendid, grand, magnificent!"

He brought us before the beautiful bust, — for it *was* beautiful, — and sprang back and struck an attitude:

"Ah, look, genteelmen! — beautiful, grand, — bust Christopher Colombo! — beautiful bust, beautiful pedestal!"

The doctor put up his eye-glass, procured for such occasions:

"Ah, — what did you say this gentleman's name was?"

"Christopher Colombo! ze great Christopher Colombo!"

"Christopher Colombo, — the great Christopher Colombo. Well, what did *he* do?"

"Discover America! — discover America, O, ze devil!"

"Discover America? No, — that statement will hardly wash. We are just from America ourselves. We heard nothing about it. Christopher Colombo, — pleasant name; — is — is he dead?"

"O corpo di Baccho! — three hundred year!"

"What did he die of?"

"I do not know. I cannot tell."

"Small-pox, think?"

"I do not know, genteelmen, — I do not know *what* he die of."

"Measles, likely?"

"Maybe, — maybe. I do *not* know, — I think he die of something."

"Parents living?"

"Im-posseeble!"

"Ah, — which is the bust and which is the pedestal?"

"Santa Maria! — *zis* ze bust! — *zis* ze pedestal!"

"Ah, I see, I see, — happy combination, — very happy

combination indeed. Is — is this the first time this gentle-was ever on a bust?"

"That joke was lost on the foreigner, — guides cannot master the subtleties of the American joke.

We have made it interesting for this Roman guide. Yesterday we spent three or four hours in the Vatican again, that wonderful world of curiosities. We came very near expressing interest sometimes, even admiration. It was hard to keep from it. We succeeded, though. Nobody else ever did, in the Vatican museums. The guide was bewildered, nonplussed. He walked his legs off, nearly, hunting up extraordinary things, and exhausted all his ingenuity on us, but it was a failure; we never showed any interest in any thing. He had reserved what he considered to be his greatest wonder till the last, — a royal Egyptian mummy, the best preserved in the world, perhaps. He took us there. He felt so sure, this time, that some of his old enthusiasm came back to him: —

"See, genteelmen! — Mummy! Mummy!"

The eye-glass came up as calmly, as deliberately as ever.

"Ah, — Ferguson, — what did I understand you to say the gentleman's name was?"

"Name? — he got no name! — Mummy! — 'Gyptian mummy!"

"Yes, yes. Born here?"

"No. *'Gyptian* mummy."

"Ah, just so. Frenchman, I presume?"

"No! — *not* Frenchman, not Roman! — born in Egypta!"

"Born in Egypta. Never heard of Egypta before. Foreign locality, likely. Mummy, — mummy. How calm he is, how self-possessed! Is — ah! — is he dead?"

"O *sacre bleu!* been dead three thousan' year!"

The doctor turned on him savagely:

"Here, now, what do you mean by such conduct as this? Playing us for Chinamen because we are strangers and trying to learn! Trying to impose your vile secondhand carcasses on *us!* Thunder and lightning! I've a notion to — to — if you've got a nice *fresh* corpse, fetch him out! — or we'll make a mummy of you!"

We make it exceedingly interesting for this Frenchman. However, he has paid us back, partly, without knowing it. He came to the hotel this morning to ask if we were up, and he endeavoured, as well as he could, to describe us, so that the landlord would know which persons he meant. He finished with the casual remark that we were lunatics. The observation was so innocent and so honest that it amounted to a very good thing for a guide to say.

Our Roman Ferguson is the most patient, unsuspecting, long-suffering subject we have had yet. We shall be sorry to part with him. We have enjoyed his society very much. We trust he has enjoyed ours, but we are harrassed with doubts.

MR. PICKWICK'S PROPOSAL TO MRS. BARDELL.

CHARLES DICKENS.

IT was evident that something of great importance was in contemplation, but what that something was not even Mrs. Bardell herself had been enabled to discover.

"Mrs Bardell," said Mr. Pickwick at last, as that amiable female approached the termination of a prolonged dusting of the apartment.

"Sir," said Mrs. Bardell.

"Your little boy is a very long time gone."

"Why, it is a good long way to the Borough, sir," remonstrated Mrs. Bardell.

"Ah," said Mr. Pickwick, "very true; so it is."

Mr. Pickwick relapsed into silence, and Mrs. Bardell resumed her dusting.

"Mrs. Bardell," said Mr. Pickwick at the expiration of a few minutes.

"Sir," said Mrs. Bardell again.

"Do you think it's a much greater expense to keep two people than to keep one?"

"La, Mr. Pickwick," said Mrs. Bardell, colouring up to the very border of her cap, as she fancied she observed a species of matrimonial twinkle in the eyes of her lodger; "La, Mr. Pickwick, what a question!"

"Well, but do you?" inquired Mr. Pickwick.

"That depends," said Mrs. Bardell, approaching the duster very near to Mr. Pickwick's elbow, which was planted on the table; "that depends a good deal upon the person, you know, Mr. Pickwick; and whether it's a saving and careful person, sir."

"That's very true," said Mr. Pickwick; "but the person I have in my eye (here he looked very hard at Mrs. Bardell) I think possesses these qualities, and has, moreover, a considerable knowledge of the world, and a great deal of sharpness, Mrs. Bardell, which may be of material use to me."

"La, Mr. Pickwick," said Mrs. Bardell, the crimson rising to her cap-border again.

"I do," said Mr. Pickwick, growing energetic, as was his wont in speaking of a subject which interested him; "I do, indeed; and, to tell you the truth, Mrs. Bardell, I have made up my mind."

"Dear me, sir!" exclaimed Mrs. Bardell.

"You'll think it not very strange now," said the amiable Mr. Pickwick, with a good-humoured glance at his companion, "that I never consulted you about this matter, and never mentioned it till I sent your little boy out this morning, — eh?"

Mrs. Bardell could only reply by a look. She had long worshipped Mr. Pickwick at a distance, but here she was, all at once, raised to a pinnacle to which her wildest and most extravagant hopes had never dared to aspire. Mr. Pickwick was going to propose, — a deliberate plan, too, — sent her little boy to the Borough to get him out of the way; how thoughtful, — how considerate!

"Well," said Mr. Pickwick, "what do you think?"

"O, Mr. Pickwick," said Mrs. Bardell, trembling with agitation, "you're very kind, sir."

"It'll save you a good deal of trouble, won't it?" said Mr. Pickwick.

"O, I never thought any thing of the trouble, sir," replied Mrs. Bardell; "and of course, I should take more trouble to please you then than ever; but it is so kind of you, Mr. Pickwick, to have so much consideration for my loneliness."

"Ah, to be sure," said Mr. Pickwick; "I never thought of that. When I am in town you'll always have somebody to sit with you. To be sure, so you will."

"I'm sure I ought to be a very happy woman," said Mrs. Bardell.

"And your little boy —" said Mr. Pickwick.

"Bless his heart," interposed Mrs. Bardell, with a maternal sob.

"He, too, will have a companion," resumed Mr. Pickwick, "a lively one, who'll teach him, I'll be bound, more tricks in a week than he would ever learn in a year." And Mr. Pickwick smiled placidly.

"O you dear!" said Mrs. Bardell.

Mr. Pickwick started.

"O you kind, good, playful dear," said Mrs. Bardell; and without more ado, she rose from her chair and flung her arms around Mr. Pickwick's neck, with a cataract of tears and a chorus of sobs.

"Bless my soul!" cried the astonished Mr. Pickwick; "Mrs. Bardell, my good woman — dear me, what a situation — pray consider, Mrs. Bardell, don't — if anybody should come —"

"O, let them come!" exclaimed Mrs. Bardell, frantically; "I'll never leave you, — dear, kind, good soul;" and, with these words, Mrs. Bardell clung the tighter.

"Mercy upon me!" said Mr. Pickwick, struggling violently, "I hear somebody coming up the stairs. Don't, don't, there's a good creature, don't." But entreaty and remonstrance were alike unavailing, for Mrs. Bardell had fainted in Mr. Pickwick's arms, and before he could gain time to deposit her on a chair, Master Bardell entered the room, ushering in Mr. Tupman, Mr. Winkle, and Mr. Snodgrass.

SAM WELLER'S VALENTINE.

CHARLES DICKENS.

"I'VE done now," said Sam, with slight embarrassment; "I've been a-writin'."

"So I see," replied Mr. Weller. "Not to any young 'ooman, I hope, Sammy."

"Why, it's no use a-sayin' it ain't," replied Sam. "It's a walentine."

"A what?" exclaimed Mr. Weller, apparently horror-stricken by the word.

"A walentine," replied Sam.

"Samivel, Samivel," said Mr. Weller, in reproachful accents, "I didn't think you'd ha' done it. Arter the warnin' you've had o' your father's wicious propensities; arter all I've said to you upon this here wery subject; arter actiwally seein' and bein' in the company o' your own mother-in-law, vich I should ha' thought was a moral lesson as no man could ever ha' forgotten to his dyin' day! I didn't think you'd ha' done it, Sammy, I didn't think you'd ha' done it." These reflections were too much for the good old man; he raised Sam's tumbler to his lips and drank off the contents.

"Wot's the matter now?" said Sam.

"Nev'r mind, Sammy," replied Mr. Weller, "it'll be a wery agonizin' trial to me at my time o' life; but I'm pretty tough, that's vun consolation, as the wery old turkey remarked ven the farmer said he vos afeerd he should be obliged to kill him for the London market."

"Wot'll be a trial?" inquired Sam.

"To see you married, Sammy; to see you a deluded wictim, and thinkin' in your innocence that it's all wery capital," replied Mr. Weller. "It's a dreadful trial to a father's feelin's, that 'ere, Sammy."

"Nonsense," said Sam, "I ain't a-goin' to get married; don't you fret yourself about that. I know you're a judge o' these things; order-in your pipe, and I'll read you the letter, — there!"

Sam dipped his pen into the ink to be ready for any corrections, and began with a very theatrical air, —

"'Lovely —'"

"Stop," said Mr. Weller, ringing the bell. "A double glass o' the inwariable, my dear."

"Very well, sir," replied the girl, who with great quickness appeared, vanished, returned, and *disappeared*.

"They seem to know your ways here," observed Sam.

"Yes," replied his father, "I've been here before, in my time. Go on, Sammy."

"'Lovely creetur',' " repeated Sam.

"'Taint in poetry, is it?" interposed the father.

"No, no," replied Sam.

"Wery glad to hear it," said Mr. Weller. "Poetry's unnat'ral. No man ever talked in poetry 'cept a beadle on boxin' day, or Warren's blackin', or Rowland's oil, or some o' them low fellows. Never you let yourself down to talk poetry, my boy. Begin again, Sammy."

Mr. Weller resumed his pipe with critical solemnity, and Sam once more commenced and read as follows:

"'Lovely creetur' i feel myself a damned —'"

"That ain't proper," said Mr. Weller, taking his pipe from his mouth.

"No; it ain't damned," observed Sam, holding the letter up to the light, "it's 'shamed,' there's a blot there; 'i feel myself ashamed.'"

"Wery good," said Mr. Weller. "Go on."

"'Feel myself ashamed, and completely cir —' I forget wot this 'ere word is," said Sam, scratching his head with the pen, in vain attempts to remember.

"Why don't you look at it, then?" inquired Mr. Weller.

"So I *am* a-lookin' at it," replied Sam, "but there's another blot; here's a 'c,' and a 'i,' and a 'd.'"

"Circumwented, p'rhaps," suggested Mr. Weller.

'No, it ain't that," said Sam; "'circumscribed,' that's it."

"That ain't as good a word as circumwented, Sammy," said Mr. Weller, gravely.

"Think not?" said Sam.

"Nothin' like it," replied his father.

"But don't you think it means more?" inquired Sam.

"Vell, p'rhaps it's a more tenderer word," said Mr. Weller, after a few moments' reflection. "Go on, Sammy."

"'Feel myself ashamed and completely circumscribed in a-dressin' of you, for you *are* a nice gal, and nothin' but it.'"

"That's a wery pretty sentiment," said the elder Mr. Weller, removing his pipe to make way for the remark.

"Yes, I think it's rayther good," observed Sam, highly flattered.

"Wot I like in that 'ere style of writin'," said the elder Mr. Weller, "is, that there ain't no callin' names in it, — no Wenuses, nor nothing o' that kind; wot's the good o' callin' a young 'ooman a Wenus or a angel, Sammy?"

"Ah! what indeed?" replied Sam.

"You might just as vell call her a griffin, or a unicorn, or a king's-arms at once, which is wery vell known to be a collection o' fabulous animals," added Mr. Weller.

"Just as well," replied Sam.

"Drive on, Sammy," said Mr. Weller.

Sam complied with the request, and proceeded as follows, his father continuing to smoke with a mixed expression of wisdom and complacency, which was particularly edifying:

"'Afore i see you i thought all women was alike.'"

"So they are," observed the elder Mr. Weller, parenthetically.

"'But now,'" continued Sam, "'now i find what a reg-'lar soft-headed, ink-red'lous turnip i must ha' been, for there ain't nobody like you, though *i* like you better than nothin' at all.' I thought it best to make that rayther strong," said Sam, looking up.

Mr. Weller nodded approvingly, and Sam resumed.

"'So i take the privilidge of the day, Mary, my dear, — as the gen'lm'n in difficulties did, ven he valked out of a Sunday, — to tell you that the first and only time i see you your likeness wos took on my hart in much quicker time and brighter colours than ever a likeness was taken by the profeel macheen, (which p'rhaps you may have heerd on Mary my dear,) altho' it *does* finish a portrait, and put the frame and glass on complete with a hook at the end to hang it up by, and all in two minutes and a quarter.'"

"I am afeerd that werges on the poetical, Sammy," said Mr. Weller, dubiously.

"No it don't," replied Sam, reading on very quickly to avoid contesting the point.

"'Except of me Mary my dear as your walentine, and think over what I've said. My dear Mary, I will now conclude.' That's all," said Sam.

"That's rayther a sudden pull up, ain't it, Sammy?" inquired Mr. Weller.

"Not a bit on it," said Sam; "she'll vish there wos more, and that's the great art o' letter writin'."

"Well," said Mr. Weller, "there's somethin' in that; and I wish your mother-in-law 'ud only conduct her conwersation on the same gen-teel principle. Ain't you a-goin' to sign it?"

"That's the difficulty," said Sam; "I don't know what *to* sign it."

"Sign it — Veller," said the oldest surviving proprietor of that name.

"Won't do," said Sam. "Never sign a walentine with your own name."

"Sign it Pickvick, then," said Mr. Weller; "it's a wery good name, and a easy one to spell."

"The wery thing," said Sam. "I *could* end with a werse; what do you think?"

"I don't like it, Sam," rejoined Mr. Weller. "I never know'd a respectable coachman as wrote poetry, 'cept one as made an affectin' copy o' werses the night afore he wos hung for a highway robbery, and *he* wos only a Cambervell man; so even that's no rule."

But Sam was not to be dissuaded from the poetical idea that had occurred to him, so he signed the letter, —

"Your love-sick
Pickwick."

PYRAMUS AND THISBE.

JOHN G. SAXE.

THIS tragical tale, which, they say, is a true one,
Is old; but the manner is wholly a new one.
One Ovid, a writer of some reputation,
Has told it before in a tedious narration;
In a style, to be sure, of remarkable fullness,
But which nobody reads on account of its dullness.

Young PETER PYRAMUS, — I call him Peter,
Not for the sake of the rhyme nor the metre,
But merely to make the name completer, —
For Peter lived in the olden times,
And in one of the worst of pagan climes
That flourish now in classical lore,
Long before either noble or boor
Had such a thing as a *Christian* name, —
Young Peter, then, was a nice young beau
As any young lady would wish to know;
In years, I ween, he was rather green,
That is to say, he was just eighteen, —
A trifle too short, a shaving too lean,
But "a nice young man" as ever was seen,
And fit to dance with a May-day queen!

Now Peter loved a beautiful girl
As ever ensnared the heart of an earl
In the magical trap of an auburn curl, —

A little Miss Thisbe, who lived next door,
(They lived, in fact, on the very same floor,
With a wall between them and nothing more, —
Those double dwellings were common of yore,)
And they loved each other, the legends say,
In that very beautiful, bountiful way,
That every young maid and every young blade
Are wont to do before they grow staid,
And learn to love by the laws of trade.
But (a-lack-a-day, for the girl and boy!)
A little impediment check'd their joy,
And gave them awhile the deepest annoy, —
For some good reason, which history cloaks,
The match didn't happen to please the old folks!
So Thisbe's father and Peter's mother
Began the young couple to worry and bother,
And tried their innocent passion to smother
By keeping the lovers from seeing each other!
But who ever heard of a marriage deterr'd
Or even deferr'd
By any contrivance so very absurd
As scolding the boy, and caging the bird?
Now, Peter, who was not discouraged at all
By obstacles such as the timid appal,
Contrived to discover a hole in the wall,
Which wasn't so thick but removing a brick
Made a passage, — though rather provokingly small.
Through this little chink the lover could greet her,
And secrecy made their courting the sweeter,
While Peter kiss'd Thisbe, and Thisbe kiss'd Peter, —
For kisses, like folks with diminutive souls,
Will manage to creep through the smallest of holes!

'Twas here that the lovers, intent upon love,
Laid a nice little plot to meet at a spot
Near a mulberry-tree in a neighbouring grove;
For the plan was all laid by the youth and the maid,

Whose hearts, it would seem, were uncommonly bold ones,
To run off and get married in spite of the old ones.
In the shadows of evening, as still as a mouse
The beautiful maiden slipp'd out of the house,
The mulberry-tree impatient to find;
While Peter, the vigilant matrons to blind,
Stroll'd leisurely out some minutes behind.

While waiting alone by the trysting-tree,
A terrible lion as e'er you set eye on
Came roaring along quite horrid to see,
And caused the young maiden in terror to flee;
(A lion's a creature whose regular trade is
Blood, — and "and a terrible thing among ladies,")
And, losing her veil as she ran from the wood,
The monster bedabbled it over with blood.

Now Peter, arriving, and seeing the veil
All cover'd o'er and reeking with gore,
Turn'd, all of a sudden, exceedingly pale,
And sat himself down to weep and to wail;
For, soon as he saw the garment, poor Peter
Made up his mind in very short metre
That Thisbe was dead, and the lion had eat her!
So breathing a prayer, he determined to share
The fate of his darling, "the loved and the lost,"
And fell on his dagger, and gave up the ghost!

Now Thisbe returning, and viewing her beau
Lying dead by her veil, (which she happen'd to know,)
She guess'd in a moment the cause of his erring;
And, seizing the knife that had taken his life,
In less than a jiffy was dead as a herring.

MORAL.

Young gentlemen: Pray recollect, if you please,
Not to make your appointments near mulberry-trees.
Should your mistress be missing, it shows a weak head

To be stabbing yourself, till you know she is dead.
Young ladies: You shouldn't go strolling about
When your anxious mammas don't know you are out;
And remember that accidents often befall
From kissing young fellows through holes in the wall!

HOW THE OLD HORSE WON THE BET.

OLIVER WENDELL HOLMES.

'TWAS on the famous trotting-ground,
The betting men were gather'd round
From far and near; the "cracks" were there
Whose deeds the sporting prints declare:
The swift g. m., Old Hiram's nag,
The fleet s. h., Dan Pfeiffer's brag,
With these a third, — and who is he
That stands beside his fast b. g.?
Budd Doble, whose catarrhal name
So fills the nasal trump of fame.
There, too, stood many a noted steed
Of Messenger and Morgan breed;
Green horses also, not a few, —
Unknown as yet what they could do;
And all the hacks that know so well
The scourgings of the Sunday swell.

Blue are the skies of opening day;
The bordering turf is green with May;
The sunshine's golden gleam is thrown
On sorrel, chestnut, bay, and roan;
The horses paw and prance and neigh;
Fillies and colts like kittens play,
And dance and toss their rippled manes
Shining and soft as silken skeins;
Wagons and gigs are ranged about,
And fashion flaunts her gay turnout:

Here stands — each youthful Jehu's dream —
The jointed tandem, ticklish team!
And there in ampler breadth expand
The splendours of the four-in-hand;
On faultless ties and glossy tiles
The lovely bonnets beam their smiles;
(The style's the man, so books avow;
The style's the woman anyhow;)
From flounces froth'd with creamy lace
Peeps out the pug-dog's smutty face,
Or spaniel rolls his liquid eye,
Or stares the wiry pet of Skye, —
O woman, in your hours of ease
So shy with us, so free with these!

"Come on! I'll bet you two to one
I'll make him do it!" "Will you? Done!"
What was it he was bound to do?
I did not hear, and can't tell you;
Pray listen till my story's through.

Scarce noticed, back behind the rest,
By cart and wagon rudely prest,
The parson's lean and bony bay,
Stood harness'd in his one-horse shay, —
Lent to his sexton for the day.
(A funeral, — so the sexton said;
His mother's uncle's wife was dead.)
Like Lazarus bid to Dives's feast,
So look'd the poor forlorn old beast;
His coat was rough, his tail was bare,
The gray was sprinkled in his hair:
Sportsmen and jockeys knew him not,
And yet they say he once could trot
Among the fleetest of the town,
Till something crack'd and broke him down, —
The steed's, the statesman's common lot!

"And are we then so soon forgot?"
Ah me! I doubt if one of you
Has ever heard the name "Old Blue,"
Whose fame through all this region rung
In those old days when I was young!

"Bring forth the horse!" Alas! he show'd
Not like the one Mazeppa rode;
Scant-maned, sharp-back'd and shaky-kneed,
The wreck of what was once a steed, —
Lips thin, eyes hollow, stiff in joints;
Yet not without his knowing points.
The sexton laughing in his sleeve,
As if 'twere all a make-believe,
Led forth the horse, and as he laugh'd
Unhitch'd the breeching from a shaft,
Unclasp'd the rusty belt beneath,
Drew forth the snaffle from his teeth,
Slipp'd off his head-stall, set him free
From strap and rein, — a sight to see!

So worn, so lean in every limb,
It can't be they are saddling him!
It is! His back the pig-skin strides,
And flaps his lank rheumatic sides;
With look of mingled scorn and mirth
They buckle round the saddle-girth;
With horsey wink and saucy toss
A youngster throws his leg across.
And so, his rider on his back,
They lead him, limping, to the track,
Far up behind the starting-point,
Too limber out each stiffen'd joint.

As through the jeering crowd he pass'd,
One pitying look old Hiram cast;
"Go it, ye cripple, while ye can!"

Cried out unsentimental Dan;
"A fast-day dinner for the crows!"
Budd Doble's scoffing shout arose.

Slowly, as when the walking-beam
First feels the gathering head of steam,
With warning cough and threatening wheeze
The stiff old charger crooks his knees;
At first with cautious step sedate,
As if he dragg'd a coach of state;
He's not a-colt; he knows full well
That time is weight and sure to tell;
No horse so sturdy but he fears
The handicap of twenty years.

As through the throng on either hand
The old horse nears the judges' stand,
Beneath his jockey's feather-weight
He warms a little to his gait,
And now and then a step is tried
That hints of something like a stride.

"Go!"—Through his ear the summons stung,
As if a battle-trump had rung;
The slumbering instincts long unstirr'd
Start at the old familiar word;
It thrills like flame through every limb,—
What mean his twenty years to him?
The savage blow his rider dealt
Fell on his hollow flanks unfelt;
The spur that prick'd his staring hide
Unheeded tore his bleeding side;
Alike to him are spur and rein,—
He steps a five-year-old again!

Before a quarter pole was pass'd,
Old Hiram said, "He's going fast."

Long ere the quarter was a half,
The chuckling crowd had ceased to laugh;
Tighter his frighten'd jockey clung
As in a mighty stride he swung,
The gravel flying in his track,
His neck stretch'd out, his ears laid back,
His tail extended all the while
Behind him like a rat-tail file!
Off went a shoe, — away it spun,
Shot like a bullet from a gun;
The quaking jockey shapes a prayer
From scraps of oaths he used to swear;
He drops his whip, he drops his rein,
He clutches fiercely for a mane;
He'll lose his hold, — he sways and reels, —
He'll slide beneath those trampling heels!
The knees of many a horseman quake,
The flowers on many a bonnet shake,
And shouts arise from left and right,
"Stick on! stick on!" "Hould tight! hould tight!"
"Cling round his neck; and don't let go, —
That pace can't hold, — there! steady! whoa!"
But, like the sable steed that bore
The spectral lover of Lenore,
His nostrils snorting foam and fire,
No stretch his bony limbs can tire;
And now the stand he rushes by,
And "Stop him! stop him!" is the cry.
"Stand back! he's only just begun, —
He's having out three heats in one!"
"Don't rush in front! he'll smash your brains;
But follow up and grab the reins!"
Old Hiram spoke. Dan Pfeiffer heard,
And sprang, impatient, at the word:
Budd Doble started on his bay,
Old Hiram follow'd on his gray,
And off they spring, and round they go,

The fast ones doing "all they know."
Look! twice they follow at his heels,
As round the circling course he wheels,
And whirls with him that clinging boy
Like Hector round the walls of Troy.
Still on, and on, the third time round!
They're tailing off! they're losing ground!
Budd Doble's nag begins to fail!
Dan Pfeiffer's sorrel whisks his tail!
And see! in spite of whip and shout,
Old Hiram's mare is giving out!
Now for the finish! At the turn,
The old horse — all the rest astern —
Comes swinging in, with easy trot;
By Jove! he's distanced all the lot!
That trot no mortal could explain;
Some said, "Old Dutchman come again!"
Some took his time, — at least, they tried,
But what it was could none decide;
One said he couldn't understand
What happen'd to his second-hand;
One said 2:10; *that* couldn't be, —
More like two twenty-two or three;
Old Hiram settled it at last:
"The time was two, — too mighty fast!"

The parson's horse had won the bet;
It cost him something of a sweat;
Back in the one-horse shay he went.
The parson wonder'd what it meant,
And murmur'd, with a mild surprise
And pleasant twinkle of the eyes,
"That funeral must have been a trick,
Or corpses drive at double quick;
I shouldn't wonder, I declare,
If Brother Murray made the prayer!"

And this is all I have to say
About the parson's poor old bay,
The same that drew the one-horse shay.

Moral for which this tale is told:
A horse *can* trot, for all he's old.

TOM'S LITTLE STAR.

FANNY FOSTER.

SWEET Mary, pledged to Tom, was fair
  And graceful, young and slim:
Tom loved her truly, and one dare
  Be sworn that she loved him;
For, twisting bashfully the ring
  That seal'd the happy fiat,
She coo'd, "When married in the Spring,
  Dear Tom, let's live *so* quiet!

Let's have our pleasant little place,
  Our books, a friend or two;
No noise, no crowd, but just your face
  For me, and mine for you.
Won't that be nice!" "It is my own
  Idea," said Tom, "so chary,
So deep and true, my love has grown,
  I worship you, my Mary."

She was a tender, nestling thing,
  A girl that loved her home,
A sort of dove with folded wing,
  A bird not made to roam,
But gently rest her little claw
  (The simile to carry)
Within a husband's stronger paw, —
  The very girl to marry.

Their courtship was a summer sea,
  So smooth, so bright, so calm,
Till one day Mary restlessly
  Endured Tom's circling arm,
And look'd as if she thought or plann'd,
  Her satin forehead wrinkled,
She beat a tattoo on his hand,
  Her eyes were strange and twinkled.

She never heard Tom's fond remarks,
  His "sweety-tweety dear,"
Or noticed once the little larks
  He play'd to make her hear.
"What ails," he begg'd, "my petsy pet?
  What ails my love, I wonder?"
"Do not be trifling, Tom. I've met
  Professor Shakespeare Thunder."

"Thunder!" said Tom; "and who is he?"
  "You goose! why, don't you know?"
"I don't. She never frown'd at me,
  Or call'd me goose. And though,"
Thought Tom, "it may be playfulness,
  It racks my constitution."
"Why, Thunder teaches with success
  Dramatic elocution."

"O! Ah! Indeed! and what is that?
  My notion is but faint."
"It's art," said Mary, brisk and pat.
  Tom thought that "art" meant *paint.*
"You blundering boy! why, art is just
  What makes one stare and wonder.
To understand *high* art you must
  Hear Shakespeare read by Thunder."

Tom started at the turn of phrase;
  It sounded like a swear.

Then Mary said, to his amaze,
  With nasal groan and glare,
"'To be or-r — not to be?'" And fain
  To act discreet yet gallant,
He ask'd, "Dear, have you any — pain?"
  "O, no, Tom; I have *talent*.

Professor Thunder told me so;
  He sees it in my eye;
He says my tones and gestures show
  My destiny is high."
Said Tom, for Mary's health afraid,
  His ignorance revealing,
"Is talent, dear, that noise you made?"
  "Why, no; that's Hamlet's feeling."

"He must have felt most dreadful bad."
  "The character is mystic,"
Mary explain'd, "and very sad,
  And very high artistic.
And you are not; you're commonplace;
  These things are far above you."
"I'm only," spoke Tom's honest face,
  "Artist enough — to love you."

From that time forth was Mary changed;
  Her eyes stretch'd open wide;
Her smooth fair hair in *friz* arranged,
  And parted on the side.
More and more strange she grew, and quite
  Incapable of taking
The slightest notice how each night
  She set Tom's poor heart aching.

As once he left her at the door,
  "A thousand times good-night,"
Sigh'd Mary, sweet as ne'er before.
  Poor Tom revived, look'd bright.

"Mary," he said, "you love me so?
We have not grown asunder?"
"Do not be silly, Tom; you know
I'm studying with Thunder.

That's from the famous Juliet scene.
I'll do another bit."
Quoth Tom, "I don't know what you mean."
"Then listen; this is it:
'Dear love, adieu.
Anon, good nurse. Sweet Montague, be true.
Stay but a little, I will come again.'
Now, Tom, say 'blessèd, blessèd night!'"
Said Tom, with hesitation,
"B-blessèd night." "Pshaw! that's not right;
You've no appreciation."

At Tom's next call he heard up-stairs
A laugh most loud and coarse;
Then Mary, knocking down the chairs,
Came prancing like a horse.
"'Ha! ha! ha! Well, Governor, how are ye? I've been down five times, climbing up your stairs in my long clothes.'
That's comedy," she said. "You're mad,"
Said Tom. "'Mad!' Ha! Ophelia!
'They bore him barefaced on his bier,
And on his grave rain'd many a tear,'"
She chanted, very wild and sad;
Then whisk'd off on Emilia:
"'You told a lie, an odious, fearful lie;
Upon my soul, a lie, a wicked lie.'"

She glared and howl'd two murder-scenes,
And mouth'd a new French *rôle*,
Where luckily the graceful miens
Hid the disgraceful soul.
She wept, she danced, she sang, she swore, —

From Shakespeare, — classic swearing;
A wild, abstracted look she wore,
And round the room went tearing.

And every word and every pause
Made Mary "quote a speech."
If Tom was sad, (and he had cause,)
She'd say, in sobbing screech,
"'Clifford, why don't you speak to me?'
At flowers for a present
She leer'd, and sang coquettishly,
"'When daises pied and violets blue.'"
Tom blurted, "That's not pleasant."
But Mary took offence at this:
"You have no soul," said she,
"For art, and do not know the bliss
Of notoriety.
The 'sacred fire' they talk about
Lights all the way before me;
It's quite my duty to 'come out,'
And all my friends implore me.

Three months of Thunder I have found
A thorough course," she said;
"I'll clear Parnassus with a bound."
(Tom softly shook his head.)
"I cannot fail to be the rage,"
(Tom look'd a thousand pities,)
"And so I'm going on the stage
To star in Western cities."

And Mary went; but Mary came
To grief within a week;
And in a month she came to Tom,
Quite gentle, sweet, and meek.
Tom was rejoiced: his heart was none
The hardest or the sternest.
"O, Tom," she sobb'd, "It look'd like fun,
But art is dreadful earnest.

Why, art means work, and slave, and bear
  All sorts of scandal too;
To dread the critics so you dare
  Not look a paper through;
O, 'art is long,' and hard." "And you
  Are short and — soft, my darling."
"My money, Tom, is gone, — it *flew*."
  "That's natural with a starling."

"I love you more than words can say,
  Dear Tom." He gave a start.
"Mary, is that from any play?"
  "No, Tom; it's from my heart."
He took the tired, sunny head,
  With all its spent ambitions,
So gently to his breast, she said
  No word but sweet permissions.

"Can you forgive me, Tom, for —" "Life,"
  He finish'd out the phrase.
"My love, you're pattern'd for a wife
  The crowded public ways
Are hard for even the strongest heart;
  Yours beats too softly human:
However woman choose her art,
  Yet art must choose its woman."

TOO LATE FOR THE TRAIN.

When they reached the depot, Mr. Mann and his wife gazed in unspeakable disappointment at the receding train, which was just pulling away from the bridge switch at the rate of a mile a minute. Their first impulse was to run after it, but as the train was out of sight and whistling for Sagetown before they could act upon the impulse, they remained in the carriage, and disconsolately turned their horses' heads homeward.

Mr. Mann broke the silence, very grimly: "It all comes of having to wait for a woman to get ready."

"I was ready before you were," replied his wife.

"Great Heavens," cried Mr. Mann, with great impatience, nearly jerking the horses' jaws out of place, "just listen to that! And I sat in the buggy ten minutes yelling at you to come along until the whole neighborhood heard me.".

"Yes," acquiesced Mrs. Mann, with the provoking placidity which no one can assume but a woman, "and every time I started down stairs you sent me back for something you had forgotten."

Mr. Mann groaned. "This is too much to bear," he said, "when everybody knows that if I were going to Europe I would rush into the house, put on a clean shirt, grab up my grip-sack, and fly, while you would want at least six months for preliminary preparations, and then dawdle around the whole day of starting until every train had left town."

Well, the upshot of the matter was that the Manns put off their visit to Aurora until the next week, and it was agreed that each one should get himself or herself ready and go down to the train and go, and the one who failed to get ready should be left. The day of the match came around in due time. The train was going at 10.30, and Mr. Mann, after attending to his business, went home at 9.45.

"Now, then," he shouted, "only three-quarters of an hour's time. Fly around; a fair field and no favours, you know."

And away they flew. Mr. Mann bulged into this room, and flew through that one, and dived into one closet after another with inconceivable rapidity, chuckling under his breath all the time to think how cheap Mrs. Mann would feel when he started off alone. He stopped on his way up stairs to pull off his heavy boots to save time. For the same reason he pulled off his coat as he ran through the dining room, and hung it on a corner of the silver closet. Then he jerked off his vest as he rushed through the hall, and tossed it on the hat-rack hook, and by the time he had reached his own room he was ready to plunge into his clean clothes. He pulled out a bureau drawer and began to paw at the things like a Scotch terrier after a rat.

"Eleanor," he shrieked, "where are my shirts?"

"In your bureau drawer," calmly replied Mrs. Mann, who was standing before a glass calmly and deliberately coaxing a refractory crimp into place.

"Well, but they ain't!" shouted Mr. Mann, a little annoyed. "I've emptied every thing out of the drawer, and there isn't a thing in it I ever saw before."

Mrs. Mann stepped back a few paces, held her head on one side, and, after satisfying herself that the crimp would do, replied, "Those things scattered around on the floor are all mine. Probably you haven't been looking into your own drawer."

"I don't see," testily observed Mr. Mann, "why you couldn't have put my things out for me when you had nothing else to do all the morning."

"Because," said Mrs. Mann, setting herself into an additional article of raiment with awful deliberation, "nobody put mine out for me. A fair field and no favours, my dear."

Mr. Mann plunged into his shirt like a bull at a red flag.

"Foul!" he shouted in malicious triumph; "No buttons on the neck!"

"Because," said Mrs. Mann, sweetly, after a deliberate stare at the fidgeting, impatient man, during which she buttoned her dress and put eleven pins where they would do the most good, "because you have got the shirt on wrong side out."

When Mr. Mann slid out of the shirt be began to sweat. He dropped the shirt three times before he got it on, and while it was over his head he heard the clock strike ten. When his head came through he saw Mrs. Mann coaxing the ends and bows of her necktie.

"Where are my shirt studs?" he cried.

Mrs. Mann went out into another room, and presently came back with gloves and hat, and saw Mr. Mann emptying all the boxes he could find in and around the bureau. Then she said, "In the shirt you just pulled off."

Mrs. Mann put on her gloves while Mr. Mann hunted up and down the room for his cuff-buttons.

"Eleanor," he snarled, at last, "I believe you must know where those cuff-buttons are."

"I haven't seen them," said the lady, settling her hat; "didn't you lay them down on the window-sill in the sitting-room last night?"

Mr. Mann remembered, and he went down-stairs on the run. He stepped on one of his boots, and was immediately landed in the hall at the foot of the stairs with neatness and dispatch, attended in the transmission with more bumps than he could count with Webb's Adder, and landed with a bang like the Hell-Gate explosion.

"Are you nearly ready, Algernon?" sweetly asked the wife of his bosom, leaning over the banisters.

The unhappy man groaned. "Can't you throw me down the other boot?" he asked.

Mrs. Mann, pityingly, kicked it down to him.

"My valise?" he inquired, as he tugged at the boot.

"Up in your dressing-room," she answered.

"Packed?"

"I do not know; unless you packed it yourself, probably not," she replied, with her hand on the door-knob; "I had barely time to pack my own."

She was passing out of the gate when the door opened, and he shouted, "Where in the name of goodness did you put my vest? It has all my money in it!"

"You threw it on the hat rack," she called. "Good-bye, dear."

Before she got to the corner of the street she was hailed again:

"Eleanor! Eleanor! Eleanor Mann! Did you wear off my coat?"

She paused and turned, after signalling the street car to stop, and cried, "You threw it in the silver-closet."

The street car engulfed her graceful form, and she was seen no more. But the neighbours say that they heard Mr. Mann charging up and down the house, rushing out of the front door every now and then, shrieking after the unconscious Mrs. Mann, to know where his hat was, and where she put the valise-key, and if she had his clean socks and undershirts, and that there wasn't a linen collar in the house. And, when he went away at last, he left the kitchen door, the side door, and the front door, all the down-stairs windows, and the front gate, wide open.

The loungers around the depot were somewhat amused, just as the train was pulling out of sight down in the yards, to see a flushed, enterprising man, with his hat on sideways, his vest unbuttoned and necktie flying, and his grip-sack flapping open and shut like a demented shutter on a March night, and a door-key in his hand, dash wildly across the platform and halt in the middle of the track, glaring in dejected, impotent, wrathful mortification at the departing train, and shaking his fist at a pretty woman who was throwing kisses at him from the rear platform of the last car.

REFLECTIONS IN THE PILLORY.

CHARLES LAMB.

SCENE, — *Opposite the Royal Exchange.*
TIME, — *Twelve to One, Noon.*

KETCH, my good fellow, you have a neat hand. Prithee adjust this new collar to my neck gingerly. I am not used to these wooden cravats. There, softly, softly! That seems the exact point between ornament and strangulation. A thought looser on this side. Now it will do. And have a care, in turning me, that I present my aspect due vertically. I now face the orient. In a quarter of an hour I shift southward, — do you mind? — and so on till I face the east again, travelling with the Sun. No half-points, I beseech you, — N. N. by W., or any such elaborate niceties.

They become the shipman's card, but not this mystery. Now leave me a little to my own reflections.

Bless us, what a company is assembled in honour of me! How grand I stand here! I never felt so sensibly before the effect of solitude in a crowd. I muse in solemn silence upon that vast miscellaneous rabble in the pit there. From my private box I contemplate, with mingled pity and wonder, the gaping curiosity of those underlings. There are my Whitechapel supporters. Rosemary Lane has emptied herself of the very flower of her citizens to grace my show. Duke's Place sits desolate. What is there in my face, that strangers should come so far from the east to gaze upon it? [*Here an egg narrowly misses him.*] That offering was well meant, but not so cleanly executed. By the tricklings, it should not be either myrrh or frankincense. Spare your presents, my friends: I am noways mercenary. I desire no missive tokens of your approbation. I am past those valentines. Bestow those coffins of untimely chickens upon mouths that water for them. Comfort your addle spouses with them at home, and stop the mouths of your brawling brats with such Olla Podridas: they have need of them. [*A brick is let fly.*] Discase not, I pray you, nor dismantle your rent and ragged tenements, to furnish me with architectural decorations, which I can excuse. This fragment might have stopped a flaw against snow comes. [*A coal flies.*] Cinders are dear, gentlemen. This nubbling might have helped the pot boil, when your dirty cuttings from the shambles at three-ha'pence a pound shall stand at a cold simmer. Now, south about, Ketch. I would enjoy Australian popularity.

What, my friends from over the water! Old benchers, — flies of a day — ephemeral Romans, — welcome! Doth the sight of me draw souls from limbo? Can it dispeople purgatory? — Ha!

What am I, or what was my father's House, that I should thus be set up a spectacle to gentlemen and others? Why are all faces, like Persians at the sunrise, bent singly on mine alone? It was wont to be esteemed an ordinary visnomy, a quotidian merely. Doubtless these assembled myriads discern some traits of nobleness, gentility, breeding, which hitherto have escaped the common observation, — some intimations, as it were, of wisdom, valour, piety, and so forth. My sight dazzles; and, if I am not deceived by the too-familiar pressure of this strange neckcloth that envelops it, my countenance gives out lambent glories. For some painter now to take me in the lucky point of expression! — the posture so convenient! — the head never shifting, but standing quiescent in a sort of natural frame. But these artisans require a westerly aspect. Ketch, turn me.

Something of St. James's air in these my new friends. How my prospects shift and brighten! Now, if Sir Thomas Lawrence be anywhere in that group, his fortune is made for ever. I think I see some one taking out of a crayon. I will compose my whole face to a smile, which yet shall not so predominate but that gravity and gayety shall contend, as it were, — you understand me? I will work up my thoughts to some mild rapture, — a gentle enthusiasm, — which the artist may transfer, in a manner, warm to the canvas. I will inwardly apostrophize my tabernacle.

Delectable mansion, hail! House not made of every wood! Lodging that pays no rent; airy and commodious; which, owing no window tax, art yet all casement, out of which men have such pleasure in peering and overlooking, that they will sometimes stand an hour together to enjoy thy prospects! Cell, recluse from the vulgar! Quiet retirement from the great Babel, yet affording sufficient glimpses into it! Pulpit, that instructs without note or sermon-book; into which the preacher is inducted without tenth or first-fruit! Throne, unshared and single, that disdainest a Brentford competitor! Honour without corrival! Or hearest thou, rather, magnificent theatre, in which the spectator comes to see and to be seen? From thy giddy heights I look down upon the common herd, who stand with eyes upturned, as if a winged messenger hovered over them; and mouths open as if they expected manna. I feel, I feel, the true Episcopal yearnings. Behold in me, my flock, your true overseer! What though I cannot lay hands, because my own are laid; yet I can mutter benedictions. True *otium cum dignitate!* Proud Pisgah eminence! pinnacle sublime! O Pillory! 'tis thee I sing! Thou younger brother to the gallows, without his rough and Esau palms, that with ineffable contempt surveyest beneath thee the grovelling stocks, which claim presumptuously to be of thy great race! Let that low wood know that thou art far higher born. Let that domicile for groundling rogues and base earth-kissing varlets envy thy preferment, not seldom fated to be the wanton baiting-house, the temporary retreat, of poet and of patriot. Shades of Bastwick and of Prynne hover over thee, — Defoe is there, and more greatly daring Shebbeare, — from their (little more elevated) stations they look down with recognitions. Ketch, turn me.

I now veer to the north. Open your widest gates, thou proud Exchange of London, that I may look in as proudly! Gresham's wonder, hail! I stand upon a level with all your kings. They and I, from equal heights, with equal superciliousness, o'erlook the plodding money-hunting tribe below, who, busied in their sordid speculations, scarce elevate their eyes to notice your ancient, or my recent, grandeur. The second Charles smiles on me from three pedestals! He closed the Exchequer: I cheated the Excise. Equal our darings, equal be our lot.

Are those the quarters? 'tis their fatal chime. That the ever-winged hours would but stand still! but I must descend, — descend from this dream of greatness. Stay, stay a little while, importunate hour-hand! A moment or two, and I shall walk on foot with the undistinguished many. The clock speaks one. I return to common life. Ketch, let me out.

ON THE DEATH OF A MAD DOG.

OLIVER GOLDSMITH.

GOOD people all of every sort,
  Give ear unto my song;
And, if you find it wondrous short,
  It cannot hold you long.

In Islington there was a man,
  Of whom the world might say
That still a godly race he ran,
  Whene'er he went to pray.

A kind and gentle heart he had,
  To comfort friends and foes;
The naked every day he clad —
  When he put on his clothes.

And in that town a dog was found,
  As many dogs there be,
Both mongrel, puppy, whelp, and hound,
  And curs of low degree.

This dog and man at first were friends;
  But, when a pique began,
The dog, to gain some private ends,
  Went mad and bit the man.

Around from all the neighbouring streets
  The wondering neighbours ran,
And swore the dog had lost his wits,
  To bite so good a man.

The wound it seem'd both sore and sad
  To every Christian eye;
And, while they swore the dog was mad,
  They swore the man would die.

But soon a wonder came to light,
  That showed the rogues they lied;
The man recover'd of the bite,
  The dog it was that died.

BETSY AND I ARE OUT.

WILL CARLETON.

DRAW up the papers, lawyer, and make 'em good and stout,
For things at home are cross-ways, and Betsy and I are out, —
We who have work'd together so long as man and wife
Must pull in single harness the rest of our nat'ral life.

"What is the matter," says you? I swan! it's hard to tell!
Most of the years behind us we've pass'd by very well:
I have no other woman, — she has no other man;
Only we've lived together as long as ever we can.

So I have talk'd with Betsy, and Betsy has talk'd with me;
And we've agreed together that we can never agree;
Not that we've catch'd each other in any terrible crime;
We've been a gatherin' this for years, a little at a time.

There was a stock of temper we both had, for a start;
Although we ne'er suspected 'twould take us two apart:
I had my various failings, bred in the flesh and bone,
And Betsy, like all good women, had a temper of her own.

The first thing, I remember, whereon we disagreed,
Was somethin' concerning Heaven, — a difference in our creed;
We arg'ed the thing at breakfast, — we arg'ed the thing at tea, —
And the more we arg'ed the question, the more we couldn't agree.

And the next that I remember was when we lost a cow;
She had kick'd the bucket, for certain, — the question was only —
  How?
I held my opinion, and Betsy another had;
And when we were done a-talkin', we both of us was mad.

And the next that I remember, it started in a joke;
But for full a week it lasted, and neither of us spoke:
And the next was when I fretted because she broke a bowl;
And she said I was mean and stingy, and hadn't any soul.

And so the thing kept workin', and all the self-same way;
Always somethin' to ar'ge, and something sharp to say, —
And down on us came the neighbours, a couple o' dozen strong,
And lent their kindest sarvice to help the thing along.

And there have been days together — and many a weary week —
When both of us were cross and spunky, and both too proud to speak;
And I have been thinkin' and thinkin', the whole of the Summer and Fall,
If I can't live kind with a woman, why, then I won't at all.

And so I've talk'd with Betsy, and Betsy has talk'd with me;
And we have agreed together that we can never agree;
And what is hers shall be hers, and what is mine shall be mine;
And I'll put it in the agreement and take it to her to sign.

Write on the paper, lawyer, — the very first paragraph, —
Of all the farm and live stock, she shall have her half;
For she has help'd to earn it, through many a weary day,
And it's nothin' more than justice that Betsy has her pay.

Give her the house and homestead; a man can thrive and roam,
But women are wretched critters, unless they have a home.
And I have always determined, and never fail'd to say,
That Betsy should never want a home, if I was taken away.

There's a little hard money besides, that's drawin' tol'rable pay,
A couple of hundred dollars laid by for a rainy day, —
Safe in the hands of good men, and easy to get at;
Put in another clause there, and give her all of that.

I see that you are smiling, sir, at my givin' her so much;
Yes, divorce is cheap, sir, but I take no stock in such:
True and fair I married her, when she was blithe and young,
And Betsy was always good to me, exceptin' with her tongue.

When I was young as you, sir, and not so smart, perhaps,
For me she mitten'd a lawyer, and several other chaps;
And all of 'em was fluster'd, and fairly taken down,
And for a time I was counted the luckiest man in town.

Once, when I had a fever, — I won't forget it soon, —
I was hot as a basted turkey and crazy as a loon, —
Never an hour went by me when she was out of sight;
She nursed me true and tender, and stuck to me day and night.

And if ever a house was tidy, and ever a kitchen clean,
Her house and kitchen was tidy as any I ever seen;
And I don't complain of Betsy or any of her acts,
Exceptin' when we've quarrell'd, and told each other facts.

So draw up the paper, lawyer; and I'll go home to-night,
And read the agreement to her, and see if it's all right;
And then in the mornin' I'll sell to a tradin' man I know;
And kiss the child that was left to us, and out in the world I'll go.

And one thing put in the paper, that first to me didn't occur;
That when I am dead at last she will bring me back to her,
And lay me under the maple we planted years ago,
When she and I was happy, before we quarrell'd so.

And, when she dies, I wish that she would be laid by me;
And, lyin' together in silence, perhaps we'll then agree;
And, if ever we meet in Heaven, I wouldn't think it queer
If we loved each other the better because we've quarrell'd here.

HOW BETSY AND I MADE UP.

WILL CARLETON.

GIVE me your hand, Mr. Lawyer; how do you do to-day?
You drew up that agreement, — I s'pose you want your pay:
Don't cut down your figures; make it an X. or a V.;
For that 'ere written agreement was just the makin' of me.

Goin' home that evenin', I tell you I was blue,
Thinkin' of all my troubles, and what I was goin' to do;
And, if my hosses hadn't been the steadiest team alive,
They'd 've tipp'd me over, certain, for I couldn't see where to drive.

No, — for I was laborin' under a heavy load;
No, — for I was travelin' an entirely different road;
For I was a-tracin' over the path of our lives ag'in,
And seein' where we miss'd the way, and where we might have been.

And many a corner we'd turn'd that just to a quarrel led,
When I ought to've held my temper, and driven straight ahead;
And the more I thought it over the more these memories came,
And the more I struck the opinion that I was the most to blame.

And things I had long forgotten kept risin' in my mind,
Of little matters betwixt us, where Betsy was good and kind;
And these things they flash'd all through me, as you know things sometimes will,
When a feller's alone in the darkness, and every thing is still.

"But," says I, "we're too far along to take another track,
And when I put my hand to the plough I do not oft turn back;
And 'taint an uncommon thing now for couples to smash in two,"
And so I set my teeth together, and vow'd I'd see it through.

When I came in sight o' the house 'twas some'at in the night,
And just as I turn'd a hill-top I see the kitchen light;
Which often a han'some pictur' to a hungry person makes,
But it don't interest a feller much that's goin' to pull up stakes.

And when I went in the house the table was set for me,—
As good a supper's I ever saw, or ever want to see;
And I cramm'd the agreement down in my pocket as well as I could,
And fell to eatin' my victuals, which somehow didn't taste good.

And Betsy she pretended to look about the house,
But she watch'd my side coat pocket like a cat would watch a mouse;
And then she went to foolin' a little with her cup,
And intently readin' a newspaper, a-holdin' it wrong side up.

And when I'd done my supper I draw'd the agreement out,
An give it to her without a word, for she know'd what 'twas about,
And then I humm'd a little tune, but now and then a note
Was bu'sted by some animal that hopp'd up in my throat.

Then Betsy she got her specks from off the mantle-shelf,
And read the article over quite softly to herself;
Read it by little and little, for her eyes is gettin' old,
And lawyers' writin' ain't no print, especially when it's cold.

And after she'd read a little she give my arm a touch,
And kindly said she was afraid I was 'lowin' her too much;
But when she was through she went for me, her face a-streamin' with tears,
And kiss'd me for the first time in over twenty years.

I don't know what you'll think, Sir, — I didn't come to inquire, —
But I pick'd up that agreement and stuff'd it in the fire;
And I told her we'd bury the hatchet alongside of the cow;
And we struck an agreement never to have another row.

And I told her in the future I would'nt speak cross or rash,
If half the crockery in the house was broken all to smash;
And she said in regard to *Heaven*, we'd try and learn its worth
By startin' a branch establishment and runnin' it *here on Earth.*

And so we sat a-talkin' three-quarters of the night,
And open'd our hearts to each other until they both grew light;
And the days when I was winnin' her away from so many men
Was nothin' to that evenin' I courted her over again.

Next mornin' an *ancient virgin* took pains to call on us,
Her lamp all trimm'd and a-burnin' to kindle another fuss;
But, when she went to pryin' and openin' of old sores,
My Betsy rose politely, and show'd her out-of-doors.

Since then I don't deny but there's been a word or two;
But we've got our eyes wide open, and know just what to do:
When one speaks cross the other just meets it with a laugh,
And the first one's ready to give up considerable more than half.

Maybe you'll think me soft, Sir, a-talkin' in this style,
But somehow it does me lots of good to tell it once in a while;
And I do it for a compliment, — 'tis so that you can see
That that there written agreement of yours was just the makin' of me.

So make out your bill, Mr. Lawyer; don't stop short of an X.;
Make it *more* if you want to, for I have got the checks:
I'm richer than a National Bank, with all its treasures told,
For I've got a wife at home now that's worth her weight in gold.

X.

DIALECTIC.

COCKNEY.

LORD DUNDREARY PROPOSING.

F. J. SKILL.

ANY fellah feelth nervouth when he knowth he'th going to make an ath of himthelf.

That's vewy twue, — I — I've often thed tho before. But the fact is, evewy fellah dothn't make an ath of himthelf, at least not quite such an ath as I've done in my time. I — don't mind telling you, but 'pon my word now, — I — I've made an awful ath of mythelf on thome occathions. You don't believe it now, — do you? I — thought you wouldn't; but I have now — *weally*. Particularly with wegard to women. To tell the twuth, that is my weakneth, — I s'pose I'm what they call a ladies' man. The pwetty cweachaws like me, — I know they do, — though they pwetend not to do so. It — it's the way with some fellahs. Let me see, — where was I? O, I rekomember, — or weckolect, — which is it? Never mind; I was saying that I was a ladies' man.

I wanted to tell you of one successful advenchaw I had, — at least, when I say successful, I mean it would have been as far as *I* was concerned, — but, of course, when two people are engaged, — or wather, when one of 'em *wants* to be engaged, one fellah by himthelf can't engage that he'll engage affections that are otherwise engaged. By the way, what a lot of 'gages that was in one thentence, and yet — it seems quite fruitless. Come, that's pwetty smart, that is — for me.

Well, as I was saying, — I mean, as I meant to have said, — when I was stopping down at Wockingham, with the Widleys, last Autumn, there was a mons'ous jolly girl staying there too. I don't mean *two* girls, you know, — only — only *one* girl — But stop a minute, — is that right? How could *one* girl be stopping there *two?* What doosid queer expressions there are in the English language! Stopping there too! It's vewy odd. *I* — I'll swear there was only one girl, — at least, the one that *I* mean was only one, — if she'd been two, of course, I should have known it, — let me see now, one is singular, and two is plural, — well, you know, she *was* a singular girl, — and she — she was one too many for me. Ah, I see now, — that accounts for it, — one *two* many — of course — I *knew* there was a two somewhere. She had a vewy queer name, Miss — miss — Missmiss, no not Miss Missmiss — I always miss the wrong — I mean the right name, — Miss Chaffingham, — that's it, — Charlotte Chaffingham.

At the top of the long walk at Wockingham there is a summer-house, — a jolly sort of place, with a lot of ferns and things about, and behind there are a lot of shrubs and bushes and pwickly plants, which give a sort of rural or *wurwal* — which is it? blest if I know — look to the place, and as it was vewy warm, I thought if I'm ever to make an ath of mythelf by pwoposing to this girl, — I won't do it out in the eye of the Sun, — it's so pwecious hot. So I pwoposed we should walk in and sit down, and so we did, and then I began:

"Miss Chaffingham, now, don't you think it doosid cool?"

"*Cool*, Lord D.," she said; "why, I thought you were complaining of the heat."

"I beg your pardon," I said, "I — I — can't speak vewy fast," (the fact is, that a beathly wasp was buthhing about me at the moment,) "and I hadn't quite finished my thentence. I was going to say, don't you think it doosid cool of Wagsby to go on laughing — at — at a fellah as he does?"

"Well, my Lord," she said, "I think so too; and I wonder you stand it. You—you have your remedy, you know."

"What remedy?" I said. "You—you don't mean to say I ought to thwash him, Miss Charlotte?"

Here she—she somehow began to laugh, but in such a peculiar way that I—I couldn't think what she meant.

"A vewy good idea," I said. "I've a vewy good mind to twy it. I had on the gloves once with a lay figure in a painter's studio,—and gave it an awful licking. It's twue, it—it didn't hit back, you know; I—*I* did all—all the hitting then. And pwaps—pwaps Wagsby would hit back. But, if—if he did any thing so ungentlemanlike as that, I could always—always—"

"Always *what*, my Lord?" said Lotty, who was going on laughing in a most hysterical manner.

"Why, I could always say it was a mithtake, and—and it shouldn't happen again, you know."

"Admirable policy, upon my word," she thaid, and began tittering again. But what the dooth amused her so *I* never could make out. Just then we heard a sort of rustling in the leaves behind, and I confess I felt wather nervouth.

"It's only a bird," Lotty said; and then we began talking of that little wobbin-wedbreast, and what a wonderful thing Nature is,—and how doosid pwetty it was to see her laws obeyed. And I said, "O Miss Chaffingham!" I said, "If I was a wobbin—"

"Yes, Dundreary," she anthered,—vewy soft and sweet. And I thought to mythelf,—Now's the time to ask her,—now's the time to—I—I was beginning to wuminate again, but she bwought me to my thenses by saying,—

"Yes?" interwoggatively.

"If I was a wobbin, Lotty,—and—and *you* were a wobbin—" I exclaimed,—with a full voice of emothun.

"Well, my Lord?"

"Wouldn't it be—jolly to have thpeckled eggs evewy morning for bweakfast?"

That wasn't *quite* what I was going to say; but just then

there was another rustling behind the summer-house, and in wushed that bwute, Wagsby.

"What's the wow, Dundreary?" said he, grinning in a dweadfully idiotic sort of way. "Come, old fellah," (I — I hate a man who calls me old fellah, — it's so beathly familiar). And then he said he had come on purpose to fetch us back, (confound him!) as they had just awanged to start on one of those cold-meat excursions, — no, that's not the word, I know, — but it has something to do with cold meat, — pic — pickles, is it? — no, pickwick? pic — I have it, — they wanted us to go picklicking, — I mean picknicking with them.

Here was a dithappointment. Just as I thought to have a nice little flirtathun with Lotty — to be interwupted in this manner! Was ever any thing so pwovoking? And all for a picnic, — a thort of early dinner without chairs or tables, and a lot of flies in the muthtard! I was in *such* a wage!

Of course I didn't get another chance to say all I wanted. I had lost my opportunity, and, I fear, made an ath of mythelf.

THE SWELL.

GEORGE W. KYLE.

I SAY! I wonder why fellahs ever wide in horse-cars? I've been twying all day to think why fellahs ever do it, weally! I know some fellahs that are in business, down town, you know, — C. B. Jones, cotton-dealer; Smith Brothers, woollen goods; Bwown & Company, stock-bwokers and that sort of thing, you know, — who say they do it every day. If I was to do it every day, my funeral would come off in about a week. 'Pon my soul, it would. I wode in a horse-car one day. Did it for a lark. Made a bet I would wide in a horse-car, 'pon my soul, I did. So I went out on the pavement before the club-house and called one. I said, "Horse-car! horse-car!" but not one of 'em stopped, weally! Then I saw that fellahs wun after them, — played tag with them, you know, as the dweadful little girls do when school is coming out. And sometimes they caught the cars, — ah — and sometimes they did not. So I wun after one, I did weally, and I caught it. I was out of breath, you know, and a fellah on the platform — a conductor fellah — poked me in the back and said, "Come! move up! make room for this lady!" Ah — by Jove he did, you know! I looked for the lady so, but I could see no lady, and I said so. There was a female person behind me, with large market basket, cwowded with, ah, — vegetables and such dweadful stuff, and another person with a bundle, and another with a baby, you know. The person with the basket prodded me in the back with it, and I said to the conductor fellah, said I, "Where shall I sit down? I — ah — I don't see any seat, you know." "The seats seem to be occupied by persons, conductor," said I. "Where shall I sit?"

He was wude, very wude, indeed, and he said, "You can sit on your thumb if you have a mind to." And when I wemonstrated with him upon the impwopwiety of telling a gentleman to sit on his thumb, he told me to go to thunder. "Go to thunder!" he did, indeed. After a while one of the persons got out, and I sat down; it was vewy disagweeable! Opposite me, there were several persons belonging to the labowing classes, with what I pwesume to be lime on their boots; and tin kettles which they carried for some mysterious purpose in their hands. There was a person with a large basket, and a coloured person. Next to me there sat a fellah that had been eating onions! 'Twas vewy offensive! I couldn't stand it! No fellah could, you know. I had heard that if any one in a car was annoyed by a fellah-passenger he should weport it to the conductor. So I said, "Conductor! put this person out of the car! he annoys me vewy much. He has been eating onions." But the conductor fellah only laughed. He did, indeed! And the fellah that had been eating onions said, "Hang yer impidence, what do ye mean by that?" "It's extwemely disagweeable, you know, to sit near one who has been eating onions," said

I. "I think you ought to resign, get out, you know." And then, though I'm sure I spoke in the most wespectful manner, he put his fist under my nose and wemarked, "You'll eat that, hang you, in a minute!" he did, indeed. And a fellah opposite said, "Put a head on him, Jim!" I suppose from his tone that it was some colloquial expwession of the lower orders, referring to a personal attack. It was vewy disagweeable, indeed. I don't see why any fellah ever wides in the horse-cars. But I didn't want a wow, you know. A fellah is apt to get a black eye, and a black eye spoils one's appeawance, don't you think? So I said, "Beg pardon, I'm sure." The fellah said, "O, hang you!" he did, indeed. He was a vewy ill-bred person. And all this time the car kept stopping, and more persons of the lower orders kept getting on. A vewy dweadful woman with a vewy dweadful baby stood right before me, intercepting my view of the street; and the baby had an orange in one hand and some candy in the other. And I was wondering why persons of the lower classes were allowed to have such dirty babies, and why Bergh or some one didn't interfere, you know, when, before I knew what she was doing, that dweadful woman sat that dweadful baby wight down on my lap! She did, indeed. And it took hold of my shirt bosom with one of its sticky hands, and took my eye-glass away with the other, and, upon my honour, I'm quite lost without my eye-glass. "You'll have to kape him till I find me money," said the woman. "Weally!" said I, "I'm not a nursery-maid, ma'am." Then the people about me laughed, they did, indeed. I could not endure it. I jumped up and dwopped the baby in the straw. "Stop the car, conductor," said I, "stop the car." What do suppose he said? "Hurry up now, be lively, be lively, don't keep me waiting all day!" And I was about to wemonstrate with him upon the impwopwiety of speaking so to a gentleman, when he pushed me off the car. That was the only time I ever wode in a horse-car. I wonder why fellahs ever do wide in horse-cars? I should think they would pwefer cabs, you know.

FRENCH.

THE FRENCHMAN AND THE FLEA-POWDER.

A Frenchman once — so runs a certain ditty —
Had cross'd the Straits to famous London city,
To get a living by the arts of France,
And teach his neighbour, rough John Bull, to dance.
But, lacking pupils, vain was all his skill;
His fortunes sank from low to lower still;
Until, at last, — pathetic to relate, —
Poor Monsieur landed at starvation's gate.
Standing, one day, beside a cook-shop door,
And, gazing in, with aggravation sore,
He mused within himself what he should do
To fill his empty maw, and pocket too.
By nature shrewd, he soon contrived a plan,
And thus to execute it straight began:
A piece of common brick he quickly found,
And with a harder stone to powder ground,
Then wrapp'd the dust in many a dainty piece
Of paper, labell'd "Poison for de Fleas,"
And sallied forth, his roguish trick to try,
To show his treasures, and to see who'd buy.
From street to street he cried, with lusty yell,
"Here's grand and sovereign *flea poudare* to sell!"
And fickle Fortune seem'd to smile at last,
For soon a woman hailed him as he pass'd,
Struck a quick bargain with him for the lot,
And made him five crowns richer on the spot.
Our wight, encouraged by this ready sale,
Went into business on a larger scale;
And soon, throughout all London, scatter'd he
The "only genuine poudare for de flea."
Engaged, one morning, in his new vocation
Of mingled boasting and dissimulation,
He thought he heard himself in anger call'd;

And, sure enough, the self-same woman bawl'd, —
In not a mild or very tender mood, —
From the same window where before she stood.
"Hey, there," said she, "You Monsher Powder-man!
Escape my clutches now, sir, if you can;
I'll let you dirty, thieving Frenchmen know
That decent people won't be cheated so."
Then spoke Monsieur, and heaved a saintly sigh,
With humble attitude and tearful eye; —
"Ah, Madame! s'il vous plait, attendez vous, —
I vill dis leetle ting *explain* to you:
My poudare gran! magnifique! why abuse him?
Aha! I show you *how to use him:*
First, you must wait until you *catch de flea;*
Den, tickle he on de petite rib, you see;
And, when he laugh, — aha! he ope his troat;
Den *poke de poudare down!* — BEGAR! HE CHOKE.

A FRENCHMAN ON MACBETH.

AN enthusiastic French student of Shakespeare thus comments on the tragedy of Macbeth:

"Ah! your Mossieu' Shak-es-pier! He is gr-aä-nd — mysterieuse — so-blime! You 'ave reads ze Macabess? — ze scene of ze Mossieu' Macabess vis ze Vitch, — eh? Superb sooblimitée! W'en he say to ze Vitch, 'Ar-r-roynt ze, Vitch!' she go away: but what she *say* when she go away? She say she will do s'omesing dat aves got no naäme! 'Ah, ha!' she say, 'I go, like ze r-r-aä-t vizout ze tail, *but* I'll do! I'll *do!* I'll DO!' *Wa't* she do? Ah, ha! — voila le graand mystérieuse Mossieu' Shak-es-pier! She not *say* what she do!"

This *was* "grand," to be sure: but the prowess of Macbeth, in his "bout" with Macduff, awakens all the mercurial Frenchman's martial ardour:

"Mossieu' Macabess, he see him come, clos' by; he say

(proud *empressement*), '*Come o-o-n*, Mossieu' Macduffs, and d—d be he who first say *Enoffs!*' Zen zey fi-i-ght—moche. Ah, ha!—voila! Mossieu' Macabess, vis his br-r-ight r-r-apier 'pink' him, vat you call, in his body. He 'ave gots mal d'estomac: he say, vis grand simplicité, '*Enoffs!*' What *for* he say 'Enoffs?' 'Cause he *got* enoffs—plaäinty; and he *ex*pire, r-r-ight away, 'mediately, pretty quick! Ah, mes amis, Mossieu' Shak-es-pier is rising man in La Belle France!"

MONSIEUR TONSON.

THERE lived, as Fame reports, in days of yore,
At least some fifty years ago or more,
  A pleasant wight in town, yclept Tom King,—
A fellow that was clever at a joke,
Expert in all the arts to tease and smoke;
  In short, for strokes of humour quite the thing.

To many a jovial club this King was known,
With whom his active wit unrivall'd shone:
  Choice spirit, grave free-mason, buck and blood,
Would crowd, his stories and *bon-mots* to hear;
And none a disappointment e'er could fear,
  His humour flow'd in such a copious flood.

To him a frolic was a high delight;
A frolic he would hunt for, day and night,
  Careless how prudence on the sport might frown:
If e'er a pleasant mischief sprang to view,
At once o'er hedge and ditch away he flew,
  Nor left the game till he had run it down.

One night, our hero, rambling with a friend,
Near famed St. Giles's chanced his course to bend,
  Just by that spot, the Seven Dials hight.
'Twas silence all around, and clear the coast,

The watch, as usual, dozing on his post,
  And scarce a lamp display'd a twinkling light.

Around this place there lived the numerous clans
Of honest, plodding, foreign artisans,
  Known at that time by name of refugees.
The rod of persecution from their home
Compell'd the inoffensive race to roam,
  And here they lighted, like a swarm of bees.

Well! our two friends were sauntering through the street,
In hopes some food for humour soon to meet,
  When, in a window near, a light they view;
And, though a dim and melancholy ray,
It seem'd the prologue to some merry play,
  So towards the gloomy dome our hero drew.

Straight at the door he gave a thundering knock,
(The time we may suppose near two o'clock.)
  "I'll ask," says King, "if Thompson lodges here."
"Thompson," cries t'other, "who the devil's he?"
"I know not," King replies, "but want to see
  What kind of animal will now appear."

After some time a little Frenchman came;
One hand display'd a rushlight's trembling flame,
  The other held a thing they call'd *culotte;*
An old striped woollen nightcap graced his head,
A tatter'd waistcoat o'er one shoulder spread;
  Scarce half awake, he heaved a yawning note.

Though thus untimely roused he courteous smiled,
And soon address'd our wag in accents mild,
  Bending his head politely to his knee, —
"Pray, sare, vat vant you, dat you come so late?
I beg your pardon, sare, to make you vait;
  Pray tell me, sare, vat your commands vid me?"

"Sir," replied King, "I merely thought to know,
As by your house I chanced to-night to go,
(But, really, I disturb'd your sleep, I fear,)
I say, I thought that you perhaps could tell,
Among the folks who in this quarter dwell,
If there's a Mr. Thompson lodges here?"

The shivering Frenchman, though not pleased to find
The business of this unimportant kind,
Too simple to suspect 'twas meant in jeer,
Shrugg'd out a sigh that thus his rest was broke,
Then, with unalter'd courtesy, he spoke;
"No, sare, no Monsieur Tonson lodges here."

Our wag begg'd pardon, and toward home he sped,
While the poor Frenchman crawl'd again to bed.
But King resolved not thus to drop the jest;
So, the next night, with more of whim than grace,
Again he made a visit to the place,
To break once more the poor old Frenchman's rest.

He knock'd, — but waited longer than before;
No footstep seem'd approaching to the door;
Our Frenchman lay in such a sleep profound.
King with the knocker thunder'd then again,
Firm on his post determined to remain;
And oft, indeed, he made the door resound.

At last King hears him o'er the passage creep,
Wondering what fiend again disturb'd his sleep:
The wag salutes him with a civil leer;
Thus drawling out to heighten the surprise,
While the poor Frenchman rubbed his heavy eyes,
"Is there — a Mr. Thompson — lodges here?"

The Frenchman falter'd, with a kind of fright, —
"Vy, sare, I'm sure I told you, sare, last night,

(And here he labour'd, with a sigh sincere,)
No Monsieur Tonson in the varld I know,
No Monsieur Tonson here, — I told you so;
Indeed, sare, dare no Monsieur Tonson here!"

Some more excuses tender'd, off King goes,
And the old Frenchman sought once more repose.
The rogue next night pursued his old career.
'Twas long indeed before the man came nigh,
And then he utter'd in a piteous cry,
"Sare, 'pon my soul, no Monsieur Tonson here!"

Our sportive wight his usual visit paid,
And the next night came forth a prattling maid,
Whose tongue, indeed, than any Jack went faster;
Anxious, she strove his errand to inquire,
He said 'twas vain her pretty tongue to tire,
He should not stir till he had seen her master.

The damsel then began, in doleful state,
The Frenchman's broken slumbers to relate,
And begg'd he'd call at proper time of day.
King told her she must fetch her master down,
A chaise was ready, he was leaving town,
But first had much of deep concern to say.

Thus urged, she went the snoring man to call,
And long, indeed, was she obliged to bawl,
Ere she could rouse the torpid lump of clay.
At last he wakes; he rises; and he swears:
But scarcely had he totter'd down the stairs,
When King attack'd him in his usual way.

The Frenchman now perceived 'twas all in vain
To his tormentor *mildly* to complain,
And straight in rage began his crest to rear:
"Sare, vat the devil make you treat me so?

Sare, I inform you, sare, three nights ago,
  Got tam — I swear, no Monsieur Tonson here!"

True as the night, King went, and heard a strife
Between the harass'd Frenchman and his wife,
  Which would descend to chase the fiend away.
At length, to *join* their forces they agree,
And straight impetuously they turn the key,
  Prepared with mutual fury for the fray.

Our hero, with the firmness of a rock,
Collected to receive the mighty shock,
  Uttering the old inquiry, calmly stood.
The name of Thompson raised the storm so high,
He deem'd it then the safest plan to fly,
  With "Well, I'll call when you're in gentler mood."

In short, our hero, with the same intent,
Full many a night to plague the Frenchman went,
  So fond of mischief was the wicked wit:
They throw out water; for the watch they call;
But King, expecting, still escapes from all.
  Monsieur at last was forced his house to quit.

It happen'd that our wag, about this time,
On some fair prospect sought the Eastern clime;
  Six lingering years were there his tedious lot.
At length, content, amid his ripening store,
He treads again on Britain's happy shore,
  And his long absence is at once forgot.

To London, with impatient hope, he flies,
And the same night, as former freaks arise,
  He fain must stroll, the well-known haunt to trace.
"Ah! here's the scene of frequent mirth," he said;
"My poor old Frenchman, I suppose, is dead.
  Egad, I'll knock, and see who holds the place."

With rapid strokes he makes the mansion roar,
And while he eager eyes the opening door,
  Lo! who obeys the knocker's rattling peal?
Why, e'en our little Frenchman, strange to say!
He took his old abode that very day, —
  Capricious turn of sportive Fortune's wheel!

Without one thought of the relentless foe,
Who, fiend-like, haunted him so long ago,
  Just in his former trim he now appears:
The waistcoat and the nightcap seem'd the same;
With rushlight, as before, he creeping came,
  And King's detested voice astonish'd hears.

As if some hideous spectre struck his sight,
His senses seem'd bewilder'd with affright,
  His face, indeed, bespoke a heart full sore;
Then, starting, he exclaim'd, in rueful strain,
"Begar! here's Monsieur Tonson come again!"
  Away he ran, and ne'er was heard of more.

GERMAN.

LEEDLE YAWCOB STRAUSS.

Charles F. Adams.

I haf von funny leedle poy
Vot gomes schust to my knee, —
Der queerest schap, der createst rogue
As efer you dit see.
He runs, und schumps, und schmashes dings
In all barts off der house.
But vot off dot? He vas mine son,
Mine leedle Yawcob Strauss.

He get der measles und der mumbs,
Und everyding dot's oudt;

He sbills mine glass off lager bier,
Poots schnuff indo mine kraut;
He fills mine pipe mit Limburg cheese, —
Dot vas der roughest chouse;
I'd dake dot vrom no oder poy
But leedle Yawcob Strauss.

He dakes der milk-ban for a dhrum,
Und cuts mine cane in dwo
To make der schticks to beat it mit, —
Mine cracious, dot vas drue!
I dinks mine hed vas schplit abart,
He kicks oup sooch a touse;
But nefer mind, der poys vas few
Like dot young Yawcob Strauss.

He asks me questions sooch as dese:
Who baints mine nose so red?
Who vos it cuts dot schmoodth blace oudt
From der hair ubon mine hed?
Und vhere der plaze goes vrom der lamp
Vene'er der glim I douse?
How gan I all dese dings eggsblain
To dot schmall Yawcob Strauss?

I somedimes dink I schall go vild
Mit sooch a grazy poy,
Und vish vonce more I gould haf rest
Und beaceful dimes enshoy:
But ven he vas ashleep in ped,
So quiet as a mouse,
I prays der Lord, "Dake anydings,
But leaf dot Yawcob Strauss."

"SOCKERY" SETTING A HEN.

MEESTER VERRIS: I see dot mosd efferpoty wrides something for de shicken pabers nowtays, and I tought praps meppe I can do dot, too; so I wride all apout vot dook blace mit me lasht Summer: you know — oder, uf you dond know, den I dells you — dot Katrina (dot is mine vrow) und me, ve keep some shickens for a long dime ago, und von tay she sait to me, "Sockery," (dot is mein name,) "vy dond you put some uf de aigs under dot olt plue hen shickens. I dinks she vants to sate." "Vell," I sait, "meppe, I guess I vill." So I bicked oud some ou de best aigs, und dook um oud do de parn fere de olt hen make her nesht in de side of de haymow, poud fife six veet up. Now you see I nefer was ferry pig up and down, but I vas pooty pig all de vay around in de mittle, so I koodn't reach up till I vent und got a parrel do stant on. Vell, I klimet me on de parrel, und ven my hed rise up py de nesht, de olt hen she gif me such a bick dot my nose runs all over my face mit plood, und ven I todge pack dot plasted olt parrel het preak, und I vent town kershlam.

Py cholly, I didn't tink I kood go insite a parrel pefore, but dere I vas, und I fit so dite dot I koodn't git me oud efferway, — my fest vas bushed vay up unter my arm-holes. Ven I fount I vos dite shtuck, I holler, "Katrina! Katrina!" Und ven she koom and see me shtuck in de parrel up to my arm-holes, mit my face all plood und aigs, by cholly, she chust lait town on de hay und laft, und laft till I got so mat I sait, "Vot you lay dere und laf like a olt vool, eh? Vy dond you koom bull me oud?" Und she set up und sait, "O, vipe off your chin, und bull your fest down"; den she lait back und laft like she vood shplit herself more as ever.

Mat as I vas, I tought to myself, Katrina, she sbeak English pooty good; but I only sait, mit my greatest dignitude, "Katrina, vill you bull me oud dis parrel?" Und she see dot I look pooty red, so she sait, "Of course I vill, Sockery." Den she lait me und de parrel town on our site, und I dook holt de door sill, und Katrina she bull on de parrel, but de first bull she mate I yellet, "Donner und blitzen, shtop dat, py golly; dere is nails in de parrel!" You see de nails bent town ven I vent in, but ven I koom oud dey schticks in me all de vay rount. Vell, to make a short shtory long, I told Katrina to go und dell naypor Hansman to pring a saw und saw me dis parrel off. Vell, he koom und he like to sphlit himself mit laf, too, but he roll me ofer und saw de parrel all de vay around off, und I git up mit half a parrel around my vaist. Den Katrina she say, "Sockery, vait a leetle till I get a battern of dot new oferskirt you haf on." But I didn't sait a vort; I shust got a nife oud, und vittle de hoops off, und shling dot confounted olt parrel in de voot pile.

Pimeby, ven I koom in de house, Katrina she said, so soft like, "Sockery, dond you go in to put some aigs under dot olt plue hen?" den I sait, in my deepest voice, "Katrina, uff you effer say dot to me again I'll git a pill from you, so help me chiminy cracious!" Und I dell you she didn't say dot any more. Vell, ven I step on a parrel now, I dond step on it, I git a pox.

IRISH.

CONNOR.

"To the memory of Patrick Connor: this simple stone was erected by his fellow-workmen."

THOSE words you may read any day upon a white slab in a cemetery not many miles from New York; but you might read them a hundred times without guessing at the little tragedy they indicate, without knowing the humble romance which ended with the placing of that stone above the dust of one poor, humble man.

In his shabby frieze jacket and mud-laden brogans, he was scarcely an attractive object as he walked into Mr. Bawne's great tin and hardware shop one day, and presented himself at the counter with an

"I've been tould ye advertized for hands, yer Honour."

"Fully supplied, my man," said Mr. Bawne, not lifting his head from his account-book.

"I'd work faithfully, sir, and take low wages, till I could do better, and I'd learn, — I would that."

It was an Irish brogue, and Mr. Bawne always declared that he never would employ an incompetent hand. Yet the tone attracted him. He turned briskly, and, with his pen behind his ear, addressed the man, who was only one of fifty who had answered his advertisement for four workmen that morning. "What makes you expect to learn faster than other folks? are you any smarter?"

"I'll not say that," said the man; "but I'd be wishing to; and that would make it aisier."

"Are you used to the work?"

"I've done a bit of it."

"Much?"

"No, yer Honour, I'll tell no lie; Tim O'Toole hadn't the like of this place; but I know a bit about tins."

"You are too old for an apprentice, and you'd be in the way, I calculate," said Mr. Bawne, looking at the brawny arms and bright eyes that promised strength and intelligence. "Besides, I know your country-men, — lazy, good-for-nothing fellows who never do their best. No, I've been taken in by Irish hands before, and I won't have another."

"The Virgin will have to be after bringing them over to me in her two arms, thin," said the man, despairingly, "for I've tramped all the day for the last fortnight, and niver a job can I get, and that's the last penny I have, yer Honour, and it's but a half one."

As he spoke, he spread his palm open, with an English half-penny in it.

"Bring whom over?" asked Mr. Bawne, arrested by the odd speech, as he turned upon his heel and turned back again.

"Jist Nora and Jamesy."

"Who are they?"

"The wan's me wife, the other me child," said the man. "O masther, just thry me. How'll I bring 'em over to me, if no one will give me a job? I want to be airning, and the whole big city seems against it, and me with arms like them."

He bared his arms to the shoulder, as he spoke, and Mr. Bawne looked at them, and then at his face.

"I'll hire you for a week," he said; "and now, as it's noon, go down to the kitchen, and tell the girl to get you some dinner, — a hungry man can't work."

With an Irish blessing, the new hand obeyed, while Mr. Bawne, untying his apron, went up stairs to his own meal. Suspicious as he was of the new hand's integrity and ability, he was agreeably disappointed. Connor worked hard, and actually learned fast. At the end of the week he was engaged permanently, and soon was the best workman in the shop.

He was a great talker, but not fond of drink or wasting money. As his wages grew, he hoarded every penny, and wore the same shabby clothes in which he had made his first appearance.

"Beer costs money," he said one day, "and ivery cent I spind puts off the bringing Nora and Jamesy over; and as for clothes, them I have must do me. Better no coat to my back than no wife and boy by my fireside; and, anyhow, it's slow work saving."

He kept his way, a martyr to his one great wish, living on little, working at night on any extra job that he could earn a few shillings by, running errands in his noon-tide hours of rest, and talking to any one who would listen to him of his one great hope, and of Nora and of little Jamesy.

At first the men who prided themselves on being all Americans, and on turning out the best work in the city, made a sort of butt of Connor, whose "wild Irish" ways and verdancy were indeed often laughable. But he won their hearts at last, and when one day, mounting a work-bench, he shook his little bundle, wrapped in a red kerchief, before their eyes, and shouted, "Look, boys; I've got the whole at last! I'm going to bring Nora and Jamesy over at last! Whorooo!! I've got it!!!" all felt sympathy in his joy, and each grasped his great hand in cordial congratulations, and one proposed to treat all round, and drink a good voyage to Nora.

They parted in a merry mood, most of the men going to comfortable homes. But poor Connor's resting-place was a poor lodging-house, where he shared a crazy garret with four other men; and in the joy of his heart the poor fellow exhibited his handkerchief, with his hard-earned savings tied up in a wad in the middle, before he put it under his pillow and fell asleep.

When he awakened in the morning, he found his treasure gone; some villain, more contemptible than most bad men, had robbed him.

At first Connor could not even believe it lost. He searched every corner of the room, shook the quilt and blankets, and begged those about him "to quit joking, and give it back." But at last he realized the truth:

"Is any man that bad that it's thaved from me?" he asked, in a breathless way. "Boys, is any man that bad?" And some one answered, "No doubt of it, Connor; it's sthole."

Then Connor put his head down on his hands and lifted up his voice and wept. It was one of those sights which men never forget. It seemed more than he could bear, to have Nora and his child "put," as he expressed it, "months away from him again."

But when he went to work that day it seemed to all who saw him that he had picked up a new determination. His hands were never idle. His face seemed to say, "I'll have Nora with me yet."

At noon he scratched out a letter, blotted and very strangely scrawled, telling Nora what had happened; and those who observed him noticed that he had no meat with his dinner. Indeed, from that moment he lived on bread, potatoes, and cold water, and worked as few men ever worked before.—It grew to be the talk of the shop; and, now that sympathy was excited, every one wanted to help Connor. Jobs were thrown in his way, kind words and friendly wishes helped him mightily; but no power could make him share the food or drink of any other workman. It seemed a sort of charity to him.

Still he was helped along. A present from Mr. Bawne, at pay-day, set Nora, as he said, "a week nearer," and this and that and the other added to the little hoard. It grew faster than the first, and Connor's burden was not so heavy.

At last, before he hoped it, he was once more able to say, "I'm going to bring them over," and to show his handkerchief, in which, as before, he tied up his earnings; this time, however, only to his friends. Cautious among strangers, he hid the treasure, and kept his vest buttoned over it night and day until the tickets were bought and sent. Then every man, woman, and child, capable of hearing or understanding, knew that Nora and her baby were coming.

The days flew by and brought at last a letter from his wife. She would start as he desired, and she was well and so was the boy; and might the Lord bring them safely to each other's arms and bless them who had been so kind to him! That was the substance of the epistle which Connor proudly assured his fellow-workmen Nora wrote herself. She had lived at service as a girl, with a certain good old lady, who had given her the items of an education, which Connor told upon his fingers. "The radin', that's one, and the writin', that's three, and, moreover, she knows all that a woman can." Then he looked up with tears in his eyes, and asked, "Do you wondher the time seems long between me an' her, boys?"

So it was. Nora at the dawn of day, Nora at noon, Nora at night, until the news came that the Stormy Petrel had come to port, and Connor, breathless and pale with excitement, flung his cap in the air and shouted.

It happened on a holiday afternoon, and half-a-dozen men were ready to go with Connor, to the steamer, and give his wife a greeting. Her little home was ready; Mr. Bawne's own servant had put it in order, and Connor took one peep at it before he started.

"She hadn't the like of that in the old counthry," he said, "but she'll know how to keep them tidy."

Then he led the way towards the dock where the steamer lay, and at a pace that made it hard for the rest to follow him. The spot was reached at last; a crowd of vehicles blockaded the street; a troop of emigrants came thronging up; fine cabin passengers were stepping into cabs, and drivers, porters, and all manner of employees were yelling and shouting in the usual manner. Nora would wait on board for her husband, he knew that.

The little group made their way into the vessel at last, and there, amid those who sat watching for coming friends, Connor searched for the two so dear to him; patiently at first, eagerly but patiently, but by-and-by growing anxious and excited.

"She would never go alone," he said, "she'd be lost entirely; I bade her wait, but I don't see her, boys; I think she's not in it."

"Why don't you see the captain?" asked one, and Connor jumped at the suggestion. In a few minutes he stood before a portly, rubicund man, who nodded to him kindly.

"I am looking for my wife, yer Honour," said Connor, "and I can't find her."

"Perhaps she's gone ashore," said the captain.

"I bade her wait," said Connor.

"Women don't always do as they are bid, you know," said the captain.

"Nora would," said Connor; "but maybe she was left behind. Maybe she didn't come. I somehow think she didn't."

At the name of Nora the captain started. In a moment he asked:

"What is your name?"

"Pat Connor," said the man.

"And your wife's name was Nora?"

"That's her name, and the boy with her is Jamesy, yer Honour," said Connor.

The captain looked at Connor's friends; they looked at the captain. Then he said huskily, "Sit down, my man! I've got something to tell you."

"She's left behind," said Connor.

"She sailed with us," said the captain.

"Where is she?" asked Connor.

The captain made no answer.

"My man," he said, "we all have our trials; God sends them. Yes, Nora started with us."

Connor said nothing. He was looking at the captain now, white to his lips.

"It's been a sickly season," said the captain; "we have had illness on board, — the cholera. You know that."

"I didn't. I can't read; they kept it from me," said Connor.

"We didn't want to frighten him," said one in a half whisper.

"You know how long we lay at quarantine?"

"The ship I came in did that," said Connor. "Did ye say Nora went ashore? Ought I to be looking for her, captain?"

"Many died, many children," went on the captain. "When we were half way here your boy was taken sick."

"Jamesy," gasped Connor.

"His mother watched him night and day," said the captain, "and we did all we could, but at last he died; only one of many. There were five buried that day. But it broke my heart to see the mother looking out upon the water. 'It's his father I think of,' said she; 'he's longing to see poor Jamesy.'"

Connor groaned.

"Keep up, if you can, my man," said the captain. "I wish any one else had it to tell rather than I. That night Nora was taken ill also; very suddenly, she grew worse fast. In the morning she called me to her. 'Tell Connor I died thinking of him,' she said, 'and tell him to meet me.' And my man, God help you, she never said any thing more, — and in an hour she was gone."

Connor had risen. He stood up, trying to steady himself, looking at the captain with his eyes as dry as two stones. Then he turned to his friends:

"I've got my death, boys," he said, and then dropped to the deck like a log.

They raised him and bore him away. In an hour he was at home on the little bed which had been made ready for Nora, weary with her long voyage. There, at last, he opened his eyes. Old Mr. Bawne bent over him: he had been summoned by the news, and the room was full of Connor's fellow-workmen.

"Better, Connor?" asked the old man.

"A dale," said Connor. "It's aisy now; I'll be with her soon. And look ye, masther, I've learnt one thing, — God is good; He wouldn't let me bring Nora over to me, but He's takin' me over to her and Jamesy over the river: don't you see it, and her standin' on the other side to welcome me?"

And with these words Connor stretched out his arms. Perhaps he did see Nora, — Heaven only knows, — and so died.

MISS MALONY ON THE CHINESE QUESTION.

MRS. MARY MAPES DODGE.

OCH! don't be talkin'. *Is it howld on ye say?* An' didn't I howld on till the heart of me was clane broke entirely, an' me wastin' that thin you could clutch me wid yer two hands? To think o' me toilin' like a nager, for the six year I've been in Ameriky, — bad luck to the day I iver left the owld counthry! to be bate by the likes o' them! (faix an' I'll sit down when I'm ready, so I will, Ann Ryan, an' ye'd better be listnin' than drawin' your remarks,) an' is it meself, with five good characters from respectable places, would be herdin' wid the haythens? The saints forgive me, but I'd be buried alive sooner'n put up wid it a day longer. Sure an' I was the granehorn not to be lavin' at onct when the missus kim into me kitchen wid her perlaver about the new waiter-man which was brought out from Californy. "He'll be here the night," says she, "an' Kitty, it's meself looks to you to be kind and patient wid him for he's a furriner," says she, a kind o' lookin' off. "Sure an' it's little I'll hinder nor interfare wid him nor any other, mum," says I, a kind o' stiff, for I minded me how these French waiters, wid their paper collars an' brass rings on their fingers, isn't company for no gurril brought up dacint an' honest. Och! sorra a bit I knew what was comin' till the missus walked into me kitchen smilin', an' says, kind o' sheared, "Here's Fing Wing, Kitty, an' you'll have too much sinse to mind his bein' a little strange."

Wid that she shoots the doore, an' I, misthrusting if I was tidied up sufficient for me fine buy wid his paper collar, looks up an' — howly fathers! may I niver brathe another breath, but there stud a rale haythen Chineser a-grinnin' like he'd just come off a tay-box. If you'll belave me, the crayture was that yallar it 'ud sicken you to see him; an' sorra a stitch was on him, but a black night-gown over his trowsers, an' the front of his head shaved claner nor a copper biler, an' a black tail a-hangin' down from behind, wid his two feet stook into the haythenestest shoes you ever set eyes on. Och! but I was up stairs before you could turn about, a-givin' the missus warnin', an' only stopt wid her by her raisin' me wages two dollars, an' playdin' wid me how it was a Christian's duty to bear wid haythins, an' taich 'em all in our power, — the saints save us! Well, the ways an' trials I had wid that Chineser, Ann Ryan, I couldn't be tellin'. Not a blissed thing cud I do, but he'd be lookin' on wid eyes cocked up'ard like two poomp-handles, an' he widdout a speck or smitch o' whishkers on him, an' his finger nails full a yard long. But it's dyin' you'd be to see the missus a-larnin' him, an' he grinnin' an' waggin' his pig-tail, (which was pieced out long wid some black stoof, the haythen chate!) an' gettin' into her ways wonderful quick, I don't deny, imitatin' that sharp, you'd be shurprised, an' ketchin' an' copyin' things the best of us will do a-hurried wid work, yet don't wan't comin' to the knowledge of the family, — bad luck to him!

Is it ate wid him? Arrah, an' would I be sittin' wid a haythen, an' he a-atin wid drum sticks, — yes, an' atin' dogs an' cats unknownst to me, I warrant you, which it is the custom of them Chinesers, till the thought made me that sick I could die. An' didn't the crayture proffer to help me a wake ago come Toosday, an' me a foldin' down me clane clothes for ironin', an' fill his haythin mouth wid water, an', afore I could hinder, squirrit it through his teeth stret over the best linen table-cloth, an' fold it up tight, as innercent now as a baby, the dirrity baste! But the worrest of all was the copyin' he'd be doin' till ye'd be dishtracted. It's yerself knows the tinder feet that's on me since iver I've bin in this counthry. Well, owin' to that, I fell into a way o' slippin' me shoes off when I'd be settin' down to pale the praties or the likes o' that, an', do ye mind? that haythen would do the same thing after me, whinivir the missus set him to parin' apples or tomaterses. The saints in Heaven couldn't have made him belave he cud kape the shoes on him when he'd be paylin' any thing.

Did I lave fur that? Faix, an' I didn't. Didn't he get me into throuble with me missus, the haythen? You're aware yersel' how the boondles comin' in from the grocery often contains more'n'll go into any thing dacently. So, for that matter, I'd now an' then take out a sup o' sugar, or flour, or tay, an' wrap it in paper, an' put it in me bit of a box tucked under the ironin' blankit, the how it cuddent be bodderin' any one. Well, what shud it be, but this blessed

Sathurday morn, the missus was a spakin' pleasant an' re-spec'ful wid me in me kitchen, when the grocer boy comes in an' stands fornenst her wid his boondles, an' she motions like to Fing Wing, (which I never would call him by that name nor any other but just haythin,) she motions to him, she does, for to take the boondles an' empty out the sugar, an' what not, where they belongs. If you'll belave me, Ann Ryan, what did that blatherin' Chineser do but take out a sup o' sugar, an' a handful o' tay, an' a bit o' chase right afore the missus, wrap them into bits o' paper, an' I spacheless wid shurprise, an' he the next minute up wid the ironin' blankit an' pullin' out me box wid a show o' bein' sly to put them in. Och, the Lord forgive me, but I clutched it, an' the missus sayin', "O Kitty!" in a way that 'ud cruddle your blood. "He's a haythin nager," says I. "I've found you out," says *she*. "I'll arrist him," says I. "It's *you* ought to be arristed," says she. "You won't," says I. "I will," says she; an' so it went till she give me such sass as I cuddent take from no lady, an' I give her warnin' an' left that instant, an' she a-pointin' to the doore.

JIMMY BUTLER AND THE OWL.

'Twas in the Summer of '46 that I landed at Hamilton, fresh as a new pratie just dug from the "ould sod," an' wid a light heart an' a heavy bundle I sot off for the township of Buford, tiding a taste of a song, as merry a young fellow as iver took the road. Well, I trudged on an' on, past many a plisint place, pleasin' myself wid the thought that some day I might have a place of my own, wid a world of chickens an' ducks an' pigs an' childer about the door; an' along in the afternoon of the sicond day I got to Buford village. A cousin of me mother's, one Dennis O'Dowd, lived about sivin miles from there, an' I wanted to make his place that night, so I inquired the way at the tavern, an' was lucky to find a man who was goin' part of the way, an' would show me the way to find Dennis. Sure he was very kind indade, an', when I got out of his wagon, he pointed me through the wood, an' tould me to go straight south a mile an' a half, an' the first house would be Dennis's.

"An' you've no time to lose now," said he, "for the Sun is low, an' mind you don't get lost in the woods."

"Is it lost now," said I, "that I'd be gittin', an' me uncle as great a navigator as iver steered a ship across the thrackless say? Not a bit of it, though I'm obleeged to ye for your kind advice, an' thank yiz for the ride."

An' wid that he drove off an' left me alone. I shouldered me bundle bravely, an', whistlin' a bit of time for company like, I pushed into the bush. Well, I went a long way over bogs, an' turnin' round among the bush an' trees till I began to think I must be well nigh to Dennis's. But, bad cess to it! all of a sudden I came out of the woods at the very identical spot where I started in, which I knew by an ould crotched tree that seemed to be standin' on its head an' kickin' up its heels to make divarsion of me. By this time it was growin' dark, an', as there was no time to lose, I started in a second time, determined to keep straight south this time, an' no mistake. I got on bravely for a while, but och hone! och hone! it got so dark I couldn't see the trees, an' I bumped me nose an' barked me shins, while the miskaties bit me hands an' face to a blister; an', after tumblin' an' stumblin' around till I was fairly bamfoozled, I sat down on a log, all of a trimble, to think that I was lost intirely, an' that maybe a lion or some other wild craythur would devour me before morning.

Just then I heard somebody a long way off say, "Whip poor Will!" "Bedad," sez I, "I'm glad it isn't Jamie that's got to take it, though it seems it's more in sorrow than in anger they are doin' it, or why should they say, 'poor Will'? an' sure they can't be Injin, haythin, or naygur, for it's plain English they're afther spakin'. Maybe they might help me out o' this," so I shouted at the top of my voice,

"A lost man!" Thin I listened. Prisently an answer came.

"Who! Whoo! Whooo!"

"Jamie Butler, the waiver!" sez I, as loud as I could roar, an', snatchin' up me bundle an' stick, I started in the direction of the voice. Whin I thought I had got near the place, I stopped an' shouted again, "A lost man!"

"Who! Whoo! Whooo!" said a voice right over my head.

"Sure," thinks I, "it's a mighty quare place for a man to be at this time of night; maybe it's some settler scrapin' sugar off a sugar-bush for the children's breakfast in the mornin'. But where's Will and the rest of them?" All this wint through me head like a flash, an' thin I answered his inquiry.

"Jamie Butler, the waiver," sez I; "an', if it wouldn't inconvanience yer Honour, would yez be kind enough to step down an' show me the way to the house of Dennis O'Dowd?"

"Who! Whoo! Whooo!" sez he.

"Dennis O'Dowd," sez I, civil enough, "an' a dacent man he is, and first cousin to me own mother."

"Who! Whoo! Whooo!" says he again.

"Me mother!" sez I, "an' as fine a woman as iver peeled a biled pratie wid her thumb nail, an' her maiden name was Molly McFiggin."

"Who! Whoo! Whooo!"

"Paddy McFiggin! bad luck to yer deaf ould head, Paddy McFiggin, I say, — do ye hear that? An' he was the tallest man in all the county Tipperary, excipt Jim Doyle, the blacksmith."

"Who! Whoo! Whooo!"

"Jim Doyle the blacksmith," sez I, "ye good for nothin' blaggard naygur, an', if yiz don't come down an' show me the way this min't, I'll climb up there an' break every bone in your skin, ye spalpeen, so sure as me name is Jimmy Butler!"

"Who! Whoo! Whooo!" sez he, as impident as iver.

I said niver a word, but lavin' down me bundle, an' takin' me stick in me teeth, I began to climb the tree. Whin I got among the branches I looked quietly around till I saw a pair of big eyes just forninst me.

"Whist," sez I, "an' I'll let him have a taste of an Irish stick," an' wid that I let drive, an' lost me balance an' came tumblin' to the ground, nearly breakin' me neck wid the fall. When I came to me sinsis I had a very sore head, wid a lump on it like a goose egg, an' half of me Sunday coat-tail torn off intirely. I spoke to the chap in the tree, but could git niver an answer at all, at all.

"Sure," thinks I, "he must have gone home to rowl up his head, for by the powers I didn't throw me stick for nothin'."

Well, by this time the Moon was up, an' I could see a little, an' I detarmined to make one more effort to reach Dennis's.

I wint on cautiously for a while, an' thin I heard a bell. "Sure," sez I, "I'm comin' to a settlement now, for I hear the church bell." I kept on toward the sound till I came to an ould cow wid a bell on. She started to run, but I was too quick for her, an' got her by the tail an' hung on, thinkin' that maybe she would take me out of the woods. On we wint, like an ould country steeple-chase, till, sure enough, we came out to a clearin', an' a house in sight wid a light in it. So, leavin' the ould cow puffin' an' blowin' in a shed, I went to the house, an', as luck would have it, whose should it be but Dennis's?

He gave me a raal Irish welcome, an' introduced me to his two daughters, — as purty a pair of girls as iver ye clapped an eye on. But, whin I tould him me adventure in the woods, an' about the fellow who made fun of me, they all laughed an' roared, an' Dennis said it was an owl.

"An ould what?" sez I.

"Why, an owl, a bird," sez he.

"Do ye tell me now?" sez I. "Sure it's a quare country and a quare bird."

An' thin they all laughed again, till at last I laughed myself that hearty like, an' dropped right into a chair between the two purty girls, an' the ould chap winked at me and roared again.

Dennis is me father-in-law now, an' he often yet delights to tell our children about their daddy's adventure wid the owl.

ITALIAN.

A SENATOR ENTANGLED.

JAMES DE MILLE.

THE Countess di Nottinero was not exactly a Recamier, but she was a remarkably brilliant woman, and the acknowledged leader of the liberal part of Florentine society.

The good Senator had never before encountered a thorough woman of the world, and was as ignorant as a child of the innumerable little harmless arts by which the power of such a one is extended and secured. At last the Senator came to this conclusion, — *La Cica* was desperately in love with him.

She appeared to be a widow. At least she had no husband that he had ever seen. Now, if the poor *Cica* was hopelessly in love, it must be stopped at once. But let it be done delicately, not abruptly.

One evening they walked on the balcony of *La Cica's* noble residence. She was sentimental, devoted, charming.

The conversation of a fascinating woman does not sound so well when it is reported as it is when uttered. Her power is in her tone, her glance, her manner. Who can catch the evanescent beauty of her expression or the deep tenderness of her well modulated voice? — who indeed?

"Does ze scene please you, my Senator?"

"Very much indeed."

"Youar countryman haf tol me zey would like to stay here alloway."

"It is a beautiful place."

"Did you aiver see any thin moaire loafely?" And the Countess looked full in his face.

"Never," said the Senator, earnestly. The next instant he blushed. He had been betrayed into a compliment.

The Countess sighed.

"Helas! my Senator, that it is not pairmitted to mortals to sociate as zey would laike."

"'Your Senator,'" thought the gentleman thus addressed; "how fond, how tender, — poor thing! poor thing!"

"I wish that Italy was nearer to the States," said he.

"How I adamiar youar style of mind, so different from ze Italiana! You are so strong, — so nobile. Yet would I laike to see moar of ze poetic in you."

"I always loved poetry, marm," said the Senator, desperately.

"Ah — good — nais — eccelente. I am plees at zat," cried the Countess, with much animation. "You would loafe it moar eef you knew Italiano. Your langua ees not sufficient musicale for poatry."

"It is not so soft a language as the *I*talian."

"Ah — no — not so soft. Very well. And what theenka you of ze Italiano?"

"The sweetest language I ever heard in all my born days."

"Ah now — you hev not heard much of ze Italiano, my Senator."

"I have heard you speak often," said the Senator, naïvely.

"Ah, you compliment! I sot you was aboove flattera."

And the Countess playfully tapped his arm with her little fan.

"What Ingelis poet do you loafe best?"

"Poet? English poet?" said the Senator, with some surprise. "O — why, marm, I think Watts is about the best of the lot."

"Watt? Was he a poet? I did not know zat. He who invented ze stim-injaine? And yet if he was a poet it is naturale zat you loafe him best."

"Steam-engine? O no! This one was a minister."

"A meeneestaire? Ah! an abbe? I know him not. Yet I have read mos of all youar poets."

"He made up hymns, marm, and psalms, — for instance, 'Watts's Divine Hymns and Spiritual Songs.'"

"Songs? Spirituelle? Ah, I mus at once procuaire ze works of Watt, which was favorit poet of my Senator."

"A lady of such intelligence as you would like the poet Watts," said the Senator, firmly. "He is the best known by far of all our poets."

"What! better zan Sakespeare, Milton, Bairon? You much surprass me."

"Better known and better loved than the whole lot. Why, his poetry is known by heart through all England and America."

"Merciful Heaven! what you tell me! ees eet possble! An yet he is not known here efen by name. It would please me mooch, my Senator, to haire you make one quotatione. Know you Watt? Tell to me some words of his which I may remembaire."

"I have a shocking bad memory."

"Bad memora! O, but you remember somethin, zis mos beautiful charm nait, — you haf a nobile soul, — you mus be affecta by beauty, — by ze ideal. Make for a me one quotatione."

And she rested her little hand on the Senator's arm, and looked up imploringly in his face.

The Senator looked foolish. He felt even more so. Here was a beautiful woman, by act and look showing a tender interest in him. Perplexing, — but very flattering, after all. So he replied, —

"You will not let me refuse any thing."

"Aha! you are vera willin' to refuse. It is difficulty for me to excitaire youar regards. You are fill with the grands ideas. But come, — will you spik for me some from your favorit Watt?"

"Well, if you wish it so much," said the Senator, kindly; and he hesitated.

"Ah, — I do wis it so much!"

"Ehem!"

"Begin," said the Countess. "Behold me. I listen. I hear every sin, and will remembaire it forava."

The only thing that the Senator could think of was a verse which had been running in his head for the last few days, its measured rhythm keeping time with every occupation:

"'My willing soul would stay —'"

"Stop one moment," said the Countess. "I weesh to learn it from you"; and she looked fondly and tenderly up, but instantly dropped her eyes.

"'Ma willina sol wooda sta —'"

"'In such a frame as this,'" prompted the Senator.

"'Een socha framas zees.' Wait — 'Ma willina sol wooda sta in socha framas zees.' Ah, appropriat! but could I hope zat you were true to zose lines, my Senator? Well?"

"'And sit and sing herself away,'" said the Senator, in a faltering voice, and breaking out into a cold perspiration for fear of committing himself by such uncommonly strong language.

"'Ansit ansin hassaf awai,'" repeated the Countess, her face lighting up with a sweetly conscious expression.

The Senator paused.

"Well?"

"I — ehem! I forget."

"Forget? Impossble!"

"I do really."

"Ah now! Forget! I see by youar face — you desave. Say on."

The Countess again gently touched his arm with both of her little hands, and held it as though she would clasp it.

"Have you fear? Ah, cruel!"

The Senator turned pale, but, finding refusal impossible, boldly finished:

"'To everlasting bliss' — there!"

"'To affarlastin blees thar.' Stop. I repeat it all: 'Ma willina sol wooda sta in socha framas zees, ansit ansin hassaf awai to affarlastin blees thar.' Am I right?"

"Yes," said the Senator meekly.

"I knew you war a poetic sola," said the Countess, confidingly. "You are honesto — true — you cannot desave. When you spik I can beliv you. Ah, my Senator! an you can spik zis poetry! — at soch a taime! I nefare knew befoare zat you wos so impassione! — an you air so artaful! You breeng ze confersazione to beauty — to poatry — to ze poet Watt, — so you may spik verses mos impassione! Ah! what do you mean? Santissima madra! how I wish you spik Italiano."

The Countess drew nearer to him, but her approach only deepened his perplexity.

"How that poor thing does love me!" sighed the Senator. "Law bless it! she can't help it, — can't help it nohow. She is a goner; and what can I do? I'll have to leave Florence."

The Countess was standing close beside him in a tender mood, waiting for him to break the silence. How could he? He had been uttering words which sounded to her like love; and she — "a widow! a widow! a widow! wretched man that I am!"

There was a pause. The longer it lasted the more awkward the Senator felt. What upon earth was he to do or say? What business had he to go and quote poetry to widows? What an old fool he must be! But the Countess was very far from feeling awkward. Assuming an elegant attitude, she looked up, her face expressing the tenderest solicitude.

"What ails my Senator?"

"Why, the fact is, marm,—I feel sad—at leaving Florence. I must go shortly. My wife has written summoning me home. The children are down with the measles."

O base fabrication! O false Senator! There wasn't a word of truth in that remark. You spoke so because you wished La Cica to know that you had a wife and family. Yet it was very badly done.

La Cica changed neither her attitude nor her expression. Evidently the existence of his wife and the melancholy situation of his unfortunate children awakened no sympathy.

"But, my Senator,—did you not say you wooda seeng yoursellef away to affarlastin blees?"

"O marm, it was a quotation,—only a quotation."

But at this critical juncture the conversation was broken up by the arrival of a number of ladies and gentlemen.

NEGRO.

CHRISTMAS-NIGHT IN THE QUARTERS.

IRWIN RUSSELL.

Abridged and arranged for public recitation.

WHEN merry Christmas-day is done,
And Christmas-night is just begun;
While clouds in slow procession drift
To wish the moon-man "Christmas gift,"
Yet linger overhead, to know
What causes all the stir below;
At Uncle Johnny Booker's ball
The darkies hold high carnival.
From all the country-side they throng,
With laughter, shouts, and scraps of song,
Their whole deportment plainly showing
That to "the frolic" they are going.

Some take the path with shoes in hand,
To traverse muddy bottom-land;
Aristocrats their steeds bestride,—
Four on a mule, behold them ride!
And ten great oxen draw apace
The wagon from " de oder place,"
With forty guests, whose conversation
Betokens glad anticipation.

In this our age of printer's ink,
'Tis books that show us how to think, —
The rule reversed, and set at nought,
That held that books were born of thought:
We form our minds by pedants' rules;
And all we know, is from the schools;
And when we work, or when we play,
We do it in an ordered way.

Untrammel'd thus, the simple race is,
That " works the craps" on cotton-places!
Original in act and thought,
Because unlearnéd and untaught,
Observe them at their Christmas party.
How unrestrain'd their mirth, how hearty!
How many things they say and do
That never would occur to you!
See " Brudder Brown" — whose saving grace
Would sanctify a quarter-race —
Out on the crowded floor advance,
To " beg a blessin' on dis dance."

O Mahsr! let dis gath'rin' fin' a blessin' in yo' sight!
Don't jedge us hard for what we does, — you knows its Chrismus night;
An' all de balunce ob de yeah, we does as right's we kin:
Ef dancin's wrong, O Mahsr! let de time excuse de sin!

We labours in de vineya'd, workin' hard, an' workin' true;
Now, shorely you won't notus, ef we eats a grape or two,

An' takes a leetle holiday, — a leetle restin'-spell, —
Bekase, nex' week, we'll start in fresh, an' labour twicet as well.

Remember, Mahsr, — min' dis now, — de sinfulness ob sin
Is pendin' 'pon de sperret what we goes an' does it in:
An' in a righchis frame ob min' we's gwine to dance an' sing;
A-feelin' like King David, when he cut de pigeon-wing.

It seems to me, — indeed it do, — I mebbe mout be wrong, —
That people raly *ought* to dance, when Chrismus comes along:
Des dance bekase dey's happy, like de birds hops in de trees;
De pine-top fiddle soundin' to de blowin' ob de breeze.

We has no ark to dance afore, like Isrul's prophet king;
We has no harp to soun' de chords, to holp us out to sing;
But cordin' to de gif's we has we does de bes' we knows,
An' folks don't 'spise de vi'let-flow'r bekase it ain't de rose.

You bless us, please sah, eben ef we's doin' wrong to-night;
Kase den we'll need de blessin' more'n ef we's doin' right;
An' let de blessin' stay wid us untell we comes to die,
An' goes to keep our Chrismus wid dem sheriffs in de sky!

Yes, tell dem preshis anjuls we's a gwine to jine 'em soon:
Our voices we's a-trainin' for to sing de glory tune;
We's ready when you wants us, an' it ain't no matter when;
O Mahsr! call yo' chillen soon, an' take 'em home! Amen.

The reverend man is scarcely through,
When all the noise begins anew,
And with such force assaults the ears,
That through the din one hardly hears
Old Fiddling Josey "sound his A," —
Correct the pitch, — begin to play, —
Stop, satisfied, — then, with the bow,
Rap out the signal dancers know:

Git yo' pardners, fust kwattilion!
Stomp yo' feet, an' raise 'em high;
Tune is, "O, dat water-million!
Gwine to git to home bime-bye."

S'lute yo' pardners! — scrape perlitely, —
Don't be bumpin' gin de res', —
Balance all! — now, step out rightly;
Alluz dance yo' lebbel bes'.

Fo'wa'd foah! — whoop up, niggers!
Back ag'in! — don't be so slow, —
Swing yo' cornahs! — min' de figgers:
When I hollers, den yo' go.

Ladies change! — shet up dat talkin':
Do yo' talkin' arter while, —
Right an' lef'! — don't want no walkin', —
Make yo' steps, an' show yo' style!

Hands around! — hol' up yo' faces,
Don't be lookin' at yo' feet!
Swing yo' pardners to yo' places!
Dat's de way, — dat's hard to beat.

And so the "set" proceeds, its length
Determined by the dancers' strength;
And all agreed to yield the palm,
For grace and skill, to "Georgy Sam,"
Who stamps so hard, and leaps so high,
"Des watch him!" is the wondering cry, —
"De nigger mus' be, for a fac',
Own cousin to a jumpin'-jack!"
On, on, the restless fiddle sounds, —
Still chorus'd by the curs and hounds, —
Dance after dance succeeding fast,
Till "supper" is announced at last.
That scene, — but why attempt to show it?
The most inventive modern poet,
In fine new words whose hope and trust is,
Could form no phrase to do it justice!
When supper ends, — that is not soon, —
The fiddler strikes the same old tune;

The dancers pound the floor again,
With all they have of might and main;

The night is spent; and, as the day
Throws up the first faint flash of gray,
The guests pursue their homeward way;
And through the field beyond the gin,
Just as the stars are going in,
See Santa Claus departing, — grieving, —
His own dear Land of Cotton leaving.
His work is done, — he fain would rest,
Where people know and love him best;
He pauses, — listens, — looks about, —
But go he must: his pass is out;
So, coughing down the rising tears,
He climbs the fence and disappears.
And thus observes a coloured youth,
(The common sentiment, in sooth,)
"O, what a blessin' 'tw'u'd ha' been,
Ef Santy had been born a twin!
We'd hab two Chrismuses a yeah,
Or p'r'aps *one* brudder'd *settle* heah!"

THE FIRST BANJO.

IRWIN RUSSELL.

Go'way, fiddle! — folks is tired o' hearin' you a-squawkin':
Keep silence fur yo' betters, — don't yo' heah de banjo talkin'?
About de 'possum's tail she's goin to lecter, — ladies, listen! —
About de ha'r what isn't dar, an' why de ha'r is missin'.

"Dar's gwine to be a oberflow," said Noah, lookin' solemn, —
Fur Noah took de *Herald*, an he read de ribber column, —
An' so he sot his hands to work a-clarin' timber-patches,
An' low'd he's gwine to build a boat to beat the steamah Natchez.

Ol' Noah kep' a-nailin', an' a-chippin', an' a-sawin';
An' all de wicked neighbours kep' a-laughin, an' a-pshawin';

But Noah didn't min' 'em, — knowin' what wuz gwine to happen:
An' forty days an' forty nights de rain it kep' a-droppin'.

Now, Noah had done catch'd a lot ob eb'ry sort o' beas'es,
Ob all de shows a-trabbelin, it beat 'em all to pieces!
He had a Morgan colt, an' sebral head o' Jarsey cattle, —
An' drew 'em board de ark as soon's he heer'd de thunder rattle.

Den sech anoder fall ob rain! — it come so awful hebby,
De ribber riz immejitly, an' busted troo de lebbee;
De people all wuz drownded out, 'cep' Noah an' de critters,
An' men he'd hired to work de boat, — an' one to mix de bitters.

De ark she kep' a-sailin', an' a-sailin', *an'* a-sailin';
De lion got his dander up, an' like to bruk de palin', —
De sarpints hiss'd, — de painters yell'd. — tell, what wid all de fussin',
You c'u'dn't hardly heah de mate a-bossin' roun' an' cussin'.

Now, Ham, de only nigger what was runnin' on de packet,
Got lonesome in de barber-shop, an' c'u'dn't stan' de racket;
An' so, for to amuse he-se'f, he steam'd some wood an' bent it,
An' soon he had a banjo made, — de fust dat wuz invented.

He wet de ledder, stretch'd it on; made bridge, an' screws, an' apron;
An' fitted in a proper neck, — 'twas berry long an' tap'rin';
He tuk some tin, and twisted him a thimble for to ring it;
An' den de mighty question riz, How wuz he gwine to string it?

De possum had as fine a tail as dis dat I's a singin';
De ha'rs so long, an' thick an' strong, — des fit for banjo-stringin';
Dat nigger shaved 'em off as short as wash-day-dinner graces;
An' sorted ob 'em by de size, frum little E's to basses.

He strung her, tuned her, struck a jig, — 'twuz "Nebber min' de wedder";
She soun' like forty-lebben bands a-playing' all togedder;
Some went to pattin'; some to dancin'; Noah call'd de figgers;
An Ham he sot an' knock'd de tune, de happiest ob niggers!

Now, sence dat time, — it's mighty strange, — dere's not de slightest showin'
Ob any ha'r at all upon de possum's tail a-growin';
An' curis, too, — dat nigger's ways! his people nebber los' 'em, —
For whar you finds de nigger, — dar's de banjo an' de 'possum.

UNCLE DAN'L'S APPARITION.

CLEMENS AND WARNER.

WHATEVER the lagging, dragging journey from Tennessee to Missouri may have been to the rest of the emigrants, it was a wonder and delight to the children, a world of enchantment; and they believed it to be peopled with the mysterious dwarfs and giants and goblins that figured in the tales the negro slaves were in the habit of telling them nightly by the shuddering light of the kitchen fire.

At the end of nearly a week of travel, the party went into camp near a shabby village which was caving, house by house, into the hungry Mississippi. The river astonished the children beyond measure. Its mile-breadth of water seemed an ocean to them, in the shadowy twilight, and the vague riband of trees on the further shore, the verge of a continent which surely none but them had ever seen before.

"Uncle Dan'l," (coloured,) aged 40; his wife, "Aunt Jinny," aged 30; "Young Miss" Emily Hawkins, "Young Mars" Washington Hawkins, and "Young Mars" Clay, the new member of the family, ranged themselves on a log, after supper, and contemplated the marvellous river and discussed it. The Moon rose and sailed aloft through a maze of shredded cloud-wreaths; the sombre river just perceptibly brightened under the veiled light; a deep silence pervaded the air, and was emphasized, at intervals, rather than broken, by the hooting of an owl, the baying of a dog, or the muffled crash of a caving bank in the distance.

The little company assembled on the log were all children, (at least in simplicity and broad and comprehensive ignorance,) and the remarks they made about the river were in keeping with their character; and so awed were they by the grandeur and the solemnity of the scene before them, and by their belief that the air was filled with invisible spirits, and that the faint zephyrs were caused by their passing wings, that all their talk took to itself a tinge of the supernatural, and their voices were subdued to a low and reverent tone. Suddenly Uncle Dan'l exclaimed:

"Chil'en, dah's sumfin a-comin'!"

All crowded close together, and every heart beat faster. Uncle Dan'l pointed down the river with his bony finger.

A deep coughing sound troubled the stillness, away toward a wooded cape that jutted into the stream a mile distant. All in an instant a fierce eye of fire shot out from behind the cape, and sent a long, brilliant pathway quivering athwart the dusky water. The coughing grew louder and louder, the glaring eye grew larger and still larger, glared wilder and still wilder. A huge shape developed itself out of the gloom, and from its tall duplicate horns dense volumes of smoke, starred and spangled with sparks, poured out and went tumbling away into the further darkness. Nearer and nearer the thing came, till its long sides began to glow with spots of light which mirrored themselves in the river, and attended the monster like a torchlight procession.

"What is it? O! what is it, Uncle Dan'l?"

With deep solemnity the answer came:

"It's de Almighty! Git down on yo' knees!"

It was not necessary to say it twice. They were all kneeling in a moment. And then, while the mysterious coughing rose stronger and stronger, and the threatening glare reached further and wider, the negro's voice lifted up its supplications:

"O Lord, we's been mighty wicked, an' we knows dat we 'zerve to go to de bad place, but good Lord, deah Lord, we ain't ready yit, we ain't ready, — let dese po' chil'en hab one mo' chance, jes' one mo' chance. Take de ole niggah if you's got to hab somebody. Good Lord, good deah Lord, we don't know whah you's a-gwine to, we don't know who you's got yo' eye on, but we knows by de way you's a-comin', we knows by de way you's a-tiltin' along in yo' charyot o' fiah, dat some po' sinner's a-gwine to ketch it. But, good Lord, dese chil'en don't 'blong heah, dey's f'm Obedstown, whah dey don't know nuffin, an' you knows yo' own sef, dat dey ain't 'sponsible.

An', deah Lord, good Lord, it ain't like yo' mercy, it ain't like yo' pity, it ain't like yo' long-sufferin' lovin' kindness, for to take dis kind o' 'vantage o' sich little chil'en as dese is, when dey's so many grown folks chuck full o' cussedness dat wants roastin' down dah. O Lord, spah de little chil'en, don't tar de little chil'en away f'm dey frens, jes' let 'em off, jes' dis once, and take it out'n de ole niggah. HEAH I IS, LORD, HEAH I IS! De ole niggah's ready, Lord, de ole —"

The flaming and churning steamer was right abreast the party, and not twenty steps away. The awful thunder of a mud-valve suddenly burst forth, drowning the prayer, and as suddenly Uncle Dan'l snatched a child under each arm and scoured into the woods with the rest of the pack at his heels. And then, ashamed of himself, he halted in the deep darkness and shouted, (but rather feebly,)

"Heah I is, Lord, heah I is!"

There was a moment of throbbing suspense, and then, to the surprise and comfort of the party, it was plain that the august presence had gone by, for its dreadful noises were receding. Uncle Dan'l headed a cautious reconnoissance in the direction of the log. Sure enough "The Lord" was just turning a point a short distance up the river; and, while they looked, the lights winked out, and the coughing diminished by degrees, and presently ceased altogether.

"H'wsh! Well, now dey's some folks says dey ain't no 'ficiency in prah. Dis chile would like to know whah we'd a ben now if it warn't fo' dat prah? Dat's it. Dat's it!"

"Uncle Dan'l, do you reckon it was the prayer that saved us?" said Clay.

"Does I reckon? Don't I know it! Whah was yo' eyes? Warn't de Lord jes' a-comin' chow! *chow!* CHOW! an' a-goin' on turrible; an' do de Lord carry on dat way 'dout dey's sumfin don't suit him? An' warn't he a-lookin' right at dis gang heah, an' warn't he jes' a-reachin' for 'em? An' d' you spec' he gwine to let 'em off 'dout somebody ast him to do it? No indeedy!"

"Do you reckon he saw us, Uncle Dan'l?"

"De law sakes, chile, didn't I see him a-lookin' at us?"

"Did you feel scared, Uncle Dan'l?"

"No sah! When a man is 'gaged in prah, he ain't 'fraid o' nuffin, — dey can't nuffin tech him."

"Well, what did you run for?"

"Well, I — I — Mars Clay, when a man is under de influence ob de sperit, he dunno what he's 'bout, — no sah; dat man dunno what he's 'bout. You mout take an' tah de head off'n dat man, an' he wouldn't scasely fine it out. Dah's de Hebrew chil'en dat went frough de fiah; dey was burnt considable, — ob course dey was; but dey didn't know nuffin 'bout it, — heal right up agin: if dey'd ben gals dey'd missed dey long haah, maybe, but dey wouldn't felt de burn."

"I don't know but what they *were* girls. I think they were."

"Now, Mars Clay, you knows better'n dat. Sometimes a body can't tell whedder you's a-sayin' what you means or whedder you's a-sayin' what you don't mean, 'case you says 'em bofe de same way."

"But how should *I* know whether they were boys or girls?"

"Goodness sakes, Mars Clay, don't de good book say? 'Sides, don't it call 'em de *He*-brew chil'en? If dey was gals wouldn't dey be de she-brew chil'en? Some people dat kin read don't 'pear to take no notice when dey do read."

"Well, Uncle Dan'l, I think that — My! here comes another one up the river! There can't be two!"

"We gone dis time, — we done gone dis time, sho'! Dey ain't two, Mars Clay, — dat's de same one. De Lord kin 'pear eberywhah in a second. Goodness, how de fiah an' de smoke do belch up! Dat mean business, honey. He comin' now like he fo'got sumfin. Come 'long, chil'en; time you's gwine to roos'. Go 'long wid you, — ole Uncle Dan'l gwine out in de woods to rastle in prah, — de ole niggah gwine to do what he kin to sabe you agin."

He did go to the woods and pray; but he went so far that he doubted, himself, if the "Lord" heard him when he went by.

SCOTCH.

CHARLIE MACHREE.

William J. Hoppin.

Come over, come over the river to me,
If ye are my laddie, bold Charlie Machree!
Here's Mary McPherson and Susy O'Linn,
Who say ye're faint-hearted, and dare not plunge in.

But the dark rolling river, though deep as the sea,
I know cannot scare you, nor keep you from me;
For stout is your back and strong is your arm,
And the heart in your bosom is faithful and warm.

Come over, come over the river to me,
If ye are my laddie, bold Charlie Machree.
I see him, I see him: he's plunged in the tide,
His strong arms are dashing the big waves aside.

O, the dark rolling water shoots swift as the sea,
But blithe is the glance of his bonny blue e'e;
His cheeks are like roses, twa buds on a bough:
Who says ye're faint-hearted, my brave laddie, now?

Ho, ho, foaming river, ye may roar as ye go,
But ye canna bear Charlie to the dark loch below!
Come over, come over the river to me,
My true-hearted laddie, *my* Charlie Machree!

He's sinking, he's sinking, — O, what shall I do!
Strike out, Charlie, boldly, ten strokes and ye're thro'
He's sinking, O Heaven! Ne'er fear, man, ne'er fear;
I've a kiss for ye, Charlie, as soon as ye're here!

He rises, I see him, — five strokes, Charlie, mair,—
He's shaking the wet from his bonny brown hair;
He conquers the current, he gains on the sea,—
Ho, where is the swimmer like Charlie Machree!

Come over the river, but once come to me,
And I'll love ye forever, dear Charlie Machree.
He's sinking, he's gone, — O God, it is I,
It is I, who have kill'd him, — help, help! — he must die

Help, help! — ah, he rises, — strike out and ye're free.
Ho, bravely done, Charlie, once more now, for me!
Now cling to the rock, now give me your hand,—
Ye're safe, dearest Charlie, ye're safe on the land!

Come rest on my bosom, if there ye can sleep;
I canna speak to ye; I only can weep.
Ye've cross'd the wild river, ye've risk'd all for me,
And I'll part frae ye never, dear Charlie Machree!

CUDDLE DOON.

ALEXANDER ANDERSON.

THE bairnies cuddle doon at nicht
  Wi' muckle faucht an' din.
"O, try and sleep, ye waukrife rogues;
  Your father's comin' in."
They never heed a word I speak:
  I try to gie a froon;
But aye I hap them up, an' cry,
  "O, bairnies, cuddle doon!"

Wee Jamie wi' the curley heid —
  He aye sleeps next the wa' —
Bangs up an' cries, "I want a piece" —
  The rascal starts them a'.
I rin an' fetch them piecés, drinks, —
  They stop a wee the soun', —
Then draw the blankets up, and cry,
  "Noo, weanies, cuddle doon!"

But, ere five minutes gang, wee Rab
  Cries oot, frae 'neath the claes,

"Mither, mak' Tam gie ower at ance;
He's kittlin' wi' his taes."
The mischief's in that Tam for tricks:
He'd bother half the toon;
But aye I hap them up, and cry,
"O, bairnies, cuddle doon!"

At length they hear their father's fit;
An', as he steeks the door,
They turn their faces to the wa',
While Tam pretends to snore.
"Hae a' the weans been gude?" he asks,
As he pits aff his shoon.
"The bairnies, John, are in their beds,
An' lang since cuddled doon."

An', just afore we bed oorsels,
We look at oor wee lambs:
Tam has his airm roun' wee Rab's neck,
An' Rab his airm roun' Tam's.
I lift wee Jamie up the bed,
An', as I straik each croon,
I whisper, till my heart fills up,
"O, bairnies, cuddle doon!"

The bairnies cuddle doon at nicht
Wi' mirth that's dear to me;
But soon the big warl's cark an care
Will quaten doon their glee:
Yet, come what will to ilka ane,
May He who sits aboon
Aye whisper, though their pows be bauld,
"O bairnies, cuddle doon!"

JOHN ANDERSON, MY JO.

ROBERT BURNS.

JOHN ANDERSON, my jo, John,
When we were first acquent,

Your locks were like the raven,
 Your bonnie brow was brent;
But now your brow is beld, John,
 Your locks are like the snaw;
But blessings on your frosty pow,
 John Anderson, my jo.

John Anderson, my jo, John,
 We clamb the hill thegither;
And mony a canty day, John,
 We've had wi' ane anither.
Now we maun totter down, John,
 But hand in hand we'll go;
And sleep thegither at the foot,
 John Anderson, my jo.

JEANIE MORRISON.

WILLIAM MOTHERWELL.

I've wander'd east, I've wander'd west,
 Through mony a weary way;
But never, never can forget
 The luve o' life's young day!
The fire that's blawn on Beltane e'en
 May weel be black gin Yule;
But blacker fa' awaits the heart
 Where first fond luve grows cule.

O dear, dear Jeanie Morrison,
 The thochts o' bygane years
Still fling their shadows ower my path,
 And blind my een wi' tears:
They blind my een wi' saut, saut tears,
 And sair and sick I pine,
As memory idly summons up
 The blithe blinks o' langsyne.

'Twas then we luvit ilk ither weel,
  'Twas then we twa did part;
Sweet time — sad time! twa bairns at scule,
  Twa bairns, and but ae heart!
'Twas then we sat on ae laigh bink,
  To leir ilk ither lear;
And tones and looks and smiles were shed,
  Remember'd evermair.

I wonder, Jeanie, aften yet,
  When sitting on that bink,
Cheek touchin' cheek, loof lock'd in loof,
  What our wee heads could think.
When baith bent down ower ae braid page,
  Wi' ae buik on our knee,
Thy lips were on thy lessons, but
  My lesson was in thee.

O, mind ye how we hung our heads,
  How cheeks brent red wi' shame,
Whene'er the scule-weans, laughin', said,
  We cleek'd thegither hame?
And mind ye o' the Saturdays,
  (The scule then skail't at noon,)
When we ran off to speel the braes, —
  The broomy braes o' June?

My head rins round and round about,
  My heart flows like a sea,
As ane by ane the thochts rush back
  O' scule-time, and o' thee.
O mornin' life! O mornin' luve!
  O lichtsome days and lang,
When hinnied hopes around our hearts
  Like simmer blossoms sprang!

O, mind ye, luve, how aft we left
  The deavin', dinsome toun,

To wander by the green burnside,
  And hear its waters croon?
The simmer leaves hung ower our heads,
  The flowers burst round our feet,
And in the gloamin' o' the wood
  The throssil whusslit sweet:

The throssil whusslit in the wood,
  The burn sang to the trees,
And we, with Nature's heart in tune,
  Concerted harmonies;
And on the knowe abune the burn
  For hours thegither sat
In the silentness o' joy, till baith
  Wi' very gladness grat.

Ay, ay, dear Jeanie Morrison,
  Tears trickled down your cheek
Like dew-beads on a rose, yet nane
  Had ony power to speak!
That was a time, a blessed time,
  When hearts were fresh and young,
When freely gush'd all feelings forth,
  Unsyllabled, — unsung!

I marvel, Jeanie Morrison,
  Gin I hae been to thee
As closely twined wi' earliest throchts
  As ye hae been to me:
O, tell me gin their music fills
  Thine ear as it does mine!
O, say gin e'er your heart grows grit
  Wi' dreamings o' langsyne?

I've wander'd east, I've wander'd west,
  I've borne a weary lot;
But in my wanderings, far or near,
  Ye never were forgot:

The fount that first burst frae this heart
  Still travels on its way;
And channels deeper, as it rins,
  The luve o' life's young day.

O dear, dear Jeanie Morrison,
  Since we were sinder'd young
I've never seen your face nor heard
  The music o' your tongue;
But I could hug all wretchedness,
  And happy could I dee,
Did I but ken your heart still dream'd
  O' bygane days and me!

SPANISH.

J. F. WALLER.

MAGDALENA, OR THE SPANISH DUEL.

  NEAR the city of Sevilla,
    Years and years ago,
  Dwelt a lady in a villa
    Years and years ago;
And her hair was black as night,
And her eyes were starry bright;
Olives on her brow were blooming,
Roses red her lips perfuming,
And her step was light and airy
As the tripping of a fairy:
When she spoke, you thought, each minute,
'Twas the trilling of a linnet;
When she sang, you heard a gush
Of full-voiced sweetness like a thrush;
And she struck from the guitar
Ringing music, sweeter far
Than the morning breezes make
Through the lime trees when they shake, —
Than the ocean murmuring o'er

Pebbles on the foamy shore.
Orphan'd both of sire and mother,
Dwelt she in that lonely villa;
Absent now her guardian brother
On a mission from Sevilla.
Skills it little now the telling
How I woo'd that maiden fair,
Track'd her to her lonely dwelling,
And obtain'd an entrance there.
Ah! that lady of the villa, —
And I loved her so,
Near the city of Sevilla,
Years and years ago.
Ay de mi! — Like echoes falling
Sweet and sad and low,
Voices come at night, recalling
Years and years ago.

'Twas an autumn eve; the splendour
Of the day was gone,
And the twilight, soft and tender,
Stole so gently on
That the eye could scarce discover
How the shadows, spreading over,
Like a vale of silver gray,
Toned the golden clouds, sun-painted,
Till they paled, and paled, and fainted
From the face of heaven away:
And a dim light, rising slowly,
O'er the welkin spread,
Till the blue sky, calm and holy,
Gleam'd above our head;
And the thin Moon, newly nascent,
Shone in glory meek and sweet,
As Murillo paints her crescent
Underneath Madonna's feet.
And we sat outside the villa

Where the waters flow
Down to the city of Sevilla, —
Years and years ago.

Seated half within a bower,
Where the languid evening breeze
Shook out odours in a shower
From oranges and citron-trees,

Sang she from a romancero,
How a Moorish chieftain bold
Fought a Spanish caballero
By Sevilla's walls of old;

How they battled for a lady,
Fairest of the maids of Spain, —
How the Christian's lance, so steady,
Pierced the Moslem through the brain.

Then she ceased: her black eyes, moving,
Flash'd, as ask'd she with a smile, —
"Say, are maids as fair and loving, —
Men as faithful, in your isle?"

"British maids," I said, "are ever
Counted fairest of the fair;
Like the swans on yonder river
Moving with a stately air:

Woo'd not quickly, won not lightly,
But, when won, forever true;
Trial draws the bond more tightly,
Time can ne'er the knot undo."

"And the men?" — "Ah! dearest lady,
Are — *quien sabe?* who can say?
To make love they're ever ready,
When they can and where they may;

Fix'd as waves, as breezes steady
In a changeful April day, —
Como brisas como rios,
No se sabe, sabe Dios."

"Are they faithful?" — "Ah! *quien sabe?*
Who can answer that they are?
While we may we should be happy."
Then I took up her guitar,
And I sang, in sportive strain,
This song to an old air of Spain:

Quien Sabe.

"The breeze of the evening that cools the hot air,
That kisses the orange and shakes out thy hair,
Is its freshness less welcome, less sweet its perfume,
That you know not the region from which it is come?
Whence the wind blows, where the wind goes,
Hither and thither and whither — who knows?
Who knows?
Hither and thither, — but whither — who knows?

The river forever glides singing along,
The rose on the bank bends down to its song;
And the flower, as it listens, unconsciously dips,
Till the rising wave glistens and kisses its lips:
But why the wave rises and kisses the rose,
And why the rose stoops for those kisses — who knows?
Who knows?
And away flows the river, — but whither — who knows?

Let me be the breeze, love, that wanders along,
The river that ever rejoices in song;
Be thou to my fancy the orange in bloom,
The rose by the river that gives its perfume.
Would the fruit be so golden, so fragrant the rose,
If no breeze and no wave were to kiss them?
Who knows?

Who knows?
If no breeze and no wave were to kiss them?
Who knows?"

As I sang, the lady listen'd,
Silent save one gentle sigh:
When I ceased, a tear-drop glisten'd
On the dark fringe of her eye.

Up I sprang. What words were utter'd
Bootless now to think or tell, —
Tongues speak wild when hearts are flutter'd
By the mighty master-spell.

"Magdalena, dearest, hear me,"
Sigh'd I, as I seized her hand; —
"Hola! Señor," very near me,
Cries a voice of stern command.

And a stalwart caballero
Comes upon me with a stride,
On his head a slouch'd sombrero,
A toledo by his side.

"Will your Worship have the goodness
To release that lady's hand?" —
"Señor," I replied, "this rudeness
I am not prepared to stand."

Then the Spanish caballero
Bow'd with haughty courtesy,
Solemn as a tragic hero,
And announced himself to me:

"Señor, I am Don Camillo
Guzman Miguel Pedrillo
De Xymenes y Ribera
Y Santallos y Herrera
Y de Rivas y Mendoza
Y Quintana y de Rosa
Y Zorilla y" — "No more, sir;

'Tis as good as twenty score, sir,"
  Said I to him, with a frown:
"Mucha bulla para nada,
No palabras, draw your 'spada;
If you're up for a duello
You will find I'm just your fellow,—
  Senior, I am Peter Brown!"

By the river's bank that night,
    Foot to foot in strife,
Fought we in the dubious light
    A fight of death or life.
Don Camillo slash'd my shoulder;
With the pain I grew the bolder,
    Close and closer still I press'd:
Fortune favour'd me at last;
I broke his guard, my weapon pass'd:
    Through the caballero's breast:
The man of many names went down,
Pierced by the sword of Peter Brown!

Kneeling down, I raised his head:
The caballero faintly said,
"Señor Ingles, fly from Spain
With all speed, for you have slain
A Spanish noble, Don Camillo
Guzman Miguel Pedrillo
De Xymenes y Ribera
Y Santallos y Herrera
Y de Rivas y Mendoza
Y Quintana y de Rosa
Y Zorilla y"—He swoon'd
With the bleeding from his wound.
If he be living still, or dead,
    I never knew, I ne'er shall know.
That night from Spain in haste I fled,
    Years and years ago.

XI.

ONOMATOPOETIC.

THE BELLS.

EDGAR A. POE.

HEAR the sledges with the bells, — silver bells;
What a world of merriment their melody foretells!
How they tinkle, tinkle, tinkle,
In the icy air of night!
While the stars, that oversprinkle
All the heavens, seem to twinkle
With a crystalline delight;
Keeping time, time, time,
In a sort of Runic rhyme,
To the tintinnabulation that so musically wells
From the bells, bells, bells, bells, bells, —
From the jingling and the tinkling of the bells.

Hear the mellow wedding-bells, — golden bells!
What a world of happiness their harmony foretells!
Through the balmy air of night
How they ring out their delight!
From the molten-golden notes,
And all in tune,
What a liquid ditty floats
To the turtle-dove that listens, while she gloats
On the moon!
O, from out the sounding cells,
What a gush of euphony voluminously wells!
How it swells! how it dwells

On the Future! how it tells
Of the rapture that impels
To the swinging and the ringing
Of the bells, bells, bells, bells, bells, —
To the rhyming and the chiming of the bells!

Hear the loud alarum bells, — brazen bells!
What a tale of terror, now, their turbulency tells!
In the startled ear of night
How they scream out their affright!
Too much horrified to speak,
They can only shriek, shriek,
Out of tune,
In a clamourous appealing to the mercy of the fire,
In a mad expostulation with the deaf and frantic fire
Leaping higher, higher, higher,
With a desperate desire,
And a resolute endeavour,
Now — now to sit or never,
By the side of the pale-faced Moon.
O, the bells, bells, bells!
What a tale their terror tells
Of despair!
How they clang, and clash, and roar!
What a horror they outpour
On the bosom of the palpitating air!
Yet the ear, it fully knows,
By the twanging and the clanging,
How the danger ebbs and flows;
Yet the ear distinctly tells,
In the jangling and the wrangling,
How the danger sinks and swells,
By the sinking or the swelling in the anger of the bells, —
Of the bells, bells, bells, bells, bells, —
In the clamour and the clangour of the bells!

Hear the tolling of the bells, — iron bells!
What a world of solemn thought their monody compels!

In the silence of the night,
How we shiver with affright
At the melancholy menace of their tone!
For every sound that floats
From the rust within their throats
Is a groan.
And the people, — ah, the people, —
They that dwell up in the steeple,
All alone,
And who tolling, tolling, tolling,
In that muffled monotone,
Feel a glory in so rolling
On the human heart a stone!
They are neither man nor woman, —
They are neither brute nor human, —
They are Ghouls:
And their king it is who tolls;
And he rolls, rolls, rolls, rolls,
A pæan from the bells!
And his merry bosom swells
With the pæan of the bells!
And he dances and he yells;
Keeping time, time, time,
In a sort of Runic rhyme,
To the tolling of the bells, bells, bells, bells, bells, —
To the moaning and the groaning of the bells.

BUGLE SONG.

ALFRED TENNYSON.

THE splendour falls on castle walls
And snowy summits old in story;
The long light shakes across the lakes,
And the wild cataract leaps in glory.
Blow, bugle, blow, set the wild echoes flying:
Blow, bugle; answer, echoes, dying, dying, dying.

O hark, O hear! how thin and clear,
And thinner, clearer, further going;
O sweet and far, from cliff and scar,
The horns of Elfland faintly blowing!
Blow, let us hear the purple glens replying:
Blow, bugle; answer echoes, dying, dying, dying.

O love, they die in yon rich sky,
They faint on hill or field or river:
Our echoes roll from soul to soul,
And grow forever and forever.
Blow, bugle, blow, set the wild echoes flying,
And answer echoes, answer, dying, dying, dying.

THE CHARCOAL MAN.

J. T. TROWBRIDGE.

THOUGH rudely blows the wintry blast,
And sifting snows fall white and fast,
Mark Haley drives along the street,
Perch'd high upon his wagon seat:
His sombre face the storm defies,
And thus from morn till eve he cries, —
"Charco'! charco'!"
While echo faint and far replies, —
"Hark, O! hark, O!"
"Charco'!" — "Hark, O!" — Such cheery sounds
Attend him on his daily rounds.

The dust begrimes his ancient hat;
His coat is darker far than that:
'Tis odd to see his sooty form
All speckled with the feathery storm;
Yet in his honest bosom lies
Nor spot nor speck, — though still he cries, —
"Charco'! charco'!"

And many a roguish lad replies, —
"Ark, ho! ark, ho!"
"Charco'!" — "Ark, ho!" — Such various sounds
Announce Mark Haley's morning rounds.

Thus all the cold and wintry day
He labours much for little pay;
Yet feels no less of happiness
Than many a richer man, I guess,
When through the shades of eve he spies
The light of his own home, and cries, —
"Charco'! charco'!"
And Martha from the door replies, —
"Mark, ho! Mark, ho!"
"Charco'!" — "Mark, ho! — Such joy abounds
When he has closed his daily rounds.

The hearth is warm, the fire is bright;
And, while his hand, wash'd clean and white,
Holds Martha's tender hand once more,
His glowing face bends fondly o'er
The crib wherein his darling lies;
And in a coaxing tone he cries,
"Charco'! charco'!"
And baby with a laugh replies, —
"Ah, go! ah, go!"
"Charco'!" — "Ah, go!" — while at the sounds
The mother's heart with gladness bounds.

Then honour'd be the charcoal man!
Though dusky as an African,
'Tis not for you, that chance to be
A little better clad than he,
His honest manhood to despise,
Although from morn till eve he cries, —
"Charco'! charco'!"

While mocking echo still replies, —
"Hark, O! hark, O!"
"Charco'!" — "Hark, O!" — Long may the sounds
Proclaim Mark Haley's daily rounds!

CREEDS OF THE BELLS.

GEORGE W. BUNGAY.

How sweet the chime of Sabbath bells!
Each one its creed in music tells,
In tones that float upon the air,
As soft as song, and pure as prayer;
And I will put in simple rhyme
The language of the golden chime:
My happy heart with rapture swells
Responsive to the bells — sweet bells.

"In deeds of love excel — excel,"
Chimed out from ivied towers a bell;
"This is the Church not built on sands,
Emblem of one not built with hands:
Its forms and sacred rites revere;
Come worship here — come worship here;
Its rituals and faith excel — excel,"
Chimed out th' Episcopalian bell.

"O, heed the ancient landmarks well,"
In solemn tones exclaim'd a bell;
"No progress made by mortal man
Can change the just, eternal plan:
With God there can be nothing new;
Ignore the false, embrace the true
While all is well — is well — is well,"
Peal'd out the good old Dutch Church bell.

"O swell, ye purifying waters, swell,"
In mellow tones rang out a bell;

"Though faith alone in Christ can save,
Man must be plunged beneath the wave,
To show the world unfaltering faith
In what the sacred Scripture saith:
O swell, ye rising waters, swell,"
Peal'd out the clear-toned Baptist bell.

"Not faith alone, but works as well,
Must test the soul," said a soft bell;
"Come here, and cast aside your load,
And work your way along the road,
With faith in God, and faith in man,
And hope in Christ, where hope began:
Do well — do well — do well — do well,"
Peal'd forth the Unitarian bell.

"Farewell! farewell! base world, farewell,"
In gloomy tones exclaim'd a bell;
"Life is a boon to mortals given,
To fit the soul for bliss in Heaven:
Do not invoke the avenging rod;
Come here, and learn the way to God:
Say to the world farewell — farewell!"
Peal'd out the Presbyterian bell.

"In after life there is no Hell!"
In raptures rang a cheerful bell;
"Look up to Heaven this holy day,
Where angels wait to lead the way;
There are no fires, no fiends, to blight
The future life; be just, do right:
No Hell! no Hell! no Hell! no Hell!"
Rang out the Universalist bell.

"To all the truth we tell — we tell,"
Shouted in ecstasies a bell;
"Come all ye weary wanderers, see!
Our Lord has made salvation free:

Repent! believe! have faith! and then
Be saved, and praise the Lord. Amen.
Salvation's free we tell — we tell,"
Shouted the Methodistic bell.

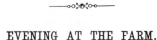

EVENING AT THE FARM.

J. T. Trowbridge.

Over the hill the farm-boy goes:
His shadow lengthens along the land,
A giant staff in giant hand;
In the poplar-tree above the spring
The katydid begins to sing;
The early dews are falling:
Into the stone-heap darts the mink,
The swallows skim the river's brink,
And home to the woodland fly the crows,
When over the hill the farm-boy goes,
Cheerily calling, —
"Co', boss! co', boss! co'! co'! co'!"
Further, further over the hill,
Faintly calling, calling still, —
"Co', boss! co', boss! co'! co'!"

Into the yard the farmer goes,
With grateful heart, at the close of day:
Harness and chain are hung away;
In the wagon-shed stand yoke and plough;
The straw's in the stack, the hay in the mow;
The cooling dews are falling:
The friendly sheep his welcome bleat,
The pigs come grunting to his feet,
The whinnying mare her master knows,
When into the yard the farmer goes,
His cattle calling, —
"Co', boss! co', boss! co'! co'! co'!"

While still the cow-boy, far away,
Goes seeking those that have gone astray, —
"Co', boss! co', boss! co'! co'!"

Now to her task the milkmaid goes;
The cattle come crowding through the gate,
Lowing, pushing, little and great;
About the trough, by the farm-yard pump,
The frolicsome yearlings frisk and jump,
While the pleasant dews are falling:
The new milch heifer is quick and shy,
But the old cow waits with tranquil eye;
And the white stream into the bright pail flows,
When to her task the milkmaid goes,
Soothingly calling, —
"So, boss! so, boss! so! so! so!"
The cheerful milkmaid takes her stool,
And sits and milks in the twilight cool,
Saying, "So, so, boss! so! so!"

To supper at last the farmer goes:
The apples are pared, the paper read,
The stories are told, then all to bed:
Without, the cricket's ceaseless song
Makes shrill the silence all night long;
The heavy dews are falling:
The housewife's hand has turn'd the lock;
Drowsily ticks the kitchen clock;
The household sinks to deep repose;
But still in sleep the farm-boy goes
Singing, calling —
"Co', boss! co', boss! co'! co'! co'!"
And oft the milkmaid, in her dreams,
Drums in the pail with the flashing streams,
Murmuring, "So, boss! so!"

THE LAST HYMN.

MRS. M. FARMINGHAM.

THE Sabbath day was ending in a village by the sea,
The utter'd benediction touch'd the people tenderly;
And they rose to face the sunset in the glowing, lighted west,
And then hasten'd to their dwellings for God's blessèd boon of rest.
But they look'd across the waters, and a storm was raging there;
A fierce spirit moved about them, — the wild spirit of the air;
And it lash'd, and shook, and tore them, till they thunder'd, groan'd, and boom'd:
And, alas! for any vessel in their yawning gulfs entomb'd.
Very anxious were the people on that rocky coast of Wales,
Lest the dawns of coming morrows should be telling awful tales,
When the sea had spent its passion, and should cast upon the shore
Bits of wreck, and swollen victims, as it had done heretofore.
With the rough winds blowing round her, a brave woman strain'd her eyes,
As she saw along the billows a large vessel fall and rise.
O! it did not need a prophet to tell what the end must be,
For no ship could ride in safety near that shore on such a sea.

Then the pitying people hurried from their homes, and throng'd the beach.
O, for power to cross the waters, and the perishing to reach!
Helpless hands were wrung in terror, tender hearts grew cold with dread,
And the ship urged by the tempest to the fatal rock-shore sped.
She has parted in the middle! O, the half of her goes down!
God have mercy! Is His Heaven far to seek, for those who drown?
Lo! when next the white, shock'd faces look'd with terror on the sea,
Only one last clinging figure on a spar was seen to be.
Nearer to the trembling watchers came the wreck toss'd by the wave,
And the man still clung and floated, though no power on Earth could save.
"Could we send him a short message? Here's a trumpet, shout away!"
'Twas the preacher's hand that took it, and he wonder'd what to say:

Any memory of his sermon? Firstly? Secondly? Ah, no!
There was but one thing to utter in that awful hour of woe.
So he shouted through the trumpet, "Look to Jesus! Can you hear?"
And "Ay, ay, sir!" rang the answer o'er the waters, faint and clear.

Then they listen'd: "He is singing, 'Jesus, lover of my soul,'"
And the winds brought back the echo, "While the nearer waters roll."
Strange indeed it was to hear him, "Till the storm of life is past,"
Singing bravely o'er the waters, "O, receive my soul at last."
He could have no other refuge, "Hangs my helpless soul on Thee."
"Leave, O! leave me not," — the singer dropp'd at last into the sea.
And the watchers looking homeward, through their eyes by tears made dim,
Said, "He pass'd to be with Jesus in the singing of that hymn."

THE LITTLE TELLTALE.

Once, on a golden afternoon,
With radiant faces and hearts in tune,
Two fond lovers in dreaming mood
Threaded a rural solitude.
Wholly happy, they only knew
That the earth was bright and the sky was blue;
That light and beauty and joy and song
Charm'd the way as they pass'd along:
The air was fragrant with woodland scents;
The squirrel frisk'd on the roadside fence;
And hovering near them, "chee, chee, chink?"
Queried the curious bobolink,
Pausing and peering with sidelong head,
As saucily questioning all they said;
While the ox-eye danced on its slender stem,
And all glad Nature rejoiced with them.
Over the odorous fields were strown
Wilting windrows of grass new-mown,

And rosy billows of clover bloom
Surged in the sunshine and breathed perfume.
Swinging low on a slender limb,
The sparrow warbled his wedding hymn;
And, balancing on a blackberry-brier,
The bobolink sang with his heart on fire, —
"Chink! If you wish to kiss her, do!
Do it, do it! You coward, you!
Kiss her! Kiss, kiss her! Who will see?
Only we three! we three! we three!"

Under garlands of drooping vines,
Through dim vistas of sweet-breathed pines,
Past wide meadow-fields lately mow'd,
Wander'd the indolent country road.
The lovers follow'd it, listening still,
And, loitering slowly, as lovers will,
Enter'd a low-roof'd bridge, that lay,
Dusky and cool, in their pleasant way.
Under its arch a smooth, bright stream
Silently glided, with glint and gleam,
Shaded by graceful elms that spread
Their verdurous canopy overhead, —
The stream so narrow, the boughs so wide,
They met and mingled across the tide.
Alders loved it, and seem'd to keep
Patient watch as it lay asleep,
Mirroring clearly the trees and sky
And the flitting form of the dragon-fly,
Save where the swift-wing'd swallow play'd
In and out in the sun and shade,
And, darting and circling in merry chase,
Dipp'd, and dimpled its clear dark face.

Fluttering lightly from brink to brink
Follow'd the garrulous bobolink,
Rallying loudly, with mirthful din,
The pair who linger'd unseen within.

And, when from the friendly bridge at last
Into the road beyond they pass'd,
Again beside them the tempter went,
Keeping the thread of his argument, —
"Kiss her! kiss her! chink-a-chee-chee!
I'll not mention it! don't mind me!
I'll be sentinel, — I can see
All around from this tall birch-tree!"
But, ah! they noted — nor deemed it strange —
In his rollicking chorus a trifling change:
"Do it! do it!" with might and main
Warbled the telltale, — "Do it *again!*"

ROBERT OF LINCOLN.

W. C. Bryant.

Merrily swinging on brier and weed,
Near to the nest of his little dame,
Over the mountain-side or mead,
Robert of Lincoln is telling his name:
Bob-o'-link, bob-o'-link,
Spink, spank, spink;
Snug and safe is that nest of ours,
Hidden among the summer flowers,
Chee, chee, chee.

Robert of Lincoln is gaily dress'd,
Wearing a bright black wedding-coat;
White are his shoulders and white his crest.
Hear him call his merry note:
Bob-o'-link, bob-o'-link,
Spink, spank, spink;
Look, what a nice new coat is mine,
Sure there never was a bird so fine.
Chee, chee, chee.

Robert of Lincoln's Quaker wife,
  Pretty and quiet, with plain brown wings,
Passing at home a patient life,
  Broods in the grass while her husband sings:
    Bob-o'-link, bob-o'-link,
    Spink, spank, spink;
Brood, kind creature; you need not fear
Thieves and robbers while I am here.
        Chee, chee, chee.

Modest and shy as a nun is she,
  One weak chirp is her only note;
Braggart and prince of braggarts is he,
  Pouring boasts from his little throat:
    Bob-o'-link, bob-o'-link,
    Spink, spank, spink;
Never was I afraid of man;
Catch me, cowardly knaves, if you can.
        Chee, chee, chee.

Six white eggs on a bed of hay,
  Fleck'd with purple, a pretty sight!
There as the mother sits all day,
  Robert is singing with all his might:
    Bob-o'-link, bob-o'-link,
    Spink, spank, spink;
Nice good wife, that never goes out,
Keeping house while I frolic about.
        Chee, chee, chee.

Soon as the little ones chip the shell,
  Six wide mouths are open for food;
Robert of Lincoln bestirs him well,
  Gathering seed for the hungry brood.
    Bob-o'-link, bob-o'-link,
    Spink, spank, spink;

This new life is likely to be
Hard for a gay young fellow like me.
Chee, chee, chee.

Robert of Lincoln at length is made
Sober with work and silent with care;
Off is his holiday garment laid,
Half forgotten that merry air:
Bob-o'-link, bob-o'-link,
Spink, spank, spink;
Nobody knows but my mate and I
Where our nest and our nestlings lie.
Chee, chee, chee.

Summer wanes; the children are grown;
Fun and frolic no more he knows;
Robert of Lincoln's a humdrum crone;
Off he flies, and we sing as he goes:
Bob-o'-link, bob-o'-link,
Spink, spank, spink;
When you can pipe that merry old strain,
Robert of Lincoln, come back again.
Chee, chee, chee.

"ROCK OF AGES."

PROF. EDWARD H. RICE.

"Rock of ages, cleft for me,"
Thoughtlessly the maiden sung:
Fell the words unconsciously
From her girlish, gleeful tongue,
Sung as little children sing,
Sung as sing the birds in June;
Fell the words like light leaves sown
On the current of the tune, —
"Rock of ages, cleft for me,
Let me hide myself in Thee."

Felt her soul no need to hide;
  Sweet the song as song could be,
And she had no thought beside:
  All the words unheedingly
Fell from lips untouch'd by care,
  Dreaming not that each might be
On some other lips a prayer,—
"Rock of Ages, cleft for me,
Let me hide myself in Thee."

"Rock of Ages, cleft for me,"—
  'Twas a woman sung them now,
Pleadingly and prayerfully;
  Every word her heart did know:
Rose the song, as storm-toss'd bird
  Beats with weary wing the air,
Every note with sorrow stirr'd,
  Every syllable a prayer,—
"Rock of Ages, cleft for me,
Let me hide myself in Thee."

"Rock of Ages, cleft for me,"—
  Lips grown agèd sung the hymn
Trustingly and tenderly,
  Voice grown weak and eyes grown dim,—
"Let me hide myself in Thee."
  Trembling though the voice, and low,
Rose the sweet strain peacefully
  As a river in its flow;
Sung as only they can sing
  Who life's thorny paths have press'd;
Sung as only they can sing
  Who behold the promised rest.

"Rock of Ages, cleft for me,"
  Sung above a coffin-lid;
Underneath, all restfully
  All life's cares and sorrows hid.

Never more, O storm-toss'd soul!
  Never more from wind or tide,
Never more from billow's roll,
  Wilt thou need thyself to hide.
Could the sightless, sunken eyes,
  Closed beneath the soft gray hair,
Could the mute and stiffen'd lips,
  Move again in pleading prayer,
Still, ay, still the words would be,
"Let me hide myself in Thee."

DRIFTING.

T. BUCHANAN READ.

My soul to-day is far away,
Sailing the Vesuvian Bay;
My wingèd boat, a bird afloat,
Swims round the purple peaks remote:

Round purple peaks it sails, and seeks
Blue inlets and their crystal creeks,
Where high rocks throw, through deeps below,
A duplicated golden glow.

Far, vague, and dim the mountains swim;
While, on Vesuvius' misty brim,
With outstretch'd hands the gray smoke stands
O'erlooking the volcanic lands.

In lofty lines, 'mid palms and pines,
And olives, aloes, elms, and vines,
Sorrento swings on sunset wings,
Where Tasso's spirit soars and sings.

Here Ischia smiles o'er liquid miles;
And yonder, bluest of the Isles,
Calm Capri waits, her sapphire gates
Beguiling to her bright estates.

I heed not, if my rippling skiff
Float swift or slow from cliff to cliff:
With dreamful eyes my spirit lies
Under the walls of Paradise.

Under the walls, where swells and falls
The Bay's deep breast at intervals,
At peace I lie, blown softly by,
A cloud upon this liquid sky.

The day, so mild, is Heaven's own child,
With earth and ocean reconciled:
The airs I feel around me steal
Are murmuring to the murmuring keel:

Over the rail my hand I trail
Within the shadow of the sail;
A joy intense, the cooling sense,
Glides down my drowsy indolence:

With dreamful eyes my spirit lies
Where Summer sings and never dies;
O'erveil'd with vines, she glows and shines
Among her future oil and wines.

Her children, hid the cliffs amid,
Are gambolling with the gambolling kid;
Or down the walls, with tipsy calls,
Laugh on the rocks like waterfalls.

The fisher's child, with tresses wild,
Unto the smooth, bright sand beguiled,
With glowing lips sings as she skips,
Or gazes at the far-off ships.

Yon deep bark goes where traffic blows,
From lands of sun to lands of snows:
This happier one, its course is run
From lands of snow to lands of sun.

O happy ship, to rise and dip,
With the blue crystal at your lip!
O happy crew, my heart with you
Sails, and sails, and sings anew!

No more, no more the worldly shore
Upbraids me with its loud uproar!
With dreamful eyes my spirit lies
Under the walls of Paradise!

XII.

FOR YOUNG FOLKS.

ANNIE AND WILLIE'S PRAYER.

MRS. SOPHIA P. SNOW.

'TWAS the eve before Christmas; "Good night" had been said
And Annie and Willie had crept into bed:
There were tears on their pillows, and tears in their eyes,
And each little bosom was heaving with sighs,
For to-night their stern father's command had been given
That they should retire precisely at seven
Instead of at eight; for they troubled him more
With questions unheard-of than ever before:
He had told them he thought this delusion a sin;
No such being as Santa Claus ever had been,
And he hoped, after this, he should never more hear
How he scrambled down chimneys with presents, each year;
And this was the reason that two little heads
So restlessly toss'd on their soft downy beds.

Eight, nine, and the clock on the steeple toll'd ten,—
Not a word had been spoken by either till then;
When Willie's sad face from the blanket did peep,
And whisper'd, "Dear Annie, is you fast asleep?"
"Why, no, brother Willie," a sweet voice replies,
"I've tried it in vain, but I can't shut my eyes;
For, somehow, it makes me so sorry because
Dear papa has said there is no Santa Claus.
Now we know that there is, and it can't be denied,
For he came every year before mamma died:
But then I've been thinking that she used to pray,
And God would hear every thing mamma would say;
And perhaps she ask'd him to send Santa Claus here,
With the sacks full of presents he brought every year."

"Well, why tant we pay dest as mamma did then,
And ask Him to send him with presents aden?"
"I've been thinking so, too;" and, without a word more,
Four little bare feet bounded out on the floor,
And four little knees the soft carpet press'd,
And two tiny hands were clasp'd close to each breast.
"Now, Willie, you know we must firmly believe
That the presents we ask for we're sure to receive:
You must wait just as still till I say the 'Amen,'
And by that you will know that your turn has come then.
Dear Jesus, look down on my brother and me,
And grant us the favour we are asking of Thee:
I want a wax dolly, a tea-set and ring,
And an ebony work-box that shuts with a spring.
Bless papa, dear Jesus, and cause him to see
That Santa Claus loves us far better than he:
Don't let him get fretful and angry again,
At dear brother Willie, and Annie, Amen!"
"Peas Desus 'et Santa Taus tum down to-night,
And bing us some pesents before it is 'ight:
I want he should div me a nice ittle sed,
With bight, shiny unners, and all painted yed;
A box full of tandy, a book and a toy,—
Amen,—and then, Desus, I'll be a dood boy."

Their prayers being ended, they raised up their heads,
And with hearts light and cheerful again sought their beds;
They were soon lost in slumber both peaceful and deep,
And with fairies in dreamland were roaming in sleep.

Eight, nine, and the little French clock had struck ten,
Ere the father had thought of his children again:
He seems now to hear Annie's half-suppress'd sighs,
And to see the big tears stand in Willie's blue eyes:
"I was harsh with my darlings," he mentally said,
"And should not have sent them so early to bed;
But then I was troubled,—my feelings found vent,
For bank stock to-day has gone down ten per cent.:
But of course they've forgotten their troubles ere this,
And that I denied them the thrice-ask'd-for kiss;
But just to make sure I'll steal up to their door,
For I never spoke harsh to my darlings before."

So saying, he softly ascended the stairs,
And arrived at the door to hear both of their prayers.
His Annie's "bless papa" draws forth the big tears,
And Willie's grave promise falls sweet on his ears.
"Strange, strange I'd forgotten," said he with a sigh,
"How I long'd when a child to have Christmas draw nigh:
I'll atone for my harshness," he inwardly said,
"By answering their prayers, ere I sleep in my bed."

Then he turn'd to the stairs, and softly went down,
Threw off velvet slippers and silk dressing-gown;
Donn'd hat, coat, and boots, and was out in the street,
A millionaire facing the cold driving sleet;
Nor stopp'd he until he had bought every thing,
From the box full of candy to the tiny gold ring.
Indeed he kept adding so much to his store,
That the various presents outnumber'd a score;
Then homeward he turn'd with his holiday load,
And with Aunt Mary's aid in the nursery 'twas stow'd.
Miss Dolly was seated beneath a pine tree,
By the side of a table spread out for a tea;
A work-box well fill'd in the centre was laid,
And on it the ring for which Annie had pray'd;
A soldier in uniform stood by a sled,
With bright shining runners, and all painted red;
There were balls, dogs and horses, books pleasing to see,
And birds of all colours were perch'd in the tree,
While Santa Claus laughing stood up in the top,
As if getting ready more presents to drop.
And, as the fond father the picture survey'd,
He thought, for his trouble he had amply been paid;
And he said to himself as he brush'd off a tear,
"I'm happier to-night than I've been for a year;
I've enjoy'd more true pleasure than ever before,—
What care I if bank stocks fall ten per cent. more?
Hereafter I'll make it a rule, I believe,
To have Santa Claus visit us each Christmas-eve."
So thinking he gently extinguish'd the light,
And tripp'd down the stairs to retire for the night.

As soon as the beams of the bright morning Sun
Put the darkness to flight, and the stars, one by one,

Four little blue eyes out of sleep open'd wide,
And at the same moment the presents espied;
Then out of their beds they sprang with a bound,
And the very gifts pray'd for were all of them found:
They laugh'd and they cried in their innocent glee,
And shouted for "papa" to come quick and see
What presents old Santa Claus brought in the night,
(Just the things that they wanted,) and left before light:
"And now," added Annie, in a voice soft and low,
"You'll believe there's a Santa Claus, papa, I know";
While dear little Willie climb'd up on his knee,
Determined no secret between them should be,
And told in soft whispers how Annie had said,
That their blessèd mamma, so long ago dead,
Used to kneel down and pray by the side of her chair,
And that God, up in Heaven, had answer'd her prayer!
"Then we dot up, and pay'd dust as well as we tould,
And Dod answer'd our payers; now wasn't he dood?"
"I should say that He was if He sent you all these,
And knew just what presents my children would please:
Well, well, let him think so, the dear little elf;
'Twould be cruel to tell him I did it myself."

Blind father! who caused your proud heart to relent,
And the hasty word spoken so soon to repent?
'Twas the Being who made you steal softly up stairs,
And made you His agent to answer their prayers.

THE DEAD DOLL.

MARGARET VANDEGRIFT.

You needn't be trying to comfort me: I tell you my dolly is dead!
There's no use in saying she isn't, with a crack like that in her head!
It's just like you said it wouldn't hurt much to have my tooth out that day;
And then, when the man most pull'd my head off, you hadn't a word to say.

And I guess you must think I'm a baby, when you say you can mend it with glue!
As if I didn't know better than that! Why, just suppose it was you!
You might make her look all mended; but what do I care for looks?
Why, glue's for chairs and tables and toys, and the backs of books!

My dolly! my own little daughter! O, but it's the awfulest crack!
It just makes me sick to think of the sound when her poor head went whack
Against that horrible brass thing that holds up the little shelf!
Now, nursey, what makes you remind me? I know that I did it myself!

I think you must be crazy! You'll get her another head!
What good would forty heads do her? I tell you my dolly is dead!
And to think I hadn't quite finish'd her elegant new spring hat!
And I took a sweet ribbon of hers last night to tie on that horrid cat!

When my mamma gave me that ribbon, — I was playing out in the yard, —
She said to me most expressly, "Here's a ribbon for Hildegarde."
And I went and put it on Tabby, and Hildegarde saw me do it;
But I said to myself, "O, never mind; I don't believe she knew it."

But I know that she knew it now; and I just believe, I do,
That her poor little heart was broken, and so her head broke too.
O, my baby! my little baby! I wish my head had been hit!
For I've hit it over and over, and it hasn't crack'd a bit!

But, since the darling is dead, she'll want to be buried, of course.
We will take my little wagon, nurse; and you shall be the horse;
And I'll walk behind, and cry; and we'll put her in this, you see, —
This dear little box, — and we'll bury her then under the maple-tree.

And papa will make me a tombstone like the one he made for my bird;
And he'll put what I tell him on it; yes, every single word.
I shall say, "Here lies Hildegarde, a beautiful doll, who is dead;
She died of a broken heart, and a dreadful crack in her head."

AN EVENING WITH HELEN'S BABIES.

J. HABBERTON.

WITH a head full of pleasing fancies, I went down to supper. My new friends, Helen's babies, were unusually good. There were two of them. Budge, the elder, was five years of age, and Toddie had seen but three Summers. Their ride seemed to have toned down their boisterousness and elevated their little souls; their appetites exhibited no diminution of force; but they talked but little, and all that they said was smart, funny, or startling, — so much so that when, after supper, they invited me to put them to bed, I gladly accepted the invitation. Toddie disappeared somewhere, and came back very disconsolate.

"Can't find my dolly's k'adle," he whined.

"Never mind, old pet," said I, soothingly. "Uncle will ride you on his foot."

"But I *want* my dolly's k'adle," said he, piteously rolling out his lower lip.

I remembered my experience when Toddie wanted to "shee wheels go wound," and I trembled.

"Toddie," said I, in a tone so persuasive that it would be worth thousands a-year to me, as a salesman, if I could only command it at will; "Toddie, don't you want to ride on uncle's back?"

"No; want my dolly's k'adle."

"Don't you want me to tell you a story?"

For a moment Toddie's face indicated a terrible internal conflict between old Adam and mother Eve, but curiosity finally overpowered natural depravity, and Toddie murmured, —

"Yesh."

"What shall I tell you about?"

"'Bout Nawndeark."

"About *what?*"

"He means Noah an' the ark," exclaimed Budge.

"Datsh what *I* shay, — Nawndeark," declared Toddie.

"Well," said I, hastily refreshing my memory by picking up the Bible, — for Helen, like most people, is pretty sure to forget to pack her Bible when she runs away from home for a few days, — "well, once it rained forty days and nights, and everybody was drowned from the face of the Earth excepting Noah, a righteous man who was saved with all his family, in an ark which the Lord commanded him to build."

"Uncle Harry," said Budge, after contemplating me with open eyes and mouth for at least two minutes after I had finished, "do you think that's Noah?"

"Certainly, Budge; here's the whole story in the Bible."

"Well, *I* don't think it's Noah one single bit," said he, with increasing emphasis.

"I'm beginning to think we read different Bibles, Budge; but let's hear *your* version."

"Huh?"

"Tell *me* about Noah, if you know so much about him."

"I will, if you want me to. Once the Lord felt so uncomfortable cos folks was bad that he was sorry he ever made anybody, or any world, or any thing. But Noah wasn't bad; the Lord liked him first-rate; so he told Noah to build a big ark, and then the Lord would make it rain so everybody should be drownded but Noah an' his little boys an' girls, an' doggies an' pussies, an' mamma-cows, an' little-boy-cows an' little-girl-cows, an' hosses, an' every thing; they'd go in the ark, an' wouldn't get wetted a bit when it rained. An' Noah took lots of things to eat in the ark; cookies, an' milk, an' oatmeal, an' strawberries, an' porgies, an' — O, yes — an' plum-puddins, an' pumpkin-pies. But Noah didn't want everybody to get drownded, so he talked to folks, an' said, 'It's goin to rain *awful* pretty soon; you'd better be good, an' then the Lord'll let you come into my ark.' An' they jus' said, 'O, if it rains we'll go in the house till it stops; an' other folks said, '*We* ain't afraid of rain; we've got an umbrella.' An' some more said, they wasn't goin' to be afraid of just a rain. But it *did* rain though, an' folks went in their houses, an' the water came in, an' they went up stairs, an' the water came up there, an' they got on the tops of the houses, an' up in big trees, an' up in mountains, an' the water went after 'em everywhere an' drownded everybody, only just except Noah and the people in the ark. An' it rained forty days an' nights, an' then it stopped; an' Noah got out of the ark, an' he an' his little boys an' girls went wherever they wanted to, and every thing in the world was all theirs; there wasn't anybody to tell 'em to go home, nor no Kindergarten schools to go to, nor no bad boys to fight 'em, nor nothin'. Now tell us 'nother story."

KATIE LEE AND WILLIE GREY.

Miss Josie R. Hunt.

Two brown heads with tossing curls,
Red lips shutting over pearls,
Bare feet, white and wet with dew,
Two eyes black, and two eyes blue;
Little girl and boy were they,
Katie Lee and Willie Grey.

They were standing where a brook,
Bending like a shepherd's crook,
Flash'd its silver, and thick ranks
Of willow fringed its mossy banks;
Half in thought, and half in play,
Katie Lee and Willie Grey.

They had cheeks like cherries red;
He was taller, — 'most a head;
She, with arms like wreaths of snow,
Swung a basket to and fro
As she loiter'd, half in play,
Chattering to Willie Grey.

"Pretty Katie," Willie said, —
And there came a dash of red
Through the brownness of his cheek, —
"Boys are strong and girls are weak,
And I'll carry, so I will,
Katie's basket up the hill."

Katie answer'd with a laugh,
"You shall carry only half";
And then, tossing back her curls,
"Boys are weak as well as girls."
Do you think that Katie guess'd
Half the wisdom she express'd?

Men are only boys grown tall;
Hearts don't change much after all;
And when, long years from that day,
Katie Lee and Willie Grey
Stood again beside the brook,
Bending like a shepherd's crook, —

Is it strange that Willie said,
While again a dash of red
Cross'd the brownness of his cheek,
"I am strong and you are weak;
Life is but a slippery steep,
Hung with shadows cold and deep.

Will you trust me, Katie dear, —
Walk beside me without fear?
May I carry, if I will,
All your burdens up the hill?"
And she answer'd with a laugh,
"No, but you may carry half."

Close beside the little brook,
Bending like a shepherd's crook,
Washing with its silver hands

Late and early at the sands,
Is a cottage, where to-day
Katie lives with Willie Grey.

In a porch she sits, and, lo!
Swings a basket to and fro, —
Vastly different from the one
That she swung in years agone;
This is long and deep and wide,
And has — *rockers at the side.*

KEEPING HIS WORD.

"ONLY a penny a box," he said;
But the gentleman turn'd away his head,
As if he shrank from the squalid sight
Of the boy who stood in the failing light.

"O sir!" he stammer'd, "you cannot know,"
(And he brush'd from his matches the flakes of snow,
That the sudden tear might have chance to fall,)
"Or I think, — I think you would take them all.

Hungry and cold at our garret-pane,
Ruby will watch till I come again,
Bringing the loaf. The Sun has set,
And he hasn't a crumb of breakfast yet.

One penny, and then I can buy the bread!"
The gentleman stopp'd: "And you?" he said;
"*I* — I can put up with them, — hunger and cold,
But Ruby is only five years old.

I promised our mother before she went, —
She knew I would do it, and died content, —
I promised her, sir, through best, through worst,
I always would think of Ruby first."

The gentleman paused at his open door,
Such tales he had often heard before;
But he fumbled his purse in the twilight drear,
"I have nothing less than a shilling here."

"O sir! if you'll only take the pack
I'll bring you the change in a moment back;
Indeed you may trust me!" "Trust you?—no!
But here is the shilling; take it and go."

The gentleman loll'd in his cozy chair,
And watch'd his cigar-wreath melt in air,
And smiled on his children, and rose to see
The baby asleep on its mother's knee.

"And now it is nine by the clock," he said,
"Time that my darlings were all a-bed;
Kiss me 'good-night,' and each be sure,
When you're saying your prayers, remember the poor."

Just then came a message,—"A boy at the door,"—
But ere it was utter'd he stood on the floor
Half-breathless, bewilder'd, and ragged and strange;
"I'm Ruby,—Mike's brother,—I've brought you the change

Mike's hurt, sir; 'twas dark; the snow made him blind,
And he didn't take notice the train was behind
Till he slipp'd on the track; and then it whizz'd by:
And he's home in the garret; I think he will die.

Yet nothing would do him, sir,—nothing would do,
But out through the snow I must hurry to you:
Of his hurt he was certain you wouldn't have heard,
And so you might think he had broken his word."

When the garret they hastily enter'd, they saw
Two arms mangled, shapeless, outstretch'd from the straw.
"You did it,—dear Ruby,—God bless you!" he said,
And the boy, gladly smiling, sank back,—and was dead.

A LEAP FOR LIFE.

WALTER COLTON.

OLD IRONSIDES at anchor lay
  In the harbour of Mahon;
A dead calm rested on the bay, —
  The waves to sleep had gone;
When little Hal, the Captain's son,
  A lad both brave and good,
In sport up shroud and rigging ran,
  And on the main truck stood!

A shudder shot through every vein,
  All eyes were turn'd on high!
There stood the boy, with dizzy brain,
  Between the sea and sky;
No hold had he above, below;
  Alone he stood in air:
To that far height none dared to go,
  No aid could reach him there.

We gazed, but not a man could speak!
  With horror all aghast;
In groups, with pallid brow and cheek,
  We watch'd the quivering mast:
The atmosphere grew thick and hot,
  And of a lurid hue; —
As riveted unto the spot,
  Stood officers and crew.

The father came on deck: he gasp'd,
  "O, God! thy will be done!"
Then suddenly a rifle grasp'd,
  And aim'd it at his son.
"Jump, far out, boy, into the wave!
  Jump, or I fire," he said,
"That only chance your life can save;
  Jump, jump!" The boy obey'd.

He sunk, — he rose, — he lived, — he moved, —
And for the ship struck out:
On board we hail'd the lad beloved,
With many a manly shout.
His father drew, in silent joy,
Those wet arms round his neck,
And folded to his heart his boy,
Then fainted on the deck.

LITTLE ROCKET'S CHRISTMAS.

VANDYKE BROWN.

I'LL tell you how the Christmas came
To Rocket; — no, you never met him,
That is, you never knew his name,
Although 'tis possible you've let him
Display his skill upon your shoes;
A bootblack, — Arab, if you choose.
Has inspiration dropp'd to zero
When such material makes a hero?

And who was Rocket? Well, an urchin,
A gamin, dirty, torn, and tatter'd,
Whose chiefest pleasure was to perch in
The Bowery gallery; there it matter'd
But little what the play might be, —
Broad farce or point-lace comedy, —
He meted out his just applause
By rigid, fix'd, and proper laws.

A father once he had, no doubt,
A mother on the Island staying,
Which left him free to knock about,
And gratify a taste for straying
Through crowded streets. 'Twas there he found
Companionship and grew renown'd.

An ash-box served him for a bed, —
  As good, at least, as Moses' rushes;
And, for his daily meat and bread,
  He earn'd them with his box and brushes.

An Arab of the city's slums,
  With ready tongue and empty pocket,
Unaided left to solve life's sums,
  But plucky always, — that was Rocket!

'Twas Christmas-eve, and all the day
  The snow had fallen fine and fast;
In banks and drifted heaps it lay
  Along the streets. A piercing blast
Blew cuttingly. The storm was past,
And now the stars look'd coldly down
Upon the snow-enshrouded town.
Ah, well it is if Christmas brings
Good-will and peace which poet sings!
How full are all the streets to-night
With happy faces, flush'd and bright!
The matron in her silks and furs,
  The pompous banker, fat and sleek,
The idle, well-fed loiterers,
  The merchant trim, the churchman meek,
Forgetful now of hate and spite,
For all the world is glad to-night!
All, did I say? Ah, no, not all,
For sorrow throws on some its pall;
And here, within the broad, fair city,
  The Christmas-time no beauty brings
To those who plead in vain for pity,
  To those who cherish but the stings
Of wretchedness and want and woe,
Who never love's great bounty know;
Whose grief no kindly hands assuage,
Whose misery mocks our Christian age.

Pray ask yourself what means to them
That Christ is born in Bethlehem!

But Rocket? On this Christmas-eve
  You might have seen him standing where
The city's streets so interweave
  They form that somewhat famous square
Called Printing-House. His face was bright,
  And at this gala, festive season
You could not find a heart more light, —
  I'll tell you in a word the reason:
By dint of patient toil in shining
  Patrician shoes and Wall-street boots,
He had within his jacket's lining
  A dollar and a half, — the fruits
Of pinching, saving, and a trial
Of really Spartan self-denial.

That dollar and a half was more
Than Rocket ever own'd before:
A princely fortune, so he thought,
  And with those hoarded dimes and nickels
What Christmas pleasures may be bought!
  A dollar and a half! It tickles
The boy to say it over, musing
Upon the money's proper using:
"I'll go a gobbler, leg and breast,
  With cranberry-sauce and fixin's nice,
And pie, mince pie, the very best,
  And puddin', — say a double slice!
And then to doughnuts how I'll freeze;
With coffee, — guess that ere's the cheese!
And after grub I'll go to see
The 'Seven Goblins of Dundee.'
If this yere Christmas ain't a buster,
I'll let yer rip my Sunday duster!"

So Rocket mused as he hurried along,
  Clutching his money with grasp yet tighter,
And humming the air of a rollicking song,
  With a heart as light as his clothes, — or lighter.
Through Centre-street he makes his way,
  When, just as he turns the corner at Pearl,
He hears a voice cry out in dismay,
  And sees before him a slender girl,
As ragged and tatter'd in dress as he,
  With hand stretch'd forth for charity.

In the street-light's fitful and flickering glare
  He caught a glimpse of the pale, pinch'd face,
So gaunt and wasted, yet strangely fair,
  With a lingering touch of childhood's grace
On her delicate features. Her head was bare,
  And over her shoulders disorder'd there hung
A mass of tangled, nut-brown hair.
  In misery old as in years she was young,
She gazed in his face; and, O! for the eyes, —
The big, blue, sorrowful, hungry eyes, —
  That were fix'd in a desperate frighten'd stare.

Hundreds have jostled her by to-night, —
  The rich, the great, the good, and the wise;
Hurrying on to the warmth and light
Of happy homes, they have jostled her by;
And the only one who has heard her cry,
Or, hearing, has felt his heartstrings stirr'd,
  Is Rocket, — this youngster of coarser clay,
This gamin, who never so much as heard
  The beautiful story of Him who lay
  In the manger of old on Christmas-day!

With artless pathos and simple speech,
  She stands and tells him her pitiful tale:
Ah, well if those who pray and preach
  Could catch an echo of that sad wail!

She tells of the terrible battle for bread,
  Tells of a father brutal with crime,
Tells of a mother lying dead,
  At this the gala Christmas-time;
Then adds, gazing up at the starlit sky,
"I'm hungry and cold, and I wish I could die."

What is it trickles down the cheek
  Of Rocket? can it be a tear?
He stands and stares, but does not speak;
  He thinks again of that good cheer
Which Christmas was to bring; he sees
  Visions of turkey, steaming pies,
The play-bills; then, in place of these,
  The girl's beseeching, hungry eyes:
One mighty effort, gulping down
  The disappointment in his breast,
A quivering of the lip, a frown,
  And then, while pity pleads her best,
He snatches forth his cherish'd hoard,
And gives it to her like a lord!

"Here, freeze to that; I'm flush, yer see;
And then you needs it more 'an me!"
With that he turns and walks away
So fast the girl can nothing say,
So fast he does not hear the prayer
That sanctifies the Winter air:
But He who bless'd the widow's mite
Look'd down and smiled upon the sight.

No feast of steaming pies or turkey,
  No ticket for the matinee;
All drear and desolate and murky,
  In truth, a very dismal day.
With dinner on a crust of bread,
  And not a penny in his pocket,

A friendly ash-box for a bed, —
  Thus came the Christmas-day to Rocket;
And yet, — and here's the strangest thing, —
  As best befits the festive season,
The boy was happy as a king, —
  I wonder can you guess the reason?

PAPA'S LETTER.

I WAS sitting in my study,
  Writing letters, when I heard,
"Please, dear mamma, Mary told me
  Mamma mustn't be 'isturb'd.

But I'se tirèd of the kitty,
  Want some ozzer fing to do.
Witing letters, is 'ou, mamma?
  Tan't I wite a letter too?"

"Not now, darling, mamma's busy;
  Run and play with kitty, now."
"No, no, mamma; me wite letter;
  Tan if 'ou will show me how."

I would paint my darling's portrait
  As his sweet eyes search'd my face, —
Hair of gold and eyes of azure,
  Form of childish, witching grace.

But the eager face was clouded,
  As I slowly shook my head,
Till I said, "I'll make a letter
  Of you, darling boy, instead."

So I parted back the tresses
  From his forehead high and white,
And a stamp in sport I pasted
  'Mid its waves of golden light.

Then I said, " Now, little letter,
  Go away and bear good news."
And I smiled as down the staircase
  Clatter'd loud the little shoes.

Leaving me, the darling hurried
  Down to Mary in his glee,
" Mamma's witing lots of letters;
  "I'se a letter, Mary, — see!"

No one heard the little prattle,
  As once more he climb'd the stair,
Reach'd his little cap and tippet,
  Standing on the entry chair.

No one heard the front door open,
  No one saw the golden hair,
As it floated o'er his shoulders
  In the crisp October air.

Down the street the baby hasten'd
  Till he reach'd the office door:
" I'se a letter, Mr. Postman;
  Is there room for any more?

'Cause dis letter's doin' to papa,
  Papa lives with God, 'ou know;
Mamma sent me for a letter;
  Does 'ou fink 'at I tan go?"

But the clerk in wonder answer'd,
  " Not to-day, my little man."
" Den I'll find anozzer office,
  'Cause I must do if I tan."

Fain the clerk would have detain'd him,
  But the pleading face was gone,
And the little feet were hastening, —
  By the busy crowd swept on.

Suddenly the crowd was parted,
People fled to left and right,
As a pair of madden'd horses
At the moment dash'd in sight.

No one saw the baby-figure,
No one saw the golden hair,
Till a voice of frighten'd sweetness
Rang out on the autumn air.

Twas too late, — a moment only
Stood the beauteous vision there;
Then the little face lay lifeless,
Cover'd o'er with golden hair.

Reverently they raised my darling,
Brush'd away the curls of gold,
Saw the stamp upon the forehead,
Growing now so icy cold.

Not a mark the face disfigured,
Showing where a hoof had trod;
But the little life was ended, —
"Papa's letter" was with God.

IN SCHOOL DAYS.

J. G. WHITTIER.

STILL sits the school-house by the road,
A ragged beggar sunning;
Around it still the sumachs grow,
And blackberry vines are running.

Within, the master's desk is seen,
Deep scarr'd by raps official;
The warping floor, the batter'd seats,
The jack-knife's carved initial;

The charcoal frescoes on its wall;
Its door's worn sill, betraying
The feet that, creeping slow to school,
Went storming out to playing.

Long years ago, a winter Sun
Shone over it at setting,
Lit up its western window-panes,
And low eaves' icy fretting.

It touch'd the tangled golden curls,
And brown eyes, full of grieving,
Of one who still her steps delay'd
When all the school were leaving.

For near her stood the little boy
Her childish favour singled,
His cap pull'd low upon a face
Where pride and shame were mingled.

Pushing with restless feet the snow
To right and left, he linger'd;
As restlessly her tiny hands
The blue-check'd apron finger'd.

He saw her lift her eyes; he felt
The soft hands' light caressing,
And heard the tremble of her voice,
As if a fault confessing, —

"I'm sorry that I spelt the word:
I hate to go above you,
Because," — the brown eyes lower fell, —
"Because, you see, I love you!"

Still memory to a gray-hair'd man
That sweet child-face is showing,
Dear girl! the grasses on her grave
Have forty years been growing.

He lives to learn in life's hard school,
How few who pass above him
Lament their triumph and his loss,
Like her, — because they love him.

SOMEBODY'S MOTHER.

The woman was old and ragged and gray,
And bent with the chill of the Winter's day;
The street was wet with a recent snow,
And the woman's feet were agèd and slow.

She stood at the crossing, and waited long,
Alone, uncared-for, amid the throng
Of human beings who pass'd her by,
Nor heeded the glance of her anxious eye.

Down the street, with laughter and shout,
Glad in the freedom of "school let out,"
Came the boys like a flock of sheep,
Hailing the snow piled white and deep.

Past the woman so old and gray
Hasten'd the children on their way,
Nor offer'd a helping hand to her, —
So meek, so timid, afraid to stir,

Lest the carriage-wheels or the horses' feet
Should crowd her down in the slippery street,
At last came one of the merry troop, —
The gayest laddie of all the group;

He paused beside her, and whisper'd low,
"I'll help you across if you wish to go."
Her agèd hand on his strong young arm
She placed, and so, without hurt or harm,

He guided the trembling feet along,
Proud that his own were firm and strong:
Then back again to his friends he went,
His young heart happy and well content.

" She's somebody's mother, boys, you know,
For all she's agèd and poor and slow;
And I hope some fellow will lend a hand
To help *my* mother, you understand,

If ever she's poor and old and gray,
When her own dear boy is far away."
And "somebody's mother" bow'd low her head
In her home that night, and the prayer she said
Was, " God, be kind to the noble boy,
Who is somebody's son and pride and joy!"

TO WHOM SHALL WE GIVE THANKS?

A LITTLE boy had sought the pump
From whence the sparkling water burst,
And drank with eager joy the draught
That kindly quench'd his raging thirst:
Then gracefully he touch'd his cap, —
"I thank you, Mr. Pump," he said,
" For this nice drink you've given me!"
(This little boy had been well bred.)

Then said the Pump, " My little man,
You're welcome to what I have done;
But I am not the one to thank, —
I only help the water run."
" O, then," the little fellow said,
(Polite he always meant to be,)
" Cold Water, please accept my thanks;
You have been very kind to me."

"Ah!" said Cold Water, "don't thank me;
  Far up the hill-side lives the Spring
That sends me forth with generous hand
  To gladden every living thing."
"I'll thank the Spring, then," said the boy,
  And gracefully he bow'd his head.
"O, don't thank me, my little man,"
  The Spring with silvery accents said,—

"O, don't thank me; for what am I
  Without the dew and summer rain?
Without their aid I ne'er could quench
  Your thirst, my little boy, again."
"O, well, then," said the little boy,
  "I'll gladly thank the Rain and Dew."
"Pray, don't thank us; without the Sun
  We could not fill one cup for you."

"Then, Mr. Sun, ten thousand thanks
  For all that you have done for me."
"Stop!" said the Sun, with blushing face;
  "My little fellow, don't thank me:
'Twas from the ocean's mighty stores
  I drew the draught I gave to thee."
"O, Ocean, thanks, then!" said the boy;
  It echo'd back, "Not unto me,—

Not unto me; but unto Him
  Who form'd the depths in which I lie;
Go, give thy thanks, my little boy,
  To Him who will thy wants supply."
The boy took off his cap, and said,
  In tones so gentle and subdued,
"O God, I thank Thee for this gift;
  Thou art the Giver of all good."

YOU PUT NO FLOWERS ON MY PAPA'S GRAVE.

C. E. L. Holmes.

With sable-draped banners, and slow measured tread,
The flower-laden ranks pass the gates of the dead;
And, seeking each mound where a comrade's form rests,
Leave tear-bedew'd garlands to bloom on his breast.
Ended at last is the labour of love:
Once more through the gateway the sadden'd lines move;
A wailing of anguish, a sobbing of grief,
Falls low on the ear of the battle-scarr'd chief:
Close crouch'd by the portals, a sunny-hair'd child
Besought him in accents which grief render'd wild:

"O sir! he was good, and they say he died brave;
Why, why did you pass by my dear papa's grave?
I know he was poor, but as kind and as true
As ever march'd into the battle with you;
His grave is so humble, no stone marks the spot,
You may not have seen it; O, say you did not!
For my poor heart will break if you knew he was there,
And thought him too lowly your offerings to share.
He didn't die lowly, — he pour'd his heart's blood,
In rich crimson streams, from the top-crowning sod
Of the breastworks which stood in front of the fight, —
And died shouting, 'Onward! for God and the right!'
O'er all his dead comrades your bright garlands wave,
But you haven't put *one* on *my* papa's grave.
If mamma were here, — but she lies by his side;
Her wearied heart broke when our dear papa died."

"Battalion! file left! countermarch!" cried the chief,
"This young orphan'd maid hath full cause for her grief."
Then up in his arms from the hot, dusty street,
He lifted the maiden, while in through the gate
The long line repasses, and many an eye
Pays fresh tribute of tears to the lone orphan's sigh.

"This way it is, — here, sir, — right under this tree;
They lie close together, with just room for me."

"Halt! Cover with roses each lowly green mound;
A love pure as this makes these graves hallow'd ground."

"O! thank you, kind sir! I ne'er can repay
The kindness you've shown little Daisy to-day;
But I'll pray for you here, each day while I live,
'Tis all that a poor soldier's orphan can give.
I shall see papa soon, and dear mamma too, —
I dream'd so last night, and I know 'twill come true;
And they both will bless you, I know, when I say
How you folded your arms round their dear one to-day;
How you cheer'd her sad heart, and soothed it to rest,
And hush'd its wild throbs on your strong noble breast;
And, when the kind angels shall call *you* to come,
We'll welcome you then to our beautiful home,
Where death never comes, his black banners to wave,
And the beautiful flowers ne'er weep o'er a grave."

THE BUTTERFLY'S BALL.

THOMAS ROSCOE.

COME, take up your hats, and away let us haste
To the butterfly's ball and the grasshopper's feast;
The trumpeter gadfly has summon'd the crew,
And the revels are now only waiting for you.

On the smooth-shaven grass by the side of the wood,
Beneath a broad oak that for ages has stood,
See the children of earth and the tenants of air
For an evening's amusement together repair.

And there came the beetle, so blind and so black,
Who carried the emmet, his friend, on his back;
And there was the gnat, and the dragonfly too,
With all their relations, green, orange, and blue.

And there came the moth, in his plumage of down,
And the hornet, with jacket of yellow and brown,

Who with him the wasp, his companion, did bring;
But they promised that evening to lay by their sting.

And the sly little dormouse crept out of his hole,
And led to the feast his blind brother the mole;
And the snail, with his horns peeping out from his shell,
Came from a great distance, — the length of an ell.

A mushroom their table, and on it was laid
A water-dock leaf, which a tablecloth made;
The viands were various, to each of their taste,
And the bee brought his honey to crown the repast.

There, close on his haunches, so solemn and wise,
The frog from a corner look'd up to the skies;
And the squirrel, well pleased such diversion to see,
Sat cracking his nuts overhead in the tree.

Then out came the spider, with fingers so fine,
To show his dexterity on the tight line;
From one branch to another his cobwebs he slung,
Then as quick as an arrow he darted along.

But just in the middle, O, shocking to tell!
From his rope in an instant poor Harlequin fell;
Yet he touch'd not the ground, but with talons outspread,
Hung suspended in air at the end of a thread.

Then the grasshopper came with a jerk and a spring,
Very long was his leg, though but short was his wing;
He took but three leaps, and was soon out of sight,
Then chirp'd his own praises the rest of the night.

With step so majestic the snail did advance,
And promised the gazers a minuet to dance;
But they all laugh'd so loud that he pull'd in his head,
And went to his own little chamber to bed.

THE SMACK IN SCHOOL.

W. P. PALMER.

A DISTRICT school, not far away,
'Mid Berkshire hills, one Winter's day,
Was humming with its wonted noise
Of three-score mingled girls and boys;
Some few upon their tasks intent,
But more on furtive mischief bent.
The while the master's downward look
Was fasten'd on a copy-book;
When suddenly, behind his back,
Rose sharp and clear a rousing smack,
As 'twere a battery of bliss
Let off in one tremendous kiss!
"What's that?" the startled master cries:
"That, thir," a little imp replies,
"Wath William Willeth, if you pleathe;
I thaw him kith Thuthanna Peathe!"
With frown to make a statue thrill,
The master thunder'd, "Hither, Will!"
Like wretch o'ertaken in his track
With stolen chattels on his back,
Will hung his head in fear and shame,
And to the awful presence came, —
A great, green, bashful simpleton,
The butt of all good-natured fun.
With smile suppress'd, and birch upraised,
The threatener falter'd: "I'm amazed
That you, my biggest pupil, should
Be guilty of an act so rude!
Before the whole set school to boot;
What evil genius put you to't?"
"'Twas she, herself, sir," sobb'd the lad;
"I did not mean to be so bad:
But, when Susannah shook her curls,
And whisper'd, I was 'fraid of girls,

And dursn't kiss a baby's doll,
I couldn't stand it, sir, at all,
But up and kiss'd her on the spot!
I know — boo-hoo — I ought to not,
But, somehow, from her looks — boo-hoo —
I thought she kind o' wish'd me to!"

MARGARET GRAY.

Charles Lamb.

It was noontide. The sun was very hot. An old gentlewoman sat spinning in a little arbour at the door of her cottage. She was blind; and her grand-daughter was reading the Bible to her. The old lady had just left her work, to attend to the story of Ruth.

"Orpah kissed her mother-in-law; but Ruth clave unto her." It was a passage she could not let pass without a *comment*. The moral she drew from it was not very new, to be sure. The girl had heard it a hundred times before; and a hundred times more she could have heard it, without suspecting it to be tedious. Rosamund loved her grandmother.

The old lady loved Rosamund too; and she had reason for so doing. Rosamund was to her at once a child and a servant. She had only *her* left in the world. They two lived together.

They had once known better days. The story of Rosamund's parents, their failure, their folly and distresses, may be told another time. Our tale hath grief enough in it.

It was now about a year and a half since old Margaret Gray had sold off all her effects, to pay the debts of Rosamund's father, — just after the mother had died of a broken heart; for her husband had fled his country, to hide his shame in a foreign land. At that period the old lady retired to a small cottage in the village of Widford in Hertfordshire.

Rosamund, in her thirteenth year, was left destitute,

without fortune or friends: she went with her grandmother. In all this time she had served her faithfully and lovingly.

Old Margaret Gray, when she first came into these parts, had eyes, and could see. The neighbours said they had been dimmed by weeping: be that as it may, she was latterly grown quite blind. "God is very good to us, child; I can *feel* you yet." This she would sometimes say; and we need not wonder to hear that Rosamund clave unto her grandmother.

Margaret retained a spirit unbroken by calamity. There was a principle *within*, which it seemed as if no outward circumstance could reach. It was religious principle; and she had taught it to Rosamund; for the girl had mostly resided with her grandmother from her earliest years. Indeed she had taught her all that she knew herself; and the old lady's knowledge did not extend a vast way.

Their library consisted chiefly in a large family Bible, with notes and expositions by various learned expositors, from Bishop Jewell downwards.

This might never be suffered to lie about like other books, but was kept constantly wrapt in a handsome case of green velvet, with gold tassels, — the only relic of departed grandeur they had brought with them to the cottage; every thing else of value had been sold off for the purpose above mentioned.

This Bible Rosamund, when a child, had never dared to open without permission; and even yet, from habit, continued the custom. Margaret had parted with none of her authority; indeed it was never exerted with much harshness; and happy was Rosamund, though a girl grown, when she could obtain leave to read her Bible. It was a treasure too valuable for indiscriminate use; and Margaret still pointed out to her grand-daughter where to read.

Rosamund's mind was pensive and reflective, rather than what passes usually for clever or acute. From a child she was remarkably shy and thoughtful: this was taken for stupidity and want of feeling; and the child has been sometimes whipt for being a *stubborn thing*, when her little heart was almost bursting with affection.

Even now her grandmother would often reprove her, when she found her too grave and melancholy; give her sprightly lectures about good-humour and rational mirth; and not unfrequently fall a-crying herself, to the great discredit of her lecture. Those tears endeared her the more to Rosamund.

Margaret would say, "Child, I love you to cry, when I think you are only remembering your poor dear father and mother: I would have you think about them sometimes, — it would be strange if you did not; but I fear, Rosamund, — I fear, girl, you sometimes think too deeply about your own situation and poor prospects in life. When you do so, you do wrong: remember the naughty rich man in the parable. He never had any good thoughts about God and His religion; and that might have been your case."

Rosamund, at these times, could not reply to her: she was not in the habit of arguing with her grandmother: so she was quite silent on these occasions; or else the girl knew well enough herself that she had only been sad to think of the desolate condition of her best friend, to see her, in her old age, so infirm and blind. But she had never been used to make excuses when the old lady said she was doing wrong.

The neighbours were all very kind to them. The veriest rustics never passed them without a bow, or a pulling-off of the hat, some show of courtesy, awkward indeed, but affectionate, — with a "Good-morrow, madam," or "young madam," as it might happen.

Rude and savage natures, who seem born with a propensity to express contempt for any thing that looks like prosperity, yet felt respect for its declining lustre.

The farmers, and better sort of people, (as they are called,) all promised to provide for Rosamund when her grandmother should die. Margaret trusted in God, and believed them.

She used to say, "I have lived many years in the world, and have never known people, *good people*, to be left without some friend; a relation, a benefactor, or *something*. God knows our wants; that it is not good for man or woman to be alone: and He always sends us a helpmate, a leaning-place, a *somewhat*." Upon this sure ground of experience did Margaret build her trust in Providence.

BETTER IN THE MORNING.

LEANDER S. COAN.

"You can't help the baby, parson,
  But still I want ye to go
Down and look in upon her,
  An' read an' pray, you know.
Only last week she was skipping around
  A-pullin' my whiskers 'n' hair,
A-climbin' up to the table
  Into her little high chair.

The first night that she took it,
  When her little cheeks grew red,
When she kiss'd good night to papa,
  And went away to bed,—
Sez she, ''Tis headache, papa,
  Be better in mornin',—bye';
An' somethin' in how she said it
  Jest made me want to cry.

But the mornin' brought the fever,
  And her little hands were hot,
An' the pretty red uv her little cheeks
  Grew into a crimson spot.
But she laid there jest ez patient
  Ez ever a woman could,
Taking whatever we give her
  Better'n a grown woman would.

The days are terrible long an' slow,
An' she's growin' wus in each;
An' now she's jest a slippin'
Clear away out uv our reach.
Every night when I kiss her,
Tryin' hard not to cry,
She says in a way that kills me,
'Be better in mornin', — bye!'

She can't get through the night, parson;
So I want ye to come an' pray,
And talk with mother a little, —
You'll know jest what to say:
Not that the baby needs it,
Nor that we make any complaint
That God seems to think He's needin'
The smile uv the little saint."

I walk'd along with the corporal
To the door of his humble home,
To which the silent messenger
Before me had also come;
And, if he had been a titled prince,
I would not have been honour'd more
Than I was with his heartfelt welcome
To his lowly cottage door.

Night falls again in the cottage;
They move in silence and dread
Around the room where the baby
Lies panting upon her bed.
"Does baby know papa, darling?"
And she moved her little face
With answer that shows she knows him;
But scarce a visible trace

Of her wonderful infantile beauty
Remains as it was before:
The unseen silent messenger
Had waited at the door.
"Papa — kiss — baby; — I's — so — tired."
The man bows low his face,
And two swollen hands are lifted
In baby's last embrace.

And into her father's grizzled beard
  The little red fingers cling,
While her husky whisper'd tenderness
  Tears from a rock would wring,
"Baby — is — so — sick — papa, —
  But — don't — want — you — to — cry :"
The little hands fall on the coverlet, —
  "Be-better — in — mornin', — bye!"

And night around baby is falling,
  Settling down dark and dense;
Does God need their darling in Heaven
  That He must carry her hence?
I pray'd, with tears in my voice,
  As the corporal solemnly knelt
With such grief as never before
  His great warm heart had felt.

O frivolous men and women!
  Do you know that around you, and nigh,
Alike from the humble and haughty
  Goeth up ever more the cry:
"My child, my precious, my darling,
  How can I let you die?"
O! hear ye the white lips whisper,
  "Be-better — in — mornin' — bye!"

TAME HARES.

WILLIAM COWPER.

THE children of a neighbour of mine had a leveret given them for a plaything; it was at that time about three months old. Soon becoming weary of their charge, they readily consented that their father should offer it to my acceptance.

I was willing enough to take the prisoner under my protection, perceiving that in the management of such an animal and in the attempt to tame it, I should find just that sort of employment which my case required. It was soon known among the neighbours that I was pleased with the present; and the consequence was that in a short time I had as many leverets offered to me as would have stocked a paddock. I undertook the care of three, called Puss, Tiney, and Bess. Immediately commencing to carpenter, I built them houses to sleep in, so contrived that they were kept perfectly sweet and clean. In the day-time they had the range of a hall, and at night retired each to his own bed, never intruding into that of another.

Puss grew presently familiar, would leap into my lap, raise himself upon his hinder feet, and bite the hair from my temples. He would suffer me to take him up, and to carry him about in my arms, and has more than once fallen fast asleep upon my knee. He was ill three days, during which time I nursed him, kept him apart from his fellows, that they might not molest him, (for, like many other wild animals, they persecute one of their own species that is sick,) and by constant care, and trying him with a variety of herbs, restored him to perfect health.

No creature could be more grateful than my patient after his recovery, a sentiment which he expressed by licking my hand, first the back of it, then the palm, then every finger separately, then between all the fingers; a ceremony which he never performed but once again upon a similar occasion. Finding him extremely tractable, I made it my custom to carry him always after breakfast into the garden, where he hid himself generally under the leaves of a cucumber-vine, sleeping or chewing the cud till evening; in the leaves also of that vine he found a favourite repast. I had not long habituated him to this state of liberty before he began to be impatient for the return of the time when he might enjoy it. He would invite me to the garden by drumming upon my knee, and by a look of such expression as it was not possible to misinterpret. If this rhetoric did not immediately succeed, he would take the skirt of my coat between his teeth and pull it with all his force. Thus Puss might be said to be perfectly tamed, the shyness of his nature was done away, and on the whole it was visible, by many symptoms which I have not room to enumerate, that he was happier in human society than when shut up with his natural companions.

Not so Tiney; upon him the kindest treatment had not the least effect. He, too, was sick, and in his sickness had an equal share of my attention; but if, after his recovery, I took the liberty to stroke him, he would grunt, strike with his fore-feet, spring forward, and bite. He was, however, very entertaining in his way; even his surliness was matter of mirth; and in his play he preserved such an air of gravity, and performed his feats with such a solemnity of manner, that in him, too, I had an agreeable companion.

Bess, who died soon after he was full grown, and whose death was occasioned by his being turned into his box, which had been washed, while it was yet damp, was a hare of great humour and drollery. Puss was tamed by gentle usage; Tiney was not to be tamed at all; and Bess had a courage and confidence that made him tame from the beginning. I always admitted them into the parlour after supper, when, the carpet affording their feet a firm hold, they would frisk, and bound, and play a thousand gambols, in which Bess, being remarkably strong and fearless, was always superior to the rest. One evening the cat, being in the room, had the hardiness to pat Bess upon the cheek, an indignity which he resented by drumming upon her back with such violence, that the cat was happy to escape from under his paws and hide herself.

I describe these animals as having each a character of his own. Such they were, in fact, and their countenances were so expressive of that character, that when I looked only on the face of either, I immediately knew which it was. It is said that a shepherd, however numerous his flock, soon becomes so familiar with their features, that he can distinguish each from all the rest, and yet, to a common observer, the difference is hardly perceptible. I doubt not that the same discrimination in the cast of countenances would be discoverable in hares, and am persuaded that among a thousand of them no two could be found exactly similar. These creatures have a singular sagacity in discovering the minutest alteration that is made in the place to which they are accustomed, and instantly apply their nose to the examination of a new object. A small hole being burnt in the carpet, it was mended with a patch, and that patch in a moment underwent the strictest scrutiny.

They seem too to be very much directed by the smell in the choice of their favourites; to some persons, though they saw them daily, they could never be reconciled, and would even scream when they attempted to touch them; but a miller coming in engaged their affections at once; his powdered coat had claims that were irresistible. It is no wonder that my intimate acquaintance with these specimens of the kind has taught me to hold the sportsman's amusement in abhorrence: he little knows what amiable creatures he persecutes, of what gratitude they are capable, how cheerful they are in their spirits, what enjoyment they have of life; and that, impressed as they seem with a peculiar dread of man, it is only because man gives them peculiar cause for it.

Bess, I have said, died young; Tiney lived to be nine years old, and died at last, I have reason to think, of some hurt in his loins by a fall; Puss is still living, and has just completed his tenth year, discovering no signs of decay, nor even of age, except that he has grown more discreet and less frolicsome than he was. I cannot conclude without observing that I have lately introduced a dog to his acquaintance, a spaniel that had never seen a hare, to a hare that had never seen spaniel. I did it with great caution, but there was no real need of it; Puss discovered no token of fear, nor Marquis the least symptom of hostility. There is, therefore, it should seem, no natural antipathy between dog and hare, but the pursuit of the one occasions the flight of the other, and the dog pursues because he is trained to it; they eat bread at the same time out of the same hand, and are in all respects sociable and friendly.

RATS.

JANE LOUDON.

A WHITE rat having been caught in some stables, and being from its colour thought a great curiosity, it was brought to a gentleman who was known to take great interest in animals. At first it was very savage, and tried to bite when left loose. It was therefore put into a turning squirrel-cage, and for two or three days kept short of food and allowed none that it would not take out of its owner's hand. At first it snapped and tried to bite through the wires, but soon learned to know his voice, and came out on hearing it; but usually it lay hid in the box at the end of the cage, and when its master took it out, it several times bit him severely. Finding at last that he always treated it kindly, it grew tame, and would let him open the box and look in, without stirring. He could soon let it out in his sitting-room, and it would come close to his feet to pick up the crumbs which he dropped for it, and in a fortnight came when called, and ate sugar from his hand.

When the rat was first brought, his little white terrier, Flora, was very anxious to get at it and kill it; but their master, holding the rat, called Flora, and showed it to her. She seemed at once to understand what he meant, and, far from harming it, thenceforward, if any stranger came in while it was loose, she stood by it, growling and showing her teeth, and the rat never failed to run up to her for protection at such times. There was a walled garden behind the house, where both rat and dog were often turned out to play together, which they did by a kind of hide-and-seek among the flowers; but if their master whistled, there was at once a race to be the first to get to him.

Scugg, as he called the rat, became so bold that he would get on the table and carry off food to share with Flora, but, if she tried to get the first bite, Scugg kept her in order by striking her on the nose with his paw. Flora took this very meekly, lapped milk out of the same saucer as Scugg, and slept on the rug with him between her paws.

Many people thought that its strange colour was the reason that the dog did not destroy it, but this was proved not to be the case. Another white rat being caught, it was set free in the room where Scugg and Flora were at play. Both the rats ran round the room with Flora after them, and in a moment one was killed by the terrier, to the great dismay of her master, who could not tell one rat from the other, so much were they alike, and thought that perhaps his pet had perished. Great was his joy to see Scugg run into a corner, and Flora follow to guard him, and she stood growling till the dead rat was taken away. The end of the poor rat was a sad one. His master gave him away, and he pined and moped, and at last was found dead in his box.

LOVE AND PRAYER.

COLERIDGE.

O, SWEETER than the marriage-feast,
'Tis sweeter far to me,
To walk together to the kirk,
And all together pray,
While each to his great Father bends,
Old men, and babes, and loving friends,
And youths and maidens gay!

Farewell, farewell! but this I tell
To thee, thou Wedding-Guest, —
He prayeth well, who loveth well
Both man and bird and beast:

He prayeth best, who loveth best
All things both great and small;
For the dear God who loveth us,
He made and loveth all.

XIII.

DRAMATIC, NOT IN THE DRAMA.

THE BEAUTIFUL SNOW.

JAMES W. WATSON.

O THE snow, the beautiful snow!
Filling the sky and earth below!
Over the house-tops, over the street,
Over the heads of the people you meet,
    Dancing, flirting, skimming along:
Beautiful snow! it can do no wrong;
Flying to kiss a fair lady's cheek,
Clinging to lips in a frolicsome freak,
Beautiful snow from the heaven above,
Pure as an angel, but fickle as love!

O the snow, the beautiful snow!
How the flakes gather and laugh as they go!
Whirling about in their maddening fun
They play in their glee with every one.
    Chasing, laughing, hurrying by,
It lights on the face and it sparkles the eye;
And even the dogs, with a bark and a bound,
Snap at the crystals that eddy around;
The town is alive and its heart in a glow,
To welcome the coming of beautiful snow!

How the wild crowd goes swaying along,
Hailing each other with humour and song!
How the gay sledges, like meteors, flash by,

Bright for a moment, then lost to the eye:
    Ringing, swinging, dashing they go,
Over the crust of the beautiful snow!
Snow so pure when it falls from the sky,
To be trampled in mud by the crowd rushing by;
To be trampled and track'd by the thousands of feet,
Till it blends with the filth in the horrible street.

Once I was pure as the snow, — but I fell!
Fell, like the snow-flakes, from Heaven to Hell;
Fell to be trampled as filth in the street;
Fell to be scoff'd, to be spit on and beat;
    Pleading, cursing, dreading to die,
Selling my soul to whoever would buy;
Dealing in shame for a morsel of bread,
Hating the living and fearing the dead:
Merciful God! have I fallen so low?
And yet I was once like the beautiful snow.

Once I was fair as the beautiful snow,
With an eye like its crystal, a heart like its glow;
Once I was loved for my innocent grace,
Flatter'd and sought for the charms of my face!
    Father, mother, sisters, all,
God and myself, I have lost by my fall;
And the veriest wretch that goes shivering by
Will make a wide swoop lest I wander too nigh;
For all that is on or about me I know
There is nothing that's pure but the beautiful snow.

How strange it should be that this beautiful snow
Should fall on a sinner with nowhere to go!
How strange it should be, when the night comes again,
If the snow and the ice strike my desperate brain;
    Fainting, freezing, dying alone,
Too wicked for prayer, too weak for my moan
To be heard in the crash of the crazy town,

Gone mad in the joy of the snow coming down,
To lie and to die in my terrible woe,
With a bed and a shroud of the beautiful snow!

BERNARDO DEL CARPIO.

MRS. HEMANS.

THE warrior bow'd his crested head, and tamed his heart of fire,
And sued the haughty king to free his long-imprison'd sire:
"I bring thee here my fortress-keys, I bring my captive train,
I pledge thee faith, my liege, my lord! — O, break my father's chain!"

"Rise, rise! even now thy father comes, a ransom'd man this day!
Mount thy good horse; and thou and I will meet him on his way."
Then lightly rose that loyal son, and bounded on his steed,
And urged, as if with lance in rest, the charger's foamy speed.

And, lo! from far, as on they press'd, there came a glittering band,
With one that 'midst them stately rode, as leader in the land:
"Now haste, Bernado, haste! for there, in very truth, is he,
The father whom thy faithful heart hath yearn'd so long to see."

His dark eye flash'd, his proud breast heaved, his cheek's hue came and went;
He reach'd that gray-hair'd chieftain's side, and there, dismounting, bent;
A lowly knee to earth he bent, his father's hand he took, —
What was there in its touch that all his fiery spirit shook?

That hand was cold, — a frozen thing; it dropp'd from his like lead!
He look'd up to the face above, — the face was of the dead!
A plume waved o'er the noble brow, — the brow was fix'd and white:
He met, at last, his father's eyes, — but in them was no light!

Up from the ground he sprang and gazed, — but who could paint that gaze?
They hush'd their very hearts that saw its horror and amaze;
They might have chain'd him, as before that stony form he stood;
For the power was stricken from his arm, and from his lip the blood.

"FATHER!" at length he murmur'd low, and wept like childhood then:
Talk not of grief till thou hast seen the tears of warlike men!
He thought on all his hopes, and all his young renown, —
He flung his falchion from his side, and in the dust knelt down.

Then, covering with his steel-gloved hands his darkly mournful brow,
"No more, there is no more," he said, "to lift the sword for, now;
My king is false, — my hope betray'd! My father, — O! the worth,
The glory and the loveliness are pass'd away from Earth!

I thought to stand where banners waved, my sire, beside thee, yet!
I would that there our kindred blood on Spain's free soil had met!
Thou wouldst have known my spirit, then: for thee my fields were won;
And thou hast perish'd in thy chains, as though thou hadst no son!"

Then, starting from the ground once more, he seized the monarch's rein,
Amidst the pale and wilder'd looks of all the courtier-train;
And, with a fierce, o'ermastering grasp, the rearing warhorse led,
And sternly set them face to face, — the king before the dead:

"Came I not forth, upon thy pledge, my father's hand to kiss? —
Be still, and gaze thou on, false king! and tell me, what is this?
The voice, the glance, the heart I sought, — give answer, where are they?
If thou wouldst clear thy perjured soul, send life through this cold clay!

Into these glassy eyes put light; — be still! keep down thine ire! —
Bid these white lips a blessing speak, — this earth is not my sire:
Give me back him for whom I strove, for whom my blood was shed! —
Thou canst not? — and a king! — his dust be mountains on thy head!"

He loosed the steed, — his slack hand fell: upon the silent face
He cast one long, deep, troubled look, then turn'd from that sad place:
His hope was crush'd, his after fate untold in martial strain:
His banner led the spears no more amidst the hills of Spain.

COUNT CANDESPINA'S STANDARD.

GEO. H. BOKER.

The King of Aragon now entered Castile, by way of Soria and Osma, with a powerful army ; and, having been met by the Queen's forces, both parties encamped near Sepulveda, and prepared to give battle.

This engagement, called, from the field where it took place, de la Espina, is one of the most famous of that age. The dastardly count of Lara fled at the first shock, and joined the Queen at Burgos, where she was anxiously awaiting the issue; but the brave Count of Candespina stood his ground to the last, and died on the field of battle. His standard-bearer, a gentleman of the house of Olea, after having his horse killed under him, and both hands cut off by sabre-strokes, fell beside his master, still clasping the standard in his arms, and repeating his war-cry of "Olea!" — *Annals of the Queens of Spain.*

SCARCE were the splinter'd lances dropp'd,
  Scarce were the swords drawn out,
Ere recreant Lara, sick with fear,
  Had wheel'd his steed about:

His courser rear'd, and plunged, and neigh'd,
  Loathing the fight to yield;
But the coward spurr'd him to the bone,
  And drove him from the field.

Gonzalez in his stirrups rose:
  "Turn, turn, thou traitor knight!
Thou bold tongue in a lady's bower,
  Thou dastard in a fight!"

But vainly valiant Gomez cried
  Across the waning fray:
Pale Lara and his craven band
  To Burgos scour'd away.

"Now, by the God above me, sirs,
  Better we all were dead
Than a single knight among ye all
  Should ride where Lara led!

Yet ye who fear to follow me,
  As yon traitor turn and fly;
For I lead ye not to win a field;
  I lead ye forth to die.

Olea, plant my standard here, —
  Here on this little mound;
Here raise the war-cry of thy House,
  Make this our rallying-ground.

Forget not, as thou hopest for grace:
  The last care I shall have
Will be to hear thy battle-cry,
  And see that standard wave."

Down on the ranks of Aragon
  The bold Gonzalez drove,
And Olea raised his battle-cry,
  And waved the flag above.

Slowly Gonzalez' little band
  Gave ground before the foe;
But not an inch of the field was won
  Without a deadly blow;

And not an inch of the field was won
  That did not draw a tear
From the widow'd wives of Aragon,
  That fatal news to hear.

Backward and backward Gomez fought,
  And high o'er the clashing steel
Plainer and plainer rose the cry,
  "Olea for Castile!"

Backward fought Gomez, step by step,
  Till the cry was close at hand, —
Till his dauntless standard shadow'd him;
  And there he made his stand.

Mace, sword, and axe rang on his mail,
  Yet he moved not where he stood,
Though each gaping joint of armour ran
  A stream of purple blood.

As, pierced with countless wounds, he fell,
  The standard caught his eye,
And he smiled, like an infant hush'd asleep,
  To hear the battle-cry.

Now one by one the wearied knights
  Have fallen, or basely flown;
And on the mound where his post was fix'd
  Olea stood alone.

"Yield up thy banner, gallant knight!
  Thy lord lies on the plain:
Thy duty has been nobly done;
  I would not see thee slain."

"Spare pity, King of Aragon!
  I would not hear thee lie:
My lord is looking down from Heaven
  To see his standard fly."

"Yield, madman, yield! thy horse is down,
  Thou hast nor lance nor shield;
Fly! — I will grant thee time." "This flag
  Can neither fly nor yield!"

They girt the standard round about,
  A wall of flashing steel;
But still they heard the battle-cry,
  "Olea for Castile!"

And there, against all Aragon,
  Full-arm'd with lance and brand,
Olea fought until the sword
  Snapp'd in his sturdy hand.

Among the foe with that high scorn
  Which laughs at earthly fears,
He hurl'd the broken hilt, and drew
  His dagger on the spears.

They hew'd the hauberk from his breast,
  The helmet from his head;
They hew'd the hands from off his limbs;
  From every vein he bled.

Clasping the standard to his heart,
  He raised one dying peal,
That rang as if a trumpet blew, —
  "Olea for Castile!"

THE FAMINE.

H. W. LONGFELLOW.

O, THE long and dreary Winter!
O, the cold and cruel Winter!
Ever thicker, thicker, thicker
Froze the ice on lake and river;
Ever deeper, deeper, deeper
Fell the snow o'er all the landscape,
Fell the covering snow, and drifted
Through the forest, round the village.
Hardly from his buried wigwam
Could the hunter force a passage;
With his mittens and his snow-shoes
Vainly walk'd he through the forest,
Sought for bird or beast and found none,
Saw no track of deer or rabbit,
In the snow beheld no footprints,
In the ghastly, gleaming forest
Fell, and could not rise from weakness,
Perish'd there from cold and hunger.

O, the famine and the fever!
O, the wasting of the famine!
O, the blasting of the fever!
O, the wailing of the children!
O, the anguish of the women!
All the earth was sick and famish'd;
Hungry was the air around them,
Hungry was the sky above them,
And the hungry stars in heaven
Like the eyes of wolves glared at them.

Into Hiawatha's wigwam
Came two other guests, as silent
As the ghosts were, and as gloomy;
Waited not to be invited,
Did not parley at the door-way,
Sat there without word of welcome
In the seat of Laughing Water;
Look'd with haggard eyes and hollow
At the face of Laughing Water.
And the foremost said, "Behold me!
I am Famine, Bukadawin!"
And the other said, "Behold me!
I am Fever, Ahkosewin!"
And the lovely Minnehaha
Shudder'd as they look'd upon her,
Shudder'd at the words they utter'd,
Lay down on her bed in silence,
Hid her face, but made no answer;
Lay there trembling, freezing, burning
At the looks they cast upon her,
At the fearful words they utter'd.

Forth into the empty forest
Rush'd the madden'd Hiawatha;
In his heart was deadly sorrow,
In his face a stony firmness,

On his brow the sweat of anguish
Started, but it froze and fell not.
Wrapp'd in furs and arm'd for hunting
With his mighty bow of ash-tree,
With his quiver full of arrows,
With his mittens, Minjekahwun,
Into the vast and vacant forest
On his snow-shoes strode he forward.

"Gitche Manito, the mighty!"
Cried he with his face uplifted
In that bitter hour of anguish,
"Give your children food, O Father!
Give us food, or we must perish!
Give me food for Minnehaha,
For my dying Minnehaha!"
Through the far-resounding forest,
Through the forest vast and vacant
Rang that cry of desolation;
But there came no other answer
Than the echo of his crying,
Than the echo of the woodlands,
"MINNEHAHA! MINNEHAHA!"

All day long roved Hiawatha
In that melancholy forest,
Through the shadow of whose thickets,
In the pleasant days of Summer,
Of that ne'er forgotten Summer,
He had brought his young wife homeward
From the land of the Dacotahs;
When the birds sang in the thickets,
And the streamlets laugh'd and glisten'd,
And the air was full of fragrance,
And the loving Laughing Water
Said with voice that did not tremble,
"I will follow you, my husband!"

In the wigwam with Nokomis,
With those gloomy guests that watch'd her,
With the Famine and the Fever,
She was lying, the belovèd,
She, the dying Minnehaha.
"Hark!" she said, "I hear a rushing,
Hear a roaring and a rushing,
Hear the Falls of Minnehaha
Calling to me from a distance!"
"No, my child!" said old Nokomis,
"'Tis the night-wind in the pine-trees."
"Look!" she said, "I see my father
Standing lonely at his door-way,
Beckoning to me from his wigwam
In the land of the Dacotahs."
"No, my child!" said old Nokomis,
"'Tis the smoke that waves and beckons."
"Ah!" she said, "the eyes of Pauguk
Glare upon me in the darkness,
I can feel his icy fingers
Clasping mine amid the darkness!
Hiawatha! Hiawatha!"

And the desolate Hiawatha,
Far away amid the forest,
Miles away among the mountains,
Heard that sudden cry of anguish,
Heard the voice of Minnehaha
Calling to him in the darkness,
"HIAWATHA! HIAWATHA!"

Over snow-fields waste and pathless,
Under snow-encumber'd branches,
Homeward hurried Hiawatha,
Empty-handed, heavy-hearted;
Heard Nokomis moaning, wailing,
"Wahonowin! Wahonowin!

Would that I had perish'd for you,
Would that I were dead as you are,
Wahonowin! Wahonowin!"
And he rush'd into the wigwam,
Saw the old Nokomis slowly
Rocking to and fro and moaning,
Saw his lovely Minnehaha
Lying dead and cold before him;
And his bursting heart within him
Utter'd such a cry of anguish
That the forest moan'd and shudder'd,
That the very stars in heaven
Shook and trembled with his anguish.

Then he sat down, still and speechless,
On the bed of Minnehaha,
At the feet of Laughing Water,
At those willing feet, that never
More would lightly run to meet him,
Never more would lightly follow.
With both hands his face he cover'd;
Seven long days and nights he sat there,
As if in a swoon he sat there,
Speechless, motionless, unconscious
Of the daylight or the darkness.

Then they buried Minnehaha;
In the snow a grave they made her,
In the forest deep and darksome,
Underneath the moaning hemlocks;
Clothed her in her richest garments,
Wrapp'd her in her robes of ermine,
Cover'd her with snow, like ermine:
Thus they buried Minnehaha;
And at night a fire was lighted,
On her grave four times was kindled
For her soul upon its journey

To the Islands of the Blessèd.
From his door-way Hiawatha
Saw it burning in the forest,
Lighting up the gloomy hemlocks;
From his sleepless bed uprising,
From the bed of Minnehaha,
Stood and watch'd it at the door-way,
That it might not be extinguish'd,
Might not leave her in the darkness.

"Farewell!" said he, "Minnehaha;
Farewell, O my Laughing Water!
All my heart is buried with you,
All my thoughts go onward with you!
Come not back again to labour,
Come not back again to suffer,
Where the Famine and the Fever
Wear the heart and waste the body.
Soon my task will be completed,
Soon your footsteps I shall follow
To the Islands of the Blessèd,
To the Kingdom of Ponemah,
To the Land of the Hereafter!"

KATE SHELLY.

EUGENE J. HALL.

HAVE you heard how a girl saved the lightning express,
Of Kate Shelly, whose father was kill'd on the road?
Were he living to-day, he'd be proud to possess
Such a daughter as Kate. Ah! 'twas grit that she show'd
On that terrible evening when Donahue's train
Jump'd the bridge and went down, in the darkness and rain!

She was only eighteen, but a woman in size,
With a figure as graceful and lithe as a doe;
With peach-blossom cheeks, and with violet eyes,
And teeth and complexion like new-fallen snow;

With a nature unspoil'd and unblemish'd by art,
With a generous soul, and a warm, noble heart!

'Tis evening; the darkness is dense and profound:
  Men linger at home by their bright-blazing fires;
The wind wildly howls with a horrible sound,
  And shrieks through the vibrating telegraph wires;
The fierce lightning flashes along the dark sky;
The rain falls in torrents; the river rolls by.

The scream of a whistle! the rush of a train!
  The sound of a bell! a mysterious light
That flashes and flares through the fast-falling rain!
  A rumble! a roar! shrieks of human affright!
The falling of timbers! the space of a breath!
A splash in the river! then darkness and death!

Kate Shelly recoils at the terrible crash;
  The sounds of destruction she happens to hear;
She springs to the window, she throws up the sash,
  And listens and looks, with a feeling of fear:
The tall tree-tops groan, and she hears the faint cry
Of a drowning man down in the river near by!

Her heart feebly flutters, her features grow wan;
  And then through her soul in a moment there flies
A forethought that gives her the strength of a man:
  She turns to her trembling old mother and cries,
"I must save the express; 'twill be here in an hour!"
Then out through the door disappears in the shower.

She flies down the track through the pitiless rain;
  She reaches the river; the water below
Whirls and seethes through the timbers. She shudders again:
  "The bridge! To Moingona God help me to go!"
Then closely about her she gathers her gown,
And on the wet ties with a shiver sinks down.

Then carefully over the timber she creeps
  On her hands and her knees, almost holding her breath.
The loud thunder peals and the wind wildly sweeps,
  And struggles to hurry her downward to death;
But the thought of the train to destruction so near
Removes from her soul every feeling of fear.

With the blood dripping down from each torn, bleeding limb,
Slowly over the timbers her dark way she feels;
Her fingers grow numb and her head seems to swim;
Her strength is fast failing; she staggers, she reels,
She falls! Ah! the danger is over at last,
Her feet touch the earth, and the long bridge is pass'd!

In an instant new life seems to come to her form;
She springs to her feet and forgets her despair:
On, on to Moingona! She faces the storm,
She reaches the station — the keeper is there.
"Save the lightning express! No, — hang out the red light!
There's death on the bridge at the river to-night!"

Out flashes the signal-light, rosy and red;
Then sounds the loud roar of the swift-coming train,
The hissing of steam; and there, brightly ahead,
The gleam of a headlight illumines the rain.
"Down brakes!" shrieks the whistle, defiant and shrill:
She heeds the red signal, she slackens! she's still!

Ah! noble Kate Shelly, your mission is done;
Your deed that dark night will not fade from our gaze;
An endless renown you have worthily won:
Let the Nation be just, and accord you its praise;
Let your name, let your fame, and your courage declare
What a woman can do, and a woman can dare.

THE GAMBLER'S WIFE.

R. Coates.

Dark is the night, how dark! No light, no fire!
Cold, on the hearth, the last faint sparks expire!
Shivering, she watches by the cradle-side
For him who pledged her *love, — last year a bride!*

"Hark! 'tis his footstep. No! 'tis past, 'tis gone!"
Tick, tick! — "How wearily the time crawls on!
Why should he leave me thus? He once was kind;
And I *believed* 'twould last! — How mad, how blind!

"Rest thee, my babe, rest on! — 'Tis hunger's cry:
Sleep! for there is no food, — the fount is dry:
Famine and cold their wearying work have done:
My heart must break! And thou!" — the clock strikes one.

"Hush! 'tis the dice-box! Yes, he's there, he's there!
For this, — for this he leaves me to despair!
Leaves love, leaves truth, his wife, *his child!* for what?
The wanton's smile, — the villain, — and the sot!

Yet I'll not curse him: no! 'tis all in vain:
'Tis long to wait, but sure he'll come again;
And I could starve, and bless him, but for *you*,
My child! — *his child!* O fiend!" — The clock strikes two.

"Hark, how the sign-board creaks! The blast howls by.
Moan! moan! A dirge swells through the cloudy sky.
Ha, 'tis his knock! he comes! — he comes once more!"
'Tis but the lattice flaps: — thy hope is o'er.

"Can he desert us thus? He knows I stay,
Night after night, in loneliness, to pray
For his return, — and yet he sees no tear.
No, no! it cannot be: he will be here!

Nestle more closely, dear one, to my heart!
Thou'rt cold! thou'rt freezing! But we *will* not part.
Husband! — I die! — Father! — It is not he!
O God, protect my child!" — The clock strikes three.

They're gone, they're gone! the glimmering spark hath fled:
The wife and child are number'd with the dead:
On the cold hearth, outstretch'd in solemn rest,
The babe lay frozen on its mother's breast.
The gambler came at last, — but all was o'er;
Dread silence reign'd around: — the clock struck four!

JOHN MAYNARD, THE HERO-PILOT.

JOHN B. GOUGH.

JOHN MAYNARD was well known in the Lake district as a God-fearing, honest, intelligent man. He was a pilot on a steamer from Detroit to Buffalo, one summer afternoon. At that time those steamers seldom carried boats. Smoke was seen ascending from below, and the captain called out, "Simpson, go down and see what that smoke is." Simpson came up with his face pale as ashes, and said, "Captain, the ship is on fire!" Then, "Fire! fire! fire! fire on shipboard!" All hands were called up. Buckets of water were dashed upon the fire, but in vain. There were large quantities of rosin and tar on board, and it was useless to attempt to save the ship. Passengers rushed forward and inquired of the pilot, "How far are we from Buffalo?" "Seven miles." "How long before we reach it?" "Three-quarters of an hour at our present rate of steam." "Is there any danger?" "Danger here, — see the smoke bursting out! Go forward, if you would save your lives!" Passengers and crew, men, women, and children, crowded the forward part of the ship. John Maynard stood at the helm. The flames burst forth in a sheet of fire, clouds of smoke arose; the captain cried out through his trumpet, "John Maynard!" "Ay, ay, sir." "Are you at the helm?" "Ay, ay, sir." "How does she head?" "Southeast by east, sir." "Head her southeast and run her on shore." Nearer, nearer, yet nearer she approached the shore. Again the captain cried out, "John Maynard!" The response came feebly, "Ay, ay, sir." "Can you hold on five minutes longer, John?" "By God's help I can." The old man's hair was scorched from the scalp; one hand disabled, his knee upon the stanchion, and his teeth set, with his other hand upon the wheel, he stood firm as a rock. He beached the ship, — every man, woman, and child was saved, as John Maynard dropped, and his spirit took its flight to his God.

LADY CLARE.

ALFRED TENNYSON.

It was the time when lilies blow,
And clouds are highest up in air,
Lord Ronald brought a lily-white doe
To give his cousin, Lady Clare.

I trow they did not part in scorn:
Lovers long-betroth'd were they:
They two will wed the morrow morn;
God's blessing on the day!

"He does not love me for my birth,
Nor for my lands so broad and fair;
He loves me for my own true worth,
And that is well," said Lady Clare.

In there came old Alice the nurse,
Said, "Who was this that went from thee?"
"It was my cousin," said Lady Clare,
"To-morrow he weds with me."

"O, God be thank'd!" said Alice the nurse,
"That all comes round so just and fair;
Lord Ronald is heir of all your lands,
And you are not the Lady Clare."

"Are ye out of your mind, my nurse, my nurse,"
Said Lady Clare, "that ye speak so wild?"
"As God's above," said Alice the nurse,
"I speak the truth: you are my child.

The old Earl's daughter died at my breast;
I speak the truth, as I live by bread!
I buried her like my own sweet child,
And put my child in her stead."

"Falsely, falsely have ye done,
  O mother," she said, "if this be true; —
To keep the best man under the Sun
  So many years from his due."

"Nay, now, my child," said Alice the nurse,
  "But keep the secret for your life,
And all you have will be Lord Ronald's,
  When you are man and wife."

"If I'm a beggar born," she said,
  "I will speak out, for I dare not lie.
Pull off, pull off the brooch of gold,
  And fling the diamond necklace by."

"Nay, now, my child," said Alice the nurse,
  "But keep the secret all ye can."
She said, "Not so; but I will know
  If there be any faith in man."

"Nay, now, what faith?" said Alice the nurse;
  "The man will cleave unto his right."
"And he shall have it," the lady replied,
  "Though I should die to-night."

"Yet give one kiss to your mother dear!
  Alas, my child, I sinn'd for thee."
"O mother, mother, mother," she said,
  "So strange it seems to me.

Yet here's a kiss for my mother dear,
  My mother dear, if this be so,
And lay your hand upon my head,
  And bless me, mother, ere I go."

She clad herself in a russet gown,
  She was no longer Lady Clare:
She went by dale, and she went by down,
  With a single rose in her hair.

The lily-white doe Lord Ronald had brought
Leapt up from where she lay,
Dropt her head in the maiden's hand,
And follow'd her all the way.

Down stept Lord Ronald from his tower:
"O Lady Clare, you shame your worth!
Why come you drest like a village maid,
That are the flower of the Earth?"

"If I come drest like a village maid,
I am but as my fortunes are:
I am a beggar born," she said,
"And not the Lady Clare."

"Play me no tricks," said Lord Ronald,
"For I am yours in word and in deed;
Play me no tricks," said Lord Ronald,
"Your riddle is hard to read."

O, and proudly stood she up!
Her heart within her did not fail:
She look'd into Lord Ronald's eyes,
And told him all her nurse's tale.

He laugh'd a laugh of merry scorn;
He turn'd and kiss'd her where she stood:
"If you are not the heiress born,
And I," said he, "the next in blood,—

If you are not the heiress born,
And I," said he, "the lawful heir,
We two will wed to-morrow morn,
And you shall still be Lady Clare."

MACLAINE'S CHILD.

CHARLES MACKAY.

"MACLAINE! you've scourged me like a hound:
You should have struck me to the ground;
You should have play'd a chieftain's part;
You should have stabb'd me to the heart.

You should have crush'd me unto death:
But here I swear with living breath
That for this wrong which you have done
I'll wreak my vengeance on your son, —

On him, and you, and all your race!"
He said, and bounding from his place,
He seized the child with sudden hold, —
A smiling infant, three years old, —

And, starting like a hunted stag,
He scaled the rock, he clomb the crag,
And reach'd, o'er many a wide abyss,
The beetling seaward precipice;

And, leaning o'er its topmost ledge,
He held the infant o'er the edge:
"In vain thy wrath, thy sorrow vain;
No hand shall save it, proud Maclaine!"

With flashing eye and burning brow
The mother follow'd, heedless how,
O'er crags with mosses overgrown,
And stair-like juts of slippery stone.

But midway up the rugged steep
She found a chasm she could not leap,
And, kneeling on its brink, she raised
Her supplicating hands, and gazed.

"O, spare my child, my joy, my pride!
O, give me back my child!" she cried:
"My child! my child!" with sobs and tears
She shriek'd upon his callous ears.

"Come, Evan," said the trembling chief, —
His bosom wrung with pride and grief, —
"Restore the boy, give back my son,
And I'll forgive the wrong you've done."

"I scorn forgiveness, haughty man!
You've injured me before the clan;
And nought but blood shall wipe away
The shame I have endured to-day."

And, as he spoke, he raised the child
To dash it 'mid the breakers wild,
But, at the mother's piercing cry,
Drew back a step, and made reply:

"Fair lady, if your lord will strip,
And let a clansman wield the whip
Till skin shall flay, and blood shall run,
I'll give you back your little son."

The lady's cheek grew pale with ire,
The chieftain's eyes flash'd sudden fire;
He drew a pistol from his breast,
Took aim, — then dropp'd it, sore distress'd.

"I might have slain my babe instead.
Come, Evan, come," the father said,
And through his heart a tremor ran;
"We'll fight our quarrel man to man."

"Wrong unavenged I've never borne,"
Said Evan, speaking loud in scorn;
"You've heard my answer, proud Maclaine:
I will not fight you, — think again."

The lady stood in mute despair,
With freezing blood and stiffening hair;
She moved no limb, she spoke no word;
She could but look upon her lord.

He saw the quivering of her eye,
Pale lips and speechless agony;
And, doing battle with his pride,
"Give back the boy, — I yield," he cried.

A storm of passions shook his mind, —
Anger and shame and love combined;
But love prevail'd, and, bending low,
He bared his shoulders to the blow.

"I smite you," said the clansman true:
"Forgive me, chief, the deed I do!
For by yon Heaven that hears me speak,
My dirk in Evan's heart shall reek!"

But Evan's face beam'd hate and joy;
Close to his breast he hugg'd the boy:
"Revenge is just, revenge is sweet,
And mine, Lochbuy, shall be complete."

Ere hand could stir, with sudden shock
He threw the infant o'er the rock,
Then follow'd with a desperate leap,
Down fifty fathoms to the deep.

They found their bodies in the tide;
And never till the day she died
Was that sad mother known to smile, —
The Niobe of Mulla's isle.

They dragg'd false Evan from the sea,
And hang'd him on a gallows tree:
And ravens fatten'd on his brain,
To sate the vengeance of Maclaine.

MOTHER AND POET.

MRS. ELIZABETH BROWNING.

LAURA SAVIO, OF TURIN, AFTER NEWS FROM GAETA, 1861.

DEAD! One of them shot by the sea in the east,
And one of them shot in the west by the sea.
Dead! both my boys! When you sit at the feast,
And are wanting a great song for Italy free,
Let none look at me!

Yet I was a poetess only last year,
And good at my art, for a woman, men said;
But this woman, this, who is agonized here,
The east sea and west sea rhyme on in her head
For ever, instead.

What art can a woman be good at? O, vain!
What art is she good at, but hurting her breast
With the milk-teeth of babes, and a smile at the pain?
Ah, boys, how you hurt! you were strong as you press'd,
And I proud, by that test.

What art's for a woman? To hold on her knees
Both darlings, to feel all their arms round her throat
Cling, strangle a little; to sew by degrees
And broider the long clothes and neat little coat;
To dream and to doat!

To teach them, — It stings there! I made them, indeed,
Speak plain the word *country.* I taught them, no doubt,
That a country's a thing men should die for at need.
I prated of liberty, rights, and about
The tyrant cast out.

And, when their eyes flash'd, — O, my beautiful eyes! —
I exulted; nay, let them go forth at the wheels
Of the guns and denied not. But then the surprise
When one sits quite alone! Then one weeps, then one kneels!
God, how the house feels!

At first happy news came, — in gay letters, moil'd
  With my kisses, — of camp-life and glory, and how
They both loved me; and, soon coming home to be spoil'd,
  In return would fan off every fly from my brow
    With their green laurel bough.

Then was triumph at Turin. Ancona was free!
  And some one came out of the cheers in the street,
With a face pale as stone, to say something to me:
  My Guido was dead! I fell down at his feet,
    While they cheer'd in the street.

I bore it; friends soothed me; my grief look'd sublime
  As the ransom of Italy. One boy remain'd
To be lean'd on and walk'd with, recalling the time
  When the first grew immortal, while both of us strain'd
    To the height he had gain'd.

And letters still came, shorter, sadder, more strong,
  Writ now but in one hand: I was not to faint, —
One loved me for two, — would be with me ere long:
  And, "*Viva l'Italia!* he died for, — our saint, —
    Who forbids our complaint."

My Nanni would add: he was safe, and aware
  Of a presence that turn'd off the balls, — was impress'd
It was Guido himself, who knew what I could bear,
  And how 'twas impossible, quite dispossess'd,
    To live on for the rest.

On which, without pause, up the telegraph line
  Swept smoothly the next news from Gaeta: *Shot.*
Tell his mother. Ah, ah, "his," "their" mother, not "mine";
  No voice says "*My* mother" again to me. What!
    You think Guido forgot?

Are souls straight so happy that, dizzy with Heaven,
  They drop Earth's affections, conceive not of woe?
I think not. Themselves were too lately forgiven
  Through that Love and Sorrow which reconciled so
    The Above and Below.

O Christ of the seven wounds, who look'dst through the dark
To the face of thy Mother! consider, I pray,
How we common mothers stand desolate, mark
Whose sons, not being Christs, die with eyes turn'd away,
And no last word to say.

Both boys dead? but that's out of nature. We all
Have been patriots, yet each house must always keep one.
'Twere imbecile, hewing out roads to a wall;
And, when Italy's made, for what end is it done
If we have not a son?

Ah, ah, ah! when Gaeta's taken what then?
When the fair wicked queen sits no more at her sport
Of the fire-balls of death, crashing souls out of men?
When the guns of Cavalli, with final retort,
Have cut the game short?

When Venice and Rome keep their new jubilee,
When your flag takes all heaven for its white, green, and red,
When you have a country from mountain to sea,
And King Victor has Italy's crown on his head,
(And I have my dead,)—

What then? Do not mock me. Ah, ring your bells low,
And burn your lights faintly! My country is there,
Above the star prick'd by the last peak of snow;
My Italy's there, with my brave civic pair,
To disfranchise despair!

Forgive me. Some women bear children in strength,
And bite back the cry of their pain in self-scorn;
But the birth-pangs of nations will wring us at length
Into wail such as this; and we sit on, forlorn,
When the man-child is born.

Dead! One of them shot by the sea in the east,
And one of them shot in the west by the sea.
Both, both my boys! If, in keeping the feast,
You want a great song for your Italy free,
Let none look at me!

PARRHASIUS AND THE CAPTIVE.

N. P. Willis.

Parrhasius stood, gazing forgetfully
Upon his canvas. There Prometheus lay,
Chain'd to the cold rocks of Mount Caucasus,
The vulture at his vitals, and the links
Of the lame Lemnian festering in his flesh;
And, as the painter's mind felt through the dim,
Rapt mystery, and pluck'd the shadows forth
With its far-reaching fancy, and with form
And colour clad them, his fine, earnest eye
Flash'd with a passionate fire, and the quick curl
Of his thin nostril, and his quivering lip,
Were like the wing'd god's, breathing from his flight.

"Bring me the captive now!
My hand feels skilful, and the shadows lift
From my waked spirit airily and swift,
And I could paint the bow
Upon the bended heavens, — around me play
Colours of such divinity to-day.

Ha! bind him on his back!
Look! — as Prometheus in my picture here!
Quick, or he faints! — stand with the cordial near!
Now, — bend him to the rack!
Press down the poison'd links into his flesh!
And tear agape that healing wound afresh!

So, — let him writhe! How long
Will he live thus? Quick, my good pencil, now!
What a fine agony works upon his brow!
Ha! gray-hair'd, and so strong!
How fearfully he stifles that short moan!
Gods! if I could but paint a dying groan!

'Pity' thee! So I do!
I pity the dumb victim at the altar;
But does the robed priest for his pity falter?
I'd rack thee, though I knew
A thousand lives were perishing in thine:
What were ten thousand to a fame like mine?

'Hereafter!' Ay,—hereafter!
A whip to keep a coward to his track!
What gave Death ever from his kingdom back
To check the skeptic's laughter?
Come from the grave to-morrow with that story
And I may take some softer path to glory.

No, no, old man! we die
Even as the flowers, and we shall breathe away
Our life upon the chance wind, even as they!
Strain well thy fainting eye;
For when that bloodshot quivering is o'er,
The light of heaven will never reach thee more.

Yet there's a deathless name!
A spirit that the smothering vault shall spurn,
And like a steadfast planet mount and burn;
And, though its crown of flame
Consumed my brain to ashes as it shone,
By all the fiery stars! I'd bind it on.

Ay,—though it bid me rifle
My heart's last fount for its insatiate thirst;
Though every life-strung nerve be madden'd first;
Though it should bid me stifle
The yearning in my throat for my sweet child,
And taunt its mother till my brain went wild;—

All,—I would do it all,—
Sooner than die, like a dull worm, to rot,—
Thrust foully into earth to be forgot!
O heavens!—but I appal

Your heart, old man! forgive — ha! on your lives
Let him not faint! — rack him till he revives!

Vain, — vain, — give o'er! His eye
Glazes apace. He does not feel you now;
Stand back! I'll paint the death-dew on his brow!
Gods! if he do not die
But for one moment, — one, — till I eclipse
Conception with the scorn of those calm lips!

Shivering! Hark! he mutters
Brokenly now, — that was a difficult breath; —
Another? Wilt thou never come, O death!
Look! how his temple flutters!
Is his heart still? Aha! lift up his head!
He shudders,— gasps, — Jove help him! — so, he's dead."

How like a mounting devil in the heart
Rules the unrein'd *ambition!* Let it once
But play the monarch, and its haughty brow
Glows with a beauty that bewilders thought
And unthrones peace forever. Putting on
The very pomp of Lucifer, it turns
The heart to ashes, and with not a spring
Left in the bosom for the spirit's lip,
We look upon our splendour and forget
The thirst of which we perish!

THE POLISH BOY.

Abridged.

ANN S. STEPHENS.

WHENCE come those shrieks so wild and shrill,
That cut, like blades of steel, the air,
Causing the creeping blood to chill
With the sharp cadence of despair?

Again they come, as if a heart
  Were cleft in twain by one quick blow,
And every string had voice apart
  To utter its peculiar woe.

Whence came they? From yon temple, where
An altar, raised for private prayer,
Now forms the warrior's marble bed
Who Warsaw's gallant armies led.

The dim funereal tapers throw
A holy lustre o'er his brow,
And burnish with their rays of light
The mass of curls that gather bright
Above the haughty brow and eye
Of a young boy that's kneeling by.

What hand is that, whose icy press
  Clings to the dead with death's own grasp,
But meets no answering caress?
  No thrilling fingers seek its clasp.
It is the hand of her whose cry
  Rang wildly, late, upon the air,
When the dead warrior met her eye
  Outstretch'd upon the altar there.

With pallid lip and stony brow
She murmurs forth her anguish now.
But, hark! the tramp of heavy feet
Is heard along the bloody street;
Nearer and nearer yet they come,
With clanking arms and noiseless drum.
Now whisper'd curses, low and deep,
Around the holy temple creep;
The gate is burst; a ruffian band
Rush in, and savagely demand,
With brutal voice and oath profane,
The startled boy for exile's chain.

The mother sprang with gesture wild,
And to her bosom clasp'd her child;
Then, with pale cheek and flashing eye,
Shouted with fearful energy,
"Back, ruffians, back! nor dare to tread
Too near the body of my dead;
Nor touch the living boy; I stand
Between him and your lawless band.
Take *me*, and bind these arms, — these hands, —
With Russia's heaviest iron bands,
And drag me to Siberia's wild
To perish, if 'twill save my child!"

"Peace, woman, peace!" the leader cried,
Tearing the pale boy from her side
And in his ruffian grasp he bore
His victim to the temple door.
"One moment!" shriek'd the mother; "one!
Will land or gold redeem my son?
Take heritage, take name, take all,
But leave him free from Russian thrall!
Take these!" and her white arms and hands
She stripp'd of rings and diamond bands,
And tore from braids of long black hair
The gems that gleam'd like starlight there;
Her cross of blazing rubies, last,
Down at the Russian's feet she cast.
He stoop'd to seize the glittering store:
Up springing from the marble floor,
The mother, with a cry of joy,
Snatch'd to her leaping heart the boy.
But no! the Russian's iron grasp
Again undid the mother's clasp.
Forward she fell, with one long cry
Of more than mortal agony.

But the brave child is roused at length,
  And, breaking from the Russian's hold,

He stands, a giant in the strength
  Of his young spirit, fierce and bold;
Proudly he towers; his flashing eye,
  So blue, and yet so bright,
Seems kindled from th' eternal sky,
  So brilliant is its light.
His curling lips and crimson cheeks
Foretell the thought before he speaks;
With a full voice of proud command
He turn'd upon the wondering band:

"Ye hold me not! no, no, nor can;
This hour has made the boy a man:
The world shall witness that one soul
Fears not to prove itself a Pole.

I knelt beside my slaughter'd sire,
Nor felt one throb of vengeful ire;
I wept upon his marble brow,—
Yes, wept,—I was a child; but now
My noble mother on her knee
Has done the work of years for me.
Although in this small tenement
My soul is cramp'd,—unbow'd, unbent,
I've still within me ample power
To free myself this very hour:
This dagger in my heart! and then
Where is your boasted power, base men?"

He drew aside his broider'd vest,
And there, like slumbering serpent's crest,
The jewell'd haft of a poniard bright
Glitter'd a moment on the sight.
"Ha! start ye back? Fool! coward! knave!
Think ye my noble father's glave
Could drink the life-blood of a slave?
The pearls that on the handle flame

Would blush to rubies in their shame:
The blade would quiver in thy breast,
Ashamed of such ignoble rest!
No; thus I rend thy tyrant's chain,
And fling him back a boy's disdain!"

A moment, and the funeral light
Flash'd on the jewell'd weapon bright;
Another, and his young heart's blood
Leap'd to the floor a crimson flood.
Quick to his mother's side he sprang,
And on the air his clear voice rang, —
"Up, mother, up! I'm free! I'm free!
The choice was death or slavery;
Up! mother, up! look on my face,
I only wait for thy embrace.
One last, last word, — a blessing, one,
To prove thou know'st what I have done!
No look? no word? Canst thou not feel
My warm blood o'er thy heart congeal?
Speak, mother, speak, — lift up thy head.
What! silent still? Then art thou dead!
Great God, I thank thee! Mother, I
Rejoice, with thee and thus, to die."
Slowly he falls: the clustering hair
Rolls back, and leaves that forehead bare:
One long, deep breath, and his pale head
Lay on his mother's bosom, dead.

VIRGINIA: A LAY OF ANCIENT ROME.

LORD MACAULAY.

OVER the Alban mountains the light of morning broke;
From all the roofs of the Seven Hills curl'd the thin wreaths of smoke;
The city gates were open; the Forum, all alive

With buyers and with sellers, was humming like a hive;
And blithely young Virginia came smiling from her home,—
Ah! woe for young Virginia, the sweetest maid in Rome.
With her small tablets in her hand, and her satchel on her arm,
Forth she went, bounding, to the school, nor dream'd of shame or harm
She cross'd the Forum, shining with the stalls in alleys gay,
And had just reach'd the very spot whereon I stand this day,
When up the varlet Marcus came; not such as when, erewhile,
He crouch'd behind his patron's heels, with the true client smile:
He came with louring forehead, swollen features, and clench'd fist,
And strode across Virginia's path, and caught her by the wrist:
Hard strove the frighten'd maiden, and scream'd with look aghast;
And at her scream from right to left the folk came running fast;
And the strong smith Muræna gave Marcus such a blow,
The caitiff reel'd three paces back, and let the maiden go;
Yet glared he fiercely round him, and growl'd, in harsh fell tone,
"She's mine, and I will have her: I seek but for mine own.
She is my slave, born in my house, and stolen away and sold,
The year of the sore sickness, ere she was twelve years old.
I wait on Appius Claudius; I waited on his sire:
Let him who works the client wrong, beware the patron's ire!"
But, ere the varlet Marcus again might seize the maid,
Who clung tight to Muræna's skirt, and sobb'd, and shriek'd for aid,
Forth through the throng of gazers the young Icilius press'd,
And stamp'd his foot, and rent his gown, and smote upon his breast,
And beckon'd to the people, and, in bold voice and clear,
Pour'd thick and fast the burning words which tyrants quake to hear.

"Now, by your children's cradles, now, by your father's graves,
Be men to-day, Quirites, or be for ever slaves!
Shall the vile fox-earth awe the race that storm'd the lion's den?
Shall we, who could not brook one lord, crouch to the wicked Ten?
O, for that ancient spirit which curb'd the Senate's will!
O, for the tents which in old time whiten'd the Sacred Hill!
In those brave days, our fathers stood firmly side by side;
They faced the Marcian fury, they tamed the Fabian pride:
But, look, the maiden's father comes,—behold Virginius here!"

. . . .

Straightway Virginius led the maid a little space aside,
To where the reeking shambles stood, piled up with horn and hide;
Hard by, a flesher on a block had laid his whittle down;
Virginius caught the whittle up, and hid it in his gown;
And then his eyes grew very dim, and his throat began to swell,
And in a hoarse, changed voice he spake, "Farewell, sweet child, farewell!
O, how I loved my darling! Though stern I sometimes be,
To thee, thou know'st, I was not so. Who could be so to thee?
And how my darling loved me! How glad she was to hear
My footsteps on the threshold, when I came back last year!
And how she danced with pleasure to see my civic crown,
And took my sword, and hung it up, and brought me forth my gown!
Now, all those things are over, — yes, all thy pretty ways, —
Thy needle-work, thy prattle, thy snatches of old lays;
And none will grieve when I go forth, or smile when I return,
Or watch beside the old man's bed, or weep upon his urn. —
The time has come! See, how he points his eager hand this way!
See, how his eyes gloat on thy grief, like a kite's upon the prey.
With all his wit he little deems that, spurn'd, betray'd, bereft,
Thy father hath in his despair one fearful refuge left.
He little deems that in this hand I clutch what still can save
Thy gentle youth from taunts and blows, the portion of the slave;
Yea, and from nameless evil, that passeth taunt and blow, —
Foul outrage which thou knowest not, — which thou shalt never know!
Then clasp me round the neck once more; and give me one more kiss;
And now, mine own dear little girl, there is no way — but — this!"
With that he lifted high the steel, and smote her in the side,
And in her blood she sank to earth, and with one sob she died!

When Appius Claudius saw that deed, he shudder'd and sank down,
And hid his face, some little space, with the corner of his gown,
Till, with white lips and blood-shot eyes, Virginius totter'd nigh,
And stood before the judgment-seat, and held the knife on high:
"O! dwellers in the nether gloom, avengers of the slain,
By this dear blood I cry to you, do right between us twain;
And, even as Appius Claudius hath dealt by me and mine,
Deal thou by Appius Claudius, and all the Claudian line!"

He writhed and groan'd a fearful groan, and then with steadfast feet,
Strode right across the market-place into the Sacred Street.

Then up sprang Appius Claudius: "Stop him, alive or dead!
Ten thousand pounds of copper to the man who brings his head!"
He look'd upon his clients, — but none would work his will;
He looked upon his lictors, — but they trembled and stood still;
And, as Virginius through the press his way in silence cleft,
Ever the mighty multitude fell back to right and left:
And he has pass'd in safety unto his woeful home,
And there ta'en horse to tell the Camp what deeds are done in Rome.

WOUNDED.

William E. Miller.

Let me lie down
Just here in the shade of this cannon-torn tree,
Here, low on the trampled grass, where I may see
The surge of the combat, and where I may hear
The glad cry of victory, cheer upon cheer:
Let me lie down.

O, it was grand!
Like the tempest we charged, in the triumph to share;
The tempest, — its fury and thunder were there:
On, on, o'er intrenchments, o'er living and dead,
With the foe under foot, and our flag overhead:
O, it was grand!

Weary and faint,
Prone on the soldier's couch, ah, how can I rest,
With this shot-shatter'd head and sabre-pierced breast?
Comrades, at roll-call when I shall be sought,
Say I fought till I fell, and fell where I fought,
Wounded and faint.

O, that last charge!
Right through the dread hell-fire of shrapnel and shell,
Through without faltering, — clear through with a yell!
Right in their midst, in the turmoil and gloom,
Like heroes we dash'd, at the mandate of doom!
O, that last charge!

It was duty!
Some things are worthless, and some others so good
That nations who buy them pay only in blood.
For Freedom and Country each man owes his part;
And here I pay my share, all warm from my heart:
It is duty.

Dying at last!
My mother, dear mother! with meek tearful eye,
Farewell! and God bless you, for ever and aye!
O that I now lay on your pillowing breast,
To breathe my last sigh on the bosom first prest!
Dying at last!

Great Heaven! this bullet-hole gapes like a grave;
A curse on the aim of the traitorous knave!
Is there never a one of you knows how to pray,
Or speak for a man as his life ebbs away?
Pray! Pray!
Our Father! our Father! why don't you proceed?
Can't you see I am dying? Great God, how I bleed!
Ebbing away!
Ebbing away! The light of the day is turning to gray.

Our Father in Heaven, — boys tell me the rest,
While I stanch the hot blood from this hole in my breast.
There's something about the forgiveness of sin;
Put that in! put that in! — and then
I'll follow your words and say an *amen*.

Here, Morris, old fellow, get hold of my hand,
And, Wilson, my comrade, — O! wasn't it grand

When they came down the hill like a thunder-charged cloud,
And were scatter'd like mist by our brave little crowd?

I am dying; bend down, till I touch you once more;
Don't forget me, old fellow: God prosper this war!
Confusion to enemies! — keep hold of my hand, —
And float our dear flag o'er a prosperous land!
Where's Wilson, — my comrade, — here, stoop down your head;
Can't you say a short prayer for the dying and dead?

Our Father which art in Heaven, hallowed be thy name. Thy kingdom come. Thy will be done in Earth, as it is in Heaven. Give us this day our daily bread. And forgive us our debts, as we forgive our debtors. And lead us not into temptation, but deliver us from evil: For thine is the kingdom, and the power, and the glory, for ever. Amen.

THE WRECK OF THE HESPERUS.

H. W. LONGFELLOW.

It was the schooner Hesperus
  That sail'd the wintry sea;
And the skipper had taken his little daughter,
  To bear him company.

Blue were her eyes as the fairy-flax,
  Her cheeks like the dawn of day,
And her bosom white as the hawthorn buds
  That ope in the month of May.

The skipper he stood beside the helm,
  His pipe was in his mouth,
And he watch'd how the veering flaw did blow
  The smoke now west, now south.

Then up and spake an old sailor, —
  Had sail'd the Spanish main, —
"I pray thee, put into yonder port,
  For I fear a hurricane.

Last night the Moon had a golden ring,
  And to-night no Moon we see!"
The skipper, he blew a whiff from his pipe,
  And a scornful laugh laugh'd he.

Colder and louder blew the wind,
  A gale from the north-east;
The snow fell hissing in the brine,
  And the billows froth'd like yeast.

Down came the storm, and smote amain
  The vessel in its strength;
She shudder'd and paused, like a frighten'd steed,
  Then leap'd her cable's length.

"Come hither! come hither! my little daughter,
  And do not tremble so;
For I can weather the roughest gale,
  That ever wind did blow."

He wrapp'd her warm in his seaman's coat
  Against the stinging blast;
He cut a rope from a broken spar,
  And bound her to the mast.

"O father! I hear the church-bells ring,
  O say, what may it be?"
"'Tis a fog-bell on a rock-bound coast!"
  And he steer'd for the open sea.

"O father! I hear the sound of guns,
  O say what may it be?"
"Some ship in distress, that cannot live
  In such an angry sea!"

"O father! I see a gleaming light,
O say, what may it be?"
But the father answer'd never a word,
A frozen corpse was he.

Lash'd to the helm, all stiff and stark,
With his face turn'd to the skies,
The lantern gleam'd through the gleaming snow
On his fix'd and glassy eyes.

Then the maiden clasp'd her hands and pray'd,
That savèd she might be;
And she thought of Christ, who still'd the wave
On the Lake of Galilee.

And fast through the midnight dark and drear,
Through the whistling sleet and snow,
Like a sheeted ghost, the vessel swept
Towards the reef of Norman's Woe.

And ever, the fitful gusts between,
A sound came from the land;
It was the sound of the trampling surf
On the rocks and the hard sea-sand.

The breakers were right beneath her bows,
She drifted a dreary wreck,
And a whooping billow swept the crew
Like icicles from her deck.

She struck where the white and fleecy waves
Look'd soft as carded wool,
But the cruel rocks, they gored her side
Like the horns of an angry bull.

Her rattling shrouds, all sheath'd in ice,
With the masts went by the board;
Like a vessel of glass, she stove and sank,
Ho! ho! the breakers roar'd!

At daybreak, on the bleak sea-beach,
  A fisherman stood aghast,
To see the form of a maiden fair
  Lash'd close to a drifting mast.

The salt sea was frozen on her breast,
  The salt tears in her eyes;
And he saw her hair, like the brown sea-weed,
  On the billows fall and rise.

Such was the wreck of the Hesperus,
  In the midnight and the snow!
Christ save us all from a death like this,
  On the reef of Norman's Woe!

GONE WITH A HANDSOMER MAN.

WILL CARLETON.

JOHN.

I've work'd in the field all day, a-plowin' the "stony streak";
I've scolded my team till I'm hoarse; I've tramp'd till my legs are weak;
I've choked a dozen swears, (so's not to tell Jane fibs,)
When the plow-pint struck a stone, and the handles punched my ribs.

I've put my team in the barn, and rubb'd their sweaty coats;
I've fed 'em a heap of hay and half a bushel of oats;
And to see the way they eat makes me like eatin' feel,
And Jane won't say to-night that I don't make out a meal.

Well said! the door is lock'd! but here she's left the key
Under the step, in a place known only to her and me:
I wonder who's dyin' or dead, that she's hustled off pell-mell;
But here on the table's a note, and probably this will tell.

Good God! my wife is gone! my wife is gone astray!
The letter it says, "Good-bye, for I'm a-going away;
I've lived with you six months, John, and so far I've been true;
But I'm going away to-day with a handsomer man than you."

A han'somer man than me! Why, that ain't much to say;
There's han'somer men than me go past here every day:
There's han'somer men than me, — I ain't of the han'some kind;
But a *loven'er* man than I was, I guess she'll never find.

Curse her! curse her! I say, and give my curses wings!
May the words of love I've spoken be changed to scorpion stings!
O, she fill'd my heart with joy, she emptied my heart of doubt,
And now, with a scratch of a pen, she lets my heart's blood out!

Curse her! curse her! say I, she'll some time rue this day;
She'll some time learn that hate is a game that two can play;
And long before she dies she'll grieve she ever was born,
And I'll plow her grave with hate, and seed it down to scorn.

As sure as the world goes on, there'll come a time when she
Will read the devilish heart of that han'somer man than me;
And there'll be a time when he will find, as others do,
That she who is false to one can be the same with two.

And when her face grows pale, and when her eyes grow dim,
And when he is tired of her and she is tired of him,
She'll do what she ought to have done, and coolly count the cost;
And then she'll see things clear, and know what she has lost.

And thoughts that are now asleep will wake up in her mind,
And she will mourn and cry for what she has left behind;
And maybe she'll sometimes long for me, — for me; but no!
I've blotted her out of my heart, and I will not have it so.

And yet in her girlish heart there was somethin' or other she had
That fasten'd a man to her, and wasn't entirely bad;
And she loved me a little, I think, although it didn't last;
But I mustn't think of these things, — I've buried 'em in the past.

I'll take my hard words back, nor make a bad matter worse:
She'll have trouble enough; she shall not have my curse;
But I'll live a life so square, — and I well know that I can, —
That she always will sorry be that she went with that han'somer man.

Ah, here is her kitchen dress! it makes my poor eyes blurr;
It seems, when I look at that, as if 'twas holdin' her.

And here are her week-day shoes, and there is her week-day hat,
And yonder's her weddin' gown: I wonder she didn't take that.

'Twas only this mornin' she came and call'd me her "dearest dear,"
And said I was makin' for her a regular paradise here:
O God! if you want a man to sense the pains of Hell,
Before you pitch him in just keep him in Heaven a spell!

Good-bye! I wish that death had sever'd us two apart:
You've lost a worshipper here, you've crush'd a lovin' heart.
I'll worship no woman again; but I guess I'll learn to pray,
And kneel as *you* used to kneel, before you run away.

And if I thought I could bring my words on Heaven to bear,
And if I thought I had some little influence there,
I would pray that I might be, if it only could be so,
As happy and gay as I was a half an hour ago.

JANE (*entering*).

Why, John, what a litter here! you've thrown things all around!
Come, what's the matter now? and what have you lost or found?
And here's my father here, a waiting for supper, too;
I've been a-riding with him,—he's that "handsomer man than you."

Ha! ha! Pa, take a seat, while I put the kettle on,
And get things ready for tea, and kiss my dear old John.
Why, John, you look so strange! come, what has cross'd your track?
I was only a-joking, you know, I'm willing to take it back.

JOHN (*aside*).

Well, now, if this *ain't* a joke, with rather a bitter cream!
It seems as if I'd woke from a mighty ticklish dream;
And I think she "smells a rat," for she smiles at me so queer;
I hope she don't; good gracious! I hope that they didn't hear!

'Twas one of her practical drives, she thought I'd understand!
But I'll never break sod again till I get the lay of the land.
But one thing's settled with me,—to appreciate Heaven well,
'Tis good for a man to have some fifteen minutes of Hell.

THE VAGABONDS.

J. T. Trowbridge.

We are two travellers, Roger and I.
Roger's my dog: — come here, you scamp!
Jump for the gentlemen, — mind your eye!
Over the table, — look out for the lamp! —
The rogue is growing a little old;
Five years we've tramp'd through wind and weather,
And slept out-doors when nights were cold,
And ate and drank — and starved together.

We've learn'd what comfort is, I tell you!
A bed on the floor, a bit of rosin,
A fire to thaw our thumbs, (poor fellow!
The paw he holds up there's been frozen,)
Plenty of catgut for my fiddle,
(This out-door business is bad for strings,)
Then a few nice buckwheats hot from the griddle,
And Roger and I set up for kings!

No, thank ye, sir, — I never drink;
Roger and I are exceedingly moral, —
Aren't we, Roger? — see him wink! —
Well, something hot, then, — we won't quarrel.
He's thirsty, too, — see him nod his head?
What a pity, sir, that dogs can't talk!
He understands every word that's said,
And he knows good milk from water-and-chalk.

The truth is, sir, now I reflect,
I've been so sadly given to grog,
I wonder I've not lost the respect
(Here's to you, sir!) even of my dog.
But he sticks by, through thick and thin;
And this old coat, with its empty pockets,
And rags that smell of tobacco and gin,
He'll follow while he has eyes in his sockets.

There isn't another creature living
  Would do it, and prove, through every disaster,
So fond, so faithful, and so forgiving,
  To such a miserable thankless master!
No, sir! — see him wag his tail and grin!
  By George! it makes my old eyes water!
That is, there's something in this gin
  That chokes a fellow. But no matter!

We'll have some music, if you're willing,
  And Roger (hem! what a plague a cough is, sir!)
Shall march a little. — Start, you villain!
  Stand straight! 'Bout face! Salute your officer!
Put up that paw! Dress! Take your rifle!
  (Some dogs have arms, you see.) Now hold your
Cap, while the gentlemen give a trifle,
  To aid a poor old patriot-soldier.

March! Halt! Now show how the traitor shakes,
  When he stands up to hear his sentence; —
Now tell us how many drams it takes
  To honour a jolly new acquaintance.
Five yelps, — that's five; he's mighty knowing!
  The night's before us, fill the glasses! —
Quick, sir! I'm ill, — my brain is going! —
  Some brandy, — thank you, — there! — it passes!

Why not reform? That's easily said;
  But I've gone through such wretched treatment,
Sometimes forgetting the taste of bread,
  And scarce remembering what meat meant,
That my poor stomach's past reform;
  And there are times when, mad with thinking,
I'd sell out Heaven for something warm
  To prop a horrible inward sinking.

Is there a way to forget to think?
  At your age, sir, home, fortune, friends,

A dear girl's love, — but I took to drink; —
  The same old story; you know how it ends.
If you could have seen these classic features, —
  You needn't laugh, sir; they were not then
Such a burning libel on God's creatures:
  I was one of your handsome men!

If you had seen her, so fair and young,
  Whose head was happy on this breast!
If you could have heard the songs I sung
  When the wine went round, you wouldn't have guess'd
That ever I, sir, should be straying
  From door to door, with fiddle and dog,
Ragged and penniless, and playing
  To you to-night for a glass of grog!

She's married since, — a parson's wife:
  'Twas better for her that we should part, —
Better the soberest, prosiest life
  Than a blasted home and a broken heart.
I have seen her? Once: I was weak and spent
  On the dusty road, a carriage stopp'd:
But little she dream'd, as on she went,
  Who kiss'd the coin that her fingers dropp'd!

You've set me talking, sir; I'm sorry;
  It makes me wild to think of the change!
What do you care for a beggar's story?
  Is it amusing? you find it strange?
I had a mother so proud of me!
  'Twas well she died before. — Do you know
If the happy spirits in Heaven can see
  The ruin and wretchedness here below?

Another glass, and strong, to deaden
  This pain; then Roger and I will start.
I wonder, has he such a lumpish, leaden,
  Aching thing, in place of a heart?

He is sad sometimes, and would weep, if he could,
  No doubt, remembering things that were, —
A virtuous kennel, with plenty of food,
  And himself a sober, respectable cur.

I'm better now; that glass was warming. —
  You rascal! limber your lazy feet!
We must be fiddling and performing,
  For supper and bed, or starve in the street. —
Not a very gay life to lead, you think?
  But soon we shall go where lodgings are free,
And the sleepers need neither victuals nor drink; —
  The sooner, the better for Roger and me!

SEARCHING FOR THE SLAIN.

HOLD the lantern aside, and shudder not so;
There's more blood to see than this stain on the snow;
There are pools of it, lakes of it, just over there,
And fix'd faces all streak'd, and crimson-soak'd hair.
Did you think, when we came, you and I, out to-night
To search for our dead, you would see a fair sight?

You're his wife; you love him, — you think so; and I
Am only his mother: my boy shall not lie
In a ditch with the rest, while my arms can bear
His form to a grave that mine own may soon share.
So, if your strength fails, best go sit by the hearth,
While his mother alone seeks his bed on the earth.

You will go? then no faintings! Give me the light,
And follow my footsteps, — my heart will lead right.
Ah, God! what is here? a great heap of the slain,
All mangled and gory! — what horrible pain
These beings have died in! Dear mothers, ye weep,
Ye weep, O, ye weep o'er this terrible sleep!

More! more! Ah! I thought I could nevermore know
Grief, horror, or pity, for aught here below.
Since I stood in the porch and heard his chief tell
How brave was my son, how he gallantly fell.
Did they think I cared then to see officers stand
Before my great sorrow, each hat in each hand?

Why, girl, do you feel neither reverence nor fright,
That your red hands turn over toward this dim light
These dead men that stare so? Ah, if you had kept
Your senses this morning ere his comrades had left,
You had heard that his place was worst of them all, —
Not 'mid the stragglers, — where he fought he would fall.

There's the Moon through the clouds: O Christ, what a scene!
Dost Thou from Thy Heavens o'er such visions lean,
And still call this cursed world a footstool of Thine?
Hark, a groan! there another, — here in this line
Piled close on each other! Ah! here is the flag,
Torn, dripping with gore; — bah! they died for this rag.

Here's the voice that we seek: poor soul, do not start!
We're women, not ghosts. What a gash o'er the heart!
Is there aught we can do? A message to give
To any beloved one? I swear, if I live,
To take it for sake of the words my boy said,
"Home," "mother," "wife," ere he reel'd down 'mong the dead.

But, first, can you tell where his regiment stood?
Speak, speak, man, or point; 'twas the Ninth. O, the blood
Is choking his voice! What a look of despair!
There, lean on my knee, while I put back the hair
From eyes so fast glazing. O, my darling, my own,
My hands were both idle when you died alone.

He's dying, — he's dead! Close his lids, let us go.
God's peace on his soul! If we only could know
Where our own dear one lies! — my soul has turn'd sick;
Must we crawl o'er these bodies that lie here so thick?
I cannot! I cannot? How eager you are!
One might think you were nursed on the red lap of War.

He's not here, — and not here. What wild hopes flash through
My thoughts, as foot-deep I stand in this dread dew,
And cast up a prayer to the blue quiet sky!
Was it you, girl, that shriek'd? Ah! what face doth lie
Upturn'd toward me there, so rigid and white?
O God, my brain reels! 'Tis a dream. My old sight

Is dimm'd with these horrors. My son! O my son!
Would I had died for thee, my own, only one!
There, lift off your arms; let him come to the breast
Where first he was lull'd, with my soul's hymn, to rest.
Your heart never thrill'd to your lover's fond kiss
As mine to his baby-touch; was it for this?

He was yours, too; he loved you? Yes, yes, you're right;
Forgive me, my daughter, I'm madden'd to-night.
Don't moan so, dear child; you're young, and your years
May still hold fair hopes; but the old die of tears.
Yes, take him again; — ah! don't lay your face there;
See, the blood from his wound has stain'd your loose hair.

How quiet you are! — Has she fainted? — her cheek
Is cold as his own. Say a word to me, — speak!
Am I crazed? Is she dead? Has *her* heart broke first?
Her trouble was bitter, but sure mine is worst.
I'm afraid, I'm afraid, all alone with these dead;
Those corpses are stirring; God help my poor head!

I'll sit by my children until the men come
To bury the others, and then we'll go home.
Why, the slain are all dancing! Dearest, don't move.
Keep away from my boy; he's guarded by love.
Lullaby, lullaby; sleep, sweet darling, sleep!
God and thy mother will watch o'er thee keep.

CLAUDIUS AND CYNTHIA.

MAURICE THOMPSON.

IT was in the mid-splendour of the reign of the Emperor Commodus. Especially desirous of being accounted the best swordsman and the most fearless gladiator of Rome, he still better enjoyed the reputation of being the incomparable archer. No one had ever been able to compete with him. His success had rendered him a monomaniac on the subject of archery, affecting him so deeply indeed that he cared more for his fame as a consummate bowman than for the dignity and honour of his name as Emperor of Rome. This being true, it can well be understood how Claudius, by publicly boasting that he was a better archer than Commodus, had brought upon himself the calamity of a public execution.

But not even Nero would have thought of bringing the girl to her death for the fault of the lover.

Claudius and his young bride had been arrested together at their wedding-feast, and dragged to separate dungeons to await the emperor's will. The rumour was abroad that a most startling scene would be enacted in the circus. The result was that all the seats were filled with people eager to witness some harrowing scene of death.

Commodus himself, surrounded by a great number of his favourites, sat on a richly-cushioned throne about midway one side of the enclosure. All was still, as if the multitude were breathless with expectancy. Presently out from one of the openings Claudius and his young bride — their hands bound behind them — were led forth upon the arena and forced to walk around the entire circumference of the place.

The youth was tall and nobly beautiful, a very Hercules in form, an Apollo in grace and charm of movement. His hair was blue-black and crisp, his eyes were dark and proud. The girl was petite and lovely beyond compare. Her eyes were gray and deep as those of a goddess; her hair was pure gold, falling to her feet, and trailing behind her as she walked.

Both were nude excepting a short girdle reaching to the knees.

At length the giant circuit was completed, and the two were left standing on the sand about one hundred and twenty feet from the emperor, who now arose and in a loud voice said:

"Behold the condemned Claudius, and Cynthia whom he lately took for his wife. They are condemned for the great folly of Claudius, that the Roman people may know that Commodus reigns supreme. The crime for which they are to die is a great one. Claudius has publicly proclaimed that he is a better archer than I, Commodus, am. I am the Emperor and the incomparable archer of Rome: whoever disputes it dies, and his wife dies with him. It is decreed."

It was enough to touch the heart of even a Roman to see the innocence of that fair girl's face, as she turned it up in speechless, tearless, appealing grief and anguish to that of her husband. Her pure bosom heaved and quivered with the awful terror suddenly generated within.

The youth, erect and powerful, set his thin lips firmly and kept his eyes looking straight out before him. Many knew him as a trained athlete and especially as an almost unerring archer: they knew him too, as a brave soldier, a true friend, an honourable citizen. Little time remained for such reflections as might have arisen, for immediately a large cage, containing two fiery-eyed and famished tigers, was brought into the circus and placed before the victims. The hungry beasts were excited to madness by the smell of fresh blood, which had been smeared on the bars of the cage for that purpose. They growled and howled, lapping their fiery tongues and plunging against the door.

A murmur of remonstrance and disgust ran all around that vast ellipse, for now every one saw that the spectacle was to be a foul murder, without even the show of a struggle.

The alert eyes of Commodus were bent on the crouching beasts.

At the same time he noted well the restlessness and disappointment of the people. He understood his subjects, and knew how to excite them. The limbs of the poor girl had begun to give way under her, and she was slowly sinking to the ground. This seemed greatly to affect Claudius, who, without lowering his fixed eyes, tried to support her with his body. Despite his efforts she fell in a helpless heap at his feet. The lines on his manly brow deepened, and a slight ashy pallor flickered on brow and eyelids. But he did not tremble. He stood like a statue of Hercules. Then a sound came from the cage which no words can describe, — the hungry howl, the clashing teeth, the hissing breath of the tigers, along with the sharp clang of the iron bars spurned by their rushing feet. The circus fairly shook with the plunge of death toward its victims. Suddenly, in this last moment, the maiden, by a great effort, writhed to her feet, and covered the youth's body with her own. Such love! It should have sweetened death to that young man. How his eyes flame, immovably fixed upon the coming demons! Those who have often turned up their thumbs in this place for men to die, now hold their breath in utter disgust and sympathy.

Look for a brief moment upon the picture; fifty thousand faces thrust forward gazing; — the helpless couple lost to every thing but the black horrors of death, quivering from from head to foot. Note the spotless beauty and unselfish love of the girl. Mark well the stern power of the young man's face. Think of the marriage vows just taken, of the golden bowl of bliss a moment ago at their young lips. And now, O, now look at the bounding tigers! See how one leads the other in the awful race to the feast. The girl is nearer than the man. She will feel the claws and fangs first. How wide those red, frothing mouths gape! How the red tongues loll! The sand flies up in a cloud from the armed feet of the leaping brutes.

There came from the place where Commodus stood a clear musical note, such as might have come from the gravest cord of a lyre, if powerfully stricken, closely followed by a keen, far-reaching hiss, like the whisper of fate, ending in a heavy blow. The multitude caught breath and stared.

The foremost tiger, while yet in mid-air, curled itself up with a gurgling cry of utter pain, and with the blood gushing from its eyes, ears, and mouth, fell heavily down dying. Again the sweet, insinuating twang, the hiss, the stroke.

The second beast fell dead or dying upon the first. This explained all. The Emperor had demonstrated his right to be called the Royal Bowman of the World.

Had the tyrant been content to rest here, all would have been well.

While yet the beasts were struggling with death he gave orders for a shifting of the scenes. He was insatiable.

For the first time during the ordeal the youth's eyes moved. The girl, whose back was turned toward the beasts, was still waiting for the crushing horror of their assault.

A soldier now approached the twain, and, seizing the arm of each, led them some paces further away from the Emperor, where he stationed them facing each other, and with their sides to Commodus, who was preparing to shoot again.

Before drawing his bow, he cried aloud, "Behold, Commodus will pierce the centre of the ear of each!"

The lovers were gazing into each other's eyes still as statues, as if frozen by the cold fascination of death. Commodus drew his bow with tremendous power, fetching the cord back to his breast, where for a moment it was held without the faintest quiver of a muscle. His eyes were fixed and cold as steel.

The arrow fairly shrieked through the air, so swift was its flight.

The girl, filled with ineffable pain, flung up her white arms, the rent thongs flying away in the paroxysms of her final struggle. The arrow struck in the sand beyond. Something like a divine smile flashed across her face. Again the bow-string rang, and the arrow leaped away to its thrilling work. What a surge the youth made! The cord leaped from his wrists, and he clasped the falling girl in his embrace. All eyes saw the arrow hurtling along the sand after its mission was done. Commodus stood like fate, leaning forward to note the perfectness of his execution. His eyes blazed with eager, heartless triumph.

"Lead them out, and set them free, and tell it everywhere that Commodus is the incomparable bowman."

And then, when all at once it was discovered that he had not hurt the lovers, but had merely cut in two with his arrows the cords that bound their wrists, a great stir began, and out from a myriad overjoyed and admiring hearts leaped a storm of thanks, while, with the clash and bray of musical instruments, and with voices like the voices of winds and seas, and with a clapping of hands like the rending roar of tempests, the vast audience arose as one person, and applauded the Emperor.

SCOTLAND'S MAIDEN MARTYR.

From the "BALTIMORE ELOCUTIONIST."

A TROOP of soldiers waited at the door,
A crowd of people gather'd in the street,
Aloof a little from them sabres gleam'd,
And flash'd into their faces. Then the door
Was open'd, and two women meekly stepp'd
Into the sunshine of the sweet May-noon,
Out of the prison. One was weak and old,
A woman full of tears and full of woes;
The other was a maiden in her morn;
And they were one in name and one in faith,
Mother and daughter in the bond of Christ,
That bound them closer than the ties of blood.

The troop moved on; and down the sunny street
The people follow'd, ever falling back
As in their faces flash'd the naked blades.
But in the midst the women simply went
As if they two were walking, side by side,
Up to God's house on some still Sabbath morn;
Only they were not clad for Sabbath day,
But as they went about their daily tasks:
They went to prison and they went to death,
Upon their Master's service.

On the shore
The troopers halted; all the shining sands
Lay bare and glistering; for the tide had
Drawn back to its farthest margin's weedy mark;
And each succeeding wave, with flash and curve,
That seem'd to mock the sabres on the shore,
Drew nearer by a hand-breadth. "It will be
A long day's work," murmur'd those murderous men,

As they slack'd rein. The leader of the troops
Dismounted, and the people passing near
Then heard the pardon proffer'd, with the oath
Renouncing and abjuring part with all
The persecuted, covenanted folk.
But both refused the oath; "because," they said,
"Unless with Christ's dear servants we have part,
We have no part with Him."

On this they took
The elder Margaret, and led her out
Over the sliding sands, the weedy sludge,
The pebbly shoals, far out, and fasten'd her
Unto the farthest stake, already reach'd
By every rising wave, and left her there:
And as the waves crept round her feet, she pray'd
"That He would firm uphold her in their midst,
Who holds them in the hollow of His hand."

The tide flow'd in. And up and down the shore
There paced the Provost and the Laird of Lag, —
Grim Grierson, — with Windram and with Graham;
And the rude soldiers, jesting with coarse oaths,
As in the midst the maiden meekly stood,
Waiting her doom delay'd, said "she would
Turn before the tide, — seek refuge in their arms
From the chill waves." But ever to her lips
There came the wondrous words of life and peace:
"If God be for us, who can be against?"
"Who shall divide us from the love of Christ?"
"Nor height, nor depth, nor any other creature."

From the crowd
A woman's voice cried a very bitter cry, —
"O Margaret! my bonnie, bonnie Margaret!
Gie in, gie in, my bairnie, dinna ye drown,
Gie in, and tak' the oath."

The tide flow'd in;
And so wore on the sunny afternoon;
And every fire went out upon the hearth,
And not a meal was tasted in the town that day.
And still the tide was flowing in:
Her mother's voice yet sounding in her ear,
They turn'd young Margaret's face towards the sea,
Where something white was floating, — something
White as the sea-mew that sits upon the wave:
But as she look'd it sank; then show'd again;
Then disappear'd; and round the shore
And stake the tide stood ankle-deep.

Then Grierson
With cursing vow'd that he would wait
No more; and to the stake the soldier led her
Down, and tied her hands; and round her
Slender waist too roughly cast the rope, for
Windram came and eased it while he whisper'd
In her ear, "Come take the test, and ye are free";
And one cried, "Margaret, say but God save
The King!" "God save the King of His great grace,"
She answer'd, but the oath she would not take.

And still the tide flow'd in,
And drove the people back and silenced them.
The tide flow'd in, and rising to her knees,
She sang the psalm, "To Thee I lift my soul";
The tide flow'd in, and rising to her waist,
"To Thee, my God, I lift my soul," she sang.
The tide flow'd in, and rising to her throat,
She sang no more, but lifted up her face,
And there was glory over all the sky,
And there was glory over all the sea,—
A flood of glory,—and the lifted face
Swam in it till it bow'd beneath the flood,
And Scotland's Maiden Martyr went to God.

JOHNNY BARTHOLOMEW.

THOMAS DUNN ENGLISH.

THE journals this morning are full of a tale
Of a terrible ride through a tunnel by rail;
And people are call'd on to note and admire
How a hundred or more, through the smoke-cloud and fire,
Were borne from all peril to limbs and to lives,—
Mothers saved to their children, and husbands to wives.
But of him who perform'd such a notable deed
Quite little the journalists give us to read:
In truth, of this hero so plucky and bold,
There is nothing except, in few syllables told,
His name, which is *Johnny Bartholomew*.

Away in Nevada,—they don't tell us where,
Nor does it much matter,—a railway is there,
Which winds in and out through the cloven ravines,
With glimpses at times of the wildest of scenes;
Now passing a bridge seeming fine as a thread,
Now shooting past cliffs that impend o'er the head,
Now plunging some black-throated tunnel within,
Whose darkness is roused at the clatter and din;

And ran every day with its train o'er the road
An engine that steadily dragg'd on its load,
And was driven by Johnny Bartholomew.

With throttle-valve down, he was slowing the train,
While the sparks fell around and behind him like rain,
As he came to a spot where a curve to the right
Brought the black, yawning mouth of a tunnel in sight;
And, peering ahead with a far-seeing ken,
Felt a quick sense of danger come over him then.
Was a train on the track? No! A peril as dire,—
The further extreme of the tunnel on fire!
And the volume of smoke, as it gather'd and roll'd,
Shook fearful dismay from each dun-colour'd fold,
But daunted not Johnny Bartholomew.

Beat faster his heart, though its current stood still,
And his nerves felt a jar but no tremulous thrill;
And his eyes keenly gleam'd through their partly-closed lashes,
And his lips—not with fear—took the colour of ashes.
"If we falter, these people behind us are dead!
So close the doors, fireman; we'll send her ahead!
Crowd on the steam till she rattles and swings!
I'll open the throttle! We'll give her her wings!"
Shouted he from his post in the engineer's room,
Driving onward perchance to a terrible doom,
This man they call Johnny Bartholomew.

Firm grasping the throttle and holding his breath,
On, on through the Vale of the Shadow of Death,
On, on through that horrible cavern of hell,
Through flames that arose and through timbers that fell,
Through the eddying smoke and the serpents of fire
That writhed and that hiss'd in their anguish and ire,
With a rush and a roar like the wild tempest's blast,
To the free air beyond them *in safety they pass'd!*
While the clang of the bell and the steam-pipe's shrill yell
Told the joy at escape from that underground hell,
Of the man they call'd Johnny Bartholomew.

Did the passengers get up a service of plate?
Did some oily-tongued orator at the man prate?
Women kiss him? Young children cling fast to his knees?
Stout men in their rapture his brown fingers squeeze?
And where was he born? Is he handsome? Has he
A wife for his bosom, a child for his knee?
Is he young? Is he old? Is he tall? Is he short?
Well, ladies, the *journals* tell nought of the sort;
And all that they give us about him to-day,
After telling the tale in a common place way,
Is—the man's *name* is Johnny Bartholomew.

XIV.

SCENES FROM POPULAR DRAMAS.

THE HUNCHBACK.

James Sheridan Knowles.

Act I. Scene II.

Characters: Julia *and her companion* Helen.

Scene: *The garden of Master* Walter's *house. Town and country life compared.* Julia *tells of her loving guardian, Master* Walter.

Enter Julia *and* Helen.

Hel. I like not, Julia, this your country life;
I'm weary on't.
Jul. Indeed? So am not I!
I know no other; would no other know.
Hel. You would no other know! Would you not know
Another relative? — another friend,
Another house, another any thing,
Because the ones you have already please you?
That's poor content! Would you not be more rich,
More wise, more fair? The song that last you learn'd
You fancy well; and therefore shall you learn
No other song? Your virginal, 'tis true,
Hath a sweet tone; but does it follow thence,
You shall not have another virginal?
You *may*, love, and a sweeter one; and so
A sweeter life may find than this you lead!

Jul. I seek it not. Helen, I'm constancy!
Hel. So is a cat, a dog, a silly hen,
An owl, a bat, that still sojourn where they
Are wont to lodge, nor care to shift their quarters.
Thou'rt constancy? I'm glad I know thy name!
The spider comes of the same family,
That in his meshy fortress spends his life,
Unless you pull it down, and scare him from it.
And so, in very deed, thou'rt constancy!
Jul. Helen, you know the adage of the tree:
I've ta'en the bend. This rural life of mine,
Enjoin'd me by an unknown father's will,
I've led from infancy. Debarr'd from hope
Of change, I ne'er have sigh'd for change. The town
To me was like the Moon, for any thought
I e'er should visit it; nor was I school'd
To think it half so fair!
Hel. Not half so fair!
The town's the Sun, and thou hast dwelt in night
E'er since thy birth, not to have seen the town!
Their women there are queens, and kings their men;
Their houses palaces!
Jul. And what of that?
Have your town-palaces a hall like this?
Couches so fragrant? walls so high-adorn'd?
Casements with such festoons, such prospects, Helen,
As these fair vistas have? Your kings and queens!
See me a May-day queen, and talk of them!
Hel. Extremes are ever neighbours. 'Tis a step
From one to th' other! Were thy constancy
A reasonable thing, — a little less
Of constancy, — a woman's constancy, —
I should not wonder wert thou ten years hence
The maid I know thee now; but, as it is,
The odds are ten to one, that this day year
Will see our May-day queen a city one.

Jul. Never! I'm wedded to a country life:
O, did you hear what Master Walter says!
Nine times in ten, the town's a hollow thing,
Where what things are, is nought to what they show;
Where merit's name laugh's merit's self to scorn;
Where friendship and esteem, that ought to be
The tenants of men's hearts, lodge in their looks
And tongues alone; where little virtue, with
A costly keeper, passes for a heap, —
A heap for none, that has a homely one;
Where fashion makes the law, — your umpire which
You bow to, whether it has brains or not;
Where Folly taketh off his cap and bells,
To clap on Wisdom, which must bear the jest;
Where, to pass current, you must seem the thing,
The passive thing, that others think, and not
Your simple, honest, independent self.

Hel. Ay; so says Master Walter. See I not
What you can find in Master Walter, Julia,
To be so fond of him!

Jul. He's fond of me.
I've known him since I was a child. E'en then
The week I thought a weary, heavy one,
That brought not Master Walter. I had those
About me then that made a fool of me,
As children oft are fool'd; but more I loved
Good Master Walter's lesson than the play
With which they'd surfeit me. As I grew up,
More frequent Master Walter came, and more
I loved to see him. I had tutors then,
Men of great skill and learning; but not one
That taught like Master Walter. What they'd show me,
And I, dull as I was, but doubtful saw,
A word from Master Walter made as clear
As day-light. When my schooling-days were o'er, —
That's now good three years past, — three years, — I vow

I'm twenty, Helen! — well, as I was saying,
When I had done with school, and all were gone,
Still Master Walter came; and still he comes,
Summer or Winter, frost or rain. I've seen
The snow upon a level with the hedge,
Yet there was Master Walter!

[*Master* WALTER *and Sir* THOMAS CLIFFORD *in the distance.*

Hel. Who comes here?
A carriage, and a gay one; — who alights?
Pshaw! Only Master Walter! What see you,
Which thus repairs the arch of the fair brow,
A frown was like to spoil? — A gentleman!
One of our town kings! Mark, — how say you now?
Wouldst be a town queen, Julia? Which of us,
I wonder, comes he for?

Jul. For neither of us;
He's Master Walter's clerk, most like.

Hel. Most like!
Mark him as he comes up the avenue:
So looks a clerk! A clerk has such a gait!
So does a clerk dress, Julia; mind his hose, —
They're very like a clerk's! a diamond loop
And button, note you, for his clerkship's hat:
O, certainly a clerk! See, Julia, see,
How Master Walter bows, and yields him place,
That he may first go in, — a very clerk!

Jul. I wonder who he is.

Hel. Wouldst like to know?
Wouldst, for a fancy, ride to town with him?
I prophesy he comes to take thee thither.

Jul. He ne'er takes me to town. No, Helen, no,
To town who will; a country life for me!

Hel. We'll see. [*Exeunt.*

ACT I. SCENE III.

An Apartment in Master WALTER'S *House.*

CHARACTERS: JULIA *and* CLIFFORD. *Love at first sight Sir* THOMAS CLIFFORD *wooes a rural maid.*

Enter JULIA *followed by* CLIFFORD.

Jul. No more! I pray you, sir, no more!
Clif. I love you!
Jul. You mock me, sir!
Clif. Then there is no such thing
On Earth as reverence. Honour filial, the fear
Of kings, the awe of Supreme Heaven itself,
Are only shows and sounds that stand for nothing.
I love you.
Jul. You have known me scarce a minute.
Clif. Say but a moment, still I say I love you.
Love's not a flower that grows on the dull earth;
Springs by the calendar; must wait for sun,
For rain; matures by parts,—must take its time
To stem, to leaf, to bud, to blow. It owns
A richer soil, and boasts a quicker seed:
You look for it, and see it not, and, lo!
E'en while you look, the peerless flower is up,
Consummate in the birth!
Jul. You're from the town:
How comes it, sir, you seek a country wife?
Clif. In joining contrasts lieth love's delight.
Complexion, stature, Nature mateth it,
Not with their kinds, but with their opposites.
Hence hands of snow in palms of russet lie;
The form of Hercules affects the sylph's,
And breasts that case the lion's fear-proof heart
Find their loved lodge in arms where tremors dwell.

So is't with habits; therefore I, indeed,
A gallant of the town, the town forsake,
To win a country bride.
Jul. Who marries me,
Must lead a country life.
Clif. The life I love!
But fools would fly from it; for, O, 'tis sweet!
It finds the heart out, be there one to find,
And corners in't where stores of pleasures lodge,
We never dream'd were there! It is to dwell
'Mid smiles that are not neighbours to deceit;
Music whose melody is of the heart,
Freely discoursed; to live on life, and feel
The soul of Nature throbbing to our own;
To con God's mercy, bounty, wisdom, power,
And see Him nearer us.
Jul. [*Aside.*] How like he talks
To Master Walter! Shall I give it o'er?
Not yet.—Thou wouldst not live one-half a year:
A quarter mightst thou for the novelty
Of fields and trees; but then it needs must be
In summer time, when they go dress'd.
Clif. Not it!
In any time,—say Winter. Fields and trees
Have charms for me in very winter time.
Jul. But snow may clothe them then.
Clif. I like them full
As well in snow.
Jul. You do?
Clif. I do.
Jul. But night
Will hide both snow and them; and that sets in
Ere afternoon is out. A heavy thing,
A country fireside in a Winter's night,
To one bred in the town, where Winter's said
To beggar shining Summer.

Clif. I should like
A country Winter's night especially!
Jul. You'd sleep by th' fire.
Clif. Not I; I'd talk to thee.
Jul. You'd tire of that!
Clif. I'd read to thee.
Jul. And that!
Clif. I'd talk to thee again.
Jul. And sooner tire
Than first you did, and fall asleep at last.
Clif. You deal too hardly with me! Matchless maid,
As loved instructor brightens dullest wit,
Fear not to undertake the charge of me:
A willing pupil kneels to thee, and lays
His title and his fortune at your feet. [*Exeunt.*

Act IV. Scene II.

Julia, *the rural maid, becomes a city belle. She embraces visions of pleasure, high life, and extravagance. Her lover, Sir* Thomas Clifford, *who accidentally overhears* Julia *boasting of her extravagance, reproves her, whereupon she becomes offended. Soon after this Sir* Thomas *loses his fortune, and becomes Secretary to the Earl of* Rochdale, *who is also a suitor for the hand of* Julia. *She, in a fit of offended pride, accepts* Rochdale, *though in truth she loves* Clifford.

Banqueting-Room in the Earl of Rochdale's *Mansion.*

A letter from the Earl of Rochdale *to* Julia, *delivered by the poor Secretary, Sir* Thomas Clifford. *Bitter anguish of* Julia. *Love overcomes pride, and* Clifford *wins.*

Jul. [*Alone.*] A wedded bride!
Is it a dream? O, would it were a dream!
How would I bless the Sun that waked me from it!

I'm wreck'd! By mine own act! What! no escape?
None: I must e'en abide these hated nuptials:
Hated? Ay! own it, and then curse thyself
That madest the bane thou loathest, for the love
Thou bear'st to one who never can be thine!
Yes, love! Deceive thyself no longer. False
To say 'tis pity for his fall; respect
Engender'd by a hollow world's disdain;
'Tis none of these: 'tis love, — or, if not love,
Why, then idolatry! Ay, that's the name
To speak the broadest, deepest, strongest passion
That ever woman's heart was borne away by.
He comes! Thou'dst play the lady, — play it now!

Enter a Servant, *conducting* CLIFFORD *attired as* ROCHDALE'S *Secretary.*

Serv. His Lordship's Secretary. [*Exit.*
Jul. [*Aside.*] Speaks he not?
Or does he wait for orders to unfold
His business? Stopp'd his business till I spoke,
I'd hold my peace forever.
[CLIFFORD *kneels, presenting a letter.*
Does he kneel?
A lady am I to my heart's content!
Could he unmake me that which claims his knee,
I'd kneel to him, — I would, I would! — Your will?
Clif. This letter from my Lord.
Jul. O fate! who speaks?
Clif. The Secretary of my Lord.
Jul. [*Aside.*] I breathe!
I could have sworn 'twas he.
[*Makes an effort to look at him, but cannot.*
So like the voice —
I dare not look, lest there the form should stand.
How came he by that voice? 'Tis Clifford's voice,

If ever Clifford spoke. My fears come back, —
Clifford the Secretary of my Lord!
Fortune hath freaks; but none so mad as that.
It cannot be — it should not be; a look,
And all were set at rest. [*Tries again, but cannot.*
So strong my fears,
Dread to confirm them takes away the power
To try and end them. Come the worst, I'll look.
[*She tries again, and is again unequal to the task.*
I'd sink before him, if I met his eye.
Clif. Will't please your ladyship to take the letter?
Jul. [*Aside.*] There Clifford speaks again! Not Clifford's breath
Could more make Clifford's voice; not Clifford's tongue
And lips more frame it into Clifford's speech.
A question, and 'tis over. — Know I you?
Clif. Reverse of fortune, lady, changes friends;
It turns them into strangers. What I am,
I have not always been!
Jul. Could I not name you?
Clif. If your disdain for one, perhaps too bold
When hollow fortune call'd him favourite, —
Now by her fickleness perforce reduced
To take a humble tone, — would suffer you —
Jul. I might?
Clif. You might.
Jul. O Clifford! is it you?
Clif. Your answer to my Lord. [*Gives the letter.*
Jul. [*Taking the letter.*] Your Lord!
Clif. [*Rising.*] Wilt write it?
Or will it please you send a verbal one?
I'll bear it faithfully.
Jul. [*Astonished.*] *You'll* bear it?
Clif. Madam,
Your pardon, but my haste is somewhat urgent.
My Lord's impatient, and to use dispatch

Were his repeated orders.

Jul. Orders! Well, [*Taking letter.*
I'll read the letter, sir. 'Tis right you mind
His Lordship's orders. They are paramount:
Nothing should supersede them — stand beside them:
They merit all your care, and have it! Fit,
Most fit they should! Give me the letter, sir.

Clif. You have it, madam.

Jul. [*Aside.*] So! How poor a thing
I look! so lost, while he is all himself!
Have I no pride? — [*She rings, the* Servant *enters.*] Paper,
and pen and ink. — [*Exit* Servant.
If he can freeze, 'tis time that I grow cold.
I'll read the letter.
[*Opens it, and holds it as about to read it.*
Mind his orders! So!
Quickly he fits his habits to his fortunes.
He serves my Lord with all his will. His heart's
In his vocation. So! Is this the letter?
'Tis upside down, — and here I'm poring on't!
Most fit I let him see me play the fool!
Shame! Let me be myself! —
[Servant *enters with materials for writing.*
A table, sir,
And chair.
[*Table and chair brought in. She sits awhile, gazing on the letter, then looks at* CLIFFORD.
How plainly shows his humble suit!
It fits not him that wears it. I have wrong'd him:
He can't be happy, — does not look it, — is not!
That eye which reads the ground is argument
Enough. He loves me! There I let him stand,
And I am sitting! — [*Rises and points to a chair.*
Pray you, take a chair.
[*He bows, declining the honour. She looks at him awhile.*
Clifford, why don't you speak to me? [*Weeps.*

Clif. I trust
You're happy.
Jul. Happy! Very, very happy!
You see, I weep, I am so happy! Tears
Are signs, you know, of nought but happiness.
When first I saw you, little did I look
To be so happy. Clifford!
Clif. Madam?
Jul. Madam!
I call thee Clifford, and thou call'st me Madam!
Clif. Such the address my duty stints me to.
Thou art the wife-elect of a proud Earl, —
Whose humble Secretary sole am I.
Jul. Most right! I had forgot: I thank you, sir,
For so reminding me; and give you joy
That what, I see, had been a burden to you
Is fairly off your hands.
Clif. A burden to me!
Mean you yourself? Are you that burden, Julia?
Say that the Sun's a burden to the Earth;
Say that the blood's a burden to the heart;
Say health's a burden, peace, contentment, joy,
Fame, riches, honours; every thing that man
Desires, and gives the name of blessing to, —
E'en such a burden Julia were to me,
Had fortune let me wear her.
Jul. [*Aside.*] On the brink
Of what a precipice I'm standing! Back,
Back! while the faculty remains to do't:
A minute longer, not the whirlpool's self's
More sure to suck thee down. One effort! [*Sits.*] There!
[*Recovers her self-possession, and reads the letter.*
To wed to-morrow night! Wed whom? A man
Whom I can never love! I should before
Have thought of that. To-morrow night! this hour
To-morrow! How I tremble! Happy bands,

To which my heart such freezing welcome gives,
As sends an ague through me! At what means
Will not the desperate snatch! What's honour's price?
Nor friends, nor lovers; no, nor life itself!—
Clifford, this moment leave me!

[CLIFFORD *retires up the stage.*

And is he gone?
O docile lover! Do his mistress' wish
That went against his own! Do it so soon!
Ere well 'twas utter'd! No good-bye to her!
No word! no look! 'Twas best that so he went.
Alas! the strait of her who owns that best
Which last she'd wish were done! What's left me now?
To weep, to weep!

[*Leans her head upon her arm, which rests upon the table, her other arm hanging listless at her side.* CLIFFORD *comes down the stage, looks a moment at her, approaches her, and kneeling, takes her hand.*

Clif. [*With stifled emotion.*] My Julia!

Jul. Here again?
Up! up! By all thy hopes of Heaven, go hence!
To stay's perdition to me! Look you, Clifford,
Were there a grave where thou art kneeling now
I'd walk into't, and be inearth'd alive,
Ere taint should touch my name. Should some one come
And see thee kneeling thus! Let go my hand!
Remember, Clifford, I'm a promised bride;
And take thy arm away: it has no right
To clasp my waist. Judge you so poorly of me,
As think I'll suffer this? My honour, sir!

[*She breaks from him, quitting her seat; he rises.*

I'm glad you've forced me to respect myself;
You'll find that I can do so!

Clif. I was bold,—
Forgetful of your station and my own.
There was a time I held your hand unchid;

There was a time I might have clasp'd your waist;
I had forgot that time was past and gone:
I pray you, pardon me.
Jul. [*Softened.*] I do so, Clifford.
Clif. I shall no more offend.
Jul. Make sure of that.
No longer is it fit thou keep'st thy post
In's Lordship's household. Give it up. A day,
An hour remain not in it.
Clif. Wherefore?
Jul. Live
In the same house with me, and I another's?
Put miles, put leagues between us! The same land
Should not contain us: oceans should divide us,
With barriers of constant tempests, such
As mariners durst not tempt! O Clifford!
Rash was the act so light that gave me up,
That stung a woman's pride, and drove her mad,
Till, in her frenzy, she destroy'd her peace:
O, it was rashly done! Had you reproved,
Expostulated, had you reason'd with me,
Tried to find out what was indeed my heart,
I would have shown it,—you'd have seen it. All
Had been as nought can ever be again!
Clif. Lovest thou me, Julia?
Jul. Dost thou ask me, Clifford?
Clif. These nuptials may be shunn'd,—
Jul. With honour?
Clif. Yes.
Jul. Then take me! Stop,—hear me, and take me then.
Let not thy passion be my counsellor!
Deal with me, Clifford, as my brother. Be
The jealous guardian of my spotless name!
Win me and wear me! May I trust thee? O,
If that's thy soul, that's looking through thine eye,
Thou lovest me, and I may!

Clif. As life is mine,
The ring that goes thy wedding finger on,
No hand save mine shall place there!

Jul. Yet a word:
By all thy hopes most dear, be true to me!
Go now; — yet stay! O Clifford! while you're here,
I'm like a bark distress'd and compassless,
That by a beacon steers; — when you're away,
That bark alone, and tossing miles at sea!
Now go! Farewell! My compass — beacon — land!
When shall mine eyes be bless'd with thee again?

Clif. Farewell! [*Exeunt.*

Act V. Scene I.

Characters: Helen *and* Modus. *The courtship of an artful girl and bashful lover.* Modus, *while at college, reads Ovid's "Art of Love," but fails in the practical part of it until taught by* Helen. *Love finally triumphs over bashfulness, with happy result.*

Helen *and* Modus *stand at opposite wings, make a long pause, then bashfully look at each other.*

Hel. Why, cousin Modus! What! will you stand by
And see me forced to marry? Cousin Modus,
Have you not got a tongue? Have you not eyes?
Do you not see I'm very — very ill?
And not a chair in all the corridor?

Mod. I'll find one in the study. [*Going.*

Hel. Hang the study!

Mod. My room's at hand. I'll fetch one thence. [*Going.*

Hel. You sha'n't! I'll faint ere you come back!

Mod. What shall I do?

Hel. Why don't you offer to support me? Well,

Give me your arm,—be quick! [MODUS *offers his arm.*] Is that the way
To help a lady when she's like to faint?
I'll drop unless you catch me!
[*Falls against him.—He supports her.*] That will do;
I'm better now. [*He offers to leave her.*] Don't leave me! is one well
Because one's better? Hold my hand. Keep so.
Well, cousin Modus?

Mod. Well, sweet cousin?

Hel. Well?
You heard what Master Walter said?

Mod. I did.

Hel. And would you have me marry? Can't you speak?
Say yes or no.

Mod. No, cousin.

Hel. Bravely said.
And why, my gallant cousin?

Mod. Why?

Hel. Ah, why—
Women, you know, are fond of reasons—why
Would you not have me marry? How you blush!
You mind me of a story of a cousin
Who once her cousin such a question asked.
He had not been to college, though; for books,
Had pass'd his time in reading ladies' eyes,
Which he could construe marvellously well.
Thus stood they once together, on a day,—
As we stand now,—discoursed, as we discourse,—
As now I question'd thee, she question'd him,
And what was his reply? To think of it
Sets my heart beating,—'twas so kind a one,
So like a cousin's answer,—a dear cousin,
A gentle, honest, gallant, loving cousin!
What did he say? A man might find it out,
Though never read he Ovid's "Art of Love."

What did he say? He'd marry her himself!
How stupid are you, cousin! Let me go!

Mod. You are not well yet.

Hel. Yes.

Mod. I'm sure you're not.

Hel. I'm sure I am.

Mod. Nay, let me hold you, cousin:
I like it.

Hel. Do you? I would wager you
You could not tell me why. Well? How you stare!
What see you in my face to wonder at?

Mod. A pair of eyes.

Hel. [*Aside.*] At last he'll find his tongue.—
And saw you ne'er a pair of eyes before?

Mod. Not such a pair.

Hel. And why?

Mod. They are so bright!
You have a Grecian nose.

Hel. Indeed!

Mod. Indeed!

Hel. What kind of mouth have I?

Mod. A handsome one.
I never saw so sweet a pair of lips:
I ne'er saw lips at all till now, dear cousin!

Hel. Cousin, I'm well,—you need not hold me now.
Do you not hear? I tell you I am well;
I need your arm no longer; take't away!
So tight it locks me, 'tis with pain I breathe:
Let me go, cousin! Wherefore do you hold
Your face so close to mine? What do you mean?

Mod. You've question'd me, and now I'll question you.

Hel. What would you learn?

Mod. The use of lips?

Hel. To speak.

Mod. Nought else?

Hel. How bold my modest cousin grows!
Why, other use know you?

Mod. I do.

Hel. Indeed!
You're wondrous wise! And pray, what is it?

Mod. This!

[*Attempts to kiss her.*

Hel. Soft! My hand thanks you, cousin; for my lips,
I keep them for a husband. Nay, stand off!
I'll not be held in manacles again.
Why do you follow me?

Mod. I love you, cousin!

Hel. O cousin, say you so? That's passing strange!
A thing to sigh for, weep for, languish for,
And die for!

Mod. Die for?

Hel. Yes, with laughter, cousin;
For truly I love you.

Mod. And you'll be mine?

Hel. I will.

Mod. Your hand upon it.

Hel. Hand and heart.
Hie to thy dressing-room, and I'll to mine,—
Attire thee for the altar,—so will I.
Whoe'er may claim me, thou'rt the man shall have me.
Away! Dispatch! But hark you, ere you go:
Ne'er brag of reading Ovid's "Art of Love"!

Mod. And cousin, stop,—one little word with you!

[*Beckons* HELEN *over to him, snatches a kiss. She runs off; he takes the book from his bosom, which he had put there in former scene, looks at it, and throws it down. Exit.*

INGOMAR, THE BARBARIAN.

FREDERICK HALM: *Translated by* MARIA LOVELL.

ACT I. SCENE I.

CHARACTERS: ACTEA, MYRON'S *wife;* PARTHENIA, *their daughter, a beautiful young Greek girl; and* POLYDOR, *a wealthy, miserly old widower, who wishes to contract for the hand of* PARTHENIA.

SCENE: *Massilia, the market-place, in front of an archway which crosses the back of the stage. In the foreground, on the right,* MYRON'S *and another house; a spinning-wheel and basket in front of* MYRON'S *house. Opposite to it the house of* POLYDOR.

Enter ACTEA, *from the House.*

Act. The Sun is nearly set; the city gates
Will quickly close, yet Myron comes not home:
Parthenia, too, wild girl! freed from her task,
Flies like a bird unfetter'd from her cage.—
Parthenia! daughter! child!

Enter PARTHENIA.

Par. Well, mother dear!
Act. Ah! truant, see, here lies thy work undone,
And evening near.
Par. I've spun enough to-day;
And yonder are our neighbours gathering olives;
I'll help them. [*Going.*
Act. No! thou shalt remain with me;
And listen, wild one: thou hast long enough
Wasted the hours in trifling children's play,—
'Tis time to end it: so now sit thee down,
And, if thou canst, be serious for once.
Par. Yes, mother dear, I hear.
[*She seats herself listlessly at the wheel.*

Act. Bethink thee, child,
This Polydor is rich, — a man in years,
'Tis true, but rich, — a widower, indeed,
But much respected, and of quality:
He asks thy hand; dost listen?

Par. [*Starting.*] Yes, O, yes.

Act. Ah, so thou always say'st; yet I may speak,
Talk by the hour, while all thy busy thoughts
Wander through fields and woods, as thou thyself,
Chasing the butterflies; but now 'tis time,
Though with spring blood, to think of coming Autumn, —
'Tis time to think of marriage; yet already
Thou hast rejected Medon.

Par. [*Coming forward.*] O! he was old,
Gray-headed, gouty, coarse, —

Act. Evander, then.

Par. Evander! Yes, he had a fox's cunning,
With a hyæna's heart, and monkey's form.

Act. Mad, foolish girl! go, trample down thy fortune,
Until repentance comes too late! Thou think'st
Thyself unequall'd, doubtless; lovely, rich.

Par. Young am I, mother; joyous, happy, too.
[*Embracing her.*
And you, you love me! what can I wish more?
Yes, you do love me!

Act. Love thee! ay, and well
Dost thou deserve our love!
Why do I fold thee thus within my arms?
We love thee, but thou lovest us not.

Par. Not love thee, mother?

Act. No; or, as our will,
So would thine own be: thou wouldst let us choose
Thy husband.

Par. No, dear mother, no, — not him.

Act. What dost thou hope for, then? Perhaps thou think'st
The Man-i'-the-moon would be thy fitting spouse:
What wait'st thou for, I say?

Par. I'll tell thee, mother: I was but a child,
And yet I mark'd it well; you sang to me
Of Hero and Leander, and their love;
And when I ask'd thee, wondering, what love was,
Then, with uplifted hands and laughing eyes,
Thou told'st me how, into the lonely heart
Love sudden comes unsought, then grows and grows,
Feeble at first, like dawn before the Sun,
Till, bursting every bond, it breaks at last
Upon the startled soul with hope and joy,
While every bounding pulse cries, "That is he
Who carries in his breast my heart, my soul:
With him, O, may I live, and with him die!"
So, when old Medon and Evander came
To woo, I laid my hand upon my heart,
And listen'd, listen'd, but, no! all was still,
All silent; no response no voice; and so
I'm waiting, mother, till my heart shall speak!

Act. [*Aside.*] Good gods! 'tis thus we let our old tongues prattle,
While young ears listen. — So, thou foolish child,
'Tis that thou waitest for, — thy heart must speak!
I prattled nonsense, a child's tale, a dream!
I tell thee, there's no second will come to thee
Like Polydor, so rich, so honourable.

Par. Honourable!
Beats down my needy father in his wares,
Higgles and bargains.

Act. That thou understandest not.
He is a careful and a saving merchant:
Think, think, my child, — say yes, — for my sake, do;
Say yes, my child.

Par. Hold, mother: I will never wander more
Through woods and fields; like other girls, will spin,
Will work, will read thy wishes in thine eyes;
But him, that Polydor, I cannot, will not —
No, never, never!

Act. Never?
Par. Thou art angry!
Act. Away! have I not cause enough for anger?
Thy parents now grow old, and long for rest;
Thy father, a poor armourer, in the fields,
Labours and toils all day;
Then must he hammer at the forge by night;
And when the tillage rests, that cannot he,
But sets out, laden heavily, as now, with arms,
To offer them for sale in neighbouring villages.
Par. Poor father!
Act. Poor, poor, indeed! Then I remain at home,
'Tis true; yet go I forth in thought, and carry
With him the burden of the goods: with him I pant
Up the rough mountain's slippery path, and feel
The pelting storms which soak his weary limbs,
And think, that even now, in the dark valley
The wild Allobroges or fierce Allemanni
Attack him, rob him, murder him, perhaps!
Par. O mother, mother!
Act. So must I weep, and weep. But thou,
Thou whom he loves, for whom he e'en would die,
For whom he risks his blood, his limbs, his life, —
Thou, thou mightst spare him from all weariness,
Mightst dry my tears, make happy our old age,
Be so thyself. But no! thou canst, yet wilt not.
Go, go, thou selfish and ungrateful child! [*Exit into house.*
Par. [*After a pause.*] Ungrateful! no, ye gods, that am I not.
Ungrateful to my father! — No! and yet
For me does the rough storm beat on his head;
For me he staggers 'neath his heavy loads,
And totters, panting up the mountain sides.
Yes, yes; I'll show my mother she is wrong;
It shall not be. But yet what would I do?
Unite myself to age, to avarice?
That is to die! to die, — 'twere better far!

But yet it must be so: — farewell, sweet dreams! [*Pauses.*
And once the future lay so bright before me:
There shone the scarce-form'd hope, the mystic joy; —
Let all be fancy, — love be but a dream; —
All is a fable that adorns our life,
And but the passing day alone is real!
Well, be it so. Parthenia wakes to duty!
And now, sweet visions of my youth, farewell!
My father now shall labour hard no more, —
Shall rest. Ah! who comes here? 'tis Polydor!
I'll fly, — yet no! I will remain: if my happiness
Must be put up for sale, then let the price
Be well secured for which I barter it.
What looks he? pride, ill-temper, avarice, —
And I his wife. It makes my heart grow cold.
[*She approaches her spinning-wheel, at which she sits to work.*

Enter POLYDOR.

Pol. [*Soliloquizing.*] This will not do, the slave impoverishes me;
There is no doing without a wife, — it must be.
Par. [*Aside.*] Does he not look as though he had the weight
O' the world upon his thoughts? and yet I wager
He only thinks on pigs and geese.
Pol. Nothing replaces Kallinike to me:
She was a true heart, — she could work, could save!
But then the armourer's daughter, — could she?
Ah, she is there herself! she's young, she's pretty:
So — yes — no — well, so be it. —
[*Approaching and addressing* PARTHENIA
Good day, fair maid. Good day!
Par. Say, rather, evening, while the Sun is sinking.
Pol. Can it be evening while thy bright eyes shine?
Par. Away, sir, with fine words! we will speak plainly.
They tell me you propose to marry me.
Pol. Ah! that is plain, — that's coming to the point. —

Alas! her fond impatience cannot wait. —
Yes, yes, such is my thought.
Par. My mother told me so: and yet I wonder
Thy choice should fall on me; how soon, it seems,
You have forgotten Kallinike!
Pol. Forgotten? No, indeed; a man like me
Forgets not gold, nor goods, nor the worth of goods,
And that was she to me; yet weighty reasons
Press on me a new choice, my children —
Par. Ay, poor orphans!
Pol. Poor they are not; but they are troublesome,
Gluttonous pigs, — wild, rude, unruly boys.
Shall I, at great expense, hire a schoolmaster
From Samos or Miletus? Gentleness
Best rules rough strength, and thou indeed art gentle.
Par. Gentle! O yes, as gentle as a lamb
Led to the sacrifice.
Pol. Besides, I'm often far from home; my business
Now calls me to the market, now to the harbour:
And shall a slave meanwhile keep house for me,
And farm, and warehouse? guard my well-fill'd coffers?
That only can a wife, only a true wife.
And then, too, I grow old, am often sick:
And who would tend me then? make ready for me
The warm room, and prepare my drink and physic?
Ah! only a fond wife.
Par. O, my poor heart!
Pol. 'Tis thou shalt be that wife, and thou shalt make me
Strong, young again; thy love, my pretty rosebud, —
Par. Away! and listen now to me:
Thou know'st my father tills the fields by day,
And at the anvil works by night, and then
Upon his shoulders carries to a distance
His wares for sale; that he is now in years,
And wants repose: say, then, when I am thine, —
Say, wilt thou think of my poor father?

Pol. Ay, certainly I will; how could I otherwise?
Yes, yes, I will, — I will think of thy father.
Par. And do? — what wilt thou do for him?
Pol. O, he shall be advanced, for he will be
My father-in-law, the father-in-law of Polydor,
Of the rich Polydor; and from the gods
My lineage springs:
Think what an honour; from the gods, my child!
Par. But honour gives not food: what wilt thou do?
Pol. Well, in the first place, buy, as hitherto,
His wares at a good price.
Par. At a good price! — That is, good for thyself.
Well, and what more?
Pol. What more! Why, then again, then will I —
Observe me now, and bear in mind, girl, — know
I'll take thee without dowry, — yes, entirely
Without a dowry; true as thou'rt alive,
I'll take thee, ay, without a drachma!
Par. But what do for my father?
Pol. Is not that
To do? and plenty, too, I think.
Par. No more?
Pol. No more! almost too much.
Par. By all the gods, yes, it is quite too much;
And so, good evening. [*Going.*
Pol. No, stay, — thou shalt not go without an answer.
Par. An answer thou shalt have, and mark it well:
Procure your children, sir, a schoolmaster
At any price, and whence you please; a slave
To guard your house, attend to bolts and bars;
Shouldst thou fall sick, there, at the corner yonder,
Go, bid the huckster sell thee wholesome herbs;
Mix for thyself thy medicine and thy drink:
But know, for me there grows no bitterer herb
On Earth than sight of thee! Now — mark it well —
This is my answer, thou poor, heartless miser!
So fare thee well, descendant of the gods! [*Exit into house.*

Pol. [*Standing looking after her for a time.*] What's
that? did I hear right? she turns me out?
Me, the rich Polydor! The armourer's child
Scorns me, the rich descendant of the gods,
As though I were her father's fellow-workman;
Disdains me! mocks me! There's no bitterer herb
On Earth than sight of me! Yes, and it shall
Be bitter to thee, and to others, too.
I'll have revenge! What shall I do? I'll take
No more swords of him, I'll buy up the rights
Of all his creditors, summon him to justice;
I will; I'll drive him from his house and home,
Ay, from the city, — him and his saucy child.
That will I! Yes; I'll force out his last drachma.
O, I'll not rest until I've had revenge! [*Exit.*

ACT II. SCENE I.

The camp of the Alemanni in the Cevennes Mountain.

CHARACTERS: INGOMAR, *the barbarian and chief of the Alemanni;* PARTHENIA, *who has given up herself to the barbarians as a ransom for her father,* MYRON. MYRON *has been sent back to Massilia, whence he was captured; and, as he is forced along amid the jeers and taunts of the Alemanni,* PARTHENIA *looks toward him, and speaks:*

Par. O, I shall never see him more!
Ing. What! have we
For a silly old man, got now a foolish
And timid weeping girl? I've had enough
Of tears.
Par. Enough, indeed, since you but mock them!
I will not, — no, I'll weep no more.
[*She quickly dries her eyes, and retires to the background*
Ing. That's good; come, that looks well:
She's a brave girl! she rules herself, and, if

She keep her word, we've made a good exchange.
"I'll weep no more." Aha! I like the girl.
And if—Ho! whither goest thou?

[*To* PARTHENIA, *who is going off with two goblets.*

Par. Where should I go? to yonder brook, to cleanse the cups.

Ing. No! stay and talk with me.

Par. I have duties to perform. [*Going.*

Ing. Stay,—I command you, slave!

Par. I am no slave! your hostage, but no slave.
I go to cleanse the cups. [*Exit.*

Ing. Ho! here's a self-will'd thing,—here is a spirit!

[*Mimicking her.*

"I will not, I'm no slave!, I've duties to perform!
Take me for hostage!" and she flung back her head
As though she brought with her a ton of gold!
"I'll weep no more,"—Aha! an impudent thing.
She pleases me! I love to be opposed;
I love my horse when he rears, my dogs when they snarl,
The mountain torrent, and the sea, when it flings
Its foam up to the stars: such things as these
Fill me with life and joy. Tame indolence
Is living death: the battle of the strong
Alone is life.

[*During this speech* PARTHENIA *has returned with the cups and a bundle of field flowers. She seats herself on a piece of rock in front.*

Ah! here she is again.—[*He approaches her, and leans over her on the rock.*

What art thou making there?

Par. I? garlands.

Ing. Garlands?—

[*Musing.*] It seems to me as I before had seen her
In a dream! How! Ah, my brother!—he who died
A child,—yes, that is it. My little Folko,—
She has his dark brown hair, his sparkling eye:
Even the voice seems known again to me:

I'll not to sleep, — I'll talk to her. — [*Returns to her.*
These you call garlands;
And wherefore do you weave them?

Par. For these cups.

Ing. How?

Par. Is't not with you a custom? With us,
At home, we love to intertwine with flowers
Our cups and goblets.

Ing. What use is such a plaything?

Par. Use? They're beautiful; that is their use:
The sight of them makes glad the eye; their scent
Refreshes, cheers. [*Fastens the half-finished garland round a cup, and presents it to him.*
There! is not that, now, beautiful?

Ing. Ay, by the bright Sun! That dark green mix'd up
With the gay flowers! Thou must teach our women
To weave such garlands.

Par. That's soon done: thy wife
Herself shall soon weave wreaths as well as I.

Ing. [*Laughing heartily.*] My wife! my wife! a woman dost thou say?
I thank the gods, not I. This is my wife, —
[*Pointing to his accoutrements.*
My spear, my shield, my sword: let him who will
Waste cattle, slaves, or gold, to buy a woman;
Not I, not I!

Par. To buy a woman? — how!

Ing. What is the matter? why dost look so strangely?

Par. How! did I hear aright? bargain for brides,
As you would slaves, — buy them like cattle?

Ing. Well, I think a woman fit only for a slave.
We follow our own customs, as you yours.
How do you in your city there?

Par. Consult our hearts.
Massilia's free-born daughters are not sold,
But bound by choice with bands as light and sweet
As these I hold. Love only buys us there.

Ing. Marry for love: — what! do you love your husbands?
Par. Why marry else?
Ing. Marry for love; that's strange!
I cannot comprehend. I love my horse,
My dogs, my brave companions, — but no woman!
What dost thou mean by love? what is it, girl?
Par. What is it? 'Tis of all things the most sweet, —
The heaven of life, — or so my mother says;
I never felt it.
Ing. Never?
Par. [*Looking at the garland.*] No, indeed.
Now look how beautiful! Here would I weave
Red flowers if I had them.
Ing. Yonder there,
In that thick wood, they grow.
Par. How sayest thou?
[*Looking off.*] O, what a lovely red! Go, pluck me some.
Ing. [*Starting at the suggestion.*] I go for thee? the master serve the slave? —
[*Gazing on her with increasing interest.*
And yet, why not? I'll go, — the poor child's tired.
Par. Dost hesitate?
Ing. No, thou shalt have the flowers
As fresh and dewy as the bush affords. [*He goes off.*
Par. [*Holding out the wreath.*] I never yet succeeded half so well.
It will be charming! Charming? and for whom?
Here among savages! no mother here
Looks smiling on it, — I'm alone, forsaken!
But no, I'll weep no more! no, none shall say I fear.

Re-enter INGOMAR, *with a bunch of flowers, and slowly advancing towards* PARTHENIA.

Ing. [*Aside.*] The little Folko, when in his play he wanted
Flowers or fruit, would so cry "Bring them to me;
Quick! I will have them, — these I'll have or none";

Till somehow he compell'd me to obey him;
And she, with the same spirit, the same fire, —
Yes, there is much of the bright child in her.
Well, she shall be a little brother to me! —
There are the flowers. [*He hands her the flowers.*

Par. Thanks, thanks. O, thou hast broken them
Too short off in the stem.

[*She throws some of them on the ground.*

Ing. Shall I go get thee more?

Par. No, these will do.

Ing. Tell me about your home: I will sit here,
Near thee.

Par. Not there: thou'rt crushing all the flowers.

Ing. [*Seating himself at her feet.*] Well, well; I'll sit here, then. And now tell me,
What is your name?

Par. Parthenia.

Ing. Parthenia!
A pretty name! and now, Parthenia, tell me
How that which you call love grows in the soul;
And what love is: 'tis strange, but in that word
There's something seems like yonder ocean — fathomless.

Par. How shall I say? Love comes, my mother says,
Like flowers i' the night, — reach me those violets; —
It is a flame a single look will kindle,
But not an ocean quench.
Foster'd by dreams, excited by each thought,
Love is a star from heaven, that points the way
And leads us to its home, — a little spot
In Earth's dry desert, where the soul may rest;
A grain of gold in the dull sand of life;
A foretaste of Elysium: but when,
Weary of this world's woes, th' immortal gods
Flew to the skies, with all their richest gifts,
Love stay'd behind, self-exiled for man's sake!

Ing. I never yet heard aught so beautiful;
But still I comprehend it not.

Par. Nor I,
For I have never felt it; yet I know
A song my mother sang, an ancient song,
That plainly speaks of love, at least to me.
How goes it? stay — [*Slowly, as trying to recollect.*

What love is, if thou wouldst be taught,
Thy heart must teach alone, —
Two souls with but a single thought,
Two hearts that beat as one.

And whence comes love? like morning's light,
It comes without thy call;
And how dies love? — A spirit bright,
Love never dies at all!

And when — and when —
[*Hesitating, as unable to continue.*

Ing. Go on.

Par. I know no more.

Ing. [*Impatiently.*] Try, try.

Par. I cannot now; but at some other time
I may remember.

Ing. [*Somewhat authoritatively.*] Now, go on, I say.

Par. [*Springing up in alarm.*] Not now, I want more roses for my wreath!
Yonder they grow, I'll fetch them for myself.
Take care of all my flowers and the wreath.
[*Throws the flowers into* INGOMAR'S *lap and runs off.*

Ing. [*After a pause, without changing his position, speaking to himself in deep abstraction.*]

Two souls with but a single thought,
Two hearts that beat as one.
[*The curtain falls.*

ACT IV. SCENE I.

CHARACTERS: INGOMAR *and* PARTHENIA.

SCENE: *The forest near Massilia.* PARTHENIA *is released from the Alemanni, and* INGOMAR *accompanies her to her home. Love conquers, and he decides to go with her to Massilia and become a Greek.*

Ing. Here, here, Parthenia, this way,—by this path.
Par. No, yonder is the way,—down there.
Ing. Hold, hold! that is to danger,—see you not?
This way,—give me thy hand.
[*They descend the path on to the stage.*
When wilt thou trust me?
Hast thou forgotten yesterday, the moor
Where, following thine own will, the ground gave way
Beneath thy feet, and, if I had not then
From off my arm thrown my broad shield, whose face
Upheld thy failing steps,—
Par. I should have sunk!
Ing. And I with thee.
Par. I think thou wouldst. Yes, yes,
I was preserved from death, and by thine arms,—
Thy shield lies i' the morass; and last night, too,
Under the bank, whose turf and moss afforded
But scanty firing, thou didst break thy spear,
And with its fragments make a cheerful blaze,
To warm and comfort me. O, thou true guide!
Ing. Then come,—this way.
Par. It seems as if that path—
Ing. Again! Why, look, the wood is ended here,
And the mountain grows more level.
Par. Ah! thou art right; the forest spreads behind us:
It seems to me I ought to know this place.
Was it not here that, when I left my home
To seek my father, on my knees I pray'd
The gods for courage, strength, and victory?
Ing. Ah! say not so. Far, far from here, I'd have
Thy home.
Par. Yes, here it was.
[*She turns to the background and recognizes Massilia*
Ah! and behold, there rolls the sea;
And yonder, shining in the purple light,

Appears Artemis' temple. — O Massilia,
My home, my home! again I throw myself [*Kneeling*
Upon the earth, with thanks, with gratitude. —
Immortal gods, who've watch'd my lonely path,
The work of love is done, and safely back
You bring me home again. O, thanks and praise!

Ing. [*Aside.*] Would that I lay beside my shield in the morass!

Par. [*Rising and coming forward, accompanied by* INGOMAR.] My father, mother, I shall see them again;
Weeping with joy shall sink into their arms,
And kiss the falling tears from their pale cheeks.
O, be saluted by me, my native city!
See how the evening light plays on each column,
Each wall, and tower, like the smile of a god.
Look, Ingomar, is it not glorious?
What ails thee? why art thou now grown sulky,
Like a vex'd child, when joy lends my soul wings?
Didst thou endure with me the burning sun,
The frost of night, and the rough path, and now
Wilt not rejoice, — now that our toil is over?

Ing. I — I rejoice?
In the dark forest, the bleak wilderness,
Alone with thee, the heavens above, around us
Loneliness and deep silence, there, — yes, there,
Where fear and danger press'd thee to my aid,
Did I rejoice; I was thy world: but here,
Where these accursèd walls cast their cold shades,
To tear our souls asunder, — here —

Par. Ah me!
Yes, I remember, — here we part. And yet
Not here; come with me to the city.

Ing. I?
Yonder, with polished Greeks, caged in dark walls?
I, the barbarian, the free man? No, yonder
Thy pathway lies, — this to my mountain home.
O, would that I had never seen thee, girl!

Enough: farewell, farewell! [*Rushes out.*

Par. Ingomar! stay, hear me! — He heeds me not;
He flies up the steep cliff; he's gone, and I
Shall never see him more! Why, how is this?
What sudden change has come upon the world?
How green, how bright, was all before! and now
How dim and dark the twilight grows! How faded
The grass, how dry the leaves! It seems to me
As if the young Spring were about to die.
What! tears? I must not weep; no, no, I must not.
Rouse thee, Parthenia, thou hast duties. Think,
Thy home awaits thee, — parents, friends, companions.
O, Ingomar! whom shall I find there like to thee?
Thou good, thou generous one! Lost — lost! [*Weeps.*

INGOMAR *re-enters and slowly approaches.*

Ing. Parthenia!

Par. Ah! come back again?

Ing. I am: I cannot, will not leave thee.
I will go with thee to the city; I —
I will become a Greek!

Par. How sayest thou?

Ing. Thou dost not despise me, Parthenia; no,
Thou'rt not ashamed of me, but only of
My nation, my rough ways: there's remedy
For that, — it can be mended. Though I am
No Greek, yet I'm a man, for 'tis the soul
That makes the man, and not his outward seeming:
My shield and spear are left in the morass,
So will I leave my nation, manners, all,
To follow thee. In yonder town, for thee
I will become a Greek. And, now I've said it,
I'm strong and well again.

Par. Thou'lt follow me?

Ing. I know I've much to learn, but thou wilt teach me,
And that will make all easy. When 'tis done,
Thou'lt love me then! thou wilt, — I feel it here;

Ay, like a sunbeam in my heart it glows;
It shouts like the loud triumph of a conqueror;
Like the voice of the high gods, it penetrates
My soul: thou'lt love me then! thou'lt love me then!
Par. [*Aside.*] If not, O Heaven! whom can I ever love!
Thou'lt follow me to Massilia. [*Exit.*

LEAH, THE FORSAKEN.

Augustin Daly.

Act IV. Scene II.

Characters: Leah, *a Jewish maiden and a fugitive to Bohemia during a persecution of her race.* Rudolf, *the son of an old Christian magistrate, falls in love with Leah, but is shortly after persuaded that she has accepted a sum of money to discard him. While labouring under this impression, he is induced by his parents to marry* Madalina, *the niece of* Father Herman, *the village priest. The marriage ceremony has just been solemnized in the church when* Leah *wanders into the church-yard.*

Scene: *Night. The churchyard behind an Austrian village church. Tombstones and graves about; at back, the side of the church, showing its stained-glass windows, and a little sacristy door leading from it to yard; among the gravestones, a little to the left of centre of stage, is a half-broken white column.*

Enter Leah, *slowly, her hair streaming over her shoulders.*

Leah. [*Sola.*] What seek I here? I know not; yet I feel I have a mission to fulfil. I feel that the cords of my soul are stretched to their utmost effort. Already seven days! So long! As the dead lights were placed about the body of Abraham, as the friends sat nightly at his feet and watched, [*Slowly sinking down.*] so have I sat for seven days, and wept over the corpse of my love! [*With painful intensity.*]

What have I done? Am I not a child of man? Is not love the right of all, like the air, the light? And, if I stretched my hands towards it, was it a crime? When I first saw him, first heard the sound of his voice, something wound itself around my heart. Then first I knew why I was created, and for the first time was thankful for my life. [*Laying her hand on her brow.*] Collect thyself, mind, and think! What has happened? I saw him yesterday,—no! eight days ago! He was full of love: "You'll come," said he. I came. I left my people. I tore the cords that bound me to my nation, my people, and came to him. He cast me forth into the night. And yet, my heart, you throb still. The Earth still stands, the Sun still shines, as if it had not gone down for ever for me. [*Low.*] By his side stood a handsome maiden, and drew him away with caressing hands. It is her he loves, and to the Jewess he dares offer gold. [*Starting up.*] I will seek him! I will gaze on his face,—[*Church lit up, windows illuminated, organ heard soft.*] that deceitful, beautiful face. I will ask him what I have done, that—[*Hides her head in her hands and weeps; organ swells louder, and then subsides again to low music.*] Perhaps he has been misled by some one,—some false tongue! His looks, his words seem to reproach me. Why was I silent? Thou proud mouth, ye proud lips, why did you not speak? [*Exultingly.*] Perhaps he loves me still. Perhaps his soul, like mine, pines in nameless agony, and yearns for reconciliation. [*Music soft.*] Why does my hate melt away at this soft voice with which Heaven calls to me? That grand music. [*Listening.*] I hear voices; it sounds like a nuptial benediction; perhaps it is a loving bridal pair. [*Clasping her hands, and raising them on high.*] Amen—amen! to that benediction, whoever you may be. [*Music stops.*] I, poor desolate one, would like to see their happy faces; I must—this window. Yes, here I can see into the church. [*Goes to window, looks in, screams, and comes down; speaks very fast.*] Do I dream? Kind Heaven, that prayer, that amen, you heard it not. I call it back. You did not hear my blessing. You were deaf. Did no blood-stained dagger drop down upon them? 'Tis he! Revenge! [*Throws off her mantle, disclosing white robe beneath; bares her arm, and rushes to the little door, but halts.*] No! Thou shalt judge! Thine, Jehovah, is the vengeance. Thou alone canst send it. [*Stands beside broken column, rests her left arm upon it, letting the other fall by her side.*

Enter RUDOLF *from the little door of church, with rose wreath in his hand.*

Rud. I am at last alone. I cannot endure the joy and merriment around me. How like mockery sounded the pious words of the priest. As I gazed towards the church windows, I saw a face, heard a muffled cry. I thought it was her face, her voice.

Leah. [*Coldly.*] Did you think so?

Rud. Leah! is it you?

Leah. Yes.

Rud. [*Tenderly.*] Leah—

Leah. [*With a gesture of contempt.*] Silence, perjured one! Can the tongue that lied still speak? The breath that called me wife now swear faith to another? Does it dare to mix with the pure air of heaven? Is this the man I worshipped? whose features I so fondly gazed upon? Ah! [*Shuddering.*] No—no! The hand of Heaven has crushed, beaten, and defaced them! The stamp of divinity no longer rests there! [*Walks away.*

Rud. Leah! hear me!

Leah. [*Turning fiercely.*] Ha! You call me back! I am pitiless now.

Rud. You broke faith first. You took the money.

Leah. Money! What money?

Rud. The money my father sent you.

Leah. Sent me money! For what?

Rud. [*Hesitating.*] To induce you to release me—to—

Leah. That I might release you. And you knew it. You permitted it?

Rud. I staked my life that you would not take it.

Leah. And you believed I had taken it?

Rud. How could I believe otherwise? I—

Leah. [*With rage.*] And you believed I had taken it? Miserable Christian, and you cast me off! Not a question was the Jewess worth. [*Subdued, but vindictive.*] This, then, was thy work: this the eternity of love which you promised me. [*Falling on her knees.*] Forgive me, Heaven, that I forgot my nation to love this Christian. Let that love be lost in hate. Love is false, unjust; hate endless, eternal.

Rud. Cease these gloomy words of vengeance,—I have wronged you. I feel it without your reproaches. I have sinned, but to sin is human, and it would be but human to forgive.

Leah. You would tempt me again? I do not know that voice.

Rud. I will make good the evil I have done; ay, an hundredfold.

Leah. [*Bitterly.*] Ay, crush the flower, grind it under foot, then make good the evil you have done. [*Fiercely.*] No, no! An eye for an eye, a tooth for a tooth, a heart for a heart.

Rud. Hold, fierce woman, I will beseech no more! Do not tempt Heaven; let it be the judge between us! If I have sinned through love, see that you do not sin through hate.

Leah. Blasphemer! and you dare call on Heaven! What commandment hast thou not broken? Thou shalt not swear falsely,—you broke faith with me! Thou shalt not steal,—you stole my heart. Thou shalt not kill,—what of life have you left me?

Rud. [*Advances towards her.*] Hold, hold! No more.

Leah. [*Repelling him.*] The old man who died because I loved you; the woman who hungered because I followed you; the infant who died of thirst because of you; may they follow you in dreams, and be a drag upon your feet forever! May you wander as I wander, suffer shame as I now suffer it! Cursed be the land you till; may it keep faith with you, as you kept faith with me! Cursed be the unborn fruit of thy marriage! may it wither as my young heart has withered! and, should it ever see the light, may its brows be blackened by the mark of Cain, and may it vainly pant for nourishment on its dying mother's breast! [*Snatching the wreath from his uplifted hand.*] Cursed, thrice cursed may you be evermore! and as my people on Mount Ebal spoke, so speak I thrice, Amen! Amen! Amen!

[RUDOLF, *who has been standing as if petrified, drops on his knees, as the curtain descends on the tableau.*

MARY STUART.

SCHILLER: *Translated by* JOSEPH MELLISH.

ACT III. SCENE IV.

CHARACTERS: ELIZABETH *of England,* MARY *of Scotland, the Earls of* LEICESTER *and* SHREWSBURY, *and* HANNAH KENNEDY, MARY'S *nurse.* MARY, *having abdicated her throne, and after an unsuccessful attempt to retrieve her fortunes, crossed over into England, threw herself on the protection of* ELIZABETH, *but was there made a prisoner for life, was removed from prison to prison, was at last tried on a charge of conspiracy against the life of* ELIZABETH, *and sentenced to death. In the hope of arresting the execution of that sentence,* MARY *solicited, and at length obtained, the privilege of an interview with* ELIZABETH. *This took place at the Castle of Fotheringay, in* 1586. *The scene opens just on the arrival of* ELIZABETH *and her retinue at the castle.*

Eliza. What seat is that, my Lord?
Leices. 'Tis Fotheringay.
Eliza. [*To* SHREWS.] My Lord, send back our retinue to London:
The people crowd too eager in the roads;
We'll seek a refuge in this quiet park.

[SHREWS. *sends the train away.*

My honest people love me overmuch:
Thus should a God be honour'd, not a mortal.

Mary. [*Who the whole time had leaned on* KENNEDY, *rises now, and her eyes meet those of* ELIZA.] O God! from out these features speaks no heart.

Eliza. What lady's that? [*A general silence.*

Leices. You are at Fotheringay,
My Liege!

Eliza. [*As if surprised.*] Who hath done this, my Lord of Leicester?

Leices. 'Tis past, my Queen: and, now that Heaven hath led
Your footsteps hither, be magnanimous,
And let sweet pity be triumphant now.

Shrews. O royal mistress! yield to our entreaties:
O, cast your eyes on this unhappy one,
Who stands dissolved in anguish.

[MARY *collects herself, and begins to advance towards* ELIZA.; *stops shuddering at half way.*

Eliza. How, my Lords!
Which of you then announced to me a prisoner
Bow'd down by woe? I see a haughty one,
By no means humbled by calamity.

Mary. Well, be it so: to this will I submit.—
Farewell high thought, and pride of noble mind!
I will forget my dignity, and all
My sufferings; I will fall before *her* feet,
Who hath reduced me to this wretchedness.—
The voice of Heaven decides for you, my sister.
Your happy brows are now with triumph crown'd;
I bless the Power Divine which thus hath raised you:
[*Kneeling.*] But in your turn be merciful, my sister;
Let me not lie before you thus disgraced:
Stretch forth your hand, your royal hand, to raise
Your sister from the depths of her distress.

Eliza. You are where it becomes you, Lady Stuart;
And thankfully I prize my God's protection,

Who hath not suffered me to kneel a suppliant
Thus at your feet, as you now kneel at mine.
Mary. Think on all earthly things, vicissitudes.
O! there are gods who punish haughty pride:
Respect them, honour them, the dreadful ones
Who thus before thy feet have humbled me!
Before these strangers' eyes, dishonour not
Yourself in me: profane not, nor disgrace
The royal blood of Tudor. In my veins
It flows as pure a stream as in your own.
O! for God's pity, stand not so estranged
And inaccessible, like some tall cliff,
Which the poor shipwreck'd mariner in vain
Struggles to seize, and labours to embrace.
Eliza. What would you say to me, my Lady Stuart?
You wish'd to speak with me; and I, forgetting
The Queen, and all the wrongs I have sustain'd,
Fulfil the pious duty of the sister,
And grant the boon you wish'd for of my presence.
Yet I, in yielding to the generous feelings
Of magnanimity, expose myself
To rightful censure, that I stoop so low:
For well you know, you would have had me murder'd.
Mary. O! how shall I begin? O, how shall I
So artfully arrange my cautious words,
That they may touch, yet not offend your heart?
I am a Queen, like you, yet you have held me
Confined in prison. As a suppliant
I came to you, yet *you* in me insulted
The pious use of hospitality;
Slighting in me the holy law of nations,
Immured me in a dungeon, tore from me
My friends and servants; to unseemly want
I was exposed, and hurried to the bar
Of a disgraceful, insolent tribunal.
No more of this: in everlasting silence
Be buried all the cruelties I suffer'd!

See, I will throw the blame of all on fate;
'Twas not your fault, no more than it was mine:
An evil spirit rose from the abyss,
To kindle in our hearts the flames of hate,
By which our tender youth had been divided:
It grew with us, and bad, designing men
Fann'd with their ready breath the fatal fire.
Now stand we face to face: now, sister, speak;
Name but my crime, I'll fully satisfy you:
Alas! had you vouchsafed to hear me then,
When I so earnest sought to meet your eye,
It never would have come to this, nor would,
Here in this mournful place, have happen'd now
This so distressful, this so mournful meeting.
Eliza. My better stars preserved me. I was warn'd.
And laid not to my breast the poisonous adder!
Accuse not fate! your own deceitful heart
It was, the wild ambition of your House.
But God is with me, and the haughty foe
Has not maintain'd the field. The blow was aim'd
Full at my head, but yours it is which falls!
Mary. I'm in the hand of Heaven. You never will
Exert so cruelly the power it gives you.
Eliza. Who shall prevent me? Say, did not your uncle
Set all the Kings of Europe the example,
How to conclude a peace with those they hate?
Force is my only surety; no alliance
Can be concluded with a race of vipers.
Mary. O, this is but your wretched, dark suspicion!
For you have constantly regarded me
But as a stranger, and an enemy.
Had you declared me heir to your dominions,
As is my right, then gratitude and love
In me had fix'd, for you, a faithful friend
And kinswoman.
Eliza. Your friendship is abroad.
Name *you* my successor! The treacherous snare!

That in my life you might seduce my people;
And, like a sly Armida, in your net
Entangle all our noble English youth;
That all might turn to the new rising Sun,
And I —

Mary. O sister, rule your realm in peace:
I give up every claim to these domains:
Alas! the pinions of my soul are lamed;
Greatness entices me no more: your point
Is gain'd; I am but Mary's shadow now;
My noble spirit is at last broke down
By long captivity: you've done your worst
On me; you have destroy'd me in my bloom!
Now end your work, my sister; speak at length
The word, which to pronounce has brought you hither;
For I will ne'er believe that you are come
To mock unfeelingly your hapless victim.
Pronounce this word; say, "Mary, you are free:
You have already felt my power; learn now
To honour too my generosity."
Say this, and I will take my life, will take
My freedom, as a present from your hands.
One word makes all undone; I wait for it:
O, let it not be needlessly delay'd:
Woe to you, if you end not with this word!
For, should you not, like some divinity
Dispensing noble blessings, quit me now,
Then, sister, not for all this island's wealth,
For all the realms encircled by the deep,
Would I exchange my present lot for yours.

Eliza. And you confess at last, that you are conquer'd.
Are all your schemes run out? no more assassins
Now on the road? will no adventurer
Attempt again, for you, the sad achievement?
Yes, madam, it is over: you'll seduce
No mortal more. The world has other cares;

None is ambitious of the dangerous honour
Of being your fourth husband: you destroy
Your wooers like your husbands.

Mary. Sister, sister!—
Grant me forbearance, all ye powers of Heaven!

Eliza. Those then, my Lord of Leicester, are the charms
Which no man with impunity can view,
Near which no woman dare attempt to stand?
In sooth, this honour has been cheaply gain'd;
She who to all is common may with ease
Become the common object of applause.

Mary. This is too much!

Eliza. You show us now, indeed,
Your real face; till now 'twas but the mask.

Mary. My sins were human, and the faults of youth;
Superior force misled me. I have never
Denied or sought to hide it: I despised
All false appearance as became a Queen:
The worst of me is known, and I can say
That I am better than the fame I bear.
Woe to you! when, in time to come, the world
Shall draw the robe of honour from your deeds.
Virtue was not your portion from your mother;
Well know we what it was which brought the head
Of Anna Boleyn to the fatal block.

Shrews. [*Stepping between them.*] O Heaven! Alas, and must it come to this?
Is this the moderation, the submission,
My Lady?—

Mary. Moderation! I've supported
What human nature can support: farewell,
Lamb-hearted resignation! passive patience,
Fly to thy native Heaven! burst at length
Thy bonds, come forward from thy dreary cave,
In all thy fury, long-suppressèd rancour!
And thou, who to the anger'd basilisk

Impart'st the murderous glance, O, arm my tongue
With poison'd darts!

Shrews. She is beside herself!
Exasperated, mad! My Liege, forgive her.

Leices. Attend not to her rage! Away, away,
From this disastrous place!

Mary. A bastard soils,
Profanes the English throne! The generous Britons
Are cheated by a juggler, whose whole figure
Is false and painted, heart as well as face!
If right prevail'd, you now would in the dust
Before me lie, for I'm your rightful monarch!

[ELIZA. *hastily quits the stage; the Lords follow her in great consternation.*

Ken. What have you done? She has gone hence in wrath.
All hope is over now!

Mary. Gone hence in wrath!
She carries death within her heart! I know it.

[*Falling on* KENNEDY'S *bosom.*

Now I am happy, Hannah! and at last,
After whole years of sorrow and abasement,
One moment of victorious revenge!
A weight falls off my heart, a weight of mountains;
I plunged the steel in my oppressor's breast!

Ken. Unhappy Lady! frenzy overcomes you:
Yes, you have wounded your inveterate foe;
'Tis she who wields the lightning, she is Queen;
You have insulted her before her minion.

Mary. I have abased her before Leicester's eyes;
He saw it, he was witness of my triumph.
How did I hurl her from her haughty height,
He saw it, and his presence strengthen'd me.

RICHELIEU; OR, THE CONSPIRACY.

LORD BULWER-LYTTON.

ACT IV. SCENE I.

CHARACTERS: LOUIS XIII., *King of France; Cardinal* RICHELIEU, *Minister of France;* JULIE DE MORTIMER, *an orphan ward to* RICHELIEU, *and afterwards wife of* ADRIAN DE MAUPRAT; JOSEPH, *a Capuchin Monk, and* RICHELIEU'S *confidant;* CLERMONT, *a courtier, and* BARADAS, *the King's favourite.* JULIE, *through the aid of the Queen, having escaped the clutches of* LOUIS XIII., *flies to the castle of Cardinal* RICHELIEU, *and seeks protection of him. She also implores* RICHELIEU *to protect her husband, who had been seized and made prisoner by* BARADAS. *The King sends* CLERMONT *to conduct* JULIE *into his presence, but* RICHELIEU *refuses to give her up. He then sends* BARADAS *to demand her presence; but* RICHELIEU, *in his hour of political helplessness, throws around his ward the holy protection of the Church, and defies the power of the King.*

Julie. [*To* RICHELIEU.] I ask thee for my home, my fate, my all!
Where is my husband?
Rich. You are Richelieu's ward,
A soldier's bride; they who insist on truth
Must out-face fear: you ask me for your husband?
There, where the clouds of heaven look darkest o'er
The domes of the Bastile!
Julie. O, mercy, mercy!
Save him, restore him, father! Art thou not
The Cardinal King? the Lord of life and death,
Art thou not Richelieu?
Rich. Yesterday I was;
To-day a very weak old man; to-morrow,
I know not what.

Julie. [*To* JOSEPH.] Do you conceive his meaning?
Alas I cannot.
Jos. The King is chafed
Against his servant. Lady, while we speak,
The lacquey of the ante-room is not
More powerless than the Minister of France.

Enter CLERMONT.

Cler. Madame de Mauprat!—
Pardon, your Eminence; even now I seek
This lady's home,—commanded by the King
To pray her presence.
Julie. [*Clinging to* RICH.] Think of my dead father,
And take me to your breast.
Rich. To those who sent you!
And say you found the virtue they would slay
Here, couch'd upon this heart, as at an altar,
And shelter'd by the wings of sacred Rome!
Be gone!
Cler. My Lord, I am your friend and servant,
Misjudge me not; but never yet was Louis
So roused against you: shall I take this answer?
It were to be your foe.
Rich. All time my foe,
If I, a priest, could cast this holy sorrow
Forth from her last asylum!
Cler. He is lost! [*Exit* CLERMONT.
Rich. God help thee, child!—She hears not! Look upon her!
The storm, that rends the oak, uproots the flower.
Her father loved me so! and in that age
When friends are brothers! She has been to me
Soother, nurse, plaything, daughter. Are these tears?
O, shame, shame! dotage! [*Places her in the arms of* JOSEPH.
Jos. Tears are not for eyes
That rather need the lightning! which can pierce
Through barrèd gates and triple walls, to smite

Crime, where it cowers in secret! The dispatch!
Set every spy to work; the morrow's Sun
Must see that written treason in your hands,
Or rise upon your ruin.

Rich. Ay, and close
Upon my corpse; I am not made to live:
Friends, glory, France, all reft from me; my star,
Like some vain holiday mimicry of fire,
Piercing imperial heaven, and falling down
Rayless and blacken'd, to the dust, — a thing
For all men's feet to trample! Yea, to-morrow
Triumph or death! — Look up, child! — Lead us, Joseph!

As they are going up, enter BARADAS.

Bar. My Lord, the King cannot believe your Eminence
So far forgets your duty, and his greatness,
As to resist his mandate. — Pray you, madam,
Obey the King; no cause for fear.

Julie. My father!

Rich. She shall not stir!

Bar. You are not of her kindred;
An orphan —

Rich. And her country is her mother.

Bar. The country is the King.

Rich. Ay, is it so?
Then wakes the power which in the age of iron
Bursts forth to curb the great, and raise the low.
Mark, where she stands: around her form I draw
The awful circle of our solemn Church!
Set but a foot within that holy ground,
And on thy head — yea, though it wore a crown —
I launch the curse of Rome!

Bar. I dare not brave you;
I do but speak the orders of my King:
The Church, your rank, power, very word, my Lord,
Suffice you for resistance; blame yourself,
If it should cost your power.

Rich. That's *my* stake. Ah!
Dark gamester! *what is thine?* Look to it well, —
Lose not a trick. By this same hour to-morrow
Thou shalt have France, or I thy head!

Bar. [*Aside.*] He cannot
Have the dispatch!

Jos. [*Aside, to* RICHELIEU.] Patience is your game;
Reflect, you have not the dispatch!

Rich. O monk!
Leave patience to the saints, for *I* am human! —
[*To* JULIE.] Did not thy father die for France, poor orphan?
And now they say thou hast *no* father! Fie!
Art thou not pure and good? if so, thou art
A part of that — the Beautiful, the sacred —
Which, in all climes, men that have hearts adore,
By the great title of their mother country!

Bar. [*Aside.*] He wanders!

Rich. So, cling close unto my breast:
Here where thou droop'st lies France! I'm very feeble, —
Of little use it seems to either now.
Well, well, we will go home. [*They go up the stage.*]

Bar. In sooth, my Lord,
You do need rest; the burdens of the State
O'ertask your health.

Rich. [*To* JOSEPH; *pauses.*] I'm patient, see!

Bar. [*Aside.*] His mind
And life are breaking fast.

Rich. [*Overhearing him.*] Irreverent ribald!
If so, beware the falling ruins! Hark!
I tell thee, scorner of these whitening hairs,
When this snow melteth there shall come a flood!
Avaunt! my name is Richelieu, — I defy thee!
Walk blindfold on; behind thee stalks the headsman. —
Ha! ha! — how pale he is! Heaven save my country!

[*Falls back in* JOSEPH'S *arms.* JULIE *kneels at his side;* BARADAS *stands*

Curtain falls.

THE SCHOOL FOR SCANDAL.

RICHARD BRINSLEY SHERIDAN.

ACT II. SCENE I.

Sir PETER TEAZLE, *a rich old bachelor, marries the daughter of a poor country squire, having been captivated by her youth, beauty, and fascinating manners. Suddenly raised from poverty to the wealth for which she marries, she plunges into every extravagance, gayety, and frivolity, much to the displeasure of Sir* PETER. *The disparity of their ages causes him to be sneered at by his acquaintances, and to be beset and perplexed by the assaults of a flippant society. This state of affairs is a constant irritant, resulting, very naturally, in many matrimonial quarrels.*

SCENE: *Sir* PETER'S *house.*

Enter Lady TEAZLE *and Sir* PETER.

Sir P. Lady Teazle, Lady Teazle, I'll not bear it!

Lady T. Sir Peter, Sir Peter, you may bear it or not, as you please; but I ought to have my own way in every thing; and, what's more, I will too. What though I was educated in the country, I know very well that women of fashion in London are accountable to nobody after they are married.

Sir P. Very well, ma'am, very well; so a husband is to have no influence, no authority?

Lady T. Authority! No, to be sure: if you wanted authority over me, you should have adopted me, and not married me; I am sure you were old enough.

Sir P. Old enough! ay, there it is! Well, well, Lady Teazle, though my life may be made unhappy by your temper, I'll not be ruined by your extravagance.

Lady T. My extravagance! I'm sure I'm not more extravagant than a woman ought to be.

Sir P. No, no, madam, you shall throw away no more sums on such unmeaning luxury. 'Slife! to spend as much to furnish your dressing-room with flowers in Winter as would suffice to turn the Pantheon into a green-house, and give a fête champêtre at Christmas!

Lady T. Sir Peter, am I to blame because flowers are dear in cold weather? You should find fault with the climate, and not with me. For my part, I'm sure, I wish it was Spring all the year round, and that roses grew under our feet!

Sir P. Oons, madam! if you had been born to this, I shouldn't wonder at your talking thus; but you forget what your situation was when I married you.

Lady T. No, no, I don't; 'twas a very disagreeable one, or I should never have married you.

Sir P. Yes, yes, madam, you were then in somewhat a humbler style, — the daughter of a plain country Squire. Recollect, Lady Teazle, when I first saw you sitting at your tambour, in a pretty figured linen gown, with a bunch of keys at your side; your hair combed smooth over a roll, and your apartment hung round with fruits in worsted, of your own working.

Lady T. O, yes! I remember it very well, and a curious life I led. My daily occupation to inspect the dairy, superintend the poultry, make extracts from the family receipt-book, — and comb my Aunt Deborah's lap-dog.

Sir P. Yes, yes, ma'am, 'twas so, indeed!

Lady T. And then, you know, my evening amusements: To draw patterns for ruffles, which I had not materials to make up; to play Pope Joan with the curate; to read a sermon to my aunt; or to be stuck down to an old spinet to strum my father to sleep after a fox-chase.

Sir P. I am glad you have so good a memory. Yes, madam, these were the recreations I took you from; but now you must have your coach — *vis-à-vis* — and three powdered footmen before your chair; and, in the Summer, a pair of white cats to draw you to Kensington Gardens. No recollection, I suppose, when you were content to ride double, behind the butler, on a docked coach-horse.

Lady T. No, I swear I never did that! I deny the butler and the coach-horse.

Sir P. This, madam, was your situation; and what have I done for you? I have made you a woman of fashion, of fortune, of rank; in short, I have made you my wife.

Lady T. Well then, and there is but one thing more you can make me, and add to the obligation, and that is—

Sir P. My widow, I suppose?

Lady T. Hem! hem!

Sir P. I thank you, madam, but don't flatter yourself; for, though your ill conduct may disturb my peace of mind, it shall never break my heart, I promise you: however, I am equally obliged to you for the hint.

Lady T. Then why will you endeavour to make yourself so disagreeable to me, and thwart me in every little elegant expense?

Sir P. 'Slife, madam! I say, had you any of these little elegant expenses when you married me?

Lady T. Lud, Sir Peter! would you have me be out of the fashion?

Sir P. The fashion, indeed! What had you to do with the fashion before you married me?

Lady T. For my part, I should think you would like to have your wife thought a woman of taste.

Sir P. Ay, there again! taste! Zounds, madam! you had no taste when you married me.

Lady T. That's very true indeed, Sir Peter; and, after having married you, I should never pretend to taste again, I allow. But now, Sir Peter, since we have finished our daily jangle, I presume I may go to my engagement at Lady Sneerwell's?

Sir P. Ay, there's another precious circumstance,—a charming set of acquaintance you have made there!

Lady T. Nay, Sir Peter, they are all people of rank and fortune, and remarkably tenacious of reputation.

Sir P. Yes, egad, they are tenacious of reputation with a vengeance; for they don't choose anybody should have a character but themselves. Such a crew! Ah! many a wretch has rid on a hurdle who has done less mischief than these utterers of forged tales, coiners of scandal, and clippers of reputation.

Lady T. What! would you restrain the freedom of speech?

Sir P. Ah! they have made you just as bad as any one of the society.

Lady T. Why, I believe I do bear a part with a tolerable grace.

Sir P. Grace, indeed!

Lady T. But I vow I bear no malice against the people I abuse. When I say an ill-natured thing, 'tis out of pure good-humour; and I take it for granted, they deal exactly in the same manner with me. But, Sir Peter, you know you promised to come to Lady Sneerwell's too.

Sir P. Well, well; I'll call in just to look after my own character.

Lady T. Then indeed you must make haste after me, or you'll be too late. So, good-bye to ye! [*Exit Lady* TEAZLE.

Sir P. So! I have gained much by my intended expostulation; yet with what a charming air she contradicts every thing I say, and how pleasingly she shows her contempt for my authority! Well, though I can't make her love me, there is great satisfaction in quarrelling with her; and I think she never appears to such advantage as when she is doing every thing in her power to plague me. [*Exit.*

ACT III. SCENE I.

SCENE: *Sir* PETER TEAZLE'S *house. More matrimonial troubles. Sir* PETER *has been bitterly reproving his ward,* MARIA, *who has just left the room.*

Sir P. Was ever man so crossed as I am? Every thing conspiring to fret me! I had not been involved in matrimony a fortnight, before her father, a hale and hearty man, died, on purpose, I believe, for the pleasure of plaguing me with the care of his daughter. [*Lady* TEAZLE *sings without.*] But here comes my helpmate! She appears in great good-humour. How happy I should be if I could tease her into loving me, though but a little!

Enter Lady TEAZLE.

Lady T. Lud! Sir Peter, I hope you haven't been quarrelling with Maria? It is not using me well to be ill-humoured when I am not by.

Sir P. Ah! Lady Teazle, you might have the power to make me good-humoured at all times.

Lady T. I am sure I wish I had; for I want you to be in a charming sweet temper at this moment. Do be good-humoured now, and let me have two hundred pounds, will you?

Sir P. Two hundred pounds! What, ain't I to be in a good-humour without paying for it? But speak to me thus, and i' faith there's nothing I could refuse you. You shall have it; [*Gives her notes.*] but seal me a bond of repayment.

Lady T. O no! there, my note of hand will do as well. [*Offering her hand.*]

Sir P. And you shall no longer reproach me with not giving you an independent settlement. I mean shortly to surprise you: but shall we always live thus, hey?

Lady T. If you please. I'm sure I don't care how soon we leave off quarrelling, provided you'll own you were tired first.

Sir P. Well, then let our future contest be, who shall be most obliging.

Lady T. I assure you, Sir Peter, good-nature becomes you. You look now as you did before we were married, when you used to walk with me under the elms, and tell me stories of what a gallant you were in your youth; and chuck me under the chin, you would; and ask me if I thought I could love an old fellow, who would deny me nothing; didn't you?

Sir P. Yes, yes; and you were as kind and attentive —

Lady T. Ay, so I was, and would always take your part, when my acquaintance used to abuse you, and turn you into ridicule.

Sir P. Indeed!

Lady T. Ay, and when my cousin Sophy has called you a stiff, peevish old bachelor, and laughed at me for thinking of marrying one who might be my father, I have always defended you, and said I didn't think you so ugly by any means.

Sir P. Thank you.

Lady T. And I dared say you'd make a very good sort of a husband.

Sir P. And you prophesied right; and we shall now be the happiest couple —

Lady T. And never differ again. [*Both sit.*]

Sir P. No, never! — though at the same time, indeed, my dear Lady Teazle, you must watch your temper very seriously; for in all our little quarrels, my dear, if you recollect, my love, you always begin.

Lady T. I beg your pardon, my dear Sir Peter; indeed, you always gave the provocation.

Sir P. Now see, my angel! take care, — contradicting isn't the way to keep friends.

Lady T. Then don't you begin it, my love!

Sir P. There, now! you — you are going on. You don't perceive, my life, that you are just doing the very thing which you know always makes me angry.

Lady T. Nay, you know if you will be angry without any reason, my dear —

Sir P. There! now you want to quarrel again.

Lady T. No, I am sure I don't; but if you will be so peevish —

Sir P. There now! who begins first?

Lady T. Why, you, to be sure. [*Both start up.*] I said nothing; but there's no bearing your temper.

Sir P. No, no, madam; the fault's in your own temper.

Lady T. Ay, you are just what my cousin Sophy said you would be.

Sir P. Your cousin Sophy is a forward, impertinent gypsy.

Lady T. You are a great bear, I'm sure, to abuse my relations.

Sir P. Now, may all the plagues of marriage be doubled on me, if ever I try to be friends with you any more.

Lady T. So much the better.

Sir P. No, no, madam; 'tis evident you never cared a pin for me, and I was a madman to marry you, — a pert, rural coquette, that had refused half the honest squires in the neighbourhood.

Lady T. And I am sure I was a fool to marry you, — an old dangling bachelor, who was single at fifty, only because he never could meet with any one who would have him.

Sir P. Ay, ay, madam; but you were pleased enough to listen to me; you never had such an offer before.

Lady T. No? didn't I refuse Sir Tivy Terrier, who everybody said would have been a better match? for his estate is just as good as yours, and he has broke his neck since we have been married.

Sir P. I have done with you, madam! You are an unfeeling, ungrateful — but there's an end of every thing. I believe you capable of every thing that is bad. Yes, madam, I now believe the reports relative to you and Charles, madam. Yes, madam, *you* and Charles are — not without grounds —

Lady T. Take care, Sir Peter! you had better not insinuate any such thing! I'll not be suspected without cause, I promise you.

Sir P. Very well, madam! very well! A separate maintenance as soon as you please! Yes madam, or a divorce! I'll make an example of myself for the benefit of all old bachelors. Let us separate, madam.

Lady T. Agreed, agreed! And, now, my dear Sir Peter, we are of a mind once more, we may be the happiest couple, and never differ again, you know, — ha! ha! ha! Well, you are going to be in a passion, I see, and I shall only interrupt you; so, bye, bye. [*Exit.*

Sir P. Plagues and tortures! Can't I make her angry, either? O, I am the most miserable fellow! but I'll not bear her presuming to keep her temper. [*Exit.*

VIRGINIUS.

JAMES SHERIDAN KNOWLES.

ACT I. SCENE II.

CHARACTERS: VIRGINIUS, *a Roman Father;* VIRGINIA, *his daughter;* SERVIA, *godmother to* VIRGINIA; ICILIUS, *a young Roman soldier, in love with* VIRGINIA; DENTATUS, *an old Decemvir.*

SCENE: VIRGINIUS' *house in Rome.*

Enter VIRGINIUS *and* SERVIA, *with some of* VIRGINIA'S *work in her hand.*

Vir. And is this all you have observed? I think
There's nothing strange in that. An L and an I,
Twined with a V. Three very innocent letters,
To have bred such mischief in thy brain, good Servia!
Come, read this riddle to me.

Serv. You may laugh,
Virginius, but I will read the riddle right.
The L doth stand for Lucius; and the I,
Icilius; which, I take it, will compose
Lucius Icilius.

Vir. So it will, good Servia.

Serv. Then, for the V; why, that is plain Virginia.

Vir. And now what conjuration find you here?

Serv. What should I find but love? The maid's in love,

And it is with Icilius. Look, the wreath
Is made of roses, that entwines the letters.
Vir. And this is all?
Serv. And is it not enough?
You'll find this figuring where'er you look:
There's not a piece of dainty work she does, —
Embroidery or painting, — not a task
She finishes, but on the skirt or border,
In needle-work or pencil, this her secret
The silly wench betrays.
Vir. Go, send her to me.
Stay! Have you spoken to her of it?
Serv. I?
Not I, indeed; I left that task to you.
Though once I ask'd her what the letters meant,
She laugh'd, and drew a scratch across them; but
Had scarce done so, ere her fair visage fell,
For grief that she had spoil'd the ciphers; and
A sigh came out, and then almost a tear;
And she did look as piteous on the harm
That she had done, as she had done it to
A thing had sense to feel it. Never after
She let me note her at the work again.
She had good reason!
Vir. Send her to me, Servia. [*Exit* SERVIA.
There's something here that looks as it would bring me
Anticipation of my wish. I think
Icilius loves my daughter, — nay, I know it;
And such a man I'd challenge for her husband,
And only waited till her forward Spring
Put on, a little more, the genial likeness
Of colouring into Summer, ere I sought
To nurse a flower, which, blossoming too early,
Too early often dies; but, if it wooes
Our hand to tend and cherish it, the growth
Is natural, and 'twere unkind to check it.
I'll ascertain it shortly: soft! she comes. [*Sits.*

Enter VIRGINIA.

Virg. Well, father, what's your will?
Vir. I wish'd to see you,
To ask you of your tasks, — how they go on;
And what your masters say of you; what last
You did. I hope you never play the truant?
Virg. The truant! No, indeed, Virginius.
Vir. I'm sure you do not. Kiss me.
Virg. O my father,
I am so happy when you're kind to me!
Vir. You are so happy when I'm kind to you!
Am I not always kind? I never spoke
An angry word to you in all my life,
Virginia! You are happy when I'm kind!
That's strange; and makes me think you have some
Reason to fear I may be otherwise than kind:
Is't so, my girl?
Virg. Indeed, I did not know
What I was saying to you!
Vir. Why, that's worse
And worse! What! when you said your father's kindness
Made you so happy, am I to believe
You were not thinking of him?
Virg. I — [*Greatly confused.*
Vir. Go, fetch me
The latest task you did. It is enough. — [*Exit* VIRGINIA.
Her artless speech, like crystal, shows the thing
'Twould hide, but only covers. 'Tis enough!
She loves, and fears her father may condemn.

Re-enter VIRGINIA *with a painting.*

Virg. Here, Sir.
Vir. What's this?
Virg. 'Tis Homer's history
Of great Achilles parting from Briseis.
Vir. You've done it well: the colouring is good;

The figure's well design'd: 'tis very well!
Whose face is this you've given to Achilles?
Virg. Whose face?
Vir. I've seen this face! Tut, tut! I know it
As well as I do my own, yet can't bethink me
Whose face it is!
Virg. You mean Achilles' face?
Vir. Did I not say so? 'Tis the very face
Of — No, no! not of him: there's too much youth
And comeliness; and too much fire to suit
The face of Siccius Dentatus.
Virg. O!
You surely never took it for his face!
Vir. Why, no; for, now I look again, I'd swear
You lost the copy ere you drew the head,
And, to requite Achilles for the want
Of his own face, contrived to borrow one
From Lucius Icilius. — My Dentatus,

Enter DENTATUS.

I'm glad to see you! [*Rises;* VIRGINIA *retires.*
Den. 'Tis not for my news, then.
Vir. Your news! What news?

Den. More violence and wrong from these new masters of ours, our noble Decemvirs, — these demi-gods of the good people of Rome! No man's property is safe from them. Nay, it appears we hold our wives and daughters but by the tenure of their will. Their liking is the law. The Senators themselves, scared at their audacious rule, withdraw themselves to their villas, and leave us to our fate. There are rumours, also, of new incursions by the Sabines.

Vir. Rome never saw such days.

Den. And she'll see worse, unless I fail in my reckoning. Is that Virginia? [*Goes to her.*] I saw her not before. — How does the fair Virginia? — Why, she is quite a woman. I was just now wishing for a daughter.

Vir. A plague, you mean.

Den. I'm sure you should not say so.
Virg. Indeed he should not; and he does not say so,
Dentatus; not that I am not a plague,
But that he does not think me one, for all
I do to weary him. I'm sure, Dentatus,
If to be thought to do well is to do well,
There's nothing I do ill. But it is far
From that! for few things do I as I ought;
Yet every thing is well done with my father,
Dentatus.
Vir. [*Goes to them.*] That's well done, is it not, my friend? [*Aside.*
But, if you had a daughter, what would you do with her?

Den. I'd give her to Içilius. I should have been just now torn to pieces, but for his good offices. The gentle citizens that are driven about by the Decemvirs' Lictors, like a herd of tame oxen, and, with the most beast-like docility, only low applauses to them in return, would have done me the kindness to knock my brains out; but the noble Icilius bearded them singly, and railed them into temper. Had I a daughter worthy of such a husband, he should have such a wife, and a Patrician's dower along with her.

Vir. I wish to speak with you, Dentatus. [*They retire.*] Icilius is a young man whom I honour, but so far only as his conduct gives me warrant. He has had, as thou knowest, a principal hand in helping us to our Decemvirs. It may be that he is what I would gladly think him; but I must see him clearly, clearly, Dentatus. [*Exeunt* VIR. *and* DEN.

Virg. How is it with my heart? I feel as one
That has lost every thing, and just before
Had nothing left to wish for! He will cast
Icilius off! — I never told it yet;
But take of me, thou gentle air, the secret,
And ever after breathe more balmy sweet,
I love Icilius! Yes, although to thee
I fear to tell it, that hast neither eye
To scan my looks, nor voice to echo me,

Nor e'en an o'er-apt ear to catch my words;
Yet, sweet invisible confidant, my secret
Once being thine, I tell thee, and I tell thee
Again, and yet again, I love Icilius!
He'll cast Icilius off! — not if Icilius
Approves his honour. That he'll ever do;
He speaks and looks and moves a thing of honour,
Or honour ne'er yet spoke, or look'd, or moved,
Or was a thing of Earth. — O, come, Icilius!
Do but appear, and thou art vindicated.

Enter ICILIUS.

Ici. Virginia! sweet Virginia! sure I heard
My name pronounced. Was it by thee, Virginia?
Thou dost not answer? Then it was by thee:
O, wouldst thou tell me why thou namedst Icilius!
Virg. My father is incensed with thee: Dentatus
Has told him of the new Decemvirate,
How they abuse their office. You, he knows,
Have favour'd their election, and he fears
May have some understanding of their plans.
Ici. He wrongs me then!
Virg. I thank the gods!
Ici. For me,
Virginia? do you thank the gods for me?
Your eye is moist, yet that may be for pity;
Your hand doth tremble, that may be for fear;
Your cheek is cover'd o'er with blushes! what,
O, what can that be for?
Virg. Icilius, leave me!
Ici. Leave thee, Virginia? O, a word, a word
Trembles upon my tongue, which, if it match
The thought that moves thee now, and thou wilt let me
Pronounce that word, to speak that thought for thee,
I'll breathe, though I expire in th' ecstasy
Of uttering it.
Virg. Icilius, will you leave me?

Ici. Love, love, Virginia, love! If I have spoke
Thy thought aright, ne'er be it said again:
The heart requires more service than the tongue
Can, at its best, perform. My tongue hath served
Two hearts; but, lest it should o'erboast itself,
Two hearts with but one thought. Virginia!
Virginia, speak. [*She covers her face with her hands.*
O, I have loved thee long:
So much the more ecstatic my delight,
To find thee mine at length!
Virg. My secret's yours.
Keep it and honour it, Icilius.

Re-enter VIRGINIUS *and* DENTATUS *behind.*

Vir. Icilius here!
Virg. I ask thee now to leave me.
Ici. Leave thee! Who leaves a treasure he has coveted
So long, and found so newly, ere he scans it
Again, and o'er again; and asks and answers,
Repeats and answers, answers and repeats,
The half-mistrustful, half-assurèd question,
And is it mine indeed?
Virg. Indeed, indeed!
Now leave me.
Ici. I must see thy father first,
And lay my soul before him.
Virg. Not to-night.
Ici. Now worse than ever, dear Virginia,
Can I endure his doubts: I'll lay my soul
Naked before him; win his friendship quite,
Or lose myself forever! [*Going, is met by* VIRGINIUS.
Vir. Stop, Icilius!
Thou see'st that hand? It is a Roman's, boy;
'Tis sworn to liberty; it is the friend
Of honour. Dost thou think so?
Ici. Do I think
Virginius owns that hand?

Vir. Then you'll believe
It has an oath deadly to tyranny,
And is the foe of falsehood! By the gods,
Knew it the lurking place of treason, though
It were a brother's heart, 'twould drag the caitiff
Forth. Darest thou take the hand?
Ici. I dare, Virginius.
Vir. Then take it! Is it weak in thy embrace?
Returns it not thy gripe? Thou wilt not hold
Faster by it than it will hold by thee.
I overheard thee say, thou wast resolved
To win my friendship quite: thou canst not win
What thou hast won already! You will stay
And sup with us to-night?
Den. To be sure, he will.
Vir. And hark you, sir:
At your convenient time, appoint a day
Your friends and kinsmen may confer with me;
There is a bargain I would strike with you.
Come to the supper-room.

Act II. Scene II.

Virginius' *house.* *Enter* Virginius, Icilius, Numitorius, Lucius, *and others.*

Vir. Welcome, Icilius! — Welcome, friends! — Icilius,
I did design to speak with you of feasting
And merriment, but war is now the word, —
One that unlovingly keeps time with mirth,
Unless war's own; whene'er the battle's won,
And, safe carousing, comrades drink to victory!
Ici. Virginius, have you changed your mind?
Vir. My mind?
What mind? How now! Are you that boy, Icilius,
You set your heart so earnestly upon
A dish of poor confections, that to baulk you

Makes you look blank? I did design to feast you
Together with your friends. The times are changed;
The march, the tent, the fight becomes us now!

Ici. Virginius!

Vir. Well?

Ici. Virginius!

Vir. How the boy
Reiterates my name!

Ici. There's not a hope
I have, but is the client of Virginius.

Vir. Well, well! I only meant to put it off:
We'll have the revel yet; the board shall smoke;
The cup shall sparkle, and the jest shall soar
And mock us from the roof. Will that content you?
Not till the war be done, though. Yet, ere then,
Some tongue, that now needs only wag to make
The table ring, may have a tale to tell
So petrifying that it cannot utter it.
I'll make all sure, that you may be my guest
At any rate; although you should be forced
To play the host for me, and feast yourself.
Look here. [*Shows him a parchment.*] How think you? Will it meet the charge?
Will it not do? We want a witness though:
I'll bring one; whom, if you approve, I'll sign
The bond. I'll wait upon you instantly. [*Exit.*

Re-enter VIRGINIUS, *with* VIRGINIA *and* NUMITORIUS.

Vir. [*Holding his daughter's hand.*] You are my witnesses,
That this young creature I present to you,
I do pronounce my profitably-cherish'd,
And most deservedly-belovèd child;
My daughter, truly filial both in word
And act, yet even more in act than word;
And — for the man who seeks to win her love —
A virgin, from whose lips a soul as pure

Exhales, as e'er responded to the blessing
Breathed in a parent's kiss. [*Kisses her.*] — Icilius! [ICIL. *rushes towards* VIR., *and kneels.*] Since
You are upon your knees, young man, look up,
And lift your hands to Heaven. You will be all
Her father has been, added unto all
A lover would be!

Ici. All that man should be
To woman, I will be to her!

Vir. The oath
Is register'd! [ICILIUS *rises.*] Didst thou but know, [*Takes a hand of each.*] young man,
How fondly I have watch'd her, since the day
Her mother died, and left me to a charge
Of double duty bound; how she hath been
My ponder'd thought by day, my dream by night,
My prayer, my vow, my offering, my praise,
My sweet companion, pupil, tutor, child;
Thou wouldst not wonder, that my drowning eye
And choking utterance upbraid my tongue,
That tells thee she is thine! [*Joins their hands.*] Icilius,
I do betroth her to thee; let but the war
Be done, you shall espouse her. Now farewell;
Your sword and buckler, boy! The foe, the foe!
Does he not tread on Roman ground? Come on,
Come on! charge on him, drive him back, or die!

ACT IV. SCENE II.

APPIUS, *enamoured of* VIRGINIA, *wishes to get possession of her; to this end he engages* CLAUDIUS *to claim her as his slave, who was sold as an infant to the wife of* VIRGINIUS; *on the trial* CLAUDIUS *produces his slave, who swears that* VIRGINIA *is her child, and* APPIUS, *who is in power, accepts this false evidence. Enter* VIRGINIUS, *leading his daughter*, VIRGINIA; NUMITORIUS, *her uncle;* ICILIUS, *her husband;* SERVIA, *her godmother; and women and children.*

SCENE: *The Forum.* APPIUS *seated on the tribunal, surrounded by his lictors and soldiers.* CLAUDIUS *stands near. A dead silence prevails.*

Vir. Does no one speak? I am defendant here:
Is silence my opponent? Fit opponent
To plead a cause too foul for speech! What brow,
Shameless, gives front to this most valiant cause,
And tries its prowess 'gainst the honour of
A girl, yet lacks the wit to know that they
Who cast off shame should likewise cast off fear,
And on the verge o' the combat wants the nerve
To stammer forth the signal?
App. You had better,
Virginius, wear another kind of carriage:
This is not of the fashion that will serve you.
Vir. [*Having left* VIRGINIA *with* ICILIUS.] The fashion,
Appius! Appius Claudius, tell me
The fashion it becomes a man to speak in,
Whose property in his own child, the offspring
Of his own body, near to him as is
His hand, his arm, — yea, nearer, closer far,
Knit to his heart, — I say, who has this property
Disputed, — and I'll speak so, Appius Claudius;
I'll speak so. Pray you, tutor me.
App. Stand forth,
Claudius! If you lay claim to any interest
I' the question now before us, speak; if not,
Bring on some other cause.
Claud. Most noble Appius —
Vir. And are you the man
That claims my daughter for his slave? Look at me,
And I will give her to thee.
Claud. She is mine, then:
Do I not look at you?
Vir. Your eye does, truly,
But not your soul. I see it through your eye,

Shifting and shrinking, turning every way
To shun me. You surprise me, that your eye
But gives the port of impudence to falsehood,
When it would pass it off for truth. Your soul
Dares as soon show its face to me! Go on,
I had forgot; the fashion of my speech
May not please Appius Claudius.

Claud. I demand
Protection of the Decemvir!

App. You shall have it.

Vir. Doubtless!

App. Keep back the people, Lictors!—What's
Your plea? You say the girl's your slave. Produce
Your proofs.

Claud. My proof is here, which, if they can,
Let them confront. The mother of the girl—

[VIRGINIUS, *about to speak, is withheld by* NUMITORIUS.

Num. Hold, brother! Hear them out, or suffer me
To speak.

Vir. Man, I must speak, or else go mad!
And if I do go mad, what then will hold me
From speaking? Were't not better, brother, think you,
To speak, and not go mad, than utter madness?
Well, well, speak thou. I'll try, and, if I can,
Be silent. [*Retires.*

Num. Will she swear she is her child?

Vir. [*Starting forward.*] Be sure she will; a most wise question that!
She not his slave? Will his tongue lie for him,
Or his hand steal, or the finger of his hand
Beckon, or point, or shut, or open for him?
To ask him if she'll swear! Will she walk or run,
Sing, dance, or wag her head? do any thing
That is most easy done? She'll swear as soon!
What mockery it is, to have one's life
In jeopardy by such a bare-faced trick!
Is it to be endured? I do protest
Against her oath!

App. No law in Rome, Virginius,
Seconds you. If she swear the girl's her child,
The evidence is good, unless confronted
By better evidence. Look you to that,
Virginius. I shall take the woman's oath.

Virg. Icilius!

Ici. Fear not, love: a thousand oaths
Will answer her.

App. [*To the slave.*] You swear the girl's your child,
And that you sold her to Virginius' wife,
Who pass'd her for her own. Is that your oath?

Slave. [*Coming round to the front of the tribunal.*] It is my oath.

App. Your answer now, Virginius.

Vir. [*Bringing* VIRG. *forward.*] Here it is!
Is this the daughter of a slave? I know
'Tis not with men, as shrubs and trees, that by
The shoot you know the rank and order of
The stem. Yet who from such a stem would look
For such a shoot? My witnesses are these, —
The friends and relatives of Numitoria. —
Speak for me, friends: have I not spoke the truth?

Women and Citizens. You have, Virginius.

App. Silence! keep silence there. No more of that!
You're very ready for a tumult, citizens. —
[*Troops appear behind.*
Lictors, make way to let these troops advance! —
We've had a taste of your forbearance, masters,
And wish not for another.

Vir. Troops i' the Forum!

App. Virginius, have you spoken?

Vir. If you've heard me,
I have; if not, I'll speak again.

App. You need not,
Virginius; I have evidence to give,
Which, should you speak a hundred times again,
Would make your pleading vain.

Vir. [*Aside.*] Your hand, Virginia!
Stand close to me.
App. My conscience will not let me
Be silent. 'Tis notorious to you all,
That Claudius' father, at his death, declared me
The guardian of his son. This cheat has long
Been known to me. I know the girl is not
Virginius' daughter.
Vir. [*Aside.*] Join your friends, Icilius,
And leave Virginia to my care.
Vir. [*Aside.*] Don't tremble, girl, don't tremble.
App. Virginius,
I feel for you; but, though you were my father,
The majesty of justice should be sacred:
Claudius must take Virginia home with him!
Vir. And, if he must, I should advise him, Appius,
To take her home in time, before his guardian
Complete the violation, which his eyes
Already have begun. — [*Turning to citizens.*] Friends, fellow citizens!
Look not on Claudius; look on your Decemvir!
He is the master claims Virginia.
The tongues that told him she was not my child
Are these, — the costly charms he cannot purchase,
Except by making her the slave of Claudius,
His client, his purveyor, that caters for
His pleasures; markets for him; picks and scents
And tastes, that he may banquet; serves him up
His sensual feast, and is not now ashamed,
In th' open, common street, before your eyes, —
Frightening your daughters' and your matrons' cheeks
With blushes they ne'er thought to meet, — to help him
To th' honour of a Roman maid! my child!
Who now clings to me, as you see, as if
This second Tarquin had already coil'd
His arms around her. Look upon her, Romans!
Befriend her! succour her! see her not polluted

Before her father's eyes! He is but one.
Tear her from Appius and his Lictors, while
She is unstain'd. Your hands! your hands! your hands!
Citizens. They're yours, Virginius.
App. Keep the people back: —
Support my Lictors, soldiers! — Seize the girl,
And drive the people back.
Ici. Down with the slaves!

[*The people make a show of resistance, but, upon the advancing of the soldiers, retreat, and leave* ICILIUS, VIRGINIUS, *and his daughter in the hands of* APPIUS *and his party.*

Deserted! — Cowards, traitors! — Let me free, —
Let me but loose a moment, if 'tis only
To rush upon your swords!
Vir. Icilius, peace!
You see how 'tis; we are deserted, left
Alone, surrounded by our enemies,
Nerveless and helpless.
App. Away with him!
Ici. Virginia! — Tyrant! — My Virginia!
App. Away with him! [ICIL. *is taken aside.*] Separate them, Lictors!
Vir. Let them forbear awhile, I pray you, Appius:
It is not very easy. Though her arms
Are tender, yet the hold is strong by which
She grasps me, Appius. Forcing them will hurt them.
They'll soon unclasp themselves. Wait but a little;
You know you're sure of her!
App. I have not time
To idle with thee; give her to my Lictors.
Vir. Appius, I pray you, wait! If she is not
My child, she hath been like a child to me
For fifteen years. If I am not her father,
I have been like a father to her, Appius,
For even such a time. Let me but take
The maid aside, I pray you, and confer

A moment with her nurse; perhaps she'll give me
Some token, will unloose a tie so twined
And knotted round my heart, that, if you break it,
My heart breaks with it.

App. Have your wish. Be brief! —
Lictors, look to them.

Virg. Do you go from me?
Do you leave? Father! Father!

Vir. No, my child;
No, my Virginia: come along with me.

Virg. Will you not leave me? Will you take me with you?
Will you take me home again? O, bless you, bless you!
My father! my dear father! Art thou not
My father?

[VIRGINIUS, *perfectly at a loss what to do, looks anxiously around the Forum; at length his eye falls on a butcher's stall, with a knife upon it.*

Vir. This way, my child. No, no! I am not going
To leave thee, my Virginia! I'll not leave thee.

App. Keep back the people, soldiers! let them not
Approach Virginius! keep the people back! —

[VIRGINIUS *secures the knife in the folds of his toga.*

Well, have you done?

Vir. Short time for converse, Appius; but
I have.

App. I hope you're satisfied.

Vir. I am —
I am — that she's my daughter!

App. Take her, Lictors!

[VIRGINIA *shrieks, and falls half dead upon her father's shoulder.*

Vir. Another moment, pray you. Bear with me
A little; 'tis my last embrace: 'twon't try
Your patience beyond bearing, if you're a man!
Lengthen it as I may, I cannot make it
Long. — My dear child! my dear Virginia! [*Kissing her.*
There is one only way to save thine honour, —

'Tis this! — [*Stabs her, and draws out the knife. She falls and dies.*] Lo, Appius! with this innocent blood,
I do devote thee to th' infernal gods! —
Make way there!

App. Stop him! Seize him!

Vir. If they dare
To tempt the desperate weapon that is madden'd
With drinking my daughter's blood, why, let them: thus
It rushes in amongst them. — Way there! Way!

[*Exit through the soldiers.*

ION; A TRAGEDY.

Sir T. N. Talfourd.

Act I. Scene I.

Characters: Agenor, Cleon, *and* Timocles, *Sages of Argos;* Medon, *High-Priest of Apollo;* Clemanthe, *his daughter;* Habra, *her attendant.* Ion, *the hero, was stolen from his nursery while an infant, by two villains, with the intent of putting him to death; but, just as they were in the act of doing this, one of the men perished through a sudden accident; which so struck the other with fear and remorse that he left the child in the Grove of Apollo, where he was found by* Medon, *and brought up as his foster-son. In the course of the play,* Ion *is discovered to have been the first-born of* Adrastus, *the tyrant king of Argos.*

Scene: *The interior of the Temple of Apollo, which is supposed to be built on a rocky eminence. Early morning.*

Present, Agenor: *To him enter* Cleon.

Cleon. Agenor, hail!
Dark as our lot remains, 'tis comfort yet
To find thy age unstricken.

Age. Rather mourn
That I am destined still to linger here
In strange unnatural strength, while death is round me.
I chide these sinews that are framed so tough
Grief cannot palsy them; I chide the air
Which round this citadel of Nature breathes
With sweetness not of this world; I would share
The common grave of my dear countrymen,
And sink to rest while all familiar things
Old custom has endear'd are failing with me,
Rather than shiver on in life behind them:
Nor should these walls detain me from the paths
Where death may be embraced, but that my word,
In a rash moment plighted to our host,
Forbids me to depart without his license,
Which firmly he refuses.

Cleon. Do not chide me
If I rejoice to find the generous Priest
Means, with Apollo's blessing, to preserve
The treasure of thy wisdom: nay, he trusts not
To promises alone; his gates are barr'd
Against thy egress: none, indeed, may pass them
Save the youth Ion, to whose earnest prayer
His foster-father grants reluctant leave
To visit the sad city at his will:
And freely does he use the dangerous boon,
Which, in my thought, the love that cherish'd him,
Since he was found within the sacred grove
Smiling amidst the storm, a most rare infant,
Should have had sternness to deny.

Age. What, Ion
The only inmate of this fane allow'd
To seek the mournful walks where death is busy!
Ion, our sometime darling, whom we prized
As a stray gift, by bounteous Heaven dismiss'd
From some bright sphere which sorrow may not cloud,
To make the happy happier! Is *he* sent

To grapple with the miseries of this time,
Whose nature such ethereal aspect wears
As it would perish at the touch of wrong?
By no internal contest is he train'd
For such hard duty; no emotion rude
Hath his clear spirit vanquish'd: Love, the germ
Of his mild nature, hath spread graces forth,
Expanding with its progress, as the store
Of rainbów colours which the seed conceals
Sheds out its tints from its dim treasury,
To flush and circle in the flower. No tear
Hath fill'd his eye save that of thoughtful joy
When, in the evening stillness, lovely things
Press'd on his soul too busily: his voice,
If, in the earnestness of childish sports,
Raised to the tone of anger, check'd its force,
As if it fear'd to break its being's law,
And falter'd into music: when the forms
Of guilty passion have been made to live
In pictured speech, and others have wax'd loud
In righteous indignation, he hath heard
With sceptic smile, or from some slender vein
Of goodness, which surrounding gloom conceal'd,
Struck sunlight o'er it: so his life hath flow'd
From its mysterious urn a sacred stream,
In whose calm depth the beautiful and pure
Alone are mirror'd; which, though shapes of ill
May hover round its surface, glides in light,
And takes no shadow from them.

Cleon. Yet, methinks,
Thou hast not lately met him, or a change
Pass'd strangely on him had not miss'd thy wonder.
His form appears dilated; in those eyes
Where pleasure danced, a thoughtful sadness dwells;
Stern purpose knits the forehead, which till now
Knew not the passing wrinkle of a care:
Those limbs which in their heedless motion own'd

A stripling's playful happiness are strung
As if the iron hardships of the camp
Had given them sturdy nurture; and his step,
Its airiness of yesterday forgotten,
Awakes the echoes of these desolate courts,
As if a hero of gigantic mould
Paced them in armour.
Age. Hope is in thy tale.
This is no freak of Nature's wayward course,
But work of pitying Heaven; for not in vain
The gods have pour'd into that guileless heart
The strengths that nerve the hero; they are ours.
Cleon. How can he aid us? Can he stay the pulse
Of ebbing life, arrest th' infected winds,
Or smite the hungry spectre of the grave?
Age. And dost thou think these breezes are our foes,
The innocent airs that used to dance around us,
As if they felt the blessings they convey'd,
Or that the death they bear is casual? No!
'Tis human guilt that blackens in the cloud,
Flashes athwart its mass in jagged fire,
Whirls in the hurricane, pollutes the air,
Turns all the joyous melodies of Earth
To murmurings of doom. There is a foe
Who in the glorious summit of the State
Draws down the great resentment of the gods,
Whom he defies to strike us; yet his power
Partakes that just infirmity which Nature
Blends in the empire of her proudest sons, —
That it is cased within a single breast,
And may be pluck'd thence by a single arm.
Let but that arm, selected by the gods,
Do its great office on the tyrant's life,
And Argos breathes again!
Cleon. A footstep! hush!
Thy wishes, falling on a slavish ear,
Would tempt another outrage: 'tis a friend, —

An honest though a crabbed one, — Timocles:
Something hath ruffled him. — Good day, Timocles! —
[TIMOCLES *passes in front.*
He will not speak to us.
Age. But he *shall* speak. —
Timocles!—nay then, thus I must enforce thee: [*Staying him.*
Thou wilt not cast from thee a comrade's hand
That may be cold ere sunset.
Tim. [*Giving his hand.*] Thou mayst school me;
Thy years and love have license: but I own not
A stripling's mastery: is't fit, Agenor?
Age. Nay, thou must tell thy wrong: whate'er it prove,
I hail thy anger as a hopeful sign,
For it revives the thought of household days,
When the small bickerings of friends had space
To fret, and Death was not for ever nigh
To frown upon Estrangement. What has moved thee?
Tim. I blush to tell it. Weary of the night
And of my life, I sought the western portal:
It open'd, when, ascending from the stair
That through the rock winds spiral from the town,
Ion, the foundling cherish'd by the Priest,
Stood in the entrance: with such mild command
As he has often smilingly obey'd,
I bade him stand aside and let me pass;
When, — wouldst thou think it? — in determined speech,
He gave me counsel to return: I press'd
Impatient onward; he, with honied phrase
His daring act excusing, grasp'd my arm
With strength resistless; led me from the gate;
Replaced its ponderous bars; and, with a look
As modest as he wore in childhood, left me.
Age. And thou wilt thank him for it soon: he comes;
Now hold thy angry purpose if thou canst!

Enter ION.

Ion. I seek thee, good Timocles, to implore
Again thy pardon. I am young in trust,

And fear lest, in the earnestness of love,
I stay'd thy course too rudely. Thou hast borne
My childish folly often: do not frown
If I have ventured with unmanner'd zeal
To guard the ripe experience of years
From one rash moment's danger.

Tim. Leave thy care.
If I am weary of the flutterer life,
Is mortal bidding thus to cage it in?

Ion. And art thou tired of being? Has the grave
No terrors for thee? Hast thou sunder'd quite
Those thousand meshes which old custom weaves
To bind us earthward, and gay fancy films
With airy lustre various? Hast subdued
Those cleavings of the spirit to its prison,
Those nice regards, dear habits, pensive memories,
That change the valour of the thoughtful breast
To brave dissimulation of its fears?
Is Hope quench'd in thy bosom? Thou art free,
And in the simple dignity of man
Standest apart untempted: do not lose
The great occasion thou hast plucked from misery,
Nor play the spendthrift with a great despair,
But use it nobly!

Tim. What, to strike? to slay?

Ion. No! not unless the audible voice of Heaven
Call thee to that dire office; but to shed,
On ears abused by falsehood, truths of power
In words immortal; not such words as flash
From the fierce demagogue's unthinking rage,
To madden for a moment and expire;
Nor such as the rapt orator imbues
With warmth of facile sympathy, and moulds
To mirrors radiant with fair images,
To grace the noble fervour of an hour;
But words which bear the spirits of great deeds
Wing'd for the Future; which the dying breath

Of Freedom's martyr shapes as it exhales,
And to the most enduring forms of Earth
Commits, to linger in the craggy shade
Of the huge valley, 'neath the eagle's home,
Till some heroic leader bid them wake
To thrill the world with echoes! But I talk
Of things above my grasp, which strangely press
Upon my soul, and tempt me to forget
The duties of my youth: pray you forgive me.

Tim. Have I not said so?

Age. Welcome to the morn!
The eastern gates unfold, the Priest approaches;

[*As* AGENOR *speaks, the great gates at the back of the scene open; the sea is discovered far beneath, the dawn breaking over it;* MEDON, *the Priest, enters attended.*

And, lo! the Sun is struggling with the gloom,
Whose masses fill the eastern sky, and tints
Its edges with dull red: but he *will* triumph;
Bless'd be the omen!

Med. God of light and joy,
Once more refresh us with thy healing beams!
If I may trace thy language in the clouds
That wait upon thy rising, help is nigh,
But help achieved in blood.

Ion. Say'st thou in blood?

Med. Yes, Ion! — why, he sickens at the word,
Spite of his new-born strength: the sights of woe
That he will seek have shed their paleness on him. —
Has this night's walk shown more than common sorrow?

Ion. I pass'd the palace where the frantic King
Yet holds his crimson revel, whence the roar
Of desperate mirth came mingling with the sigh
Of death-subdued robustness, and the gleam
Of festal lamps, 'mid spectral columns hung
Flaunting o'er shapes of anguish, made them ghastlier.
How can I cease to tremble for the sadness
He mocks, and him the wretchedest of all?

Tim. And canst thou pity him? Dost thou discern,
Amidst his impious darings, plea for him?

Ion. Is he not childless, friendless, and a king?
He's human; and some pulse of good must live
Within his nature: have ye tried to wake it?

Med. Yes, I believe he felt our sufferings once;
When, at my strong entreaty, he dispatch'd
Phocion my son to Delphos, there to seek
Our cause of sorrow; but, as time dragg'd on
Without his messenger's return, he grew
Impatient of all counsel; to his palace
In awful mood retiring, wildly call'd
The reckless of his Court to share his stores,
And end all with him. When we dared disturb
His dreadful feastings with a humble prayer
That he would meet us, the poor slave who bore
The message flew back smarting from the scourge,
And mutter'd a decree that he who next
Unbidden met the tyrant's glance should die.

Age. I am prepared to brave it.

Cleon. So am I.

Tim. And I.

Ion. O Sages! — do not think my prayer
Bespeaks unseemly forwardness, — send me:
The coarsest reed that trembles in the marsh,
If Heaven select it for its instrument,
May shed celestial music on the breeze
As dearly as the pipe whose virgin gold
Befits the lip of Phœbus. Ye are wise,
And needed by your country; ye are fathers:
I am a lone stray thing, whose little life
By strangers' bounty cherish'd, like a wave
That from the summer sea a wanton breeze
Lifts for a moment's sparkle, will subside
Light as it rose, nor leave a sigh in breaking.

Med. Ion, no sigh!

Ion. Forgive me if I seem'd

To doubt that thou wilt mourn me if I fall;
Nor would I tax thy love with such a fear;
But that high promptings, which could never rise
Spontaneous in my nature, bid me plead
Thus boldly for the mission.

Med. My brave boy!
It shall be as thou wilt. I see thou'rt call'd
To this great peril, and I will not stay thee.
When wilt thou be prepared to seek it?

Ion. Now.
Only, before I go, thus, on my knee
Let me in one word thank thee for a life
Made by thy love one cloudless holiday;
And, O my more than father! let me look
Up to thy face as if indeed a father's,
And give me a son's blessing.

Med. Bless thee, son!
I should be marble now: let's part at once.

Ion. If I should not return, bless Phocion for me;
And, for Clemanthe, may I speak one word,
One parting word with my fair playfellow?

Med. If thou wouldst have it so, thou shalt.

Ion. Farewell, then!
Your prayers wait on my steps: the arm of Heaven,
I feel, in life or death will be around me. [*Exit.*

Med. O, grant it be in life! Let's to the sacrifice.
[*Exeunt.*

SCENE II.: *An Apartment of the Temple.*

Enter CLEMANTHE *followed by* HABRA.

Clem. Is he so changed?

Habra. His bearing is so alter'd,
That, distant, I scarce knew him for himself;
But, looking in his face, I felt his smile
Gracious as ever, though his sweetness wore
Unwonted sorrow in it.

Clem. He will go
To some high fortune, and forget us all,
Reclaim'd — be sure of it — by noble parents:
Me he forgets already; for five days,
Five melancholy days, I have not seen him.
Habra. Thou know'st that he has privilege to range
Th' infected city; and 'tis said he spends
The hours of needful rest in squalid hovels
Where death is most forsaken.
Clem. Why is this?
Why should my father, niggard of the lives
Of agèd men, be prodigal of youth
So rich in glorious prophecy as his?
Habra. He comes to answer for himself. I'll leave you.
[*Exit.*
Clem. Stay! —Well, my heart may guard its secret best
By its own strength.

Enter ION.

Ion. How fares my pensive sister?
Clem. How shall I fare but ill when the pale hand
Draws the black foldings of th' eternal curtain
Closer and closer round us; Phocion absent,
And thou, forsaking all within thy home,
Wilt risk thy life with strangers, in whose aid
Even thou canst do but little?
Ion. It is little;
But, in these sharp extremities of fortune,
The blessings which the weak and poor can scatter
Have their own season. 'Tis a little thing
To give a cup of water; yet its draught
Of cool refreshment, drain'd by fever'd lips,
May give a shock of pleasure to the frame
More exquisite than when Nectarean juice
Renews the life of joy in happiest hours.
It is a little thing to speak a phrase
Of common comfort which by daily use

Has almost lost its sense ; yet, on the ear
Of him who thought to die unmourn'd, 'twill fall
Like choicest music ; fill the glazing eye
With gentle tears ; relax the knotted hand
To know the bonds of fellowship again ;
And shed on the departing soul a sense,
More precious than the benison of friends
About the honour'd death-bed of the rich,
To him who else were lonely, that another
Of the great family is near and feels.

Clem. O, thou canst never bear these mournful offices !
So blithe, so merry once ! Will not the sight
Of frenzied agonies unfix thy reason,
Or the dumb woe congeal thee ?

Ion. No, Clemanthe :
They are the patient sorrows that touch nearest !
If thou had'st seen the warrior, when he writhed
In the last grapple of his sinewy frame,
With conquering anguish strive to cast a smile
(And not in vain) upon his fragile wife,
Waning beside him ; and, his limbs composed,
The widow of the moment fix her gaze
Of longing, speechless love upon the babe,
The only living thing which yet was hers,
Spreading its arms for its own resting-place,
Yet with attenuated hand wave off
Th' unstricken child, and so embraceless die,
Stifling the mighty hunger of the heart ;
Thou couldst endure the sight of selfish grief
In sullenness or frenzy : but to-day
Another lot falls on me.

Clem. Thou wilt leave us !
I read it plainly in thy alter'd mien :
Is it forever ?

Ion. That is with the gods !
I go but to the palace, urged by hope,
Which from afar hath darted on my soul,

That to the humbleness of one like me
The haughty King may listen.
Clem. To the palaçe!
Know'st thou the peril, nay, the certain issue
That waits thee? Death! the tyrant has decreed it,
Confirm'd it with an oath; and he has power
To keep that oath: for, hated as he is,
The reckless soldiers who partake his riot
Are swift to do his bidding.
Ion. I know all:
But they who call me to the work can shield me,
Or make me strong to suffer.
Clem. Then the sword
Falls on thy neck! O Gods! to think that thou,
Who in the plenitude of youthful life
Art now before me, ere the Sun decline,
Perhaps in one short hour, shalt lie cold, cold,
To speak, smile, bless no more! Thou shalt not go!
Ion. Thou must not stay me, fair one; even thy father,
Who (blessings on him!) loves me as his son,
Yields to the will of Heaven.
Clem. And he can do this!
I shall not bear his presence if thou fall'st
By his consent; so shall I be alone.
Ion. Phocion will soon return, and juster thoughts
Of thy admiring father close the gap
Thy old companion left behind him.
Clem. Never!
What will to me be father; brother, friends,
When thou art gone, the light of our life quench'd,
Haunting like spectres of departed joy
The home where thou wert dearest?
Ion. Thrill me not
With words that, in their agony, suggest
A hope too ravishing, or my head will swim,
And my heart faint within me.
Clem. Has my speech

Such blessèd power? I will not mourn it then,
Though it hath told a secret I had borne
Till death in silence. How affection grew
To this, I know not: day succeeded day,
Each fraught with the same innocent delights,
Without one shock to ruffle the disguise
Of sisterly regard which veil'd it well,
Till thy changed mien reveal'd it to my soul,
And thy great peril makes me bold to tell it.
Do not despise it in me!

Ion. With deep joy
Thus I receive it. Trust me, it is long
Since I have learn'd to tremble 'midst our pleasures,
Lest I should break the golden dream around me
With most ungrateful rashness. I should bless
The sharp and perilous duty which hath press'd
A life's deliciousness into these moments, —
Which here must end. I came to say farewell,
And the word must be said.

Clem. Thou canst not mean it!
Have I disclaim'd all maiden bashfulness,
To tell the cherish'd secret of my soul
To my soul's master, and in rich return
Obtain'd the dear assurance of his love,
To hear him speak that miserable word
I cannot, will not echo?

Ion. Heaven has call'd me,
And I have pledged my honour. When thy heart
Bestow'd its preference on a friendless boy,
Thou didst not image him a recreant; nor
Must he prove so, by thy election crown'd.
Thou hast endow'd me with a right to claim
Thy help through this our journey, be its course
Lengthen'd to age, or in an hour to end;
And now I ask it! bid my courage hold,
And with thy free approval send me forth
In soul apparell'd for my office!

Clem. Go!
I would not have thee other than thou art,
Living or dying; and, if thou shouldst fall, —
Ion. Be sure I shall return.
Clem. If thou shouldst fall,
I shall be happier as th' affianced bride
Of thy cold ashes, than in the proudest fortunes.
Thine, — ever thine — [*She faints in his arms.*
Ion. [*Calls.*] Habra! — So best to part. —

Enter HABRA.

Let her have air; be near her through the day;
I know thy tenderness: should ill news come
Of any friend, she will require it all. —
[HABRA *bears* CLEMANTHE *out.*
Ye Gods, that have enrich'd the life ye claim
With priceless treasure, strengthen me to yield it! [*Exit.*

DON CARLOS.

Translated by BOYLAN.

ACT III. SCENE IX.

CHARACTERS: PHILIP THE SECOND, *King of Spain, and the* MARQUESS DE POSA. *The* KING, *having heard that of* POSA *which made him curious to see and study the man, face to face, has had him summoned to an interview.*

SCENE: *The* KING'S *Cabinet.*

The MARQUESS *alone.*

Marq. How came I here? Is it caprice or chance
That shows me now my image in this mirror?
Why, out of millions, should it picture me,—
The most unlikely,—and present my form

To the King's memory? Was this but chance?
Perhaps 'twas something more! What else is chance
But the rude stone which from the sculptor's hand
Receives its life? Chance comes from Providence,
And man must mould it to his own designs.
What the King wants with me but little matters;
I know the business I shall have with him.
Were but one spark of truth with boldness flung
Into the despot's soul, how fruitful 'twere
In the kind hand of Providence! and so
What first appear'd capricious act of chance,
May be designed for some momentous end.
Whate'er it be, I'll act on this belief.

Enter the KING.

[*The* MARQUESS, *as soon as he sees the* KING, *comes forward and sinks on one knee; then rises and remains standing before him.*

King. We've met before, then?
Marq. No.
King. You did my Crown
Some service: why, then, do you shun my thanks?
My memory is throng'd with suitors' claims:
One only is Omniscient. 'Twas your duty
To seek your monarch's eye! Why did you not?
Marq. Two days have scarce elapsed since my return
From foreign travel, Sire.
King. I would not stand
Indebted to a subject: ask some favour.
Marq. I enjoy the laws.
King. So does the murderer!
Marq. Then how much more the honest citizen!
My lot contents me, Sire.
King. [*Aside.*] By Heavens, a proud
And dauntless mind! That was to be expected.
Proud I would have my Spaniards; better far

The cup should overflow than not be full.—
They say you've left my service.
Marq. To make way
For some one worthier, I withdrew.
King. 'Tis pity:
When spirits such as yours make holiday,
The State must suffer. But perchance you fear'd
To miss the post best suited to your merits.
Marq. O no! I doubt not the experienced judge,
In human nature skill'd, — his proper study, —
Will have discover'd at a glance wherein
I may be useful to him, wherein not.
With deepest gratitude, I feel the favour
Wherewith, by so exalted an opinion,
Your Majesty is loading me; and yet — [*He pauses.*
King. You hesitate?
Marq. I am, I must confess,
Sire, at this moment unprepared to clothe
My thoughts, as the world's citizen, in phrase
Beseeming to your subject. When I left
The Court for ever, Sire, I deem'd myself
Released from the necessity to give
My reasons for this step.
King. Are they so weak?
What do you fear to risk by their disclosure?
Marq. My life at farthest, Sire, were time allow'd
For me to weary you; but, this denied,
Then truth itself must suffer. I must choose
'Twixt your displeasure and contempt; and, if
I must decide, I rather would appear
Worthy of punishment than pity.
King. Well?
Marq. I cannot be the servant of a prince.
[*The* KING *looks at him with astonishment.*
I will not cheat the buyer. Should you deem
Me worthy of your service, you prescribe
A course of duty for me; you command

My arm in battle and my head in council:
Then, not my actions, but th' applause they meet
At Court becomes their object. But, for me,
Virtue possesses an intrinsic worth:
I would myself create that happiness
A monarch, with my hand, would seek to plant;
And duty's task would prove an inward joy,
And be my willing choice. Say, like you this?
And, in your own creation, could you bear
A new creator? For I ne'er could stoop
To be the chisel, where I fain would be
The sculptor's self. I dearly love mankind,
My Gracious Liege, but in a monarchy,
I dare not love another than myself.

King. This ardour is most laudable. You wish
To do good deeds to others; how you do them,
Is but of small account to patriots,
Or to the wise. Choose, then, within these realms
The office where you best may satisfy
The noble impulse.

Marq. 'Tis not to be found.

King. How!

Marq. What your Majesty would spread abroad,
Through these my hands, is it the good of men?
Is it the happiness that my pure love
Would to mankind impart? Before such bliss
Monarchs would tremble. No! Court policy
Has raised up new enjoyments for mankind,
Which she is always rich enough to grant;
And waken'd, in the hearts of men, new wishes
Which such enjoyments only can content.
In her own mint she coins the truth, — such truth
As she herself can tolerate! all forms
Unlike her own are broken. But is that
Which can content the Court enough for me?
Must my affection for my brother pledge
Itself to work my brother injury?

To call him happy, when he dare not think?
Sire, choose not me, to spread the happiness
Which you have stamp'd for us: I must decline
To circulate such coin. I cannot be
The servant of a prince.

King. You are, perhaps,
A Protestant?

Marq. Our creeds, my liege, are one. [*A pause.*
I am misunderstood: I fear'd as much.
You see the veil torn by my hand aside
From all the mysteries of Majesty.
Who can assure you I shall still regard
As sacred that which ceases to alarm me?
I may seem dangerous, because I think
Above myself. I am not so, my Liege;
My wishes lie corroding here. [*Laying his hand on his breast.*
The rage
For innovation, which but serves t' increase
The heavy weight of chains it cannot break,
Shall never fire my blood! The world is yet
Unripe for my Ideal; and I live
A citizen of ages yet to come.
But does a fancied picture break your rest?
A breath of yours destroys it.

King. Say, am I
The first to whom your views are known?

Marq. You are.

King. [*Aside.*] This tone, at least, is new; but flattery
Exhausts itself; and men of talent still
Disdain to imitate: so let us test
Its opposite for once. Why should I not?
There is a charm in novelty. — Should we
Be so agreed, I will bethink me now
Of some new State employment, in whose duties
Your powerful mind —

Marq. Sire, I perceive how small,
How mean, your notions are of manly worth,

Suspecting, in an honest man's discourse,
Nought but a flatterer's artifice: methinks
I can explain the cause of this your error.
Mankind compel you to it: with free choice
They have disclaim'd their true nobility,
Lower'd themselves to their degraded state.
Before man's inward worth, as from a phantom,
They fly in terror, and, contented with
Their poverty, they ornament their chains
With slavish prudence, and they call it virtue,
To bear them with a show of resignation.
Thus did you find the world, and thus it was
By your great father handed o'er to you.
In this debased condition, how could you
Respect mankind?

King. Your words contain some truth.

Marq. Alas, that, when from the Creator's hand
You took mankind, and moulded him to suit
Your own ideas, making yourself the god
Of this new creature, you should overlook
That you yourself remained a human being,
A very man, as from God's hands you came!
Still did you feel a mortal's wants and pains;
You needed sympathy; but to a God
One can but sacrifice, and pray, and tremble.
Wretched exchange! Perversion most unblest
Of sacred nature! Once degrade mankind,
And make him but a thing to play upon,
Who then can share the harmony with you?

King. [*Aside.*] By Heaven, he moves me!

Marq. But this sacrifice
To you is valueless. You thus become
A thing apart, a species of your own:
This is the price you pay for being a god!
'Twere dreadful were it not so, and if you
Gain'd nothing by the misery of millions
As if the very freedom you destroy'd

Were the sole blessing that could make you happy!
Dismiss me, Sire, I pray you; for my theme
Bears me too far; my heart is full; too strong
The charm, to stand before the only man
To whom I may reveal it.

King. Nay, continue.

Marq. I feel, Sire, all the worth — [*He pauses.*

King. Proceed; you had
Yet more to say to me.

Marq. Your Majesty,
I lately pass'd through Flanders and Brabant,
So many rich and blooming provinces,
Fill'd with a valiant, great, and honest people.
To be the father of a race like this
I thought must be divine indeed! and then
I stumbled on a heap of burnt men's bones!

[*He stops, and fixes a penetrating look on the* King.

True, you are forced to act so; but that you
Could dare fulfil your task, this fills my soul
With shuddering horror! O, 'tis pity that
The Victim, weltering in his blood, must cease
To chant the praises of his sacrificer!
And that mere men — not beings loftier far —
Should write the history of the world. But soon
A milder age will follow that of Philip,
An age of truer wisdom: hand in hand,
The subjects' welfare and the Sovereign's greatness
Will walk in union. Then the careful State
Will spare her children, and necessity
No longer glory to be thus inhuman.

King. When, think you, would that blessèd age arrive,
If I had shrunk before the curse of this?
Behold my Spain; see here the burgher's good
Blooms in eternal and unclouded peace.
A peace like this will I bestow on Flanders.

Marq. The churchyard's peace! And do you hope to end
What you have now begun? Say, do you hope

To check the ripening change of Christendom,
The universal Spring, that shall renew
The Earth's fair form? Would you alone, in Europe,
Fling yourself down before the rapid wheel
Of destiny, which rolls its ceaseless course,
And seize its spokes with human arm? Vain thought!
Already thousands have your kingdom fled
In joyful poverty: the honest burgher,
For his faith exiled, was your noblest subject.
See, with a mother's arms, Elizabeth
Welcomes the fugitives, and Britain blooms
In rich luxuriance from our country's arts.
Bereft of the new Christian's industry,
Grenada lies forsaken, and all Europe,
Exulting, sees its foe oppress'd with wounds,
By its own hands inflicted! You would plant
For all eternity; and yet the seeds
You sow around you are the seeds of death!
This hopeless task, with Nature's laws at strife,
Will ne'er survive the spirit of its founder.
You labour for ingratitude in vain;
With Nature you engage in desperate struggle;
In vain you waste your high and royal life
In projects of destruction. Man is greater
Than you esteem him: he will burst the chains
Of a long slumber, and reclaim once more
His just and hallow'd rights. With Nero's name,
And fell Busiris', will he couple yours:
And — ah! you once deserved a better fate.
King. How know you that?
Marq. In very truth you did, —
Yes, I repeat it, — by the Almighty power!
Restore us all you have deprived us of,
And, generous as strong, let happiness
Flow from your horn of plenty; let man's mind
Ripen in your vast empire; give us back
All you have taken from us; and become

Amidst a thousand kings, a king indeed!
O, that the eloquence of all those myriads
Whose fate depends on this momentous hour
Could hover on my lips, and fan the spark
That lights thine eye into a glorious flame!
Renounce the mimicry of godlike powers
Which levels us to nothing; be, in truth,
An image of the Deity himself!
Never did mortal man possess so much,
For purpose so divine. The kings of Europe
Pay homage to the name of Spain: be you
The leader of these kings: one pen-stroke now,
One motion of your hand, can new create
The Earth! but grant us liberty of thought.
[*Casts himself at his feet.*

King. Enthusiast most strange! arise; but I—

Marq. Look round on all the glorious face of Nature:
On freedom it is founded; see how rich,
Through freedom, it has grown. The great Creator
Bestows upon the worm its drop of dew,
And gives free-will a triumph in abodes
Where lone corruption reigns. See *your* creation,
How small, how poor! The rustling of a leaf
Alarms the powerful lord of Christendom:
Each virtue makes you quake with fear; while He,
Rather than mar blest freedom's sacred rule,
Lets evil blemish and untune His order.
Th' Almighty works through universal laws,
Himself unseen: the sceptic, seeing these,
And owning nought beyond his vision, asks,
"Wherefore a God? the world goes of itself,
It needs no God." And ne'er did Christian worship
More praise Him than this scoffer's blasphemy.

King. And will you undertake to raise up this
Exalted standard of weak human nature
In my dominions?

Marq. You can do it, Sire!
Who else? Devote to your own people's bliss
The kingly power, which has too long enrich'd
The greatness of the throne alone: restore
The prostrate dignity of human nature;
And let the subject be, what once he was,
The end and object of the monarch's care,
Bound by no duty save a brother's love.
And, when mankind is to itself restored,
Roused to a sense of its own innate worth;
When freedom's lofty virtues proudly flourish;
Then, Sire, when you have made your own wide realms
The happiest in the world, it then may be
Your duty to subdue the Universe.
King. I've heard you to the end: far differently,
I find, than in the minds of other men
The world exists in yours. And you shall not
By foreign laws be judged: I am the first
To whom you have your secret self disclosed;
I know it, so believe it. For the sake
Of this forbearance, — that you have till now
Conceal'd these sentiments, although embraced
With so much ardour, — for this cautious prudence,
I will forget, young man, that I have learn'd them,
And how I learn'd them. Rise! I will confute
Your youthful dreams by my matured experience,
Not by my power as king: such is my will;
And therefore act I thus. Poison itself
May, in a worthy nature, be transform'd
To some benignant use. But, Sir, beware
My Inquisition! 'Twould afflict me much —
Marq. Indeed!
King. [*Aside.*] Ne'er met I such a man as this! —
No, Marquess, no! you wrong me! Not to you
Will I become a Nero, — not to you!
All happiness shall not be blasted round me;

And you, at least, beneath my very eyes
May dare continue still to be a man.
Marq. And, Sire! my fellow subjects? Not for me,
Nor my own cause, I pleaded. Sire, your subjects —
King. Nay, if you know so well how future times
Will judge me, let them learn at least from you
That, when I found a man, I could respect him.
Marq. O, let not the most just of kings at once
Be the most unjust! In your realm of Flanders
There are a thousand better men than I.
But you, — Sire, may I dare to say so much? —
For the first time perhaps, see liberty
In milder form portray'd.
King. No more of this,
Young man! you would, I know, think otherwise
Had you but learn'd to understand mankind
As I. But, truly, I would not this meeting
Should prove our last. How can I hope to win you?
Marq. Pray, leave me as I am. What value, Sire,
Should I be to you, were you to corrupt me?
King. This pride I will not bear. From this day forth
I hold you in my service. No remonstrance,
For I will have it so. But how is this?
What would I now? Was it not truth I wish'd?
But here is something more. Marquess, so far
You've learn'd to know me as a King; but yet
You know me not as man. Just such a man
As you I long have wish'd for: you are kind,
Cheerful, and deeply versed in human nature;
Therefore I've chosen you —
Marq. [*Surprised and alarmed.*] Me, Sire!
King. You stand
Before your King and ask no special favour, —
For yourself nothing! — that is new to me;
You will be just; ne'er weakly swayed by passion.
Retire. [*Exit the Marquess*

INDEXES.

I. INDEX TO SCENES FROM SHAKESPEARE.

[In this Index, we have endeavoured to collect and arrange for convenient reference those scenes which are best suited to public readings, and which will give the clearest idea of the dominant characters and dramatic situations of the plays. The scenes embrace all the varieties of matter and purpose as discriminated in the table of contents, but no attempt is made to range them under characteristic headings; though the cast and spirit of each scene are meant to be indicated by the statement here given of its special subject. — For the sake of convenience in the class-room and the social circle, and also because a standard edition with expurgated text is highly desirable for such use, the references here made are to the Rev. H. N. Hudson's series of "Annotated English Classics," as far as that series extends, and to his Harvard Edition of Shakespeare for the rest of the plays.]

ANTONY AND CLEOPATRA.

AS YOU LIKE IT.

CORIOLANUS.

CYMBELINE.

HAMLET.

I. 2. Hamlet's anguish at the death of his father, his mother's shameful disrespect to the memory of his father, and his surprise on learning of the appearance of his father's ghost. From "*Ham.* O, that this too-too solid flesh would melt." ..62–68

I. 4. The platform scene. Hamlet's surprise and awe when the Ghost first appears to him. His determination to follow and question it. To "*Ham.* I say, away!—Go on; I'll follow thee." Omit the twenty-two lines, from "This heavy-headed revel" to "To his own scandal."........................75–80

I. 5. The Ghost reveals to Hamlet the crime of Claudius. To "*Ham.* I have sworn 't."..................................80–86

II. 2. Hamlet reviles and storms at himself for not killing Claudius. From "*Ham.* Now I am alone." 121–124

III. 1. Hamlet's soliloquy on death, and his dialogue with Ophelia. From "*Ham.* To be, or not to be," to "*Ophe.* T' have seen what I have seen, see what I see!"................127–132

III. 2. Hamlet's advice to the players, his friendship for Horatio, and his artful refusal to be entrapped by the King's spies. To "*Ham.* I will speak daggers to her, but use none."....133–151
Omit all after "I must be idle; get you a place," to "Come, some music!"......................................137–147

III. 4. The closet scene. Hamlet's interview with his mother; the death of Polonius; the re-appearance of the Ghost. To "*Ham.* Thus bad begins, and worse remains behind."....156–165
Omit the lines beginning "That monster, custom," and ending "With wondrous potency."......................... 164

IV. 2. Ophelia's madness. To "*King.* It springs all from her father's death."......................................177–180

V. 1. The grave-digging scene. Colloquy of the two Clowns; Hamlet's talk with one of them; and the burial of Ophelia. To "The cat will mew, the dog will have his day."......199–211

V. 2. The catastrophe. Death of the Queen; Laertes falls, and makes known his treacherous plotting with the King against Hamlet's life; Hamlet kills Claudius, forgives Laertes, and dies. From "*King.* Come, Hamlet, come, and take this hand," to "*Hor.* And flights of angels sing thee to thy rest!"..224–230

KING HENRY THE FOURTH, PART FIRST.

I. 2. Prince Henry and Pointz lay plans by which they may have some merriment at the expense of Falstaff...........59–69

KING HENRY THE FOURTH, PART SECOND.

KING HENRY THE FIFTH.

V. 1. Henry wooing the Princess Catharine. From "*King Hen.* Fair Catharine, and most fair!" to "*K. Henry.* I am content."..161–169

KING HENRY THE EIGHTH.

II. 4. Catharine earnestly pleads for justice at the hands of the King. From "*Cath.* Sir, I desire you do me right and justice," to "In any of their courts."....................95–100

III. 1. Catharine's indignation at the proposal by ambassadors that she admit the justice of the divorce. "Nothing but death shall e'er divorce my dignities." From "*Cath.* How now!"..106–112

III. 2. Wolsey's downfall and depression. From "*Wol.* Farewell, a long farewell, to all my greatness!".................129–133

IV. 2. The death of Queen Catharine........................140–148

JULIUS CÆSAR.

I. 2. The scheming Cassius instigates Brutus to join in a conspiracy against Cæsar. From "*Bru.* What means this shouting?" to "*Cass.* As easily as a king!".............49–53

II. 1. Portia's anxious appeal to learn the cause of Brutus' abstraction. From "*Portia.* Brutus, my lord!" to "*Bru.* And by-and-by thy bosom shall partake the secrets of my heart." 85–89

III. 1. Antony's wily dissimulation in the presence of the assassins when they "render him their bloody hands." His mourning over the dead body of Cæsar. From "*Bru.* But here comes Antony.—Welcome, Mark Antony," to "*Ant.* With carrion men groaning for burial."................110–116

III. 2. The orations of Brutus and Antony over the body of Cæsar. From "*Bru.* Be patient till the last," to "*Ant.* Take thou what course thou wilt!".........................117–129

IV. 3. The quarrel of Brutus and Cassius. To "*Bru.* He'll think your mother chides and leave you so."................137–143

KING JOHN.

III. 1. Lady Constance's extreme surprise and contempt for the marriage of Louis and Blanch. She gives expression to her distress in the most stinging and bitter reproaches. To "*Const.* And hang a calf's skin on those recreant limbs."..74–79
Omit the seven lines beginning "Or, if it must stand still.". 78

III. 4. The grief of Constance at the loss of her son Arthur. To "*Const.* My widow-comfort, and my sorrows' cure!".......92–96

KING LEAR.

MACBETH.

MERCHANT OF VENICE.

MIDSUMMER-NIGHT'S DREAM.

MUCH ADO ABOUT NOTHING.

OTHELLO.

KING RICHARD THE SECOND.

KING RICHARD THE THIRD.

ROMEO AND JULIET.

COMEDY OF ERRORS.

HARVARD EDITION, VOL. I.

KING HENRY THE SIXTH, PART FIRST.

HARVARD EDITION, VOL. VIII.

KING HENRY THE SIXTH, PART SECOND.

HARVARD EDITION, VOL. VIII.

KING HENRY THE SIXTH, PART THIRD.

HARVARD EDITION, VOL. IX.

LOVE'S LABOUR LOST.

HARVARD EDITION, VOL. II.

II. 1. A merry war of wit and coquetry in the Court of Navarre, 23–33

MEASURE FOR MEASURE.

HARVARD EDITION, VOL. VI.

V. 1. Isabella proves her innocence, and, with the aid of the Duke and Provost, rescues her brother Claudio from death. Omit "I find an apt remission in myself," and what follows, 242

MERRY WIVES OF WINDSOR.

HARVARD EDITION, VOL. VI.

III. 3. The trick of the Merry Wives. In order to conceal Falstaff from their husbands, they put him in a basket of clothes, and the servants "empty it in a muddy ditch close by the Thames." 60–68

III. 5. Falstaff's comical description of the situation. To "*Fal.* Think of that, Master Brook!" 72–76

IV. 2. Falstaff's second exploit. This time he escapes detection by disappearing in a woman's dress 80–87

V. 1. Falstaff resolves to make a third adventure with Mrs. Ford, 97–98

PERICLES.

HARVARD EDITION, VOL. XIX.

V. 1. Marina, with her singing, awakens Pericles from his trance, and, "by her own most clear remembrance, makes known herself his daughter." The surprise and joy of Pericles. From "*Hel.* Sure, all's effectless," to "[*Exeunt all but* PERICLES." 90–98

V. 2. Pericles goes to Ephesus to offer sacrifice to Diana, and while in the temple is transported with joy at meeting with his Queen, whom he supposed to be dead. To "*Enter* GOWER." 100–103

THE TAMING OF THE SHREW.

HARVARD EDITION, VOL. II.

II. 1. Petruchio's humorous wooing of Catharine. From "*Pet.* Signior Baptista, my business asketh haste," to "*Pet.* And kiss me, Kate; we will be married o' Sunday." 177–184

V. 2. The astonishment of the company when Petruchio wins the wager by the prompt and cheerful obedience of his wife 234–241

TIMON OF ATHENS.

HARVARD EDITION, VOL. XV.

TITUS ANDRONICUS.

HARVARD EDITION, VOL. XIII.

TROILUS AND CRESSIDA.

HARVARD EDITION, VOL. XVI.

TWO GENTLEMEN OF VERONA.

HARVARD EDITION, VOL. I.

IV. 2. Julia is cast off by Proteus. Disguised as a boy, she becomes his servant. He sends her to woo Silvia for him. She recounts to Silvia the grief and loneliness of Julia. From "*Pro.* Sebastian is thy name? I like thee well."..228–235

II. INDEX TO READINGS FROM THE BIBLE.

[The following selections are made with reference to their adaptation to public reading. We do not claim that this list covers the whole ground, or includes all the choice readings from the Scriptures, but that the selection and classification have been carefully made. In many cases, marked differences of sentiment occur in the same chapter; so that it is not always easy to decide just where, in our order, a given chapter should be placed; but it is believed that, on the whole, the selections are assigned to those places which best fit their general character. — The brief titles we give to the chapters are intended merely to announce the subject in as few words as possible. — The numerals on the right hand of the page refer to the characteristic headings under which the matter of the volume is distributed, as set forth in the Table of Contents.]

III. INDEX TO HYMNS.

[As the titles of hymns are not always the same in the different denominational hymn-books, and as we do not wish to quote any particular hymn-book in preference to others, we make this an index to the first lines. We have chosen the hymns best adapted to use in reading rather than those which have become popular from the tunes they are commonly sung to. We do not claim that the whole of each hymn has the character of the division to which it is referred ; for it often happens that the first part of a hymn is in a joyous, triumphant mood, while the latter part is a solemn prayer; but the general sentiment of the selection will be found to accord with the classification here given.]

I. NARRATIVE, DESCRIPTIVE, DIDACTIC.

II. LOVE, BEAUTY, TRANQUILLITY.

"Forever with the Lord!" .... *James Montgomery.*
Hail, sweetest, dearest tie that binds .... *Sutton.*
How blest the righteous when he dies! .... *Mrs. A. L. Barbauld.*
How happy is the Christian's state ....
How sweet the hour of closing day .... *William H. Bathurst.*
How sweet the name of Jesus sounds .... *John Newton.*
I love to steal awhile away .... *Mrs. P. H. Brown.*
More love to Thee, O Christ .... *Mrs. Elizabeth P. Prentiss.*
My days are gliding swiftly by .... *David Nelson.*
My hope is built on nothing less .... *Edward Mote.*
Nearer, my God, to Thee! .... *Mrs. Sarah F. Adams.*
One more day's work for Jesus .... *Anna B. Warner.*
Only waiting till the shadows .... *Mrs. F. L. Mace.*
Since I can read my title clear .... *Isaac Watts.*
Sister, thou wast mild and lovely .... *S. F. Smith.*
Softly now the light of day .... *George W. Doane.*
Vain, delusive world, adieu .... *Charles Wesley.*
What a friend we have in Jesus .... *Horatius Bonar.*
When I survey the wondrous cross .... *Isaac Watts.*
When shall the voice of singing .... *James Edmeston, alt.*
Yield to me now, for I am weak . ... *Charles Wesley.*

III. GRAVE, SOLEMN, SERIOUS, PATHETIC.

Alas! and did my Saviour bleed .... *Isaac Watts.*
Approach, my soul, the mercy-seat .... *John Newton.*
Arise, my soul, arise .... *Charles Wesley.*
Beyond the smiling and the weeping . ... *Horatius Bonar.*
Come, Thou Fount of every blessing .... *Robert Robinson.*
Depth of mercy! can there be .... *Charles Wesley.*
Did Christ o'er sinners weep .... *Benj. Beddone.*
Friend after friend departs .... *James Montgomery.*
From every stormy wind that blows .... *H. Stowell.*
He leadeth me! O blessed thought .... *J. H. Gilmore.*
Holy Bible; book divine .... *John Burton.*
How tedious and tasteless the hours .... *John Newton.*
I know that my Redeemer lives .... *Charles Wesley.*
I would not live always .... *W. A. Muhlenberg.*
Jerusalem, my happy home ....
Jesus, I my cross have taken .... *Henry F. Lyte.*
Late, late, so late! and dark the night .... *Alfred Tennyson.*
Let us gather up the sunbeams .... *Mrs. Albert Smith.*
Love for all, and can it be .... *S. Longfellow.*

IV. REVERENCE, DEVOTION, ADORATION.

Pass me not, O gentle Saviour! ....*F. C. Van Alstyne.*
Rock of Ages, cleft for me.................*Augustus M. Toplady, alt.*
Saviour, breathe an evening blessing................*James Edmeston.*
Saviour, like a shepherd lead us..................*Dorothy A. Thrupp.*
Show pity, Lord, O Lord forgive ....*Isaac Watts.*
The day of wrath, that dreadful day................*Sir Walter Scott.*
When all thy mercies, O my God ....*Joseph Addison.*

V. GRAND, BOLD, SUBLIME.

All hail the power of Jesus' name!.................*Edward Perronet.*
Blow ye the trumpet, blow.............................*Charles Wesley.*
Come, let us join our cheerful songs....................*Isaac Watts.*
Come, let us join our friends above ....*Charles Wesley.*
Come, ye that love the Lord ....*Isaac Watts.*
Earth has a joy unknown in heaven..................*A. L. Hillhouse.*
From all that dwell below the skies.....................*Isaac Watts.*
From Greenland's icy mountains ....*Reginald Heber.*
Hark! ten thousand harps and voices ....*Thomas Kelly.*
Holy, holy, holy, Lord God Almighty! .. ..*Reginald Heber.*
Jesus, and shall it ever be...........................*Joseph Gregg.*
Lift your glad voices in triumph....................*Henry Ware, Jr.*
Lo, He comes with clouds descending ....*Charles Wesley.*
O for a thousand tongues, to sing...................*Charles Wesley.*
On Jordan's stormy banks I stand ....*Samuel Stennett.*
Our country's voice is pleading.............*Mrs. Maria F. Anderson.*
Praise the Lord! ye heavens adore him ....*John Kempthorne.*
Roll on, thou mighty ocean! ....
Sinners, turn, why will ye die ....*John Wesley.*
When through the torn sail ....*Reginald Heber.*

VI. RELIGIOUS PATRIOTISM.

Awake my soul, stretch every nerve................*Philip Doddridge.*
Fling out the banner! let it float......................*G. W. Doane.*
Forward! be our watchword.........................*Henry Alford.*
Go forward, Christian soldier ....*Laurence Tuttiett.*
Go forth, ye heralds, in my name.........................*John Logan.*
Ho! reapers of life's harvest...................................
Labourers of Christ, arise.................*Mrs. Lydia H. Sigourney.*
My country! 'tis of thee..........................*Samuel F. Smith.*
Onward, Christian soldiers! ....*Sabine Baring-Gould.*
Soldiers of Christ, arise...........................*Charles Wesley.*

VII. LIVELY, JOYOUS, GAY.

IV. ALPHABETICAL INDEX OF SELECTIONS.

[NOTE. This Index is for the general reader who would find an alphabetical list more convenient than that given in the first part of the book. The numerals on the left hand of the page refer to the characteristic headings under which the selections are classed. See page vii.]

A.

B.

T.

U.

V.

W.

SCENES FROM POPULAR DRAMAS.